New York State Regents Review U.S. HISTORY AND GOVERNMENT

Dr. Andrew Peiser
Associate Professor of Education, Mercy College, New York

Michael Serber
Founding Principal, Academy of American Studies, New York

Senior Education Fellow, Emeritus, Gilder Lehrman Institute of American History, New York

AMSCO SCHOOL PUBLICATIONS, INC.,
a division of Perfection Learning®

Dr. Andrew Peiser is an Associate Professor of Education at Mercy College, New York. His previous positions included Dean of the School of Education, Mercy College, and Chair of the Social Studies Department at Sheepshead Bay High School, Brooklyn, New York.

Michael Serber served as a Senior Education Fellow at the Gilder Lehrman Institute of American History, and was the Founding Principal of the Academy of American Studies in Long Island City, New York. He served as chair of the Social Studies Department at Taft High School, Bronx, New York, and Forest Hills High School, Queens, New York.

Dr. Andrew Peiser dedicates this book to his wife, Barbara; his children, Richard, Jacqueline, and Brett; his daughter-in-law, Emmy; his son-in law Brian; and his grandchildren, Jack, Matteah, and Nicholas, for all their love and support; and to the memory of his mother, Marianne.

Michael Serber dedicates this book to his wife, Adele; his children, Ellen, Richard, and Jeff; and his grandchildren, Daniel, Noah, and Jared, for all their love and support; and to the memory of his parents.

Student's Study Guide prepared by ***Stephen A. Shultz,*** Social Studies Coordinator, Rocky Point Public Schools, New York

Answer Key Prepared by ***Ross Bloomfield,*** Social Studies Teacher, Queens High School for the Sciences, New York City

Reviewers

John M. Schmalbach, Adjunct Professor, Temple University, former Social Studies Department Head, Abraham Lincoln High School, Philadelphia, Pennsylvania

Brian E. Walsh, History Dept. Chair, Altmar-Parish-Williamstown High School, NY

Richard Rose, AP U.S. History Teacher, Elwood John Glenn High School, East Northport, NY

Florence Caragine, Chairman, History Dept., Sacred Heart High School, Yonkers, NY

Text design and cover by Joseph A. Piliero
Photo research by Tobi Zausner
New art by Eric Hieber
Composition by Brad Walrod/Kenoza Type

Please visit our websites at:
www.amscopub.com and ***www.perfectionlearning.com***

When ordering this book, please specify:
ISBN 978-1-56765-696-1 or **1350201**

31 32 33 34 35 PP 23 22 21 20 19

Printed in the United States of America

Preface

New York State Regents Review: U.S. History and Government is a review text for students preparing to take the 11th-grade New York State Regents examination. In the front of the book is a *Student's Study Guide* for reviewing the entire course. It provides proven test-taking strategies for multiple-choice, thematic essay, and document-based questions.

Chapter 1 describes the founding of the republic, Chapter 2 treats the drafting of the Constitution and Bill of Rights, and Chapter 3 analyzes the federal government and state and local governments as they exist today.

Chapters 4 through 9 present a concise review from the colonial period to industrialization in the post–Civil War United States.

Since an understanding of 20th- and early 21st-century trends and events is critical if Americans are to cope successfully with the changes ahead in this century, the remaining 13 chapters deal with events since 1900.

Throughout, historical topics are presented in *outline form*, arranged in three levels of headings. This format is intended to enhance review work.

The following text features are designed to enhance the visibility of the book:

- a *chapter-opening overview* in three parts: documents, laws, and Supreme Court cases; events; and people and groups
- numerous *tables*, *diagrams*, *graphs*, *maps*, *illustrations*, and *cartoons*—for interest, information, and skill building
- mid-chapter *In Reviews* to target important subjects and concepts
- *Chapter Reviews* of actual Regents multiple-choice questions (many testing comprehension of visuals and readings), Regents-style thematic essays, and document-based questions (DBQs).

Three important features comprise the final portion of the book. (1) For reinforcement, a *glossary* succinctly defines every important vocabulary term that appears in bold type in the text. (2) A comprehensive *index* facilitates easy reference to the content of the text. (3) The book concludes with two of the most recent U.S. history and government Regents examinations to test student competency.

Our nation derives its unique identity and character from the contributions of many people over centuries of history. As teachers and writers of that remarkable history, we feel privileged to present it to you in a solid review format.

Andrew Peiser
Michael Serber

Contents

	Preface		iii
	Student's Study Guide		vii
UNIT I	**Constitutional Foundations of American Society**		
	Chapter 1	Origins of the Constitution	1
	Chapter 2	The Constitution and Bill of Rights	19
	Chapter 3	The Federal Government and the State Governments	35
	Chapter 4	Implementing Principles of the New Constitution	56
	Chapter 5	Nationalism and Sectionalism	69
	Chapter 6	Western Expansion and Civil War	89
UNIT II	**Industrialization of the United States**		
	Chapter 7	The Reconstructed Nation	109
	Chapter 8	Rise of American Business, Labor, and Agriculture	124
	Chapter 9	Impact of Industrialization	144
UNIT III	**The Progressive Era**		
	Chapter 10	Reform in America	167
	Chapter 11	Rise of American Power	185
UNIT IV	**Prosperity and Depression**		
	Chapter 12	War and Prosperity: 1917–1929	207
	Chapter 13	The Great Depression	221
UNIT V	**The United States in an Age of Global Crises**		
	Chapter 14	Peace in Peril: 1933–1950	239
	Chapter 15	Peace With Problems: 1945–1960	256
UNIT VI	**The World in Uncertain Times**		
	Chapter 16	Containment and Consensus: 1945–1960	273
	Chapter 17	Liberalism at Home: 1961–1969	289
	Chapter 18	The Continuing Cold War, 1961–1974	312
	Chapter 19	A Decade of Moderation: 1969–1980	328
	Chapter 20	The Triumph of Conservatism: 1981–1992	344
	Chapter 21	Toward a Postindustrial World: 1993–2001	371
	Chapter 22	A New Century: 2000–Present	394
	Glossary		423
	Index		431
	Acknowledgments		443
	Regents Examinations		445

A Practical Plan for Success on the Regents Examination

In order to receive a NYS high school diploma, you will need to pass a Regents exam in U.S. history. This Study Guide and the whole book *New York State Regents Review: U.S. History and Government* are intended to help increase your chances of passing this important test. If there is a recipe for passing the test, the two most important ingredients are study and practice. If you read this chapter carefully and practice the suggested techniques for answering both the multiple-choice and essay questions, you will improve your chances of passing the Regents exam and earning a higher grade.

Success, however, cannot be based on one chapter. The content of each chapter should be read carefully. Notes should be taken to help you remember important events and individuals. Answering the Regents questions at the end of each chapter, checking your answers, re-reading what do you not know, and re-writing essay answers will all help you gain the knowledge and skills to do well.

Success on a Regents exam, as in any endeavor, requires thought and effort throughout the school year.

Strategies for Studying for the Regents Exam

1. Review Frequently

Review daily or several times a week the material covered in class, and do all your homework assignments. Such periodic reviews will help you understand the connections among the different events studied, without the need for cramming the day before a test.

2. Initial Preparation

There is no substitute for adequate, regular preparation. Your teacher will probably review highlights of your study of U.S. history and government. But this is not enough. In-class review merely suggests what you need to study and know.

Allow yourself four to six weeks of study time before the Regents exam is given. It is better to study half an hour daily over this period than to cram for many hours several days before the examination. To review effectively, try the following suggestions:

- Separate your studying into separate historical sections or periods. On average, two to four days should be spent on each one.
- Plan a daily study schedule. This will help you adequately cover the entire U.S. history and government course.
- Spend a short time reviewing the previous day's work to reinforce what you have already covered.
- Study when you are alert rather than after exercise or a big meal.
- Avoid distractions (television, radio, phone, the Internet, etc.)
- Take a five-minute break each study hour to help you stay fresh and retain what you have learned.

3. Knowing How and What to Study

Take a practice Regents examination before you begin your course of study. This will help you identify areas of study that need special attention. After reviewing for several weeks, take a different Regents examination. How far have you progressed, and what material still needs more review? (Your teacher should be able to supply you with past Regents examinations.)

4. Knowing the Examination Format

Use the practice Regents examinations to familiarize yourself with how each part of the test is structured. Understanding the form of each group of questions and how best to answer each one will help you maximize your score.

5. Learn Important Vocabulary Terms and Names

You will not remember every term and name discussed during the course, but you should be familiar with important terms that apply to all periods of U.S. history and government, as well as terms and names related to particular historical eras. As you proceed through your course of study, make a list of these terms and names for periodic review.

Here are some tips for identifying such terms and names:

- **Check off familiar names.** Keeping track of the number of them that you already know will boost your confidence.
- **Identify recurring vocabulary terms.** Words such as federalism, checks and balances, states' rights, neutrality, judicial review, and due process come up again and again in a U.S. history and government course. Identify them as they are repeated throughout the course.
- **Review areas for which you know the fewest terms.** Your check-off will identify areas in which you need more help. The glossary in this book will give you basic definitions.

- **Make appropriate connections.** Linking related words, names, and terms is an effective way to reinforce the details in a large amount of material.
- **Do not try to learn every term.** Trying to memorize everything is frustrating and practically impossible. Build a list designed to reacquaint yourself with key names and terms in U.S. history and government. The concepts they represent will likely be test subjects.
- **Identifications are more important than definitions.** A definition gives you only the meaning of a term. An identification of a term's historical significance is a building block that will help you link one important concept with another.

6. Create Broad Questions That Focus on Key Themes

By recasting the material under study into questions or problems, you will create an outline for study and understanding. Here are several examples from the passages on immigration from Chapter 9, pages 151–157.

Why was Chinese labor essential to the development of the West?
How was anti-Chinese sentiment reflected in America's immigration laws?
List *three* reasons for emigration to America and explain which you think was the most important?
Describe the terms assimilation, melting pot theory, and cultural pluralism.
How did nativist views of immigrants clash with non-nativist views?
Would you consider the Literacy Test and Quota Acts to be pro- or anti-immigrant? Explain.

Learning to write such probing questions will teach you to arrange the material into smaller units of study and help you anticipate possible test questions.

7. Review Graphics Provided in Class and Your Textbook

Illustrations will be included in the Regents examination. Familiarity with graphs, maps, tables, charts, drawings, paintings, cartoons, and photographs will help you interpret and analyze them. (Specific suggestions for developing skills with graphics are given in the multiple-choice section under the heading "Analyzing the Regents Exam.")

8. Review "In Review" and "Chapter Review" Questions

"In Review" questions in this book reinforce your understanding of the key topics, section by section. "Chapter Review" questions in this book simulate questions on the Regents examination (or are actual Regents questions, in the case of the multiple-choice questions). As you answer the Chapter

Review questions, you will become familiar with the Regents questions format.

9. Determine Cause-and-Effect Relationships

When you understand *chronology*—the order of historical events—you will better understand why events have taken place. This is called the *cause-and-effect relationships.*

Consider the following statements:

- The issues of nullification, states' rights, and slavery resulted in the Civil War.
- Jim Crow laws developed in the South as a result of the end of Reconstruction.

Each statement contains a *cause* and *effect.* The first statement says that nullification, states' rights, and slavery were causes of the Civil War; in other words, the Civil War was an effect of these causes.

The second statement says that Jim Crow laws were the effect of the end of Reconstruction; in other words, that Reconstruction's end helped cause Jim Crow laws.

Ask yourself (a) what past events caused the event you are studying to take place and (b) what were the later effects of that event. Thus, you will realize that history appears to flow from one topic to another, and that no event occurs in isolation.

Take notes on what you do not understand. Turn back to those pages in the textbook and re-read the content. If necessary, ask your teacher to explain the significance of the event

Analyzing the Regents Exam

The Regents examination is a three-hour test consisting of three parts: 50 multiple-choice questions, worth 55 percent of the score; one thematic essay, worth 15 percent; and one document-based question (DBQ), worth 30 percent.

Part I: Multiple Choice

Standard Multiple Choice Most multiple-choice questions are like those you have regularly answered in high school. A question or statement requires completion. There are four possible choices. Here are strategies for answering standard multiple-choice questions:

- Read all the choices. There are often one or more "decoy" choices. That is, they seem correct but, in fact, are not.

- Note such words as "all," "none," "always," and "never," which often signal an incorrect choice. Such words allow for no exceptions.
- Note key terms that often point to the correct answer.
- Weed out incorrect choices by the process of elimination.
- Do not get stalled by a particular question. Answer first the questions you know. Then attack questions that you can narrow down to two choices. Tackle the rest of the questions last.

Now put these strategies to work by answering the following multiple-choice questions from past Regents examinations:

QUESTION 1: The framers of the U.S. Constitution showed the strongest commitment to democratic principles in regard to the (1) method for choosing Cabinet members (2) election of members of the House (3) election of senators (4) selection of U.S. Supreme Court justices.

The key word is "democratic." To evaluate the best choice, determine which one gave the most power to citizens.

In choice 1, the president chooses Cabinet members with the "advice and consent" of the Senate. This may appear to be correct because it reflects checks and balances, but remember that the question asks for the *strongest commitment to democratic principles.* (Also keep in mind that the Founders did not foresee that a president would form a Cabinet.)

Choice 2 refers to the election of members of the House, which is a democratic process.

Choice 3 refers to the election of senators as the *framers of the U.S. Constitution* designed it. This is not a good choice because state legislatures, not the people, originally elected senators.

Concerning choice 4, Supreme Court justices, like Cabinet members, are appointed by the president and approved by the Senate.

Careful thought will convince you that choice 2 answers the question best.

QUESTION 2: What is the most frequent criticism of the Electoral College system? (1) An excessive number of third-party candidates are encouraged to run for office. (2) Electors frequently ignore the vote of the people. (3) The person who wins the popular vote is not always elected president. (4) The electors are not chosen by political parties.

The Electoral College resulted from the Founders' fear of the mob, or ordinary citizens—that the majority of voters could not select the best person as president.

Choice 1 deals with third-party candidates and has no relationship to the Electoral College.

Choice 2 can be eliminated because each elector in each state is pledged to a particular candidate.

Choice 4 is incorrect because, although the voters determine who will be electors, the major political parties choose who runs for the Electoral College.

Choice 3 is the correct answer. The Electoral College's choice of president did not reflect the popular vote in three elections—Hayes-Tilden (1876), B. Harrison-Cleveland (1888), and Bush-Gore (2000).

Multiple Choice and Interpreting Graphics Some multiple-choice questions ask you to interpret an illustration, graph, or chart. This requires the development of special skills, such as identifying the meaning of symbols, the artist's point of view, and the underlying significance of the figures in a scene. The following political cartoon and question are from the January 1999 Regents examination:

QUESTION 3: Base your answer on the following cartoon and on your knowledge of U.S. history and government.

The cartoon makes the point that Supreme Court decisions (1) sometimes do not resolve controversial issues (2) are usually accepted by both sides in a controversy (3) avoid dealing with controversial issues (4) ignore public opinion.

This cartoon provides several hints to the answer. Both women disagree with a Supreme Court decision on abortion, but their beliefs about what is the proper decision are opposite.

Choice 2 is incorrect because neither woman is satisfied.

The cartoon also shows that Choice 3 is incorrect because the abortion issue is shown to be very controversial.

Your decision is thus narrowed to choice 1 or 4. The cartoon shows that the decision has not resolved a controversial issue (choice 1). It also shows that the Court apparently did not take into account public opinion (choice 4). Therefore, you must decide which choice best reflects the cartoonist's point of view.

Obviously, this controversial abortion issue has not been resolved; it is so sensitive that there is no clear-cut public opinion. Choice 4, it turns out, is a decoy after the correct answer. The cartoon's main point is best illustrated by choice 1.

Some questions call for interpreting a table or chart. Consider the following chart and question from the January 1999 Regents examination:

QUESTION 4: Base your answer to the question on the following table and on your knowledge of U.S. history and government.

Life Expectancy of U.S. Men and Women

Year	*Men*	*Women*
1900	46.3	48.3
1950	65.6	71.1
1960	66.6	73.1
1970	67.1	74.7
1980	70.0	77.4
1990	71.8	78.8
1998	73.9	79.4

A valid conclusion based on the data in the table is that (1) men have received better medical attention than women (2) Americans are healthier than people in any other country (3) the average life expectancy increased steadily during the 20th century (4) most of the change in the average life span for men and women has occurred after 1950.

It is not the purpose of this type of question to require sophisticated mathematical calculations. Rather it tests the ability to understand and interpret information in a table, chart, or graph. Therefore, search for trends within the table. This table shows two trends taking place between 1900 and 1998:

- Life expectancy increased during the 20th century.
- Women tend to live longer than men.

The first trend is the subject of choice 3.

Choice 1 must be incorrect because (a) American men have tended not to live as long as American women, and (b) the table provides no information on medical care.

Choice 2 should be eliminated because the table gives no information about people living outside of the United States.

Choice 4 is incorrect because the table gives no information for the years 1901 to 1949.

The best answer is choice 3.

QUESTION 5: A correct conclusion based on the map is that (1) territorial boundaries were maintained as new states were created (2) all territories were acquired through wars and other conflicts (3) U.S. expansion generally occurred in a westerly direction (4) Southern territories were the last areas to be acquired.

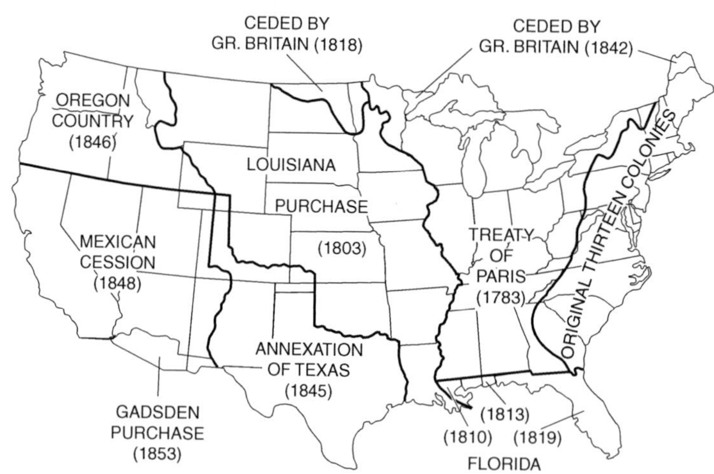

The map shows that present-day state boundaries (the gray lines) do not always match territorial boundaries (the black lines). Thus, choice 1 must be eliminated.

Choice 2 is suspicious because it contains the world "all." A choice containing "all," "never," "none," or "always" might be correct, but even one exception would make the choice incorrect. And, in fact, choice 2 is incorrect because the map gives no information about how territories were acquired. (The statement is also historically inaccurate, as shown by the labels "Louisiana Purchase" and "Gadsden Purchase.")

Choice 4 is incorrect because the map shows that territories in the South (Florida and Texas) were acquired before 1853 when the final acquisition (the Gadsden Purchase) was made.

The map supports choice 3 because it shows that most territories were acquired in chronological order from left to right, or east to west—Treaty of Paris (1783), Louisiana Purchase (1803), and Annexation of Texas (1845). There are, however, some exceptions: the Oregon Territory was acquired two years before the Mexican Cession, the Gadsden Purchase was made after the Mexican Cession, and Florida was acquired in no apparent chronological pattern. But because choice 3 includes the word "generally," allowing for a few exceptions, it is still correct.

Part II: Thematic Essay

The thematic essay focuses on a theme spanning several periods or linking several events in U.S. history and government. It asks you to show how well you understand the theme's importance and its role in the course. Examples of themes include nationalism, sectionalism, imperialism, geography, technology, warfare, peacekeeping, equality, checks and balances, and federalism.

In developing your answers to the essays in Parts II and III B, keep the following definitions in mind:

- **Discuss** means "to make observations about something, using facts, reasoning, and argument; to present in some detail."
- **Describe** means "to illustrate something in words or tell about it."
- **Evaluate** means "to examine and judge the significance, worth, or condition of; to determine the value of."

The following thematic essay might appear on the Regents examination:

DIRECTIONS: Write a well-organized essay that includes an introduction, several paragraphs addressing the task, and a conclusion.

THEME: *Presidential Decisions.* During the last 100 years, U.S. presidents have made important decisions in an effort to solve crucial problems.

TASK: From your study of U.S. history and government, identify *two* important presidential decisions made during the last 100 years. For each decision:

- state *one* goal the president hoped to accomplish by the decision.
- discuss the historical circumstances surrounding the decision.
- discuss *one* immediate or *one* long-term effect of the decision on U.S. history and government.

You may use any important presidential decision in 20th-century U.S. history and government. Some suggestions include: (a) Woodrow Wilson seeks ratification of the Versailles Treaty (1918), (b) Franklin D. Roosevelt institutes the New Deal program (1933), (c) Harry S. Truman decides to drop atomic bombs on Japan (1945), (d) Dwight D. Eisenhower sends federal troops to Little Rock, Arkansas (1957), (e) John F. Kennedy places a naval blockade around Cuba (1962), (f) Lyndon Johnson proposes the Great

Society program (1965), and (g) Jimmy Carter meets with Anwar Sadat and Menachem Begin at Camp David (1978).

ESSAY GUIDELINES: Be sure to:

- Address all aspects of the task.
- Analyze, evaluate, or compare and/or contrast issues and events whenever possible.
- Fully support the theme with relevant facts, examples, and details.
- Write a well-developed essay that is consistently logical and clearly organized.
- Establish an initial framework that is more than a restatement of the task.
- Conclude with a strong summation of the theme.

Key words and phrases in the task are: (a) *identify* two *important presidential decisions*; (b) *for each decision*; *goal*; (c) *historical circumstances*; and (d) one *immediate or* one *long-term effect.* By jotting them down, you create a checklist for organizing the thematic essay.

Observe the following seven additional guidelines:

1. **ANALYZE THE QUESTION:** Be sure you understand the theme and directions —the key words and phrases.

2. **ORGANIZE THE INFORMATION:** Add the general information you plan to write about to your checklist to create an *instant outline.* For the sample thematic essay, you might include:

Two Presidential Decisions

1: Truman drops A-bombs on Japan (1945)
Goal: Force quick Japanese surrender
Historical Circumstances: Western European war over. Long war in Pacific continues; many casualties
Extent of Goal Achieved: Immediate Japanese surrender
Immediate/Long-Term Effect: Nuclear arms race begins

2: Eisenhower sends federal troops to Little Rock, Ark. (1957)
Goal: Desegregate Central High School
Historical Circumstances: Enforce *Brown* v. *Board of Education* (1954) on separate educational facilities
Extent of Goal Achieved: Black students admitted to school
Immediate/Long-Term Effect: Federal enforcement gives impetus to civil rights movement

Notice how you have expanded your checklist with ideas to flesh out your essay. The outline should take only five minutes.

3. **DEVELOP THE THESIS:** Use the theme or task to create an original thesis, such as the following thought-provoking one: "The president of the United States must often make difficult and controversial decisions that will have major effects on the nation both at the time the decision is made and for many years into the future."

4. **WRITE THE INTRODUCTORY PARAGRAPH:** The introductory paragraph should include the thesis statement and background of your essay. Introduce examples taken from the instant outline and to be used in the essay. Include the decision by Truman to drop atomic bombs on Japanese cities and the decision by Eisenhower to enforce *Brown* v. *Board of Education* (1954) by sending federal troops to Little Rock, Arkansas.

5. **WRITE THE SUPPORTING PARAGRAPHS:** These paragraphs *explain* your answer with facts, details, and examples. Elaborate on the facts from your instant outline. Be as specific as possible. *Do not use* meaningless facts or information unrelated to your theme.

6. **WRITE THE CONCLUDING PARAGRAPH:** The concluding paragraph should restate the thesis in a fresh, interesting manner and briefly summarize the essay. A good concluding paragraph to the sample essay would be:

   > Both presidents Truman and Eisenhower made decisions that had enormous impacts on our nation's 20th-century history. Truman's decision to drop atomic bombs on Hiroshima and Nagasaki in 1945 ended World War II, but at the cost of many civilian lives and the start of a nuclear arms race. Eisenhower's decision to use federal troops to desegregate Central High School in Little Rock, Arkansas, in 1957 gave hope to African Americans and helped foster the growing civil rights movement.

7. **CHECK THE ESSAY:** If time permits, reread your essay to correct grammar, spelling, punctuation, sentence structure, and errors in fact. Does your essay read clearly and make sense? Rereading the essay can improve your grade for the thematic essay portion of the Regents examination.

Generic Thematic Essay Rubrics Those who score your thematic essay will use the following guidelines, or scoring scale:

5 Thoroughly develops all aspects of the task evenly and in depth
Is more analytical than descriptive (analyzes, evaluates, and/or creates information)
Richly supports the theme with many relevant facts, examples, and details
Demonstrates a logical and clear plan of organization; includes an introduction and a conclusion that are beyond a restatement of the theme

4 Develops all aspects of the task but may do so somewhat unevenly
Is both descriptive and analytical (applies, analyzes, evaluates, and/or creates information)
Supports the theme with relevant facts, examples, and details
Demonstrates a logical and clear plan of organization; includes an introduction and a conclusion that are beyond a restatement of the theme

3 Develops all aspects of the task with little depth or develops most aspects of the task in some depth
Is more descriptive than analytical (applies, may analyze, and/or evaluate information)
Includes some relevant facts, examples, and details; may include some minor inaccuracies
Demonstrates a satisfactory plan of organization; includes an introduction and a conclusion that may be a restatement of the theme

2 Minimally develops all aspects of the task or develops some aspects of the task in some depth
Is primarily descriptive; may include faulty, weak, or isolated application or analysis
Includes few relevant facts, examples, and details; may include some inaccuracies
Demonstrates a general plan of organization; may lack focus; may contain digressions; may not clearly identify which aspect of the task is being addressed; may lack an introduction and/or a conclusion

1 Minimally develops some aspects of the task
Is descriptive; may lack understanding, application, or analysis
Includes few relevant facts, examples, or details; may include inaccuracies
May demonstrate a weakness in organization; may lack focus; may contain digressions; may not clearly identify which aspect of the task is being addressed; may lack an introduction and/or a conclusion

0 Fails to develop the task or may only refer to the theme in a general way; OR includes no relevant facts, examples, or details; OR includes only the theme, task, or suggestions as copied from the test booklet; OR is illegible; OR is a blank paper

Part III: Document-Based Questions (DBQs)

This essay calls for you to write a general essay after interpreting a variety of documents about the topic (including maps, pictures, cartoons, graphs, charts). One or more questions on each document test your understanding of it. Here is a sample DBQ:

DIRECTIONS: This document-based question consists of Part A and Part B. In Part A, you are to read each document and answer the question or questions that follow it. In Part B, you are to write an essay based on the information in the documents and your knowledge of U.S. history and government.

HISTORICAL CONTEXT: After the Civil War, the United States became much more industrialized. Between 1865 and 1910, industrialization improved life in many ways. Industrialization, however, also created social problems.

Part A

DOCUMENT 1 (see the following table)

Impact of Industrialization (1870–1910)

Year	*GNP per Capita*	*Employed Children Under 15 Years of Age (millions)*	*% of U.S. Population*		*Infant Mortality Rate (deaths under 1 Year of Age per 1,000)*	*High School Graduates (% of 17- year-olds with diplomas)*	*Telephone Usage (number of telephones per 1,000)*	*Steel Prod. (1,000 short tons)*
			Rural (%)	*Urban (%)*				
1870	$ 531	0.70	74	26	170	2.0	0	77
1880	744	1.10	72	28	161	2.5	1	1,400
1890	836	1.50	65	35	163	3.5	4	4,780
1900	1,011	1.75	60	40	141	6.5	18	11,220
1910	1,299	1.63	54	46	117	9.0	82	28,330

1*a*. Identify *one* aspect of American life shown in the table that improved between 1870 and 1910.

1*b*. Identify *one* aspect of American life shown in the table that worsened between 1870 and 1910.

DOCUMENT 2

> The groundwork principle of America's labor movement has been to recognize that first things must come first. . . . Our mission has been the protection of the wage-worker, now, to increase his wages; to cut hours off the long workday, which was killing him; to improve the safety and the sanitary conditions of the workshop; to free him from the tyrannies, petty or otherwise. . . .
>
> —Samuel Gompers

2. According to Samuel Gompers, why should workers organize into unions?

Document 3

The houses of the ward, for the most part wooden, were originally built for one family and are now occupied by several. Many houses have no water supply save [except] the faucet in the back yard, there are no fire escapes, the garbage and ashes are placed in wooden boxes.... The streets are inexpressibly dirty, the number of schools inadequate, sanitary legislation unenforced, the street lighting bad, the paving miserable and altogether lacking in the alleys and small streets, and the stables foul beyond description.

—Jane Addams, *Twenty Years at Hull-House*

3. How was the life of the poor affected by the conditions described by Jane Addams?

Document 4

The sweatshop is a place where ... a "sweater" assembles journeymen tailors and needlewomen, to work under his supervision. He takes a cheap room outside the ... crowded business center and within the neighborhood where the workpeople live. This is rent saved to the employer, and time and travel to the employed. The men can work more hours than was possible under the centralized system, and their wives and children can help.... For this service, ... they cannot earn more than from 25 to 40 cents a day.... In one such place there were fifteen men and women in one room, which contained also a pile of mattresses on which some of the men sleep at night....

—Joseph Kirkland, *Among the Poor of Chicago*, 1895

4. According to Joseph Kirkland, what were conditions like in a sweatshop?

Document 5

After the feast, the workingman gets what is left!

5a. According to the cartoon, what is one way in which the rich treated the workingman?

5*b*. What is one way in which such cartoons influenced public opinion toward the rich?

DOCUMENT 6

From John D. Rockefeller's testimony before a congressional commission investigating industrial combinations, 1899:

> Q: What are . . . the chief advantages from industrial combinations [trusts, monopolies, and so on] . . . to the public?
>
> A:. . . Much that one man cannot do alone two can do together. . . . [Industrial combinations] are a necessity . . . if Americans are to have the privilege of extending their business in all the States of the Union, and into foreign countries as well. . . . Their chief advantages are:. . .
>
> - Improvements and economies which are derived from knowledge of many interested persons of wide experience.
> - Power to give the public improved products at lower prices and still make a profit for stockholders.
> - Permanent work and good wages for laborers. . . .
>
> —U.S. Industrial Commission, *Preliminary Report on Trusts and Industrial Combinations*

6*a*. According to John D. Rockefeller's testimony, what did he believe was an advantage of industrial combinations?

6*b*. What was one reason why John D. Rockefeller would testify in favor of industrial combinations?

DOCUMENT 7

7. According to the cartoon, what did Andrew Carnegie do with much of his wealth?

Part B

TASK: Using information from the documents and your knowledge of U.S. history and government, write an essay in which you discuss the advantages and disadvantages of industrialization to American society between 1865 and 1910. In your essay, include a discussion of how industrialization affected different groups in American society.

ESSAY GUIDELINES: Approach the DBQ as you would any other essay question. Use the same guidelines as for the thematic essay (page xvii), with one addition: Add references from *most* of the documents.

Look again at the seven documents in the sample DBQ. (Most DBQs have between six and nine documents.) Notice that there are two cartoons. The DBQ usually includes two or more graphic documents—cartoons, tables, charts, graphs, or pictures. Note that the documents contain a variety of ideas and perspectives on the topic—in this case, the advantages and disadvantages of American industrialization, and industrialization's effects on different groups. Some documents may be contradictory. This is not done to confuse you but to assess how well you analyze different points of view. (When you prepare your essay response, you will need to account for some of the differences of opinion.)

Now look at the questions following the documents. They test your understanding of the main idea of each document. All questions must be answered. Your answers may help you organize your essay response.

Generic Document-Based Question Rubric Those who score your document-based questions and essay will use the following guidelines, or scoring scale:

5 Thoroughly develops all aspects of the task evenly and in depth
Is more analytical than descriptive (analyzes, evaluates, and/or creates information)
Incorporates relevant information from at least xxx documents
Incorporates substantial relevant outside information
Richly supports the theme with many relevant facts, examples, and details
Demonstrates a logical and clear plan of organization; includes an introduction and a conclusion that are beyond a restatement of the theme

4 Develops all aspects of the task but may do so somewhat unevenly
Is both descriptive and analytical (applies, analyzes, evaluates, and/or creates information)
Incorporates relevant information from at least xxx documents
Incorporates relevant outside information

Supports the theme with relevant facts, examples, and details
Demonstrates a logical and clear plan of organization; includes an introduction and a conclusion that are beyond a restatement of the theme

3 Develops all aspects of the task with little depth or develops most aspects of the task in some depth
Is more descriptive than analytical (applies, may analyze, and/or evaluate information)
Incorporates some relevant information from some of the documents
Incorporates limited relevant outside information
Includes some relevant facts, examples, and details; may include some minor inaccuracies
Demonstrates a satisfactory plan of organization; includes an introduction and a conclusion that may be a restatement of the theme

2 Minimally develops all aspects of the task or develops some aspects of the task in some depth
Is primarily descriptive; may include faulty, weak, or isolated application or analysis
Incorporates limited relevant information from the documents or consists primarily of relevant information copied from the documents
Presents little or no relevant outside information
Includes few relevant facts, examples, and details; may include some inaccuracies
Demonstrates a general plan of organization; may lack focus; may contain digressions; may not clearly identify which aspect of the task is being addressed; may lack an introduction and/or a conclusion

1 Minimally develops some aspect of the task
Is descriptive; may lack understanding, application, or analysis
Makes vague, unclear references to the documents or consists primarily of relevant and irrelevant information copied from the documents
Presents no relevant outside information
Includes few relevant facts, examples, or details; may include inaccuracies
May demonstrate a weakness in organization; may lack focus; may contain digressions; may not clearly identify which aspect of the task is being addressed; may lack an introduction and/or a conclusion

0 Fails to develop the task or may only refer to the theme in a general way; *OR* includes no relevant facts, examples, or details; *OR* includes only the historical context and/or task as copied from the test booklet; *OR* includes only entire documents copied from the test booklet; *OR* is illegible; *OR* is a blank paper

Note the requirements for category 5. All aspects of the task must be developed, the essay must be more analytical than descriptive, and incorporate substantial, relevant outside information. The theme must be supported with many relevant facts, examples, and details.

Final Reminders

You have done everything possible to prepare for the Regents examination. Now get a good night's sleep. Arriving well rested at the testing room is the best preparation at this point.

After you finish the exam, check your answers and re-read your essays. For example, if the question listed a particular time period (1900–1914) make sure your response fell within that era. Leave room at the end of each essay answer in case you want to add additional information or change what you have written. Better to go over your answers than to rush out of the room. Take all the allotted time you need and to which you are entitled. Finally, make sure your handwriting is legible and easy to read.

UNIT I
Constitutional Foundations of American Society

CHAPTER 1
Origins of the Constitution

DOCUMENTS AND LAWS
Magna Carta (1215) • Iroquois Confederacy (about 1570) • Mayflower Compact (1620)
Habeas Corpus Act (1679) • English Bill of Rights (1689) • Stamp Tax (1765)
Coercive Acts (1774) • Declaration of Independence (1776)
New York State Constitution (1777) • Articles of Confederation (1781)
Northwest Ordinance (1787) • U.S. Constitution (written 1787; ratified 1789)

EVENTS
Glorious Revolution (1688) • Zenger case (1735) • French and Indian War (1754–1763)
Boston Massacre (1770) • Boston Tea Party (1773) • Battles of Lexington and Concord (1775)
Revolutionary War (1775–1783) • Battle of Saratoga (1777) • Battle of Yorktown (1781)
Shay's Rebellion (1786–1787)

PEOPLE/GROUPS
John Adams • Samuel Adams • Crispus Attucks • Benjamin Franklin • Patrick Henry
Thomas Jefferson • John Locke • Baron Montesquieu • Jean-Jacques Rousseau • Voltaire
George Washington • Patriots • Tories

OBJECTIVES

- To explain the influence of the Enlightenment on U.S. political rights and institutions.
- To describe the experiences of various groups in the American colonies.
- To explain events leading up to the American Revolution.
- To evaluate the Declaration of Independence.
- To describe the strengths and weaknesses of the Articles of Confederation.

Historical Foundations of Representative Government

In a **democracy**, the people govern themselves. In a form of democracy called a **republic**, people elect representatives to make and carry out laws that benefit them. The philosophers of the Enlightenment, as well as events in Britain and its American colonies, influenced the development of U.S. representative democracy.

European Philosophers of the Enlightenment

During the Age of Enlightenment (1600s and 1700s), the leading thinkers in Western Europe thought that society should be ruled by natural laws rather than the divine right of absolute monarchs.

- *John Locke* (1632–1704), an English philosopher, wrote *Two Treatises of Government* (1690). He stated that life, liberty, and property were **natural rights** that all persons are born with. A government should protect these natural rights. The people have a right to overthrow a ruler who fails to do so. Locke's ideas influenced the American Founding Father Thomas Jefferson. When he wrote the *Declaration of Independence* (1776), he claimed that all people have the right to "life, liberty, and the pursuit of happiness."
- *Baron Montesquieu* (1689–1755), a French philosopher, wrote *The Spirit of Laws* (1748). In it, he argued that government should be separated into three branches: a legislative branch to pass laws, an executive branch to carry out laws, and a judicial branch to interpret laws. Such separation would prevent a person or group from gaining total control of the government. Montesquieu's ideas are the basis of the *U.S. Constitution.*
- *Voltaire* (1694–1778), a French writer, wrote essays, plays, and letters that attacked the French monarchy, class privileges, torture, slavery, censorship, and religious intolerance. Voltaire argued that the best form of government is a monarchy with a constitution, a strong parliament, and civil rights for all—an idea based on the British monarchy. Many characteristics of British government were incorporated in the U.S. form of democracy.
- *Jean-Jacques Rousseau* (1712–1778), a Swiss-born philosopher, wrote *The Social Contract,* in which he stated that the will of the people should guide the decisions of government. He felt that people are born good but corrupted by society. Rousseau's ideas had a profound influence on the writers of the U.S. Constitution.

Key English Limitations on Government

Over the centuries, English kings lost some of their power.

- *Magna Carta.* In 1215, a group of nobles compelled England's King John to sign the *Magna Carta.* This document guaranteed (a) trial by a jury of the accused's equals and (b) the right of the Grand Council (a group of nobles) to approve a monarch's proposed taxes.

- *Parliament.* In 1295, King Edward I called on representatives of both the English nobility and the middle class to meet as a **parliament** (advisory group) to consider laws and taxes. Parliament became a check on the monarch's power to make laws and impose taxes. In 1679, Parliament passed the *Habeas Corpus Act* to protect people against unjust imprisonment. It required a judge to rule whether a person should be held in jail.
- *Glorious Revolution.* In 1688, Parliament forced King James II to give up his throne to King William and Queen Mary. The *English Bill of Rights* (1689) then guaranteed such benefits as the right to a speedy jury trial, protection against excessive **bails** (money to obtain release pending trial) and fines, and Parliament's consent for collecting taxes, suspending laws, and keeping an army.

People in the American Colonies

The three main groups in the American colonies were the Native Americans, the Africans, and the European immigrants.

Native Americans

Origins Native Americans are descendants of Asian peoples who probably migrated from Siberia to North America between 40,000 and 20,000 years ago.

Contact With Spaniards The first contact between Native Americans and Spaniards occurred mainly in Spanish America during and after the voyages of Christopher Columbus in the 1490s. Spain gradually colonized much of the Native-Americans' lands. The colonists forced Native Americans to work in mines, on **plantations** (large farms with many workers), and in Roman Catholic **missions**. Harsh treatment and European diseases killed off large numbers of Native Americans.

Contact With the British The first long-term contact between the British and Native Americans occurred in Jamestown, Virginia, in the early 1600s. Many colonists starved to death during the winter of 1609–1610, but some survived on corn provided by Native Americans. One English leader, John Rolfe, learned how Native Americans grew tobacco. The export of tobacco to England improved conditions in Jamestown. As the colonists sought more land, conflicts arose with Native Americans. Rolfe won a short period of peace when he married a Native-American princess, Pocahontas. But war erupted when the colonists continued to take over Native-American land.

Much farther north, Native Americans also helped the English Pilgrims, a religious community, survive their first, harsh New England winter. In time, however, the Pilgrims also aroused Native-American anger by expanding into their territory. The colonists, aided by firearms, easily defeated the Native Americans in battle. Moreover, smallpox brought from Europe wiped out entire Native-American villages.

When the Quakers, another religious group, settled in Pennsylvania, their leader, William Penn, set a policy of living peaceably with the Delaware Indians of the region.

French and Indian War Between 1754 and 1763, Great Britain and France fought for control of North America in the French and Indian War. Both countries arranged alliances with Native-American groups. The British were allied with the Iroquois nation; the French, with the Hurons. The British victory gained them control of much of North America, including Canada.

Africans

Enslaved Africans were taken to the British colonies in America against their will. They had labored in Spanish America as early as the 1500s as replacements for Native Americans who had died from disease and overwork.

Global Slave Trade, 1700s

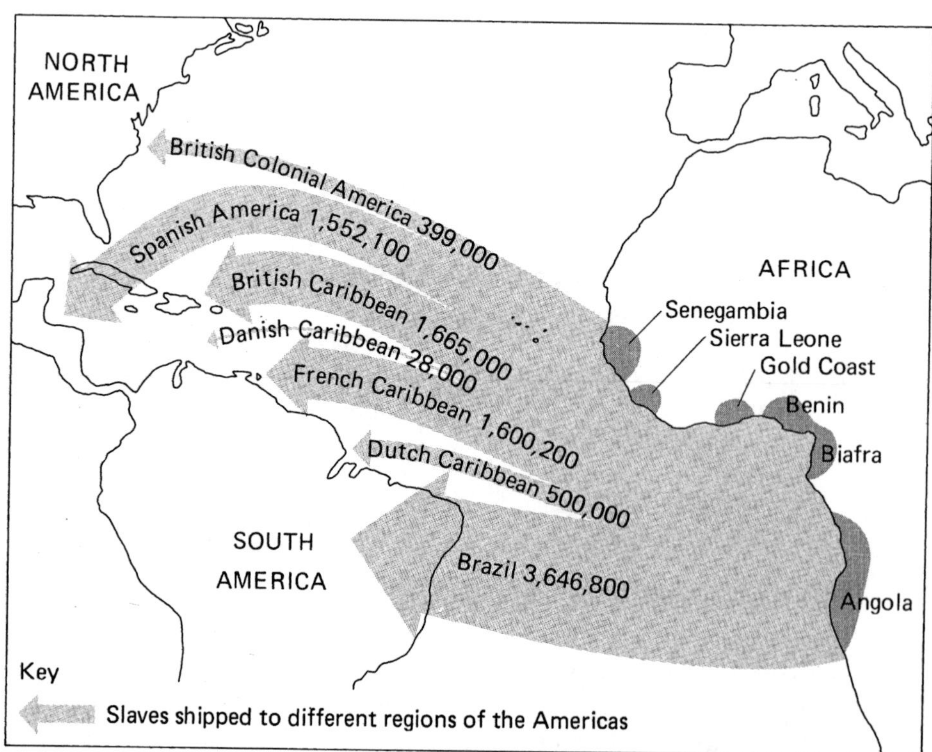

The Africans sold to the British colonists in North America represented about 6 percent of the total number shipped to the Americas from Africa. The first enslaved Africans in the British colonies arrived in Jamestown, Virginia, in 1619. By the time of the American Revolution, African Americans in the original 13 states made up about 20 percent of the population.

European Immigrants

A majority of immigrants to the British colonies from 1607 to 1776 came from the British Isles. The Puritans came to escape religious persecution in England. The Quakers sought religious freedom in Pennsylvania under the leadership of William Penn. James Oglethorpe helped criminals, debtors, and the poor seeking new economic opportunities to settle Georgia. Some immigrants came as **indentured servants**, people who agreed to work for a number of years in return for their passage to America.

Non-British immigrants came chiefly from France, Germany, Holland, and Sweden.

Difficulties for Immigrants European immigrants experienced many difficulties:

- separation from family, friends, and familiar surroundings
- city dwellers learning to farm
- diseases
- attacks from Native Americans
- dependence on supplies shipped from England.

Ethnic Groups in the United States, 1790

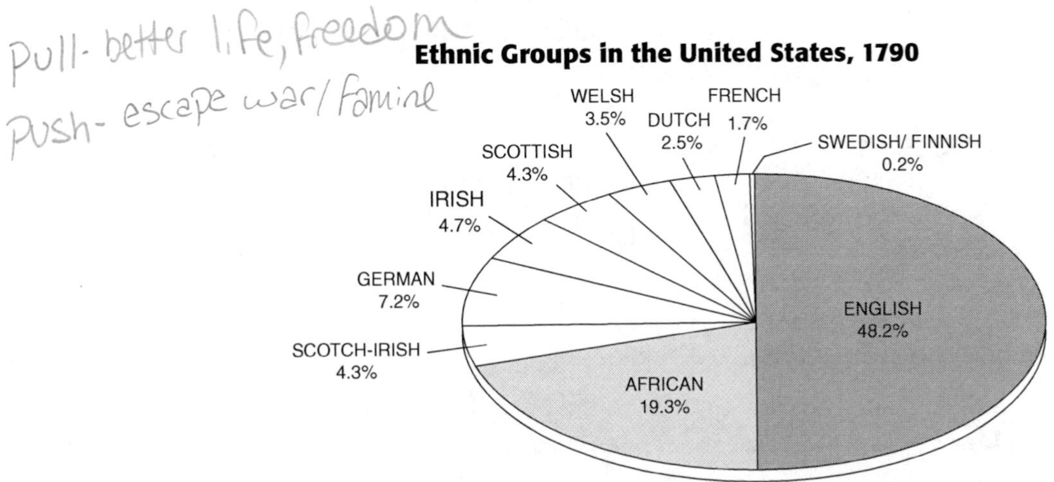

Which was the largest ethnic group in 1790?

IN REVIEW

1. How did the Enlightenment influence the development of the United States?
2. Describe *three* important events in British history that limited the power of government.
3. Contrast the experiences of Native Americans, Africans, and European immigrants in colonial America.

Colonial Experience

The experiences of British colonists in America involved different forms of government, different economic systems, and different cultures.

Charters and Self-Government

House of Burgesses/Mayflower Compact In 1619, the settlers of Jamestown, Virginia, founded the *House of Burgesses,* America's first representative assembly for making laws. In 1620, the Pilgrims drew up the *Mayflower Compact.* It stated that the laws of Plymouth, Massachusetts, would be subject to the colonists' consent. Subsequently, New England townspeople regularly held **town meetings** to discuss problems and to vote directly on laws.

Although English monarchs appointed governors for the colonies founded during the next 150 years, popularly elected assemblies made most of the colonies' laws. By 1760, colonial assemblies enjoyed the **power of the purse**—the right to approve or reject new tax proposals.

Colonial democracy was limited. Only property-owning males had the right to vote. Women, slaves, and free males without property could not vote.

Albany Plan of Union In 1754, representatives from Britain, from seven of the colonies, and from the Iroquois nation met in Albany to discuss a plan of defense against France. Benjamin Franklin, the representative from Pennsylvania, proposed the *Albany Plan of Union.* It was based on the *Iroquois Confederacy,* in which six Native-American peoples had united for mutual defense. The Albany Plan of Union aimed to bring colonial representatives together in a council led by a representative of the British crown, but it was rejected.

Business and Property Laws

Colonial land was privately owned and purchased through legally binding contracts. The monarch gave **joint-stock companies** exclusive rights to trade in specific areas of the colonies. People invested in these businesses in hopes of making a profit.

Under a system called **mercantilism**, colonies were expected to produce crops and sell only to England and to buy everything else they needed from England. England did not enforce this policy until the 1760s.

Franklin's 1754 cartoon advocating colonial union

Native-American Governments

At first, Native Americans were loyal to their village or clan. In time, however, several villages formed tribal councils to better defend themselves. Loyalty to the tribe rather than to the village increased. Warriors became the most important members of a tribe.

In colonial New York, the six nations of the Iroquois Confederacy had prompted the Albany Plan for Union and may have influenced the plan of government created by the Articles of Confederation, adopted in 1781 (discussed on pages 14–15).

Slavery

The South Slavery in the United States first developed in Chesapeake, an area that included both Virginia and Maryland. As demand for the region's major crop—tobacco—grew, so did the demand for slaves. The economies of South Carolina and Georgia depended on the production of rice. As rice exports to Europe grew from approximately 15,000 pounds in 1700 to 80 million pounds in the 1770s, both colonies became reliant on slave labor.

Slavery also developed in the French territory of Louisiana. Enslaved Africans worked on rural rice and tobacco plantations and in such cities as New Orleans as crafts workers and domestic servants.

The North The North had few large agricultural enterprises except farms that produced wheat and **provisioning plantations** that produced food and lumber for sugar plantations in the West Indies. Both kinds of spreads used some slave labor. In Northern cities, slaves served as laborers and skilled artisans. Because the slavery system was less advantageous to the Northern economy, it never became as important as in the South.

African Culture

Among other things, Africans introduced the following to the Americas:

- music with "call-and-response" features
- wood carvings, folk medicines, and charms
- mixture of Christianity and **animism**, the African belief in nature spirits

- African names
- slave houses modeled after West African houses
- pottery similar to that found in Nigeria and Ghana.

Slavery and Democracy During the American Revolution, opponents of the rebellion noted that the revolutionaries demanded their own freedom while denying it to others. Between the end of the Revolution in 1783 and 1800, slavery was made illegal and ended in the Northern states. At the same time, it expanded in the South. There, plantation owners expanded the enslaved labor force as cotton production grew more profitable and increased, largely due to the invention of the cotton gin in 1793.

Freedom of the Press

The *Zenger case* expanded colonial rights. When John Peter Zenger published an article criticizing the governor of New York, he was arrested in 1734 for **libel** (writing a false and unfavorable opinion about another person). At his trial in 1735, Zenger's lawyer argued that the article was true. The jury agreed and declared him innocent of libel. This ruling established the principle of freedom of the press, an important part of the First Amendment to the U.S. Constitution.

Rights of English Citizens

Prior to the French and Indian War, Britain had practiced **salutary neglect** in its colonies. That is, it usually allowed the colonists to govern

Growth of African Colonial Population, 1700s

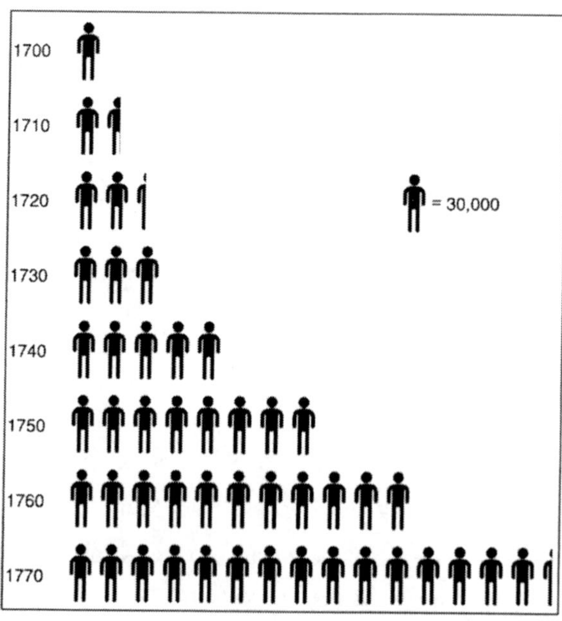

themselves, did not enforce laws requiring the colonies to trade only with England, did not collect taxes, and allowed the establishment of popular assemblies. It did not, however, allow colonists to elect representatives to Britain's Parliament.

American Revolution

Great Britain won the French and Indian War (1754–1763) and gained control of French Canada. This victory would lead the 13 American colonies to revolt against Britain.

Causes

Change in Colonial Policy The French and Indian War put Britain in debt just when it needed money and greater political control to maintain its expanded empire. The government decided to enforce its trade laws, station a permanent military force in the colonies, and collect new taxes there.

Closing of the Frontier The growing movement of colonists west of the Appalachian Mountains provoked Native Americans into attacking new

American Colonies, 1763 and 1774

settlements and British forts in the region. Britain's *Proclamation of 1763* forbade such Western settlements and even visits there by colonists without permission. Colonists, eager for new land and opportunities in the West, were furious. (See the map on the previous page.)

Resistance to British Taxation Parliament taxed the colonies without their assemblies' consent. The colonists protested against (1) the *Stamp Tax* (1765) on colonial newspapers and legal documents and (2) import taxes (1767) on tea, glass, and other articles from Britain. Resistance took the form of **boycotts** (refusal to buy British goods), riots against tax collectors, and the *Boston Tea Party* (dumping British tea into Boston Harbor in 1773).

British Retaliation The British soon retaliated. In the *Boston Massacre* (1770), British troops fired on a crowd and killed five colonists, including an African American named Crispus Attucks. As punishment for the Boston Tea Party, the *Coercive Acts* or Intolerable Acts (1774) closed Boston Harbor to shipping.

First Battles: Lexington and Concord On April 19, 1775, British troops marched into Lexington, Massachusetts, and fired upon a small band of armed Americans. The British moved on to nearby Concord, where farmers, firing from behind trees and stone walls, drove back the British, who retreated to Boston.

Boston Massacre, 1770, as depicted by Paul Revere

Revolutionary Ideology

In the earliest stages of the war, most Americans wanted only to defend their rights, not to gain independence. *Common Sense* (1776), a pamphlet by Thomas Paine, however, changed the minds of many. Paine wrote that it made no sense for a small island kingdom like Great Britain to rule over the vastly larger American lands at a great distance.

On two occasions, delegates met in Philadelphia to plan a defense of their rights. This body of delegates, known as the *Continental Congress*, served as the governing body for the American revolutionaries. The *First Continental Congress* (1774) unsuccessfully petitioned the British government to repeal its taxes and other harsh measures. In 1776, the year after the British and Americans had clashed at Lexington and Concord and at Bunker Hill outside Boston (1775), the *Second Continental Congress* declared the independence of a new nation, the United States.

General Arguments for Independence Drawing on the theories of John Locke, Thomas Jefferson drafted the Declaration of Independence. In it, he stated that governments must be (1) representative of the people and (2) limited in power by a recognition of basic human rights. If any government violates people's natural rights, then they have the right to "alter or to abolish" that government.

Specific Arguments for Independence Specific grievances against the British king demonstrated that the colonists' rights had been repeatedly violated. These grievances included (1) dissolving colonial assemblies, (2) stationing British troops in the colonies, and (3) "imposing taxes without [the colonists'] consent."

THE DECLARATION OF INDEPENDENCE

...That whenever any form of government becomes destructive of these ends, it is the right of the people to alter or to abolish it, and to institute new government, laying its foundation on such principles and organizing its powers in such form as to them shall seem most likely to effect their safety and happiness. Prudence, indeed, will dictate that governments long established should not be changed for light and transient causes; and, accordingly, all experience hath shown that mankind are more disposed to suffer, while evils are sufferable, than to right themselves by abolishing the forms to which they are accustomed. But when a long train of abuses and usurpations, pursuing invariably the same object, evinces a design to reduce them under absolute despotism, it is their right, it is their duty, to throw off such government, and to provide new guards for their future security.

Continuing Importance of the Declaration People in many nations have used the Declaration to justify their own struggles against oppressive governments. Since it states that all men are created equal, the Declaration would serve as an important document in the fight to end slavery in the United States.

Revolutionary Leaders

Among the *Patriots* (those colonists who favored separation from Britain) were these born leaders:

- *Benjamin Franklin* assisted in writing of the Declaration of Independence and represented the Continental Congress in France during the Revolutionary War. He helped set up a republican form of government in the United States.
- *George Washington* commanded the Continental Army. He was elected the first president of the United States and served for two terms.
- *Samuel Adams* organized a boycott of British goods. He set up the *Committee of Correspondence* by which colonists shared their opinions and activities with one another. He served as a Massachusetts delegate to the Second Continental Congress.
- *John Adams* served as a Massachusetts delegate to the First Continental Congress and argued against Britain's right to tax the colonies. He served with Thomas Jefferson on the committee that wrote the Declaration of Independence. He was elected second president of the United States.
- *Patrick Henry* was a Virginia delegate to the First and Second Continental Congresses. His speeches urging independence influenced many colonists to support revolution.

War for Independence

Early Defeats At first, Washington's troops, disorganized and untrained, suffered many defeats. By the end of 1776, British troops had occupied Boston and New York. The American capital, Philadelphia, fell to the British the following year. Some of the *Tories* (those colonists who opposed independence) aided the British troops.

Turning Points: Trenton and Saratoga American hopes were failing when Washington launched a successful surprise attack on Trenton, New Jersey, on Christmas Night, 1776. A decisive American victory at Saratoga, New York, in October 1777 against British General John Burgoyne convinced France to give the Americans military and naval assistance. This news helped the needy Continental Army survive the severe winter of 1777–1778 at Valley Forge, Pennsylvania.

United States in 1783

Victory at Yorktown Aided by French troops and ships, Washington's army defeated Britain's commanding general, Lord Cornwallis, at Yorktown, Virginia (1781). Two years later in Paris, American and British delegates signed a peace treaty ending the war. In it, Great Britain recognized the United States as an independent nation. The western border of the new nation was to be the Mississippi River.

Contributions of African Americans Approximately 5,000 free and enslaved African Americans fought against Britain in the Revolutionary War. After Britain offered freedom to any slaves who fought the colonists, the revolutionists made the same promise to slaves who fought with them. Thus, African Americans fought on both sides. After the war, some ex-slaves who had fought for the British emigrated to the West Indies or England.

IN REVIEW

1. How did political developments during the colonial period increase the rights of colonists?
2. Explain how slavery influenced the economies of the Southern colonies.
3. Identify *three* acts of Parliament that led to protests in the American colonies.

4. Discuss the ways the Declaration of Independence expressed ideas of representative government and limited government.

Early U.S. Government

After 1776, both the country as a whole and the states were experimenting with new governments.

State Constitutional Governments

During the Revolutionary War, all 13 former colonies declared themselves states and wrote **constitutions** (written plans of government). These documents provided that final authority rested with the people.

New York State Constitution The *New York State Constitution* (1777) exemplified other state constitutions. It provided for a **bicameral** (two-house) legislative branch, an executive branch, a judicial branch, and a bill of rights. The bill of rights was to guarantee freedom of religion and many of the rights found in the English Bill of Rights (discussed on page 3). Such republican principles were later incorporated in the U.S. Constitution.

Abolition of Slavery in the North In 1799, New York passed an act designed to gradually achieve **abolition** of slavery. This law freed future-born males at age 28 and future-born females at age 25. By 1800, all the Northern states had passed laws to end slavery. By 1810, most African Americans in the North were free citizens.

Articles of Confederation

During and after the Revolution, delegates from the 13 states to the Continental Congress drew up the *Articles of Confederation*. This document, describing the new government's official powers, was approved by the states in 1781:

- *Organization.* The one-house lawmaking body was the Continental Congress. There was no executive branch to enforce the laws or national court system to interpret them. Each state delegation could cast one vote on each issue.
- *Powers.* Congress could declare war, make peace, and conduct foreign affairs.
- *Achievements.* Congress under the Articles brought the Revolutionary War to a successful end. It passed the *Northwest Ordinance* (1787), a workable plan for governing the territories between the Appalachian

Mountains and the Mississippi River: The ordinance also prohibited slavery there and set up rules for forming new states.

- *Weaknesses.* Since Congress could not impose taxes, it relied on money donated by the states to pay expenses. Laws had to be approved by a two-thirds majority of the states. Congress could not regulate commerce between the states. It issued paper currency that would become nearly worthless. Unanimous agreement by the states was necessary to change the Articles.

In the 1780s, economic and political troubles exposed the inadequacy of a weak central government. An alarming example was *Shay's Rebellion* (1786–1787), a violent protest by Massachusetts farmers against the collection of a state tax.

IN REVIEW

1. What features from state constitutions were incorporated into the U.S. Constitution?
2. Describe how the national government was organized under the Articles of Confederation.
3. Summarize why state governments were stronger than the national government under the Articles of Confederation.

CHAPTER REVIEW

MULTIPLE-CHOICE QUESTIONS

1 In writing the *Declaration of Independence*, Thomas Jefferson was influenced most by John Locke's idea of
(1) due process of law
(2) natural rights
(3) the rights of the accused
(4) the right to privacy

2 "No freeman shall be . . . imprisoned . . . or in any way harmed . . . except by the lawful judgment of his peers. . . ."
—MAGNA CARTA, 1215

This statement is the basis for the democratic principle of the right to
(1) trial by jury
(2) freedom from cruel and unusual punishment
(3) freedom from double jeopardy
(4) protection against self-incrimination

3 The Mayflower Compact, New England town meetings, and the Virginia House of Burgesses are examples of
(1) early colonial efforts in self-government
(2) colonial protests against British taxation
(3) governments imposed by Parliament
(4) attempts to limit democracy

Base your answer to question 4 on the following map and on your knowledge of social studies.

Slavery in the Colonies, 1775

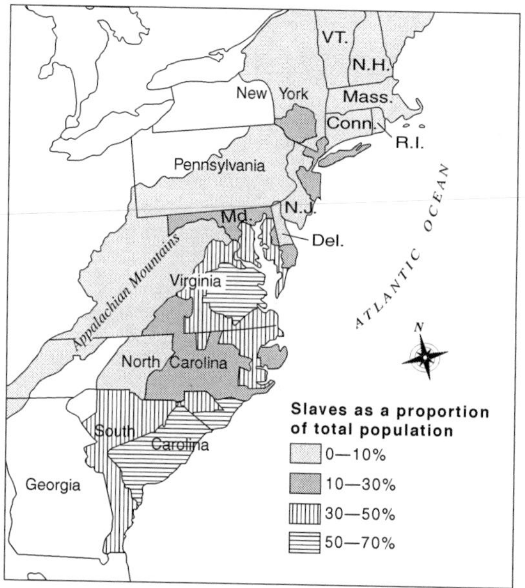

4 A conclusion supported by the information on the map is that slavery in the American colonies was
   (1) declining by the start of the Revolutionary War
   (2) concentrated in areas suitable for large plantations
   (3) becoming illegal in the Northern colonies
   (4) growing fastest in the New England colonies

5 In its economic relationship with its North American colonies, Great Britain followed the principles of 18th-century mercantilism by
   (1) outlawing the African slave trade
   (2) limiting the colonies' trade with other nations
   (3) encouraging the development of manufacturing in the colonies
   (4) establishing laws against business monopolies

6 The main reason Great Britain established the Proclamation Line in 1763 was to
   (1) avoid conflicts between American colonists and Native American Indians
   (2) make a profit by selling the land west of the Appalachian Mountains
   (3) prevent American industrial development in the Ohio River valley
   (4) allow Canada to control the Great Lakes region

Base your answer to question 7 on the time line below and on your knowledge of social studies.

7 Which title is most accurate for this time line?
   (1) Forms of Colonial Protest
   (2) Effects of British Navigation Laws
   (3) Causes of the American Revolution
   (4) Abuse of Power by Colonial Legislatures

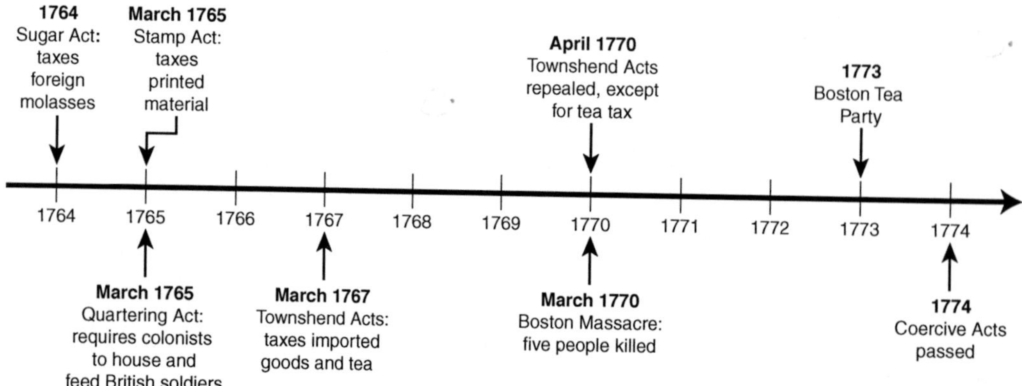

8 During the Revolutionary War period, Thomas Paine's *Common Sense* was important because it
(1) described a military plan for the defeat of England
(2) convinced many Americans who had been undecided to support independence
(3) contained a detailed outline for a new form of government
(4) argued for the addition of a bill of rights to the Constitution

9 Which principle of government is proposed in the Declaration of Independence?
(1) Political power originates with a strong central government.
(2) The primary function of government is to protect natural rights.
(3) A system of checks and balances is the most effective way to prevent governmental abuse of power.
(4) Individual liberties must be guaranteed by a strong bill of rights.

10 A major weakness of government under the Articles of Confederation was that
(1) the large states received more votes in Congress than the small states did
(2) the national government could not enforce its laws
(3) too much power was given to the president
(4) state governments could not coin money

THEMATIC ESSAYS

1 **Theme:** *Colonial Democracy and Self-Government.* The 13 American colonies established traditions of democracy and self-government before the Declaration of Independence was written.

Task: Describe the extent to which there was democracy and/or self-government in colonial America prior to 1776.

You may use any example from your study of American history and government. Some suggestions include the Mayflower Compact, the House of Burgesses, New England town meetings, and the Zenger trial.

2 **Theme:** *Immigration to Colonial America.* People came for a variety of reasons:

- to improve their economic opportunities
- to find political or religious freedom
- because they had no choice.

Task: Choose *two* of the above reasons for immigration. For each, name the group and describe why they left their home country.

DOCUMENT-BASED QUESTION

Read each document and answer the question that follows it. Then read the **Task** and write your essay. Include references to most of the documents and additional information you retain about U.S. history and government.

Historical Context: By the 1760s and 1770s, a number of events and the colonial tradition of self-government had led to a debate about independence from Britain.

Document 1: From John Locke, *Second Treatise of Government* (1690):

> Whenever the legislators endeavor to take away and destroy the property of the people, or to reduce them to slavery... they put themselves into a state of war with the people, who are thereupon absolved from any further obedience and are left to the common refuge which God hath provided for all men against violence.

Question: How does Locke feel that rulers should be treated when they disregard people's rights?

can be subject to being overthrown

DOCUMENT 2: From Thomas Paine, *Common Sense* (1776):

> Small islands not capable of protecting themselves are the proper objects for kingdoms to take under their care; but there is something very absurd in supposing a continent to be perpetually governed by an island. In no instance hath nature made the satellite larger than its primary planet; and as England and America, with respect to each other, reverse the common order of nature, it is evident that they belong to different systems. England to Europe: America to itself.

QUESTION: Why does Paine feel that the colonies should declare independence?

GB shouldn't govern a huge continent

DOCUMENT 3: From Lord Mansfield, debate in the House of Lords, 1766, on repealing the Stamp Act:

> It must be granted that they migrated with leave [permission] as colonies and therefore from the very meaning of the word were, are, and must be subjects, and owe allegiance and subjection to their mother country [England].

QUESTION: How does Lord Mansfield feel about the relationship between colonies and the "mother country"?

TASK: Using the documents and your knowledge of causes of the American Revolution, write an essay about whether the American Revolution was inevitable.

You are debted to England

CHAPTER 2
The Constitution and Bill of Rights

DOCUMENTS AND LAWS
Great Compromise, or the Connecticut Plan (1787) • New Jersey Plan (1787)
Virginia Plan (1787) • *The Federalist* (1787–1788) • Bill of Rights (1791)
Amendments 11 to 27 (1798–1992) • *Schenck* v. *United States* (1919)
Mapp v. *Ohio* (1961) • *Engel* v. *Vitale* (1962) • *Gideon* v. *Wainwright* (1963)
School District of Abington Township v. *Schempp* (1963) • *Escobedo* v. *Illinois* (1964)
Miranda v. *Arizona* (1966) • *Katz* v. *United States* (1967)
Tinker v. *Des Moines School District* (1969) • *Furman* v. *Georgia* (1972)
Gregg v. *Georgia* (1976) • *Collin* v. *Smith* (1978) • *Texas* v. *Johnson* (1989)

EVENTS
Constitutional Convention (1787)

PEOPLE/GROUPS
Samuel Adams • Alexander Hamilton • Federalists • Anti-Federalists • Patrick Henry
Oliver Wendell Holmes • John Jay • James Madison • Earl Warren • George Washington

OBJECTIVES

- To identify and understand the importance of key clauses in the Constitution.
- To define and illustrate basic principles of the U.S. Constitution—federalism, separation of powers, checks and balances.
- To know the main provisions of the U.S. Bill of Rights.
- To evaluate selected landmark cases of the Supreme Court.
- To understand that the Constitution is a living document that has changed over time.

Constitutional Convention

Delegates from every state except Rhode Island went to Philadelphia in the summer of 1787 to amend the Articles of Confederation. Among them were Benjamin Franklin, James Madison, and Alexander Hamilton. The Constitutional Convention was headed by George Washington.

James Madison framed a new plan of government, and he and other Virginia delegates persuaded the Convention to replace the Articles with this new constitution. The delegates took the document back to their states for **ratification** (approval).

Conflict and Compromise

The delegates to the Convention disagreed sharply on three issues:

Representation Virginia drew up a plan by which the number of a state's representatives in Congress was proportional to its population. New Jersey's plan called for the same number of representatives per state. The larger states favored the Virginia Plan; the smaller ones, the New Jersey Plan.

Slavery Many Southern delegates owned slaves. They proposed that slaves be counted for purposes of representation but not for taxes. Northern delegates wanted just the opposite. Moreover, most Northerners wanted to end the slave trade. Southerners, fearing that this action could end slavery, opposed this proposal.

Trade Since the South relied heavily on imported goods from Britain, Southern delegates were against taxing foreign commerce. Since some Northerners manufactured goods that competed with imports, Northern delegates favored taxing foreign goods. Since the South shipped large quantities of cotton and tobacco to Britain, Southern delegates opposed a tax on exports.

Compromises

The delegates would have never agreed to a new constitution without some key compromises.

Great Compromise, or Connecticut Plan Congress was to have two houses. In the House of Representatives, states would be represented in proportion to their populations. In the Senate, all states would be represented equally.

Compromises on Slavery

This controversial subject was resolved in the following manner:

- Three-fifths of a state's slaves would be counted for purposes of both taxation and representation.
- Congress could not end the slave trade for 20 years, until 1808.
- The tax on imported slaves could not exceed $10 a person.

Compromise on Trade Congress was given the power to tax imports but not exports.

Main Parts of the Constitution

The Constitution consists of the *Preamble*, a main body of seven articles, the Bill of Rights, and 17 other amendments adopted at later intervals.

Signers of the Constitution, Philadelphia, 1787

Preamble

The Preamble asserts that the new U.S. government was established by "we the people" (the entire nation) rather than by the individual states. It also identifies the following goals:

> We the people of the United States of America, in order to form a more perfect Union, establish justice, insure domestic tranquility, provide for the common defense, promote the general welfare, and secure the blessings of liberty to ourselves and our posterity, do ordain and establish this Constitution of the United States of America.

Three Branches

Articles I, II, and III establish the **separation of powers** by dividing the powers of government among three branches—legislative, executive, and judicial.

Legislative Branch Article I describes the legislative, or lawmaking, branch—the U.S. Congress. It consists of two groups: the House of Representatives and the Senate. Besides listing the laws that Congress may make, this article describes (1) methods for electing members of each house, (2) qualifications for running for office, (3) terms of office in the House and Senate, and (4) lawmaking procedures.

Executive Branch Article II concerns the executive, or law-enforcing branch. It describes (1) powers of the **chief executive**, or president, (2) the term limit (four years), (3) the method for electing the president and vice president, and (4) the method for removing the president by **impeachment** (accusation of wrongdoing) and trial. It says little about the responsibilities of the vice president.

Judicial Branch Article III describes the federal court system of "inferior" courts (lower courts) and a Supreme Court that interprets the laws in specific cases.

The article describes (1) the term of office for federal judges (life) and (2) Congress's power to establish new courts. Each court is assigned its **jurisdiction** (area of authority). Some cases are to go directly to the Supreme Court (the highest court), and some are to be heard first by lower federal courts.

Other Provisions

Interstate Relations Article IV describes relations among states and their obligations to one another. A person charged with breaking the laws of one state and fleeing to another is subject to **extradition** (return) to the original state. The article also describes (1) how U.S. territories may become states and (2) the government's responsibility for protecting states from invasion and "domestic violence" (rioting).

Amendment Process Article V describes ways to amend the Constitution (discussed on page 49).

Supreme Law The **supremacy clause** in Article VI states that "the Constitution and the laws of the United States . . . shall be the supreme law of the land." Historic decisions of the Supreme Court making federal laws supreme over state laws were based on this clause.

Ratification Article VII describes how the Constitution was to be submitted to the states in 1787 for ratification.

Debate on Ratification

The Constitution describes government by a **federal system**, one in which political power is divided between a national government and state governments. The *Federalists* favored the ratification of the Constitution and the federal system, while the *Anti-Federalists* opposed them.

Federalist Arguments

James Madison, Alexander Hamilton, and John Jay wrote essays called "Federalist Papers," explaining the need to replace the Articles of Confederation with a federal system. These *Federalists* favored ratification of the Constitution, saying that a representative government with powers evenly distributed among three branches would strengthen the nation and protect personal liberties. These "Federalist Papers" were published as a book entitled *The Federalist.*

THE FEDERALIST. 217

Nothing remains but the landed intereſt; and this in a political view, and particularly in relation to taxes I take to be perfectly united from the wealthieſt landlord to the pooreſt tenant. No tax can be laid on land which will not affect the propietor of millions of acres as well as the proprietor of a ſingle acre. Every land-holder will therefore have a common intereſt to keep the taxes on land as low as poſſible; and common intereſt may always be reckoned upon as the ſureſt bond of ſympathy. But if we even could ſuppoſe a diſtinction of intereſt between the opulent land-holder and the middling farmer, what reaſon is there to conclude that the firſt would ſtand a better chance of being deputed to the national legiſlature than the laſt? If we take fact as our guide, and look into our own ſenate and aſſembly we ſhall find that moderate proprietors of land prevail in both; nor is this leſs the caſe in the ſenate, which conſiſts of a ſmaller number than in the aſſembly, which is compoſed of a greater number. Where the qualifications of the electors are the ſame, whether they have to chooſe a ſmall or a large number their votes will fall upon thoſe in whom they have moſt confidence; whether theſe happen to be men of large fortunes or of moderate property or of no property at all.

It is ſaid to be neceſſary that all claſſes of citizens ſhould have ſome of their own number in the repreſen-

Page from Jefferson's copy of *The Federalist*

Anti-Federalist Arguments

Anti-Federalists Patrick Henry and Samuel Adams feared that the central government under the Constitution might not respect people's liberties or the rights of states. They opposed ratification of the Constitution, saying that it lacked a bill of rights.

Federalist Victory

Each state called a convention to vote for or against the Constitution. Large majorities in Delaware, Pennsylvania, and New Jersey voted for the Constitution. In Massachusetts and Virginia, the delegates were opposed unless it included a bill of rights. New York voted to ratify by the slim majority of 30 to 27. Ratification by the required nine states was accomplished in June 1788.

Strengths and Weaknesses of the Constitution

Strengths Some constitutional scholars cite the following features of the Constitution as its strengths:

- The Constitution is flexible enough to allow for changes required by new generations but still merits respect for its traditional values and principles.
- The Preamble states that the Constitution is a document of the people, not of the states.
- Separation of powers and checks and balances prevent one branch of government from gaining absolute power (see below).

Weaknesses The original Constitution needed amendments to guarantee individual liberties and omissions with regard to equality:

- Without a bill of rights, the federal government could abuse its power and deny personal freedoms.
- Women were denied equality—the right to vote, hold property in their own names, and act as legal guardians of their children.
- The Constitution failed to abolish slavery.
- In some states, white males (the only group allowed to vote) had to meet property qualifications for voting.
- Several amendments were needed to extend voting rights to all groups of adult age.

Checks and Balances in the Federal Government

The president acts . . .

The president acts . . .	Another branch checks . . .
1 Makes a treaty with a foreign government.	The Senate rejects the treaty (fails to ratify it by a two-thirds vote).
2 Commits certain "crimes and misdemeanors."	The House impeaches the president; the Senate votes to remove the president from office.
3 Vetoes an act of Congress.	Congress overrides the veto by a two-thirds vote of each house.
4 Makes an appointment to a Cabinet post.	The Senate rejects the president's nominee.

Congress acts . . .

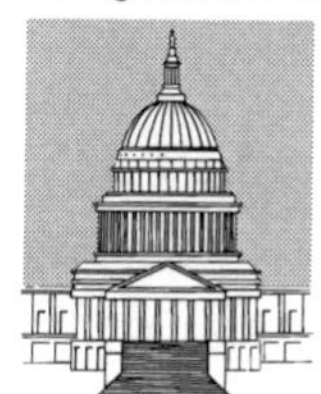

Congress acts . . .	Another branch checks . . .
1 Enacts a bill.	The president vetoes Congress's act.
2 Enacts a bill that is signed by the president.	The Supreme Court declares Congress's act to be unconstitutional.

The Supreme Court acts . . .

The Supreme Court acts . . .	Another branch checks . . .
1 Declares an act of Congress unconstitutional.	Congress proposes a constitutional amendment.
2 Declares an action of the president unconstitutional.	The president appoints a new justice to the Supreme Court (if there is a vacancy).

IN REVIEW

1. Describe *two* conflicts at the Constitutional Convention and the compromise that settled *each* conflict.
2. How did the Preamble give authority to the people rather than the states?
3. Describe the major function of *each* branch of the federal government.

Bill of Rights

A **bill of rights** identifies actions that government may *not* take. Its purpose is to prevent abuses of power and to protect personal liberties. In 1789, soon after the Constitution was adopted, Congress proposed ten amendments known as the U.S. Bill of Rights. They were ratified in 1791. Originally, they protected citizens from the federal government but were later applied to state governments as well.

Main Provisions

Freedom of Religion Congress may not interfere with a person's choice of worship (First Amendment).

Separation of Church and State Congress may not show special support to any church, synagogue, or other religious institution (First Amendment).

Freedom of Speech, Press, Assembly, Petition Congress may not make any law that interferes with the free expression of ideas in speech and writing. Government officials may not stop **peaceful assemblies** (demonstrations). People may not be punished for making **petitions** (requests in writing) seeking a change in government policy (First Amendment).

Right to Keep and Bear Arms Citizens may not be denied the right to carry weapons for use in a **state militia**, or group of volunteer soldiers for the common defense (Second Amendment).

Protection Against Quartering Citizens are not required to house and feed soldiers in times of peace and, in times of war, must do so only as provided by law (Third Amendment).

Searches and Seizures Government officials must obtain a **search warrant** (judge's permission) before searching a suspect's property. The warrant must describe "the place to be searched and the persons or things to be seized." A judge may issue the warrant only when convinced that there is "probable cause" of criminal evidence being found (Fourth Amendment).

Rights of Accused Persons The Fifth and Sixth amendments make the following guarantees for accused persons:

- **Indictments** (accusations) in federal court must be made by a **grand jury**.
- If acquitted by a **petit jury**, accused persons cannot incur **double jeopardy** (being tried again on the same charge).
- They cannot be forced to give testimony or evidence that may be used against them at trial.
- They will have "a speedy and public trial."
- They will be tried by an impartial jury.
- They will be informed of the criminal charges against them.
- They will be represented by a lawyer, and the government will help produce defense witnesses.

Sources of Major Ideas in the Constitution and Bill of Rights

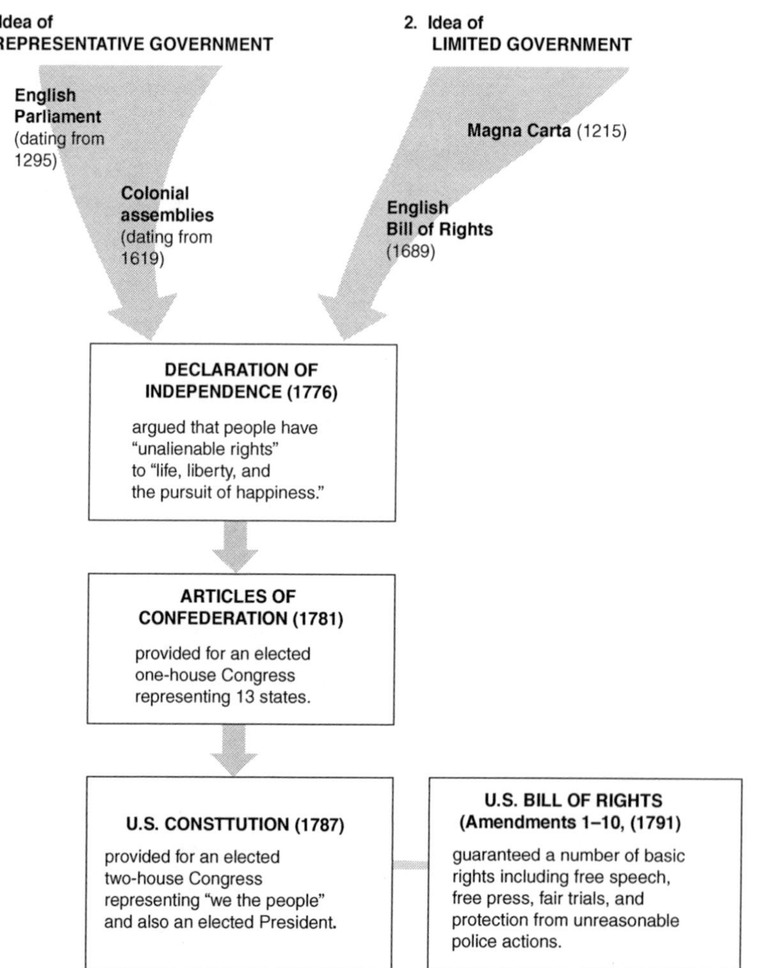

Due Process No person may be deprived of "life, liberty, or property without due process of law" (Fifth Amendment).

Bail and Punishment A person awaiting trial may not be charged excessive bail. A person convicted of a crime may not be punished in "cruel and unusual" ways (Eighth Amendment).

Rights Reserved to the States Powers neither delegated to the federal government nor denied to the states belong to the state governments and to the American people (Tenth Amendment).

Additional Amendments

After the adoption of the Bill of Rights, the Constitution was amended 17 times, from 1798 (Eleventh Amendment) to 1992 (Twenty-seventh Amendment). The most important are as follows:

- The Twelfth Amendment modifies how the president and vice president are elected.
- The Thirteenth Amendment abolishes slavery.
- The Fourteenth Amendment guarantees equal rights of citizenship to all groups. (The next section treats this crucial amendment in more detail.)
- The Fifteenth Amendment guarantees equal voting rights to citizens of all races.
- The Sixteenth Amendment provides for the collection of a federal income tax.
- The Nineteenth Amendment guarantees voting rights for women.
- The Twenty-sixth Amendment guarantees voting rights to people aged 18 or older.

For a summary of all of the amendments, see pages 29–31.

Fourteenth Amendment The first ten amendments protected citizens from abuses of the federal government only. The Fourteenth Amendment was adopted in 1868, after the Civil War. Northerners wanted, in particular, to protect freed slaves against unfair state laws, but the provisions applied to all Americans.

The amendment provides that no state may deny its citizens either "due process of law" (from the Fifth Amendment) or "equal protection of the laws." Often in the 20th century, the Supreme Court used the due process clause to apply the protections of the first ten amendments to state laws.

Interpreting the Bill of Rights

In the 20th century, many of the Supreme Court's **landmark** (most important) **decisions** applied the Bill of Rights to specific situations.

Decisions on First Amendment Rights

The First Amendment guarantees every citizen freedom of religion, freedom of speech, freedom of the press, freedom of assembly, and freedom of petition.

Separation of Church and State The First Amendment states that Congress may "make no law respecting an establishment of religion," that is, to give preference to any religious practice or group.

- In *Engel* v. *Vitale* (1962), the Supreme Court ruled that prayer in public schools violated separation of church and state and was unconstitutional.
- In *School District of Abington Township* [Pennsylvania] v. *Schempp* (1963), the Court ruled against Bible reading in public schools.

Freedom of Speech and the Press Although no one may be penalized for criticizing government officials and policies, under certain circumstances that threaten public safety, free expression of ideas may be limited.

- In *Schenck* v. *United States* (1919), Justice Oliver Wendell Holmes said that speech that presented a "clear and present danger" could be limited. "Free speech would not protect a man falsely shouting fire in a theater and causing a panic," he said.
- In *Tinker* v. *Des Moines School District* (1969), the Court ruled that students could not be penalized for wearing black armbands to school to protest the Vietnam War.
- In the controversial case *Texas* v. *Johnson* (1989), the Court decided that a person who protested by setting fire to an American flag could not be punished by state officials, because flag burning was a form of symbolic speech.

Freedom of Assembly The people have the right to assemble peacefully and petition the government "for a redress of grievances."

- In *Collin* v. *Smith* (1978), the Court ruled that the American Nazi Party had a right to march in Skokie, Illinois, even if this "peaceable assembly" offended other people.

Decisions of the Fourth, Fifth, and Sixth Amendments

In the 1960s, the Supreme Court, under Chief Justice Earl Warren, decided a number of cases that tested the Fourth, Fifth, and Sixth amendments.

Search and Seizure The Fourth Amendment protects citizens against "unreasonable" police searches and seizures of personal property.

- In *Mapp* v. *Ohio* (1961), the Court ruled that evidence obtained without a search warrant may not be admitted into a state court.
- In *Katz* v. *United States* (1967), the Court ruled that wiretapping requires a search warrant, because the Fourth Amendment protects privacy as well as property.

Rights of Accused Persons The Fifth and Sixth amendments protect arrested persons from unfair treatment.

- In *Gideon* v. *Wainwright* (1963), the Court ruled that if an accused person cannot afford a lawyer, the state must provide and pay for one.
- In *Escobedo* v. *Illinois* (1964), the Court ruled that a person questioned at a police station has the right to be represented by a lawyer.
- In *Miranda* v. *Arizona* (1966), the Court ruled that an arrested person must be told of the right to remain silent before police questioning and have an attorney present during such questioning.

"Cruel and Unusual Punishments"

The Eighth Amendment bans "cruel and unusual punishments." Does this ban include the execution of someone found guilty of a violent crime?

- In *Furman* v. *Georgia* (1972), the Court ruled that the death penalty is constitutional only if a state has clear and consistent rules for the execution of people of all races and social classes.
- In *Gregg* v. *Georgia* (1976), the Court ruled that the death penalty is constitutional if imposed solely because of the nature of the crime.

Summary of the 27 Amendments to the U.S. Constitution

Amendment	*Year Adopted*	*Main Provisions*
First	1791	People have freedom of religion, speech, press, assembly, and petition.
Second	1791	People may carry arms for use in a state militia.
Third	1791	People cannot be forced to *quarter* (house and feed) soldiers during times of peace.
Fourth	1791	People are protected against unfair police searches and seizures.
Fifth	1791	The indictment by a federal court of a civilian citizen of the United States must be made by a grand jury. If acquitted, a person cannot be tried again on the same charge (no double jeopardy).

		People cannot be forced to give testimony or evidence that may be used against them at a trial. People cannot be deprived of life, liberty, or property without due process of law. Private property cannot be taken for public use without just compensation.
Sixth	1791	People have the right to a jury trial in criminal cases.
Seventh	1791	People have the right to a jury trial in *civil* (noncriminal) *cases.*
Eighth	1791	Accused persons are protected against excessive bail while awaiting trial. Accused persons are also protected against cruel and unjust punishments.
Ninth	1791	People have rights that are not specified in the Constitution.
Tenth	1791	Powers not delegated to the federal government or denied to the states belong to state governments and to the American people.
Eleventh	1798	Citizens of other states or foreign countries cannot sue a state in federal court without that state's consent.
Twelfth	1804	Electors from each state shall cast two separate ballots—one for president, one for vice president.
Thirteenth	1865	Slavery is abolished in the United States.
Fourteenth	1868	All persons born in the United States are U.S. citizens and entitled to due process of law and equal protection of the laws.
Fifteenth	1870	No government in the United States may prevent citizens from voting because of race.
Sixteenth	1913	Congress has the power to collect income taxes without dividing them among the states according to population.
Seventeenth	1913	The two U.S. senators from each state shall be elected by direct vote of the state's people.
Eighteenth	1919	(Prohibition) Manufacture and sale of intoxicating beverages in the United States is prohibited.
Nineteenth	1920	No government in the United States may prevent citizens from voting because of gender.
Twentieth	1933	("Lame Duck" Amendment) The terms of office of president and vice president end at noon, January 20. The terms of office of members of Congress end at noon, January 3.
Twenty-first	1933	The Eighteenth Amendment is repealed.
Twenty-second	1951	No person may be elected more than twice to the office of president.
Twenty-third	1961	Residents of the District of Columbia may vote for president and vice president by choosing electors, the number (at present, three) to be determined by population.
Twenty-fourth	1964	No government in the United States may collect a poll tax from citizens who want to vote.
Twenty-fifth	1967	If the Cabinet and Congress determine that the president is disabled, the vice president will temporarily assume the duties of president.

Twenty-sixth	1971	No government in the United States may prevent persons age 18 or older from voting on account of age.
Twenty-seventh	1992	No law increasing compensation of Congress may take effect until an election of representatives intervenes.

IN REVIEW

1. Define separation of church and state and due process of law.
2. Explain how the Fourteenth Amendment extended the protections of the Bill of Rights.
3. List *three* landmark Supreme Court cases and describe the right that is protected by *each* case.

CHAPTER REVIEW

MULTIPLE-CHOICE QUESTIONS

1 What was the primary reason for holding the Constitutional Convention of 1787?
(1) outlaw slavery in both the North and the South
(2) place taxes on imports and exports
(3) revise the Articles of Confederation
(4) reduce the power of the federal government

2 The Great Compromise at the Constitutional Convention of 1787 was important because it
(1) established suffrage for all males over the age of twenty-one
(2) ended the controversy over slavery
(3) created a single-house national legislature
(4) balanced the interests of states with large and small populations

3 The purpose of the Three-fifths Compromise, which was adopted by the Constitutional Convention of 1787, was to
(1) balance power between states with large populations and those with smaller populations
(2) provide a means of deciding disputed Presidential elections
(3) allow Congress to override a Presidential veto of an act passed by both Houses
(4) reduce the fear of loss of representation by Southern states with large slave populations

4 "We, the people of the United States, in order to form a more perfect union, establish justice,... and secure the blessings of liberty... do ordain and establish this Constitution for the United States of America."
—PREAMBLE TO THE UNITED STATES CONSTITUTION

This quotation from the Preamble illustrates the constitutional principle that people
(1) have a right to a trial by jury
(2) are guaranteed an adequate standard of living
(3) are the true source of political power
(4) have the right to assemble

5 The term *supreme law of the land* refers to which document?
(1) Fundamental Orders of Connecticut
(2) Constitution of the United States
(3) Articles of Confederation
(4) Declaration of Independence

6 "...it is the opinion of this committee that a national government ought to be established consisting of a Supreme Legislature, Judiciary, and Executive...."

—RESOLUTION SUBMITTED BY EDMUND RANDOLPH, DELEGATE TO THE CONSTITUTIONAL CONVENTION, 1787

In adopting this resolution, the framers of the Constitution showed their belief in the idea of
(1) judicial review
(2) an elastic clause
(3) states' rights
(4) separation of powers

7 The United States Government is considered a federal system because
(1) national laws must be passed by both houses of Congress
(2) powers are divided between the state and national governments
(3) the states are guaranteed a republican form of government
(4) the President is selected by the Electoral College

8 "...Now, one of the most essential branches of English liberty is the freedom of one's house. A man's house is his castle; and whilst he is quiet, he is as well guarded as a prince in his castle...."

—JAMES OTIS, *AGAINST THE WRITS OF ASSISTANCE*, 1761

Which provision in the Bill of Rights includes this same belief?
(1) right to a fair trial
(2) protection against unreasonable search and seizure
(3) guarantee against double jeopardy
(4) prohibition of cruel and unusual punishment

9 In the United States Supreme Court case *Engel* v. *Vitale* (1962), concerning the separation of church and state, the Court banned
(1) state-required student prayer in public schools
(2) the study of religions in public schools
(3) released time for religious instruction for public school students
(4) transportation of students to parochial schools at public expense

10 The United States Supreme Court decision in *Miranda* v. *Arizona* (1966) shows that the Court can
(1) suspend civil liberties in times of national crisis
(2) increase the power of state governments
(3) expand the constitutional rights of individuals
(4) limit the powers of Congress and the President

THEMATIC ESSAYS

1 **THEME:** *Compromise as a Foundation to the U.S. Constitution.* The Constitution would never have been written without compromises by all sides. The nation, therefore, was founded on the give-and-take of debate, discussion, and problem solving.

TASK: Choose *two* areas of disagreement among delegates to the Constitutional Convention. For *each* area of disagreement:
- Describe the disagreement by discussing all sides of the problem.
- Explain how the disagreement was resolved through compromise.

You may use any examples of compromise at the Convention, including representation, slavery, the slave trade, and foreign trade.

2 **THEME:** *Interpreting the Bill of Rights.* The U.S. Supreme Court has ruled in many disputes concerning interpretation of the Bill of Rights. These disputes often involve freedom of speech, separation of church and state, the right to assemble,

freedom from illegal search and seizure, rights of accused persons, and freedom from cruel and unusual punishments.

TASK: Choose *two* of the above issues. For *each*:

- Describe a dispute over the issue.
- Discuss how the Supreme Court interpreted the Bill of Rights in order to resolve each dispute.

You must use *two* different issues and cases in answering the question. You may, however, use any example from your study of the Supreme Court cases in this chapter.

DOCUMENT-BASED QUESTION

Study each document and answer the question that follows it. Then read the **Task** and write your essay. Include references to most of the documents and additional information you retain about U.S. history and government.

HISTORICAL CONTEXT: A "Critical Period" followed the American Revolution. As a result, a new constitution was created to replace the Articles of Confederation.

DOCUMENT 1: Patrick Henry, at a debate in the Virginia Ratifying Convention, June 5, 1788:

> The Confederation . . . carried us through a long and dangerous war; it rendered us victorious in that bloody conflict with a powerful nation; it has secured us a territory greater than any European monarch possesses: and shall a government which has been thus strong and vigorous, be accused of imbecility and want of energy? Consider what you are about to do before you part with the government. . . .

QUESTION: Why does Patrick Henry feel that the Articles should not be replaced?

DOCUMENT 2: From James Madison in *The Federalist*, Number 10, 1787:

> Complaints are everywhere heard . . . that our governments are too unstable. . . . [I]t may be concluded that a pure democracy . . . can admit of no cure for the mischiefs of faction. . . . A republic . . . promises the cure for which we are seeking. . . .
>
> The effect is . . . to refine and enlarge the public views, by passing them through the medium of a chosen body of citizens, whose wisdom may best discern the true interest of their country. . . . On the other hand, men of factious [dissenting] tempers, of local prejudices may . . . betray the interests of the people. . . . The influence of factious leaders may kindle a flame within their particular States, but will be unable to spread a general conflagration [revolution] through the other States.

QUESTION: Why does Madison feel that the new constitution will better serve the people than the Articles?

DOCUMENT 3: Benjamin Franklin on the actions of politicians:

> Few men in public affairs act from a mere view of the good of their country, whatever they may pretend; and though their activity may bring real good to their country, they do not act from a spirit of benevolence.

QUESTION: What dangers does Benjamin Franklin feel exist in any form of government?

TASK: Using the documents and your knowledge of the issues involved in ratifying the U.S. Constitution, write an essay in which you:

- compare and contrast arguments for and against the new constitution
- explain why you favor either the arguments for or against ratification.

CHAPTER 3
The Federal Government and the State Governments

DOCUMENTS AND LAWS
Article I of Constitution (1788) • Article III of Constitution (1788)
Article IV of Constitution (1788) • Federal Judiciary Act (1789) • Election of 1800
Marbury v. *Madison* (1803) • *McCulloch* v. *Maryland* (1819) • *Gibbons* v. *Ogden* (1824)
Election of 1912 • Twenty-second Amendment (1951) • *Baker* v. *Carr* (1962)
Twenty-fifth Amendment (1967)

EVENTS
Great Depression (1929–1942) • World War II (1941–1945)

PEOPLE
Bill Clinton • Dwight D. Eisenhower • Andrew Johnson • Lyndon Johnson • John Kennedy
John Marshall • Richard Nixon • Franklin D. Roosevelt • Theodore Roosevelt • William H. Taft
Harry S. Truman • George Washington • Woodrow Wilson

OBJECTIVES

- To understand how the legislative, executive, and judicial branches of the U.S. government are organized.
- To know how government officials are elected or chosen.
- To evaluate selected landmark cases of the Supreme Court.
- To understand the organization and responsibilities of state and local governments.

Congress

As a bicameral organization, Congress is divided into two houses: the House of Representatives and the Senate. Each house votes separately on all bills.

Number of Seats in Congress

The House is affected by population change, but the Senate is not. Every ten years, a **census** counts the population of the 50 states. In a process called **reapportionment**, a state that has gained population relative to other states might gain seats in the House, and one that has lost population relative to other states might lose seats. The total number of House seats is 435. The total number of Senate seats is 100—two for each state.

Elections to Congress Elections to Congress are held in every even-numbered year. All House members are elected at the same time. One-third of the senators, who serve six years, are elected at one time; the second third are elected two years later; and the final third, two years after that.

Special Powers and Rules of the Senate

Only the Senate gives "advice and consent" to (approval or rejection of) treaties made by the executive branch. Only the Senate votes on whether to accept the president's nominations of key federal officials.

Senators are allowed unlimited debate. A small group may attempt to defeat a bill favored by the majority by a **filibuster**—nonstop speech to delay a vote on the bill and weaken the majority's will to pass it. Sixty votes are needed to end a filibuster.

Powers of Congress

Article I of the Constitution gives Congress power to collect taxes, borrow money, regulate trade, coin money, declare war, raise and support armed forces, and establish a post office.

Elastic Clause The **elastic clause** is the final legislative power in Article 1. It allows Congress to make all laws necessary and proper to carrying out its other powers. Thus, Congress can use **implied powers** to make laws on matters not considered in 1789—airplane traffic, speed limits on interstate highways, minimum wages. Such regulations are viewed as "necessary and proper" means of, for instance, regulating **interstate commerce** (trade crossing state lines) as conditions change. (The Constitution does not mention interstate commerce.)

U.S. Capitol, Home of Senate and House

Differences Between the Houses of Congress

	House of Representatives	*Senate*
Number of members	435; seats apportioned to each state according to its population	100; each state represented by two senators
Term of member	Two years; may be reelected to unlimited number of terms; all members elected at same time	Six years; may be reelected to unlimited number of terms; one-third of Senate seats subject to election in same year
Member's qualifications	At least 25 years old; U.S. citizen for at least seven years; resident of state from which elected	At least 30 years old; U.S. citizen for at least nine years; resident of state from which elected
Member's **constituency** (people represented)	Citizens residing in given congressional district of state	All citizens of state
Presiding officer	Speaker of the House	Vice president of the United States

Limits on Power The Constitution denies Congress the power to (1) impose taxes on exports, (2) grant titles of nobility, (3) favor the ports of one state over those of another, or (4) suspend the **writ of habeas corpus**, which protects citizens from being jailed without good reason.

Procedures for Making Laws

Committees and Subcommittees Committees in the House and Senate specialize in different areas of lawmaking, including agriculture, foreign affairs, armed services, commerce, and labor. Such **standing** (permanent) **committees** consider a bill before the House or Senate votes on it. Committees often divide into smaller **subcommittees** that study a bill and report back to the full committee. The full committee then votes on whether to approve the bill, approve an amended version, or defeat it.

Floor Votes A bill with committee approval goes to the House or Senate for debate and vote. Senators or representatives may debate a bill's merits and propose amendments. To be *enacted* (passed), the bill must be approved by a majority of those present. After passage by one house, the bill goes to the other house for consideration and vote.

Conference Committee The two houses may pass similar but not identical bills. Members from both houses then iron out differences in a **conference committee.** When a compromise is reached, two identical bills return to the House and Senate for final votes.

Action by the President A bill enacted by both houses goes to the president, who may sign it into law or **veto** (reject) it, as follows:

- If Congress is in session longer than ten days after passing an act, the president must promptly return it to Congress explaining the veto. Congress can override the veto by a two-thirds vote in each house.
- If Congress is in session fewer than ten days after passing an act, the president can leave it unsigned, defeating it by **pocket veto.**

Influence of Pressure Groups

How members of Congress vote on a bill can influence their reelection, because they must face the voters on Election Day. Voters can exert pressure

How a Bill Becomes a Law

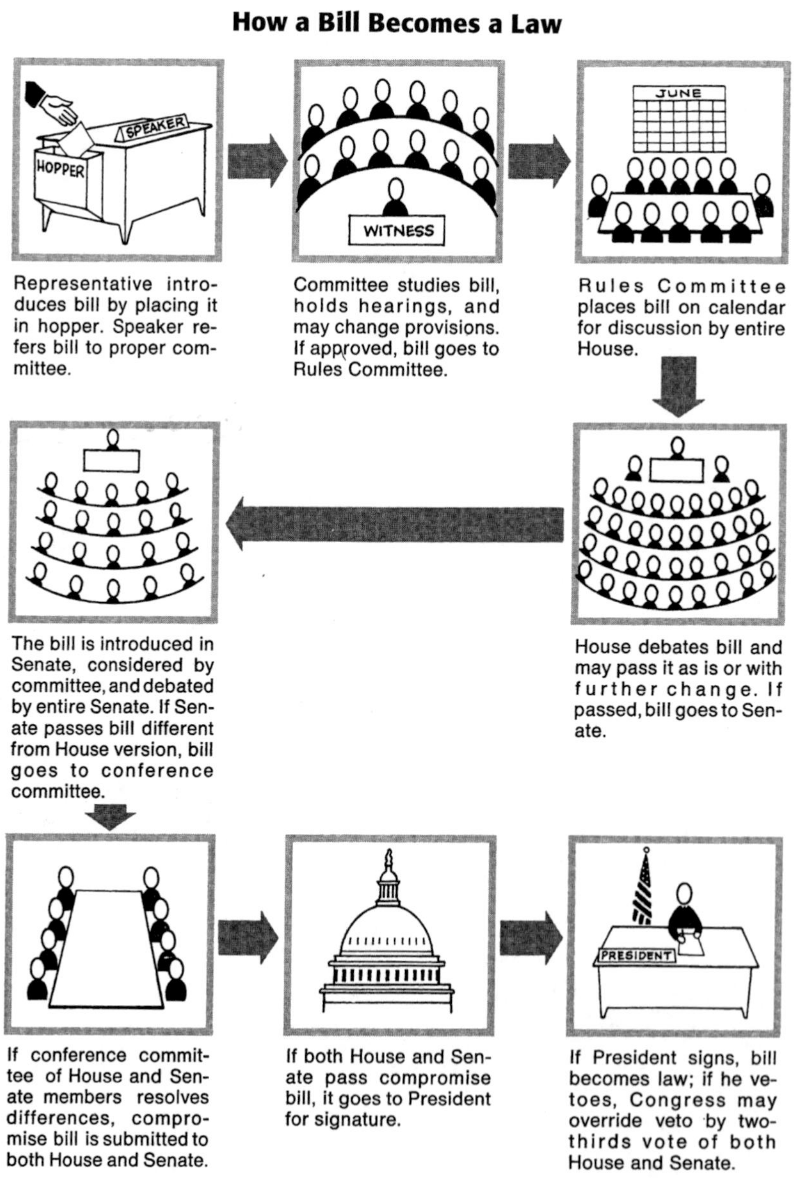

on the lawmaking process either as individuals or as members of **special-interest groups**.

Individual Action Citizens can e-mail and write letters to lawmakers, or visit their district offices in the home state. Some members of Congress often use mass mailings to constituents to ask their opinions on public issues. Increasingly, the Internet is becoming a means of communication between elected officials and their constituents

Group Action Many businesses, labor unions, and other organizations have a special interest in influencing congressional decisions. Special-interest groups organize letter-writing campaigns, place advertisements, and hire **lobbyists** (professional advocates) to visit members of Congress. Many groups form **political action committees (PACs)** to give money to the election campaigns of those they favor. These PACs have grown in importance as elections have become more expensive.

President

The writers of the Constitution wanted the executive branch to be equal in power to the other two branches. Many modern historians believe that the presidency has become the most powerful element.

Presidential Leadership

Chief Executive As chief executive, the president directs Cabinet heads and supervises agencies of the executive branch. The president is responsible for enforcing all federal laws and programs.

Among government agencies assisting the president are:

- *Office of Management and Budget (OMB)*, which prepares an annual government spending plan
- *Central Intelligence Agency (CIA)*, which gathers information on foreign matters affecting national security
- *National Aeronautics and Space Administration (NASA)*, which directs space exploration.

The president's **Cabinet** comprises heads of the departments of the federal government: Agriculture, Commerce, Defense, Education, Energy, Health and Human Services, Homeland Security, Housing and Urban Development, Interior, Justice, Labor, State, Transportation, Treasury, and Veterans Affairs.

Military Leader The president is commander in chief of the armed forces. Important military decisions must be approved by the president.

Legislative Leader The president uses the annual "State of the Union" address to recommend new laws. The president can call Congress into special session after adjournment. The president signs or vetoes acts of Congress.

Diplomatic Leader As the chief maker of U.S. foreign policy, the president (1) makes treaties (with approval of two-thirds of the Senate), (2) recognizes other countries by receiving ambassadors, and (3) nominates U.S. ambassadors to other countries (with the approval of a majority of the Senate).

Chief of State: Ceremonial Leader The president, as chief of state, speaks for the nation when abroad and strives to inspire Americans to honor their traditions and ideals. Once each year, the president comes before Congress to speak to the nation on the "State of the Union."

Judicial Role The president may grant either a **pardon** (forgiveness for a federal crime) or **reprieve** (delay of punishment). When a seat on the U.S. Supreme Court is vacant, the president nominates a new justice and submits the choice to the Senate for **confirmation** (approval).

Election Process

Election of a president and vice president occurs every four years on the second Tuesday in November.

Nomination of Candidates Presidential candidates seek the **nomination** (selection) of the Democratic Party, Republican Party, or a minor party. The first step is a state **primary election**, at which a party's voters choose a candidate and delegates to a national convention.

In the summer before the election, each party holds its convention, at which delegates from the 50 states make nominations for candidates for president. The candidate chosen in a state primary receives most of that state's delegate votes. In recent elections, a single candidate in each party usually wins enough primaries to be assured of nomination. The presidential nominee of each party usually then selects a vice-presidential running mate.

Fall Campaign The nominees travel across the nation making speeches and appear on televised debates seeking votes in the November election.

Electoral College Voters on Election Day do not actually vote for president and vice president. Instead, they vote for **electors**, who are authorized by the Constitution to cast ballots for president and vice president.

Electors are assigned to each state according to the size of its congressional delegation. In 2008, Nevada, with three representatives and two senators, had five electors. California, with 53 representatives and 2 senators, had 55 electors.

In all but two states, the candidate who wins a *plurality*, or most, of a state's *popular votes* (those cast by the people) wins all the state's electoral votes. All of the states' electors make up the **Electoral College**. The electors cast ballots for president and vice president one month after the popular election. Almost always, electors cast their ballots for the candidate favored by the plurality of voters.

Lack of a Majority If there are more than two major candidates and no one wins a majority (more than 50 percent) of electoral ballots, the election is decided in the House of Representatives. Each state has one vote. The candidate who wins a majority of the House vote is elected president.

Unusual Elections

Election of 1800: Tie Vote Broken by House Thomas Jefferson and Aaron Burr had an equal number of electoral votes (73). The House of Representatives broke the tie and elected Jefferson.

Election of 1824: Defeat of the Most Popular Candidate

Candidate	*Popular Vote*	*Electoral Vote*
Andrew Jackson	153,544	99
John Quincy Adams	108,740	88
William H. Crawford	46,618	41
Henry Clay	47,136	37

Since no candidate had an electoral majority, the election was decided by the House. The winner was John Quincy Adams.

Election of 1912: Three-way Race

Candidate	*Popular Vote*	*Electoral Vote*
Woodrow Wilson	6,296,547	435
Theodore Roosevelt	4,118,571	88
William H. Taft	3,486,720	8

Wilson, the winner, had less than a majority of the popular vote but a huge majority of electoral votes.

Election of 2000: Defeat of the More Popular Candidate

Candidate	*Popular Vote*	*Electoral Vote*
Albert Gore, Jr.	50,996,116	266
George W. Bush	50,456,169	271

The winner, Bush, had less than a majority of the popular vote.

Presidential Campaign 2004: Massachusetts Senator John Kerry (left) and President George W. Bush and First Lady Laura Bush greeting their supporters.

Rules of Succession

The **rules of succession** ensure an orderly procedure to replace the chief executive in case of illness or death.

Presidential Succession By a 1947 act of Congress, the vice president automatically succeeds a president who dies. If both die at the same time, the following order of succession applies:

- Speaker of the House
- President pro tempore of the Senate
- Cabinet members in the order in which their departments were created, beginning with the secretary of state.

Twenty-second Amendment (1951) No president may serve more than two elected terms.

Twenty-fifth Amendment (1967) A disabled president may notify Congress of the inability to carry out presidential powers and duties. In this case:

- The vice president then serves temporarily.
- The vice president, supported by a majority of the Cabinet, may notify Congress that the president is unable to "discharge the powers and duties of his office."
- The vice president then serves as acting president.
- If the president claims renewed capability of carrying out presidential duties and the vice president and a Cabinet majority disagree, the president may be overruled by a two-thirds vote of Congress.

Impeachment

The House of Representatives may decide by majority vote on articles of impeachment, accusing a president of "high crimes and misdemeanors." The Senate then meets as a trial court presided over by the chief justice of the United States. A two-thirds vote of the Senate is necessary for conviction and removal.

Two presidents, Andrew Johnson (1868) and Bill Clinton (1998), were impeached and acquitted. Richard Nixon (1974) resigned from office before the House voted.

Growth of Presidential Power

In 1789, the United States had 4 million inhabitants, a new and untried government, an agricultural economy, and a tiny army and navy. Today, it is a mighty industrial nation and a superpower.

Leadership in Domestic Affairs In the early 1900s, three successive presidents—Theodore Roosevelt, William H. Taft, and Woodrow Wilson—championed reforms to make the government more honest and efficient (discussed in Chapter 10). In the 1930s and 1940s, Franklin D. Roosevelt led the nation from the Great Depression to victory in World War II. In the 20th century, the civil rights movement of the 1950s and 1960s enhanced the central role of four presidents—Truman, Eisenhower, Kennedy, and Johnson.

Leadership in Foreign Affairs As leader of the world's strongest nation, the president meets often with other world leaders at **summit conferences**.

In this age of jet planes, nuclear weapons, and computer-controlled missiles, the response to military attack must usually be entrusted to the commander in chief rather than to the slower deliberation of Congress.

Debating the Electoral College

Arguments For	*Arguments Against*
Democratic; electors vote per majority in each state.	Less democratic than direct vote by the people. There is no need for a second election by small number of electors.
Carries out federal system by voting state by state.	Possible danger that electors will vote contrary to the popular plurality.
Good for large urban states, where candidates must appeal to minorities.	Good chance that election involving three or more candidates will be decided by the House.
Good for lightly populated states, which are guaranteed at least four electoral votes.	Gives lightly populated states more weight in election than they deserve.

Additional Factors Owing to modern technology, the president can address the entire nation and be seen on television and the Internet.

Through appointments to federal agencies, the president influences many aspects of our lives.

IN REVIEW

1. Explain the elastic clause.
2. How does a bill become law?
3. Describe the differences between the electoral vote and the popular vote.

Supreme Court and Lower Courts

Article III of the Constitution empowers a U.S. Supreme Court but leaves the responsibility of organizing lower courts to Congress.

Supreme Court Jurisdictions

Original Jurisdiction In a few cases—involving ambassadors and disputes between states—the Supreme Court acts as a trial court, with **original jurisdiction**.

Appellate Jurisdiction When the Supreme Court reviews cases appealed from lower courts, it has **appellate jurisdiction**. It may decide either to uphold the decision of a lower court or overturn it.

Justices of the Supreme Court Congress determines the number of justices on the Supreme Court. The first Court had six; today, there are nine, one chief justice and eight associate justices. Cases are decided by majority vote. One of the majority usually gives a constitutional explanation for the decision. A justice in the minority may write a **dissenting opinion**.

Organization of Federal Courts

The Federal Judiciary Act of 1789 organized the federal court system, with three **circuit courts** (courts of appeal) to review district court decisions. Now there are 94 district courts, 12 circuit courts, and 1 federal circuit court.

Trial Courts For most trials involving federal laws, district courts have original jurisdiction.

Appeals Process A district court's decision may be appealed to a circuit court. A circuit court's decision may be appealed to the Supreme Court, "the court of last resort." The Supreme Court may also hear cases begun

Federal and State Courts: Appeals Process

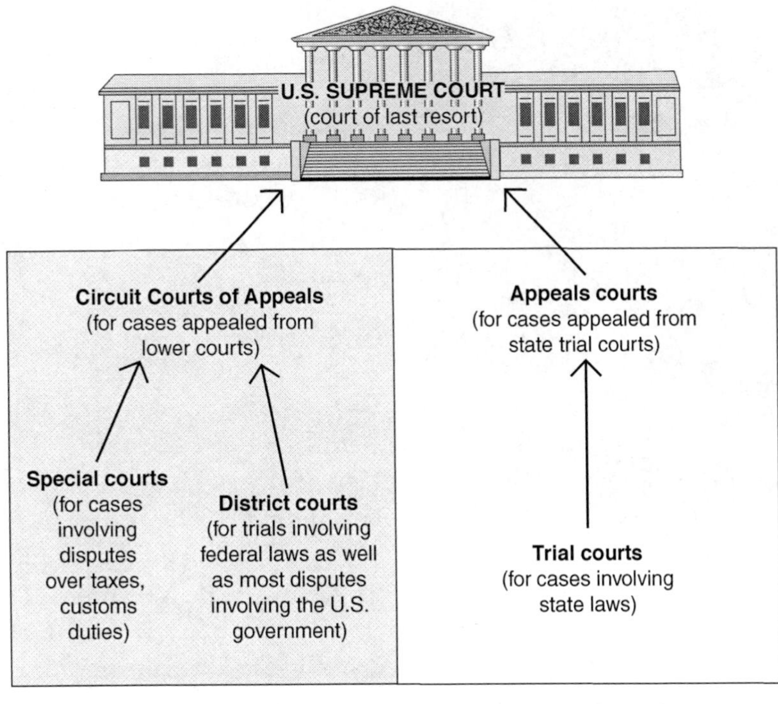

and appealed in state courts. The Supreme Court decides whether to hear a case on appeal.

Life Tenure A federal judge holds office for life, voluntary retirement, or impeachment and removal for wrongdoing. This relieves pressure to make decisions favoring politicians or voters.

Landmark Decisions of the Marshall Court

John Marshall was the fourth chief justice of the United States (1801–1835). He made the Supreme Court an independent and influential force in the federal government.

***Marbury* v. *Madison* (1803)** Before leaving office, President John Adams appointed William Marbury as a federal court judge. Thomas Jefferson, the next president, ordered Secretary of State James Madison to ignore the appointment. Marbury appealed to the Supreme Court, arguing that the Judiciary Act of 1789 gave the Supreme Court power to force Madison to grant the appointment. Chief Justice Marshall argued that that section of the law was unconstitutional—null and void.

His decision established the principle of **judicial review**, the power of the Court to rule on the constitutionality of federal and state laws. Each

Chief Justice John Marshall

case that the Court hears involves how the Constitution applies to a unique set of circumstances, because times change. Many cases of the 1880s and 1890s involved the regulation of railroads and oil companies—issues unknown to the Constitution's framers. In the late 20th century, the Constitution was applied to abortion, the death penalty, minority rights, and computer technology.

***McCulloch* v. *Maryland* (1819)** Maryland wished to collect a tax from a bank chartered by the U.S. government. Marshall argued that states could not tax a federal agency because the Constitution held the federal government to be supreme: "The power to tax is the power to destroy." Marshall also argued that Congress's powers could be interpreted loosely to authorize the creation of a national bank.

This decision permitted **nullification** (cancellation) of a state law that conflicted with a federal law.

***Gibbons* v. *Ogden* (1824)** New York State granted one steamship company the exclusive right to operate on an interstate waterway, the Hudson River. Marshall stated that trade is commerce, commerce between states is controlled by Congress, and so New York's law was invalid.

This ruling clarified the concept of interstate commerce and increased federal authority to regulate it.

Impact of the Marshall Court Many cases decided under Chief Justice Marshall increased federal power in relation to the states. By repeated application of judicial review, Marshall greatly expanded the power and influence of the Court.

Basic Constitutional Principles

The most basic constitutional principles are separation of powers, checks and balances, and federalism.

The Separation of Powers

The Constitution prevents domination by one branch of government by distributing legislative, executive, and judicial powers among three branches. This separation of powers gives each one a special area of responsibility.

Separation of Powers in the U.S. and State Systems

Checks and Balances

Definition and Purpose Each branch has some power to participate in decisions of the others. Thus, each branch must try to gain approval for its policies and decisions. This system of **checks and balances** allows each branch to block actions of the other branches (see diagram on page 24).

Federalism: Powers of the Central and State Governments

Federalism is the principle by which political power is divided between a central government and state governments.

Division of Powers Since the central government under the Articles of Confederation was ineffective, the framers of the Constitution increased its powers while reserving others for the states.

Delegated Powers The Constitution *enumerates* (names) the powers given to the central government. These **delegated powers** include collecting taxes, coining money, maintaining the armed forces, regulating trade, and making treaties.

Reserved Powers The **reserved powers** granted to the states and people by the Tenth Amendment are those not delegated to the federal government nor denied to the states, including such matters as health and safety, marriage and divorce, regulation of businesses, and licensing of professions.

Concurrent Powers **Concurrent powers** are those exercised by both the federal and state governments, including building roads and highways, borrowing money, collecting taxes, and operating courts.

IN REVIEW

1. Define judicial review.
2. Describe *two* important decisions of the Supreme Court under Chief Justice John Marshall.
3. Define separation of powers, checks and balances, and federalism.

The Constitution: A "Living Document"

The U.S. Constitution is a "living document" because it is flexible enough to be changed either by formal amendment or informal adjustments and decision making.

Most Common Method of Amending the Constitution

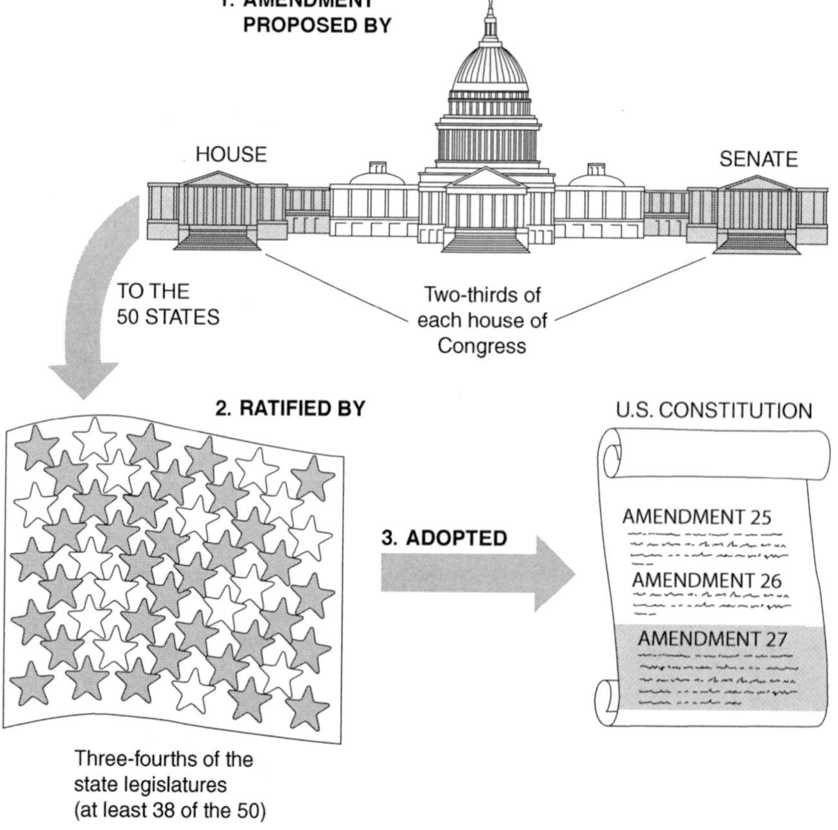

Formal Amendment

Article V of the Constitution describes formal procedures for proposing and ratifying amendments, the most common of which are:

- Congress proposes an amendment by a two-thirds vote of each house.
- The proposed amendment is considered by state legislatures. If three-fourths of them ratify the proposal, it is added to the Constitution (see the art on previous page).

Informal Change

Congress and the Elastic Clause The elastic clause in Article I of the Constitution empowers Congress to legislate on a vast number of subjects that were unknown when the Constitution was written (discussed on page 36).

Presidency and the Unwritten Constitution

The **unwritten constitution** refers to traditions that have become part of the American political system. For example:

- Most elected officials are either Republican or Democratic, even though the Constitution does not mention political parties.
- George Washington declined to serve more than two terms, and later presidents followed suit. This tradition was broken when Franklin Roosevelt won a third term (1940) and a fourth term (1944). The Twenty-second Amendment (1951) limited future presidents to two elected terms.
- The Constitution mentions no Cabinet, but after George Washington began to meet with four key advisers, presidents relied on a Cabinet and added new positions to it.

States in the Federal System

Citizens of the United States are also citizens of their states. Our 50 state governments are organized like the national government and have authority to deal with local issues. Each one has a constitution, which provides for separation of powers.

Admission of New States

Thirty-seven states were admitted to the Union after the Constitution was written in 1787. Article IV empowers Congress to admit new states, as follows:

- A territory applies to Congress for statehood.
- The territory submits a proposed constitution approved by its people.
- Congress may accept or reject a territory's application by majority vote.

Congress may attach conditions to statehood. When Utah applied for statehood in 1875, it had to disavow **polygamy** (having multiple marriage partners).

The last states, Hawaii and Alaska, were admitted in 1959.

New York State Legislature

New York State has a representative legislature whose members debate and vote on bills affecting such issues as (1) expenditures for education, (2) penalties for criminal behavior, and (3) funding mass transit and highways.

Bicameral Organization Most state legislatures have two houses, both of which approve bills by majority vote. In New York State, the larger house is the Assembly, and the smaller is the Senate.

Redistricting The process of changing district lines for representation in the legislature (called **redistricting**) reflects shifts in population. The New York State legislature can vote on the new district boundaries set by redistricting.

In a common practice called **gerrymandering**, members of a majority party often draw a district so as to favor their party. The U.S. Supreme Court ruled in *Baker* v. *Carr* (1962) that district lines must reflect "one man, one vote." That is, districts must be about equal in population so that all residents are equally represented. Nevertheless, occasional gerrymandering still helps candidates of one party win an election.

New York State Executive

New York State's chief executive is the governor, whose primary role is to enforce state laws. Executive departments and agencies are responsible for various functions. A highway department maintains state roads, and an education department supervises education in the state.

Governor's Influence on Legislation The governor proposes a series of bills and tries to persuade a majority of the legislature to vote for it. The governor can veto any bills passed.

Every year, the governor of New York recommends a state **budget** (income and spending plan). The governor tries to win approval of the budget by use of executive authority, access to the media, and political influence with party leaders.

Other Duties The governor nominates heads of executive departments and agencies. In many states, the governor also appoints state judges. Usually, such appointments require approval of one of the two houses of the legislature.

The governor is commander in chief of the state **national guard** (military force of citizen volunteers). In times of natural disaster or riot, the governor can order it into action and may ask the president for federal troops as well.

The governor may grant a pardon to a person convicted of a state crime.

New York State Judiciary

New York State's court system consists of the New York State Supreme Court (which tries cases) and the New York State Court of Appeals (a higher court that hears appeals).

Function State courts hear criminal cases involving state laws, settle legal disputes between citizens, and resolve cases involving interpretation of the state constitution.

Judicial Process Before a criminal case goes to trial, a grand jury decides whether there is enough evidence to indict an accused person. If so, that person is tried by a petit jury, which decides on guilt or innocence. A convicted person may ask to appeal the case to a state appeals court. A case involving a federal issue or interpretation of the U.S. Constitution ultimately may be appealed to the U.S. Supreme Court.

In handing down decisions, state courts are guided not only by the state constitution but also by the U.S. Constitution's guarantees of rights.

Interstate Relations

Each state is free to make its own laws and regulations, which may conflict with those of other states. Provisions of the U.S. Constitution and interstate agreements help to ease this problem.

"Full Faith and Credit" Article IV of the Constitution requires that states give "full faith and credit" to each other's laws, licenses, and official documents. Thus, the validity of automobile licenses and high school diplomas is recognized from state to state. "Full faith and credit," however, is limited. A state may refuse to acknowledge out-of-state certificates in such professions as medicine, law, and education.

Interstate Compacts Bordering states often recognize a mutual interest in solving common problems. By signing **interstate compacts**, governors of neighboring states set up **regional agencies**. An example is the Port Authority of New York and New Jersey, which operates interstate bridges and tunnels that cross the Hudson River.

Local Governments

Counties, villages, towns, and municipalities (cities) have their own governments. Most municipalities, for example, operate their own police, fire, sanitation, and health departments.

Local Officials Local chief executives—mayors, city managers, county executives—supervise departments of the municipal or county government. City councils and county boards of supervisors (in some places, called freeholders) make local regulations called **ordinances**. Legislative and executive decisions must conform to state laws.

Finances Public schools and other local institutions are funded mainly by property taxes on the value of land, homes, and other buildings. Grants from the state and federal governments supplement these revenues.

IN REVIEW

1. Explain why the Constitution is a "living document."
2. Describe *two* examples of the unwritten constitution.
3. Explain the principle of redistricting and how it may be abused.

CHAPTER REVIEW

MULTIPLE-CHOICE QUESTIONS

1 To provide for change, the authors of the United States Constitution included the amendment process and the
(1) commerce clause
(2) elastic clause
(3) supremacy clause
(4) naturalization clause

Base your answer to question 2 on the cartoon below and on your knowledge of social studies.

Ed Gamble © 1996. King Features Syndicate, Inc.

2 What is the main idea of this cartoon?
(1) Wealthy persons should be discouraged from running for public office.
(2) Efforts to limit political contributions from special interest groups are not successful.
(3) Special interest groups from foreign nations have too much influence on American politics.
(4) Placing limits on terms in office for elected officials would solve campaign funding problems.

Base your answer to question 3 on the following graphs and on your knowledge of social studies.

3 Which generalization is supported by the information provided by the graphs?
(1) The electoral vote often fails to reflect the popular vote.
(2) The House of Representatives settles Presidential elections in which third party candidates participate.
(3) The Electoral College system weakens the two-party system.
(4) Electoral College members often vote against their party's candidates.

4 In the United States Constitution, the power to impeach a federal government official is given to the
(1) House of Representatives
(2) president
(3) state legislatures
(4) Supreme Court

5 What was one outcome of the Supreme Court decision in *Marbury* v. *Madison* (1803)?
(1) State governments could now determine the constitutionality of federal laws.
(2) The principle of judicial review was established.
(3) Congress expanded its delegated powers.
(4) A method to approve treaties was developed.

6 The power of judicial review allows the Supreme Court to
(1) repeal amendments to the Constitution
(2) determine the constitutionality of a law
(3) break tie votes in the Electoral College
(4) impeach the president and other high-level officials

7 Which principle of the United States Constitution is intended to ensure that no one branch of government has more power than another branch?
(1) checks and balances
(2) federalism
(3) limited government
(4) rule of law

Presidential Election Results, 1992

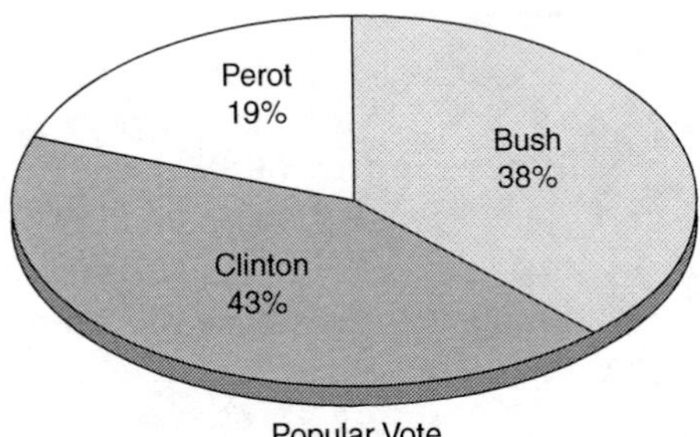

Popular Vote

Electoral Vote

8 The United States Constitution grants certain powers only to the Federal Government. For example, only Congress can declare war. These powers are called
(1) police powers
(2) reserved powers
(3) delegated powers
(4) concurrent powers state + federal

9 • The United States government taxes gasoline.
• New York State law requires a sales tax on many goods.

These two statements best illustrate the principle of
(1) concurrent powers
(2) property rights
(3) reserved powers
(4) popular sovereignty

10 The creation of the presidential Cabinet and political parties are examples of
(1) the unwritten constitution
(2) separation of powers
(3) the elastic clause
(4) judicial review

THEMATIC ESSAYS

1 **THEME:** *Powers of the President.* Presidential power has increased over time to meet new challenges in the nation and the world.

TASK: Choose *two* instances in which a problem, crisis, or emergency demanded increased presidential power. For *each* situation:
- Describe the problem, crisis, or emergency.
- Demonstrate how the solution increased presidential power.

You may use any two situations from your study of the Constitution, the presidency, and U.S. history and government. You may wish to include civil rights, economic depression, need for honest and efficient government, and national emergencies such as war or rebellion.

2 **THEME:** *State and Federal Powers.* The Constitution provides for a federal system that delegates certain powers to the federal government, reserves others for the states, and provides for concurrent powers between the federal and state governments.

TASK: Choose *one* power that illustrates *each* of the following:
- powers delegated to the federal government
- powers reserved for the state governments
- powers concurrent between federal and state governments.

Explain why the writers of the Constitution created *each* power that you selected.

DOCUMENT-BASED QUESTION

Study each document and answer the question that follows it. Then read the **Task** and write your essay. Include references to most of the documents and additional information you retain about U.S. history and government.

HISTORICAL CONTEXT: The writers of the Constitution created a government designed to meet the new nation's needs without the exercise of abusive power.

DOCUMENT 1: From the Constitution of the United States:

> The Congress shall have power . . . to make all laws which shall be necessary and proper for carrying into execution the foregoing powers and all other powers vested by this Constitution in the government of the United States, or in any department or officer thereof.

QUESTION: How does the elastic clause help Congress pass needed laws?

DOCUMENT 2: From the Supreme Court's decision in *McCulloch* v. *Maryland* (1819), by John Marshall:

> We admit, as all must admit, that the powers of the government are limited, and that its limits are not to be transcended. But we think the sound construction of the Constitution must allow to the national legislature that discretion, with respect to the means by which the powers it confers are to be carried into execution, which will enable that body to perform the high duties assigned to it, in the manner most beneficial to the people. Let the end be legitimate, let it be within the scope of the Constitution, and all means which are appropriate, which are plainly adapted to that end, which are not prohibited, but consistent with the letter and spirit of the Constitution, are constitutional....

QUESTION: What decision did the Supreme Court reach about the power of Congress?

DOCUMENT 3: From the Supreme Court's decision in *Gideon* v. *Wainwright* (1963), by Hugo Black:

> We accept *Betts* v. *Brady*'s assumption... that a provision of the Bill of Rights which is "fundamental and essential to a fair trial" is made *obligatory* [binding] upon the States by the Fourteenth Amendment. We think the Court in *Betts* was wrong, however, in concluding that the Sixth Amendment's guarantee of counsel is not one of those fundamental rights....
>
> Reason and reflection require us to recognize that... any person [brought into] court, who is too poor to hire a lawyer, cannot be assured a fair trial unless counsel is provided....
>
> The judgment is reversed....

QUESTION: Why did the Supreme Court reverse a lower court's decision?

TASK: Using the documents and your knowledge of U.S. history and government, write an essay that illustrates how the Constitution has been adapted to the needs of changing times but kept secure against abusive power.

CHAPTER 4
Implementing Principles of the New Constitution

DOCUMENTS AND LAWS
Alien and Sedition Acts (1798) • Twelfth Amendment (1804) • Monroe Doctrine (1823)

EVENTS
Whiskey Rebellion (1794) • French Revolution (1789–1799) • XYZ Affair (1797)
Election of 1800 • Napoleonic Wars (1804–1815) • War of 1812 (1812–1815)
Hartford Convention (1814) • Election of 1824

PEOPLE/GROUPS
John Adams • John Quincy Adams • Alexander Hamilton • Andrew Jackson • Thomas Jefferson
Democratic-Republicans • Francis Scott Key • Henry Knox • James Madison • James Monroe
Napoleon • Edmund Randolph • Tecumseh • George Washington • National Republicans
Democrats • War Hawks

OBJECTIVES

- To identify important policies of early presidents and evaluate their effects.
- To understand Hamilton's financial plan.
- To investigate the unwritten constitution under Washington, Adams, and Jefferson.
- To evaluate early obstacles to a stable political system.
- To analyze early U.S. foreign policy.

The U.S. Constitution was only a framework for government. The first five presidents worked out practical details necessary to the systematic operation of government.

Unwritten Constitution Under Washington, Adams, and Jefferson

During his two terms as president (1789–1797), George Washington influenced U.S. government more than any other president. John Adams, the second president, and his successor, Thomas Jefferson, also made major decisions that became part of the unwritten constitution.

First Cabinet (1789)

Officials of a president's Cabinet meet to advise the chief executive. This group is not mentioned in the Constitution. Washington established the Cabinet as a permanent executive institution when, in 1789, he appointed a secretary of state (Thomas Jefferson), a secretary of the treasury (Alexander

Hamilton), a secretary of war (Henry Knox), and an attorney general (Edmund Randolph).

Hamilton's Financial Plan

Alexander Hamilton immediately drew up plans to strengthen the new country's economic position and finances:

- a system for repaying debts of the states and national government
- establishment of a national bank in which to deposit tax revenues and private loans to the U.S. government
- **tariffs** (taxes on imports) to protect new American industries from foreign competition.

Southerners Thomas Jefferson and James Madison opposed these policies as favoring Northern business interests over Southern agrarian interests. In addition, Jefferson believed that Hamilton's plan would give the federal government too much power. Over such objections, Congress enacted the plan, which proved successful.

President Washington (inset) and his first Cabinet: (left to right) Henry Knox, Thomas Jefferson, Alexander Hamilton, Edmund Randolph

Stabilizing the Political System

Political Parties While expecting differences of opinion within the Cabinet, Washington hoped to avoid the formation of political parties, which the Constitution does not mention. Nevertheless, they soon came into being and form the basis of the current U.S. political system. Over time, the president came to be viewed as the head of his party as well as the official head of state.

Federalists Conflict over Hamilton's financial plan was one reason why two political parties emerged in the 1790s. Hamilton and Jefferson each became a leader of a party. The policies of Hamilton's party, the Federalists, favored Northern merchants and, to a lesser extent, large plantation owners in the South. The merchants, in particular, liked Hamilton's plan:

- It would stabilize and strengthen the national government.
- A national bank would be a source of loans for new businesses.
- Tariffs would protect new domestic industries from foreign competition.

Concerning interpretation of the Constitution, the Federalists argued for **loose construction:** Government had many powers implied by the elastic clause.

Democratic-Republicans The policies of Thomas Jefferson's party, the *Democratic-Republicans*, favored the interests of small farmers and the common people. It opposed Hamilton's financial plan:

- Full payment of the national debt, achieved by buying back government bonds would benefit **speculators.** Many of them had bought government bonds at a reduced rate and would make a fortune if the government bought them back at full value.
- A national bank would more readily give loans to Northern merchants than to Southern and Western farmers.

The Democratic-Republicans argued for **strict construction** of the Constitution: Government should do no more than what the Constitution specified. Jefferson, as president, softened this position when he purchased the vast Louisiana Territory from France (see the map on page 67).

Whiskey Rebellion (1794) To raise revenue, Congress placed a federal **excise tax** (one made on the sale of a domestic product) on the distilling of whiskey. When whiskey-producing farmers in western Pennsylvania organized an armed revolt, Washington sent troops to put down their rebellion. He thus demonstrated that a federal government was more effective than a confederate government, which had been helpless during Shays' Rebellion.

Alien and Sedition Acts (1798) During the presidency of John Adams (1797–1801), a Federalist majority in Congress enacted two laws to intimidate supporters of the Democratic-Republicans. The *Alien Act* authorized the president to deport foreigners thought to endanger public safety. The *Sedition Act* authorized the government to fine and imprison newspaper editors who printed "scandalous and malicious writing" about the government.

The Virginia and Kentucky legislatures passed resolutions protesting these acts, claiming the right to **nullify** (disregard) them as unconstitutional. These resolutions expressed the views of Thomas Jefferson, who argued that the Alien and Sedition Acts violated citizens' basic rights.

End of the Federalist Era

Election of 1800 During the administrations of Washington and Adams, the Federalists were in control. In 1800, Adams was defeated by two Democratic-Republican candidates, Thomas Jefferson and Aaron Burr. Because Jefferson and Burr had the same number of electoral votes, the election went to the House of Representatives, where Jefferson emerged the winner with Hamilton's support.

Congress then proposed the Twelfth Amendment to change the Electoral College system. The original Constitution had provided that each elector cast two ballots, both for president. The Twelfth Amendment (1804)

Election of 1800

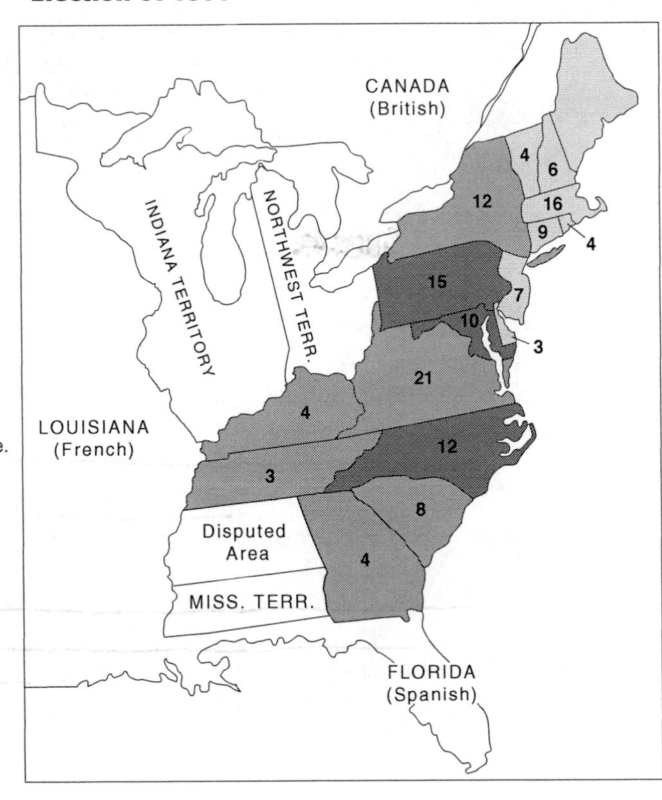

First Political Parties

	Federalists	*Democratic-Republicans*
Leaders	Alexander Hamilton John Adams John Marshall	Thomas Jefferson James Madison James Monroe
Geographic strength	Strong support among Northeastern merchants	Strong support among farmers of South and West
Position on Hamilton's financial plan	In favor of national bank, funding the debt, protecting new industries	Opposed to all these features
Position on constitutional issues	Favored loose construction to maximize federal power	Favored strict construction to limit federal power and safeguard rights of states
Position on foreign policy	Partial to the British but supportive of Washington's Proclamation of Neutrality	Partial to France but supportive of Jefferson's attempts to remain neutral during Napoleonic wars

provided that each elector cast one ballot for president and a second ballot for vice president.

IN REVIEW

1. How did Hamilton propose to increase the economic strength of the new U.S. government?
2. Explain why the Cabinet and political parties are examples of the unwritten constitution.
3. Contrast Hamilton's and Jefferson's views of the Constitution.

Neutrality and National Security

Foreign policies under the first five presidents aimed for the following goals:

- **neutrality** (taking no sides in a foreign war)
- recognition of U.S. **sovereignty** (independence)
- support for Latin Americans struggling for independence.

Washington stated in his *Proclamation of Neutrality* that the United States should remain neutral in European conflicts. In his "Farewell Address" he stated that the nation should "steer clear of permanent alliances." Washington pursued his policy of neutrality in order to allow the country time to develop its economic and military strength. The new nation had a small army and navy, and was bordered on the north by British Canada, on the south by Spanish Florida, and on the west by the Mississippi River, controlled by Spain.

Washington and the French Revolution (1789–1799)

A revolution in France overthrew the monarchy in 1789. Viewing the French republic as a threat to their own monarchies, Britain, Austria, and Spain sent armies to invade France and crush the republican government there. Although U.S. public opinion was divided, Washington followed a policy of neutrality on this issue, as he did throughout his two terms.

John Adams and the XYZ Affair (1797)

John Adams adopted Washington's policy of neutrality. During his presidency, the French navy seized American ships and France sent diplomats (identified as X, Y, and Z) who demanded bribes to stop the French abuses. Angered by the *XYZ Affair*, many Americans called for retaliation. Adams avoided war, but in 1798 French and U.S. warships clashed. Adams and Napoleon, the new head of the French government, then reached a temporary settlement.

Jefferson and the Napoleonic Wars (1804–1815)

Jefferson as president (1801–1809) also chose neutrality. In 1804, Napoleon ended the French republic and crowned himself emperor. France was soon at war with Britain. British warships searched U.S. merchant ships, removed cargo, and forced American sailors into British service by **impressment**. Since the French navy thus also violated U.S. rights as a neutral nation, Congress in 1807 placed an **embargo** (trade ban) on shipping American goods to all of Europe. The purpose of the *Embargo Act* was to help maintain U.S. neutrality and avoid going to war. New England merchants and shipbuilders, whose businesses were damaged, protested. Thus, the embargo was lifted in 1809.

War of 1812

The fourth president, James Madison (1809–1817), also tried to defend U.S. rights at sea without going to war. But U.S.-British tensions increased. As settlers took over Native-American lands near the Great Lakes, the leader Tecumseh led his people in 1811 against the settlers, who complained that Britain was arming the Native Americans. Moreover, a congressional faction of Southerners and Westerners—the "War Hawks"—argued that the United States could gain Canada if it went to war against Britain. Congress declared war in 1812.

Protest in New England

In December 1814, however, members of the Federalist Party met in Hartford, Connecticut, to protest the continuing war. The delegates to this *Hartford Convention* discussed New England's **secession** (withdrawal from the Union) but took no action.

Consequences of War

An 1815 treaty ending the war said nothing about U.S. neutrality rights and awarded no territory or money to either side. Great Britain, however, stopped seizing American cargoes, and the United States emerged as a respected sovereign nation.

The War of 1812 boosted **nationalism** (loyalty to and support of one's country). Inspired by watching a battle at Fort McHenry near Baltimore in 1814, Francis Scott Key wrote the poem "The Star-Spangled Banner," which was later set to music as the national anthem. For his 1815 victory at New Orleans, General Andrew Jackson became a hero. Historians have found out much about the War of 1812 through their study of primary sources, such as battle plans, letters, and presidential documents.

The British burned Washington, D.C., during the War of 1812.

Era of Good Feelings

The Federalist Party, widely condemned for its antiwar stance, ceased to be a major force in U.S. politics. The next Democratic-Republican candidate for president, James Monroe, easily won two terms as president (1817–1825). This period has been called the *Era of Good Feelings.*

Monroe and Latin America

Inspired by the American and French revolutions, rebels in South and Central America revolted successfully against Spain, Portugal, and France. Monroe and his secretary of state, John Quincy Adams, warned European powers not to recolonize any part of Latin America. This *Monroe Doctrine* of 1823 stated:

- The Western Hemisphere was closed to further colonization by Europeans.
- The United States would firmly oppose European intervention in the Western Hemisphere.

Latin America: Dates of Independence From European Rule

- The United States would not involve itself politically in the affairs of Europe.

Great Britain and the new Latin American nations supported the Monroe Doctrine, and it became the foundation of U.S. policy toward Europe and Latin America.

The Monroe Doctrine reflected neutrality, **isolationism** (noninvolvement with foreign entanglements or organizations), and the U.S. concern to end European expansion in the Western Hemisphere. It also protected the interests of the Latin American republics.

Onset of Sectional Conflict

During the Era of Good Feelings, two disputes revealed sectional resentments. One, the *Missouri Compromise*, concerned slavery (discussed on page 81).

The second concerned party politics. By 1824, the Democratic-Republican Party had split into several groups, each favoring a different candidate for president. Andrew Jackson, a hero of the War of 1812, had more popular votes than the other three candidates. But none had the majority of electoral votes required to win. John Quincy Adams, with the support of candidate Henry Clay, won the election in the House of Representatives. Jackson then charged that the election had been stolen. After this rift, supporters of Adams and Clay called themselves *National Republicans*. Supporters of Jackson took the name of *Democrats*.

IN REVIEW

1. How did the election of 1800 lead to changes in the Constitution?
2. Explain the major causes and results of the War of 1812.
3. To what extent did the Monroe Doctrine reflect sentiments of neutrality and isolationism?

CHAPTER REVIEW

MULTIPLE-CHOICE QUESTIONS

1 Which action is an example of the unwritten constitution?
(1) formation of the first Cabinet by President George Washington
(2) admission of Vermont and Kentucky as states
(3) enforcement of the Alien and Sedition Acts by President John Adams
(4) declaration of war by Congress in 1812

2 One major reason that Alexander Hamilton proposed a national bank was to
(1) improve the economic position of the United States government

(2) help state governments collect taxes
(3) make loans available to owners of small farms
(4) reduce foreign investment in the United States

3 Which presidential role resulted from practice and custom rather than from constitutional authority?
(1) commander in chief
(2) chief executive
(3) head of his political party
(4) head of state

4 On what grounds would strict constructionists of the United States Constitution have questioned the purchase of the Louisiana Territory?
(1) It violated the guarantee of states' rights.
(2) The president was not specifically given the power to purchase new land.
(3) Congress was opposed to expansion west of the Mississippi River.
(4) The Constitution applied only to the original thirteen states.

5 Which action during Washington's administration led to the Whiskey Rebellion in western Pennsylvania?
(1) passage of a new excise tax
(2) establishment of a presidential Cabinet
(3) creation of the Bank of the United States
(4) ban on slavery in the Northwest Territory

6 • Alien and Sedition Acts
• Virginia and Kentucky Resolutions

These pieces of legislation reflected the conflict between
(1) Congress and the president
(2) states' rights and federal supremacy
(3) the military and the civilian government
(4) the United States Supreme Court and state courts

7 President George Washington pursued a foreign policy of neutrality during his administration primarily because he believed that
(1) the United States needed time to gain economic and military strength
(2) treaties were prohibited by the Constitution
(3) the United States should not expand by force
(4) alliances should be established with both France and England

8 An example of a primary source of information about the War of 1812 would be a
(1) battle plan for the attack on Fort McHenry
(2) historical novel on the Battle of New Orleans
(3) movie on the life of President James Madison
(4) textbook passage on the naval engagements of the war

9 A primary goal of the Monroe Doctrine (1823) was to
(1) prevent European intervention in Latin America
(2) create an opportunity for the annexation of Canada
(3) protect the site of a canal across Central America
(4) help European nations establish new Western Hemisphere colonies

10 Washington's Proclamation of Neutrality (1793), Jefferson's Embargo Act (1807), and the Monroe Doctrine (1823) were all efforts to
(1) avoid political conflicts with European nations
(2) directly support European revolutions
(3) aid Great Britain in its war against France
(4) promote military alliances

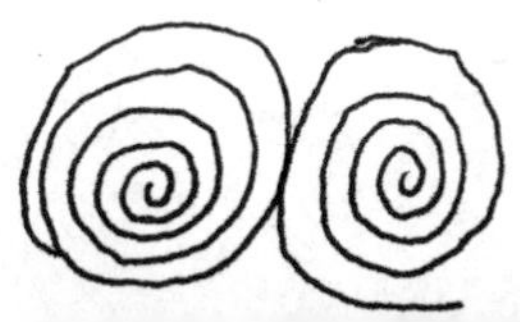

THEMATIC ESSAY

Theme: *Neutrality as Foreign Policy.* President Washington decided that it would be best for the new nation to pursue a foreign policy of neutrality. Succeeding presidents followed his lead with varying degrees of success.

Task: Show how *two* situations required U.S. presidents to enforce neutrality. For each situation:

- describe the events that led the president to enforce neutrality
- evaluate how successful the U.S. policy of neutrality was.

You may use any event you have studied. Some presidents and events you may wish to use are John Adams and the XYZ Affair, Thomas Jefferson and the Napoleonic wars, James Madison and the War of 1812, and James Monroe and the issuance of the Monroe Doctrine.

DOCUMENT-BASED QUESTION

Study each document and answer the question that follows it. Then read the **Task** and write your essay. Include references to most of the documents and additional information you retain about U.S. history and government.

Historical Context: Even though our early presidents followed a policy of neutrality, they could not ignore the rest of the world.

Document 1: From George Washington's "Farewell Address":

> Europe has a set of primary interests which to us have no or a very remote relation.... [T]herefore, it must be unwise to implicate ourselves by artificial ties.... [I]t is our true policy to steer clear of permanent alliances with any portion of the foreign world....

Question: Why did Washington favor U.S. noninvolvement in European affairs?

Document 2: Anonymous author's "Open Letter to George Washington," 1793:

> Had you... consulted the general sentiments of your fellow citizens, you would have found them... firmly attached to the cause of France.... Had even no written treaty existed between France and the United States, still would the strongest ties of amity [friendship] have united the people of both nations; still would the republican citizens of America have regarded Frenchmen, contending for liberty, as their brethren.

Question: Why does the writer tell Washington that the nation should support France against Britain?

Document 3: Thomas Jefferson on France's possible acquisition of the Louisiana Territory (1802):

> The day France takes possession of New Orleans... we must marry ourselves to the British fleet and nation.... This is not a state of things we seek and desire.

Question: What would Jefferson have to do if France controlled New Orleans?

Document 4: Refer to the map on the next page.

Question: How did the Louisiana Purchase prevent the United States from "marrying" the British fleet?

Document 5: Study the cartoon on the next page.

Question: How does the cartoonist feel the embargo is affecting New England?

Louisiana Purchase (1803)

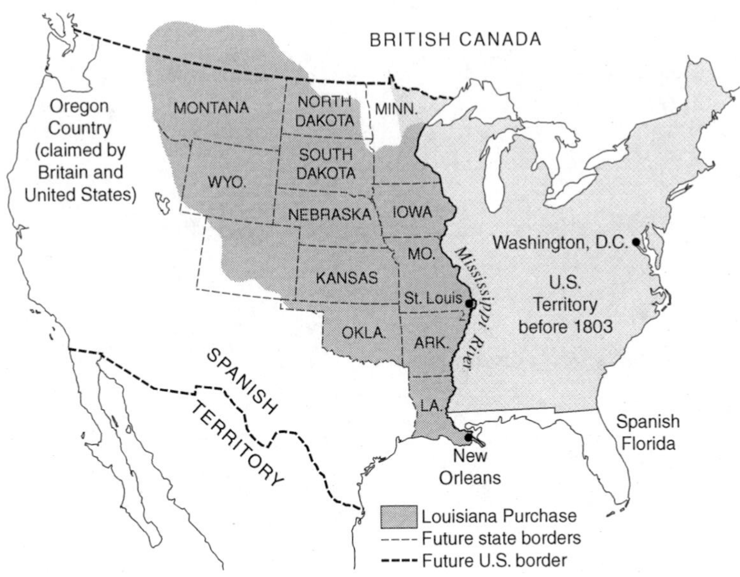

Snapping turtle "Ograbme" ("embargo" spelled backward) stops shipment of U.S. goods to Britain.

DOCUMENT 6: From James Madison, War Message to Congress, 1812:

> British cruisers have been . . . violating the American flag on the great highway of nations [the Atlantic Ocean], and . . . seizing and carrying off per sons sailing under it.

> . . . British cruisers have been . . . violating the rights and peace of our coasts. They . . . harass our entering and departing commerce [which] has been plundered in every sea. . . .

QUESTION: Why was Madison recommending a declaration of war on Britain?

TASK: Using the documents and your knowledge of early U.S. foreign affairs, write an essay in which you explain:

- why the United States long followed a policy of neutrality
- why public opinion made it difficult to maintain neutrality
- how world affairs placed neutrality in jeopardy.

CHAPTER 5
Nationalism and Sectionalism

DOCUMENTS AND LAWS
Missouri Compromise (1820) • "Tariff of Abominations" (1828)
Ordinance of Nullification (1832) • Compromise of 1850 • Fugitive Slave Act (1850)
Dred Scott v. *Sanford* (1857)

EVENTS
Opening of Erie Canal (1825) • Resettlement Act (1830) • "Trail of Tears" (1838)
Irish Potato Famine (1845–1852) • Seneca Falls Convention (1848) • Harpers Ferry raid (1859)

PEOPLE/GROUPS
abolitionists • Henry Barnard • John Brown • John C. Calhoun • Henry Clay • nativists
Know-Nothings • Whigs • Dorothea Dix • Frederick Douglass • Robert Fulton
William Lloyd Garrison • Andrew Jackson • Horace Mann • Lucretia Mott
Elizabeth Cady Stanton • Harriet Beecher Stowe • Harriet Tubman • Nat Turner
Denmark Vesey • Eli Whitney •

OBJECTIVES

- To identify the geographic and economic factors contributing to sectionalism.
- To explain living conditions under slavery.
- To identify early immigrant groups and their impact on the nation.
- To identify important policies of Andrew Jackson and evaluate their political effects.
- To describe how U.S. expansion affected Native Americans.
- To describe reform movements during the Age of Jackson.
- To compare and contrast attempts to preserve the Union.

Between 1789 and 1861, several forces preserved national unity and a general feeling that Americans were citizens of the country rather than of individual states. The Marshall Court rulings established federal supremacy over state governments and federal power to regulate interstate commerce. By supporting one of the major political parties, most Americans were organized into two groups rather than many different factions. Finally, industrialization and the building of roads and canals promoted economic interdependence within the United States.

Other forces, however, provoked **sectionalism** (strong loyalty to one region within a nation), which, in 1861, led to the Civil War. The underlying cause was that the North, South, and West had different kinds of economies.

Industrial North

Geography, abundance of natural resources, technology, and U.S. economic policy helped the North industrialize.

Geography

The North's many rivers (1) provided waterpower to drive machinery and (2) served as natural highways for transporting goods. A network of roads and canals were built to connect the rivers. Completion of the *Erie Canal* in 1825 enabled merchants and farmers to ship goods without transfer between New York City and Lake Erie ports. The North also had ocean ports that facilitated easy and profitable trade with Europe. Agriculture in New England, however, was limited because of the region's short growing season and rocky soil.

Technology

The invention of the steamboat by Robert Fulton and others in the early 1800s speeded up water transportation. In the 1830s and 1840s, railroads began to transport goods efficiently by land.

Major Canals and Roads, 1820–1850

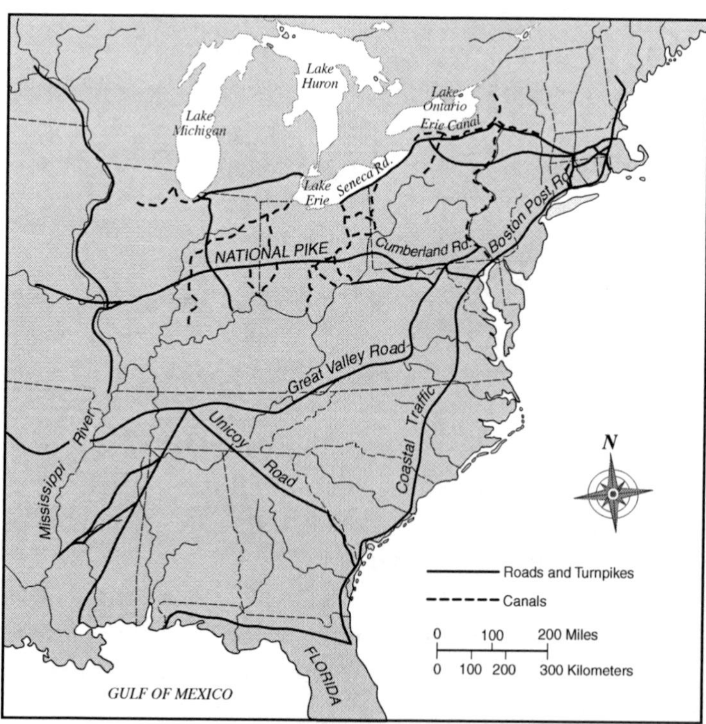

Economic Policies

Alexander Hamilton's national bank benefited Northern merchants. An 1816 tariff act that taxed imports allowed American textile mills to compete with those in Britain. Also in 1816, the Second Bank of the United States, which replaced Hamilton's national bank, helped industrial growth by providing loans to businesses.

Factory System

New technology spurred the growth of factories. Eli Whitney invented tools to make each part of a musket a standard size. Manufacture of these **interchangeable parts** into muskets became much faster. Similar systems of interchangeable parts were then used in other industries. The thousands of immigrants arriving every year in Boston and New York provided cheap labor for the new factories.

Women and Children Workers Most workers in New England's textile mills were women and children under the age of 12. At first, working conditions were reasonable, but mill owners soon instituted 12- to 14-hour daily shifts, six days a week. Wages were low and conditions unhealthy and dangerous. Critics of the factory system compared mill workers to slaves.

Urban Problems

Farm people and immigrants flocked to cities in the Northeast, swelling their populations. As the poorer sections grew crowded, open sewers polluted the streets and fresh water became scarce. Diseases such as typhoid and cholera spread rapidly.

Competition for jobs between poor whites and free blacks sometimes resulted in riots. With the influx of poor people, the middle and upper classes moved to different neighborhoods.

Family Life

Middle-class families had comfortable homes. Working-class families crowded in cramped **tenements** (multifamily buildings with few amenities). In general, middle-class men supported their families while the women ran households and raised children. Their children did not work. In contrast, working–class men, women, and children all worked long hours for low wages and had little leisure time.

Free Blacks

Most blacks living in the pre–Civil War North were free, but they did not have full rights of citizenship. Except in New England, most cities and towns denied them the vote. Throughout the North, African Americans were usually segregated: Black children went to separate schools, and white churches rarely welcomed black members. In some Northern states, blacks could not serve on juries or testify in criminal cases.

Development of the South

While the North took the lead in developing railroads and industry, the South's economy remained largely agricultural. Cotton was the South's main crop.

Role of Cotton

Even in the 1780s and 1790s, the South exported a lot of cotton to British textile mills. By the early 1800s, this region of many plantations had become economically dependent on this single crop.

Cotton grew easily in the South. But removing the seeds from cotton by hand was a slow process. Then, in 1793, Eli Whitney invented the **cotton gin**, which separated seeds from cotton mechanically. This device and the ever-increasing demand for cotton by British and Northern mills (where it was processed) made Southern planters wealthy.

Old Southwest

Cotton's one drawback was that it wore out the soil. In search of large tracts of new farmland, Southerners began to move into the Old Southwest—Alabama, Mississippi, Louisiana, Arkansas, and Texas. As a result, Southern wealth and leadership spread to plantation owners in the new regions.

Women on Plantations

White women on plantations were expected to supervise activities in the large home on the plantation and entertain relatives, friends, and business associates. Their style of living depended to a great extent on the efforts of their slaves.

Slavery

Laws Most work on plantations was done by African slaves. Southern laws gave plantation owners free reign over their slaves. Beatings were common. Children born into slavery were the property of their owners. It was legal and common to sell slaves and thus separate slave families.

Women Slaves Enslaved women worked along with the men in the fields, maintained homes, and raised families. Women house slaves were cooks, seamstresses, and caretakers of their owners' children. Some male owners expected slave women to have sex with them. Historians believe that

Thomas Jefferson had at least one child with Sally Hemings, a slave with whom he had a long relationship.

Child Slaves By the age of six or eight, slave children were expected to work. In his autobiography, escaped slave Frederick Douglass stated that he and other black children were poorly fed, inadequately clothed and protected against cold, and kept illiterate. Some, including Douglass, were separated early from one or both parents and their siblings.

Labor As the demand for cotton grew, so did the demand for slaves to plant and pick it. Plantation owners largely ignored the 1808 law against importing slaves. For them, slavery was an economic necessity. Besides serving as field hands and servants, slaves worked as blacksmiths, carpenters, and barrel makers, enabling plantations to be nearly self-sufficient.

Slavery and Religion Slaves were permitted to attend religious services. Most of them became Baptists or Methodists, like the majority of white Southerners. The form of Christianity that they practiced, however, retained many elements from African religions—charms, love potions, and folk medicines. Slaves were particularly attracted to Old Testament stories about the freeing of Hebrew slaves and their return to the Promised Land. When blacks and whites attended the same church, blacks sat in separate pews.

Resistance Some slaves revolted against lifelong bondage, even though it was usually hopeless and the penalty was death. In 1822, an uprising planned by Denmark Vesey, a South Carolina slave, was discovered before it began. Nat Turner's 1831 revolt in Virginia resulted in 59 deaths but was quickly put down. Turner was tried and hanged.

Spirituals (religious songs of an emotional nature) composed by slaves such as "Go Down Moses" and "Michael, Row the Boat Ashore" expressed the intense desire for freedom. Some songs, such as "Follow the Drinking Gourd," served as codes about escape plans.

Slaveholding Southerners—and Whites with No Slaves

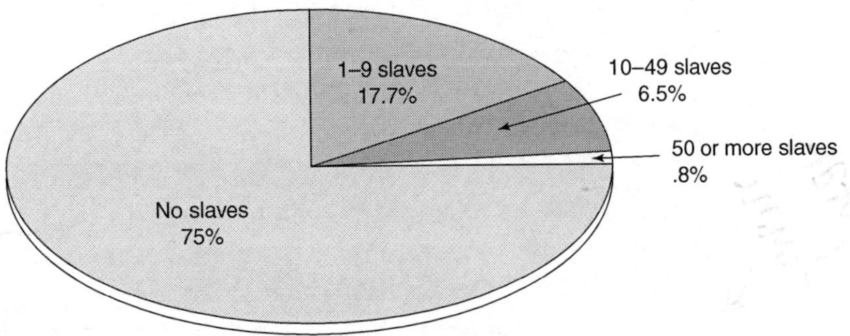

In daily life, slaves often slowed their cotton picking. When owners, eager for profits, offered rewards for quicker work, many slaves risked punishment by refusing.

Some slaves fled. Runaways in the deep South were more easily caught than those farther north. Frederick Douglass disguised himself as a free black seaman and took a train north from Maryland. "Box Henry" hid himself in a box with a Northern address and was shipped to freedom.

Most escaped slaves left on the *Underground Railroad*, a system of routes and safe havens in the homes of white *abolitionists* (persons opposed to slavery). "Conductors" guided escapees to Northern states or to Canada.

U.S. Labor Force, 1800–1860 (in thousands)

Year	*Free*	*Slave*	*Total*
1800	1,330	530	1,860
1810	1,590	740	2,330
1820	2,185	950	3,135
1830	3,020	1,180	4,200
1840	4,180	1,480	5,660
1850	6,280	1,970	8,250
1860	8,770	2,340	11,110

Pre-Civil War Immigration

In the decades before the Civil War, the three main groups of immigrants were the British, Germans, and Irish.

- The British came mainly for economic reasons. Unable to find factory work at home, they hoped to do better in the United States.
- The Germans, including many Jews, came in large numbers after 1848. Some were political refugees from the failed 1848 revolution in Germany. Others sought better economic opportunities. As a group, Germans supported the antislavery movement and public education. Many became farmers in the Midwest.
- The Irish were the largest immigrant group before the Civil War. Their numbers soared after 1845, when blight killed the potato crop that the Irish relied on for food. Many escaped famine only by coming to the United States. They made up the first large-scale group of Roman Catholics in American society. Many Irish built the nation's new canals and roads. In the 1860s, Irish immigrants helped build the Union Pacific

Routes and "Stations" on the Underground Railroad

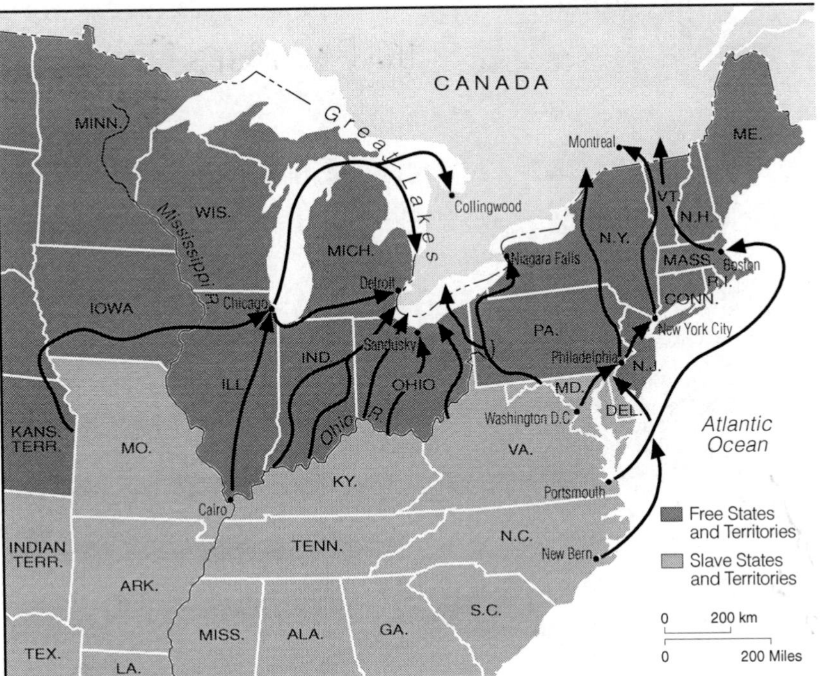

Railroad. After the Civil War, many worked in coal mines and became active in the campaign for better working conditions there.

Nativist Reactions A *nativist* believes that foreign-born people threaten the majority culture. During the 19th century, nativists tried to exclude Irish Catholics, Jews from Eastern Europe, Italians, Chinese, and Japanese.

In the 1850s, Irish Catholic immigrants were the first targets of nativist anger. Groups of American-born Protestants organized a secret society. As a political party, it worked to elect candidates who were in favor of banning or limiting immigration. Members were called *Know-Nothings* because, when asked about their society, they answered, "I know nothing."

IN REVIEW

1. Compare and contrast patterns of life in the North and the South.
2. How did the nativist movement affect new immigrants?
3. How did African slaves resist their owners?

Age of Jackson

In the election of 1828, Andrew Jackson, a Democrat, decisively won the popular and electoral votes. His presidency (1829–1837) became known as the *Age of Jackson*. Although remembered for reforms, it was also marked by the expansion of slavery, persecution of Native Americans, and sectional conflict.

Reform and Political Change

Universal Suffrage for White Males Between 1800 and 1830, state after state removed property requirements for voting. By the Age of Jackson, most white males aged 21 or older could vote.

Election Campaigns As voting rights were extended, candidates developed new techniques to reach voters. Political parties (at this time, the *Whigs* and Democrats) used banners, rallies, speeches, and debates. **Caucuses** (meetings of party leaders) were replaced by **nominating conventions**, where party delegates from many states voted for candidates.

Spoils System After his election, Jackson soon put into effect his motto "To the victor belong the spoils." Under the **spoils system**, his supporters took over most federal jobs in the belief that giving them to "the common man" rather than to the educated and privileged was a democratic reform. Later presidents, Whigs and Democrats alike, followed Jackson's example.

Bank Issue The Second Bank of the United States provoked a bitter dispute. Jackson accused the bank of granting loans to Northeastern businesspeople and denying them to Western farmers. In 1832, he vetoed an act to renew the bank's charter. Henry Clay, Jackson's Whig opponent in the

U.S. Population by Region, 1790–1860

Year	*Northeast*[1]	*North Central*[2]	*South*[3]	*West*[4]
1790	1,968,040	–	1,961,174	–
1800	2,635,576	51,006	2,621,901	–
1810	3,486,675	292,107	3,461,099	–
1820	4,359,916	859,305	4,419,232	–
1830	5,542,381	1,610,473	5,707,848	–
1840	6,761,082	3,351,542	6,950,729	–
1850	8,626,951	5,403,595	8,982,612	178,818
1860	10,594,268	9,096,716	11,133,361	618,976

[1] Maine, New Hampshire, Vermont, Massachusetts, Rhode Island, Connecticut, New York, New Jersey, Pennsylvania

[2] Ohio, Indiana, Illinois, Michigan, Wisconsin, Minnesota, Iowa, Missouri, and the territories of Kansas Nebraska

[3] Delaware, Maryland, Virginia, North Carolina, South Carolina, Georgia, Florida, Kentucky, Tennessee, Alabama, Mississippi, Arkansas, Texas, Louisiana, the Oklahoma Territory

[4] all area west of the states and territories listed for Northeast, North Central, South.

Indian Removal in the 1830s

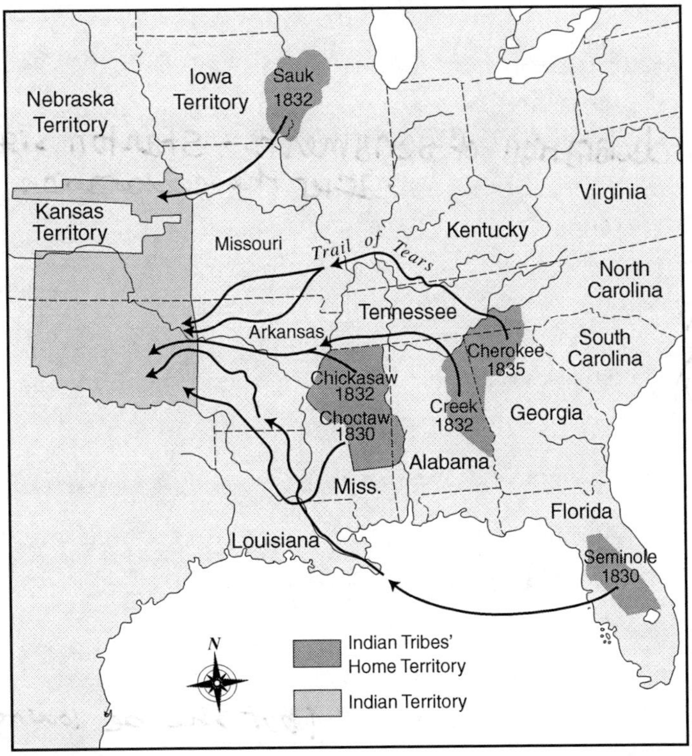

presidential election of 1832, came out in support of the bank. Jackson won reelection by a huge majority.

Native Americans

Immigrants swelled the number of Americans who, in search of land and economic opportunity, kept pushing Native Americans farther west. Outnumbered and facing superior weapons, Native Americans tried several survival strategies. Some adopted European culture. Others maintained and strengthened their own heritage. At times, they united in an attempt to stop the incursions into their territories.

When conflicts arose, Jackson favored the settlers over the Native Americans by initiating *Indian Removal*. The *Resettlement Act* (1830), for example, forced Native Americans to abandon their villages and move hundreds of miles west, where whites had not yet settled.

The worst forced removal was the "*Trail of Tears*" (1838). Some 15,000 Cherokees from Georgia were made to trek westward 800 miles through cold and rain; many of them died from exposure and starvation. Chief Justice John Marshall had earlier ruled that the Cherokees had a right to their land, but Jackson ignored the ruling.

Birth of the Reform Tradition

Some Americans of the 1830s and 1840s worked for women's rights and were also extremely active in other reform movements.

Women's Rights

Lucretia Mott and Elizabeth Cady Stanton objected to the "male-only" political meetings that were common in the reform movements. To discuss such injustices, Stanton called a convention in Seneca Falls, New York (1848). Delegates drafted a declaration based on the assumption that "all men and women are created equal." It stipulated the following rights:

- the right of women to vote and hold office
- the right of married women to hold property in their names
- the right of women wage earners to manage their incomes
- the right of women to be legal guardians of their children.

Stanton fought for laws to grant women long-denied rights and was president of the National Woman Suffrage Association (1869–1890).

Control of Alcohol

In the 1840s, some women led an antidrinking campaign called the **temperance movement**. They persuaded several states to prohibit the production and sale of alcoholic beverages in an effort to stop heads of households from spending money on liquor rather than on supporting their families.

Educational Reform

Until the 1830s, education was primarily for privileged boys whose parents paid for them to attend private schools. Such reformers as Horace Mann and Henry Barnard argued that democracy depends on people who can read, write, and reason. They advocated public education paid for by the states. Massachusetts and New York established the first free schools for children from eight to fourteen. Attendance was compulsory. By 1850, New York's public education system offered instruction from grade one to grade twelve.

Institutions for the Mentally Ill

A former schoolteacher, Dorothea Dix, discovering that the mentally ill were often chained and beaten, called public attention to these horrors. As a result, several states set aside "asylums" where patients received humanitarian care.

Abolitionists (left to right): Harriet Beecher Stowe, Frederick Douglass, Harriet Tubman, John Brown, William Lloyd Garrison

Abolition Movement

Political Conflict In the early days of slavery, some Southerners as well as many Northerners wanted it abolished by law. But as slave labor became critical to the economy of the South, most whites there viewed slaves as property whose ownership was permitted by the Constitution. Northern states banned slavery, and a small group of abolitionists, mostly Northerners, demanded that slavery end everywhere in the United States. A more moderate group wanted to stop the spread of slavery only beyond the Mississippi.

Abolitionist Leaders

Some of the abolitionist leaders were:

- *Harriet Beecher Stowe*, a white woman from Connecticut, wrote *Uncle Tom's Cabin* (1852). This novel is about a kind old slave abused by a vicious slave overseer, Simon Legree. The book aroused intense indignation among Northerners and deep resentment among Southerners, who claimed that it depicted Southern society falsely.
- *Harriet Tubman* escaped slavery as a young woman and became a principal organizer and guide on the Underground Railroad. She also helped free hundreds of slaves during the Civil War and was an advocate of women's rights after the war.
- *Frederick Douglass*, an escaped slave and skillful orator, argued for abolition. He founded the *North Star*, a newspaper written by African

Americans, and wrote his autobiography. During the Civil War, he recruited black soldiers for the Union Army.

- *William Lloyd Garrison*, a white reformer, helped launch the abolitionist movement by publishing an antislavery newspaper, *The Liberator*, beginning in 1831. He demanded an immediate end to slavery without compensation to owners.
- *John Brown*, a white abolitionist, believed in using violence to fight slavery. In Kansas in 1856, Brown and his sons murdered five supporters of slavery in retaliation for the deaths of abolitionist settlers. In 1859, he led an attack at Harpers Ferry, Virginia (now West Virginia), a federal arsenal, probably hoping to arm slaves in the area. After Brown was captured and hanged, abolitionists considered him a martyr, while proslavery Southerners saw him as a crazed fanatic.

IN REVIEW

1. How did democracy expand in the first half of the 19th century?
2. How did Andrew Jackson resolve his differences with supporters of a national bank?
3. How did abolitionists attempt to end slavery?

Federal Supremacy Versus States' Rights

Until the Civil War ended, one of the great constitutional debates concerned nullification, a state's purported right to disregard laws passed by the federal government. An early example occurred in 1798 when Virginia and Kentucky passed resolutions nullifying the Federalist-dominated Congress's Alien and Sedition Acts.

Tariff of Abominations

During Jackson's presidency, the debate heated up over tariffs. During the War of 1812, when Americans could no longer import goods from Britain, factories in the North sprang up and became profitable. To maintain this advantage after the war, Congress raised tariff rates in 1816, 1818, 1824, and 1828. Besides reducing foreign competition, the tariffs encouraged Northern manufacturers to raise prices paid by its U.S. consumers.

The tariffs also reduced the market for British-made cotton cloth. This meant that the South sold less cotton to Britain, its chief customer. When Congress again raised the tariff in 1828, Southerners resisted, calling it the "*Tariff of Abominations.*"

Jackson's vice president, John C. Calhoun of South Carolina, led the resistance. He wrote that every state had a right to nullify an act of Congress that it deemed unconstitutional, and that the Tariff of 1828 should be nullified because it benefited one section of the country at the expense of another. Jackson declared that Calhoun's ideas were treasonable.

In 1832, Congress reduced the tariff in part, but Southerners remained dissatisfied. South Carolina's *Ordinance of Nullification* threatened the state's secession if the federal government tried to collect tariffs in Southern ports.

Jackson threatened to use U.S. troops to enforce the tariff. Senator Henry Clay of Kentucky then proposed a compromise: Congress would pass a new tariff in 1833, providing for a gradual reduction of rates, if South Carolina repealed its ordinance. The compromise was accepted.

Free and Slave States

As new Western territories were added to the United States, arguments about slavery in them became more heated.

Missouri Compromise Slave owners who moved to the Missouri Territory usually brought along their slaves. In 1819, Missouri applied for admission as a state that would permit slavery. After much debate, Congress passed the *Missouri Compromise* (1820), which maintained the balance between slave and free states:

- Missouri would enter the Union as a slave state.
- Maine would enter the Union as a free state.
- All the rest of the Louisiana Purchase north of the 36°30′ line of latitude would be closed to slavery.

The agreement did not solve the crisis but merely put it off for two decades.

Missouri Compromise of 1820

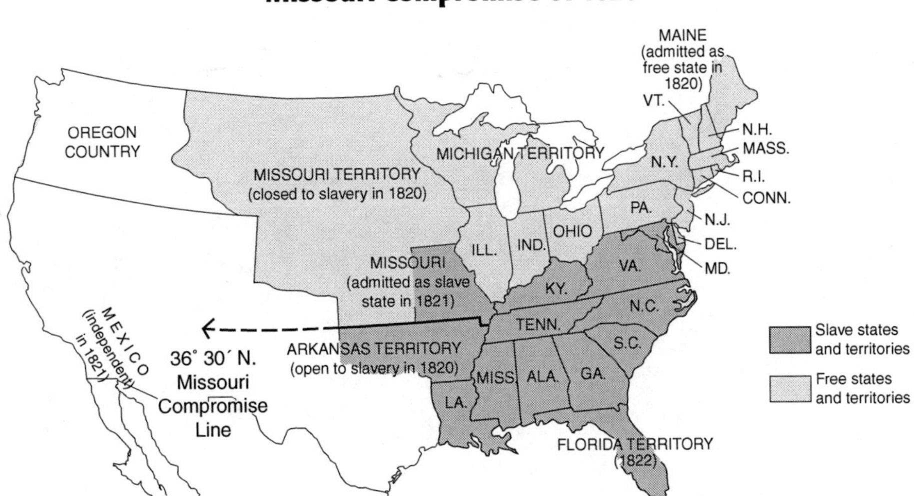

Compromise of 1850

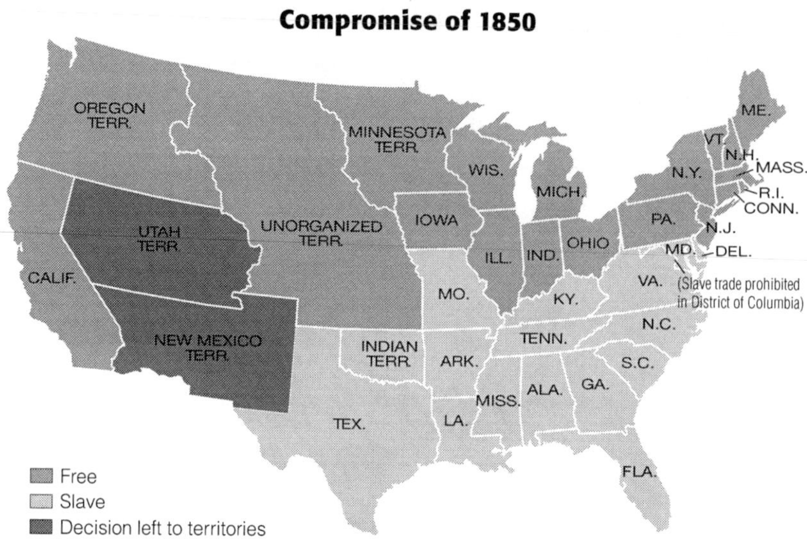

California After the Mexican War (1846–1848), the United States acquired a large tract of land that included present-day California. Settlement there soared after the gold rush of 1849, and California applied for admission as a free state. Southerners were opposed because its admission would upset the balance between free and slave states, as established by the Missouri Compromise, and give the North majorities in the Senate and House. They feared that the Northern majority might prevent them from taking slaves into other territories won from Mexico.

Compromise of 1850 Senator Clay proposed another compromise:

- California would be admitted as a free state. In other parts of the *Mexican Cession* (lands ceded by Mexico to the United States), including Arizona, New Mexico, Utah, and Nevada, settlers would decide by **popular sovereignty** (majority vote) whether to allow slavery.
- Buying and selling slaves at public auction would be abolished in Washington, D.C.
- A *Fugitive Slave Act* would require Northern officials to assist in the capture and return of escaped slaves. Although Congress finally passed the compromise, widespread resistance among Northern abolitionists to the Fugitive Slave Act continued.

Dred Scott v. Sanford (1857)

Facts Dred Scott was a slave from Missouri before his owner took him to Wisconsin, a free territory. Scott returned to Missouri and asked a court there to declare him a free citizen on the grounds that he had lived in a free territory. His case eventually was appealed to the Supreme Court.

Supreme Court Decision In 1857, Chief Justice Roger Taney, a Southerner, ruled as follows:

- Free African Americans were not citizens and could not sue in federal courts.
- Slaves brought into free territory remained slaves because they were property, and owners could not be denied property without due process of law.
- The Missouri Compromise's ban on slavery in free territory was unconstitutional because it had denied slave owners their property rights.

Public Reaction Southerners rejoiced that the Supreme Court had confirmed their views. Many Northerners were shocked at a decision that threw all territories in the West open to slavery.

IN REVIEW

1. How did the tariff issue heat up the nullification debate during Jackson's administration?
2. How did *each* of the following attempt to resolve the slavery issue? (a) Missouri Compromise and (b) Compromise of 1850.
3. What were the facts, issues, and decision in *Dred Scott* v. *Sanford*?

CHAPTER REVIEW

MULTIPLE-CHOICE QUESTIONS

1 During the early 1800s, which factor contributed the most to the start of the Industrial Revolution in the United States?
   (1) a restriction on European immigration
   (2) the end of the slave labor system
   (3) an abundance of natural resources
   (4) the availability of electricity

2 During the first half of the 1800s, geographic factors influenced the economy of New England by
   (1) encouraging the establishment of large plantations
   (2) promoting the growth of trade and manufacturing
   (3) increasing the region's reliance on slave labor
   (4) supporting rice and indigo farming

3 What was an immediate effect of the completion of the Erie Canal in 1825?
   (1) Prices increased for food products along the Atlantic Coast.
   (2) Farmers could more easily ship grain to eastern markets.
   (3) A territorial conflict began with Canada over the Great Lakes.
   (4) Railroads were forced to reduce their shipping rates.

4 The climate and topography of the southeastern United States had a major impact on the history of the United States before 1860 because the region
   (1) became the center of commerce and manufacturing
   (2) developed as the largest domestic source of steel production

(3) was the area in which most immigrants chose to settle
(4) provided agricultural products that were processed in the North and in Europe

5 President Andrew Jackson's policy toward Native American Indians was created to
(1) encourage Native American Indians to become part of mainstream American society
(2) force Native American Indians to move west of the Mississippi River
(3) improve educational opportunities for Native American Indians
(4) grant citizenship to Native American Indians

Base your answer to question 6 on the poster below and on your knowledge of social studies.

100 DOLLARS REWARD!

Ranaway from the subscriber on the 27th of July, my Black Woman, named

EMILY,

Seventeen years of age, well grown, black color, has a whining voice. She took with her one dark calico and one blue and white dress, a red corded gingham bonnet; a white striped shawl and slippers. I will pay the above reward if taken near the Ohio river on the Kentucky side, or THREE HUNDRED DOLLARS, if taken in the State of Ohio, and delivered to me near Lewisburg, Mason County, Ky.

THO'S H. WILLIAMS.

August 4, 1853.

6 Prior to the Civil War, abolitionists reacted to the situation described in the poster by
(1) supporting the Underground Railroad
(2) opposing the Emancipation Proclamation
(3) banning freed slaves from Northern states
(4) proposing a stricter fugitive slave law

7 In the 1850s, why did many runaway slaves go to Canada?
(1) They feared being drafted into the Northern army.
(2) The Fugitive Slave Act kept them at risk in the United States.
(3) More factory jobs were available in Canada.
(4) Northern abolitionists refused to help fugitive slaves.

8 Which statement about the Missouri Compromise (1820) is most accurate?
(1) Slavery was banned west of the Mississippi River.
(2) Unorganized territories would be governed by the United States and Great Britain.
(3) The balance between free and slave states was maintained.
(4) The 36°30′ line formed a new boundary between the United States and Canada.

9 Which Supreme Court decision created the need for a constitutional amendment that would grant citizenship to formerly enslaved persons?
(1) *Marbury* v. *Madison*
(2) *McCulloch* v. *Maryland*
(3) *Worcester* v. *Georgia*
(4) *Dred Scott* v. *Sanford*

Base your answer to question 10 on the following map and on your knowledge of social studies.

10 What is the most accurate title for this map?
(1) Closing the Frontier
(2) Results of Reconstruction
(3) A Nation Divided
(4) Compromise of 1850

THEMATIC ESSAYS

1 **THEME:** *Sectionalism in the North and South.* Between 1800 and 1850, the United States became increasingly divided by sectional differences in the North and South.

TASK: Explain *three* ways in which the sections differed, and explain the differences. Refer to historical events that contributed to the growth of these differences. Consider such factors as people, geography, work, and lifestyles.

2 **THEME:** *Expansion as a Cause of Nationalism and Sectionalism.* The expansion of the Western frontier resulted in events that encouraged both the unity of nationalism and the disunity of sectionalism.

TASK: Describe *one* circumstance that promoted nationalism and *another* that resulted in sectionalism. For *each* example, include the following:

- background of the circumstance
- how nationalism or sectionalism became an outcome.

You may use such examples as Eli Whitney's cotton gin and system of interchangeable parts, the Missouri Compromise, the Compromise of 1850, and the Dred Scott case.

DOCUMENT-BASED QUESTION

Study each document and answer the question that follows it. Then read the **Task** and write your essay. Include references to most of the documents and additional information you retain about U.S. history and government.

HISTORICAL CONTEXT: While the period between the 1820s and the 1840s saw democracy expand, many people still had no control over their lives or were second-class citizens.

DOCUMENT 1: Refer to the cartoon below.

"Box Henry" Brown arriving in the North

QUESTION: What does the cartoon show about the extremes to which slaves would go to gain freedom?

DOCUMENT 2: From Lucretia Mott and Elizabeth Cady Stanton's "Declaration of Sentiments," 1848:

> The history of mankind is a history of repeated injuries . . . on the part of man toward woman, having in the direct object the establishment of an absolute tyranny over her. To prove this, let facts be submitted to a candid world:
>
> He has never permitted her to exercise her inalienable right to the elective franchise.
>
> He has compelled her to submit to laws, in the formation of which she had no voice. . . .

QUESTION: What complaints did Mott, Stanton, and other women have about men's treatment of women throughout history?

DOCUMENT 3: Examine the painting *The Trail of Tears* below.

QUESTION: What does the painting show about the government's treatment of Native Americans?

DOCUMENT 4: Refer to the following cartoon of American slaves and American and British working people.

"The Trail of Tears"—Cherokees' forced journey to an unknown land

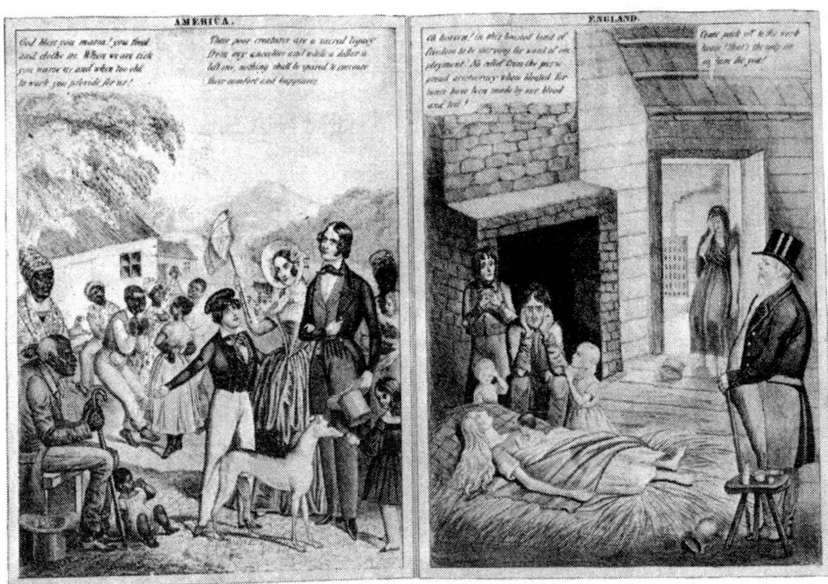

1840s cartoon contrasting Southern slavery with Northern and British "wage slavery"

QUESTION: What attitude does the artist express in comparing British and Northern factory labor and Southern slavery?

DOCUMENT 5: Refer to the cartoon below.

QUESTION: How does the cartoon illustrate the view of some Americans about immigrants during the early to mid-1800s?

DOCUMENT 6: Harriet Martineau, a British author, describes her 1834 visit to the United States:

In an 1800s nativist cartoon, new citizens—an Irishman and a German—steal the ballot box.

> I had been less than three weeks in the country and was in . . . awe at the prevalence of . . . not only external competence, but intellectual ability. The striking effect . . . of witnessing . . . the absence of poverty, of gross ignorance, or all servility, of all insolence of manner cannot be exaggerated. I had seen every man . . . an independent citizen [or] a landowner. I had seen that the villages had their newspapers, the factory girls their libraries. I had witnessed [candidates'] controversies . . . on some difficult subjects, of which the people were to be the judges. With all these things in my mind, and with evidence of prosperity about me, . . . I was thrown into painful amazement by being told that the grand question of the time was "whether the people should be encouraged to govern themselves, or whether the wise should save them from themselves."

QUESTION: How did Martineau feel about life in the United States in 1834?

DOCUMENT 7: Look at the painting *Canvassing for a Vote* below.

QUESTION: What does the painting show about election campaigns in the Age of Jackson?

TASK: Using the documents and your knowledge of U.S. history and government, write an essay in which you show how the period of the early and mid-1800s had both democratic and undemocratic aspects.

Canvassing for a Vote: Politicians from the Jacksonian era onward sought the common man's vote.

CHAPTER 6
Western Expansion and Civil War

DOCUMENTS AND LAWS
Kansas-Nebraska Act (1854) • Homestead Act (1862) • Emancipation Proclamation (1863)
National Banking Act (1863) • Thirteenth Amendment (1865)

EVENTS
Independence of Texas (1836–1845) • Annexation of Texas (1845) • Treaty of 1846
Mexican War (1846–1848) • Mexican Cession (1848) • Gadsden Purchase (1853)
"Bleeding Kansas" (1855) • Election of 1860 • South Carolina secession (1860)
Firing on Fort Sumter (1861) • Civil War (1861–1865) • Battle of Antietam (1862)
Gettysburg Address (1863) • Surrender of Vicksburg (1863)
Sherman's March to the Sea (1864) • Surrender at Appomattox Court House (1865)
Assassination of Lincoln (1865)

PEOPLE/GROUPS
Santa Ana • Clara Barton • John Wilkes Booth • John Brown • Henry Clay • Jefferson Davis
Dorothea Dix • Stephen Douglas • Ulysses S. Grant • Thomas J. "Stonewall" Jackson
Robert E. Lee • Abraham Lincoln • George B. McClellan • George G. Meade • Mormons
James K. Polk • Republicans • Sacajawea • Antonio López de Santa Anna • William T. Sherman
Harriet Beecher Stowe

OBJECTIVES

- To explain the impact of Western expansion on Native Americans and Mexicans.
- To examine how the dispute over Oregon was settled peacefully, while others over Texas and the Southwest resulted in war.
- To identify the causes and consequences of the Mexican War.
- To compare the Northern and Southern viewpoints on the slavery issue.
- To identify causes and consequences of the Civil War.
- To analyze why Lincoln was a great president.

Territorial Expansion

As a Democratic-Republican, Jefferson was committed to states' rights. Yet his prime presidential duty was to strengthen the nation. Because of his decision to buy the vast Louisiana Territory, he had to modify his view of the Constitution.

Louisiana Purchase

Thomas Jefferson

The treaty ending the American Revolution set the Mississippi River as the western boundary of the new nation. The Mississippi—2,348 miles long—is the largest U.S. river. With its **tributaries** (rivers flowing into it), it drains almost the entire area from the Appalachian Mountains to the Rockies. It pours into the Gulf of Mexico near New Orleans, Louisiana. The Mississippi was a means of transport for Native Americans and European explorers into the heartland of America. It served as a major highway for trade. At that time, New Orleans and the unexplored expanse of Louisiana to the west were under French rule. By 1800, pioneers had moved into Kentucky, Tennessee, and Ohio, all east of the Mississippi. No more expansion was possible until, in 1803, Napoleon Bonaparte offered to sell New Orleans and the Louisiana Territory to the United States for the bargain price of about $15 million.

Jefferson's Dilemma No clause in the Constitution authorized the federal government to expand U.S. borders. As a strict constructionist, Jefferson could not justify buying Louisiana.

Jefferson finally yielded to the arguments of opponents in the Federalist Party. They insisted that the elastic clause implied many powers not specifically listed in the Constitution. In 1803, Jefferson asked the Senate to ratify the Louisiana Purchase. (Map is on page 107.)

Exploring and Settling the West

Louisiana more than doubled the U.S. land area. In 1804, Jefferson sent Meriwether Lewis and William Clark to explore the new lands. The following year, they reached the Columbia River, which was a water route to the Pacific Ocean. Because of these explorations, the United States claimed the whole territory of Oregon. On their journey, Lewis and Clark were fortunate to secure the help of a Native American, Sacajawea. Serving as a

Lewis and Clark stop at a Native-American village.

North Wind Picture Archives

guide and translator, she was of significant help to the explorers. In 1806, they returned with a full report, maps, and drawings of the region.

American fur trappers soon went to the so-called Oregon Country. Known as "mountain men," they became trailblazers for new settlers and for missionaries who wished to convert the Native Americans there to Christianity. By the 1840s, several thousand Americans were living in the Oregon Country.

Mormons were among new settlers in the West. Joseph Smith had founded the Mormon Church (Church of the Latter-Day Saints) in western New York State. The growing Mormon congregation tried to set up communities in the Midwest but were persecuted for their beliefs, particularly the practice of polygamy. Led by Brigham Young, the Mormons traveled to Utah, where they founded Salt Lake City.

Spaniards, Mexicans, and Native Americans Present-day Texas, New Mexico, Arizona, and California were earlier explored and settled by the Spaniards. Spreading northward from Mexico City, they claimed and occupied much of the Southwest and established forts, missions, ranches, villages, and towns.

Spanish missions were surrounded by farmlands. The missionaries gave small plots to Native-American converts.

Some Native Americans challenged Spanish control of the Southwest. In 1680, the Pueblos drove the Spaniards from Santa Fe, New Mexico. Within a dozen years, however, the region was again under Spanish control.

IN REVIEW

1. With what constitutional dilemma did the opportunity to purchase Louisiana present Jefferson?
2. Discuss the long-term effects of the Louisiana Purchase.
3. Describe the significance of the Lewis and Clark expedition.

Motives for Expansion and Western Settlement

By the 1800s, many Americans believed in a self-evident U.S. right to expand to the Pacific coast and dominate North America. They called it **manifest destiny**. Mexicans, who had already settled large parts of the West, viewed manifest destiny as a threat. So did the Native Americans there.

To encourage Western settlement, Henry Clay proposed, and Congress adopted, the **American System**. It called for building roads and canals to the West and placing a high tariff on European imports. The tariff would

Pre-Civil War Agriculture, Mining, and Manufacturing

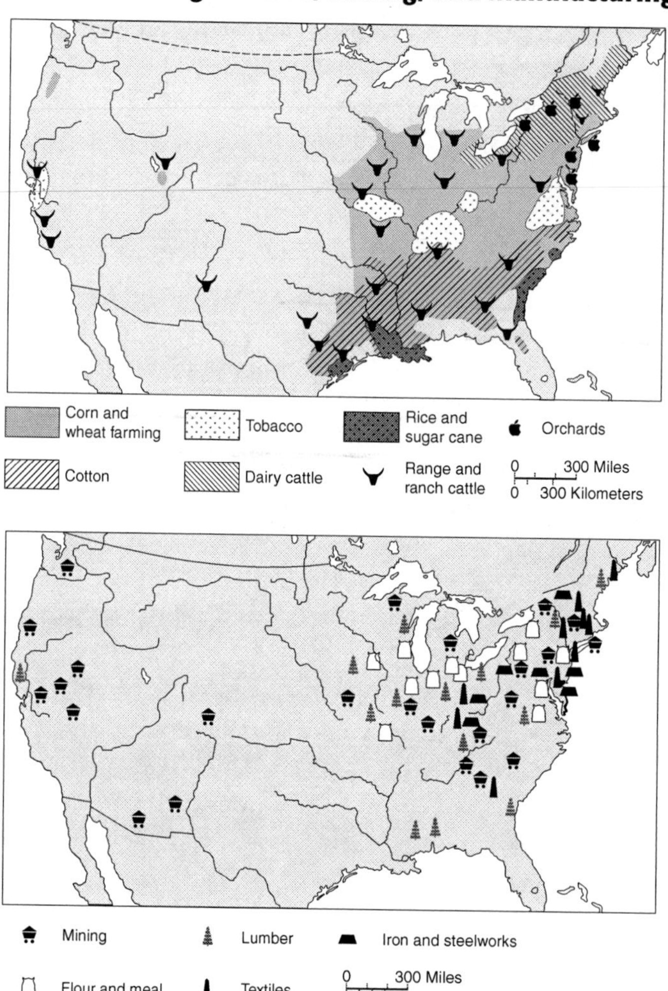

encourage Westerners to buy from Eastern manufacturers. By aiding both the West and East, Clay hoped to unite the nation's economy.

Politics of Expansion

In colonial times, the lands from Texas to California had been Spanish. When the Mexicans revolted in 1821, Texas and California became the northern part of independent Mexico.

Texan Independence and Annexation

In the 1820s, only a few thousand Mexicans lived in Texas, and the Mexican government did not immediately object when U.S. pioneers began to move in. By the mid-1830s, however, more Americans than Mexicans lived there. Americans often defied Mexican laws, including the ban against slavery. When Mexico tried to end this immigration, the American settlers revolted and declared Texas independent (1836).

Mexico's president, General Antonio López de Santa Anna, led troops into Texas and defeated the Texan defenders occupying the Alamo, a mission serving as a fort. Soon afterward, however, the Texans captured Santa Anna and forced him to recognize their independence.

From 1836 to 1845, Texas was an independent nation. Many Texans wanted Texas to become part of the United States. But the issue of slavery delayed its **annexation** (formal addition) into the Union. Southerners supported it, but Northerners were opposed to gaining another slave state. In 1845, Congress annexed Texas.

Dispute Over Oregon

In the Pacific Northwest, both the United States and Britain claimed the Oregon Country. President James K. Polk and other expansionists wanted this forested land as far north as the 54°40′ line of latitude in present-day Canada. Thus, in 1845 their supporters adopted the slogan, "Fifty-four forty or fight!" War with Britain loomed.

Settlement British-American compromise resulted in the *Treaty of 1846*, which divided the Oregon Country roughly in two; the northern half went to Britain and the southern half (below the 49th parallel of latitude) to the United States. The treaty both extended the U.S.-Canadian border to the Pacific and improved U.S. relations with Britain.

Cartoon of "John Bull" (Britain) laughing at "Yankee Doodle" (United States) in the Oregon dispute

Oregon Country, 1848

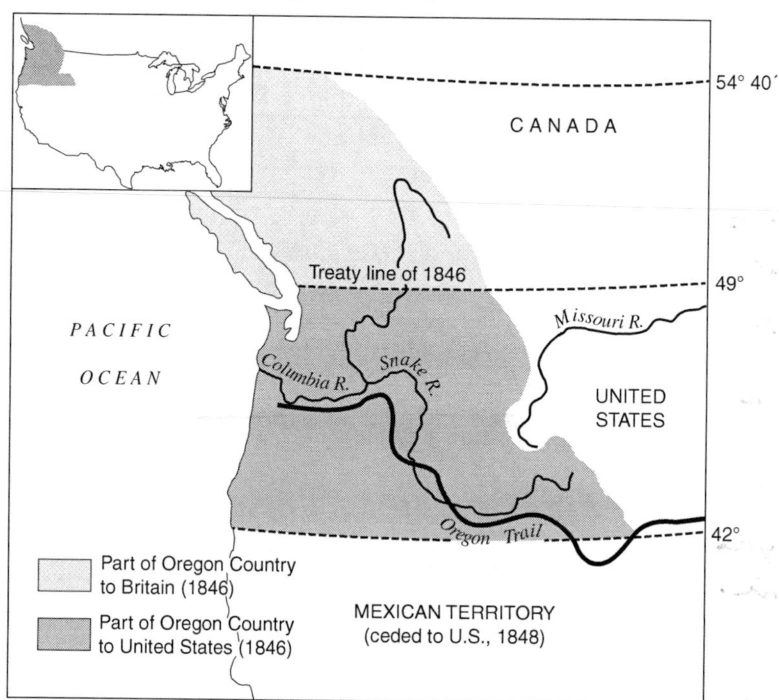

Mexican War (1846–1848)

Mexico still held present-day Arizona, New Mexico, Utah, Nevada, and California. When the United States offered to buy these lands, Mexico, angry about the annexation of Texas, refused.

Causes of War The expansionism of President Polk was largely responsible for the U.S. war with Mexico. The immediate cause was a disputed Texas-Mexico boundary. When Mexican troops fired on U.S. troops in the area, Polk asked Congress to declare war, stating that Mexico had "shed American blood on American soil."

Peace Terms The Mexican War ended after U.S. troops captured Mexico City and the territory of California. By terms of the *Treaty of Guadalupe Hidalgo* (1848), the United States paid a mere $15 million for all the land west of Texas to the California coast (the *Mexican Cession*).

California Gold Rush

Soon afterward, an American settler in California discovered gold. Fortune hunters poured into California. As a result of the 1849 gold rush, California's population grew rapidly, and it soon applied for admission as a nonslave state. The South opposed its admission.

Gadsden Purchase

In 1853, the United States made a final purchase of land from Mexico for $10 million. Called the *Gadsden Purchase*, it consisted of land along the southern border of New Mexico and Arizona.

Impact of Expansion on Mexicans and Native Americans

The Mexican War deprived Mexico of much of its land and natural resources. Mexicans who found themselves living within the United States lost their farms and ranches and took low-paying jobs on farms, in mines, or on railroads. Many other Americans looked down on the Mexicans whom they had dispossessed.

Western expansion severely reduced the Native-American population. U.S. settlers brought diseases, such as measles and smallpox, against which Native Americans had no immunity. The great buffalo herds on which Plains people depended for survival were destroyed. As the settlers advanced, Native Americans fought to defend their territory. They were no match for the well-equipped U.S. Army, however, and were forced to move to **reservations** (government land set aside for them).

IN REVIEW

1. What did Americans mean by manifest destiny?
2. Identify the causes of conflict between (a) Mexico and American settlers of Texas in 1836, (b) Britain and the United States in 1845, and (c) the United States and Mexico in 1846.
3. Summarize the impact of Western expansion on Mexicans and Native Americans.

United States Divided

The slavery issue continued to divide the country in the 1850s.

Western Expansion and Slavery

The territories of Kansas and Nebraska were both north of the 36°30′ line, so they were, according to the Missouri Compromise of 1820, slave-free. In the 1850s, Senator Stephen Douglas of Illinois proposed, and Congress passed, the *Kansas-Nebraska Act* (1854), which stated:

- The Missouri Compromise no longer applied to Kansas and Nebraska.
- The states would decide by popular sovereignty whether to allow slavery.

"Bleeding Kansas" Fighting broke out in Kansas between Southern, proslavery settlers and Northern, antislavery settlers. "*Bleeding Kansas*" became a clear omen of civil war.

Disintegration of the Whig Party From the early to mid-1800s, Whigs comprised one of the two major political parties. Having supporters in both the North and South, they took no initial stand on slavery. In the 1850s, however, legislation such as the Compromise of 1850 and the Kansas-Nebraska Act pointed up the deep division between Northern and Southern Whigs.

In 1852, the Whig candidate for president won only four states. As the party divided, many Northern Whigs joined the Know-Nothings or American Party, which campaigned against immigration and Catholicism. But the new Republican Party replaced the Whigs as the country's second major party.

Rise of the Republican Party

Founded in 1854 by such antislavery groups as Whigs, Northern Democrats, and abolitionists, the Republican Party drew its support from the North and West. The Democratic Party's strength was more widespread—North, West, and South.

The Republican platforms of 1856 and 1860 included the following goals:

- keep slavery out of Western territories
- enact a high protective tariff to encourage Northern industries
- build a transcontinental railroad (stretching from the Atlantic to the Pacific).

John Brown's Harpers Ferry raid and the Dred Scott decision increased the Republicans' popularity in the North. In the election of 1856, the Republican presidential candidate, John C. Frémont, came in second nationwide and first in the North.

Abraham Lincoln

Abraham Lincoln began his political career in Illinois. As a state legislator, he opposed the expansion of slavery and supported internal improvements and a high tariff. Lincoln joined the Republican Party as the Whig Party began to disintegrate. In 1858, he became the Republican candidate for the U.S. Senate.

Lincoln-Douglas Debates Lincoln and his opponent, Stephen Douglas, the Democratic leader in the Senate, debated the issue of slavery in the new

Lincoln-Douglas debate

Western states. Douglas supported the idea of popular sovereignty in these new states. Lincoln, by contrast, believed that slavery was wrong and should not be allowed to spread under any circumstances. Douglas was reelected to the Senate in 1858, but Lincoln's strong arguments in the debate and the closeness of the election earned Lincoln national attention.

Election of 1860 In 1860, the *Republicans* nominated Lincoln for president. A majority of Democrats nominated Stephen Douglas, whose views on slavery were moderate. Southern Democrats nominated John Breckinridge, who was a proslavery Southerner. The new Constitutional Union Party nominated John Bell. Lincoln won this race with only 40 percent of the popular vote (the heavily populated North gave him enough electoral votes).

Secession of the South

One month after Lincoln's election, South Carolina seceded from the Union. These were the reasons:

- *Slavery.* Most Southern whites owned no slaves but supported slavery. More and more Northerners viewed slavery as immoral and unprincipled. The differing views of North and South became more divided as a result of the Kansas-Nebraska Act, violent conflicts in Kansas, John Brown's raids, the Dred Scott decision, and the birth of the Republican Party. As white Southerners attempted to justify slavery, more and more white Northerners regarded it as immoral and unprincipled.
- *Economic Differences.* Southern plantation life was based on one family's ownership of land worked by many slaves, while the industrialized North had many small farms. The North also had many more factories than the South. These differing economies conflicted on important political issues such as the tariff.

- *Regional Loyalties.* Nationalism was weaker in the South, where people were attached to their region and jealously guarded states' rights.
- *Belief in "Cotton Is King."* Many Southerners believed that the North would not go to war over secession since it needed Southern cotton for its mills. Even if war came, Southerners believed, the foreign (especially British) demand for their cotton would result in European support for their cause.
- *Lack of National Leadership.* Recent presidents—Millard Fillmore, Franklin Pierce, and James Buchanan—were not strong leaders, and congressional leadership was weak, too. Two important nationalist senators, Henry Clay and Daniel Webster, died in the early 1850s.

Efforts at Compromise A compromise plan, the *Crittenden Proposal,* called for federal protection of slavery in any U.S. territory below the 36°30′ line of latitude, thus allowing slavery in any Southern territory. Territories north of the line would be slave-free. On becoming a state, any territory could choose admittance as a slave or free state. Lincoln opposed the expansion of slavery into the territories and rejected the compromise. However, he promised to allow the Southern states to maintain slavery.

Fort Sumter U.S. forces had long held Fort Sumter, an island fortress in the harbor of Charleston, South Carolina. Now South Carolina demanded its surrender, but Lincoln refused. A month after the president's inauguration in March 1861, Southern guns bombarded the fort. The Civil War had begun.

Election of 1860

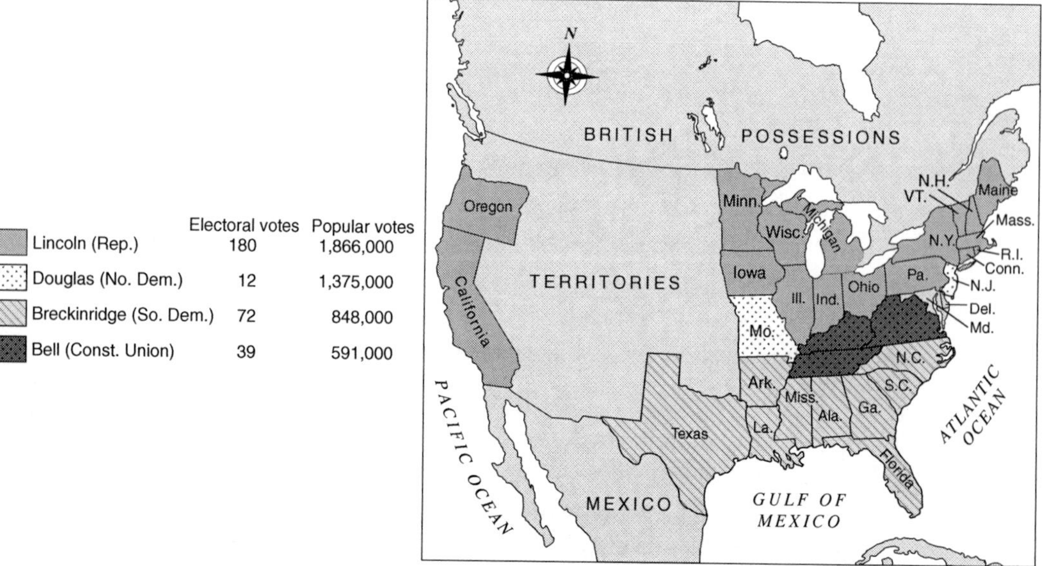

IN REVIEW

1. Explain the major reasons for the decline of the Whigs and rise of the Republicans.
2. List key reasons for Lincoln's victory in the election of 1860.
3. Describe the major steps that led to the Civil War.

Civil War

By the spring of 1861, a total of 11 Southern states had seceded and loosely joined together under their own constitution and central government, the Confederate States of America. Between 1861 and 1865, Southerners fought for independence and Northerners fought to save the Union and put down the "rebellion."

At first, the South had a better officer corps. The North, however, had a large population and the economic resources needed to win a long war.

Military Strategy and Major Battles

Both the North and the South believed that it would win the war quickly. The South relied on its strength as defender of its own territory. The North

United States at the Outbreak of the Civil War, 1861

expected that its numerically huge advantage in troops and equipment would defeat the South.

Lincoln's Strategy Lincoln planned to capture the Mississippi River and then defeat Southern armies in the West and East separately. He intended to stop the export of cotton and import of supplies and weapons by imposing a blockade. Finally, he hoped that the Union army would inflict major losses on the smaller Confederate army.

Antietam The South won most of the important initial battles. In 1862, however, Union general George McClellan stopped a Confederate advance by General Robert E. Lee in Maryland at the *Battle of Antietam*, with important consequences. England and France decided not to intervene, and Lincoln issued the Emancipation Proclamation (discussed on page 103).

Gettysburg With war supplies running low, Lee invaded the North. After a three-day battle near Gettysburg, Pennsylvania (July 1–3, 1863), Confederate troops were badly defeated by well-protected Union troops, and Lee retreated South. Both sides had lost thousands of men, but General George G. Meade had won the Union's first major battle and stopped the only Confederate attempt to invade the North.

Vicksburg One day later, Union general Ulysses S. Grant forced the *surrender of Vicksburg*, a key Confederate port on the Mississippi River. One of the South's main supply routes was now blocked.

Sherman's March to the Sea In 1864, Union general William T. Sherman led a campaign of destruction from Tennessee to the Georgia coast and then northward through the Carolinas. For the first time, destruction of civilian property became Union wartime policy, as numerous Southern mansions and farmhouses were put to the torch.

Richmond and Appomattox Richmond, in central Virginia, was the Confederate capital. On April 2, 1865, a Union army marched into the city, and seven days later, the Civil War ended when Lee surrendered to Grant at *Appomattox Court House*, Virginia.

Impact on the Home Front

Civil Liberties During the war, Lincoln made the defeat of the South his priority and suspended the writ of habeas corpus. Hundreds of people in Maryland, including Baltimore's mayor and police chief and members of the state legislature, were arrested for disloyalty but not tried. Lincoln feared that they posed a threat to nearby Washington, D.C.

By the end of the war, 15,000 individuals had been arrested and imprisoned without trial. Some civilians were tried and convicted by military

North and South in the Civil War

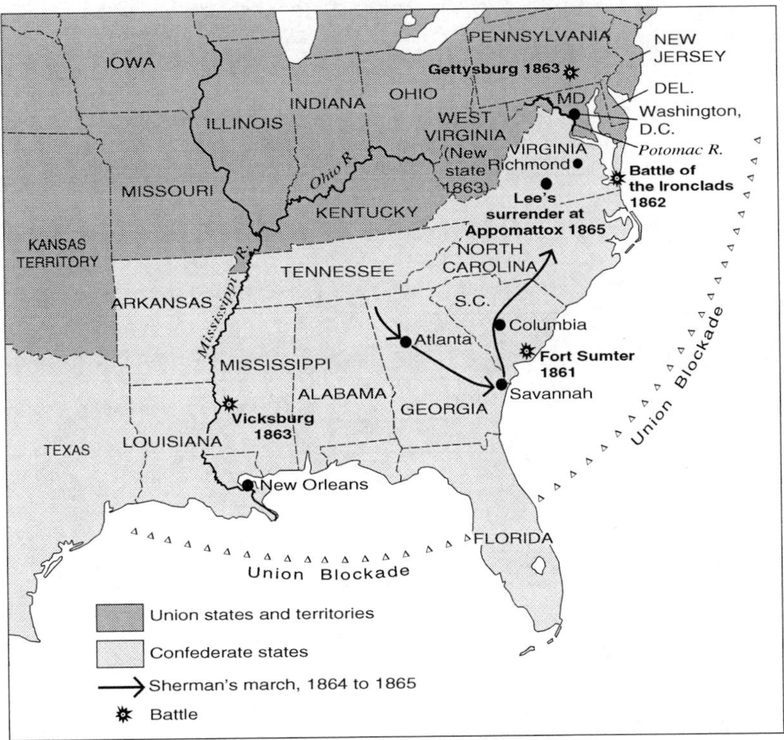

courts. After the war, the Supreme Court held that military courts could not try civilians where state and federal courts are functioning.

Scholars still disagree about Lincoln's actions. Supporters hold that the Constitution allows the suspension of habeas corpus "when in cases of rebellion or invasion the public safety may require it" (Article I, Section 9). Opponents believe that only Congress may suspend habeas corpus and that such strong use of presidential power could lead to a **dictatorship** (one-person rule).

Women's Roles Women factory workers, already accustomed to long hours, worked even harder to fill the labor gap left by the fighting men. They earned as little as 25 cents a day producing uniforms, weapons, and other war goods.

The need for nurses opened up the profession to women. Under the leadership of Dorothea Dix and Clara Barton, women volunteers cared for the wounded on battlefields and in hospitals. After the war, Clara Barton organized the American Red Cross (1881).

The wives and mothers of soldiers on both sides supported the war effort by writing their men letters of comfort and encouragement.

IN REVIEW

1. Explain how Lincoln's wartime strategies were related to Northern advantages.
2. Was Lincoln right to limit civil liberties during the Civil War? Explain.
3. "Although women did not fight, they played a major role during the Civil War." Do you agree with this statement? Explain.

Wartime Policy

Finances The North financed the war effort by increasing tariffs on imports and excise taxes on domestic goods (such as alcoholic beverages), issuing "greenbacks" (paper money), and selling government bonds. Government bonds brought in the most money and rose in value as the Union Army began to win.

Resources of the North and South

	North: Union	*South: Confederacy*
Population	22 million (1860)	6 million free citizens, 3 million slaves
Economic resources	Many factories and farms to produce war goods and food supplies; superior railroad system; control of 70% of nation's wealth	Little industry; farms for growing cotton, not food; poor railroad system; control of 30% of nation's wealth
Strategic position	Difficult: forces required to launch risky offensives on enemy territory	Relatively easy: forces deployed on home ground in defensive positions
Morale	Poor: many civilians initially indifferent to or against war; troops far from home and family	Good: most civilians behind war effort; troops fighting in defense of homes and families
Preparation	Mostly undertrained, raw recruits with no military tradition	Strong military tradition; general expertise in riding and shooting
Military leadership	Inexperienced officers; mediocre or uncooperative generals (e.g., George B. McClellan) until later years (e.g., Ulysses S. Grant)	Experienced officers and superior generals (e.g., Robert E. Lee and Thomas J. "Stonewall" Jackson)
Naval strength	Strong navy able to blockade Southern ports and cut off vital supplies	Few ships; dependence on blockade-runners
Political leadership	President Abraham Lincoln: tireless, active, militarily astute	President Jefferson Davis: intelligent, aloof, overly cautious
Foreign relations	Universal recognition as legitimate government	Lack of support and recognition from other nations

The South had few ways to raise money. The Union blockade deprived it of foreign goods and limited tariff collections. Dedicated to states' rights, the Southern states opposed taxation by the Confederate government, which instead printed a large amount of paper currency backed by little gold. As the Southern cause worsened, Confederate money lost value.

National Currency The *National Banking Act* (1863) gave banks in the national banking system the right to issue paper money backed by government bonds. The federal government's success in selling U.S. Treasury bonds reinforced the soundness of the new currency.

Homestead Act The *Homestead Act* (1862) provided free public lands to those willing to settle on them. Any citizen or immigrant aspiring to citizenship could acquire 160 acres of federal land simply by farming it for five years.

Emancipation

Although opposed to slavery, Lincoln waited two years before acting on the issue. In September 1862, after the Battle of Antietam, he announced that he would issue an emancipation order in the new year. The *Emancipation Proclamation* (January 1, 1863) declared that slaves in Confederate states were free. In border states that had remained loyal, slavery could remain legal.

Slaves throughout the South made their way to Union lines seeking freedom. The Emancipation Proclamation gave the war a moral basis. Thus, Great Britain, which had abolished slavery in the 1830s, was now reluctant to aid the South even though it desired Southern cotton.

Gettysburg Address

Thousands of soldiers died at Gettysburg. A military cemetery was then dedicated there to honor the Union dead. In his *Gettysburg Address* (1863), Lincoln demonstrated that the Union was fighting not only for victory but also for universal values. His speech ends thus: "... that we here highly resolve that these dead shall not have died in vain; that this nation, under God, shall have a new birth of freedom; and that government of the people, by the people, for the people, shall not perish from the earth."

African Americans in the War

At first, neither the North nor the South allowed African Americans in its armed forces. As the war progressed, the Union allowed both emancipated slaves and free blacks to serve in army units under a system of **segregation** (separation by race). At first, they were assigned nonfighting duties. In 1863, African-American troops (usually commanded by white officers) were trained for combat and sent into battle. By the war's end, more than

African-American Union regiment during the Civil War

180,000 African Americans had joined the Union Army and about 38,000 of those had lost their lives. Sixteen African Americans won the nation's highest military honor, the Medal of Honor.

Draft Riots in the North In 1863, Congress passed a **draft**, which compelled young men of a certain age to join the military. In New York City, whites unwilling to serve rioted by targeting the black population. During four days of violence, countless African Americans were beaten and some **lynched** (hanged).

Thirteenth Amendment

The *Thirteenth Amendment* (1865), passed by two-thirds of Congress and ratified by three-quarters of the states, made slavery illegal in every state. This amendment was strongly supported by Lincoln. It is the only amendment in U.S. history signed by a president.

Second Term

Lincoln won reelection as president in 1864, defeating General McClellan. In his "Second Inaugural Address," he saw the war as divine retribution for 250 years of American slavery. In his concluding paragraph, he called for a fair and generous peace, saying that now was the time to "bind up the nation's wounds... to do all which may achieve and cherish a just and a lasting peace among ourselves and with all nations."

Lincoln's Leadership

Historians consider Lincoln one of the greatest presidents, for the following reasons:

- *Firm political purpose.* All of Lincoln's actions and decisions were focused on saving the Union.

- *Political shrewdness and courage.* He had a keen sense of when to bend to political pressure and when to risk an unpopular decision. He gave many other generals a chance before deciding on Grant's superior capability.
- *Achievements.* He steadily pursued the war when others might have tried compromise. He kept the Union together. He overcame sectionalism. He freed 4 million people from slavery.

In April 1865, an actor and Southern sympathizer, John Wilkes Booth, assassinated Lincoln as he and his wife, Mary Todd Lincoln, watched a play at Ford's Theater in Washington, D.C.

IN REVIEW

1. Why did the Union have an advantage over the South in financing the war?
2. Explain why *each* of the following events was a turning point in the Civil War: (a) Battle of Antietam, (b) Union victory at Gettysburg, (c) Union victory at Vicksburg.
3. Historians consider Lincoln one of the greatest U.S. presidents. Do you agree with this assessment? Explain.

CHAPTER REVIEW

MULTIPLE-CHOICE QUESTIONS

1 In the early 1800s, the Mississippi River was important to the United States because it
(1) served as a major highway for trade
(2) led to wars between Great Britain and Spain
(3) divided the Indian territories from the United States
(4) served as a border between the United States and Mexico

2 The Louisiana Purchase initially presented a dilemma for President Thomas Jefferson because he believed it would
(1) lead to war with Great Britain
(2) bankrupt the new nation
(3) force Native American Indians off their lands
(4) violate his strict constructionist view of the Constitution

3 The principal goal of the supporters of Manifest Destiny in the 1840s was to
(1) convince Canada to become part of the United States
(2) expand United States territory to the Pacific Ocean
(3) build a canal across Central America
(4) acquire naval bases in the Caribbean

4 The foreign policies of President James Polk involving Texas, California, and the Oregon Territory were all efforts to
(1) remain neutral toward western territories
(2) continue traditional American isolationism
(3) weaken the Monroe Doctrine
(4) fulfill the goal of manifest destiny

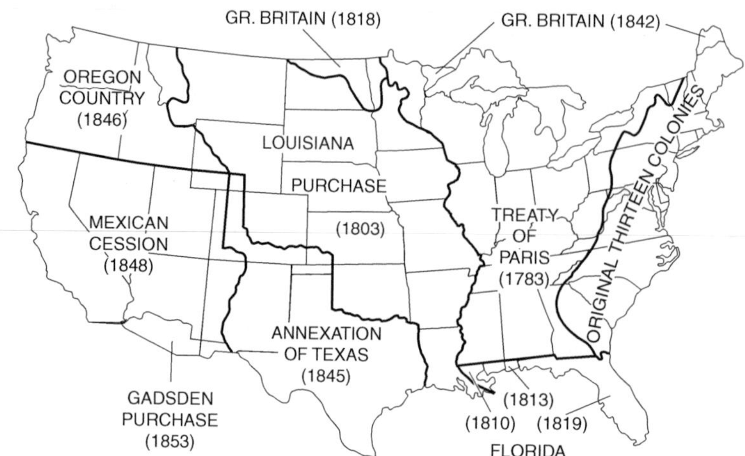

Base your answers to questions 5 and 6 on the map above and on your knowledge of social studies.

5 What would be the best title for this map?
(1) British North America Before 1850
(2) United States Territorial Expansion
(3) Colonial North America
(4) Wartime Land Acquisitions

6 The Louisiana Purchase was important to the United States because it
(1) expanded the nation's boundary to the Pacific Ocean
(2) removed the Spanish from North America
(3) closed the western territories to slavery
(4) secured control of the Mississippi River

7 Which term refers to the idea that settlers had the right to decide whether slavery would be legal in their territory?
(1) nullification
(2) sectionalism
(3) popular sovereignty
(4) Southern secession

8 In the 1850s, the phrase "Bleeding Kansas" was used to describe clashes between
(1) proslavery and antislavery groups
(2) Spanish landowners and new American settlers
(3) Chinese and Irish railroad workers
(4) Native American Indians and white settlers

9 Which situation was the most immediate result of Abraham Lincoln's election to the presidency in 1860?
(1) Kansas and Nebraska joined the Union as free states.
(2) A constitutional amendment was adopted to end slavery.
(3) Missouri entered the Union as a slave state.
(4) Several Southern states seceded from the Union.

Base your answer to question 10 on the quotation below and on your knowledge of social studies.

> . . . With malice toward none, with charity for all, with firmness in the right as God gives us to see the right, let us strive on to finish the work we are in, to bind up the nation's wounds, to care for him who shall have borne the battle and for his widow and his orphan, to do all which may achieve and cherish a just and lasting peace among ourselves and with all nations.

—Abraham Lincoln, Second Inaugural Address, March 4, 1865

10 This statement reveals President Lincoln's support for
(1) a new peace treaty with Great Britain
(2) universal male suffrage
(3) a fair and generous peace
(4) harsh punishment for Confederate leaders

THEMATIC ESSAYS

1 **THEME:** *Slavery and the Civil War.* The controversy over slavery's moral justification and expansion into new territories led to sectional conflict and ultimately to civil war.

TASK: Choose *two* events that caused serious controversy and helped lead to the Civil War. For *each* event:

- describe the circumstances causing the event
- explain how the events helped lead to the Civil War.

Some events that you may use are the Mexican War, Compromise of 1850, Kansas-Nebraska Act, Dred Scott decision, and John Brown's raid at Harpers Ferry.

2 **THEME:** *States' Rights and the Civil War.* Although the Civil War was fought over the morality of slavery, it was also fought to determine if the powers of the federal government (the Union) were greater than states' rights.

TASK: Choose *two* issues that created great controversy and helped lead to the Civil War. For *each* issue, *specifically* discuss how states' rights versus federal powers played a part in leading to the Civil War.

Some ideas that you may wish to discuss are the Fugitive Slave Act, popular sovereignty, and the Dred Scott decision.

DOCUMENT-BASED QUESTION

Study each document and answer the question that follows it. Then read the **Task** and write your essay. Include references to most of the documents and additional information you retain about U.S. history and government.

HISTORICAL CONTEXT: Although the United States was originally an Atlantic coast nation, its future rested in expansion westward.

DOCUMENT 1: Study the map below.

Louisiana Purchase (1803)

QUESTION: How did the United States change as a result of the Louisiana Purchase?

DOCUMENT 2: Study the map below.

Indian Removal in the 1830s

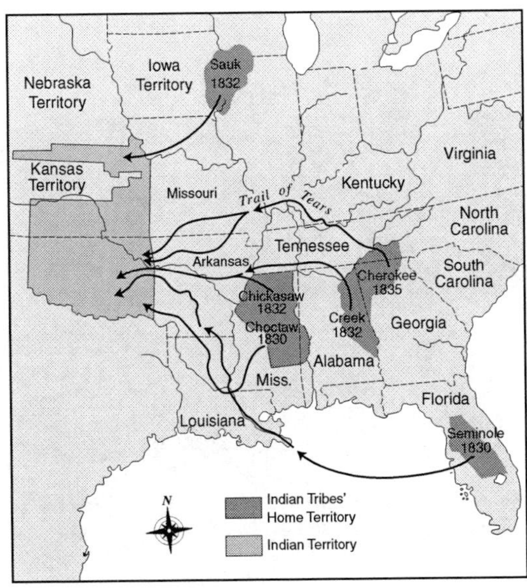

QUESTION: How did the United States remove Native Americans from their tribal homelands?

DOCUMENT 3: Study the map below.

Annexation of Texas, Mexican Cession, and Gadsden Purchase

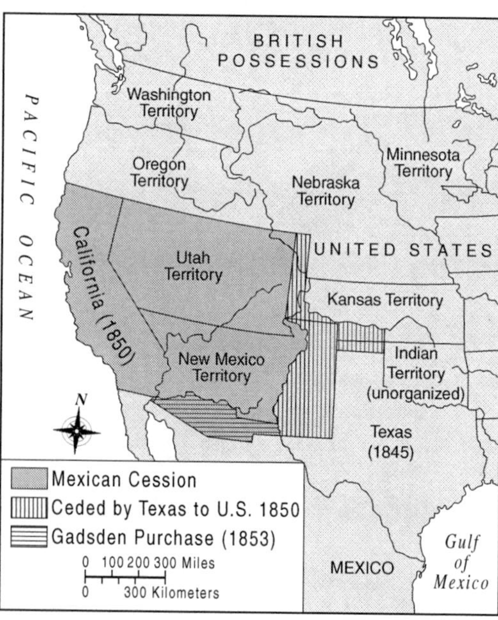

QUESTION: How did war with Mexico affect U.S. territory?

DOCUMENT 4: Look at the cartoon below.

"Plucked"—bird symbolizing Mexico before and after its territories were taken by the United States

QUESTION: How does the cartoonist feel about what happened to Mexico as a result of war with the United States?

DOCUMENT 5: Study the map below.

United States After the Kansas-Nebraska Act, 1854

QUESTION: How did the acquisition of Western lands further aggravate the controversy over slavery?

TASK: Using the documents and your knowledge of U.S. history and government, write an essay in which you:

- describe the opportunities that acquiring land in the West provided for the United States
- explain how territorial expansion also resulted in issues that had serious consequences for the nation.

UNIT II
Industrialization of the United States

CHAPTER 7
The Reconstructed Nation

DOCUMENTS AND LAWS
Black Codes (1865) • Thirteenth Amendment (1865) • Freedmen's Bureau (1865)
Civil Rights Act (1866) • Military Reconstruction (1867) • Tenure of Office Act (1867)
Fourteenth Amendment (1868) • Fifteenth Amendment (1870) • Force Acts (1870–1871)
Amnesty Act (1872) • Civil Rights Acts (1866, 1875) • Compromise of 1877
"Jim Crow" laws (1881–mid-1900s) • Civil Rights cases (1883) • *Plessy* v. *Ferguson* (1896)

EVENTS
Reconstruction (1865–1877) • Impeachment of Andrew Johnson (1868)
Completing the Transcontinental Railroad (1869) • Election of 1876

PEOPLE/GROUPS
carpetbaggers • W. E. B. Du Bois • Ulysses S. Grant • Jeremiah Haralson • John Harlan
Rutherford B. Hayes • Matthew Perry • Radical Republicans • Hiram Revels • scalawags
William Seward • Robert Smalls • Edwin Stanton • Thaddeus Stevens • Samuel Tilden
Booker T. Washington

OBJECTIVES

- To evaluate various plans for readmitting Southern states to the Union after the Civil War.
- To understand the changing nature of American society, especially Southern society, from 1865 to 1895.
- To describe why African Americans did not achieve full freedom after their emancipation.
- To compare Northern and Southern viewpoints during Reconstruction.
- To describe the weakening of Northern Republican control and increase of Southern Democratic control in the post-Reconstruction South.

Plans of Reconstruction

After the Civil War, the U.S. government faced the problem of how to rebuild the governments of Southern states and readmit them to the Union. The era of Reconstruction lasted from 1865 to 1877.

The Civil War had taken the lives of more than 600,000 soldiers (adding the totals from both the North and the South). It had damaged vast amounts of property in the South. Moreover, Southern planters had lost a labor force of 4 million slaves, now freed.

Meanwhile, U.S. leaders debated two major problems: (1) On what terms should Southern states be readmitted to the Union? and (2) How would the rights of former slaves be protected?

Lincoln's Plan

President Lincoln wanted seceded states to rejoin the Union on a status equal to those of the North. He proposed two conditions: (1) Ten percent of a state's voters would have to take an oath of allegiance to the United States, and (2) Each state had to guarantee the end of slavery.

Andrew Johnson's Plan

After Lincoln's assassination, Vice President Andrew Johnson became president (1865–1869). Many Northern Republicans distrusted him because he had been a Democrat from the slaveholding state of Tennessee.

Johnson's Reconstruction plan was the same as Lincoln's, with one addition: A state had to deny important Confederate leaders the right to vote, while granting it to all other Southern white men.

Both presidents favored full participation in Congress by the Southern states.

Congressional Reconstruction

A large group in Congress, the *Radical Republicans*, devised a plan to protect former slaves and punish the South:

- No state could deprive citizenship to any native-born American or withhold the right to vote because of race or former slave status.
- No Confederate military leader or officeholder could hold any office without congressional pardon.
- The U.S. Army would occupy and govern a state until its new constitution was acceptable to Congress.

Post–Civil War Amendments The Radical Republicans got Congress to pass three constitutional amendments to grant long-denied rights to African Americans:

- The *Thirteenth Amendment* (1865) declared slavery illegal in every state.

- The *Fourteenth Amendment* (1868) defined the rights of U.S. citizenship: "All persons born or naturalized in the United States, and subject to the jurisdiction thereof, are citizens of the United States and of the state wherein they reside." It also itemized three prohibitions to ensure that rights protected by the Constitution applied to state and federal governments alike:
  1. States could not interfere with the "privileges and immunities" of citizens.
  2. States could not deprive a person of life, liberty, or property without due process of law.
  3. States could not deny a citizen equal protection of the law.
- The *Fifteenth Amendment* (1870) stated that voting rights could not be denied because of "race, color, or previous condition of servitude."

Impeachment and Trial of Andrew Johnson

President Johnson antagonized the Radical Republicans in Congress by vetoing each step in their Reconstruction plan. The lawmakers overrode each veto.

In 1867, Congress tried to redesign the system of checks and balances in Congress's favor. The *Tenure of Office Act* prohibited a president from

Congressional Reconstruction, 1865–1877

firing a Cabinet officer without Senate approval. Johnson, believing the act unconstitutional, fired Secretary of War Edwin Stanton. In 1868, the House of Representatives impeached the president. At his trial, the Senate fell one vote short of the two-thirds majority needed to convict him, so Johnson completed his term.

IN REVIEW

1. How were the Radical Republicans' Reconstruction plans more "radical" than those of Lincoln and Johnson.
2. Summarize the Thirteenth, Fourteenth, and Fifteenth amendments.
3. Why did the Radical Republicans impeach Johnson? How did this conflict illustrate the system of checks and balances?

Reconstructed Nation

Southern whites considered Union control of their state governments an insult and continued to champion states' rights. For blacks, Reconstruction was an all too brief period of freedom and equal opportunity under federal law.

Northern Viewpoint

After the war, thousands of Northerners moved to the South in search of economic gain and political power. Shielded by federal troops, they ran for election to the legislatures created by the new state constitutions.

Republican Victories Seven Southern states held elections in 1868. Supported by freed blacks, Northern Republicans won four of seven governorships, ten of 14 seats in the Senate, and 20 of 35 seats in the House of Representatives.

The new legislatures' chief task was to rebuild what had been destroyed by war. Republican legislators voted large sums of money for this purpose, and some used some of these funds for personal use.

Southern Viewpoint

Southern whites wanted (1) a revived economy, (2) recontrol of state governments, and (3) a reduction of the political power of Southern blacks.

"Carpetbaggers" and "Scalawags" Southerners called Northerners who descended on them *carpetbaggers* (fortune hunters carrying their belongings in one travel bag). Southern whites who cooperated with the Northerners were called *scalawags* (by their critics) and deemed to have only one motive —a share in corrupt, moneymaking schemes.

Secret societies such as the Knights of the White Camellia and the Ku Klux Klan (KKK) used violence against blacks and scalawags alike.

Poster of the Ku Klux Klan championing white supremacy

Economic and Technological Impacts

The Civil War had accelerated industrialization and the growth of an urban middle class in the North but devastated infant Southern industries. After the war, the North broke all records for output, inventions, and business growth. Historians disagree about whether the business boom would have happened anyway or if the war was a major stimulus for investment.

Trade With Europe

The United States and Europe became more industrialized in the postwar period. Increased output by manufactures boosted their need for buyers. Industrialized nations also needed more raw materials—cotton, coal, iron, oil, and so on. The resource-rich United States exported its raw goods to Europe, simultaneously building up its industries.

Trade With Asia

Through much of the 1800s, American merchants were frustrated by the refusal of the Chinese court to import cheap, factory-made U.S. goods. At the same time, Chinese teas, porcelains, and silks were in great demand in the United States.

Japan long shared China's lack of interest in trading with Europeans and Americans. In 1853, however, Commodore Matthew Perry arrived in Japan with a U.S. fleet. He persuaded the Japanese to initiate mutual trade. When new leadership in Japan decided to industrialize the nation, it eagerly sought Western technologies. Trade with Japan increased after the U.S. Civil War. Nevertheless, the United States imported more from Asia than it exported to there.

Purchase of Alaska

In 1867, Secretary of State William Seward purchased Alaska from Russia for $7.2 million. Many people thought the purchase was a waste, calling it "Seward's Folly." However, this vast expanse, larger than the state of Texas, proved later to be valuable when gold and oil were discovered there. Alaska would be made a state in 1959.

Transcontinental Railroad

After the Civil War, internal improvements increased at a rapid rate. A great postwar achievement was the building of a transcontinental railroad across the Western plains to the Pacific Coast. Completed in 1869 by two private companies, the Union Pacific and the Central Pacific Railroads, the project had considerable federal help.

The railroad was designed to open the West to settlers. The route passed over sparsely settled territory. Congress made huge land grants along the route to the railroad companies. The government kept other plots of land along the route to sell to ordinary Americans.

Other Western railroads were soon completed too. Between 1865 and 1900, U.S. railroad tracks increased from 35,000 to 260,000 miles.

Need for Labor Immigrants made U.S. industrial growth possible. Most immigrants settled in the North, where factory jobs for unskilled workers were plentiful. They built the first transcontinental railroad. They turned Midwest prairies and forests into prosperous farms. In New York, they worked at construction or in garment factories. Many opened small retail stores, a few of which grew into large department stores. Immigrant workers went down into mines or manned the steel mills of Pittsburgh, Pennsylvania, and Birmingham, Alabama. Immigrants also became the technicians, inventors, and scientists necessary for industrial development.

Women joined the workforce because men's wages seldom covered family needs. In the early postwar years, women took low-paying jobs in factories or as servants. New technologies of the 1880s and 1890s, however, opened up jobs for typists and telephone operators, which were often women.

IN REVIEW

1. Define carpetbagger. Describe how Southern whites viewed them.
2. In what ways did the North benefit economically after the Civil War?
3. Describe trade with Europe and Asia after the Civil War.

The New South

In the South during and after Reconstruction, whites owned most of the land, while blacks worked it as tenants and sharecroppers.

Farm Owners After the war, few plantation owners could afford to keep their huge properties intact. Some were broken up into small sections and sold as farms. Most buyers were white, although there were a few black landowners.

Tenant Farmers Some plantation owners rented parts of their land to **tenant farmers**, who provided their own seed, mules, and provisions.

Sharecroppers The poorest Southerners, white and black, were **sharecroppers**. In return for farming a piece of land, they gave some of the crop to a landlord. Worn-out land, low prices for cotton, and high prices for farm supplies kept many sharecroppers in debt. Thus, in spite of the Thirteenth Amendment, many Southerners were in a kind of bondage.

Status of Freedmen

Economic and Political Hopes In the early years of Reconstruction, Congressman Thaddeus Stevens and other Radical Republicans wanted to give land to freed slaves. The Fifteenth Amendment made African Americans believe that the federal government would protect their right to vote.

Economic and Political Reality Congress never acted on land distribution. At first, Northern troops protected the right of blacks to vote, but the determination of many white Southerners to end this right eventually prevailed.

Participation in Reconstruction Governments From 1868 to 1872, many African Americans won seats in Southern legislatures. In one house of South Carolina's legislature, black men were in the majority.

African Americans in Congress During Reconstruction, 14 Southern African Americans served in Congress, among them Senator Hiram Revels of Mississippi, Congressman Robert Smalls of South Carolina, and Congressman Jeremiah Haralson of Alabama. Half of the black lawmakers were former slaves; half had attended college. As a group, they championed civil rights and federal aid to education.

Senator Hiram Revels (far left) and Congressman Robert Smalls

From Exclusion to Segregation Many white Americans regarded blacks as inferior. In some Northern and Southern cities, blacks were forbidden to mix with whites in public.

The *Civil Rights Act of 1875* prohibited railroads, restaurants, and other public places from segregating African American customers. For a time, the law was generally obeyed. Beginning in 1881, however, Southern states adopted **Jim Crow laws** enforcing segregation. By the 1890s, these laws applied to every part of life—marriage, education, health care, public accommodations, even burial in cemeteries.

Struggle for Political Control

Black Codes In 1865, Southerners holding state conventions to organize new governments drew up measures to restrict the rights of former slaves. These **Black Codes** prohibited blacks from (1) carrying firearms, (2) starting businesses, (3) appearing outside after sunset, (4) renting or leasing farmland, and (5) traveling without a permit.

Radical Republican Laws for the South To protect the blacks and punish the whites, Radical Republican leaders pushed through a series of laws.

- *Freedmen's Bureau (1865).* This agency helped more than 3 million **freedmen** (former slaves) adjust to freedom. They were provided with necessities of life and new educational facilities. As a result, thousands attended school and college for the first time.
- *Civil Rights Act of 1866.* Congress moved against the Black Codes by empowering the federal government to protect the civil rights of blacks.
- *Military Districts.* Congress divided the South into five military districts, each occupied by federal troops responsible to a military governor.

- *Conditions for Readmission of a Seceded State.* Congress made the state conventions of 1865 illegitimate. A state had to draw up a constitution that recognized the Fourteenth Amendment, including the provisions that former Confederate officers could not hold office.
- *Force Acts (1870–1871).* Federal troops were authorized to break up organizations that intimidated black voters, such as the Ku Klux Klan.

Civil Rights Cases (1883) African-American citizens challenged Jim Crow laws on the grounds that they violated the Fourteenth Amendment's equal protection clause.

In a series of cases, the U.S. Supreme Court ruled that Jim Crow laws *were* constitutional because property owners had the right to choose their customers. The Fourteenth Amendment, the Court said, applied only to government officials.

Debating the Role of African Americans Between 1890 and 1910, two African-American leaders took opposite positions on segregation.

- *Booker T. Washington.* Washington was freed from slavery at the age of nine. In 1881, he founded the Tuskegee Institute in Alabama to provide industrial and vocational training to African Americans. Washington thought that blacks should not seek social acceptance by whites but rather improve their economic position by learning higher-paying job skills.
- *W. E. B. Du Bois.* Du Bois was younger than Washington and had earned a Ph.D. from Harvard. In *The Souls of Black Folk* (1903), he stated that education for economic success was important, but not as important as achieving political and civil rights. He urged firm opposition to Jim Crow laws.

Former slaves and their children being educated at the Freedmen's Bureau

IN REVIEW

1. How did the Southern economy change after the Civil War?
2. What new forms of discrimination against African Americans developed after the Civil War?
3. Compare and contrast the strategies of Booker T. Washington and W. E. B. Du Bois for achieving equality for African Americans.

End of Reconstruction

Northern Republican control of Southern state governments began to weaken in 1869, when those states began to elect governments dominated by Democrats. By 1877, there were no more Reconstruction governments.

Reasons

- *Change in Public Opinion.* Northern whites became less concerned about African-American rights and more about their own affairs. By 1875, many wanted to withdraw U.S. troops from the South.
- *Amnesty Act.* Toward the end of Ulysses S. Grant's first term as president (1869–1873), Congress enacted the *Amnesty Act* (1872), restoring voting rights to 160,000 former Confederates.
- *Increased Terrorism.* Extremist groups such as the Ku Klux Klan grew stronger, and the federal government either could not or would not enforce civil rights laws. Many frightened Southern blacks stopped trying to vote.

Election of 1876

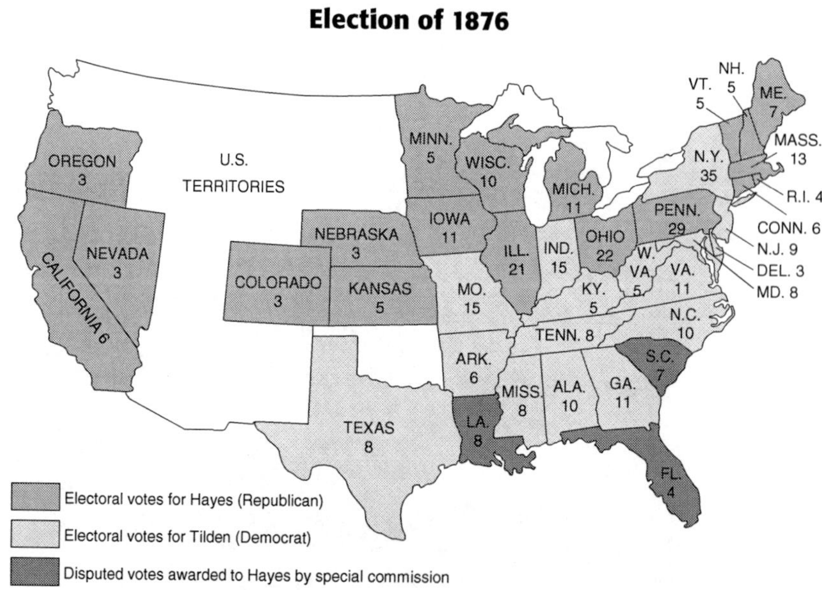

- *Election of 1876.* In the election year of 1876, federal troops still occupied South Carolina, Florida, and Louisiana, where the Republican presidential candidate, Rutherford B. Hayes, won. The other Southern states gave their electoral votes to the Democratic candidate, Samuel Tilden of New York. Tilden, however, claimed victory in the occupied states, citing Democratic voting returns that contradicted Republican ones. A federal commission, called to decide the winner, had a majority of Republicans and went for Hayes. Southern Democrats talked of another civil war.
- *Compromise of 1877.* In secret, Republican and Democratic leaders agreed to support Hayes's claim. In exchange, Hayes would remove federal troops from the South, abandoning Southern blacks to the rule of the white majority.

Restoration of White Control

Solid South Southern whites blamed Republicans for their hardships. After Reconstruction, the South became the *Solid South*, a Democratic-controlled region. From 1880 to 1924, Democratic candidates for president won all the electoral votes of the Southern states.

Disenfranchisement The Fourteenth Amendment had briefly punished Confederate officers with **disenfranchisement** (cancellation of voting rights). After Reconstruction, the South disenfranchised black citizens to ensure control by the Democratic Party.

***Plessy* v. *Ferguson* (1896)** After Reconstruction, the Supreme Court became less protective of African-American civil rights. Homer Plessy, a black man, sued a railroad for denying him entry into a car set aside for whites. In a landmark decision, the Supreme Court ruled that because the railroad provided "separate but equal" facilities for blacks, the equal

Methods of Disenfranchisement

Method	*Law*	*Discriminatory Use of Law*
Literacy test	Voters must pass reading and writing test.	Slaves had not been taught literacy skills. State examiners deliberately passed whites and failed blacks.
Poll tax	Citizens must pay state tax before voting.	Most blacks were too poor to pay the tax.
Grandfather clause	Men whose grandfathers had voted before 1867 could vote without taking literacy test.	Only white males had grandfathers who voted before 1867.

protection clause in the Constitution had not been violated. One justice, John Harlan, dissented, arguing that segregation threatened personal liberty and equality of rights. For many years, however, the Court's majority used "separate but equal" to justify racial segregation.

IN REVIEW

1. How did the Compromise of 1877 contribute to segregation?
2. How and why did the Solid South emerge?
3. How did the Supreme Court's ruling in *Plessy* v. *Ferguson* establish a legal basis for segregation?

CHAPTER REVIEW

MULTIPLE-CHOICE QUESTIONS

1 The Reconstruction plans of President Abraham Lincoln and President Andrew Johnson included a provision for the
(1) resumption of full participation in Congress by Southern states
(2) long-term military occupation of the Confederacy
(3) payment of war reparations by Southern states
(4) harsh punishment of former Confederate officials

Base your answers to questions 2 and 3 on the cartoon at right and on your knowledge of social studies.

The Strong Government, 1869–1877

Source: J. A. Wales, *Puck*, May 12, 1880 (adapted)

2 What is the main idea of this cartoon from the Reconstruction Era?
(1) Southern society was oppressed by Radical Republican policies.
(2) Military force was necessary to stop Southern secession.
(3) United States soldiers forced women in the South to work in factories.
(4) Sharecropping was an economic burden for women after the Civil War.

3 Which congressional action led to the Southern viewpoint expressed in this cartoon?
(1) passage of the Homestead Act
(2) strengthening of the Fugitive Slave Laws
(3) military occupation of the former Confederate states
(4) ending the Freedmen's Bureau

4 What was a common purpose of the three amendments added to the United States Constitution between 1865 and 1870?
(1) extending suffrage to Southern women
(2) reforming the sharecropping system
(3) granting rights to African Americans
(4) protecting rights of Southerners accused of treason

5 The underlying reason for the impeachment of President Andrew Johnson was
(1) the Credit Mobilier scandal
(2) a power struggle with Congress over Reconstruction
(3) his refusal to appoint new justices to the Supreme Court
(4) his policies toward Native American Indians

6 What effect did the system of sharecropping have on the South after the Civil War?
(1) It kept formerly enslaved persons economically dependent.
(2) It brought investment capital to the South.
(3) It encouraged Northerners to migrate south.
(4) It provided for a fairer distribution of farm profits.

7 During Reconstruction, the Black Codes passed by Southern states were attempts to
(1) provide land to former slaves
(2) punish former Confederate leaders
(3) repeal the Jim Crow laws
(4) deny equal rights to African Americans

8 Booker T. Washington stated that the best way for formerly enslaved persons to advance themselves in American society was to
(1) leave their farms in the South and move to the North
(2) run for political office
(3) pursue economic gains through vocational training
(4) form a separate political party

9 In *Plessy* v. *Ferguson* (1896), the Supreme Court ruled that
(1) states may not secede from the Union
(2) racial segregation was constitutional
(3) slaves are property and may not be taken from their owners
(4) all Western territories should be open to slavery

10 The most direct effect of poll taxes and literacy tests on African Americans was to
(1) prevent them from voting
(2) limit their access to public facilities
(3) block their educational opportunities
(4) deny them economic advancements

THEMATIC ESSAYS

1 **THEME:** *Reconstruction and Balance of Power.* An intense struggle for power between Andrew Johnson and the Radical Republicans took place between 1865 and 1868.

TASK: Complete *both* of the following tasks:
- Compare and contrast Johnson's Reconstruction plan with that of the congressional Radical Republicans.
- Show how the dispute between Johnson and the Radical Republicans ended in the impeachment of the president, and describe the outcome.

You may include in your answer differing views on secession, amnesty, pardon, and procedures for readmitting secessionist states to the Union. In addition, describe the controversy over the Tenure of Office Act, which led to Johnson's impeachment.

2 **THEME:** *Outcomes of the Civil War and Reconstruction.* The Civil War and Reconstruction resulted in change but left serious problems unresolved.

TASK: Complete *all* of the following tasks:
- Describe *one* change that resulted from the Civil War and/or Reconstruction.

- Show how *one* problem remained unresolved after the end of Reconstruction.
- Based on information you have given, react to the following statement: "In some ways, the Civil War was both a victory for the North and a draw for the South."

In writing your essay, you may refer to federal-state relations, the development of Northern industry, the Compromise of 1877, *Plessy* v. *Ferguson* (1896), sharecropping, and tenant farming.

DOCUMENT-BASED QUESTION

Study each document and answer the question that follows it. Then read the **Task** *and write your essay. Include references to most of the documents and additional information you retain about U.S. history and government.*

HISTORICAL CONTEXT: In spite of emancipation, many former slaves were given freedom only briefly. As Reconstruction ended, African Americans in the South became segregated from white society, with no real rights as U.S. citizens.

DOCUMENT 1: The Thirteenth and Fifteenth amendments:

Amendment 13: *Abolition of Slavery (1865)*

[Slavery Forbidden] Neither slavery nor involuntary servitude [compulsory service], except as a punishment for a crime whereof the party shall have been duly convicted, shall exist within the United States, or any place subject to their jurisdiction.

[Enforcement Power] Congress shall have power to enforce this article [amendment] by appropriate [suitable] legislation.

Amendment 15: *Right of Suffrage (1870)*

[African Americans Guaranteed the Right to Vote] The right of citizens of the United States to vote shall not be denied or abridged by the United States or by any state on account of race, color, or previous condition of servitude [slavery].

[Enforcement Power] The Congress shall have power to enforce this article by appropriate legislation.

QUESTION: According to the Thirteenth and Fifteenth amendments, what responsibilities was Congress given on behalf of freedmen?

DOCUMENT 2: Refer to the illustration below.

Freedmen voting in the South

QUESTION: What change had taken place in the South by 1868?

DOCUMENT 3: From the writings of "Pitchfork" Ben Tillman, a Southerner:

> ...We organized the Democratic Party with one plank...that "this is a white man's country, and white men must govern it....
>
> ...President Grant sent troops to maintain the carpetbag government in power and to protect the Negroes in the right to vote. He merely obeyed the law....Then it was that "we stuffed ballot boxes" because desperate diseases require desperate remedies and having resolved to take the state away, we hesitated at nothing....
>
> I want to say now that we have not shot any Negroes...on account of politics since 1876. We have not found it necessary. Eighteen hundred and seventy-six happened to be the hundredth anniversary of the Declaration of Independence, and the action of the white men...in taking the [government] away from the Negroes we regard as a second declaration of independence from African barbarism.

Question: How did Southern white Democrats justify their actions?

Document 4: From *Plessy* v. *Ferguson* (1896):

> Legislation is powerless to eradicate racial instincts or to abolish distinctions based upon physical differences, and the attempt to do so can only result in accentuating the difficulties of the present situation. If the civil and political rights of both races be equal, one cannot be inferior to the other civilly or politically. If one race be inferior to the other socially, the Constitution of the United States cannot put them upon the same plane.

Question: What did *Plessy* v. *Ferguson* decide regarding segregation?

Document 5: Refer to the illustration below.

Cartoon of Southern railroad car

Question: What does the illustration show about Reconstruction and the period immediately following?

Task: Using the documents and your knowledge of U.S. history and government, write an essay in which you:

- describe in what ways former slaves obtained temporary freedom and equality.
- explain how the post-Reconstruction era left Southern African Americans in a segregated and inferior status.

CHAPTER 8
Rise of American Business, Labor, and Agriculture

DOCUMENTS AND LAWS
Homestead Act (1862) • Morrill Act (1862) • *Munn* v. *Illinois* (1877)
Wabash, St. Louis, and Pacific Railway v. *Illinois* (1886) • Interstate Commerce Act (1887)
Sherman Antitrust Act (1890) • *United States* v. *E. C. Knight* (1895)
Sixteenth Amendment (1913) • Seventeenth Amendment (1913)

EVENTS
Industrial Revolution (c. 1750–present) • Grange Movement founded (1867)
First continental railroad (completed 1869) • Knights of Labor organized (1869)
American Federation of Labor founded (1886) • Haymarket riot (1886)
Homestead strike (1892) • Populist Party organized (1892) • Pullman strike (1894)
Election of 1896 • International Ladies' Garment Workers' Union founded (1900)
National Women's Trade Union League founded (1903) • Lawrence strike (1912)

PEOPLE/GROUPS
Horatio Alger • Alexander Graham Bell • Henry Bessemer • William Jennings Bryan
Andrew Carnegie • Grover Cleveland • Eugene V. Debs • Thomas Edison • Henry Ford
Samuel Gompers • William McKinley • Samuel F. B. Morse • Mary Kenney O'Sullivan
Terence Powderly • John D. Rockefeller • Adam Smith • James Watt • James Weaver
Anarchists • Grangers • Populists •

OBJECTIVES

- To understand how U.S. industrialization was part of a worldwide economic revolution.
- To know how American business changed from 1865 to 1920.
- To understand the federal responses to industrialization and business growth.
- To evaluate labor's struggle to organize and improve working conditions.
- To explain the causes of farmers' discontent and evaluate their political program.

Economic Change

The **Industrial Revolution**, which began about 1750, persists today. It has involved the invention of machines and systems to mass-produce goods for domestic and foreign markets. Manufacturing started within homes but now takes place in large factories.

Great Britain

The making of textiles such as cotton cloth was the first industry revolutionized by machinery and mass production. British inventors created machines for spinning cotton thread. In 1782, James Watt invented the steam engine, which supplied power for various machines. Beginning in 1786, the steam-powered loom speeded up the weaving of thread into cloth.

Machine-made cloth cost less to produce than handmade cloth and could be sold more cheaply at home and abroad. Manufacturers made great profits from textiles, but only after investing large sums to buy machines, build factories, and pay workers.

U.S. Advantages in Industrialization

The United States was rich in the resources necessary for industrialization —land and raw materials, labor, and **capital** (tools, machinery, and money for investment). Supporting these advantages was a belief in capitalism.

Capitalism is an economic system that relies on economic freedom. The tools, machinery, and factories are privately owned and managed by competing businesses. In his book *The Wealth of Nations*, written in 1776, Adam Smith developed the idea that **laizzez-faire**, a belief that government should not interfere with business competition, would lead to increased economic growth and output.

Post–Civil War Growth of U.S. Industry

Each region of the nation contributed to economic growth after the Civil War. The South continued to produce cotton but also developed a small industrial base that in Birmingham, Alabama, included iron and steel. The Midwest provided corn and wheat that would be shipped east on new railroad lines. In addition, the Midwest had centers of heavy industry, including iron and steel processing and the manufacture of farm equipment and machine tools. Mining was widespread throughout the West. In the 20th century, the discovery of oil in Texas and Oklahoma would further spur industrial growth. With its many harbors and ports, the East was the center of trade with Europe and the entry point for many immigrants. New York City, in particular, would emerge as the financial capital of the nation. Northern industries had already made great strides before the Civil War and its cities were already linked by railroads. After the war, production of pig iron (crudely cast iron) increased, and the steel industry developed around Pittsburgh, Pennsylvania. In addition, many other industries developed in the East.

In the early 1900s, Henry Ford utilized the assembly line to build cars near Detroit, Michigan. As cars moved on conveyor belts past a line of workers, each worker did one job in the assembly process. Thus, workers became specialized, faster, and produced more. The rate in turning out goods is called **productivity**. Higher productivity lowers costs.

Proprietorships, Partnerships, and Consolidation Early U.S. businesses were usually a **proprietorship** (single ownership) or **partnership** (multiple ownership). Because a proprietor or partner was *liable* (responsible) for all business debts, raising money for risky enterprises was difficult.

Incorporation By the late 19th century, many businesses were organizing as **corporations**, which were chartered under state laws. To raise capital, a corporation sells ownership **shares**, or **stock**, to the public. **Stockholders** (buyers of stock) can lose no more money than they have originally invested. If the corporation goes bankrupt, its stockholders are not personally liable for its debts.

Investment in Transportation Railroad and canal companies were also organized as corporations and sold their stock to the public to finance their costly operations. Many people invested in canals and railroads because these improved ways of transporting freight over long distances were key to the nation's industrial future. Railroads became important for transporting people too.

Consolidation After the Civil War Businesses minimized competition through consolidation, by which several businesses joined together and operated under one management. A more extreme step was to set up a monopoly by consolidating all competing businesses. Because a monopoly became the only seller of a product and controlled its manufacture, it was able to charge high prices.

Cartoon of "King Monopoly" and his subjects

Expanding Markets

Domestic Markets Investors and business leaders began to create products that could be sold nationwide. Railroads shipped goods from Eastern factories to the South, Midwest, and West. Meat and wheat from the Midwest and West were shipped east to feed the workers in big cities there.

International Markets Global trade increased as the United States was challenged by competition in the international textile, steel, machinery, and shipbuilding markets. Western European nations, the United States, and Japan engaged in **imperialism** by gaining foreign territories for their own economic benefit. Imperialism also encouraged railroad building and the shipment of consumer goods throughout the world. Thus, new markets were opened for American goods. In order to prevent European manufacturers from challenging American industries, industrial leaders called for higher tariffs (taxes on imports) in order to increase prices on those goods.

Business and Industrial Growth

Economic growth in the second half of the 19th century was spurred by developments in the transportation, steel, and energy industries.

Transportation

Prior to the Civil War, roads, rivers, and canals made up the U.S. transportation system.

Railroads The steam locomotive, first built in 1804 in England, led to vast new transportation networks. Although the earlier means of transportation remained important, the new railroad networks truly united the nation. After completion of the first transcontinental (coast-to-coast) railroad in 1869, other Western railroads followed. By the end of the century, the United States was tied together by more miles of railroad track than existed in all of Europe.

Steel

For a long time, people knew that steel was stronger and more durable than iron. But it was time-consuming and costly to make. In 1855, a British industrialist, Henry Bessemer, invented a process for producing steel with no impurities by blowing cold air through molten iron. An American industrialist, Andrew Carnegie, adopted the Bessemer process in 1867. By 1901, the United States was leading the world in steel production.

Energy Sources

Coal Coal became important in the 1800s when it replaced wood to power locomotives. Coal was mined in the Allegheny Mountains, from Pittsburgh,

Transcontinental Railroads, 1865–1900

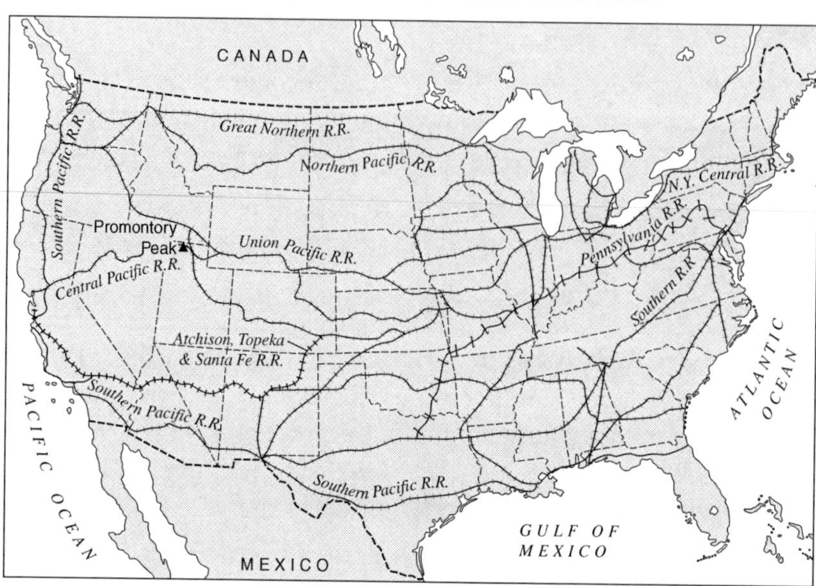

Pennsylvania, to Birmingham, Alabama. Growing industrialization led to an increase in coal production—from approximately 30 million tons in 1870 to more than 200 million tons by 1900.

Oil Before the Civil War, homes were lighted mainly by lamps that burned whale oil or vegetable oil. In the 1850s, kerosene from petroleum (oil) was discovered to be a relatively clean fuel for home lighting. In 1859, Edwin Drake of Titusville, Pennsylvania, accidentally discovered a source of oil while drilling a well for water. Drilling oil wells and processing oil into kerosene became a big business.

Electricity Among the nation's most prolific inventors was Thomas Edison. One of his key inventions was the lightbulb (1879), which gives off light when an electric current passes through a filament inside. In addition to the Victrola (early phonograph) and the motion picture camera, Edison devised a system in which talented people work together on research projects. His "invention factory" of the 1870s and 1880s was the forerunner of modern industrial laboratories.

Communications

The use of electricity to send messages greatly speeded up business communications. Before the Civil War, telegraph wires connected American cities. After the war, Alexander Graham Bell's main invention, the telephone (1874–1876), allowed people to talk with each other over long distances.

IN REVIEW

1. What advantages enabled the United States to industrialize rapidly?
2. What advantages do corporations have over proprietorships and partnerships?
3. How did railroads affect the United States in the 19th century?

Work Methods for Success

Admirers of U.S. business growth in the late 19th century cite three factors in its success: entrepreneurship, a work ethic, and philanthropy.

Entrepreneurship

John D. Rockefeller In 1865, John D. Rockefeller invested in an oil-refining company. Oil refining was a fiercely competitive industry. To ensure his company's survival, Rockefeller tried to drive all competitors out of business. In 1870, when Rockefeller organized the Standard Oil Company, he had 200 competitors. Ten years later, Standard Oil refined 90 percent of U.S. oil.

Rockefeller crushed his competitors by these means:

- He persuaded railroads to give Standard Oil **rebates**—that is, they returned to the company a portion of their shipping charges. Rockefeller was then able to charge the lowest prices for oil.
- Rockefeller offered to buy struggling competitors.
- To eliminate railroad shipping charges, Rockefeller built pipelines to carry his oil from one place to another.

Andrew Carnegie Andrew Carnegie, a poor immigrant from Scotland, at first worked in a cotton mill. He then got a job working for the president

John D. Rockefeller (left) and Andrew Carnegie

of the Pennsylvania Railroad and invested his savings in railroad sleeping cars, iron mills, and steel. By the 1870s, he owned his own steel company. He paid low wages, drove hard bargains with railroads over their shipping prices, and tried to bankrupt competitors. In 1901, his steel company was worth nearly $500 million.

Work Ethic

When the Pilgrims and Puritans arrived here from England in the early 1600s, they brought with them a religious belief in a strong **work ethic**. Hard work and material success were signs that a person was predestined for a good afterlife. Two Americans who helped solidify this tradition were:

- *Cotton Mather.* A Puritan minister of Boston's North Church, Mather preached and wrote about the importance of a strong work ethic.
- *Horatio Alger.* In the post–Civil War era, Alger wrote popular books for young people in which poor boys, by hard work and lucky breaks, rose from rags to riches (as Andrew Carnegie did).

Public Good Versus Private Gain

Carnegie and Rockefeller made their industries the biggest and most productive ever. They took huge risks with no guarantee of success. As **philanthropists**, they both made huge donations for libraries, schools, hospitals, and other institutions. For their achievements, they were called "captains of industry."

Carnegie, Rockefeller, and other business leaders of their time were also known as "robber barons." They paid low wages, did not tolerate strikes, and used every available means—including secret agreements with railroads and temporary price cuts—to put competitors out of business.

Business Practices and Controls

According to the laissez-faire theory developed by Adam Smith, government regulations are harmful to economic growth and the development of capitalism The U.S. government observed laissez-faire in protecting and encouraging businesses. It applied the Fourteenth Amendment's provision that no state may "deprive any person of life, liberty, or property without due process of law" to corporations. Thus, corporations enjoyed the same protections as individuals and won favorable rulings in many judicial decisions.

Business Practices

Pooling Railroad lines that had once cut fares to attract business began to engage in **pooling** (that is, different lines secretly agreed to charge the same high fares). They also shared profits and divided up their once-competitive market. One railroad often had a monopoly on lines servicing small towns and could thus charge higher prices for short trips from one town to another than for longer trips between cities.

Competition and Consolidation

Three forms of business consolidation emerged in the late 1800s: mergers, trusts, and holding companies.

Mergers During the 1870s and 1880s, competition declined as businesses **merged** (several companies joined together). If enough companies merged, they could become a monopoly.

Trusts Rockefeller created a super corporation called a **trust**. After nearly ruining competitors, he let them exchange their company stock for trust certificates and share in the trust's profits. Other business leaders followed his example, and soon there was a steel trust, a tobacco trust, a sugar-refining trust, and so on.

Holding Companies In the 1890s, corporations were formed that had only one function—to hold the stocks of several businesses in the same industry. By controlling a majority of each company's stock, such **holding companies** could dictate common policy.

Government and Trusts

Congress made an effort to control trusts, but the Supreme Court did not always back it up.

1889 cartoon showing business trusts controlling the Senate

Changes in Business and Industry

	Age of Jackson (1825–1845)	*Mid-century (1845–1865)*	*After Civil War (1865–1900)*
Business organization and manufacturing advances	• growth of textile mills • increase in corporations	• Isaac Singer's sewing machine plant (1853) • Bessemer steel-making process (1855)	• Standard Oil Trust (1882) • trend toward business consolidation
Inventions in transportation and communication	• Peter Cooper's first locomotive (1830) • Samuel Morse's telegraph (1844)	• laying of New York–London transatlantic cable (1859–1865) • first oil pipeline (1865)	• cable streetcars in San Francisco (1873) • Alexander Graham Bell's telephone (1876) • Thomas Edison's phonograph (1878)

Sherman Antitrust Act (1890) This act provided that "every contract, combination in the form of a trust or otherwise, or conspiracy, in restraint of trade or commerce . . . is hereby declared to be illegal." Such terms as "trust," "conspiracy," and "restraint of trade," however, were not defined, and no trusts were successfully prosecuted in the 1890s. But the Sherman Antitrust Act did establish the principle that the government should break up trusts and other forms of monopoly.

***United States v. E.C. Knight* (1895)** The weakness of the Sherman Antitrust Act was demonstrated in the government's attempt to break up E.C. Knight and Co.'s control of sugar refining. The Supreme Court ruled that the federal government had no authority to do so. The Court defined interstate commerce as a business involved in trade or transportation. The sugar refinery, located within only one state, did not qualify.

IN REVIEW

1. What methods did Rockefeller use to maximize profits, reduce costs, and eliminate competition?
2. Discuss whether Rockefeller and Carnegie were captains of industry or robber barons.
3. How did Supreme Court rulings affect efforts to regulate business?

Labor Organization

To minimize costs, most manufacturers kept wages low. Workers had to put in 60- to 70-hour workweeks in unventilated factories—cold in winter and hot in summer. Accidents from unsafe machinery were common and blamed on the operator. Unable on their own to persuade corporate giants to better conditions, workers organized large labor unions.

National Labor Unions

The Knights of Labor (1869) The Knights of Labor, led by Terence Powderly, was the first important union. Unlike earlier ones, it was open to skilled **craft workers** and unskilled **industrial workers** alike, as well as to African Americans, women, and the foreign born.

For years, the Knights of Labor tried to settle disputes through **arbitration** (judgment by an impartial person). It established cooperatives (discussed on page 137). Its most important goal was to win an eight-hour workday.

Changing tactics in 1885, the Knights of Labor initiated (and won) a major strike against a railroad company. Membership soared to 700,000. Then, in 1886, a bombing in Chicago's Haymarket section killed several police officers and civilians. Because the Knights of Labor was wrongly blamed for the incident, workers left in droves. By the 1890s, the union was almost defunct.

The Haymarket bombing was the work of **anarchists**, those who believed that capitalism and its allied political system could not be reformed and should be ended through violence.

American Federation of Labor (A.F. of L.) Founded in 1886, this organization, in altered form, survives to this day as the largest American labor organization. Its first leader, Samuel Gompers, brought craft unions together in one large, loose organization. This federation permitted unions of cigar makers, carpenters, and so on to exist as independent groups. The A.F. of L. leadership set overall policy for achieving common objectives.

Membership grew steadily. By 1900, half a million workers belonged to A.F. of L. craft unions.

Gompers focused on the crucial goals of higher wages, shorter hours, and better working conditions. This was to be achieved through **collective bargaining** (negotiations between management and union workers). If a strike seemed the best means to these ends, Gompers approved it.

Most unions in the A.F. of L. discriminated against black workers. The few that admitted African Americans segregated them. Employers often used the excluded blacks to fill the jobs of striking union members. Black workers' reputations as "strike breakers" increased racial prejudice within the membership.

The A.F. of L. also excluded women. Mary Kenney O'Sullivan, an activist in the labor movement, persuaded thousands of garment workers in New York City and Troy, New York, to join local unions. In 1903, she founded an organization for women called the *National Women's Trade Union League.*

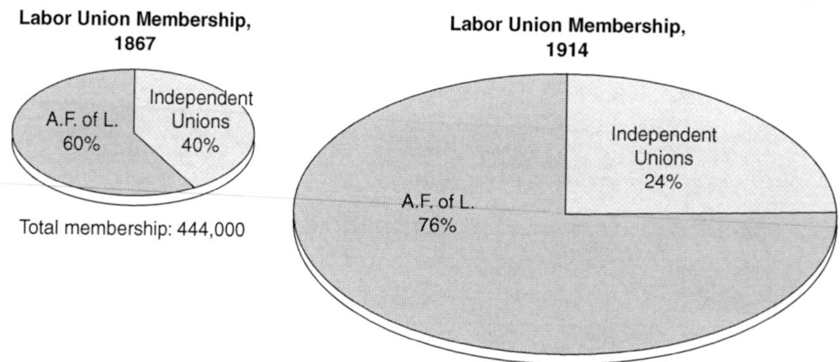

International Ladies' Garment Workers' Union (ILGWU) This union, representing workers in the women's clothing industry, protested low pay, long hours, and unsafe working conditions. Most members were Jewish immigrants employed in **sweatshops**—small manufacturing establishments with unsafe and unsanitary conditions. In 1909 and 1910, the ILGWU organized garment strikes and won pay raises, a shorter workweek, and paid holidays. In 1911, after a fire in the Triangle Shirtwaist Company in New York City killed 146 workers, the New York State legislature established strict fire safety codes in factories.

Struggle and Conflict

Homestead Strike In 1892, a union of steel workers refusing to accept a wage reduction struck the Homestead, Pennsylvania, steel plant owned by Andrew Carnegie. Henry Clay Frick, the chairman of Carnegie Steel, called in guards from the Pinkerton National Detective Agency to protect the plant and the replacement workers. Fighting broke out between the guards and the strikers, and many on both sides were killed. After the governor called out the state militia, workers went back to work at lower wages, the union was crushed, and unionization of the steel industry was hindered until the 1930s.

Pullman Strike In 1894, George Pullman, inventor and manufacturer of the Pullman sleeping car, announced a reduction in his workers' wages, but no reduction in their rents or groceries in the **company town**—one in which workers are dependent on one business for employment, housing, and supplies. Supported by the American Railway Union and its leader, Eugene V. Debs, the Pullman workers went on strike, picketed Pullman's railway cars, and prevented them from entering or leaving Chicago. Debs called for a boycott of Pullman cars, and railway workers nationwide refused to handle trains using them, which stopped interstate commerce and the transport of U.S. mail. A federal court granted an **injunction** (court order) against the picketing, and President Grover Cleveland sent federal troops to end the strike. When Debs and other union officials refused to comply, they were jailed and the railway union was broken. The Supreme Court upheld the injunction by ruling that the federal government may prevent "all obstructions to the freedom of interstate commerce or the transportation of the mails."

Lawrence Strike In 1912, the Industrial Workers of the World (IWW) struck the American Woolen Company in Lawrence, Massachusetts. It was led by Joseph Ettor, "Big Bill" Haywood, and Elizabeth Gurley Flynn. Founded in 1905, the IWW was a radical (extreme) labor organization opposed to capitalism and promoting **socialism** (the belief that major industries should be owned and operated by the government). The issue in Lawrence was low wages. Although the governor called in the state militia, the strikers won raises and were not punished for their actions.

Anti-Union Ploys Employers sometimes threatened pro-union workers with a loss of jobs by **blacklisting** them (circulating their names among other employers). Another anti-union method used by some employers was the **yellow dog contract**. It is an employment contract that requires workers to agree not to join a union as a condition of employment.

Public Policy and Public Opinion Most Americans viewed strike leaders as revolutionaries who challenged society's traditional values. But a growing minority sympathized with the unions and recognized that workers were being treated unfairly.

IN REVIEW

1. Explain how the growth of labor unions was a response to the growth of business.
2. How did the Knights of Labor and the A.F. of L. differ?
3. For the Homestead, Pullman, and Lawrence strikes, prepare a chart listing the (a) conditions that led to the strike, (b) tactics used by both sides, (c) union leadership, (d) role of state or federal government, and (e) outcome of the strike.

Agrarian Organization

American agriculture was influenced by cheap land and dependence on businesses. Farmers organized into social, economic, and political groups.

Cheap Land

Homestead Act (1862) This law provided that any citizen or immigrant intending to become a citizen could acquire 160 acres of federal land by farming it for five years.

Morrill Act (1862) This act gave huge tracts of federal land to the states on condition that they use it for colleges that taught agricultural and mechanical arts. These land-grant colleges taught farmers new technology for increasing crop yields.

Dependence on Railroads, Merchants, and Banks

Although farmland was cheap, machines, tools, buildings, seeds, horses, and crop storage and transportation were not. Farmers needed capital to buy these. To that end, farmers sought bank loans and credit from merchants. Several years of bad weather, poor crops, and low prices, however, would leave a farmer unable to repay these debts. The bank would then take possession of the farm by **foreclosure**.

During the 1870s, 1880s, and 1890s, an agricultural revolution led to increased farm production to feed the newly arrived immigrants and other urban dwellers. An agricultural revolution is the shift from hand labor to the use of machinery in farming. Crops were good, but prices for farm products fell, as dictated by the **law of supply and demand**. As formulated by Adam Smith, this economic law states that if supply of an item is low, sellers can charge a high price for it. When supply increases, the price is lowered in the competition for customers. As farm products' prices sank, farm debts soared.

Grange Movement

The Grange was founded in 1867 to bring farm families together for social purposes. Its meetings, however, soon focused on economic problems.

Agricultural Innovations

	Age of Jackson (1825–1845)	*Mid-century (1845–1865)*	*After Civil War (1865–1900)*
Inventions in agriculture	• John Deere's steel plow (1837) • Cyrus McCormick's reaper (1831)	• introduction of grain elevators (1850s) • mowing, threshing, and haying machines (1850s)	• giant harvester-and-thresher combine (1880s) • corn-shucking machine (1890s)

Rising Wheat Production (left) and Falling Farm Prices, 1867–1900

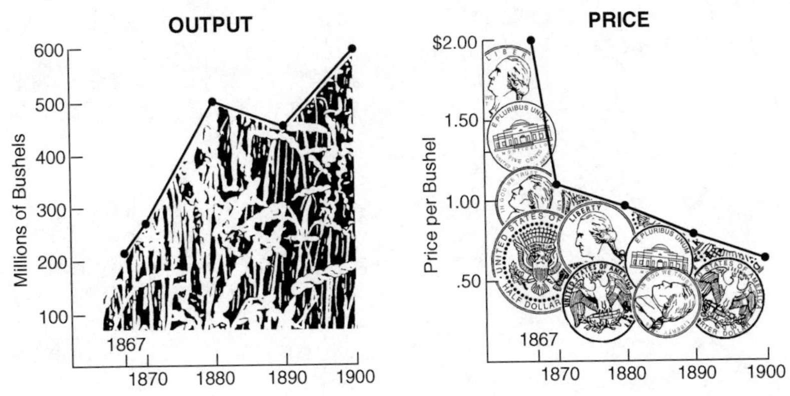

Grievances Farmers complained about the cost of transporting goods by rail. Railroads competed for business over long routes and therefore charged low rates. They made up their losses by overcharging farmers who had to ship over less competitive short routes. They also charged farmers high rates for storing their wheat and corn in railroad-owned grain elevators.

Cooperatives Grange members set up their own grain elevators by contributing money to a **cooperative** (an enterprise owned and operated by those using its services). Besides giving farmers access to low-cost storage, Grange cooperatives lowered prices for supplies by buying them in large quantities.

Laws To fight high railroad rates, the *Grangers* persuaded several state legislatures in the 1870s to regulate railroad freight and storage rates.

Supreme Court Decisions Companies facing such regulation challenged the Granger laws. In the landmark case of *Munn* v. *Illinois* (1877), the Supreme Court decided that a state could set maximum rates for grain storage. The Court reversed itself in 1886 in the case of *Wabash, St. Louis, and Pacific Railway* v. *Illinois* by ruling that railroads were a part of interstate commerce and their rates could be regulated only by the federal government. The next year, Congress enacted the *Interstate Commerce Act*, which created the Interstate Commerce Commission. It was in existence for more than a century (discussed on page 139).

Populism

As farm prices fell in the late 1880s, some farmers joined a movement that became a new political party—the *Populist Party*.

Platform of 1892

In 1892, the new party announced its **platform** (statement of political ideas), which was radical for the time:

- **graduated income tax** (the higher the income, the higher the tax rate)
- establishment of savings banks in U.S. post offices
- government ownership and operation of railroads
- government ownership and operation of telephone and telegraph companies
- election of U.S. senators by direct vote of the people rather than by state legislatures
- eight-hour workday for all factory workers
- state laws granting the **initiative** (voters can initiate ideas for new laws) and **referendum** (voters can mark ballots for or against proposed laws).

Monetary Policy

Between 1873 and 1890, the U.S. government had minted and circulated only coins of gold. Because gold was more valuable than silver, these coins were often hoarded (kept and not spent). As money became scarce, farmers saw a connection between the scarcity of money and the low prices they got for cotton and corn. The *Populists* felt that if the government coined 16 silver dollars for every gold dollar, farm prices would rise. In effect, the Populists wanted the government to create **inflation** (constantly rising prices). Silver miners and farmers liked this idea and became enthusiastic Populists.

Early Triumphs

The coinage of silver and other Populist reforms appealed to voters. The 1892 Populist presidential candidate, James Weaver, won more than a million votes (almost 9 percent of the total) as well as 22 electoral votes. Other Populists were elected to seats in Congress and in state legislatures of the South and West—an impressive showing for a new party.

Elections of 1892 and 1896

In 1892, Grover Cleveland, a Democrat, was elected president. He believed that gold was "sound money" and that silver coins would damage business confidence. Most Democrats of the North and East supported his stand, while those of the South and West favored the "free and unlimited coinage of silver."

Democratic Nomination of Bryan At the Democratic nominating convention of 1896, Congressman William Jennings Bryan of Nebraska thrilled the "silver Democrats" with his rousing "Cross of Gold" speech. Declaring that farmers would prevail over city bankers, he brought the convention to its feet with his last sentence: "You shall not press down upon the brow of labor this crown of thorns; you shall not crucify mankind upon a cross of gold." Bryan easily won the nomination.

Populist Nomination of Bryan The Populist Party also nominated Bryan as the candidate most able to rally the nation behind the cause of silver.

Republican Victory Nevertheless, Bryan lost to the Republican candidate, William McKinley, who supported the gold standard. Bryan carried the South and much of the West but failed to win crucial Eastern electoral votes. Many Eastern workers feared inflation and believed McKinley's prediction that silver money would cause high prices, a depression, and the loss of jobs.

Contributions

Bryan's defeat, the discovery of gold in Alaska, and improved farm prices after 1896 caused a rapid decline of the Populist Party. After 1900, no more Populists were elected to Congress.

Nevertheless, many Populist reforms were adopted. Two Populist ideas became the basis for constitutional amendments:

- graduated income tax—Sixteenth Amendment (1913)
- popular election of U.S. senators—Seventeenth Amendment (1913).

Early Regulation of Business

Until 1887, the federal government encouraged business growth through tariffs, land grants, and patents but did little to regulate business practices. Then, however, Congress, in responding to public pressure, enacted a law that marked the beginning of government regulation of business.

Interstate Commerce Act (1887)

To regulate certain practices of railroad companies, Congress created the *Interstate Commerce Commission (ICC)*, with power to enforce the following rules:

- Railroad rates had to be "reasonable and just."
- Pools were illegal.
- Rebates to favored customers was illegal.
- Railroads could not charge more for a short haul than for a long haul.

Later amendments to the law expanded the commission's powers.

IN REVIEW

1. What problems did small farmers experience, and what economic solutions did the Grangers propose?
2. To what extent was the Populist Party successful in resolving the problems of the farmers?
3. What features of the Populist agenda were eventually legislated?

CHAPTER REVIEW

MULTIPLE-CHOICE QUESTIONS

1 The principal reason Congress raised tariff rates in the late 1800s and early 1900s was to
(1) increase personal income taxes
(2) lower prices for American consumers
(3) guarantee high wages to American workers
(4) protect United States businesses from foreign competition

2 One reason John D. Rockefeller, Andrew Carnegie, and J. Pierpont Morgan were sometimes called robber barons was because they
(1) robbed from the rich to give to the poor
(2) made unnecessarily risky investments
(3) used ruthless business tactics against their competitors
(4) stole money from the federal government

3 In the late 1800s, the theory of laissez-faire capitalism was used by many industrialists to
(1) petition the government for assistance during times of financial crisis
(2) oppose colonial expansion in Africa and Asia
(3) argue against government regulation of business practices
(4) defend limits on the number of immigrants allowed to work in factories

4 A goal of the Granger and Populist movements was to
(1) expand rights for African Americans
(2) help Western farmers fight unjust economic practices
(3) provide support for the banking industry
(4) enable big business to expand without government interference

5 During the late 1800s, presidents and governors most often used military force during labor-management conflicts as a way to
(1) support industrialists and end strikes
(2) make employers sign collective bargaining agreements
(3) protect workers from the private armies of employers
(4) replace striking factory workers with soldiers

Base your answers to questions 6 and 7 on the cartoon at right and on your knowledge of social studies.

6 What is the main idea of this cartoon from the 1800s?
(1) Labor is gaining power over big business.
(2) Most Americans support the labor movement.
(3) Business has advantages over labor.
(4) Government should support the expansion of railroads.

7 The American Federation of Labor responded to the situation shown in the cartoon by
  (1) organizing skilled workers into unions
  (2) encouraging open immigration
  (3) forming worker-owned businesses
  (4) creating a single union of workers and farmers

8 In the late 1800s, free and unlimited coinage of silver was supported by farmers primarily because they hoped this policy would
  (1) make foreign crop prices less competitive
  (2) allow farmers to grow a greater variety of crops
  (3) increase crop prices and make it easier to repay loans
  (4) bring about political equality between rural and urban residents

9 The national income tax, free and unlimited coinage of silver, and the direct election of senators were proposals that were included in the
  (1) Declaration of Sentiments
  (2) Republican plan for Reconstruction
  (3) Populist Party platform
  (4) Federal Reserve System

10 The Interstate Commerce Act and the Sherman Antitrust Act were attempts by Congress to
  (1) regulate the activities of big business
  (2) protect consumers against unsafe products
  (3) impose government regulations on agricultural production
  (4) bring transportation activities under government ownership

THEMATIC ESSAYS

1 **THEME:** *The Federal Government as a Partner of Big Business.* In spite of its policy of laissez-faire, the federal government cooperated with and assisted in the growth and development of private business.

TASK: Compete *both* of the following tasks:

- Discuss *two* specific ways in which the government helped private business expand.

- Evaluate how *each* example had a positive or negative impact on a *specific* group in the United States.

You may discuss land grants, railroad subsidies, and tariff and monetary policies, with their impact on any group, including farmers, Native Americans, consumers, and industrial workers.

2 **THEME:** *Impact of Railroads on the Nation.* Completion of the transcontinental railroad in 1869 marked a major change for the people in the states and territories.

TASK: Choose *two* groups and show how railroads caused major changes in their lives.

Examples you may choose are farmers, immigrants, city dwellers, and Native Americans.

DOCUMENT-BASED QUESTION

Study each document and answer the question that follows it. Then read the ***Task*** *and write your essay. Include references to most of the documents and additional information you retain about U.S. history and government.*

HISTORICAL CONTEXT: Because of excesses by businesses, banks, and the federal government, industrial workers and farmers organized unions and political parties to make their voices heard.

DOCUMENT 1: Refer to the illustration below.

QUESTION: Who does the man raising his fist represent and why is he making this gesture?

DOCUMENT 2: An infamous sign in a sweatshop:

> IF YOU DON'T COME
> IN SUNDAY,
>
> DON'T COME TO WORK
> MONDAY!

QUESTION: How were the factory owners who posted the sign taking advantage of their workers?

DOCUMENT 3: From Samuel Gompers's "Letter on Labor" in *Industrial Society Forum,* September 1894:

Government troops putting down the Pullman strike, 1894

> . . . man's liberties are trampled underfoot [by] corporations and trusts, rights are invaded and laws perverted . . . wherever a tyrant has shown himself he has always found some willing judge to clothe that tyranny in . . . legality, and modern capitalism has proven no exception. . . .

QUESTION: How does Gompers feel about government's attitude toward labor and the common people?

DOCUMENT 4: Refer to the cartoon below.

Cartoon showing effects of the railroad monopoly on farmers

QUESTION: How does the cartoonist feel about the railroads' treatment of farmers?

DOCUMENT 5: From a speech by Populist orator Mary Lease in 1890:

> This is a nation of inconsistencies. The Puritans fleeing from oppression became oppressors. We fought England for our liberty and put chains on four million blacks. We wiped out slavery and by our tariff laws and national banks began a system of white wage slavery worse than the first.
>
> . . . It is no longer a government of the people, by the people, and for the people, but a government of Wall Street, by Wall Street, and for Wall Street. . . .
>
> . . . Kansas suffers from two great robbers, the Santa Fe Railroad and the loan companies. The common people are robbed to enrich their masters. . . .

QUESTION: How was Lease comparing the problems of Kansas farmers to those of slaves?

DOCUMENT 6: From William Jennings Bryan's "Cross of Gold" speech at the Democratic National Convention, 1896:

> You . . . tell us that the great cities are in favor of the gold standard; we reply that the great cities rest upon our broad and fertile prairies. Burn down your cities and leave our farms, and your cities will spring up again as if by magic; but destroy our farms and the grass will grow in the streets of every city. . . .
>
> . . . We will answer their demand for a gold standard by saying to them: You shall not press down upon the brow of labor this crown of thorns, you shall not crucify mankind upon a cross of gold.

QUESTION: Why does Bryan say that the gold standard will destroy both farms and cities?

TASK: Using the documents and your knowledge of U.S. history and government, write an essay describing how, between the late 1800s and early 1900s, farmers and factory workers organized labor unions and political parties to gain an effective voice in politics.

CHAPTER 9
Impact of Industrialization

DOCUMENTS AND LAWS
Chinese Exclusion Act (1882) • Dawes Act (1887) • Gentlemen's Agreement (1907–1908)
Literacy test law (1917) • Immigration quota laws (1882–1924)
Indian Reorganization Act (1934)

EVENTS
Gold rushes (1849, 1859) • Women's suffrage in Wyoming (1869) • Gilded Age (1869–1896)
Battle of Little Bighorn (1876) • Dedication of Statue of Liberty (1886)
Battle at Wounded Knee (1890) • End of the frontier (1890) • Red Scare (1919–1920)
Protest at Wounded Knee (1973)

PEOPLE/GROUPS
Apache • Willa Cather • Charles Darwin • William Randolph Hearst • Helen Hunt Jackson
Henry James • Scott Joplin • Chief Joseph • Emma Lazarus • Nez Percé • Joseph Pulitzer
Theodore Roosevelt • Sioux • Herbert Spencer • Tammany Hall • Frederick Jackson Turner
Mark Twain • Thorstein Veblen • Edith Wharton • Woodrow Wilson

OBJECTIVES

- To understand the impact of industrialization and urbanization on American life.
- To trace how industrialization changed the role of women.
- To appreciate how immigrants contributed to American life in a pluralistic society.
- To examine prejudice and discrimination against ethnic minorities.
- To understand how Western settlement affected Native Americans and U.S. society.

Urban Growth

In the late 1800s, millions of people—native-born Americans from rural areas, freed slaves seeking to escape social and economic bondage in the South, and immigrants from Europe and Asia—flocked to Eastern and Midwestern cities.

Attractions of Urban Life

Jobs Industrialists built factories near transportation centers such as railroad terminals and steamship ports. Workers moved near these hubs to get factory jobs. Near the factories, **entrepreneurs** (business investors) rented housing to the workers and opened shops to supply their needs. As city populations increased, so did the variety of goods and services available there.

Public Education City schools were larger, better-equipped, and offered more complete courses of study than rural ones. To serve growing populations, cities raised money for new elementary schools and high schools. Between 1865 and 1900, elementary school enrollments more than doubled. The number of U.S. high schools rose from about 400 in 1860 to more than 6,000 in 1900. Schools also improved in quality as more teachers received professional training. As schools and school districts increased in size, the "factory system" became the model for school systems. In high schools, students would move from room to room in large factory-like buildings and take specialized subjects in time periods designated by the ringing of bells. School principals and superintendents would oversee instruction. Boards of education would be responsible for making policies, hiring superintendents, and having general oversight.

Earlier educators had concentrated on teaching reading, writing, and arithmetic. After 1900, however, occupational training and citizenship education were considered equally important.

Culture Urban cultural resources—libraries, museums, and concert halls—enriched the education of city children. Moreover, urban life offered a variety of cultural experiences. For example, in the late 1800s, as now, New Yorkers had their choice of restaurants, theaters, beaches and parks, sporting events, and amusement centers.

Urban Problems

Slums As disadvantaged people crowded into cities, they could afford to live only in **slums**—poor neighborhoods with crowded streets and rundown buildings.

Increased Crime Poverty encouraged crime. As cities grew, so did the number of murders, burglaries, and robberies. Tenement youths organized rival gangs.

Major Cities and Industrial Areas, 1900

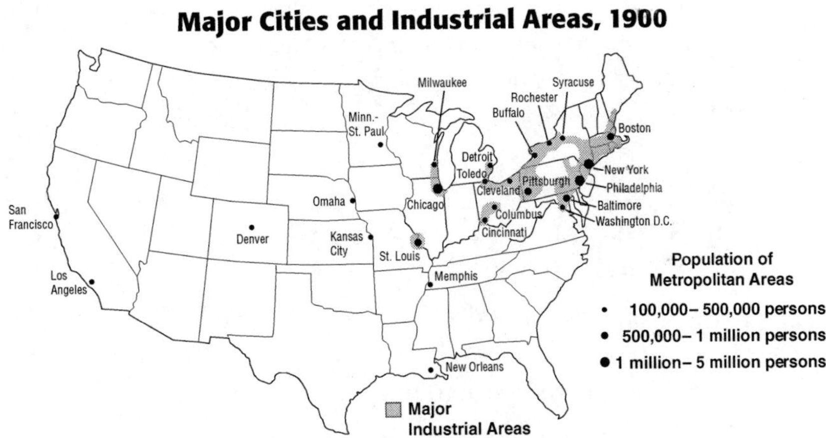

Inadequate Water and Sanitation Cities dumped sewage into rivers and lakes that provided drinking water. As a result, there were frequent outbreaks of typhoid fever, transmitted by polluted water. Lacking bathtubs and running water, tenement dwellers could not keep clean. Factory smokestacks polluted the air. Horse droppings fouled the streets.

New Urban Architecture

Skyscrapers and Elevators The invention of electric elevators made it possible to erect higher buildings. The first skyscraper, built in Chicago in 1884, was ten stories high.

Urban and Rural Population, 1870–1900

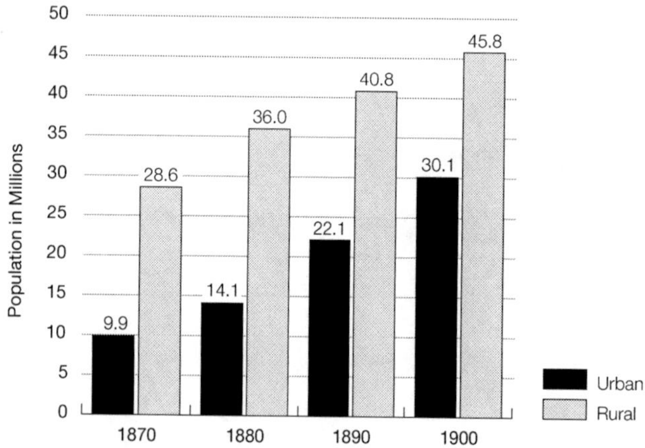

Tenements The tenements that dotted the slums were cheaply constructed buildings five or six stories high, without elevators. They were breeding grounds for vermin and disease, and built so closely together that fire could spread through an entire neighborhood in minutes. In New York City, many tenements were located on the lower east side of Manhattan.

Social Classes

Social Darwinism The British biologist Charles Darwin advanced the theory that lower forms of life evolved into higher forms as the result of evolution and an ongoing struggle for survival. The survivors were the "fittest" of the species. The British philosopher Herbert Spencer adapted this theory as **social Darwinism**: It is for the good of society that the strongest and most efficient businesses survive while weaker ones die out. In Spencer's words: "The American economy is controlled for the benefit of all by a natural aristocracy . . . brought to the top by a competitive struggle that weeded out the weak, incompetent, and unfit and selected the wise and able."

Class Divisions

The division among the social classes seemed more apparent in the last decades of the 1800s.

- *Working-class hardship.* A laborer's wages seldom covered family expenses, so the wife and children also had to work. Women and children were paid lower wages than men.

- *Middle-class contentment.* The middle class had sufficient income to live in modest comfort. After the Civil War, the middle class included shopkeepers, well-educated professionals (doctors, lawyers, teachers, and so on), and office workers.
- *Upper-class display and philanthropy.* In the late 1800s—the so-called *Gilded Age*—the families of people who had made great fortunes from corporations and trusts comprised the upper class. Such men as Andrew Carnegie and John D. Rockefeller flaunted their wealth and built enormous mansions filled with masterpieces of art and cared for by many servants. The economist Thorstein Veblen called their buying habits **conspicuous consumption**.

The rich also donated millions for public causes such as libraries, museums, universities, and medical research.

Work and Workers

Factories and People During the late 1800s, skilled craft workers were replaced by semiskilled and unskilled workers in the new factories. Most factory workers could not better their positions because unskilled work taught them little that was useful. Their wages were so low that even ambitious, clever workers could seldom raise enough capital to start a business. In large factories, business owners and their managers had too little contact with workers to recognize those with promise.

Immigrant Patterns of Settlement Immigrants tended to move to cities, where there were jobs. Since many immigrants arrived at New York City, many stayed there. Others settled in cities such as Philadelphia, Boston, and

Gilded Age: The very rich (left) and very poor

Chicago. Wherever they settled, immigrants usually moved into neighborhoods peopled by their own nationality. In New York, people still refer to such neighborhoods as Little Italy and Chinatown.

Insecurity After 1865, the plight of factory workers increased. Appeals to employers were useless, and those who joined unions or participated in strikes were fired. Replacement workers were plentiful—immigrants, women and children, youths fresh from farms, and African Americans who had migrated north.

Jobs were also threatened by new machines that were cheaper and faster than humans. Depressions and financial panics sometimes ended business booms abruptly, and there was no unemployment insurance for those who were fired or laid off.

Women, Families, and Work

Traditional Roles From the mid- to late 1800s, middle-class women were completely under male protection and expected to be wives and mothers rather than professional workers. Many single women became teachers, the one calling in which women outnumbered men.

Working-class women had to provide some of the family income. Farm women worked with their husbands, sons, and brothers in the fields. City women became mill or factory hands, servants, or laundresses and did their own housework in the evenings.

Emerging Family Patterns The long hours of working-class women strained family ties, but their incomes were badly needed to supplement their husbands' low wages. Additional strains arose when men wasted their salaries on gambling or drinking.

African-American women could generally find work only as domestic help.

Children, the Elderly, and the Disabled Prior to the Civil War, children under 12 earned pennies a day in textile mills. In 1900, about 1.7 million children between the ages of 10 and 15 earned pennies an hour in mines and factories.

Unprotected by law, the elderly and the disabled were often unemployed. Some relied heavily upon support from family members and charity.

Religion in a Pluralistic Society

Degree of Tolerance The Pilgrims and Puritans had come to America seeking religious freedom, but they did not grant it to others. They were particularly intolerant of Quakers, who were forced to leave the Massachusetts Bay Colony. In the 1800s, Americans of British descent considered their culture and Protestant faith superior. Religious intolerance—always a problem—increased when many Catholics from Italy, Poland, and Ireland arrived. Eastern Orthodox Christians from Greece and Jews from Poland and Russia also arrived in the United States in large numbers.

Influence of Puritan Beliefs and Values In colonial New England, most Protestant ministers were Puritans, who had split from the Church of England. Their beliefs in predestination, hard work, and the careful management of property are still a part of American values.

Religion and Party Politics Throughout the 1800s, elected leaders on both national and state levels were generally Protestants. As more Catholics and Jews arrived in the late 1800s and early 1900s, they began to influence Democratic politics in New York City, Boston, and Chicago. Party leaders sought to win the support of new immigrants at the polls by providing them with financial assistance and social welfare.

Threatened by the number of Catholic immigrants, some Protestants believed that the pope had sent the new arrivals to take over the country. Such extremists joined the American Protective Association, as others like them had joined the Know-Nothings decades earlier.

Since **political machines** (organized control of elected officials by party leaders) in Northern cities were usually controlled by Catholics and Jews, and overcrowding provided more votes for these politicians, Protestants set up religious reform groups aimed at lessening overcrowding and improving living conditions of the poor, and thereby reducing the influence of political

North Wind Picture Archives

Thomas Nast cartoon about Tammany Hall corruption

machines such as *Tammany Hall* in New York. These reform goals influenced the emerging Progressive movement of the early 1900s.

Changes in Lifestyle

Buying and Selling Goods New methods of commercial financing encouraged urban middle-class consumers to buy the new products created by industrialization. People who could not afford a new Singer sewing machine could buy it on **credit** and pay for it sometime in the future. Or they could put down part of the price and pay off the rest monthly on the **installment plan**.

Sports and Recreation City dwellers who could not hunt and fish could enjoy sports as spectators. In 1846, one of the first amateur baseball games was played in Hoboken, New Jersey. Cincinnati had the first professional team—the Red Stockings (today's Cincinnati Reds)—formed in 1869. College football became popular in the 1870s. A teacher in Springfield, Massachusetts, invented basketball in 1892.

Health and Life Expectancy Doctors developed cures for diphtheria and other contagious diseases that raged through the crowded, dirty cities. New city hospitals met the needs of a growing population. Improved health care raised the average life expectancy in the United States from the 35.5 years in 1800 to 47.3 in 1900.

Literature and Music As prosperity gave the urban middle class more leisure, some turned to the arts. Thus, more American writers, musicians, and artists were able to make a living. Samuel Clemens, the author of *The Adventures of Tom Sawyer* (1876) and *The Adventures of Huckleberry Finn* (1884), became a celebrity under the pen name Mark Twain. Willa Cather achieved fame for *My Ántonia* (1918), a novel of Midwestern life. Henry James's *Washington Square* (1880) and Edith Wharton's *The Age of Innocence* (1920) depicted earlier and later manners of upper-class New Yorkers.

In 1883, the Metropolitan Opera House opened in New York City. Scott Joplin, the son of a former slave, composed original, distinctly American music. His piano compositions, such as "Maple Leaf Rag" (1899), were in the style known as ragtime. Its lively, rhythmic musical style had a marked influence on the development of jazz.

Popular Culture One-penny and two-penny newspapers circulated daily in every city. New York publishers such as William Randolph Hearst and Joseph Pulitzer appealed to the urban masses by featuring articles on team sports and sensational crimes. Some publishers issued dime novels on such exciting subjects as the outlaws of the West.

IN REVIEW

1. How was Darwin's theory of evolution applied to the business world?
2. Compare the impact of industrialism on a working-class family and a middle-class family.
3. Identify *three* ways in which the growth of cities affected American cultural life.

Immigration: 1850–1924

While European immigrants were settling mainly in the East and Midwest, Chinese and Japanese immigrants were settling on the West Coast. By 1910, more than 300,000 Chinese and more than 150,000 Japanese immigrants lived and worked in the United States.

Italians Italians began a mass emigration in the late 1800s. By 1898, some 205,000 emigrated every year. Between 1898 and 1914, the arrival number increased to about 750,000 a year.

The main cause of this huge emigration from Italy was poverty. In the 1880s, an agricultural crisis caused, in part, by increased competition from American farmers, resulted in a decline in the standard of living in Italy. The price of farm products there fell and unemployment increased. Peasants spent about three-fourths of their income on food. In addition, Italy was a country where few could vote or gain an education.

Photographer and writer Jacob Riis set up scenes like this to portray the horrors of slums in New York City.

Chinese The Chinese first arrived in California in 1849. They hoped to discover gold and return home rich. They were the first nonwhites to arrive in large numbers of their own free will. Viewed with hostility, Chinese immigrants were prevented from owning property or gaining citizenship.

Chinese labor was essential in the development of the West. Agents of the Central Pacific Railroad recruited thousands to build the western half of the first transcontinental railroad. Thus, Chinese workers dynamited the tunnels through the rugged Sierra Nevada. Overworked and underprotected from both the elements and hazardous working conditions, many Chinese lost their lives.

When a depression hit the nation in the 1870s, Chinese laborers became **scapegoats** (people unfairly blamed for an event or condition). Further resentment arose when bosses replaced striking workers with Chinese laborers. Anti-Chinese sentiment led to the passage of the *Chinese Exclusion Act* (1882), which halted further immigration. The law also prevented all Chinese and their American-born children from becoming citizens. (For information on the Japanese exclusion, see page 156.)

The Chinese Exclusion Act, the first major restriction on U.S. immigration, was not fully repealed until 1943, when China was an ally in World War II. Chinese immigrants, however, had challenged the law in the U.S. Supreme Court. In 1897, the Court established for the first time the legal right of citizenship by birth for all Americans.

Russian Jews Abraham Cahan was one of many Jews who arrived from Russia. He wrote about the experiences of immigrant Russian Jews in an article, "The Lower East Side in 1898," in *The Atlantic Monthly* (see page 165).

European Immigrants: When They Came and Why

Nationality	*Period of Greatest Immigration*	*Reasons*
Irish	1840s–1850s	Failure of potato crop and resulting famine
Germans	1840s–1880s	Economic depression; oppression following failed revolutions
Scandinavians (Danes, Swedes, Norwegians, Finns)	1870s–1900s	Poverty; shortage of farmland
Italians	1880s–1920s	Poverty; shortage of farmland
Jews from Eastern Europe (including Poles and Russians)	1880s–1920s	Political oppression; religious persecution; poverty

Reasons for Emigration

Population Pressures As Europe industrialized, it became overcrowded. A population of 140 million in 1750 grew to 260 million in 1850 and 400 million in 1914. Farmland was much scarcer than in the United States.

Recruitment Railroad companies with Western lands to sell and steamship companies seeking passengers sent agents abroad to promote emigration. Steamship lines offered tickets to New York City for as little as $25 a person.

Economic Conditions From generation to generation, European farm families divided their land to provide for their sons. Eventually, most farms had become too small to be profitable. After 1880, poor farmers in Italy, Sweden, and Norway found it almost impossible to earn a living.

American Attractions

Labor Shortage Because of rapid industrialization in the United States, Europeans thought that American factory jobs would be plentiful and better-paying than those at home.

Liberty and Freedom Jews in Russia and Poland lived in fear of **pogroms** —sudden violent attacks on their communities. In many Eastern European countries, laws required boys of 15 and 16 to do military service.

Ghettos Distinct immigrant groups gathered in **ghettos**—city neighborhoods made up mostly of one nationality or **ethnicity** (common cultural bond uniting a large group of people).

The tenement apartments of poor immigrants were known as "railroad flats" because their rooms were arranged in a straight line, one after the other. Families often shared an already crowded apartment with relatives and friends newly arrived.

"Americanization"

Ghetto life helped immigrants preserve their customs and language, and the adults often had difficulty adapting to strange new ways. Although they tried to learn English, only the children usually adapted readily.

Society pressured new immigrants to undergo "Americanization." School lessons were taught only in English. Sometimes, a teacher changed a student's name to one that was easier for a native-born American to pronounce.

Most immigrants supported the Democratic Party, which, on the local level, provided services for the urban poor in return for their support in elections. Since most cities had large immigrant populations, Democratic politicians usually won city elections.

Immigration by Nationality, 1840s–1920s

Nationality	*Number (approximate)*
German	6 million
Italian	4.75 million
Irish	4.5 million
English, Scots, Welsh	4.2 million
From Austro-Hungarian Empire	4.2 million
From Russian Empire	3.3 million
Scandinavian	2.3 million

Growing Diversity and Reaction

Between the 1840s and the 1920s, approximately 37 million immigrants arrived in the United States. Until the 1870s, Germans and Irish predominated.

After 1890, the "new immigration"—those from Southern and Eastern Europe—began to exceed those from other regions. Between 1900 and 1910, total immigration averaged close to a million people a year. Of the total arriving in 1910, about 700,000 people came from Southern and Eastern Europe and only about 300,000 from all other areas.

English-speaking Protestant Americans, as guardians of the dominant culture, feared that the "new immigrants" would not easily adapt to it. Although American values differed from region to region, several were generally agreed upon and cherished:

- *Individualism.* Each American was completely responsible for his or her actions. People attained economic success because of strength of character. Failure resulted from weakness of character.

U.S. Population Distribution, 1900

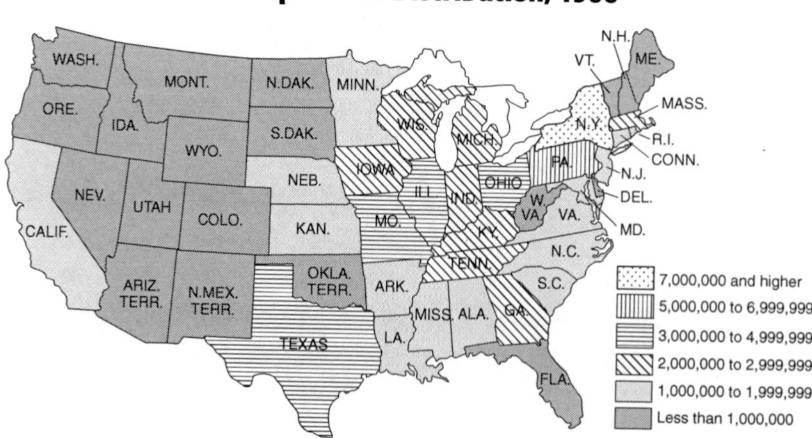

- *Rough social equality.* Americans of European descent tended to view one another as social equals deserving of mutual cooperation, especially on the Western frontier.
- *White superiority.* Most American whites believed in the superiority of their "race" and culture. They saw that they had a mission to bring Western civilization to other world regions and peoples.

Methods of Adaptation

During the peak immigration years (1901–1910), Americans debated three points of view about how immigrants should adapt to their new country:

- *Assimilation.* Immigrants should quickly learn English and adopt all aspects of American culture.
- *"Melting pot" theory.* Immigrants would gradually and naturally blend into a new American culture that combined the best elements of many cultures and nationalities.
- *Cultural pluralism.* There are no superior cultures, and each ethnic group should practice its own customs, respect unfamiliar customs, and adjust to the ways of a larger society.

Resurgence of Nativism

Nativist feelings had not disappeared (discussed on page 75). Faced with the "new immigrants," nativists had four main fears:

- *Economic.* Immigrants would deprive native-born Americans of jobs by accepting lower wages.
- *Cultural.* The dominant culture deserved to be protected against foreign influences.
- *Psychological.* Native-born Americans of European descent were superior by race and nationality, and inferior newcomers from Eastern and Southern Europe would produce a class of criminals and paupers.
- *Political.* The "new immigrants" might be connected with radical and revolutionary causes.

Non-nativists voiced their opposition. A New York writer, Emma Lazarus, poetically expressed her recognition of the contributions of immigrants:

> ... "Give me your tired, Your poor,
> Your huddled masses yearning to breathe free,
> The wretched refuse of your teeming shore.
> Send these, the homeless, the tempest-tossed, to me,
> I lift my lamp beside the golden door!

Lazarus's complete poem is inscribed at the base of the Statue of Liberty, which began welcoming immigrant ships to New York Harbor in 1886.

Cartoon of anti-immigrant citizens and their "shadows"–their immigrant ancestors

Limits on Immigration

Between 1870 and 1920, there were few restrictions on European immigration as a result of the need for workers in the new factories. However, in the 1870s, anti-Chinese riots broke out to protest the "yellow peril"—the unfounded fear that Asian immigrants would overwhelm American culture. Two new laws reflected such nativist fear and prejudice:

- The *Chinese Exclusion Act* (1882) declared that no more Chinese would be allowed into the United States.
- Japanese schoolchildren in San Francisco were ordered to attend segregated classes. When the Japanese government expressed resentment, President Theodore Roosevelt arranged a compromise, the *Gentlemen's Agreement* of 1907–1908. California would end its offensive school policy, and Japan would stop further immigration of Japanese workers into the United States.

Literacy Testing In 1917, Congress overrode President Woodrow Wilson's veto and passed a *literacy test law*. It provided that those unable to pass a reading test in their native language (or any other language) were prohibited from immigrating. The law aimed to reduce emigration from Southern and Eastern Europe.

Red Scare In 1917, the Communist-backed revolution in Russia fueled nativist fears that Communists (Reds) and other foreign-born radicals might overthrow the U.S. government. During the **Red Scare** of 1919 and 1920, President Wilson's attorney general, A. Mitchell Palmer, organized raids, often without search warrants, to arrest and deport immigrants suspected of disloyalty.

Quota Acts of 1921 and 1924 The *Emergency Quota Act* (1921) limited the yearly emigration from any country to 3 percent of the number arriving from that country in 1910. The *Immigration Restriction Act* (1924) limited the yearly emigration from any country to 2 percent of the number arriving from that country in 1890.

These quota laws were designed to cut sharply the number of emigrants from Italy, the Soviet Union (formerly Russia), and other countries of Southern and Eastern Europe. They were also meant to halt emigration from Asia. Between 1901 and 1910, more than eight million immigrants had arrived, most from Southern and Eastern Europe. In the 1930s, immigrants numbered fewer than 350,000.

Summary of Immigration Laws

Date	*Law*
1882	Chinese Exclusion Act: Chinese immigration was prohibited.
1882	Paupers, convicts, and mentally defective persons were prohibited.
1891	Prostitutes, polygamists, and diseased persons were prohibited.
1917	Literacy test. Those unable to pass a reading test in their native language (or any language) were prohibited.
1921	Emergency Quota Act: Yearly emigration from a country was limited to 3 percent of the number arriving from that country in 1910.
1924	Immigration Restriction Act: (a) Yearly emigration from a country was limited to 2 percent of the number arriving from that country in 1890; (b) no more than 150,000 immigrants were to be admitted yearly from a single country; (c) no Asians would be admitted.

IN REVIEW

1. Why did the “new immigrants” leave their countries for the United States?
2. How did the “new immigrants” contribute to American society?
3. What conflicts between American ideals and reality are illustrated by the following laws? (a) Chinese Exclusion Act, (b) Gentlemen’s Agreement, (c) literacy test law of 1917, (d) Emergency Quota Act and (e) Immigration Restriction Act.

The Frontier: 1850–1900

The U.S. **frontier** was an imaginary line separating settled areas from the wilderness. As trappers, miners, and farmers moved west, the frontier moved with them.

Westward From the Missouri River

Plains and Desert Before 1850, the region between Missouri and California was somewhat inacurrately called the Great American Desert because it seemed dry, barren, and impossible to farm. It consisted of:

- the *Great Plains*—flat grasslands in the central United States, from the banks of the Missouri River to the slopes of the Rocky Mountains, from Texas into Canada. The more western Great Plains are drier than the Central Plains.
- the *Great Basin*—a dry area between the Rocky Mountains and the Sierra Nevada.

Settlement of the West

Beginning around 1850, Easterners began to realize that the so-called Great American Desert was rich in resources.

Mining Frontier In 1859, news of a gold strike on Pikes Peak in Colorado touched off a rush westward similar to the one in California ten years earlier. Later, many others were lured elsewhere in the Rockies by news of silver in Nevada and copper in Montana, and to the Black Hills of the Dakotas for gold.

Cattle Frontier During the 1860s and 1870s, settlers began to raise cattle on the grassy plains of Texas. The herds were privately owned, but the open range was used by all.

Farming Frontier The 1862 Homestead Act (discussed on page 136) attracted "homesteaders," who set up farms on the Great Plains. Speculators took over some of the newly available land.

Violence in the "Wild West"

Ranchers Versus Farmers The barbed wire that farmers used to fence in their homesteads angered cattle owners, who regarded the grasslands as open range. Gun battles broke out between the factions. In the 1880s, the ranchers conceded defeat and began to fence in their own grazing lands.

Vigilantes Versus Outlaws For many adventurers, it was easier to steal a miner's gold or rustle a rancher's cattle than work for them. Most Westerners carried guns to protect their property and, sometimes, to settle personal quarrels.

Remote towns could not rely on government officials to capture thieves. Therefore, they carried out the law as **vigilantes** (a self-appointed police force). Suspected outlaws were sometimes hanged without a full trial—or any trial at all.

Westward Movement of the Frontier, 1700–1850

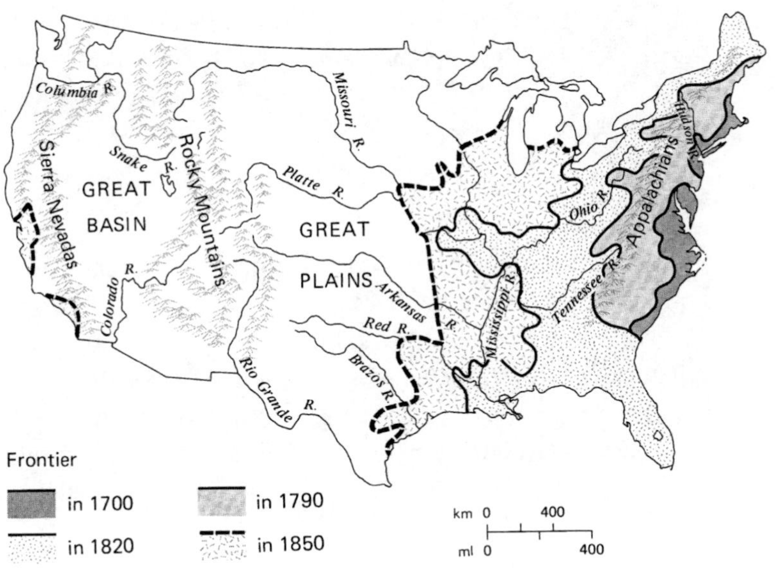

Industrialization and the West

Railroads and Investment Railroad companies were even more eager than the U.S. government to encourage farmers to go west. A railroad's chief business was transporting freight. Settlers on the plains would expand business.

Railroads were crucial to the **cattle drives** from Texas. At the end of the cowboys' long journey north were the railroad depots in Abilene and Dodge City, Kansas, from which cattle were shipped to Chicago for slaughter. The meat was then sent east. Cattle ranchers needed railroads. In the 1860s, a steer worth $3 in Texas could bring between $30 and $40 when sold to a Chicago meatpacker.

Urban Centers Chicago grew into a great city and the world's largest meatpacking center. Abilene and Dodge City fared well, too. Their stockyards charged cowboys to house their cattle before shipment. During their stay, cowboys spent money at hotels, restaurants, stores, and other businesses. With their prosperity, the towns' populations grew. Soon, **railheads**, as such stopovers were called, became bustling urban centers.

Technology Farmers on the Great Plains faced three problems. (1) Rainfall was slight, (2) there was a scarcity of trees for rail fences to enclose their animals, and (3) the soil was dry, hard, and full of tough grass roots. *Windmills* provided the power for pumping up groundwater. *Barbed wire* (invented in 1874) enabled farmers to fence their lands. With improved *steel plows*, they could cut deep into the hard ground.

Cultural Diversity

Mexicans who had lost their land in the Mexican War often worked as cowboys on American ranches. African Americans, many recently freed from slavery, became ranchers and farmers. In the 1860s and 1870s, many emigrants from Europe joined the movement west.

Lifestyles

Sod Houses and Dugouts Lacking trees, homesteaders built their first homes out of bricks made from the prairie sod, with blankets and hides covering doors and windows. On hilly sites, they dug these homes into the hillside. When it rained, the sod roof leaked. In long dry spells, crops withered and dust covered everything. Separated by great distances, farmers only rarely got together. Many farm families on the plains soon moved back east.

Women Women farmed, fed the livestock, milked cows, churned butter, cooked, sewed linens and clothing, and reared children—often, ten or more of them. It was common for a woman to work all morning, give birth in the afternoon, and return to chores the next morning.

In spite of this drudgery, women were a civilizing influence that could turn a rough mining camp or cow town into a more settled, peaceful community. They called for libraries, schools, even theaters. They worked as teachers, missionaries, librarians, and, occasionally, doctors and dentists.

Women of the Wyoming Territory first achieved the right to vote in 1869. By 1910, women in most Western states were voting in large numbers, while Eastern women were still fighting for suffrage.

Impact on American Life

In 1890, the U.S. Census Bureau reported that the frontier had ceased to exist. Frederick Jackson Turner, a historian, then wrote an essay about the effects of the frontier on American society.

Turner observed that frontier life was more democratic than life in settled areas. People on the frontier judged one another not by social rank but by ability and strength of character. They felt that everyone had an equal chance for success. For people from crowded Eastern cities, the frontier was a new starting point where hardworking people could get land cheaply.

Some scholars, who feel that American democracy owes more to British colonial influences than to the frontier, point out that few poor people could afford covered wagons and supplies necessary for the trip west.

Native Americans

Plains Indians The Great Plains were filled with plants and animals that supported the Native-American way of life. Huge buffalo herds supplied Plains Indians with meat for food, hides for clothing and shelter, bones

Native Americans in the West, Late 1800s

for tools, and dried manure for fuel. Buffalo-hunting tribes (the Blackfeet, Cheyenne, Comanche, and Sioux) believed that the land and the life it supported were sacred. They could not conceive of dividing land into private plots and using it for personal gain.

Pressures of White Settlement By 1890, most Native Americans had been placed on reservations and had lost their rights to the land. White people hunted the buffalo herds of the plains for hides and sometimes merely for sport. By 1890, the once-teeming buffalo numbered fewer than a thousand herds.

Reservations Often located in otherwise sparsely populated areas of the West, reservations were usually barren and supported little wildlife for hunting. Native Americans there were reduced to poverty and hopelessness. U.S. agents who ran the reservations often pocketed funds intended for the inhabitants.

In 1887, Congress passed the *Dawes Act*, which offered 160-acre plots on reservations to the heads of Indian households. Lawmakers viewed it as a form of Americanization by which Indians would adopt the lifestyle of self-supporting white farmers. Many Native Americans, however, followed a nomadic hunting culture, and many of them rented or sold their plots to white settlers.

Treaties and Legal Status U.S. treaties had guaranteed Native Americans the right to their own land. But as settlers moved west in the 1850s, these treaties were ignored. Often, the U.S. Army supported the takeover of Native-American land. Some of the troops were African Americans (whom the Indians called "buffalo soldiers"), and they fought against Native Americans as well.

A reformer named Helen Hunt Jackson published *A Century of Dishonor* (1881), describing how often the U.S. government had violated its treaties with Native Americans.

Indian Wars: 1850–1900 The Sioux of Wyoming were the first Plains people to attack U.S. military posts. In an 1876 battle on the Little Bighorn

River in Montana, the Sioux, led by Chief Crazy Horse, killed 210 U.S. soldiers, including Lieutenant Colonel George Custer. In 1890, the U.S. Army retaliated by killing about 300 Sioux at Wounded Knee Creek in South Dakota. This massacre, in which even women and children were killed, ended Sioux resistance. They moved to a South Dakota reservation.

Chief Joseph, around 1870

Other Native-American resistance also failed. In 1877, some 500 members of the Oregon Nez Percé fled toward Canada to escape being forced onto a reservation. They were turned back by U.S. troops. So thorough was their defeat that their leader, Chief Joseph, declared that his people's fight was finished forever.

The Apaches of Arizona, who submitted in 1900, were the last Native Americans to engage U.S. troops.

Western Native Americans lost their wars against settlers and U.S. troops for three reasons:

- They usually fought as separate tribes, rather than uniting.
- Most tribes numbered fewer than a thousand people.
- Though equipped with bows and arrows and rifles, they lacked such advanced weapons as cannons and machine guns.

Indian Civil Rights

Early in the 20th century, two laws somewhat improved the status of Native Americans. In 1924, Congress granted Native Americans full citizenship. In 1934, the *Indian Reorganization Act* permitted Indian peoples to own land in common as tribal property rather than as separate farms. At the same time, reservation schools began to teach scientific farming.

IN REVIEW

1. How did the Industrial Revolution contribute to the economic development of the Great Plains?
2. Identify (a) Homestead Act, (b) Wounded Knee, and (c) Frederick Jackson Turner.
3. Summarize the federal government's attempts to address Native-American rights from 1887 to 1934.

CHAPTER REVIEW

MULTIPLE-CHOICE QUESTIONS

1 During the late 1800s, what was a major effect of industrialization on workers in the United States?
(1) Membership in labor unions declined.
(2) Workers migrated to rural regions.
(3) Most factory jobs became service industry jobs.
(4) Skilled craftsmen were replaced by semiskilled machine operators.

2 "Society advances when its fittest members are allowed to assert themselves with the least hindrance."

The idea expressed in this statement is most consistent with the
(1) principles of Social Darwinism
(2) concept of assimilation
(3) goals of the Progressive movement
(4) melting pot theory of American culture

3 Between 1870 and 1920, the federal government placed relatively few restrictions on immigration primarily because it wanted to
(1) sell land in the West
(2) recruit men for the military
(3) ensure that there would be workers for the factories
(4) avoid offending foreign governments

4 Between 1880 and 1920, the majority of the "new immigrants" to the United States came from
(1) Northern and Western Europe
(2) Southern and Eastern Europe
(3) Canada and Latin America
(4) China and Southeast Asia

5 What was the experience of most of the "new immigrants" who arrived in the United States in the late 1800s and early 1900s?
(1) They lived in urban areas and most held low-paying jobs.
(2) They obtained free land in the West and became farmers.
(3) They became discouraged with America and returned to their homelands.
(4) They were easily assimilated into mainstream American culture.

Base your answers to questions 6 and 7 on the speakers' statements below and on your knowledge of social studies.

Speaker A: "Our nation has grown and prospered from the ideas and labor of immigrants. The nation has been enriched by immigrants from different nations who brought new ideas and lifestyles, which have become part of American culture."

Speaker B: "United States industries are competing with established European manufacturers. To prosper, American industries need the vast supply of unskilled labor that is provided by immigrants."

Speaker C: "Immigrants are taking jobs at low wages without regard for long hours and workers' safety. American workers must unite to end this unfair competition."

Speaker D: "Immigrants arrive in American cities poor and frightened. They are helped to find jobs or housing. These newcomers should show their gratitude at voting time."

6 Which speaker is most clearly expressing the melting pot theory?
(1) A (3) C
(2) B (4) D

7 Speaker *D* is expressing an opinion most like that of a
(1) labor union member
(2) religious leader
(3) factory owner
(4) political party boss

8 The Chinese Exclusion Act (1882) and the Gentlemen's Agreement with Japan (1907) are examples of
(1) international humanitarian programs
(2) actions that reflected widespread nativist sentiment
(3) successful negotiations to encourage trade
(4) United States attempts to stay out of foreign wars

9 In the late 1800s and early 1900s, many members of Congress supported legislation requiring literacy tests for immigrants in an attempt to
(1) stop illegal immigration from Latin America
(2) provide highly skilled workers for industry
(3) limit the power of urban political machines
(4) restrict immigration from Southern and Eastern Europe

10 The passage of the Dawes Act in 1887 was primarily an attempt by the United States government to
(1) limit the power of the Bureau of Indian Affairs
(2) return Eastern land to Native American Indian tribes
(3) encourage Native American Indians to give up their traditional cultures
(4) hire Native American Indians as military scouts

THEMATIC ESSAYS

1 **THEME:** *Urbanization.* The gradual U.S. population shift from rural to urban areas created new problems that demanded new solutions.

TASK: Choose *one* change resulting from the growth of cities that created a problem. For this change:
- describe in detail the problem created
- show how people attempted to solve the problem
- evaluate the success of the attempted solution.

You may wish to consider changes in the areas of housing, immigration, and working conditions.

2 **THEME:** *The Shrinking Frontier.* As the U.S. frontier moved west, it shrank and disappeared.

TASK: Complete *all* of the following tasks:
- Define "frontier" and show how its movement west resulted in its disappearance.
- Explain *two* factors that caused the frontier to shrink and disappear.
- Describe *one* outcome of the shrinking frontier.

Some factors to consider in explaining the shrinking frontier are the discovery of gold in California, Homestead Act, development of railroads, and role of technology.

Outcomes of the shrinking frontier might include, but are not limited to, its impact on Native Americans, immigrants, the environment, and living styles.

DOCUMENT-BASED QUESTION

*Study each document and answer the question that follows it. Then read the **Task** and write your essay. Include references to most of the documents and additional information you retain about U.S. history and government.*

HISTORICAL CONTEXT: The "new immigration" presented special challenges for newcomers to New York City and other urban centers.

DOCUMENT 1: Refer to the following graph.

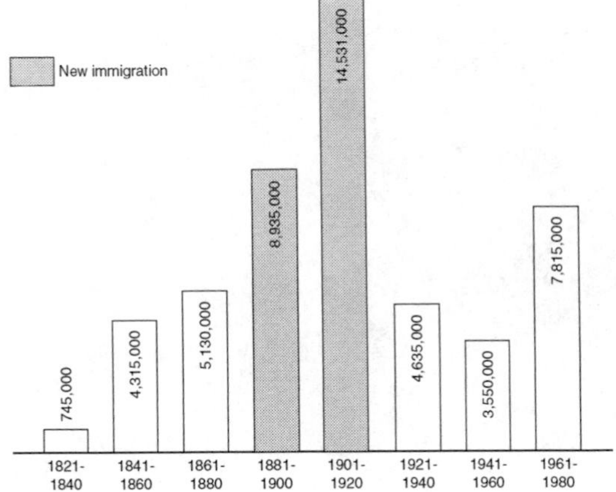

Question: What happened to the number of immigrants from 1881 through 1920?

Document 2: Refer to the map below.

Question: During the period shown on the map, where did most immigrants come from?

Document 3: From the excerpt "The Lower East Side in 1898" by Abraham Cahan, published first in *The Atlantic Monthly.*

> Sixteen years have elapsed. . . . The Jewish population has grown . . . to about one million. Scarcely a large American town but [it] has . . . an educated Russian-speaking minority forming a colony within a **Yiddish**-speaking colony [Yiddish is the language of many European Jews], while . . . New York, Chicago, Philadelphia, and Boston have each a ghetto rivaling . . . the largest Jewish cities in Russia, Austria, and Rumania. The [Jews] in Manhattan [number] 250,000, making it the largest center of Hebrew population in the world. . . .
>
> The grammar schools of the Jewish quarter are overcrowded. . . . For progress and deportment, [immigrant children] are raised with the very best in the city. At least 500 of 1,677 students at New York City College, where tuition and books are free, are Jewish boys from the East Side. . . .
>
> The 5,000,000 Jews . . . in Russia had not a single Yiddish daily paper . . . , while their fellow countrymen and coreligionists . . . in America publish six dailies . . . , not to mention the countless Yiddish weeklies and monthlies. . . . New York [is] the largest Yiddish book market in the world.

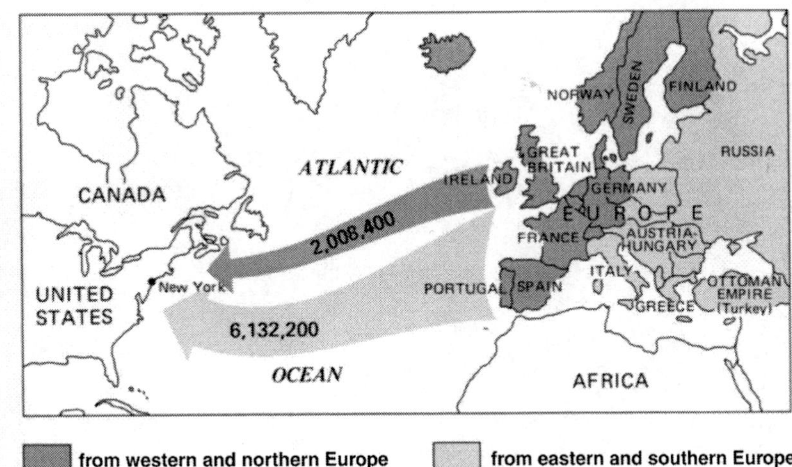

Early 20th-century immigrants arriving at Ellis Island, New York City

Question: In Cahan's view, how did life in the United States compare with that in Russia?

Document 4: Refer to the photograph above.

Question: What feelings does this photo convey to you?

Document 5: Refer to the photograph below.

Question: What conditions did many immigrants live in when they first arrived in U.S. cities?

Task: Using the documents and your knowledge of U.S. history and government, write an essay in which you:

- describe some challenges faced by immigrants who arrived during the late 1800s and early 1900s
- explain why most immigrants decided to remain in spite of the challenges facing them.

New York City's Lower East Side, 1900

UNIT III
The Progressive Era

CHAPTER 10
Reform in America

DOCUMENTS AND LAWS
Sherman Antitrust Act (1890) • Newlands Reclamation Act (1902) • Elkins Act (1903)
Northern Securities Company v. *United States* (1904) • *Lochner* v. *New York* (1905)
Hepburn Act (1906) • Meat Inspection Act (1906) • Pure Food and Drug Act (1906)
Inland Waterways Act (1907) • *Muller* v. *Oregon* (1908) • Payne-Aldrich Tariff (1909)
Sixteenth Amendment (1913) • Seventeenth Amendment (1913) • Underwood Tariff (1913)
Federal Reserve Act (1913) • Clayton Antitrust Act (1914)
Federal Trade Commission Act (1914) • Eighteenth Amendment (1919)
Nineteenth Amendment (1920)

EVENTS
Seneca Falls Convention (1848) • Women's suffrage in Wyoming (1869)
Progressive Era (1890–1917) • Pennsylvania Coal Strike (1902)
National Association for the Advancement of Colored People (NAACP), formed 1909
Election of 1912

PEOPLE/GROUPS
Jane Addams • Susan B. Anthony • Louis Brandeis • Eugene V. Debs • W. E. B. Du Bois
Marcus Garvey • Florence Kelly • Robert La Follette • John Muir • Frank Norris • Gifford Pinchot
Jacob Riis • Margaret Sanger • Upton Sinclair • Lincoln Steffens • William H. Taft • Ida Tarbell
Lillian Wald • Ida B. Wells • muckrakers • suffragists • progressives

OBJECTIVES

- To evaluate progressive reforms.
- To identify movements to protect consumers, workers, the environment, and the rights of women and minorities.
- To describe how women and African Americans brought about democratic reforms.
- To compare the reform politics of presidents Theodore Roosevelt, William H. Taft, and Woodrow Wilson.

Pressures for Reform

The *Progressive Era* began in the 1890s. Reformers in this movement aimed to solve problems of industrial growth and change.

Government Power and Reform

Should government regulate businesses? **Progressives** and their conservative opponents actively debated this question.

Conservative View Conservatives believed in laissez-faire—government should not restrain businesses from free competition.

Progressive View Progressives wanted to (1) stop unfair competition by businesses and (2) protect consumers and the public from the bad effects of industrialism.

Developing Technologies

New technologies of the late 19th century helped industry grow. Using the Bessemer process, Andrew Carnegie's steel company outproduced all competitors. High-quality steel tracks replaced weaker iron ones as railroads expanded westward. The Westinghouse air brake made railroads safer, and the Pullman car made them more comfortable. Refrigeration enabled railroads to carry shipments of food long distances without spoilage.

Improved transportation helped farmers and miners move west. At the same time, immigrants poured into American cities and brought about the increasing urbanization of the nation. By 1920, more people lived in cities than in rural areas.

The typewriter, Dictaphone, and telephone opened up new jobs for women, which created the foundation for social and political change.

Conservative (left) and progressive views of government's role in business

Business Practices and Working Conditions

Reformers weighed the effects of long working hours on women's health. A Chicago social worker, Florence Kelley, helped bring about an Illinois law that limited women's workdays to eight hours. Women in Massachusetts persuaded the legislature to pass a minimum wage law in 1912.

In response, businesses argued in court that state regulatory laws infringed on property rights and were unconstitutional.

***Lochner* v. *New York* (1905)** A New York law prohibited bakers from working more than a 60-hour week or 10-hour day. The U.S. Supreme Court ruled the law unconstitutional, saying it violated the Fourteenth Amendment's protection of a business owner's right not to be deprived of the use of property without "due process of law."

***Muller* v. *Oregon* (1908)** An Oregon law provided that women could not work more than ten hours a day in factories and laundries. Lawyer Louis Brandeis successfully defended the law before the Supreme Court by showing scientifically that long hours of physical labor could injure a woman's health. He later became the first Jew to serve on the Court.

Increasing Inequities

From 1865 through the early 1900s, the gap between great wealth and great poverty widened and became a target for progressive reformers. Railroad millionaires such as Leland Stanford and Cornelius Vanderbilt were able to handsomely endow the universities that bear their names. Rockefeller and Carnegie grew fabulously rich. When Carnegie sold his steel company to J. P. Morgan, he donated most of the proceeds to new libraries and other institutions—notably, New York City's 42nd Street Library and Carnegie Hall. Other multimillionaires of the era included meatpackers Gustavus Swift and Philip Armour.

The new millionaires defended their fortunes by citing social Darwinism (discussed on page 146).

In contrast were the millions who labored long hours for low wages. In the late 1800s, steelworkers worked 12-hour shifts, often seven days a week. Women and children toiled in New York City's garment industry. In Chicago, immigrants earned low wages in dangerous meatpacking jobs. From 1880 to 1900, the number of women working (usually for pennies a day) increased from 2.5 million to almost 9 million.

Influence of the Middle Class and Newspapers Progressive politicians depended on support from middle-class voters and city newspapers.

The middle class read books, newspapers, and magazines that influenced their economic and political views. Proud of tradition and patriotic in their civic duties, middle-class men voted regularly, and the women joined clubs, charities, and, often, reform movements.

New inventions helped publishers sell more newspapers. By the 1870s, machine-driven presses had replaced earlier hand presses. Publishers schemed to increase readership and advertising income. Joseph Pulitzer's *New York World* and William Randolph Hearst's *New York Journal* competed to reach a large public by selling newspapers for only a penny and running scandalous and sensational feature stories. Such methods were known as **yellow journalism**.

Social and Economic Reform/Consumer Protection

Many writers reported on corruption in city government and the shocking living and working conditions of the poor. These journalists, dedicated to exposing immorality in business and politics, came to be called **muckrakers**.

The *Ladies' Home Journal* and *McClure's* were among the magazines that published muckraking articles. The most influential writers were:

- *Lincoln Steffens.* In *The Shame of the Cities* (1904), he revealed how corrupt city politicians of his time were.
- *Ida Tarbell.* Her investigation of John D. Rockefeller's monopolistic methods was first a series of articles and then a book, *History of the Standard Oil Company* (1904).

North Wind Picture Archives

Cartoon of President Theodore Roosevelt as a muckraker cleaning up the meat scandal.

- *Frank Norris.* His novel *The Octopus* (1901) dealt with the struggle of California wheat growers against a monopolistic railway.
- *Upton Sinclair.* His novel *The Jungle* (1906) exposed unhealthy conditions in Chicago's meatpacking plants (quoted on page 183).

Legislation

The public outcry following publication of *The Jungle* led to the Meat Inspection Act and the Pure Food and Drug Act.

- The *Meat Inspection Act* (1906) gave officials the power to check the quality of meats shipped in interstate commerce.
- The *Pure Food and Drug Act* (1906) banned the manufacture and sale of impure foods, drugs, and liquors. It also required the truthful labeling of commercial medicines.

Social Justice Movement

Other reformers wanted to help people who lived in slums:

- *Jacob Riis.* A New York City newsman, Riis wrote *How the Other Half Lives* (1890), exposing the misery of slum life and prompting efforts by the New York State legislature to reduce tenement overcrowding and lack of sanitation.
- *Jane Addams and Lillian Wald.* These women knew about urban poverty and persuaded state legislatures to protect children against harsh labor. They ran **settlement houses** (Addams's Hull House in Chicago and Wald's Henry Street Settlement in New York City), where immigrants received help in adjusting to American life and poor children were safe from the dangers of city streets. These institutions also offered free adult education in English, the arts, literature, and music.

Women's Rights

Suffrage Movement Male and female activists for women's **suffrage** (voting rights) were known as *suffragists.* The movement, begun at the Seneca Falls Convention in 1848 (first discussed on page 78), continued into the Progressive Era. One leader, Susan B. Anthony, wanted to amend the Constitution so as to guarantee voting rights for women in every state. When the amendment was introduced in Congress in 1878, the all-male lawmakers rejected it. Suffragists introduced it during every session for the next 40 years. Despite setbacks on the national level, many territories and states in the West provided for a woman's right to vote before 1919.

Suffragists asked how a democracy could fail to grant women the vote. A new generation led by Alice Paul and Carrie Chapman Catt replaced Susan B. Anthony and Elizabeth Cady Stanton. Support for a constitutional

Suffragists marching in Washington, D.C., in 1913 in favor of a constitutional amendment guaranteeing women the right to vote

amendment grew as a result of Americans' appreciation of women's contributions to the war effort during World War I.

Margaret Sanger and Birth Control A nurse to immigrant families in New York City, Margaret Sanger saw that frequent pregnancies increased hardships for poor women. She began publishing a magazine on birth control in 1914, opened the first U.S. birth-control clinic, in Brooklyn, and wrote *What Every Girl Should Know* (1916). Her ideas and work gained strength in later decades.

Black Movement

The best-known African Americans of the Progressive Era were Booker T. Washington and W. E. B. Du Bois. (For their points of view about racial segregation, see page 117.) White business leaders and politicians conferred

Reformer and educator Booker T. Washington (left) and W. E. B. Du Bois, African-American activist against racial discrimination

with Washington about preparing young black people for skilled industrial jobs. Washington was a frequent adviser to President Theodore Roosevelt.

In 1905, Du Bois launched the *Niagara Movement* at a meeting of black reformers in Niagara Falls, Canada. Its focus was to publicize and protest injustice against African Americans.

NAACP In 1909, members of the Niagara Movement and white reformers organized the *National Association for the Advancement of Colored People (NAACP)*. Its aims were to protect the civil rights of African Americans, end segregation, and defend black suspects unfairly accused of crimes because of race. Its magazine, the *Crisis*, was edited by Du Bois.

The NAACP won a number of civil rights cases in the Supreme Court, which between 1915 and 1917 declared the following unconstitutional:

- "grandfather clause" (discussed on page 119)
- segregated housing
- denying African Americans the right to serve on juries
- denying African Americans the right to run for office in party primaries.

Ida Wells One of the NAACP's founders was a Tennessee reporter named Ida B. Wells. She wrote a book about lynchings—between 1900 and 1914, more than 1,100 African Americans had been lynched by white mobs—and dedicated her career to racial justice.

Marcus Garvey In 1916, Marcus Garvey came to the United States from Jamaica. He was deeply offended by the second-class status of African Americans. In Jamaica, he had organized the *Universal Negro Improvement Association (UNIA)* and its "Back to Africa" movement. In the United States, he attracted about 500,000 followers to these causes. Garvey urged African Americans to shun the white majority, build their own institutions, and return to Africa. His leadership ended in 1925 when he was convicted of mail fraud. In 1927, he was deported to Jamaica.

Temperance/Prohibition

The many women of the temperance movement urged people not to drink alcohol and wanted public sale of it banned. Drinking alcohol, they argued, increased working-class poverty. The most famous crusaders were Frances Willard and Carrie Nation. In 1919, the *Eighteenth Amendment* was passed, and, until its repeal in 1933, the manufacture and sale of alcohol in the United States was prohibited.

Anti-Defamation League (1913)

Jewish immigrants from Europe were so often the target of nativist prejudices that Jewish Americans organized the *Anti-Defamation League* in 1913. Its purpose was to combat unfair statements made about Jews.

IN REVIEW

1. How did the Supreme Court both assist and retard progressive reforms?
2. Define progressivism, muckraker, social justice, settlement house, and suffragist.
3. Describe the efforts of women and African Americans to bring about democratic reforms.

Progressivism and Government Action

From about 1890 to 1900, progressives focused on enacting laws at the local and state levels.

Urban Middle Class and Political Reform

Unlike the Populist Party, progressives were concerned with reform in the cities. By 1900, approximately 30 million of the 75 million Americans lived in urban areas. As urban populations grew, so did the middle class—lawyers, doctors, middle-management employees, shopkeepers, teachers, and clerical workers.

Municipal Reform In the late 1800s, many cities were controlled by political machines. Government provided no unemployment insurance or welfare for the poor. Instead, the poor looked to the local party boss for help paying rent and buying food in exchange for loyalty at the polls. Political leaders took bribes for contracts and jobs.

Large cities badly needed bridges, subways, electric trolley cars, gas and electricity, and telephones. Reformers feared that the growth in services would lead to more corruption in government. The urban middle class supported progressive attempts to break the power of party bosses, reduce the cost of government, lower taxes, and end corruption.

In the early 1900s, progressive mayors in several large cities broke the power of political machines. Two Ohio mayors, Tom Johnson in Cleveland and Samuel ("Golden Rule") Jones in Toledo, provided efficient transportation and honest government. Often, however, reform politicians could not keep power when they failed to meet the needs of growing ethnic minorities.

State Reform

Wisconsin: Robert La Follette In Wisconsin, as elsewhere, railroads, political bosses, and business interests had great influence. Governor Robert ("Battling Bob") La Follette challenged them. Besides providing tax reform, business regulation, and technical expertise, he fought for the following:

- The **direct primary**: Instead of state nominating conventions, voters would nominate candidates by direct popular vote in a *primary election* (an early election before the general election in November).
- The **initiative**: By signing a petition, a small percentage of voters could force the state legislature to consider a proposed law.
- The **referendum**: A proposed law could be submitted to the people and voted on in an election.
- The **recall**: The people, by special election, could vote on whether to remove an elected official from office before term's end.

For all these reforms, Wisconsin became known as a "laboratory for democracy."

New York: Theodore Roosevelt As president of the New York Board of Police Commissioners, Theodore Roosevelt tried to end police corruption. As governor of the state in the late 1890s, his dedication to civil service reform angered several important state politicians. They were happy to have him selected as the vice-presidential candidate on the 1900 Republican ticket (along with William McKinley) and get him away from the state arena.

Political Reforms Elsewhere Oregon was the first state to use the initiative and referendum. Many states also adopted the **Australian ballot** (also known as the secret ballot), whereby voters could mark in secret a ballot printed not by a political party but by the state.

Economic, Environmental, and Social Reforms By 1914, most states had enacted child labor laws. As more children attended school, mandatory education requirements were set. Engineers and urban planners were developing new methods of sanitation and garbage removal, designing bridges and tunnels, and installing street lighting. Building codes, which increased safety in new housing, were introduced.

President Theodore Roosevelt (1901–1909)

At the age of 42, following the assassination of President McKinley, Theodore Roosevelt became the youngest president in U.S. history. He promised a *Square Deal* to all Americans—labor and business, poor and rich.

Stewardship Theory Throughout the late 1800s, government policy toward business was laissez-faire. When presidents intervened at all, they favored big business. Roosevelt, however, believed that presidents should be stewards (guides) of the nation's economy and politics. A depression in the 1890s had convinced him to try to improve conditions.

Roosevelt demonstrated the Square Deal when Pennsylvania coal miners struck in 1902. He did not call in troops to support the mining company;

he invited union and company leaders to the White House to talk. The coal company agreed to a shorter workday and a 10 percent wage increase, and the strike was settled.

Railroad Regulation and Consumer Protection Roosevelt persuaded Congress to enact the following laws to reform railroads:

- The *Elkins Act* (1903) allowed the Interstate Commerce Commission to punish railroads that granted rebates.
- The *Hepburn Act* (1906) empowered the Interstate Commerce Commission to fix railroad rates and limit free passes for politicians and business owners.

Roosevelt also persuaded Congress to pass the Pure Food and Drug Act and the Meat Inspection Act (discussed on page 171).

Trust-Busting Many monopolies in the late 1800s and early 1900s were organized as trusts. Using the Sherman Antitrust Act for the first time, Roosevelt prosecuted the Northern Securities Company, a powerful holding company controlling several Western railroads. In *Northern Securities Company* v. *United States* (1904), the Supreme Court ruled the president's move to break up Northern Securities constitutional. Roosevelt broke up other business combinations as well, including Standard Oil.

Theodore Roosevelt and John Muir in Yosemite Valley, 1906

Popularly known as a **trustbuster** (breaker of monopolies), Roosevelt was not an enemy of big business. He encouraged "good trusts," ones that acted responsibly, and broke up "bad trusts," ones that ignored the public interest.

Conservation of Nature, Land, and Resources

Roosevelt was wary of mining and lumbering companies exploiting the wilderness. He sought public support for **conservation**—wise management and careful use of the natural environment. Thus, Congress passed two major conservation laws:

- The *Newlands Reclamation Act* (1902) set aside money from the sale of Western desert lands for irrigation projects.
- The *Inland Waterways Act* (1907) provided that a commission be appointed to study how major rivers were being used.

Using an already existing law, the *Forest Reserve Act*, Roosevelt established 149 publicly owned national forests totaling more than 190 million acres, to be controlled by the new U.S. Forest Service.

Gifford Pinchot and John Muir

Two individuals were especially important to Roosevelt's conservation efforts:

- *Gifford Pinchot.* Theodore Roosevelt appointed Gifford Pinchot head of the U.S. Forest Service. Pinchot tried to get private lumber companies to plant new trees to replace those cut down. He insisted that only full-grown trees be cut down.
- *John Muir.* Prior to joining Roosevelt's administration, John Muir had supported bills to create a national park in Yosemite Valley, California. Under Roosevelt, he realized that dream and the establishment of other national parks in Mesa Verde, Colorado, and the Grand Canyon, Arizona.

Controversy Under President Taft (1909–1913)

Roosevelt chose his secretary of war, William Howard Taft, as Republican presidential nominee for president in 1908. Taft easily won the election.

Taft was often a zealous progressive. He prosecuted 90 businesses for antitrust violations. (Roosevelt had prosecuted 44.)

But Taft did not please progressives who favored lower tariffs and better conservation measures. Over the protests of progressives in Congress, he signed the *Payne-Aldrich Tariff* (1909), which resulted in higher prices on many products.

Even more upsetting was Taft's firing of Gifford Pinchot. Roosevelt was especially angered over that move.

Progressivism and the Election of 1912 In the 1912 election, the Republican party was split. Conservative Republicans nominated Taft. Progressive Republicans and others supported Roosevelt and formed the *Progressive Party*—also known as the "Bull Moose" Party because Roosevelt described himself as "strong as a bull moose."

Woodrow Wilson, the popular and progressive governor of New Jersey, won the Democratic nomination.

The Socialist Party had gained strength and numbers by championing industrial workers and proposing that major industries be owned and operated by the government. Its presidential candidate was labor leader Eugene Debs.

In this race of four self-acclaimed reformers, Wilson won over the divided Republicans with 435 electoral votes.

Woodrow Wilson (1913–1921)

In 1912, Wilson was only the second Democrat (after Grover Cleveland) elected president after the Civil War. In his inaugural address of 1913, he announced a program called the *New Freedom*, including a lower tariff, more effective business regulation, and a reformed banking system.

Underwood Tariff Wilson appealed for lower tariffs. The *Underwood Tariff* (1913) had the effect of lowering prices of many consumer goods and depriving big business of protections it had long enjoyed.

Graduated Income Tax The *Sixteenth Amendment* (1913) empowered Congress to collect an income tax that was *not* apportioned according to state populations. At first, it was collected only from people with very high incomes. Called a **graduated income tax**, its rate schedule rose as reported income increased.

Clayton Antitrust Act Wilson persuaded Congress to enact the *Clayton Antitrust Act* (1914). It strengthened the Sherman Antitrust Act by making illegal such business practices as (1) holding companies that prevented competition, (2) **interlocking directorships** (the same people serving as directors of several companies), and (3) secret agreements to fix an industry's prices. In addition, labor unions could no longer be prosecuted as monopolies.

Federal Trade Commission Under pressure from Wilson, Congress passed the *Federal Trade Commission Act* in 1914. It created the Federal Trade Commission (FTC) to (1) investigate suspicious business practices, and (2) order companies to "cease and desist" from illegal acts.

Election of 1912

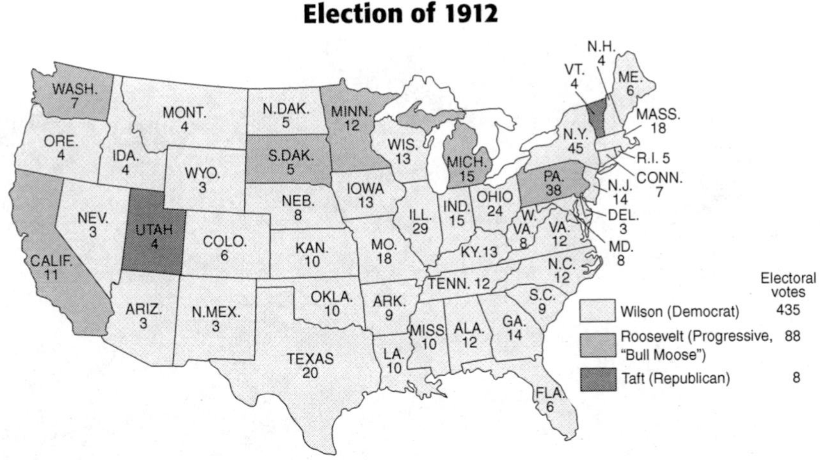

Federal Reserve System Before Wilson, there was no federal system to control the supply of *currency* (money) needed by business. Thus, private banks often had too little currency *in reserve* (kept in their vaults). If many customers withdrew their money at the same time, a bank with a low reserve might fail. The failing of many banks at once would cause an economic depression.

Wilson supported the progressives who called for a federal reserve system. In such a system, private banks would deposit cash reserves in 12 regional banks. Officials of the Federal Reserve Board would supervise those regional banks, which could make loans to private banks at interest rates set by the board. The loans would be in the form of paper currency printed by the government as Federal Reserve notes (dollar bills). Americans have used such currency ever since the *Federal Reserve Act* was passed in 1913.

Under the act, the nation's money supply may be increased or decreased according to need. The Federal Reserve Board does this by setting interest rates that affect member banks and, therefore, the national economy. In a recession, for example, the Federal Reserve might act to stimulate economic growth by decreasing interest rates.

Expanding and Contracting Democracy

Direct Election of Senators The *Seventeenth Amendment* (1913) required that senators be elected by the voters of their state rather than state legislatures. This reduced the influence of special interests, particularly big business.

Women's Suffrage Women's struggle for voting rights ended with the ratification of the *Nineteenth Amendment* (1920). It stated: "The right of citizens of the United States to vote shall not be denied or abridged by the United States or by any state on account of sex."

The Progressive Movement: Causes and Effects

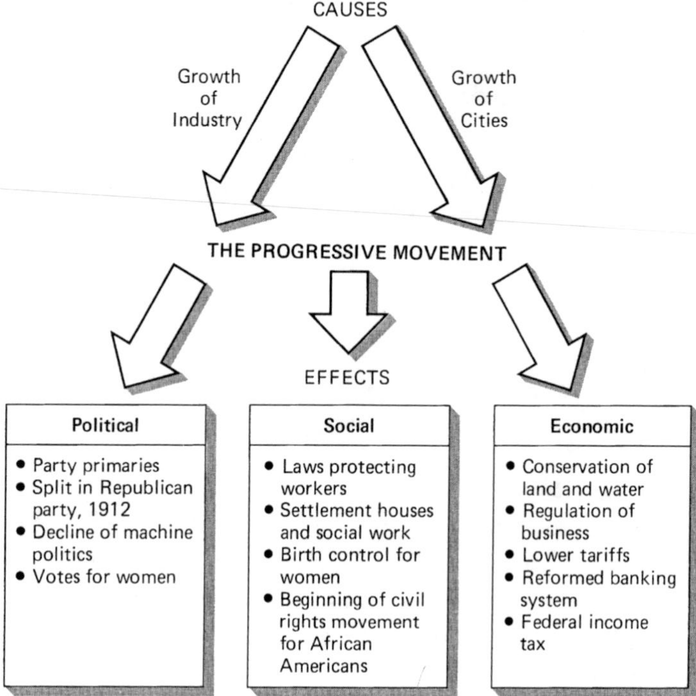

Segregation Under Woodrow Wilson Rights of African Americans did not expand under Wilson. In fact, he ordered the segregation of the washrooms in federal buildings in the nation's capital, and he angrily dismissed a group of African Americans who came to the White House to protest.

World War I and Domestic Reform

In 1917, the United States entered World War I. Government and big business cooperated to produce the greatest amount of war supplies in the shortest time. Government regulation of business ceased. After the war, most citizens were more interested in goods and services than reform. As a result, the three conservative Republican presidents after Wilson returned to a policy of laissez-faire.

IN REVIEW

1. Define initiative, referendum, recall, direct primary, and Australian ballot.
2. For *each* of the following concerns, describe a progressive reform associated with it: (a) consumer safety, (b) trusts, (c) natural resources, (d) tariffs, (e) banks.
3. Describe the main features of Theodore Roosevelt's Square Deal and Woodrow Wilson's New Freedom.

CHAPTER REVIEW

MULTIPLE-CHOICE QUESTIONS

1 A major purpose of the Progressive movement was to
(1) stimulate the economy
(2) support government control of factory production
(3) encourage immigration from Southern and Eastern Europe
(4) correct the economic and social abuses of industrial society

2 During the early 1900s, the term *muckrakers* was used to describe
(1) pacifists who demonstrated against war
(2) writers who exposed the evils in American society
(3) newspaper columnists who reported on celebrities
(4) politicians who criticized Progressive Era presidents

Base your answer to question 3 on the table below and on your knowledge of social studies.

Progressive Era Legislation

Date	*Legislation*	*Purpose*
1905	United States Forest Service established	Manage the nation's water and timber resources
1906	Meat Inspection Act	Regulate meat processing to ensure clean conditions
1906	Pure Food and Drug Act	Outlaw dishonest labeling of food and drugs
1913	Department of Labor established	Promote the interests of working people

3 The common purpose of these legislative acts was to
(1) protect the nation's natural resources
(2) improve conditions for recent immigrants to the United States
(3) advance the growth of big business
(4) promote the general welfare of the American public

Base your answer to question 4 on the chart below and on your knowledge of social studies.

States and Territories Fully Enfranchising Women Prior to the 19th Amendment

State	*Date Begun*
Territory of Wyoming	1869
Wyoming	1890
Colorado	1893
Utah	1896
Idaho	1896
Arizona	1912
Washington	1910
California	1911
Kansas	1912
Oregon	1912
Territory of Alaska	1913
Montana	1914
Nevada	1914
New York	1917
Michigan	1918
Oklahoma	1918
South Dakota	1918

Source: Alexander Keyssar, *The Right to Vote,* Basic Books, 2000 (adapted)

4 Which conclusion about women's suffrage is best supported by the information in the chart?
(1) Congress did not allow women to vote in the territories.
(2) Before 1919, many of the Western states had granted women the right to vote.
(3) The United States Supreme Court had to approve a woman's right to vote in each state.
(4) Women were permitted to vote only in state elections.

5 During the early 1900s, the initiative, recall, and referendum were changes made in many states to give
(1) citizens the right to choose presidential candidates
(2) voters greater direct participation in government
(3) workers more rights in the collective bargaining process
(4) business leaders more control over their industries

6 President Theodore Roosevelt's policy regarding big business was to
(1) replace private ownership with public ownership
(2) encourage a laissez-faire attitude toward business
(3) support the deregulation of business
(4) distinguish between "good" and "bad" trusts

7 A graduated (progressive) income tax is based on the idea that tax rates should
(1) be the same for all individuals and businesses
(2) be adjusted to achieve a balanced federal budget
(3) rise as individual or business incomes rise
(4) increase more rapidly for business profits than for personal incomes

8 President Woodrow Wilson supported creation of the Federal Reserve System in 1913 to
(1) balance the federal budget
(2) regulate the amount of money in circulation
(3) serve as a source of loans for farmers
(4) solve the financial problems of the Great Depression

9 When the Federal Reserve Board lowers interest rates, it is most likely attempting to
(1) stimulate consumer spending
(2) lower prices
(3) encourage saving
(4) reduce investment

10 During the Progressive Era, an amendment to the United States Constitution provided for greater representative democracy by changing the method of selecting the
(1) members of the United States Senate
(2) Electoral College
(3) President's Cabinet
(4) judges for federal courts

THEMATIC ESSAYS

1 **THEME:** *Progressive Era and Reform.* The Progressive Era involved broad reforms that had far-reaching effects on the society at large.

TASK: Choose *two* areas in which reform was attempted. For *each* reform chosen:
- describe the problem trying to be corrected
- show how the reform tried to correct the problem
- evaluate the success of the reform.

You may wish to include in your answer consumer protection, poverty and immigration, women's rights, and the attempts of African Americans to gain civil rights.

2 **THEME:** *Progressive Era and Presidential Power.* According to some historians, the Progressive Era was brought about largely through activism by presidents Roosevelt and Wilson.

TASK: Select *one* example of presidential activism by Roosevelt and *another* by Wilson.
- Show how *each* president tried to correct a specific problem. (Do not treat the same problem for both presidents.)
- Demonstrate how *each* president expanded federal power.

You may select trust busting and conservation for Roosevelt, and tax reform and monetary policy for Wilson.

DOCUMENT-BASED QUESTION

*Study each document and answer the question that follows it. Then read the **Task** and write your essay. Include references to most of the documents and additional information you retain about U.S. history and government.*

HISTORICAL CONTEXT: Progressive reforms were a response to many problems resulting from the Civil War, industrialization, and urbanization.

DOCUMENT 1: From *Lochner* v. *New York* (1905):

> Statutes... [that limit] hours in which grown and intelligent men may... earn their living,... [meddle with] rights of the individual, and [cannot be defended] by the claim that they are passed in the exercise of the police power and upon the subject of [an individual's] health..., unless there be some fair ground... to say that there is material danger to the public health, or to the health of the employees, if the hours... are not curtailed.

QUESTION: Why did the Supreme Court declare the New York State law limiting bakers' hours unconstitutional?

DOCUMENT 2: From *Muller* v. *Oregon* (1908):

> ...as healthy mothers are essential to vigorous offspring, the physical well-being of woman becomes an object of public interest and care in order to preserve the strength and vigor of the race....
>
> ...Differentiated by these matters from the other sex, she is properly placed in a class by herself and legislation designed for her protection may be sustained, even when [it] is not necessary for men....

QUESTION: Why did the Supreme Court rule to protect female workers?

DOCUMENT 3: From Upton Sinclair's *The Jungle*:

> ...There [came] back from Europe old sausage that had been rejected... moldy and white—it would be dosed with borax and glycerine... and made over again for home consumption.... Meat... tumbled out on the floor, in the dirt and sawdust, where the workers had tramped and spit.... Meat [was] stored in rooms, and the water from leaky roofs would drip over it, and thousands of rats would race about on it.... A man could... sweep off handfuls of the dried dung of rats [who were then poisoned]; they would die, and then rats, bread, and meat would go into the hoppers together. ...There were things that went into the sausage in comparison with which a poisoned rat was a tidbit.

QUESTION: What was Sinclair telling his readers about the meatpacking industry?

DOCUMENT 4: Refer to the cartoon below.

Dreadful tenement conditions—in this case, cholera confronting a slumlord

QUESTION: Why does the cartoonist feel that cholera might spread?

DOCUMENT 5: Refer to the graph below.

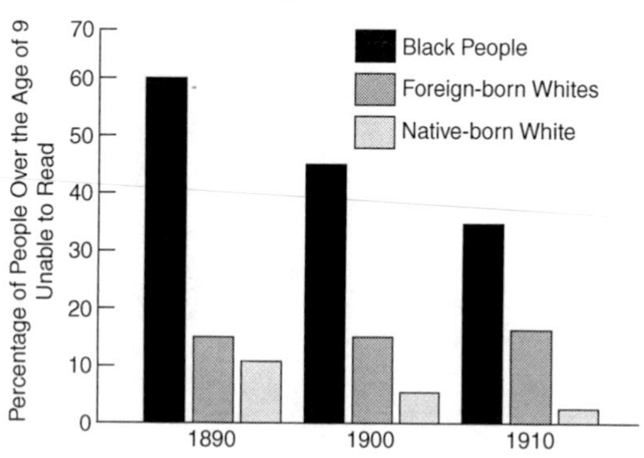

QUESTION: How does the graph show *both* progress and problems for African Americans between 1890 and 1910?

DOCUMENT 6: Refer to the following cartoon.

"Teddy" Roosevelt, trust buster

QUESTION: How does the cartoon show what President Roosevelt did about "bad trusts"?

TASK: Using the documents and your knowledge of U.S. history and government, write an essay in which you:

- describe *two* problems existing at the end of the 19th and beginning of the 20th century.
- choose *one* problem you selected and show to what extent it was solved or remained a problem.

CHAPTER 11
Rise of American Power

DOCUMENTS AND LAWS
Monroe Doctrine (1823) • "Open Door" Notes (1899–1900) • Foraker Act (1900)
Platt Amendment (1901) • Roosevelt Corollary (1904) • Selective Service Act (1917)
Fourteen Points (1918) • Sedition Act (1918) • *Schenck* v. *United States* (1919)
Treaty of Versailles (1919) • Kellogg-Briand Pact (1928)

EVENTS
Acquisition of Hawaii (1898) • Sinking of the *Maine* (1898) • Spanish-American War (1898)
Battle of Manila Bay (1898) • Battles of San Juan Hill and El Caney (1898)
Boxer Rebellion (1900) • Russo-Japanese War (1904–1905)
Construction of Panama Canal (1907–1914)
U.S. intervention in Haiti and Dominican Republic (1904, 1915–1934)
Assassination of Archduke Francis Ferdinand (1914) • World War I (1904, 1914–1918)
Fourteen Points (1918) • Sinking of the *Lusitania* (1915) • Russian Revolution (1917)
Zimmermann Telegram (1917) • League of Nations established (1920)
Washington Naval Conference (1921–1922) • Statehood for Hawaii (1959)

PEOPLE
Bernard Baruch • Bolsheviks • Venustiano Carranza • Grover Cleveland • Dupuy de Lôme
George Dewey • Cyrus Field • George W. Goethals • William C. Gorgas • Warren G. Harding
John Hay • Oliver Wendell Holmes • Herbert Hoover • Victoriano Huerta • Henry Cabot Lodge
William McKinley • Alfred Thayer Mahan • John J. Pershing • Josiah Strong • William H. Taft
Pancho Villa

OBJECTIVES

- To analyze reasons for U.S. involvement in Asia and Latin America, 1890–1920.
- To evaluate arguments for and against U.S. intervention in Latin America.
- To identify causes of World War I.
- To explain why U.S. foreign policy changed from neutrality to involvement.
- To understand how war affected the civil liberties of Americans.
- To evaluate U.S. contributions to peace after the war.

New U.S. Power and Diplomacy (1865–1900)

After the Civil War, U.S. leaders were better able to consider foreign interests. American businesses and farmers were looking for markets for their goods. And others wanted to expand U.S. power and prestige.

Communications Technology

Before the Civil War, the telegraph and Morse Code led to speedier long-distance communication. After the war, Cyrus Field successfully completed a transatlantic cable. As rapid messages between North America and Europe became possible, the two continents seemed closer than ever.

Attitudes Toward an International Role

After years of industrialization, U.S. leaders considered a policy of imperialism.

Arguments for Expansion The arguments for expansion include the following:

- *Economics.* As the frontier disappeared, business leaders looked for new markets and investment opportunities abroad. Belief in manifest destiny (discussed on page 91) justified increasing the U.S. role in world affairs.
- *Culture.* Many Protestant ministers, Josiah Strong among them, argued that undeveloped regions would benefit from contact with advanced Western civilization. Their belief that Christianity and American civilization were linked benefits was based on a variation of social Darwinism —superior nations and cultures survive, while weaker ones die out.
- *Strategy.* In the 1890s, Alfred Thayer Mahan, a U.S. naval captain, pointed out that U.S. security depended on having a strong navy like Britain's. Because ships were powered by coal, the nation had to establish strategic island bases in the Atlantic and Pacific where ships could pick up coal. Moreover, increased U.S. trade with Asia and Latin America would require naval protection against rivals.

Arguments Against Expansion Of course, there were also arguments against expansion, which included the following:

- *Morality.* Some Americans felt that the cause of democracy would suffer from a U.S. takeover of foreign lands and their people. Many also believed that manifest destiny had rightly ended with American expansion to the Pacific Ocean.
- *Practicality.* Some Americans feared that foreign involvement would lead to foreign wars. Such wars would do more to harm overseas trade than to help.

"Opening" of Japan (1854)

Japan had avoided trading with the West. In 1853, however, Commodore Matthew Perry arrived there with a U.S. fleet. To persuade the Japanese to open trade and assist shipwrecked U.S. sailors, he gave gifts exemplifying industrial technology and fired the fleet's guns as a show of force.

In 1854, Japan signed a trade treaty with the United States. Soon

Spheres of Influence in China, 1900

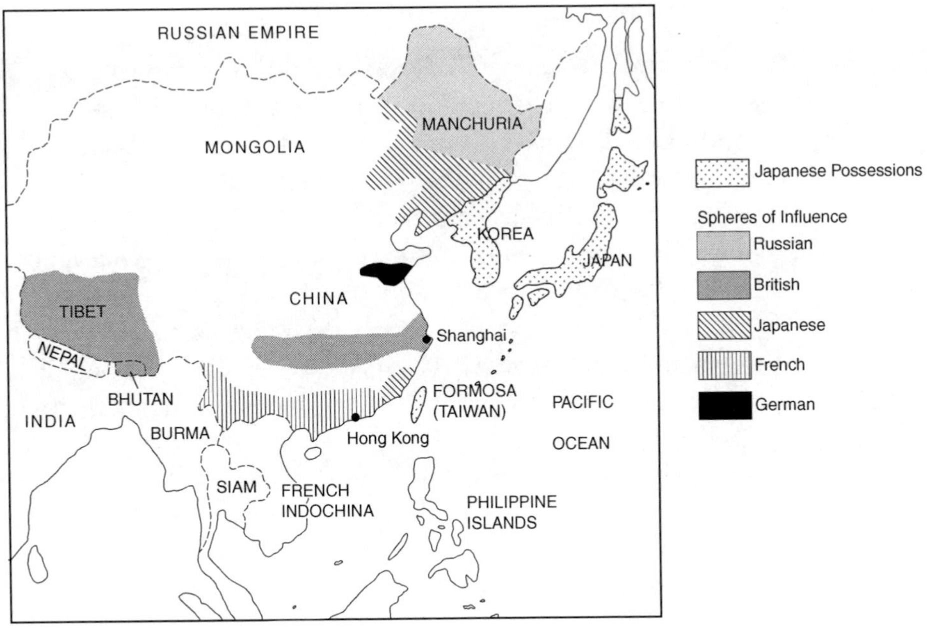

afterward, new Japanese leadership, eager to industrialize the nation, sought Western technologies.

Imperialism and China

Japan's 1895 defeat of China in the *Sino-Japanese War* showed two things: (1) China could not withstand imperialism, and (2) the newly industrialized Japan was a major power in East Asia. Japan then occupied Korea and the Chinese island of Taiwan and won economic control of Manchuria in northern China.

Manchuria became a Japanese **sphere of influence** (area dominated by an imperialistic power). Russia also claimed the right to control parts of Manchuria until 1904, when Japan defeated Russia in the *Russo-Japanese War*.

Other Spheres of Influence France, Germany, Russia, and Great Britain also forced China to grant them spheres of influence. As a result, the U.S. government feared that its trade with China might be cut off.

"Open Door" Notes U.S. Secretary of State John Hay, therefore, wrote two diplomatic notes. In one (1899), he asked the European powers and Japan to agree to an *Open Door Policy*; all nations would have "equal trading rights" in China and pay equal port fees and taxes. In the second note (1900), he suggested that all powers in East Asia respect China's **territorial integrity**; that is, no nation would compel China to give up control of any territory. The other nations' replies to U.S. demands were intentionally vague and evasive.

The U.S. government maintained this policy until the early 1940s, when Japanese troops occupied much of China.

Boxer Rebellion Many Chinese, resentful of Western imperialism, joined a secret terrorist organization, the Boxers. In 1900, they attacked Westerners and their embassies to drive the "foreign devils" from China. Many Christian missionaries, including some Americans, lost their lives. To rescue those trapped in the capital of Peking (now Beijing), the United States, Japan, and the European powers formed an international army and crushed the *Boxer Rebellion.*

Most of the foreign victors threatened China with harsh terms and demanded an **indemnity** (payment to cover damages and deaths). But the United States remained committed to the territorial integrity of China and insisted that the others do likewise. It also returned its portion of the indemnity, which so impressed China's government that it applied the money to scholarships for Chinese students attending U.S. colleges and universities.

Other Pacific Overtures

Acquisition of Hawaii In 1893, a group of American sugar growers in Hawaii, helped by U.S. Marines, overthrew Queen Liliuokalani. President Grover Cleveland opposed imperialism and rejected a plan to turn Hawaii over to the United States. Hawaii remained independent for a few more years. In 1898, however, President William McKinley pushed to make Hawaii a U.S. territory, which the U.S. Senate approved in 1900. (Hawaii became the 50th state in 1959.)

Naval Bases in Samoa A group of Pacific islands, Samoa lies far southwest of Hawaii. The United States, Germany, and Britain all wanted Samoa as a naval base. In the 1880s, Germany and the United States almost went to war over Samoa. But in the late 1890s, Germany and the United States agreed to divide Samoa, each taking control of a different set of islands.

Spanish-American War

In 1895, Cubans rebelled against Spanish rule. Three years later, the United States sided with Cuba by declaring war against Spain. The swift and decisive U.S. victory demonstrated American military and economic power.

Causes

Americans' sympathy for the Cuban rebels played a large role in bringing about the war. Several factors accounted for that sympathy.

Yellow Journalism Hearst's and Pulitzer's New York City newspapers specialized in yellow journalism (discussed on page 170). Both publishers sensationalized the conflict in Cuba. Reporters described, and sometimes exaggerated, the terrible suffering of Cubans and the brutal acts of Valeriano Weyler, a Spanish general nicknamed "Butcher" Weyler.

De Lôme Letter Early in 1898, Hearst's *New York Journal* printed a stolen letter written by the Spanish minister to the United States, Dupuy de Lôme. Its description of President McKinley as "weak and a bidder for the admiration of the crowd" outraged many Americans.

Sinking of the *Maine* A few days later, the USS *Maine*, a battleship anchored in the harbor of Havana, Cuba, exploded and sank, killing abut 250 of the crew. The cause was never discovered, but the newspapers suggested Spain's guilt. Editorials called for the U.S. liberation of Cuba from Spain.

Additional Reasons

- *Strategy.* Military and naval planners saw in Cuba an ideal naval base for U.S. ships, and they argued that an island 90 miles from Florida should not belong to a European power.
- *Economics.* By replacing a hostile Spanish government with a friendly Cuban one, Americans could protect their $50 million of investments in Cuba's sugar and tobacco plantations.

Decision for War

Some U.S. business leaders feared that the war might destroy American-owned properties in Cuba. Moreover, after the sinking of the *Maine*, Spain had agreed to all U.S. demands, including Cuba's eventual independence.

Cuba as a pawn in the U.S.-Spanish power play

Nevertheless, President McKinley decided that most Americans wanted war and persuaded Congress to declare war against Spain in April 1898.

"Splendid Little War"

The *Spanish-American War* lasted four months, and the United States won every major battle. One American called it a "splendid little war."

In Cuba, the Rough Riders, led by Theodore Roosevelt, won instant glory by charging up San Juan Hill. African Americans took part in the charge and also spearheaded another attack in El Caney. The battles of San Juan Hill and El Caney forced the Spanish to surrender the port of Santiago. Neighboring Puerto Rico—a Spanish island colony since 1508—also fell to the Americans.

In the Pacific, the U.S. Navy under Commodore George Dewey decisively defeated the Spanish fleet in Manila Bay, the Philippines. Filipinos—like Cubans—had already been fighting for independence from Spain. After Manila Bay, they were bitterly disappointed by the U.S.-Spanish peace treaty.

Results of the War

The terms of the treaty, signed in December 1898, were as follows:

- The United States gained Puerto Rico in the Caribbean and Guam in the Pacific.
- Spain granted Cuba independence.
- Spain sold the Philippines to the United States for $20 million.

The United States was now regarded as a major power.

Puerto Rico For economic reasons, most Puerto Ricans wanted to be part of the U.S. empire. The *Foraker Act* (1900) allowed Puerto Ricans to elect their legislators, but their governor would be appointed by the U.S. president.

Cuba The U.S. position on Cuba's independence was unclear. McKinley and Congress finally decided to allow it under conditions listed in the *Platt Amendment* (1901):

- Cuba would sell or lease a piece of land for use as a U.S. naval and coaling station. (The United States still occupies the Guantánamo Bay facility.)
- Cuba would permit no other power to acquire Cuban territory.
- Cuba would allow U.S. intervention (when needed) to protect American citizens there.

Cubans strongly protested these terms, but the Cuban government finally accepted them when the United States made them firm conditions for removing its troops. Cuba became a U.S. **protectorate** (a nation whose foreign policy is partly controlled by a foreign power).

Debate About the Philippines

Some Americans wanted the Philippines to become a U.S. territory. Others wanted the islands to become independent.

Anti-Imperialist Argument William Jennings Bryan led those Americans who favored Filipino independence. These anti-imperialists warned that the United States would abandon its commitment to democracy by ruling overseas territory. And they feared that possession of Asian islands would lead to involvement in Asian politics and wars.

Imperialist Argument Imperialists, including Theodore Roosevelt, argued that acquisition of Pacific islands would ensure the U.S. reputation as a great world power. They also felt that the Philippines would likely fall under some other foreign influence and that U.S. control would be more democratic than control by Germany or Russia, for example.

Filipino Rebellion Unwilling to trade one colonial power for another, Philippine rebels rose up against U.S. forces in 1899. As a result, McKinley sent in 70,000 additional troops. After nearly three years of fighting, U.S. troops finally forced the last rebel band to surrender in 1902. The Philippines remained a U.S. territory until July 4, 1946, when it gained independence.

Constitutional Issues

Did citizens of colonial U.S. territories have the same rights as U.S. citizens, including the right to protection? In the *Insular Cases*, the Supreme Court in 1901 ruled that the Constitution did not fully apply to possessions. The extent to which it did apply would be determined by Congress.

Latin American Affairs

In addition to the Spanish-American War, U.S. leaders had other foreign affairs interests.

Interventions by Roosevelt, Taft, and Wilson (1900–1920)

Roosevelt Corollary to the Monroe Doctrine Implied in the Monroe Doctrine of 1823 was the idea that the United States would protect Latin America from outside interference (discussed on page 63). Also implied was the U.S. right to send troops into a threatened country there. The Platt Amendment making Cuba a protectorate was one example.

Roosevelt added a *corollary* (logical extension) to the Monroe Doctrine when several Latin American countries failed to repay funds borrowed from Britain, Germany, and other European nations. Roosevelt, fearing that the Europeans might use the debts as an excuse for taking over Latin American territory, announced that the United States might intervene in Latin America when debts were overdue. Thus, the United States would serve as the policeman of the Western Hemisphere. The *Roosevelt Corollary* reads:

> Chronic wrongdoing may in America, as elsewhere, ultimately require intervention. In the Western Hemisphere the adherence of the United States to the Monroe Doctrine may force the United States, however reluctantly, in flagrant cases of such wrongdoing...to the exercise of an international police power.

Many Latin Americans saw in this an unfair expansion of U.S. military power into their affairs—not for their protection but to maintain U.S. dominance. Roosevelt liked to repeat the African proverb, "Speak softly and carry a big stick; you will go far."

West Indies Protectorates Applying his corollary in 1904, President Roosevelt sent troops to the Dominican Republican, an island nation in the Caribbean. The troops stayed until the Dominican Republic paid its debts.

Haiti, which shared the same island, was also treated as an American protectorate.

Roosevelt and the Panama Canal

Intervention is a policy by which a nation's military and naval power achieves its political goals in another country. Roosevelt used this policy to build the Panama Canal.

Early Attempts In the 1850s, there were vague but ambitious plans to dig a canal through the Isthmus of Panama, a 30-mile-wide strip of Central American land between the Atlantic and Pacific oceans. Such a canal would cut in half sailing time between New York and San Francisco, help international trade, and eliminate the dangerous voyage around the tip of South America. Jungle diseases and inadequate funds frustrated a French attempt to construct such a canal in the 1880s. During and after the Spanish-American War, U.S. interest in such a canal increased as a result of the new territories the United States acquired in the Pacific.

Quarrel With Colombia When Roosevelt became president in 1901, he was eager to begin construction on a canal through either Nicaragua or Panama, a province of Colombia. Preferring the Panama route, he offered Colombia $10 million to lease the land. Colombia's refusal angered Roosevelt, who in 1903 decided to support a Panamanian rebellion.

Acquisition The uprising lasted only a few hours. U.S. naval forces blocked Colombian interference, and Roosevelt immediately recognized the new Republic of Panama, which quickly agreed to U.S. terms for a **canal zone**.

The United States (Theodore Roosevelt) as the world's policeman

A ten-mile wide, U.S.-administered strip of land within which the canal would be built. Work began soon afterward.

Evaluating Roosevelt's Intervention Roosevelt boasted: "I took Panama," but Colombians called the move imperialist robbery. Years later, President Woodrow Wilson persuaded Congress to award Colombia $25 million in compensation.

Construction The building of the canal began in 1907. A marvel of the 20th century, it was supervised by George W. Goethals, a U.S. Army engineer. A 10-mile-wide strip of jungle had to be cleared, a huge dam built to control the canal's water level, and towns raised for workers.

Two mosquito-transmitted diseases—malaria and yellow fever—threatened the enterprise. Dr. William C. Gorgas, who had curbed the breeding of deadly mosquitoes in Cuba during the Spanish-American War, came to Panama. Although he saved many lives, thousands died of malaria and yellow fever—most of them African Americans (they accounted for 4,500 of the 5,500 canal workers).

Taft's Dollar Diplomacy

Roosevelt's successor as president, William H. Taft, believed that the United States should protect its business investments in Latin America and that the United States had the right to force a Latin American country to repay its debts. This policy, called *dollar diplomacy*, resulted in U.S. intervention in Nicaragua in 1912, where civil war threatened to prevent repayment of a large U.S. loan.

U.S. Territories and Protectorates, 1917

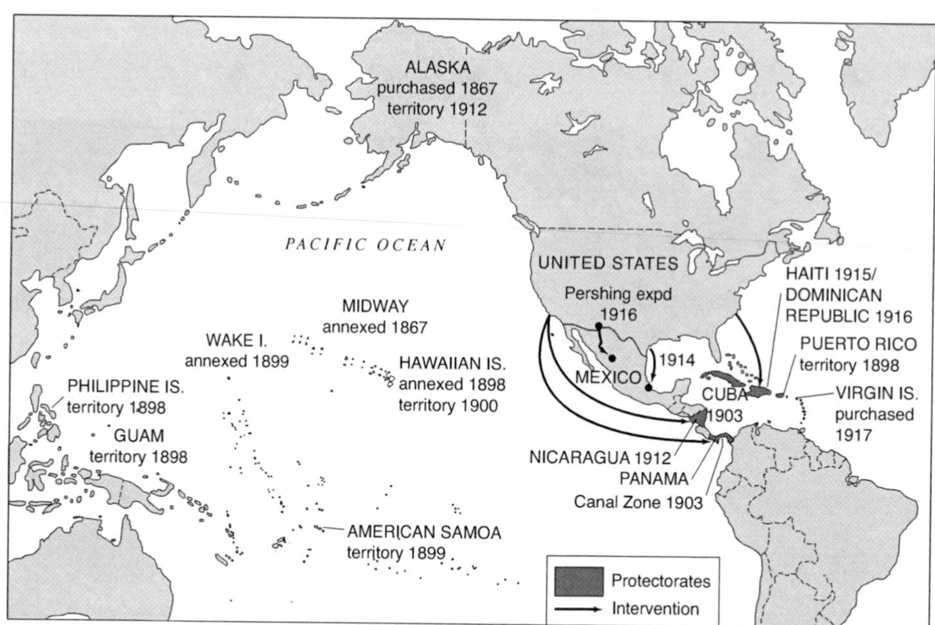

Wilson's Continued Intervention

The next president, Woodrow Wilson, disavowed dollar diplomacy but believed in keeping order in areas near the United States. In 1915, he sent U.S. Marines to quell a civil war in Haiti. Two years later, he intervened in the Dominican Republic for the same reason. The latter remained occupied until 1925; Haiti, until 1934. Latin Americans deeply resented such interventions.

The Mexican Revolution began in 1910. Wilson distrusted the new ruthless Mexican dictator Victoriano Huerta. Instead of recognizing Huerta's government, Wilson followed a policy of *Watchful Waiting* to see if Huerta would be overthrown.

In 1914, several U.S. sailors in Mexico were jailed, which gave Wilson a reason to take action against Huerta. U.S. occupation of the Mexican port of Vera Cruz greatly offended both Huerta and his enemies. Wilson withdrew the troops after the "ABC Powers" (Argentina, Brazil, and Chile) urged Huerta to resign. The new Mexican president, Venustiano Carranza, was immediately challenged by rebels under Pancho Villa.

In 1916, Villa raided a town in New Mexico, killing 19 Americans. A punitive U.S. expedition entered northern Mexico to chase Villa, but war with Mexico was averted in 1917 when Wilson withdrew the troops and recognized the Carranza government. Bitter memories of these U.S. interventions led to poor Mexican-U.S. relations for many years.

IN REVIEW

1. Define sphere of influence, Open Door Policy, Boxer Rebellion, de Lôme Letter, Platt Amendment, anti-imperialist, protectorate, Roosevelt Corollary, and Watchful Waiting.
2. Evaluate (a) the U.S. decision to go to war with Spain and (b) the U.S. decision to take possession of the Philippines.
3. Describe Latin American reaction to U.S. interventions in Mexico, Nicaragua, and Haiti.

World War I

This major war had both long-range and short-range causes.

Long-Range Causes

The long-range causes of World War I were nationalism, imperialism, and **militarism** (a nation's policy of glorifying its armed forces and aggressive spirit). In addition, a system of alliances made it more likely that a war between two European nations would grow into a larger war involving the allies of each nation.

Before 1914, tensions between rival European powers had been building. Britain worried about Germany's colonial ambitions, strong navy, and growing industrial strength. Austria-Hungary worried about rebellious Serbs and other Slavs within its empire—and especially about Russia's support of Serbia. Russia worried about Germany's support for Austria-Hungary.

Short-Range Causes

The immediate cause of World War I was the assassination in June 1914 of the heir to the Austro-Hungarian throne, Archduke Francis Ferdinand, and his wife in Sarajevo (present-day capital of Bosnia-Herzegovina). The assassin was a Serbian terrorist committed to independence for Serbs within the empire.

Austria-Hungary presented Serbia with an **ultimatum** (final demands). Even though Serbia mostly agreed, Austria-Hungary declared war.

The allies of each side became involved. By early August, all major powers in Europe were at war—Britain, Russia, and France against Germany and Austria-Hungary.

Neutrality (1914–1916) and "Preparedness"

In 1914, most Americans, including President Wilson, believed that the war in Europe did not involve U.S. interests. The Atlantic Ocean shut the United States off from European problems. Many remembered President George Washington's advice against permanent alliances.

As a neutral country, the United States traded with all the countries of

Europe. But a German victory largely depended on keeping supplies from reaching its enemies. German submarines began sinking passenger and merchant ships nearing Britain. Many carried American cargo and passengers. The United States protested this use of submarines as a violation of freedom of the seas.

In May 1915, a German submarine torpedoed the British liner *Lusitania*, and more than 1,000 people, including 128 Americans, were killed. Wilson's protests persuaded Germany to stop sinking unarmed ships without warning.

But after Germany resumed submarine warfare in 1916 and 1917, sinking a number of passenger ships, Wilson accepted the need for "preparedness." He asked Congress for funds to build up the armed forces and established a *Council of National Defense* to increase cooperation between the military and private industry.

Long-Range Causes of U.S. Involvement

Sympathy for Britain and France Most Americans felt strong ties to Britain and France—sharing a common language with Britain and remembering French aid during the Revolutionary War. Both countries also had democratic governments, while Germany and Austria-Hungary were directly ruled by monarchs. Moreover, most U.S. trade during the period of neutrality was with Britain and France.

Fear of German Power U.S. military leaders worried about American security and trade if Germany controlled the Atlantic Ocean. Would Germany then hesitate to intervene in South America?

British and French Propaganda Germany's military aggressiveness was stressed by British and French **propaganda** (facts, ideas, and rumors spread to help one cause and harm an opposing one). Invented stories of German cruelty were widely reprinted in U.S. newspapers.

Conditions in Europe By the end of 1916, millions of soldiers had died from artillery fire, poison gas, tank attacks, and machine-gun bullets, without significant gains on either side. Civilians suffered as much as soldiers. The Germans and Russians were near starvation.

Short-Range Causes of U.S. Involvement

Submarine Warfare In January 1917, Germany announced a renewal of submarine attacks without warning in British waters. Germany knew that it risked provoking U.S. entry on Britain's side but hoped to win the war before U.S. troops could be trained for combat.

Zimmermann Telegram The German foreign secretary, Arthur Zimmermann, telegraphed a German diplomat in Mexico with the message that Germany might help Mexico regain lost territories in the American Southwest if Germany and Mexico both declared war on the United States. After the telegram was intercepted and published in American newspapers, anger toward Germany soared.

Revolution in Russia In March 1917, the terrible suffering in Russia led to the overthrow of the czar, who was replaced by a constitutional government. Thus, Wilson felt that he could lead the United States to war on the side of democracies.

Decision for War

In April 1917, Wilson, arguing that "the world must be made safe for democracy," asked Congress for a declaration of war against Germany. Congress voted almost unanimously for the declaration.

Mobilization

Wilson recognized that all the nation's resources had to be a part of the national war effort. For an entire year after U.S. entry into the war, its main contributions to the Allies were large supplies of food, guns, ships, airplanes, and other goods.

Factories Business leaders were asked to coordinate the war effort. Bernard Baruch, head of the new *War Industries Board*, told thousands of corporation presidents how to convert their products and methods to wartime needs. Soon American factories produced vast quantities of war materials.

Food Supply Herbert Hoover, head of the new *Food Administration*, sent out pamphlets to Americans explaining how to save food badly needed by

During the war, many American women took jobs for the first time. This woman worked as a welder.

the British. Americans responded by having a "meatless" day and "wheatless" day every week.

Jobs for Women and Minorities As young men entered the armed forces, women took their places in shipyards and factories. African Americans, who had begun to migrate north before the war, were drawn in increasing numbers by new wartime job opportunities.

Between 1917 and 1920, about 100,000 Mexicans settled permanently in Texas, New Mexico, Arizona, and California to replace enlisted Americans as farmworkers.

Fighting the War

Weapons New weapons included (1) machine guns, (2) poison gas carried by the wind, (3) armored tanks, (4) submarines, and (5) airplanes that fought one another in the sky and detected enemy positions on the ground.

Final Campaigns and Armistice In 1918, large numbers of U.S. soldiers, led by General John J. Pershing, were sent into combat in France. After several months, they began to play a major role in forcing a German retreat. The Allied push continued until Germany was defeated and signed an armistice conceding defeat on November 11, 1918.

United States and the Russian Revolution

In November 1917, a second revolution in Russia overthrew the new democratic government. The victorious revolutionaries were *Bolsheviks* (also known as Communists). In 1918, to lessen Russian suffering, Russia made peace with Germany. This enabled Germany and Austria-Hungary to concentrate their strength on the Western Front.

In 1918, U.S. troops went to the aid of Russian forces known as the "Whites" in their attempt to overthrow the new Communist government of the "Reds." The U.S. troops failed and eventually withdrew.

In 1921, Herbert Hoover organized a program to send millions of tons of food to help the starving Russians.

In 1922, the Communist government in Russia renamed the country the Soviet Union in recognition of the fact that (in addition to Russians) it was made up of many nationalities.

IN REVIEW

1. Describe the U.S. response to Germany's submarine policy from 1915 to 1917.
2. Identify the *two* causes of U.S. involvement in World War I that you think were most important. Explain each choice.
3. Describe the effects of U.S. participation in the war on (a) women and minorities and (b) industry.

Wartime Constitutional Issues

Most Americans supported the war, but a few **dissenters** openly disagreed and refused to cooperate. The First Amendment protects a person's rights to speak on any issue in peacetime. When national security is at stake, however, the Constitution may be interpreted differently.

Draft Issue

An army can be recruited by (a) calling for volunteers and (b) compelling service by a draft of persons from every social class and ethnic group.

Believing that the draft was more efficient and democratic, Wilson got Congress to pass the *Selective Service Act* in May 1917. All male citizens age 21 to 30 were required to register. If drafted, those who passed a medical examination were required to serve.

Some Americans opposed the draft as a threat to democracy and a step toward militarism. Many socialists and anarchists thought war was a capitalist scheme to make money. Still others—**pacifists**—regarded all wars as legalized murder.

Espionage and Sedition Acts

Congress passed the *Espionage Act* (1917) and the *Sedition Act* (1918). They imposed heavy fines and prison sentences for (1) spying and aiding the enemy, (2) interfering with recruitment, (3) speaking against the sale of government bonds, (4) urging resistance to U.S. laws, and (5) using "disloyal, profane, scurrilous, or abusive language" about the government, flag, or military uniform. In addition, the U.S. Post Office was empowered to remove antiwar materials from the mails.

About 1,500 dissenters were arrested. The socialist Eugene Debs was sentenced to ten years in prison for giving antiwar speeches. The anarchist Emma Goldman received a two-year prison term for antiwar activities.

Schenck v. *United States*

Another jailed dissenter, Charles Schenck, had mailed leaflets urging draftees to refuse to serve. Convicted of violating the Espionage Act, Schenck appealed to the Supreme Court, arguing that his First Amendment rights to freedom of speech had been denied.

In *Schenck* v. *United States* (1919), the Court ruled against Schenck. Justice Oliver Wendell Holmes noted that speech must be judged according to circumstances. Thus, the First Amendment "would not protect a man in falsely shouting fire in a theatre and causing a panic." The question to be asked was whether speech posed "clear and present danger" to the public. When there is a clear and present danger to the national interest or the security of the nation, individual rights may be limited.

Postwar Peace and Arms Control

In January 1918, President Woodrow Wilson announced the *Fourteen Points,* which he considered integral to any peace settlement and to avoid future conflicts. The key points were:

- an end to secret treaties
- freedom of the seas for all nations in peace and war
- the reduction of numbers of weapons
- **self-determination** in Europe, whereby people with a common culture could unite as an independent nation
- the establishment of a *League of Nations* to resolve international disputes
- the placing of European colonies in Africa, Asia, and Latin America under the League's control.

Treaty of Versailles

Wilson sailed to France to meet with the Allied leaders and negotiate a peace treaty. The discussions took place in Paris.

Allies' Revenge The British, French, and Italian leaders wanted to punish Germany and Austria-Hungary. They were determined that Germany remain weak militarily and pay heavy war damages.

Treaty Provisions The peace treaty with Germany was signed in June 1919 in the Palace of Versailles, near Paris. The *Treaty of Versailles* contained the following provisions:

- Alsace-Lorraine, seized by Germany in 1871, would be returned to France.
- Poland would be independent and gain from Germany the Polish Corridor, a strip of land connecting Poland to the Baltic Sea.
- Germany would lose its colonies, including Cameroon, German West Africa, and German East Africa, as well as islands in the Pacific.
- Germany's Saar Basin, a major coal-producing region, would be controlled by France for 15 years.
- Germany would pay huge **reparations** (payments in exchange for wrongs and losses).
- Germany would disband its armed forces.
- Germany would be forbidden to manufacture and import war materials.
- Germany would accept full responsibility for the war.
- The League of Nations would be created as an institution designed to reduce the chance of future wars.

A separate treaty with Austria ended the Austro-Hungarian Empire, reduced Austrian territory, and created several new nations, including Hungary.

Analysis Wilson regarded the treaty as harsh and at odds with his Fourteen Points. He was somewhat appeased that formation of the League of Nations was part of the treaty.

League of Nations

All U.S. treaties must be approved in the Senate by a two-thirds vote. Wilson's Democratic Party generally supported the Versailles Treaty, but many Republican senators feared that a clause concerning the League of Nations might draw the United States into a war that Congress had not voted for and thus threaten U.S. sovereignty. Opponents of the treaty included (a) isolationists, who felt that it involved too many commitments abroad, and (b) reservationists, who would accept the treaty only if it contained some modifying clauses. Senator Henry Cabot Lodge, a Republican opponent of Wilson's, was the leading reservationist.

New Nations of Eastern Europe, 1919

Votes in the Senate In 1920, a majority voted in favor of Senator Lodge's reservations. But because Wilson instructed Democrats to vote against it, this form of the treaty did not win two-thirds approval. A vote for the treaty without reservations also failed.

The United States thus also rejected the League of Nations. A separate U.S. peace treaty with Germany was signed by Republican president Warren Harding in 1921. Since it contained nothing about the League of Nations, this treaty was approved by the U.S. Senate.

U.S. Postwar Foreign Policy

Washington Naval Conference President Warren G. Harding called the *Washington Naval Conference* (1921–1922) to reduce international military rivalry. The United States and other naval powers agreed to limits on ship construction according to the following ratio: United States (5), Great Britain (5), Japan (3), France (1.67), Italy (1.67). The ratios helped reduce U.S. and British expenses but did not limit potentially dangerous competition among the naval powers. Japan had wanted full **parity** (equality) with its Western rivals and, in the 1930s, ignored the agreed limits by building a navy strong enough to challenge both U.S. and British forces.

Reparations and War Debts The Allies fixed German reparations at $33 billion. U.S. leaders thought that sum was too high. But the United States was unable to propose a smaller sum because its new policy of isolationism did not allow it to participate in the discussions.

During World War I, the European Allies had borrowed more than $10 billion from the United States to purchase war materials. Thus, the United States in the 1920s became the world's greatest *creditor nation* (one to which debts are owed). France, for one, argued that its debts should be canceled since it had lost more lives and fought longer than the Americans. U.S. presidents, however, insisted on a sizable repayment of Allied debt.

Kellogg-Briand Pact In 1928, the United States signed the *Kellogg-Briand Pact*, by which participating nations agreed to "renounce war as an instrument of national policy." Unfortunately, it was unenforceable because it contained no requirement that the signers had to act against aggression.

World Court The Permanent Court of International Justice, or World Court, was a branch of the League of Nations. Nations could settle disputes peacefully by arguing their cases before the Court's judges. The United States could have joined the World Court without joining the League, but isolationist senators feared that even an "advisory opinion" of the Court might draw the United States into a war.

IN REVIEW

1. Explain the significance of the draft, dissenters, *Schenck* v. *United States*, self-determination.
2. What factors contributed to the Senate's failure to ratify the Treaty of Versailles?
3. To what extent did the Treaty of Versailles and postwar diplomacy reflect Wilson's principles?

CHAPTER REVIEW

MULTIPLE-CHOICE QUESTIONS

1 The main reason the United States implemented the Open Door policy in China was to
(1) promote immigration
(2) expand democratic reforms
(3) encourage religious freedom
(4) guarantee access to markets

2 Which 1890s headline is the best example of yellow journalism?
(1) "President Supports Child Labor Legislation"
(2) "McKinley Asks Congress To Annex Hawaii"
(3) "Populists Demand Change in the Gold Standard"
(4) "Spanish Authorities Butcher Innocent Cubans"

3 One result of the Spanish-American War of 1898 was that the United States was
(1) recognized as a world power
(2) committed to isolationism
(3) drawn into World War II
(4) forced into an economic depression

4 The principle that the United States has the right to act as the "policeman of the Western Hemisphere" and intervene in the internal affairs of Latin American nations was established by the
(1) Good Neighbor policy
(2) Open Door policy
(3) Roosevelt Corollary to the Monroe Doctrine
(4) Marshall Plan

5 What was a major reason the United States entered World War I (1917)?
(1) The Japanese had occupied Manchuria.
(2) Foreign troops had landed on American soil.
(3) The Austro-Hungarian Empire had invaded Belgium.
(4) Germany had resumed unrestricted submarine warfare.

6 The "clear and present danger" ruling of the United States Supreme Court in *Schenck* v. *United States* established that
(1) third political parties must suspend their activities during wartime
(2) accused persons must be advised of their rights
(3) due process of law does not apply to the military
(4) certain circumstances may limit the exercise of free speech

7 The Fourteen Points proposed by President Woodrow Wilson are best described as a
(1) statement of principles that would govern the postwar world
(2) program the United States could follow to achieve victory in World War I

(3) list of reasons for the United States to remain neutral in World War I
(4) policy dealing with the threat of international communism

8 Many United States senators refused to support membership in the League of Nations because they believed that it would
(1) endanger United States economic growth
(2) force the United States to give up its colonies
(3) grant the president the power to annex new territory
(4) involve the United States in future foreign conflicts

Base your answers to questions 9 and 10 on the map below and on your knowledge of social studies

9 The main purpose of this map is to illustrate the
(1) sources of important natural resources
(2) development of United States imperialism
(3) growth of the Atlantic slave trade
(4) results of the Spanish-American War

10 The conclusion that can best be supported by the information on this map is that construction of the Panama Canal was motivated by the desire of the United States to
(1) raise the living standards of Latin American people
(2) increase naval mobility and expand overseas markets
(3) improve relations with Latin American and Asian nations
(4) maintain a policy of collective security

THEMATIC ESSAYS

1 **THEME:** *Spanish-American War.* The war was, to a great extent, a "newspaperman's war," which led to acquisition of overseas territory.

TASK: Complete *both* of the following tasks.

U.S. Territories and Leases, 1857–1903

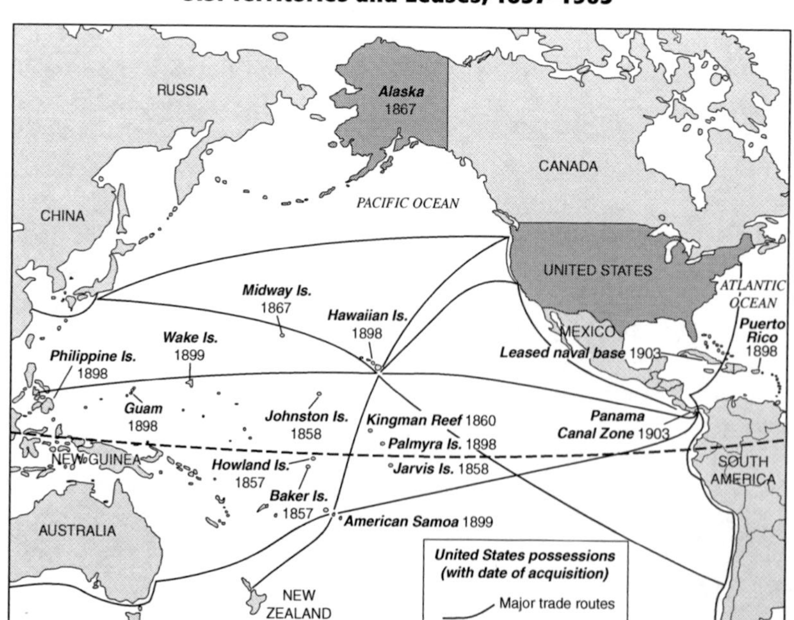

- Describe how newspapers influenced the U.S. government to declare war on Spain.
- Explain how the results of the war represented a second phase of manifest destiny.

2 **Theme:** *Emerging U.S. Global Involvement.* Overseas involvement took place mainly in Latin America, the Caribbean, and Asia.

Task: Select *one* example of overseas involvement in Latin America or the Caribbean and *another* in Asia. For *each* example:
- describe circumstances leading to involvement
- show whether the involvement had a positive or a negative impact on each area chosen.

You may use, but are not limited to, Panama, the "big stick," and dollar diplomacy (for Latin America and the Caribbean); Commodore Perry, the Open Door Policy, and acquisition of the Philippines (for Asia).

DOCUMENT-BASED QUESTION

Study each document and answer the question that follows it. Then read the **Task** *and write your essay. Include references to most of the documents and additional information you retain about U.S. history and government.*

Historical Context: U.S. entry into World War I marked a consensus among citizens unprecedented in U.S. history.

Document 1: Refer to the poster at right.

Question: How did the poster encourage young men to support the war?

Document 2: Senator Robert La Follette in the *Congressional Record*, 1917:

> The President proposes alliance with Great Britain, . . . which is a hereditary monarchy, with a hereditary ruler, . . . with a hereditary House of Lords, with a hereditary landed system, with a limited . . . suffrage for one class and a multiplied suffrage . . . for another, and with grinding industrial conditions for all the wageworkers. The President has not suggested that we make our support . . . conditional [on home rule in] Ireland, or Egypt, or India. We rejoice in the establishment of democracy in Russia, but [if Russia were still autocratic], we would [still] be asked to [ally] with her. . . . [All] of the countries with whom we are to enter into alliance, except France and . . . Russia, are still of the old order. . . .
>
> This war is being forced upon our people without their knowing why and without their approval.

Question: Why does Senator La Follette oppose U.S. entry into the war?

In a 1917 poster, Uncle Sam backs up the draft.

DOCUMENT 3: Refer to the cartoon below.

In a 1917 cartoon, Germany's Kaiser honors Senator La Follette for his antiwar stance.

QUESTION: How does the cartoonist feel about Senator La Follette's opposition?

DOCUMENT 4: From a release by George Creel, Director of the U.S. Committee for Public Information, 1918:

> Now let us picture what a sudden invasion of the United States by these Germans would mean....
>
> ...While their fleet blockades the harbor [of New York City] and shells the city...their troops land...and advance toward the city in order to cut its rail communications, starve it into surrender and then plunder it....
>
> ...They pass through Lakewood, ...New Jersey....They first demand wine...and beer....They pillage and burn....They demand $1,000,000 from the residents. One feeble old woman tries to conceal $20....She is taken out and hanged....The Catholic priest and Methodist minister are thrown into a pig-sty....Officers quarter themselves in a handsome house,...insult the ladies of the family, and destroy and defile the contents of the house.
>
> ...Robbery, murder, and outrage run riot....Most of the town and beautiful pinewoods are burned, and then the troops move on to treat New Brunswick in the same way....
>
> This is not just a snappy story.... The general plan of campaign against America has been announced repeatedly by German military men. *And every horrible detail is just what the German troops have done in Belgium and France.*

QUESTION: What is Creel saying could happen if Germany invades the United States?

TASK: Using the documents and your knowledge of U.S. history and government, write an essay in which you:

- describe how the U.S. government promoted and encouraged conformity to make victory in World War I more likely.
- explain how some people opposed to the war were treated.

UNIT IV
Prosperity and Depression

CHAPTER 12
War and Prosperity: 1917–1929

DOCUMENTS AND LAWS
Eighteenth Amendment (1919) • Nineteenth Amendment (1920)
Village of Euclid, Ohio v. *Ambler Realty Company* (1926) • Twenty-first Amendment (1933)

EVENTS
Harlem Renaissance (1920s) • Sacco-Vanzetti case (1921–1927) • Scopes trial (1925)

PEOPLE
Calvin Coolidge • Countee Cullen • F. Scott Fitzgerald • Henry Ford • Sigmund Freud
Ernest Hemingway • Langston Hughes • James Weldon Johnson • Sinclair Lewis • Carrie Nation
Paul Robeson • Edith Wharton

OBJECTIVES

- To describe social changes in the 1920s.
- To examine positive and negative changes in the lives of women, African Americans, and other minorities.
- To examine the economic policies of the 1920s.
- To understand the effects of mass consumption on cultural values.
- To describe constitutional and legal issues that arose between 1917 and 1929.

Impact of War

After World War I, the United States enjoyed prosperity, its government resumed a policy of laissez-faire, and its citizens ceased promoting progressive reforms.

During World War I, as men fought in Europe, women filled their jobs at home—as factory workers, railroad conductors, farmers, and so on. They served as U.S. Army and Navy nurses. As more telephone operators, secretaries, and salespeople were needed, women comprised the majority in these occupations.

African-American men had fought for their country and, more than ever, resented treatment as second-class citizens. During the 1920s, confrontations between blacks and whites increased, and organizations challenging discriminatory practices became strong and numerous.

The 1920s were a difficult time for immigrants. Many from Eastern Europe were thought to be Communist sympathizers. Those from Asia, whose numbers were increasing, were distrusted by much of the white population.

Northern Migration of African Americans Between 1910 and 1930, the number of African Americans in the North grew from 1 million to 2.5 million. Southern blacks moved north partly to find good-paying work and partly to escape Jim Crow laws. Blacks who defied such laws risked jail or lynching. In 1927, for example, 24 lynchings occurred in the South.

Race Riots The arrival of blacks in large numbers threatened many Northern whites. Segregation was as strict and common in the North and at times led to race riots. In 1919, a riot on a segregated Chicago beach resulted in the deaths of 38 people, black and white.

Similar confrontations also rocked Southern cities. One of the most serious took place in Tulsa, Oklahoma, in 1921. A rumor that a black man had attacked a white woman sent an army of whites on the offense in the black section of the city. Many black-owned homes and businesses were burned, and many people were killed, most of them black.

Politics and Economics of the 1920s

During World War I, prices of many goods exported or used by the military increased. Wages, however, remained low. By 1920, wartime production was in decline, unemployment was rising, and many businesses were failing. Neither the employed nor unemployed could afford many goods and services. Farm income also declined as European farmers resumed raising crops that had been imported during the war. The U.S. **recession** (period of business decline) lasted from 1920 to 1922. Then, the economy experienced a business boom, which, nevertheless, masked problems that would lead to disaster in 1929.

Return to "Normalcy"

In 1920, the Republican presidential candidate, Warren G. Harding, won by a huge majority. He had promised to lead the nation back to "*normalcy*"—the

What is the cartoonist saying about the fate of the American farmer compared to that of industries in the 1920s?

quieter time before the war and before Wilson's progressive politics. In fact, Harding's laissez-faire policy toward business recalled the 1880s and 1890s. Such a domestic policy failed to take into account that society and the economy were changing fast. In foreign affairs, the return to normalcy looked toward a more isolationist policy (especially with less involvement in European affairs).

Prosperity Under Coolidge Vice President Calvin Coolidge became president when Harding died suddenly in 1923, and he was reelected in his own right in 1924.

"The business of America is business," summed up Coolidge's support of unregulated big business, high protective tariffs, less government spending, and lower taxes.

Farmers and Workers in Trouble

The general prosperity of the 1920s did not include farmers or the urban working poor.

Productivity, Mortgages, and Technology During World War I, European farmlands were turned into battlefields. American farmers expanded production to meet the growing demand for crops, and farm income reached new heights. After 1921, foreign demand for U.S. farm products fell, as did U.S. farm prices. Use of improved farm machinery, which produced wheat and corn surpluses, also lowered prices. Moreover, to buy the new machinery,

Gains in Productivity and Wages, 1909–1929

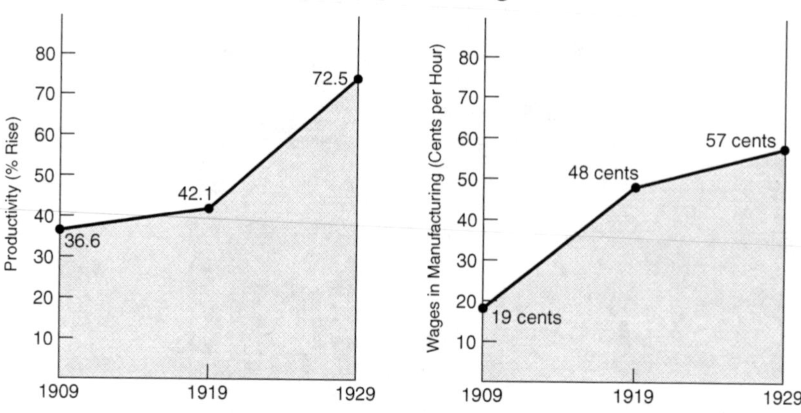

What happened to worker productivity and wages, 1909–1929?

many farmers took **mortgages** (money borrowed against the value of property) on their land and homes. Lower prices for crops often made it impossible to repay such loans, and many farmers lost their land by foreclosure.

Decreased Government Supports Laissez-faire hurt urban workers as well. The government was no longer committed to improving working conditions and wages. Union efforts to force factory owners to raise wages usually failed. Union membership declined greatly from 1920 to 1925.

Business Boom and Wider Investment

During the 1920s, there was no trust busting. By 1929, the 200 largest U.S. corporations controlled 49 percent of all corporate wealth.

New machinery and new work methods resulted in greatly increased productivity, which reduced the cost of manufacture. Workers' wages also increased in the 1920s, but far less than increases in productivity.

This business boom encouraged Americans with average incomes to invest in major corporations. As people invested more in the stock market, stock prices rose to record levels in a great **bull market** (condition when public confidence in stocks causes stock prices to soar). These investments led to **speculation** (making risky investments) as people gambled that stock prices would continue to increase.

IN REVIEW

1. Describe the effects of World War I on women and African Americans.
2. What were the causes and effects of the African-American migration north after World War I?
3. How did uneven distribution of wealth and farm overproduction show that the prosperity of the 1920s did not include everyone?

Effect of Mass Consumption

While prosperity lasted, most Americans cared more about exciting new amusements than about politics. Movies, major league sports, new dance steps, and fast-paced jazz music—the last one, mainly the creation of African Americans—became very popular. As a result, the decade became known as the *Roaring Twenties.*

Automobile

Model of Productivity Henry Ford mass-produced his Model T cars so that they could be sold cheaply. His assembly-line method (discussed on page 125) saved time, cut production costs, and lowered the Model T's price ($400 in 1916, down from $500). Ford's methods were widely copied.

The number of American cars manufactured increased from 1.5 million in 1919 to 4.7 million in 1929. By 1930, Americans owned more than 25 million cars. The success of the automobile industry helped other industries to grow. The rubber industry produced more tires. The oil and gasoline industries provided fuel. The steel industry produced millions of tons for auto bodies. Roadside hotels and restaurants that catered to motorists sprang up everywhere.

Problems The automobile brought problems as well: drunken driving, fatal accidents, parking problems—and later, polluted air. But in the 1920s, most Americans welcomed the mobile way of life made possible by the automobile.

Installment Buying

Only in the 1920s did technological marvels such as the telephone and automobile become widely available to American consumers. To encourage sales, businesses advertised extensively and encouraged customers to buy on the installment plan (discussed on page 150). Many people went so deeply into debt that they had to use all their resources to make monthly payments on what they had already bought.

Real Estate Boom and Suburban Development

Subways, buses, and electric trolleys made urban transportation easy. By the 1920s, the residents in cities outnumbered those in rural areas.

To escape city crowds, many people moved to the **suburbs** (residential communities near cities) and commuted to their city jobs by car. Land outside the city became more valuable, the real estate business flourished, and new roads to serve the suburbs became a construction priority. New

How does this advertisment in a 1920s magazine differ from today's car advertisements?

railroad lines also connected suburban and urban areas. Better urban-suburban transportation encouraged businesses to move to the suburbs as well.

Regional Politics and Economics

Counties, small cities, and towns developed alternate forms of government. In Suffolk County, Long Island, New York, for example, county boards and executives regulated property taxes, road building, environmental codes, and schools. Town governments provided police protection, welfare, clean water, and garbage removal, and town residents elected boards of education. Thus, political parties developed new areas of influence.

Suburban **zoning** became increasingly important. Local governments regulated business and home locations, land use, and allowable acreage for building sites. Zoning sometimes became a means to limit housing in areas for only the well-to-do. The Supreme Court usually upheld zoning regulations. In *Village of Euclid, Ohio* v. *Ambler Realty Company* (1926), the Court agreed that municipalities had a right to regulate health and safety through zoning.

Entertainment and a Common Culture

By 1920, popular entertainment had undergone a revolution to include phonograph records of classical and popular music, radio broadcasts, and bigger and better motion pictures, produced in the new movie capital, Hollywood, California. Such stars as Charlie Chaplin and Mary Pickford acted in early silent movies. In 1927, Al Jolson starred in *The Jazz Singer*, the first "talkie."

The new entertainment created a common culture. Americans everywhere enjoyed the same movies and radio programs and, with one voice, idolized such celebrities as the aviator Charles Lindbergh, the movie actor Rudolph Valentino, and the baseball hero Babe Ruth.

Repeated magazine and radio advertising made Americans feel that they had a culture in common. Some people expressed fear that regional differences would disappear, blended into a uniform way of life.

Issues About Differing Rural and Urban Values

Although life in the 1920s was generally good for the white middle class, it was otherwise for ethnic minorities and the foreign born. Rural people, especially, often distrusted urban Italian and Jewish immigrants. Nativists held them responsible for city slums and crime even though they were usually hardworking and law abiding.

Threats to Civil Liberties

The Communist revolution in Russia made nativists fearful that foreign-born radicals would try to overthrow the U.S. government (discussed on pages 156–157). Such fears persisted throughout most of the 20th century.

Urban and Rural Population, 1860–1920

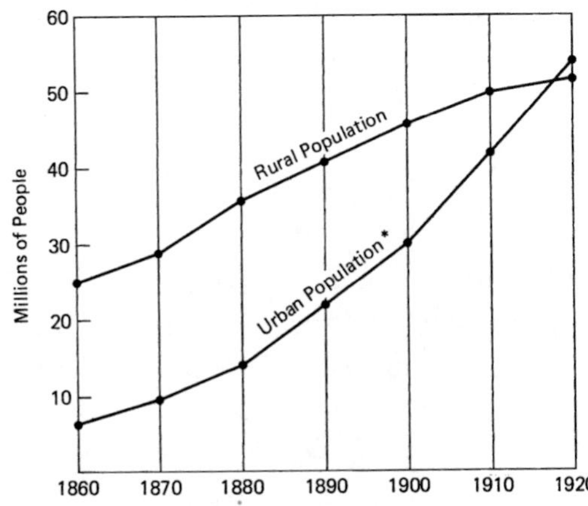

*Urban areas were defined by the U.S. Census Bureau as places with at least 2,500 inhabitants.

In the 1920s, the Ku Klux Klan (first discussed in Chapter 7) made a comeback. The revived Klan's targets were African Americans, Roman Catholics, Jews, and immigrants. As its membership grew, it became important in the politics of many states. The governors of Oregon and Indiana owed their election to Klan support.

In 1921, Nicola Sacco and Bartolomeo Vanzetti were convicted by Massachusetts of armed robbery and murder. The evidence of guilt was weak, and the judge appeared biased against them. Liberals blamed antiforeign prejudice for their conviction. In spite of worldwide protests and appeals for clemency, Sacco and Vanzetti were executed in 1927.

"The Only Way to Handle It": cartoon of U.S. immigration quotas in the 1920s

Prohibition and the Volstead Act

The work of temperance reformers such as Carrie Nation bore fruit with the adoption of the Eighteenth (Prohibition) Amendment (1919), which prohibited the manufacture and sale of alcoholic beverages in the United States. Congress passed the National Prohibition Act (Volstead Act) to enforce the amendment.

Supporters (many from rural areas) believed that Prohibition would reduce crime and make Americans healthier. Instead, it caused millions of otherwise law-abiding citizens to drink illegally. Alcohol was either manufactured illegally or smuggled across the border from Canada. **Bootleggers** (suppliers of illegal beverages) made huge profits, and organized gangs evaded the law by bribing the police. In addition to a huge increase in organized crime, many Americans were poisoned from contaminated liquor produced illegally and without quality control. In 1933, the Eighteenth Amendment was *repealed* (abolished) by the Twenty-first Amendment.

Prohibitionist disposing of a dandelion that might be processed into homemade wine

Scopes Trial

In 1925, another clash between urban and rural cultures arose in a famous trial. John Scopes, a biology teacher, defied a Tennessee law against the teaching in public schools of Darwin's theory of evolution. Darwin's ideas offended fundamentalist Protestants, many of them rural, who interpreted the Bible strictly. Many city people tended to support the theory. The following is a portion of the examination by Clarence Darrow, Scopes's defense lawyer, of the prosecution's chief witness, William Jennings Bryan:

Mr. Darrow: Do you claim that everything in the Bible should be literally interpreted?

Mr. Bryan: I believe [it] should be accepted [as is]; some of the Bible is given illustratively. For instance: "Ye are the salt of the earth." I would not insist [on a literal reading]. . . . It is used in the sense of salt as saving God's people.

Mr. Darrow: But when you read that Jonah swallowed the whale—or that the whale swallowed Jonah . . . how do you literally interpret that? . . .

Mr. Bryan: One miracle is just as easy to believe as another. . . .

Mr. Darrow: Perfectly easy to believe that Jonah swallowed that whale? . . .

Mr. Bryan: Your honor. . . . [Mr. Darrow's] only purpose . . . is to slur at the Bible, but I will answer his question. . . . I want the world to know that this man, who does not believe in God, is trying to use a court. . . .

Mr. Darrow: I object. . . .

Mr. Bryan: [Continuing] to slur at it. . . .

Mr. Darrow: I object. . . . I am examining you on your fool ideas that no intelligent Christian on earth believes.

Scopes was convicted but fined only a token $100, and a higher court later reversed the verdict. In recent years, the conflict between teaching science versus religion in the classroom has reemerged.

Shifting Cultural Values

Fads are vivid, usually frivolous forms of social expression that last only briefly. One fad of the 1920s was a fast dance called the "Charleston." Another was the slang expression "23 skiddoo" (good-bye).

Flappers Many young women of the 1920s shocked their elders by bobbing their hair, raising their hemlines, dancing to ragtime, and smoking in public. Traditionalists worried that the new freedoms of these "flappers" would lead to a breakdown of the family.

Freud Sigmund Freud was an Austrian psychiatrist whose ideas became popular in the United States. He held that people could resolve emotional problems through **psychoanalysis**, which involved a "talking cure" of free association, reliving troubling experiences, and recalling and interpreting dreams. Freud's theory that sexual repression was a major cause of emotional problems found a receptive audience during the newly liberated 1920s.

Women's Changing Roles

Suffrage The Nineteenth Amendment gave all American women the right to vote. During their struggle for suffrage, women had organized public demonstrations and used such tactics as petitioning, picketing, and hunger strikes. They had succeeded in influencing public policy.

Women in the Workforce After World War I, women were reluctant to give up working and keep house again. Such labor-saving appliances as refrigerators, washing machines, and vacuum cleaners enabled middle-class women to enter the workforce in the 1920s in record numbers. Most jobs were in support services, such as secretary or typist to a male boss. Other jobs that became available were telephone operator, clerk, and teacher. Women earned less than men doing the same work and were expected to stop working when they got married. Nevertheless, jobs gave young women the chance to live on their own and experience independence.

Women's health improved as they exchanged heavy physical labor such as farmwork for less strenuous white-collar work. Moreover, as city dwellers, they had better access to doctors and medical facilities.

Literature and Music

During the 1920s, a number of writers wrote about American life. Sinclair Lewis, in his novel *Main Street* (1920), exposed the attitudes of smug small-town Americans. In *The Sun Also Rises* (1926), Ernest Hemingway depicted Americans abroad who cast off traditional values but found no alternatives to help them understand themselves or the world. In *The Age of Innocence* (1920), Edith Wharton satirized the social manners and arrogance of upper-class New Yorkers. In his novel *The Great Gatsby* (1925), F. Scott Fitzgerald lent a tragic note to the American dream of material success and social acceptance.

Harlem Renaissance In the 1920s, a number of talented African Americans brought new acclaim to Harlem, a black neighborhood of New York City. Their creativity became known as the *Harlem Renaissance*. Their achievements increased pride in African-American culture. Best known of the Harlem poets were James Weldon Johnson, Langston Hughes, and Countee Cullen. Hughes's poem "What happens to a dream deferred?" expresses the frustration of African Americans still living in an age of segregation.

Paul Robeson, a black actor and singer, starred in several Eugene O'Neill plays. He also appeared in Jerome Kern's 1927 hit *Showboat,* the first American musical to (1) highlight problems faced by black Americans and (2) bring black and white performers together on the same stage. Josephine Baker sang and danced in nightclubs in Philadelphia, New York, and Paris. Eubie Blake and W. C. Handy composed songs that are still popular today.

African-American musicians began playing jazz in New Orleans around 1900. By the 1920s, this music was also popular in Chicago and New York City. Among the greatest of the jazz musicians were bandleader and songwriter Duke Ellington, trumpet player and singer Louis Armstrong, and blues singer Bessie Smith.

Discrimination in the Entertainment Industry In spite of their popularity, African-American entertainers often faced discrimination. In the movies, they were cast in stereotypical roles as servants and figures of fun. Chorus lines were generally all-white.

IN REVIEW

1. Explain the significance of installment buying, the Eighteenth Amendment, Sigmund Freud, the Nineteenth Amendment, and the Harlem Renaissance.
2. How did the growth of the automobile industry stimulate growth in other industries? How did it influence American lifestyles?
3. How did each of the following contribute to the literary scene during the 1920s: Sinclair Lewis, Ernest Hemingway, Edith Wharton, F. Scott Fitzgerald, and Langston Hughes?

CHAPTER REVIEW

MULTIPLE-CHOICE QUESTIONS

Base your answer to question 1 on the poem below and on your knowledge of social studies.

One Way Ticket

I am fed up
With Jim Crow laws,
People who are cruel
And afraid,
Who lynch and run,
Who are scared of me
And me of them.

I pick up my life
And take it away
On a one way ticket—
Gone up North,
Gone out West,
Gone!

—LANGSTON HUGHES, 1926

1 The author states that he has "Gone" because
(1) jobs were available in Northern industries
(2) there was no racial prejudice in the West
(3) farmland was more available in the North
(4) racial discrimination drove him away

2 A main reason that demand for American farm goods dropped dramatically in the 1920s was that
(1) European need for imported farm products declined after World War I
(2) fashion styles required less cotton material than previous styles
(3) Americans refused to buy foods that were genetically altered
(4) people left the cities to return to the farms

3 Henry Ford's use of the assembly line in the production of automobiles led directly to
(1) a decrease in the number of automobiles available
(2) a decrease in the cost of automobiles
(3) an increase in the unemployment rate
(4) an increase in the time needed to produce a single automobile

4 The convictions of Sacco and Vanzetti in the 1920s most closely reflected the
(1) increase in nativist attitudes
(2) federal government's war on crime
(3) corruption of political machines
(4) rise in labor unrest

5 The influence of nativism during the 1920s is best illustrated by the
(1) increase in the popularity of the automobile
(2) emergence of the flappers
(3) expansion of trusts and monopolies
(4) growth of the Ku Klux Klan

6 National Prohibition, as authorized by the 18th amendment, stated that
(1) Americans must be 18 years old to purchase alcoholic beverages
(2) only imported alcoholic beverages would be sold
(3) alcoholic beverages could be sold only in government-run stores
(4) the manufacture and sale of alcoholic beverages were banned

7 The Scopes Trial of 1925 is an example of
(1) the effects of assimilation on American culture
(2) a clash between scientific ideas and religious beliefs
(3) an increase in violence in American society
(4) government intervention in racial conflicts

8 A study of the "flappers" of the 1920s would indicate that
(1) some women rejected traditional feminine roles
(2) many women were elected to national political office
(3) women were fired from traditionally male occupations
(4) the earning power of women was equal to that of men in the same occupation

9 The Harlem Renaissance of the 1920s can best be described as
(1) an organization created to help promote African-American businesses
(2) a movement that sought to draw people back to the inner cities
(3) a relief program to provide jobs for minority workers
(4) a period of great achievement by African-American writers, artists, and performers

Base your answer to question 10 on the chart below and on your knowledge of social studies.

Rural and Urban Populations in the United States

Year	*Rural*	*Urban*
1860	25,226,803	6,216,518
1870	28,656,010	9,902,361
1880	36,059,474	14,129,735
1890	40,873,501	22,106,265
1900	45,997,336	30,214,832
1910	50,164,495	42,064,001
1920	51,768,255	54,253,282

Source: Bureau of the Census

10 Which generalization about population growth is supported by information in this chart?
(1) For every census listed, rural population exceeded urban population.
(2) By 1920, more people lived in cities than in rural areas.
(3) The Civil War significantly slowed the rate of population growth.

(4) Most urban population growth was due to people migrating from rural areas.

THEMATIC ESSAYS

1 **Theme:** *Tradition Versus Change.* The 1920s were a time of great change in the United States. Changes, however, provoked resistance to change and a longing for "the good old days."

Task: Complete *both* of the following tasks:

- Choose *one* change during the 1920s. Describe its cause and impact on the United States.
- Give *one* example of how some Americans tried to resist a change and evaluate their success in stopping or slowing it. (You may use the same change or a different one.)

You may wish to discuss migration of African Americans, women's roles, and mass consumption.

Some examples of resistance to change are attitudes toward immigrants, Prohibition, and the fundamentalist response to science.

2 **Theme:** *Return to "Normalcy."* During the presidential election campaign of 1920, soon-to-be-elected Republican candidate Warren G. Harding promised a "return to normalcy."

Task: Complete *both* of the following tasks:

- Describe what Harding meant by "normalcy."
- Choose *two* events or circumstances from the 1920s. For each, explain how it stemmed, in part, from U.S. participation in World War I.
- Use *each* example to evaluate whether the United States had returned to "normalcy."

You may use, but are not limited to, the treatment of immigrants, stock speculation, foreign policy, mass consumption, and changing cultural values.

DOCUMENT-BASED QUESTION

Study each document and answer the question that follows it. Then read the ***Task*** *and write your essay. Include references to most of the documents and additional information you retain about U.S. history and government.*

Historical Context: World War I left an aftereffect of fear for some and hope for others.

Document 1: Refer to the cartoon below.

The Red Scare

Question: What does the cartoon say about immigrants and foreigners?

Document 2: From Hiram W. Evans, Imperial Wizard of the Ku Klux Klan, in *North American Review,* 1926:

> The greatest achievement so far has been to formulate and [recognize] the idea of preserving and developing America . . . for the benefit of the children of pioneers. . . . The Klan [did not create] this idea—it has long been a vague stirring in [plain people's] souls. But the Klan can fairly claim to have given it purpose, method, direction. . . .
>
> . . . there are three great racial instincts . . . [in] the Klan slogan: "Native, white, Protestant supremacy."

QUESTION: Whom does Evans feel that the nation was created to benefit?

DOCUMENT 3: Refer to the photo below.

QUESTION: How does the photo show that women's role had started to change by the end of World War I?

DOCUMENT 4: From James Weldon Johnson in *Harper's*, November 1928:

> . . . [T]here is a common, widespread, and persistent [stereotype of] the Negro, and it is that he is here only to receive; to be shaped into something new and unquestionably better. The common idea is that the Negro reached America intellectually, culturally, and morally empty, and that he is here to be filled . . . with education, filled with religion, filled with morality, filled with culture. . . .
>
> Through his artistic efforts the Negro is smashing this . . . stereotype. . . . He is [showing] that he [has] a wealth of natural endowments and that he has long been a generous giver to America; . . . that he is an active and important force in American life; that he is a creator as well as a creature; that he . . . is the potential giver of larger and richer contributions.
>
> In this way the Negro . . . has placed himself in an entirely new light. . . . Through artistic achievement the Negro has found a means of getting at the very core of the prejudice against him by challenging the Nordic superiority complex. A great deal has been accomplished in this decade of "renaissance."

QUESTION: Why does Johnson feel that there was a change in attitude toward African Americans following World War I?

TASK: Using the documents and your knowledge of U.S. history and government, write an essay in which you:

- describe why Americans were *both* fearful and hopeful immediately following World War I.
- show how *one* of the fears or hopes is still important in the 21st century.

Women ship construction workers, Puget Sound, Oregon, 1919

CHAPTER 13
The Great Depression

DOCUMENTS AND LAWS
Federal Farm Board (1929) • Hawley-Smoot Tariff (1930) • New Deal legislation (1933–1938)
Reconstruction Finance Corporation (1932) • Indian Reorganization Act (1934)
Schechter Poultry Corp. v. *United States* (1935) • Wagner Act (1935)
Fair Labor Standards Act (1938) • Twenty-second Amendment (1951)

EVENTS
Stock Market crash (1929) • Great Depression (1929–1942) • Bonus Army (1932)
Congress of Industrial Organizations (C.I.O.) established (1938)

PEOPLE
Marion Anderson • Mary McLeod Bethune • Father Charles Coughlin • Amelia Earhart
William Faulkner • Lillian Hellman • John L. Lewis • Huey Long • Frances Perkins
Eleanor Roosevelt • Franklin D. Roosevelt • Alfred E. Smith • Norman Thomas
Dr. Francis Townsend • John Steinbeck • Robert Weaver

OBJECTIVES

- To examine causes of the Great Depression and its effect on people and institutions.
- To understand worldwide financial and economic interdependence.
- To examine how Herbert Hoover and Franklin D. Roosevelt responded to the Depression.
- To evaluate the impact of the New Deal on the U.S. economy.
- To examine cultural life during the Depression.

ONSET OF THE DEPRESSION

A **depression** is a severe, long-term economic decline marked by business failures, high unemployment, and low production levels and prices.

Weak Economy

Overproduction/Underconsumption A nation's economic strength depends on whether its citizens can afford what factories and farms produce. As wages in the 1920s failed to keep up with productivity, many goods went unsold and many businesses failed.

Much of the nation's wealth belonged to a small number of people. The richest 5 percent had 25 percent of total income.

Overexpansion of Credit In the 1920s, it was a common practice among those who bought stocks to do so *on margin*, that is, to pay a small percent of the purchase price and finance the rest with a loan.

Stock Market Crash

Herbert Hoover succeeded Calvin Coolidge as president in 1929. Economic prosperity continued for about six months, and Hoover ran the executive branch well.

The bull market on New York City's Wall Street crested in September 1929. Then stock prices started to drop. Bankers tried to halt the decline in stock prices, but on October 29—"Black Tuesday"—thousands of stockholders panicked and ordered their brokers to sell at any price. A record 16.5 million shares were traded, almost all at a loss. By the end of December, the combined prices of Wall Street stocks had lost one-third of their peak value in September.

There were four harmful consequences. (1) Billions of dollars that people had invested in stocks were wiped out. (2) Many investors had bought on margin and went bankrupt. (3) Banks failed because loans were not repaid. (4) People lost confidence in the economy and, for years afterward, preferred savings over investments.

Worldwide Financial Interdependence World War I produced an imbalance in the world economy. The peace treaty forced Germany to pay the Allies huge reparations. The European Allies owed vast sums to the United States for wartime consumption of American goods. In the 1920s, the United States became the world's largest creditor nation.

By 1930, most nations were linked financially. The United States lent money to Germany so that Germany could pay reparations to England and France. England and France then repaid war debts to the United States.

How U.S. Loans Financed International Prosperity, 1924–1929

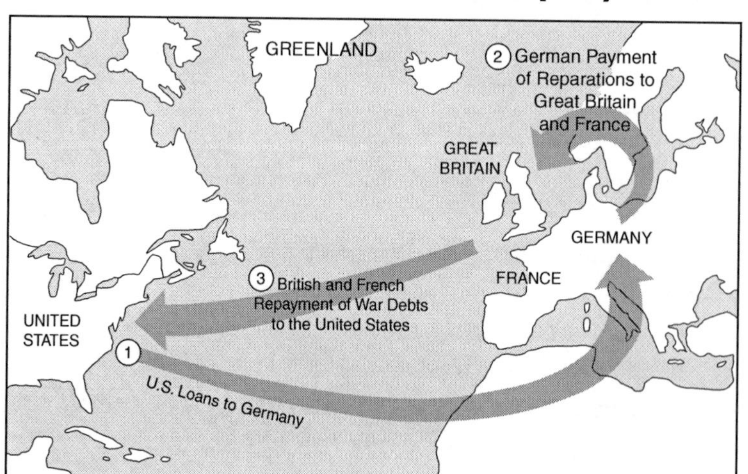

Interdependent Banking American bank and business loans enabled Europeans to pay war debts to the U.S. government. This arrangement sustained prosperity as long as U.S. banks had enough money to make foreign loans. With the collapse of the stock market, the worldwide cycle of debt payments ended.

International Trade The lifeblood of the international economy was trade. Protective tariffs hurt all nations, including the United States. Nevertheless, in 1930 many in Congress hoped to protect domestic industries from foreign competition with the *Hawley-Smoot Tariff*, which increased import taxes on more than 1,000 items. European nations, in turn, raised their own tariffs, and U.S.-European trade dropped by half. Partly because of the tariff war, the worldwide depression deepened.

Political Repercussions

Hoover's Response Herbert Hoover was president during the worst years of the *Great Depression*, 1930–1932. His attempts to revive the economy included the following:

- cutting taxes to encourage consumerism
- greatly increasing government expenditure on public projects—dams, highways, harbors, and so forth
- persuading Congress to establish the *Federal Farm Board* (1929) to buy farm goods and keep up prices
- persuading Congress to establish the *Reconstruction Finance Corporation* (1932) to fund banks, railroads, and insurance companies threatened with bankruptcy (Hoover's most successful program)
- declaring a **debt moratorium** (temporary halt on the payment of debts) to fight the worldwide spread of the Depression.

"Rugged Individualism" Hoover did not believe that government should directly aid the poor. His creed was "rugged individualism"—decisions by businesses and individuals on how best to help themselves. Moreover, he felt that when businesses succeed, everyone benefits indirectly from profits that "trickle down" to wage earners.

IMPACT OF THE DEPRESSION

In 1932, approximately 12 million workers—25 percent of the U.S. labor force—were unemployed. The employed worked for much lower wages than in the 1920s. Prices paid to farmers were desperately low. Factories produced

Rising Unemployment and Falling Prices, 1929–1932

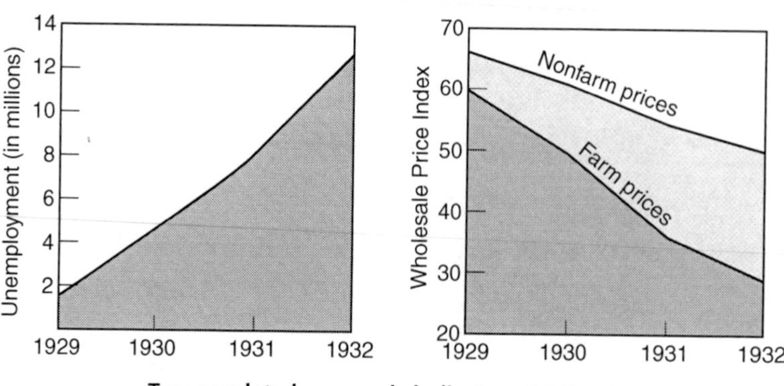

Two unrelated economic indicators, 1929–1932

only half of their 1929 output. About 5,000 banks had closed their doors, forever cutting off depositors from their savings.

"Bonus Army" In the summer of 1932, 17,000 unemployed veterans of World War I marched to Washington, D.C. They wanted the government to pay them immediately the bonuses owed to them at a later time. This "*Bonus Army*" set up shacks near the Capitol. When the protesters ignored President Hoover's order to leave, he sent federal troops to break up their encampment.

Desperate Conditions All over the country, jobless people who became homeless slept in tents and shacks clustered in areas called **Hoovervilles**. They also hid in railroad boxcars and traveled in search of jobs or handouts. Men and women sold apples on city street corners.

Women and Minorities

As the Great Depression deprived women of job opportunities, they again concentrated on family needs.

African Americans suffered the full impact of the Depression. Last to be hired, they were usually first to be fired.

Native Americans continued to live in poverty on reservations.

Nativist distrust of immigrants and opposition to immigration continued as jobs became scarce.

Much of the lands of Great Plains farmers turned into a *Dust Bowl*, for several reasons—poor farming practices, long drought, and high winds that pulled moisture from the soil. As the farmers lost income and land, they took to the open road looking for work as migrant farmworkers. So many came from Oklahoma that almost all of them became known as "Okies."

IN REVIEW

1. Summarize basic economic weaknesses that contributed to the Stock Market crash and the Great Depression.

2. Explain how Hoover responded to the Depression.
3. Identify the following: rugged individualism, trickle-down economics, Reconstruction Finance Corporation, Bonus Army, Hoovervilles.

FRANKLIN D. ROOSEVELT'S NEW DEAL

In 1932, Hoover lost the presidential election by a huge margin to his Democratic presidential challenger, Franklin D. Roosevelt. Roosevelt's plan was to help people directly by giving them government jobs. Federal paychecks would give them hope and purchasing power, which would put money back into the economy.

Roosevelt tried out many ideas for solving the economic crisis. During his first and part of his second term (1933–1938), he favored programs that came to be known as the *New Deal.*

Roosevelt and his advisers—the "brain trust"—had three main goals —*relief, recovery, and reform*: Relieve the misery of the poor and unemployed, bring about the recovery of businesses, and reform the economic system to prevent mistakes in the future like those that had caused the Great Depression. In order to achieve these goals, the government would have to use **deficit spending** (spending borrowed money) to stimulate economic growth.

Relief of Suffering

In Roosevelt's first three months in office—almost 100 days—more important laws were enacted than had been during all of the 1920s. The President believed that the times called for bold measures, and the Democratic majority in Congress gave the president almost all that he asked for. The laws passed during these *Hundred Days* had a long-lasting effect on the country.

Bank Holiday After the Stock Market crash, many Americans lost faith in banks and withdrew their money. Banks that could not produce all the cash called for failed. In 1933, Roosevelt declared a nationwide "*bank holiday.*" Then Congress passed the *Emergency Banking Act*, which allowed sound banks to reopen. The drain on banks stopped and public confidence was restored.

Federal Emergency Relief Act This 1933 law created the *Federal Emergency Relief Administration (FERA).* The organization gave federal money to the states to set up projects that provided jobs to people.

Strategies Against Unemployment

Congress passed several laws that established organizations to fight unemployment.

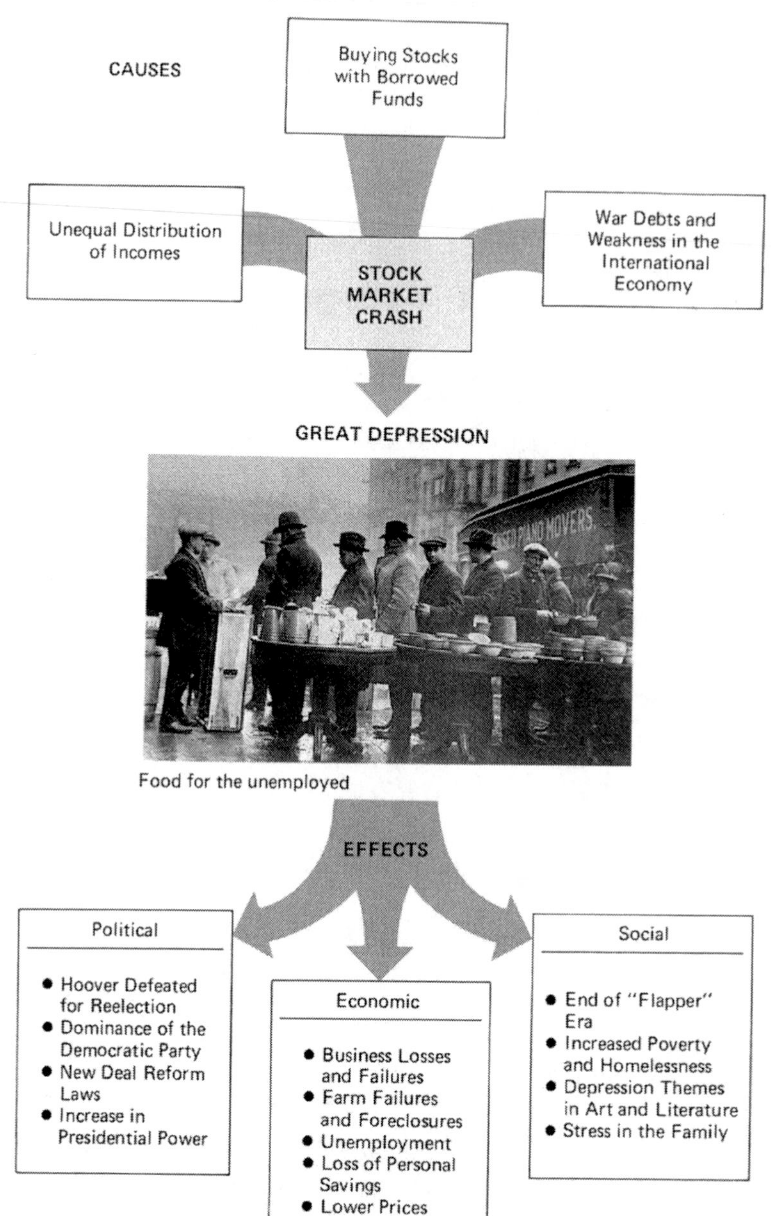

Food for the unemployed

- The *Public Works Administration (PWA),* set up in 1933, put people to work building roads, bridges, libraries, hospitals, schools, courthouses, and other public projects.
- *The Civilian Conservation Corps (CCC),* set up in 1933, employed men between 18 and 25 in flood control, soil conservation, forest replanting, and park construction. To encourage workers to save some money to send home, they lived in camps or dorms and ate together.

- *The Works Progress Administration (WPA)*, set up in 1935, organized public projects and paid workers to do them. Only the head of a family—usually a man—could qualify. Women who headed families were given less-skilled jobs. Workers who had been offered private employment were ineligible.

Recovery

Fair Competition In 1933, the *National Industrial Recovery Act* (*NIRA*) set up the *National Recovery Administration* (*NRA*) to encouraged businesses and labor organizations to draw up **codes of fair practices**—maximum work hours, minimum wages, productivity, and prices. The codes were to help businesses control production and raise prices, and to help labor by putting people to work and raising wages. The NRA gave workers the right to form unions.

Relief

Mortgages For homeowners who could not meet mortgage payments, Congress created the *Home Owners' Loan Corporation (HOLC)* in 1933. The *Federal Housing Administration (FHA)*, which followed in 1934, insured bank loans for the construction of new housing and the repair of old homes, and reduced the required down payment for buying homes.

Scarcity and Parity The *Agricultural Adjustment Act (AAA)* of 1933 paid farmers to limit production and raise farm prices. The money came from a "processing tax" on the industries that made raw products into finished goods. Farmers had to destroy a portion of their crops and livestock to raise their farm prices to **parity** (the higher, prewar price level for farm products).

Search for Effective Reform

Banking The *Glass Steagall Act* (1933) created the *Federal Deposit Insurance Corporation (FDIC)*, which backed and insured bank deposits up to a certain amount, thus making them risk free to consumers.

Stock Market The *Securities and Exchange Commission (SEC)* of 1934 regulated the pricing of stocks and bonds and required publication of basic financial data about them. A major goal was to curb margin buying in order to reduce risk and speculation.

Social Security The *Social Security Act* (1935) established old-age insurance through a joint tax on employers and employees. Workers thus received a monthly income at age 65. The act also gave laid-off workers compensation while they job-hunted and provided grants to the states for the care of the disabled, the blind, and dependent children.

Gross National Product (GNP), 1929–1941

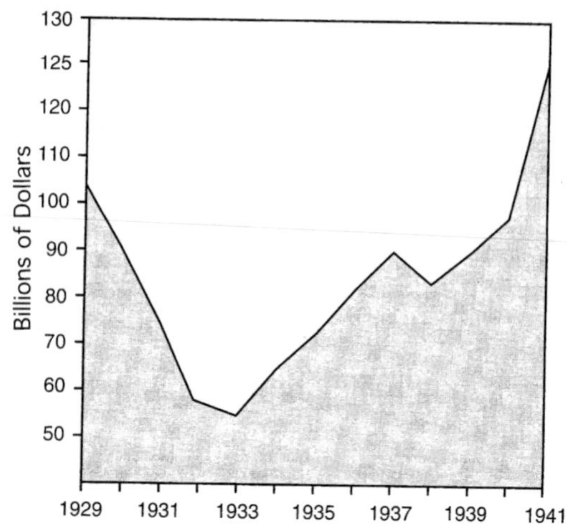

Unemployment, 1929–1941

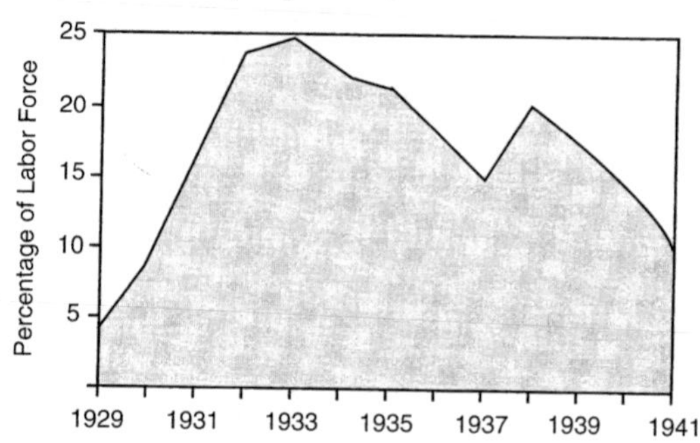

What happened to the unemployment rate as GNP went down? As GNP went up?

Labor and Unions The *Wagner Act* (1935) guaranteed workers the right to unionize and engage in collective bargaining (process by which workers and employers work out differences about wages, hours, and working conditions). The *National Labor Relations Board* could force employers to deal fairly with a union representing the majority of workers. Firing anyone for joining a union was illegal. From 1935 to 1940, more than 5 million workers joined unions, doubling total union membership.

The *Fair Labor Standards Act* (1938) set minimum wages (increased from 25 to 40 cents an hour) and maximum hours (reduced from 44 to 40 hours a week) in industries engaged in interstate commerce. Time and a half was to be paid for overtime. Children under 16 were prohibited from working in such industries.

In 1935, the most powerful union within the A.F. of L. was the *United Mine Workers.* Its leader, John L. Lewis, objected to A.F. of L policy of favoring skilled crafts workers over less-skilled workers. He favored the creation of one large industrial organization to represent all American workers (black and white, skilled and unskilled). In 1938, it became a separate union called the C.I.O. (Congress of Industrial Organizations).

Unions in the C.I.O. devised **sit-down strikes**, ones in which workers occupy a factory and refuse to work or leave until demands are met. One such strike shut down General Motors automobile factories in the winter of 1936–1937. The company ended up yielding to most of the union's demands.

Model Yardstick

The lands watered by the Tennessee River were often flooded. Farmers had no electric power and were desperately poor. In 1933, Congress created the *Tennessee Valley Authority (TVA)* to accomplish the following goals:

- to build dams to control floods
- to build power plants and provide electricity
- to charge fair prices for TVA-generated electricity
- to build reservoirs to hold needed water.

Many viewed the TVA as a model for Roosevelt's plan of relief, recovery, and reform. Throughout the region, people experienced relief in the form of TVA jobs, recovery in the form of electric power, and reform through flood control and water conservation.

NEW DEAL CONTROVERSIES

In the mid-1930s, unemployment still remained high and business activity slow. Opposition to the New Deal intensified.

Constitutional Issues

Supreme Court and the NRA In *Schechter Poultry Corp.* v. *United States* (1935), a chicken-raising company challenged the law that had created the National Recovery Administration (first discussed on page 227) by arguing that industry codes under this law gave legislative power to the executive branch. The U.S. Supreme Court agreed and declared the act unconstitutional.

Supreme Court and the AAA In 1936, the Court considered whether the processing tax discussed on page 227 could be collected to pay farmers under the Agricultural Adjustment Act of 1933. After the Court ruled against the tax and the law, Congress passed a new Agricultural Adjustment Act (1938). It (1) replaced the tax with direct federal payments to farmers, (2) tried to stabilize farm prices by storing surplus produce and releasing it in times of scarcity, (3) provided for soil conservation, (4) allowed marketing quotas for certain crops, and (5) insured wheat crops against natural disasters.

Election Mandate?

Before the 1930s, Republicans had usually been in the majority. Democrats had relied on Southerners for support—and they were usually conservative in everything except anti-Republicanism. The New Deal, however, appealed to many Northerners—industrial workers, immigrants, African Americans, ethnic Americans, and liberals. It also appealed to the farmers it had helped. These groups formed a majority, and Roosevelt was reelected in 1936 by a landslide.

"Court-Packing" Proposal Angered by the Supreme Court's anti–New Deal decisions, Roosevelt proposed increasing the number of justices from

THE INGENIOUS QUARTERBACK!

9 to 15—in effect, enabling him to appoint six politically sympathetic justices. The President was accused by many of trying to "pack" the court, so Congress defeated his plan in 1937. This action (by a Democratic-controlled Congress) demonstrated the meaning of checks and balances.

Third-Term Controversy In 1940, Roosevelt was elected to a third term and in 1944, to a fourth. Republicans accused him of breaking the two-term tradition. After Roosevelt's death in 1945, Congress proposed the Twenty-second Amendment limiting future presidents to two full terms. It was ratified in 1951.

Opposition to the New Deal

Conservative business leaders and politicians in both parties criticized Roosevelt. New Deal programs such as the TVA, they complained, undermined free enterprise. "Creeping socialism" was being substituted for the "rugged individualism" that had made the United States great, they said. They also stated that the constitutional principle of division of powers was threatened by the expanding powers of the federal government. Later, conservatives would note that the Depression did not fully end until the beginning of World War II, and claimed that war ended the Depression.

While conservatives voiced strong opposition to Roosevelt and his programs, radical groups who wanted to do away with free enterprise in part or altogether also targeted him:

- *Alfred E. Smith.* Al Smith was a Roman Catholic Democrat who had run for president against Herbert Hoover. At first, he supported Roosevelt. By 1934, however, Smith had turned against the president and his New Deal and helped form the Liberty League, a conservative antilabor organization.
- *Huey Long.* The most serious challenge to Roosevelt's leadership came from Governor Huey Long of Louisiana. Long called for the rich to give up their fortunes to provide every American family with $5,000. Through this "Share Our Wealth" program, each family would also be guaranteed an annual income of $2,500. (These were considerable sums at the time.) Long was assassinated in 1935.
- *Father Charles Coughlin.* Father Coughlin, a Roman Catholic priest, used **racism** (prejudice and discrimination based on the supposed superiority of some groups over others) to attack the New Deal on national radio. He accused Jews of controlling banks worldwide and of causing the Great Depression. Though false, these charges gained Coughlin some popularity until the Catholic Church removed him from the radio.
- *Dr. Francis Townsend.* A California physician, Dr. Townsend won a following by proposing that the government provide $200 monthly to each unemployed citizen over 60. The recipients would have to spend the money within the same month. Although impractical, Dr. Townsend's plan was a forerunner of Social Security.
- *Radical Reformers.* Norman Thomas, a Socialist, ran for president in 1928, 1932, and 1936. Thomas wanted changes more radical than New Deal reforms, and he thought that such changes could be achieved peacefully, through elections. Communists, who were more extreme, felt that only a violent revolt of the working class would bring about reform.

Support for the New Deal

Defenders of the New Deal argued that Roosevelt had saved democracy and free enterprise. His programs of economic relief had prevented extremists from tearing the nation apart. Moreover, New Deal reforms (Social Security, regulated banking, minimum wages) extended reforms of the Progressive Era. They were intended to avoid some bad effects of capitalism (bank failures, economic insecurity, possible depressions) while preserving good effects (freedom of choice, inventiveness, economic growth). The New Deal firmly established the principle that government must accept responsibility for the well-being of its citizens.

THE ROOSEVELTS: KEEPING THE PEOPLE IN MIND

By 1920, Franklin Roosevelt had become crippled by polio. Nevertheless, he seemed a pillar of strength to many Americans, who drew confidence from his statement (in his "First Inaugural Address") that "... the only thing we have to fear is fear itself...." To explain his New Deal programs to as many as possible and calm their anxieties, he gave regular radio "fireside chats."

President Roosevelt speaks to the nation.

Eleanor Roosevelt

FDR's wife, Eleanor Roosevelt, championed liberal causes. Acting as the president's eyes and ears, she visited areas hard-hit by the Depression. Speaking out boldly on public issues, she came to symbolize the "new woman"—one active in national and world affairs.

New Deal and Women

Women of the 1930s achieved fame in various fields. Amelia Earhart was the first woman to fly a plane across the Atlantic. As secretary of labor, Frances Perkins became the first woman in the Cabinet, administered many New Deal relief programs, and helped abolish child labor.

New Deal and African Americans

"Among American citizens there should be no forgotten man and no forgotten races." This is how Roosevelt expressed his awareness that the government had long neglected African Americans. New Deal programs provided them with what they most needed—jobs.

Roosevelt organized a "Black Cabinet" of distinguished African-American leaders, such as Robert Weaver, an expert on urban housing, and Mary McLeod Bethune, an expert in education.

When the African-American opera singer Marian Anderson was denied the right to perform in a concert space in Washington, D.C., Eleanor

Roosevelt invited her to sing at the Lincoln Memorial. Such gestures led thousands of African Americans to become Democrats.

The Roosevelts' personal sympathies did not wipe out racism and discrimination. The industrial codes of the NRA allowed white workers higher wages than black ones. Moreover, TVA administrators were far more likely to hire whites than African Americans.

Indian Reorganization Act

In 1934, Congress passed the *Indian Reorganization Act* in an effort to improve the status of Native Americans. The government stressed tribal over individual ownership of reservation land and encouraged the preservation of Native-American culture. Reservation schools began to stress scientific farming. Nevertheless, by 1941 Native Americans were still desperately poor and had few job opportunities on or away from the reservations.

CULTURE OF THE DEPRESSION

During the 1930s and 1940s, the novelist William Faulkner created characters who exemplified social tensions in Southern society. So did the playwright Lillian Hellman, who, in addition, treated both domestic and international social issues of the time.

The Great Depression inspired John Steinbeck to depict American people's struggles against hardship. His novel *The Grapes of Wrath* (1939) creates an unforgettable picture of Oklahoma sharecroppers ("Okies"), who set out for the fruit orchards of California. Steinbeck's novel shows these people pitted against cruel and impersonal economic forces.

The WPA hired writers, artists, actors, and musicians to write, paint, and perform. One historical WPA project involved interviews with former slaves and the children of slaves in order to better document slavery in America.

The "hot jazz" of the Roaring Twenties gave way to the "swing" of the 1930s. Band leaders such as Glenn Miller led white musicians playing music mostly by white composers. But Benny Goodman's band included such great African-American musicians as vibraphonist Lionel Hampton and pianist Teddy Wilson.

During this period, however, most bands were segregated. The bands of Cab Calloway, Duke Ellington, and Count Basie played music by African-American composers.

Popular Culture

During the Depression, movies became more popular than ever. For a few cents, people could escape from their troubles and watch stars such as Shirley

Temple, Clark Gable, James Stewart, and Judy Garland perform in a make-believe world of romance and opulence. Such hits as *The Wizard of Oz* (1939) satisfied people's needs for both fantasy and fun. Other classics of the time treated serious social themes.

Comic books first appeared in the United States in the 1930s. *Superman* paved the way for *Batman, Captain Marvel, Wonder Woman*, and *Spider-Man.*

IN REVIEW

1. Explain how *each* of the following New Deal acts or programs contributed to relief, recovery, or reform: (a) Emergency Banking Act, (b) Federal Emergency Relief Act, (c) Works Progress Administration, (d) Public Works Administration, (e) Civilian Conservation Corps, (f) National Recovery Administration, (g) Home Owners' Loan Corporation, (h) Federal Housing Administration, (i) Agricultural Adjustment acts, (j) Federal Deposit Insurance Corporation, (k) Securities and Exchange Commission, (l) Social Security Act, (m) National Labor Relations Board, (n) Fair Labor Standards Act, (o) Tennessee Valley Authority.
2. Summarize the effects of the Great Depression and the New Deal on (a) labor unions, (b) women, (c) African Americans, (d) Native Americans.
3. Describe the programs of *three* opponents of the New Deal. Why were these ideas popular?

CHAPTER REVIEW

MULTIPLE-CHOICE QUESTIONS

1 Which combination of factors contributed most to the start of the Great Depression of the 1930s?
(1) immigration restrictions and a lack of skilled workers
(2) high taxes and overspending on social welfare programs
(3) United States war debts and the declining value of the dollar
(4) overproduction and the excessive use of credit

2 "Europeans can't buy goods from Americans because Europeans can't sell goods in the American market. Obviously, they don't have the chance to earn the money they need to buy our goods."

This statement focuses on which cause of the Great Depression?
(1) restriction of credit by banks
(2) high protective tariffs
(3) low wages of American workers
(4) overspeculation on the stock market

3 President Franklin D. Roosevelt believed that declaring a bank holiday and creating the Federal Deposit Insurance Corporation (FDIC) would help the nation's banking system by
(1) restoring public confidence in the banks
(2) reducing government regulation of banks
(3) restricting foreign investments
(4) granting tax relief to individuals

4 During the New Deal, the Federal Government attempted to improve conditions for farmers by
(1) ending the practice of sharecropping
(2) supporting the formation of farm-worker unions
(3) raising tariffs on farm imports
(4) paying farmers to take land out of production

5 The National Labor Relations Act of 1935 (Wagner Act) affected workers by
(1) protecting their right to form unions and bargain collectively
(2) preventing public employee unions from going on strike
(3) providing federal pensions for retired workers
(4) forbidding racial discrimination in employment

Base your answers to questions 6 and 7 on the cartoon below and on your knowledge of social studies.

"The Spirit of '37": FDR berating the Supreme Court for opposing the New Deal

6 What is the main idea of this cartoon?
(1) The legislative branch disagreed with the executive branch during the presidency of Franklin D. Roosevelt.
(2) President Franklin D. Roosevelt wanted the Supreme Court to support his programs.
(3) Justices of the Supreme Court were not asked for their opinion about New Deal programs.
(4) The three branches of government agreed on the correct response to the Great Depression.

7 President Roosevelt responded to the situation illustrated in the cartoon by
(1) calling for repeal of many New Deal programs
(2) demanding popular election of members of the judicial branch
(3) asking voters to elect more Democrats to Congress
(4) proposing to increase the number of justices on the Supreme Court

8 In 1944, Franklin D. Roosevelt was elected to a fourth term as President. Which action was taken to prevent future Presidents from breaking the two-term tradition?
(1) Both major political parties agreed to nominate a new candidate for President after an incumbent's second term.
(2) A constitutional amendment was adopted, placing term limits on the Presidency.
(3) The Supreme Court ruled that a President could serve for only eight years.
(4) An unwritten agreement was made by Presidential candidates that they would serve for no more than two terms.

9 A lasting effect of the New Deal has been a belief that government should
(1) own the principal means of producing goods and services
(2) allow natural market forces to determine economic conditions
(3) maintain a balanced federal budget during hard economic times
(4) assume responsibility for the well-being of its citizens

10 Critics charged that New Deal policies favored socialism because the federal government
(1) took ownership of most major industries
(2) favored farmers over workers and business owners
(3) increased its responsibility for the welfare of the economy
(4) declined to prosecute business monopolies

THEMATIC ESSAYS

1 **THEME:** *Causes of the Great Depression.* The 1920s business boom masked weaknesses in the economy that ultimately helped trigger the Great Depression.

TASK: Complete *both* of the following tasks:
- Choose *two* areas of economic weakness during the 1920s. Show how *each* weakness helped lead the United States into the Great Depression.
- Describe how developing world interdependence after World War I helped make the Great Depression a global crisis.

You may wish to select economic weaknesses such as overproduction, easy credit, and the unequal distribution of wealth.

A discussion of international trade and banking may help illustrate how the Great Depression grew to worldwide proportions.

2 **THEME:** *New Deal.* Roosevelt's New Deal was marked by dramatic action by the federal government to fight the ravages of the Great Depression.

TASK: Select *two* New Deal programs. For *each* one:
- describe the problem that it was designed to correct
- evaluate its effectiveness.

You may include programs dealing with banking, labor, the stock market, or any other aspect of the economy.

3 **THEME:** *New Deal and Constitutional Issues.* Although the New Deal did much to counter effects of the Great Depression, it was constitutionally controversial.

TASK: Choose *two* ways in which the New Deal caused controversy. For *each* one:
- describe the controversy
- explain how it was resolved.

Areas to consider may involve checks and balances, federalism, presidential power, and the proper role of government.

DOCUMENT-BASED QUESTIONS

*Study each document and answer the question that follows it. Then read the **Task** and write your essay. Include references to most of the documents and additional information you retain about U.S. history and government.*

HISTORICAL CONTEXT: The 1932 presidential election entailed a fundamental disagreement over the degree of federal involvement proper to solve the severe problems of the Depression.

DOCUMENT 1: From a speech by President Hoover at Madison Square Garden, New York City, October 31, 1932:

> . . . you can not extend the master of government over the daily lives of a people . . . making it master of . . . souls and thoughts.
>
> Expansion of government in business means that . . . to protect itself from the political consequences of its errors [government] is driven . . . to greater and greater control of . . . press and platform. Free speech does not live many hours after free industry and free commerce die. . . .
>
> Even if [government's] conduct of business could give us . . . maximum . . . instead of least efficiency, it would be purchased at the cost of freedom.

QUESTION: Why did Hoover choose to avoid most direct federal involvement with private business during the Depression?

DOCUMENT 2: Refer to the photograph below.

"Hooverville" in Washington, D.C.

QUESTION: Why did people call the settlement shown in the photo a "Hooverville"?

DOCUMENT 3: From President Roosevelt's "First Inaugural Address," March 4, 1933:

> . . . Plenty is at our doorsteps, but a generous use of it languishes in the very sight of the supply. . . .
>
> . . . Our greatest primary task is to put people to work. . . . It can be accomplished in part by direct recruiting by the government itself, treating the test as we would treat the emergency of a war, but at the same time, through this employment, accomplishing greatly needed projects to stimulate and reorganize the use of our national resources.

QUESTION: How did Roosevelt propose to fight the unemployment caused by the Depression?

TASK: Using the documents and your knowledge of U.S. history and government, write an essay in which you:

- describe the differing philosophies of President Herbert Hoover and his presidential challenger in 1932, Franklin D. Roosevelt.
- explain why Roosevelt won the election of 1932 by an overwhelming majority of the popular vote.

UNIT V
The United States in an Age of Global Crises

CHAPTER 14
Peace in Peril: 1933–1950

DOCUMENTS AND LAWS
U.S. Neutrality Acts (1935–1939) • Destroyers-for-Bases Agreement (1940)
Atlantic Charter (1941) • Lend-Lease Act (1941) • Executive Order 9066 (1942)
Korematsu v. *United States* (1944) • Taft-Hartley Act (1947)

EVENTS
Japanese invasions of Manchuria and China (1931–1937)
Italian invasion of Ethiopia (1935–1936) • German invasion of Rhineland (1936)
Spanish Civil War (1936–1939)
German annexation of Austria, Czechoslovakia, and Poland (1938–1939)
Holocaust (1941–1945) • Japanese attack on Pearl Harbor (1941)
Allied invasion of Normandy (1944) • Germany's unconditional surrender (1945)
Atomic bombings of Hiroshima and Nagasaki (1945) • Nuremberg Trials (1945–1946)

PEOPLE/GROUPS
Winston Churchill • Thomas E. Dewey • Dixiecrats • Albert Einstein • Dwight D. Eisenhower
Fascists • Adolf Hitler • Douglas MacArthur • Benito Mussolini • Republicans (Spanish)
Hideki Tojo • Harry S. Truman • Strom Thurmond • Henry Wallace

OBJECTIVES

- To review U.S. isolationism and assess its impact on foreign policy in the 1930s.
- To recognize how military aggression increasingly threatened U.S. security before 1941.
- To examine the impact of World War II on various groups.
- To summarize U.S. military participation in World War II.
- To analyze the impact of World War II on domestic policy.

Isolationism and Neutrality

Traditional U.S. policy toward Europe had been isolationism and neutrality. When World War I began in 1914, for example, Wilson's first move was to proclaim U.S. neutrality. Among other factors, German submarine attacks on American shipping forced him—reluctantly—to ask for a declaration of war. Wilson became an internationalist in the effort to win public approval for the League of Nations.

The Senate, however, reverted to a policy of isolationism and rejected the League. Tired of international politics and disillusioned with war, most Americans in the 1920s agreed. Pacifists in particular disapproved of military buildups and support for **belligerents** (nations involved in war).

Rise of Dictatorships

A type of government called **fascism** glorifies war, preaches extreme nationalism, and calls for obedience to an all-powerful dictator. In Italy, the Fascist Party, led by Benito Mussolini, seized power in 1922. Anyone who criticized Mussolini's regime was at risk.

The Treaty of Versailles imposed crushing reparations on Germany, took from it the Saar Valley with its profitable coal mines, and made Germany accept complete responsibility for World War I. Germany, its pride wounded, also faced economic ruin.

Adolf Hitler, leader of the fascistic Nazi Party, turned German rage and frustration against the Jews. After being legally appointed chancellor (prime minister) of Germany in 1933, Hitler illegally seized absolute power and became a dictator.

Hitler (left) and Nazi troops in Berlin

Neutrality Acts of 1935–1937

U.S. Neutrality Acts, intended to avoid the policies that had drawn the United States into World War I, included the following:

- no sale or shipment of arms to belligerents
- no loans or credits to belligerents
- no travel by U.S. citizens on belligerents' ships
- the purchase of nonmilitary goods by belligerents to be paid in cash and transported in their ships—the **cash-and-carry** principle (sell to whomever pays the money).

Spanish Civil War

Beginning in 1936, *Fascists* in Spain tried to overthrow the Republican government. The Soviet Union sent military support to the *Republicans*, while Germany and Italy aided the Fascists.

For Germany and Italy, the civil war was a testing ground for new weapons—tanks and airplanes. The Republicans, including some Communists and Socialists, also looked to Western democracies for help. An American volunteer unit, the Abraham Lincoln Brigade, answered the call. Soviet assistance and volunteer fighters, however, were no match for the new German-supplied weapons. In 1939, Spain fell to fascism.

FDR's "Quarantine" Speech

President Franklin Roosevelt was concerned about aggression by Germany, Italy, Fascist Spain, and Japan. After Japan invaded China in 1937, Roosevelt gave his "Quarantine" speech, proposing that democratic nations "quarantine" aggressors to "protect the health of the [international] community against the spread of the disease." Isolationists warned about possible U.S. involvement in a war. Polls showed that most Americans agreed with them, and Roosevelt gave no direct assistance to Europe's democracies.

Triumph of Aggression

The timid policies of the democracies led to the triumph of aggression and the failure of peace efforts.

Germany, Japan, Italy (1932–1940) Hitler violated the Treaty of Versailles by ordering German troops into the demilitarized Rhineland (1936). In 1938, Germany invaded Austria, and Hitler announced his intention of seizing Czechoslovakia's Sudetenland, where many Germans lived.

Meanwhile, Mussolini sent Italian troops to conquer Ethiopia in Africa. It fell in 1936.

The military leaders dominating Japan's government used similar methods. Japanese troops marched into Manchuria in 1931 and invaded China's heartland in 1937.

Munich Conference **Appeasement** is the policy of yielding to an aggressor's demands in order to avoid armed conflict. In 1938, British and French leaders applied this policy at the Munich Conference, where they gave in to Hitler's annexation of the Sudetenland. Hitler claimed that this was the last act of expansionism he would make.

A few months later, Germany occupied all of Czechoslovakia and threatened Poland. By 1939, it was clear that Hitler could be stopped only by force.

Start of World War II

In September 1939, Germany invaded Poland in a swift advance of troops, tanks, and planes called a **blitzkrieg**. Britain and France declared war on Germany.

"The Other Road"
from *Straight Herblock* (Simon & Schuster, 1964)

During the first two years of World War II (1939–1941), Britain, France, and their allies suffered a series of defeats. Germany forced the surrender of Poland in 30 days. Its armies then swept over Denmark and Norway. France fell to the Nazis in June 1940.

In 1939, Soviet leader Joseph Stalin had signed a prewar nonaggression pact with Hitler—a pledge that if war broke out, the two countries would not attack each other. With France beaten and the Soviet Union uninvolved, Britain alone had to try and stop Germany and Italy from conquering the rest of Europe. Planning an invasion of England in September 1940, Hitler ordered the heavy bombing of British cities to weaken them. The British RAF (air force) downed so many German planes that Hitler called off the invasion.

Gradual U.S. Involvement

With the outbreak of war and early German successes, Americans began to understand that a German victory in Europe would threaten U.S. security.

Neutrality Act of 1939 In 1939, Roosevelt persuaded Congress to pass a new Neutrality Act. U.S. war supplies could now be sold to belligerents under the cash-and-carry principle.

Destroyers Deal/Lend-Lease Roosevelt gave Britain 50 U.S. destroyers to use against submarines. In exchange, Britain gave the United States eight naval and air bases in North and South America. The exchange was called the *Destroyers-for-Bases Agreement* (1940).

But Britain needed more supplies than could be obtained by cash-and-carry. Roosevelt persuaded Congress to authorize the lending of war materials to Britain. The 1941 *Lend-Lease Act* ended U.S. neutrality. Although not yet at war, the United States had committed huge economic resources to fighting Germany and had become what Roosevelt called the "arsenal of democracy."

Atlantic Charter In 1940, Roosevelt had been reelected to a third term in good part because there was a war going on in Europe. In August 1941, Roosevelt and the British prime minister, Winston Churchill, met aboard a ship near Newfoundland to formulate the *Atlantic Charter*, with the following aims:

- the right of all nations to self-determination
- neither the United States nor Britain would seek territory from the war
- **disarmament** (removal of weapons) of aggressor nations
- "a permanent system of general security" in the future.

IN REVIEW

1. Define and explain isolationism, fascism, appeasement, Neutrality Acts, "Quarantine" speech, Lend-Lease Act, and Atlantic Charter.
2. Give *one* example of aggression committed in the 1930s by (a) Germany, (b) Italy, and (c) Japan.
3. Describe the causes that led to a change in U.S. policy from isolationism in 1939 to involvement in 1940 and 1941.

United States in World War II

Throughout the 1930s, the United States viewed Japanese aggressions in China as violations of the Open Door Policy (discussed on page 187). In 1940, the United States placed an embargo on those U.S. exports to Japan that had helped it maintain its war machine—oil, aviation gasoline, scrap iron, and steel.

By 1941, Japanese leaders believed that U.S. entry into the war might block their planned invasion of Indonesia. Therefore, they decided to launch a surprise attack on the U.S. Pacific fleet.

On December 7, 1941, Japanese planes bombed the U.S. naval base at Pearl Harbor, Hawaii, sinking 19 ships, destroying 150 planes, and killing 2,335 soldiers and sailors.

The next day, President Roosevelt, calling December 7 "a date which will live in infamy," asked a willing Congress to declare war on Japan. Germany and Italy then declared war on the United States. The American people abandoned isolationism and rallied to the war effort.

Human Dimensions

"Arsenal of Democracy" Allied hopes for victory depended largely on how fast U.S. factories could turn out war goods. Government officials encouraged every industry to stop production of consumer goods and retool for ships, planes, bombs, bullets, and other military supplies.

Role of Women As young men entered the armed forces, women became the chief producers of ships, aircraft, and other war supplies. The number of women in the labor force went from about 15 million in 1941 to about 19 million in 1945.

"Rosie the Riveter Steps Out" in defiance of her traditional role as homemaker

Women also enlisted in support (but not in combat) units of the armed services. Many retired workers, too old for armed service, returned to industrial work. When the war came to an end, many women and retirees would be replaced by returning servicemen.

Mobilization Congress enacted a draft (selective service) law in 1940. Every man between 21 and 35 was required to register for possible service. By 1945, some 12.5 million men and women—about one out of three of those eligible—were in uniform.

More than a million African Americans served, about half of them overseas. Hopes for equal treatment were again dashed when they were placed in segregated units. Many black civilians held relatively high-paying jobs in Northern defense plants. Such opportunities greatly increased African-American migration from the South.

Financing the War As spending on the war effort rose to billions of dollars, the government debt grew daily, and people were encouraged to buy war bonds. This action raised money for the war effort but increased the national debt. Hollywood stars promoted bond sales nationwide. Popular entertainers such as Bob Hope organized shows that took movie and recording stars around the globe to entertain U.S. soldiers.

Rationing As industry shifted from consumer to wartime production, clothing, sugar, meat, rubber, gasoline, and other goods became scarce and were subject to **rationing**. Americans received coupon books that limited their purchases of a rationed item. The *Office of Price Administration* made sure that retail prices of scarce products did not exceed allowable limits and cause inflation.

Military Service Those in the service were sent far from home and often lived in regulated, sometimes harsh, conditions. Those in battle faced death at every turn. The death of friends and the obligation to kill an enemy often caused severe psychological problems. The wounded were often disabled for life. For some, adjustment to military life was difficult. Most in the services, however, understood that they were in a war to save democracy.

Allied Strategy and Leadership

Assistance to the Soviet Union In June 1941, Hitler broke his nonaggression pact with Stalin by making a massive assault against the Soviet Union. In response, the United States provided military aid to the Soviets and followed it up with Lend-Lease assistance of U.S. military equipment.

Europe First Despite Japan's attack on Pearl Harbor, the Allies' strategy was to defeat Nazi Germany first. They took more than three years to win back the territories taken by Germany and Italy in the first two years of war.

After initial successes, the Germans in the Soviet Union suffered a crushing defeat at Stalingrad (1942–1943). In the North African desert,

World War II in Europe, 1943–1945

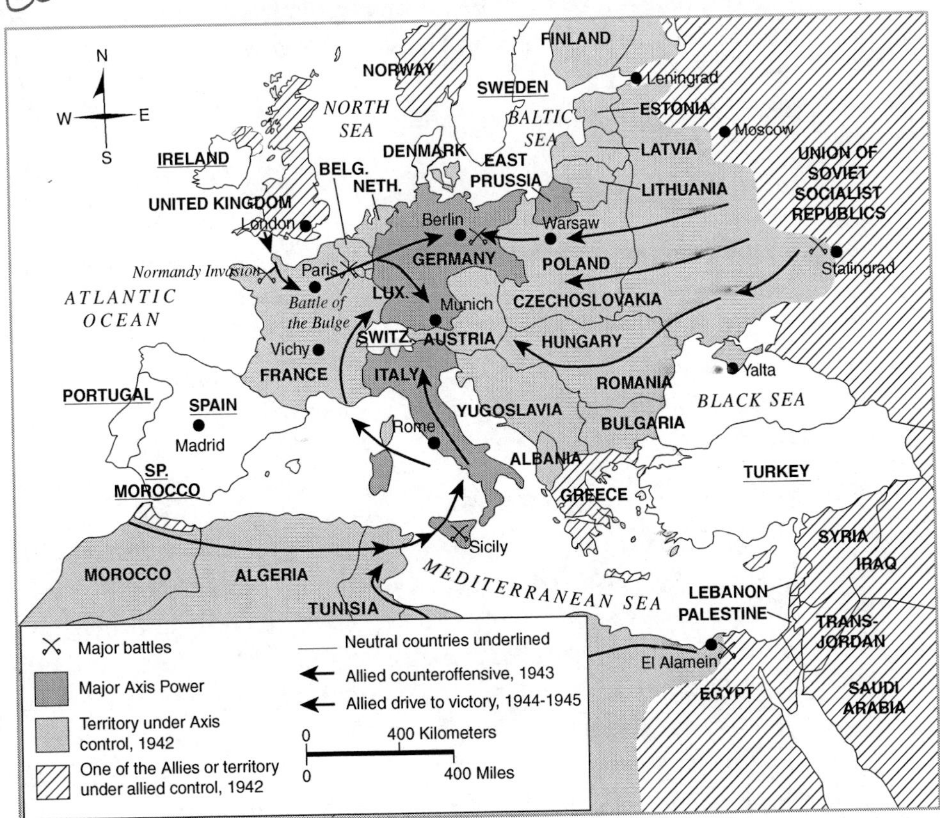

the British defeated the Germans at El Alamein (1942). In 1943, combined assaults by the British and Americans forced the surrender of Germany's North African army. From their African bases, the Allies invaded Sicily and began a long campaign to liberate Italy.

On June 6, 1944 (code name: *D-day*), the Allies began the liberation of France and thereby opened up a new front—the Western Front. The largest *amphibious* (sea-to-land) force in history crossed the English Channel to secure beachheads on the coast of Normandy (in northern France). From these strongholds, General Dwight D. Eisenhower, Supreme Allied Commander in Western Europe, led the fight to control Normandy and then all of France. Paris was liberated in August, and the push to Germany began.

Soviet troops also moved rapidly toward Germany and its capital, Berlin, from the other direction. In April 1945, U.S. and Soviet troops met on German soil. With the end near, Hitler committed suicide, and Germany surrendered unconditionally on May 7, 1945 (*V-E day*), ending the war in Europe.

Two-Front War By 1942, Japan had occupied much of Asia and the islands of the South Pacific. Forced by Japan's successes to fight a two-front war, U.S. leaders developed a Pacific strategy known as **island hopping**. U.S. forces concentrated on winning back only those islands that put them within striking distance of Japan. The Americans defeated the Japanese in several major battles. A turning point in the war at sea was the U.S. victory at Midway (1942). Although battles raged in both Europe and Asia, the United States was protected by its geographic location.

Atomic Bomb

Manhattan Project When Hitler initiated a program to exterminate Jewish citizens, the great German-Jewish scientist Albert Einstein, among others, fled to the United States. Einstein advised Roosevelt to develop an atomic bomb before Germany could do so. Roosevelt committed funds to the *Manhattan Project* (code name for the project to develop an atomic bomb) in Los Alamos, New Mexico.

Decision to Use the Bomb President Roosevelt died in 1945. His successor, Harry S. Truman, planned on achieving final victory by an invasion of Japan. Persuaded that an invasion might result in the deaths of hundreds of thousands of American soldiers, Truman chose another option—to save American lives by using the atomic bomb. His decision knowingly condemned thousands of Japanese civilians to death, but he reasoned that the bomb's very destructiveness would force a Japanese surrender.

On August 6, 1945, a U.S. plane dropped an atomic bomb on Hiroshima. Three days later, a second bomb fell on Nagasaki. The two explosions

World War II in the Pacific, 1941–1945

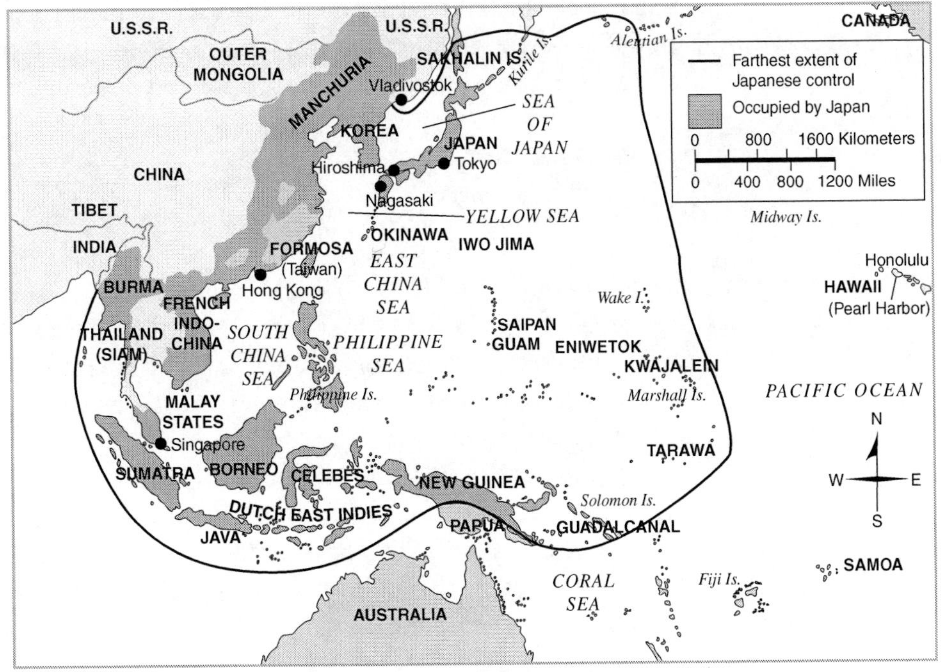

instantly killed more than 100,000 Japanese. (Many thousands of others died later from effects of nuclear radiation.) Japan surrendered immediately. Thus, ended the most destructive war in history. The total death toll for all nations was 17 million military deaths and probably more than twice that number of civilian deaths. The U.S. death toll was about 600,000.

Was the United States justified in dropping the bombs?

- Although more than 100,000 people died from the atomic explosions, many times that number (including Japanese civilians and soldiers) might have died during a U.S. invasion.
- Instead of dropping atomic bombs on civilian targets, the United States could have demonstrated the new weapons' power by dropping them over the ocean close to Japan.
- The United States dropped a bomb on Nagasaki less than a week after the first drop on Hiroshima. It could have waited a little longer for a Japanese surrender.

U.S. Occupation of Japan

General Douglas MacArthur, Supreme Commander of the U.S. forces occupying Japan in 1945, was responsible for (1) demilitarizing the country (making it incapable of waging war) and (2) democratizing it. He supervised adoption of a new constitution (1947) that took away all power from the emperor, guaranteed free elections and a representative government, banned a Japanese army and navy, and declared Japan averse to war forever. Millions of dollars were spent rebuilding Japan's economy. By 1955, it was a prosperous nation closely allied with the Western democracies.

War's Impact on Minorities

Japanese Americans Thousands of Japanese Americans served loyally in the U.S. armed forces. Even so, Roosevelt yielded to nativist prejudice by signing *Executive Order 9066* (1942), which mandated the forced removal of 110,000 Japanese Americans from their homes in California and other Western states to barbed-wire "relocation centers." Most were released before the war's end, but about 18,000 suspected of disloyalty were kept in a California relocation center until Japan surrendered.

In spite of this harsh violation of Japanese-American civil rights, the Supreme Court, in *Korematsu* v. *United States* (1944), ruled that the removal was justified by military necessity and national security. In recent years, Japanese Americans thus mistreated have received formal apologies from the government and some financial compensation.

Segregation in the Military Segregation of African Americans in the armed forces did not end until after World War II.

Holocaust

As U.S. troops moved across Germany, they came upon concentration camps whose inmates, mainly European Jews, had barely survived Hitler's policy of **genocide** (extermination of an entire people). The Nazis had captured Jews in occupied European countries and murdered them or worked them to death in such camps. About six million Jews were killed in the **Holocaust**, the systematic Nazi slaughter of Jews. About the same number of other peoples—Slavs, Gypsies, political prisoners, handicapped individuals, and gays—were also exterminated in the camps.

Many Jews fleeing the Nazis tried to enter the United States. About 175,000 were accepted, but hundreds of thousands more were rejected although the immigration quota for Germany remained unfilled.

Adjusting to Peace

From November 1945 to October 1946, a unique trial took place in Nuremberg, Germany. The defendants were former Nazi military and political leaders accused of war crimes, especially the mass murders of Jews. Judges at this first *Nuremberg Trial* represented the Allies. Of 24 defendants, 19 were convicted and 10 of them executed. These decisions established the precedent that national leaders could be held responsible for "crimes against humanity."

Thus, at war crimes trials held in Japan, seven Japanese officers, including wartime leader Hideki Tojo, were sentenced to execution.

Demobilization

U.S. **demobilization** (reduction of armed forces in peacetime) proceeded rapidly. In just two years, 11 million soldiers were released from service.

Inflation and Strikes

During the war, the government had tried to prevent inflation by imposing price controls to regulate what businesses could charge for products. After the war, such goods as cars, gasoline, and rubber products were once more available, and consumers were eager to buy them. Most businesses wanted the controls removed. Reluctantly, President Truman complied. Without controls, prices increased by 25 percent from mid-1945 to mid-1946.

Businesses raised prices but not wages. Thus, one union after another struck for higher pay. Strikes in the steel, automobile, coal, and railroad industries threatened to cripple the economy. In response to a 1946 coal strike, Truman, otherwise a friend to labor; threatened to order U.S. troops

Military and Civilian Deaths in World War II

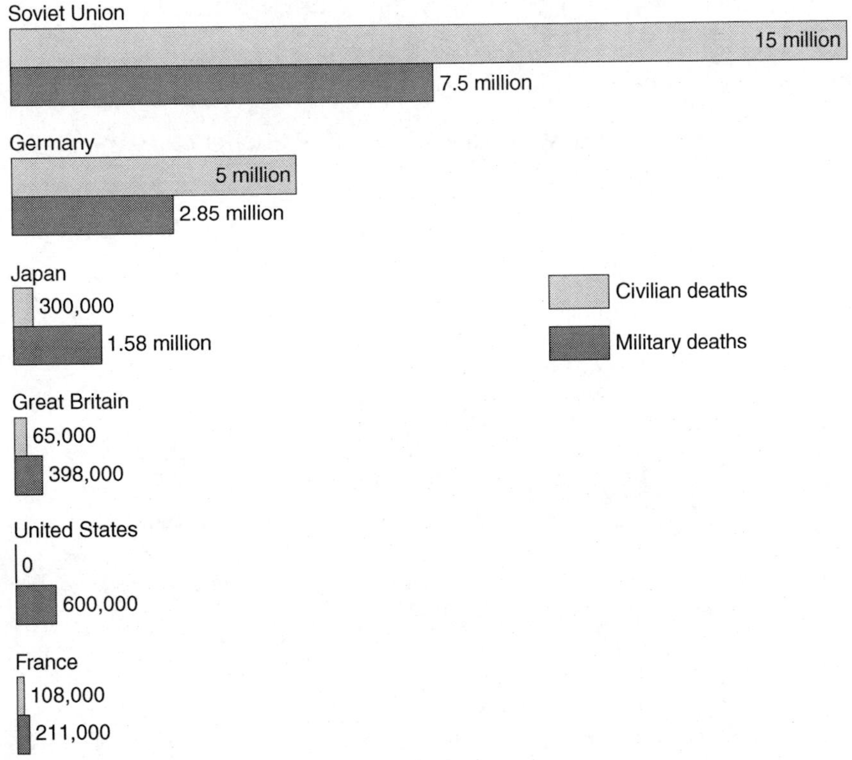

to operate the mines, and he also proposed drafting striking railroad workers and ordering them to work the trains as soldiers. Both strikes were settled without these actions.

GI Bill of Rights

In 1944, Congress enacted a measure known as the *GI Bill of Rights.* It entitled veterans to free hospital care, grants and loans for college, and guaranteed loans for buying homes and investing in businesses. The law also gave a boost to colleges, universities, and the housing industry.

Truman's Fair Deal

As vice president, Truman succeeded Roosevelt, who died in 1945. Truman was elected president in his own right in 1948. Truman's domestic program, known as the *Fair Deal,* added to the reform ideas of the New Deal.

Partisan Problems With Congress

The war years had been characterized by **bipartisanship** (two parties acting together for the national good). During Truman's presidency, however, Republicans and Democrats were again at odds over almost every domestic issue.

Congress passed some parts of the Fair Deal while rejecting others. It approved the following measures:

- an increase in the minimum wage from 40 to 75 cents an hour
- an extension of Social Security benefits to 10 million people not originally covered
- funds for low-income housing and slum clearance
- increased funds for flood control, irrigation projects, and electrical-power projects.

Congress rejected the following measures:

- national health insurance
- federal aid to education
- legal protection of African-American civil rights.

Over Truman's veto, the Republican-controlled Congress enacted the *Taft-Hartley Act* (1947). Designed to limit the power of unions, it provided for the following:

- Union leaders had to sign loyalty oaths that they were not Communists and did not advocate violent overthrow of the government.

- A labor union could no longer demand a **closed shop**, one in which an employer can hire only dues-paying members of one union.
- A labor union could not conduct a **secondary boycott**, by which strikers refuse to buy products from companies doing business with their employer.
- An employer could sue a union for **breach of contract** (failure to carry out a contract's terms).
- The president could call for an 80-day "cooling-off" period to delay a strike that threatened the economy or national security.

Upset Election of 1948

In the 1948 presidential election, Truman faced opposition within his own party. A liberal group of Democrats led by former Vice President Henry Wallace thought Truman's foreign policy was too tough on the Soviets. The conservative *Dixiecrats,* led by Governor Strom Thurmond of South Carolina, objected to Truman's support of civil rights for African Americans. Polls showed that the Republican candidate, Governor Thomas E. Dewey of New York, was far ahead of Truman. However, Truman's energetic campaign and the strong support of labor unions, farmers, and minorities carried him to victory in a close election.

Truman and Civil Rights

Continued Difficulties for Minorities Conditions remained difficult for African Americans. In the South, schools were segregated by law (***de jure* segregation**). In the North, housing patterns, not law, often imposed segregation in schools (***de facto* segregation**).

Truman's Policy Truman recognized that a democracy cannot deny fundamental rights to a large group of citizens. One of his first acts as president was to issue an executive order to end segregation in the armed forces. He also established a *Fair Employment Board* to ensure African Americans equal opportunity to hold civil service jobs.

Truman urged Congress to enact laws to abolish poll taxes and punish those guilty of lynching African Americans. Congress refused to enact such laws, but Truman's stance paved the way for civil rights laws adopted later in the 1950s and 1960s.

IN REVIEW

1. Identify *each* of the following and give its significance: (a) Pearl Harbor, (b) "arsenal of democracy," (c) D-day, (d) "island hopping," (e) Manhattan Project, (f) *Korematsu* v. *United States,* (g) Holocaust, (h) Nuremberg Trials, (i) GI Bill of Rights, (j) Fair Deal, (k) Taft-Hartley Act.

2. How did the need to wage total war alter the nature of American society?
3. Describe how *each* of the following were moral issues arising from the war experience: (a) integration of the armed forces, (b) nuclear warfare, (c) Japanese Americans' civil rights, (d) Holocaust, and (e) war crimes trials.

CHAPTER REVIEW

MULTIPLE-CHOICE QUESTIONS

Base your answers to questions 1 and 2 on the cartoon below and on your knowledge of social studies.

Ho Hum! No Chance of Contagion.

Source: *PM*, May 15, 1941 (adapted)

1 In the cartoon, most of the "diseases" refer to the
(1) military dictatorships of the 1930s
(2) Allied powers of World War II
(3) nations banned from the United Nations after World War II
(4) Communist bloc countries in the Cold War

2 Which action is most closely associated with the situation shown in the cartoon?
(1) signing of the Atlantic Charter
(2) passage of the Neutrality Acts of 1935–1937
(3) first fireside chat of Franklin D. Roosevelt
(4) declaration of war on Japan

3 The policy of Cash and Carry, the Destroyers for Naval Bases Deal, and the Lend-Lease Act were all designed to
(1) contribute to the success of the Axis powers
(2) relieve unemployment caused by the Great Depression
(3) guarantee a third term to President Franklin D. Roosevelt
(4) aid the Allies without involving the United States in war

4 Which change in American society occurred during World War II?
(1) African Americans were granted equality in the armed forces.
(2) Women were allowed to enter combat units for the first time.
(3) Congress enacted the first military draft.
(4) Women replaced men in essential wartime industries.

5 Rationing was used in the United States during World War II as a way to
(1) ensure adequate supplies of scarce natural resources
(2) increase the number of imports
(3) raise production of consumer goods
(4) provide markets for American-made products

6 To help pay for World War II, the United States government relied heavily on the
(1) money borrowed from foreign governments
(2) sale of war bonds
(3) sale of United States manufactured goods to neutral nations
(4) printing of additional paper money

7 President Harry Truman's decision to use atomic bombs against Japan was primarily based on his belief that
(1) an invasion of Japan would result in excessive casualties
(2) Germany would refuse to surrender in Europe
(3) an alliance was developing between Japan and the Soviet Union
(4) Japan was in the process of developing its own atomic weapons

8 "...The Director of the War Relocation Authority is authorized and directed to formulate and effectuate [implement] a program for the removal, from the areas designated from time to time by the Secretary of War or appropriate military commander under the authority of Executive Order No. 9066 of February 19, 1942, of the persons or classes of persons designated under such Executive Order, and for their relocation, maintenance, and supervision...."

—EXECUTIVE ORDER 9102, MARCH 18, 1942

Shortly after this executive order was signed, federal government authorities began to
(1) move Japanese Americans to internment camps
(2) deport German and Italian aliens
(3) detain and interrogate Chinese immigrants
(4) arrest the individuals who planned the attack on Pearl Harbor

Base your answer to question 9 on the following quotation and on your knowledge of social studies.

Korematsu was not excluded from the military area because of hostility to him or his race. He was excluded because we are at war with the Japanese Empire, because the...authorities feared an invasion of our West Coast and felt constrained to take proper security measures.

—JUSTICE HUGO BLACK, *KOREMATSU* v. *UNITED STATES*, 1944

9 Which generalization is supported by this quotation?
(1) Individual rights need to be maintained in national emergencies.
(2) The Supreme Court lacks the power to block presidential actions taken during wartime.
(3) Individual rights can be restricted under certain circumstances.
(4) Only the Supreme Court can alter the constitutional rights of American citizens.

10 In 1948, President Harry Truman showed his support for civil rights by issuing an executive order to
(1) end the immigration quota system
(2) assure equal status for women in military service
(3) ban racial segregation in the military
(4) guarantee jobs for Native American Indians

THEMATIC ESSAYS

1 **THEME:** *Fighting World War II: War Experience and Morality.* The experience of fighting World War II made Americans face a number of moral issues.

TASK: Select *two* moral issues that World War II brought into focus. For *each* issue:
- show how World War II made the issue a major moral question
- describe the decision that was made to deal with the issue and the explanation given for reaching that decision.

You may wish to consider use of atomic weapons, trying war criminals, and the conflict between national security and Japanese Americans' rights.

2 **THEME:** *The United States and the Coming of World War II.* Necessity demanded that the U.S. government under President Roosevelt practice neutrality while, in fact, assisting the British and preparing for its own entry into the war.

TASK: *Specifically* describe how the U.S. government practiced neutrality while preparing itself for and becoming involved in World War II. You may wish to include the Neutrality Acts, Lend-Lease, public opinion, and the Atlantic Charter.

DOCUMENT-BASED QUESTION

*Study each document and answer the question that follows it. Then read the **Task** and write your essay. Include references to most of the documents and additional information you retain about U.S. history and government.*

HISTORICAL CONTEXT: Opening hostilities of World War II forced the United States to decide whether to aid the democratic nations fighting the forces of dictatorship, oppression, and militarism.

DOCUMENT 1: From the agreement forming the Rome-Berlin-Tokyo Axis, 1940:

> The governments of Germany, Italy, and Japan consider it a condition precedent of a lasting peace, that each nation of the world be given its own proper place....
>
> ARTICLE 1. Japan recognizes and respects the leadership of Germany and Italy in the establishment of a new order in Europe.
>
> ARTICLE 2. Germany and Italy recognize and respect the leadership of Japan in the establishment of a new order in Greater East Asia.
>
> ARTICLE 3. Germany, Italy, and Japan agree to cooperate... on the aforesaid basis [and] assist one another with all political, economic, and social means, if one of the three Contracting Parties is attacked by a Power at present not involved in the European war or in the Chinese-Japanese conflict.

QUESTION: Why was Roosevelt concerned about the German-Italian-Japanese agreement?

DOCUMENT 2: From an address by President Roosevelt, 1941:

> Suppose my neighbor's home catches fire, and I have a length of garden hose four or five hundred feet away. If he can take my garden hose and connect it up with his hydrant, I may help him to put out his fire. Now, what do I do? I don't say to him before that operation, "Neighbor, my garden hose cost me $15; you have got to pay me $15 for it".... I don't want $15—I want my garden hose back after the fire is over.... If it goes through the fire all right,... he gives it back to me.... But suppose it gets smashed up .... He says, "All right, I will replace it." Now, if I get a nice garden hose back, I am in pretty good shape.
>
> In other words, if you lend certain munitions and get [them] back... you are all right. If they have been damaged... it seems to me you come out pretty well if you have them replaced by the fellow to whom you have lent them.

QUESTION: How was Roosevelt suggesting we help the British in their fight against the Nazis?

DOCUMENT 3: Refer to the cartoon below.

"Hands Across the Sea": FDR with a fist for Hitler and the helping hand of Lend-Lease for Britain

QUESTION: How does the cartoon show the purpose of Roosevelt's Lend-Lease Act?

DOCUMENT 4: Charles Lindbergh, as quoted in *The New York Times*, April 24, 1941:

> We have weakened ourselves . . . [and] divided our own people, by this dabbling in Europe's wars. [Instead of] concentrating on American defense, we have been forced to argue over foreign quarrels. We must turn our eyes and our faith back to our own country [so that] a different vista opens before us.
>
> Practically every difficulty we would face in invading Europe becomes an asset to us in defending America. Our enemy, and not we, would then have the problems of transporting millions of troops across the ocean and landing them on a hostile shore. . . .

QUESTION: Why did Charles Lindbergh feel that the United States should remain neutral?

DOCUMENT 5: From an editorial in *The New York Times*, April 30, 1941, in answer to Charles Lindbergh:

> . . . That conqueror [Hitler] does not need to attempt at once an invasion of continental United States in order to place this country in deadly danger. We shall be in deadly danger the moment British sea power fails; the moment the eastern gates of the Atlantic are open to the aggressor; the moment we are compelled to divide our one-ocean Navy between two oceans simultaneously. . . .

QUESTION: Why did the editor of *The New York Times* disagree with Charles Lindbergh?

TASK: Using the documents and your knowledge of U.S. history and government, write an essay in which you:

- explain the arguments that supported and rejected U.S. neutrality during the opening years of World War II.
- describe how the United States participated in World War II before entering the war as a combatant.

CHAPTER 15
Peace With Problems: 1945–1960

DOCUMENTS AND LAWS

Smith Act (1940) • Truman Doctrine (1947) • Universal Declaration of Human Rights (1948)
Point Four Program (1949) • McCarran Act (1950) • *Dennis et al.* v. *United States* (1951)
Yates v. *United States* (1957) • *Watkins* v. *United States* (1957)

EVENTS

United Nations established (1945) • Yalta and Potsdam conferences (1945)
"Iron curtain" speech (1946) • Hiss case (1948) • Berlin Airlift (1948–1949)
Marshall Plan (1948–1951) • Chinese Communist defeat of Nationalists (1949)
NATO established (1949) • Soviet Union A-bomb test (1949) • Rosenberg case (1950)
Korean War (1950–1953) • Oppenheimer case (1954) • European Economic Community (1957)
European Union (1994)

PEOPLE

Jiang Jieshi • George Kennan • George Marshall • Joseph McCarthy • Mao Zedong
Joseph Stalin • Adlai Stevenson

OBJECTIVES

- To understand how U.S. involvement with the UN ended U.S. isolationism.
- To describe U.S. global commitments after World War II.
- To explain the origins of the cold war.
- To compare U.S. postwar policies toward Europe and Asia.
- To describe cold-war conflicts in Berlin, China, and Korea.
- To analyze how the cold war affected U.S. domestic policy.

International Peace Efforts

Representatives of the United States and its allies met in San Francisco in April 1945 to replace the League of Nations with the *United Nations (UN)*. In this new peacekeeping organization, representatives from member nations would meet to settle disputes and stop aggressions like those that had led to World War II.

According to the *UN Charter* (constitution), all members could vote in the *General Assembly*. The *Security Council* consisted of five permanent members—the Soviet Union, Britain, France, China, and the United States —and ten nonpermanent members, each serving two-year terms. In the event of an international crisis, a unanimous vote of the permanent members of the Security Council, along with four votes from nonpermanent members, would allow the UN to take military action.

An *Economic and Social Council* would attempt to reduce hunger and improve health care in poor countries. A *Trusteeship Council* would decide on the futures of former colonies of Japan and Germany. An *International Court of Justice* would hear legal cases involving disputes between nations.

In 1945, by a vote of 89 to 2, the Senate approved U.S. membership in the UN. Isolationism was at an end. As the world's mightiest nation and only atomic power, the United States prepared to play a leading role in international affairs.

Eleanor Roosevelt's Role In 1945, Eleanor Roosevelt was appointed U.S. representative to the UN, where she served until 1953. Elected chairperson of the Human Rights Commission in 1946, she was largely responsible for passage of the *Universal Declaration of Human Rights.* In 1948, the UN General Assembly approved the Declaration, which cited such civil and political rights as freedom of speech and religion, freedom of movement and **asylum** (protection by a government of a person fleeing danger or mistreatment), equality before the law, and the rights to a fair trial, participation in government, and freedom from torture. It cited such economic, social, and cultural rights as the right to food, clothing, housing, medical care, education, social security, a decent standard of living, and work, as well as to form labor unions, marry and raise a family, and maintain one's culture.

Displaced Persons

The fascism of the 1930s and the widespread fighting of World War II created many **refugees** (people who flee life-threatening conditions or persecution in their own countries). In 1951, the UN General Assembly created the *United Nations High Commissioner for Refugees* to safeguard the well-being and rights of refugees, help them return to their countries or settle elsewhere, and coordinate international action to end refugee problems.

Expansion and Containment in Europe

In 1945, Franklin Roosevelt, Winston Churchill, and Joseph Stalin—the "Big Three"—held a summit conference at Yalta in the Soviet Union. After Roosevelt's death in July of that year, President Truman represented the United States at a similar conference at Potsdam, Germany. The "Big Three" agreed to a number of principles about how to treat Germany and Japan in defeat:

- Germany would be disarmed.
- Germany—and its former capital, Berlin—would be divided into four zones of occupation (British, U.S., French, and Soviet).
- War criminals in both countries would be put on trial.
- Japan would be occupied chiefly by U.S. troops.
- Polish territory would be granted to the Soviet Union.

The agreement about Poland was made at Yalta. Critics complain that Roosevelt conceded too much to the Soviets by allowing the occupation of Poland, which led to the Soviet domination of Eastern Europe. Others point out that the Soviets also made an important concession—they agreed that after the defeat of Germany, they would fight Japan. Furthermore, Soviet troops were already in Eastern Europe at the time of Yalta. In effect, the region was already theirs.

Origins of the Cold War

Western leaders believed that the Soviet Union intended to gain control over other nations by supporting Communist revolutions.

The Soviet government feared the United States because it (1) uniquely possessed nuclear weapons and (2) was part of a **coalition** (alliance for joint action) of Western capitalistic democracies.

The postwar U.S.-Soviet rivalry was based on opposing **ideologies** (belief systems). It was known as the **cold war** because the nations never

Division of Germany and Berlin After World War II

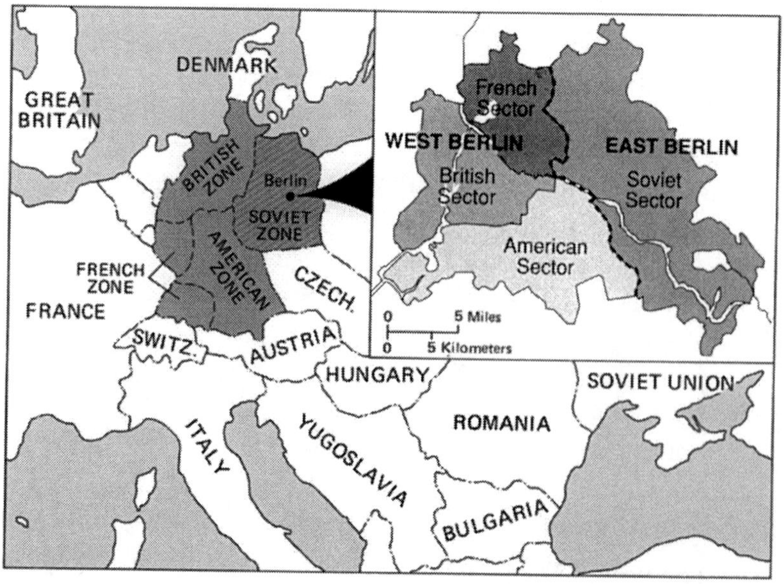

fought each other directly, but rather showed their hostility in the following ways:

- an arms race to build the most powerful nuclear weapons
- aid to rebel or government forces in local and regional wars, depending on which side leaned toward communism or democracy
- **espionage** (spying)
- propaganda to smear and condemn the opposition's way of life
- space race to impress world public opinion with "firsts" in space exploration
- mutual condemnation during meetings of the UN General Assembly and Security Council.

Soviet Satellites

At Yalta and Potsdam, Stalin had agreed that postwar governments in Eastern Europe should have free and fair elections. Instead, it was not long before Communist parties supported by occupying Soviet armies took control of the police, newspapers, and radio stations. Communist candidates came to power in rigged elections.

Communist parties controlling Eastern European countries took orders from the Soviet Union. The one exception was Communist-controlled

Soviet Satellites in Eastern Europe After World War II

Yugoslavia. In effect, almost all Eastern European states became Soviet **satellites**; that is, their policies were dictated by the Soviet Union.

Each of the major wartime Allies was to occupy, briefly, one zone of Germany, after which the country would be united under a democratically elected government. Instead, Germany became divided into two parts—a democratic West Germany and East Germany, a Soviet satellite. Thus, the United States set up a long-term military presence in West Germany in order to stop Soviet expansion in Europe.

"Iron Curtain" In a 1946 speech at Fulton, Missouri, Winston Churchill said that an "iron curtain" had descended across Europe. In other words, he said that there would be little contact between the Soviet satellites, which were no longer free countries, and the democracies of Western Europe.

Postwar Uses of U.S. Power

Many Americans wanted Europe to resolve its own postwar problems. President Truman and congressional leaders, however, believed that a Europe weakened by war was open to Soviet domination. Therefore, the administration initiated a policy conceived by U.S. diplomat George Kennan and labeled **containment**. It called for U.S. military and economic efforts to prevent Soviet influence and expansion from spreading.

Truman Doctrine In 1947, Greece was in danger of being overthrown by Greek Communists. If it became a Soviet satellite, Turkey might follow. Truman asked Congress for $400 million in military aid for both nations. His statement, the *Truman Doctrine*, said in part: "The free peoples of the world look to us for support in maintaining their freedoms. If we falter in our leadership we may endanger the peace of the world—and we shall surely endanger the welfare of our own nation." Congress passed a foreign aid bill, the first of many during the cold war. Thus, Greece and Turkey turned back the Communist threat.

Marshall Plan In 1947, Western Europe was still in desperate economic shape. Communist parties in France and Italy won many supporters. Truman's secretary of state, George Marshall, proposed an ambitious program designed to promote recovery and contain communism in Europe. Under this *Marshall Plan*, Congress approved $12 billion for economic assistance to Europe. The aid seemed to work. By 1951, Communists had little hope of controlling France or Italy, although they remained strong. (The United States had offered Marshall Plan aid to *all* nations in Europe, but the Soviet Union and its satellites refused.)

Berlin Airlift In Germany, the Soviets controlled the zone that surrounded Berlin. In 1948, they announced a closing of the land routes to West Berlin, the part of the city under British, French, and U.S. control.

As commander in chief, Truman ordered the U.S. Air Force to deliver food and other vital supplies to West Berlin by air. The *Berlin Airlift* became a daily routine for almost a year. In 1949, the Soviets ended their ineffectual blockade.

Soviet A-Bomb and H-Bomb Tests

In 1949, the Soviet Union exploded its first atomic bomb (*A-bomb*). By 1952, the United States had developed the hydrogen bomb (*H-bomb*), which was thousands of times more destructive than the atomic bomb. The next year, the Soviet Union successfully tested an H-bomb. The world now witnessed an arms race as the two most powerful nations competed to produce more and more nuclear weapons. One by-product of the competition was the building of bomb shelters in the 1950s by Americans fearful of a nuclear war.

Cartoon comment on the sorry state of the planet after an atomic war

Western European Organizations

Common Market/European Community/European Union After World War II, Western European countries gradually restored their economies. The most important factors were: (1) U.S. economic aid—the Marshall Plan; (2) Western Europe's skilled workforce; (3) strong demand for European consumer goods such as new cars and appliances; and (4) the reduction of regional trade barriers.

In 1952, France, West Germany, the Netherlands, Belgium, Luxembourg, and Italy formed the *European Coal and Steel Community.* They hoped to increase prosperity by removing tariffs on coal, iron ore, and steel, and by regulating their production.

In 1957, the same six countries created the *Common Market* or *European Economic Community (EEC)* to eliminate all tariff barriers among members. Eventually, Britain, Greece, Portugal, Spain, Ireland, Denmark, Austria, Finland, and Sweden joined.

Member nations of the Common Market then set up the *European Community (EC)* to promote the free flow of goods, services, people, and capital among members. In 1991, the EC met in Maastricht, the Netherlands, and agreed to launch a common currency (the **euro**), establish a European Parliament to set common foreign policies, and work toward a common defense policy. In 1994, the EC became known as the *European Union (EU)*. In 1998, the *European Central Bank* was established. There are now 27 European Union countries, and 16 have changed over completely to the euro. Most of the new members are from Eastern Europe, and a number of other nations have applied to join the union. However, the widespread economic problems of 2007–2010 caused a reevaluation by the member nations of the financial regulations and requirements for EU membership and adoption of the euro.

North Atlantic Treaty Organization (NATO) The Soviet Union and its satellites posed a threat to Western Europe's security. For the first time, the United States joined a military alliance in peacetime. In 1949, Truman signed, and the Senate approved, a treaty with 11 other nations (Britain, France, Italy, Belgium, the Netherlands, Denmark, Norway, Iceland, Portugal, Luxembourg, and Canada). It created the *North Atlantic Treaty Organization (NATO)*, whose purpose was to discourage Soviet aggression and thus avoid war. The allies agreed "that an armed attack against one or more of them . . . shall be considered an attack against all." NATO's strategy rested on a shield-and-sword concept: European and U.S. ground troops would be a "shield" against Soviet attack. U.S. nuclear weapons would be the "sword." Over the decades, membership in NATO has increased considerably beyond its original 12 founding nations.

IN REVIEW

1. Explain the significance of Senate approval for U.S. membership in the UN.
2. Summarize the origins of the cold war.
3. Define and explain the significance of *each* of the following: UN Declaration of Human Rights, refugees, Yalta and Potsdam conferences, satellite nation, iron curtain, containment, Truman Doctrine, Marshall Plan, Common Market.

Containment in Asia, Africa, and Latin America

In his 1949 inaugural address, Truman announced his *Point Four Program*, a foreign policy of economic aid to fight the cold war in underdeveloped regions of the world. Congress thereafter voted for foreign aid to developing countries in Asia, Africa, and Latin America.

United States and China

After the defeat of Japan in 1945, U.S. policy makers hoped that China would become a strong and prosperous democracy. But China fell under control of a Communist government.

Cartoonist's view of U.S. international alliances and commitments after World War II

Rise of Mao Zedong During the 1920s and 1930s, a Communist army led by Mao Zedong fought against China's government army led by Jiang Jieshi, head of the Nationalist Party. The fighting ceased when Japan attacked China during World War II but continued after the war.

Flight of Chiang Kai-Shek The United States gave economic and military aid to the Nationalists, and the Soviet Union did likewise for Mao's Communist forces. Mao attracted peasant recruits by the millions, and they defeated Chiang Kai-Shek, also known as Jiang Jieshi, and his Nationalists in 1949. The Nationalists thus fled to the island of Taiwan.

"Hot War" in Korea At the close of World War II, the Japanese fled from Korea as Soviet armies moved in from the north and U.S. armies from the south. The two forces agreed on the 38th Parallel of latitude as a temporary line between their zones of occupation. As the cold war developed, though, the 38th Parallel became a permanent border between North Korea with its Soviet-backed Communist government and South Korea with its U.S.-supported government.

In 1950, North Korean troops marched into South Korea. Truman ordered U.S. troops into South Korea and called on the UN to defend its government. (The Soviet Union had temporarily withdrawn its UN representative and thus lost veto power in the Security Council.) As a result, for the first time the UN used military force against an aggressor nation.

As commander in chief, Truman pursued an undeclared war in Korea, calling it a "police action" (see the map on page 272).

Chinese Involvement U.S. General Douglas MacArthur commanded the UN forces in Korea. After a series of defeats, his forces made a surprise attack behind enemy lines and pushed the North Koreans back toward the Yalu River on the Chinese border. As MacArthur pursued them, China sent thousands of its soldiers across the Yalu. Overwhelmed by this assault, UN South Korean forces retreated south of the 38th Parallel.

Truman, MacArthur, and "Limited War" MacArthur urged Truman to let him bomb Chinese bases in Manchuria to stop the Chinese attack. Recognizing the danger of a larger war, Truman refused. MacArthur then tried to persuade congressional leaders to back the bombing of China. Truman, determined to keep to a "limited war," removed MacArthur as commander of UN forces.

Cold War at Home

Because of the postwar Communist takeover of Eastern Europe and China, many Americans feared that their own country might also be targeted by Communist spies and sympathizers.

During the presidencies of Harry S. Truman and Dwight D. Eisenhower, the government tried to determine the loyalty of its employees and others by measures that restricted free speech.

Truman and Loyalty Checks

In 1946, newspapers reported that Canadian government workers had given secrets about the U.S. atomic bomb to the Soviet Union. In the United States, President Truman began a system of **loyalty checks** of federal employees: He ordered the Federal Bureau of Investigation (FBI) and the Civil Service Commission to find out if such persons had ever belonged to a Communist or other **subversive** organization. (The U.S. government defined "subversive" as someone seeking to overthrow the government.) The U.S. attorney general listed 90 possibly subversive organizations, although, in many cases, he failed to prove the charge. Between 1947 and 1951, 3 million government workers were investigated. More than 200 lost their jobs as "security risks."

Anti-Communist Legislation

Smith Act Enacted before U.S. entry into World War II, the *Smith Act* prohibited any group from advocating or teaching violent overthrow of the government. It also prohibited anyone from belonging to such a group. In effect, since Communists advocated the overthrow of capitalist governments (not necessarily by violence), the Smith Act was used to make the Communist Party illegal in the United States.

U.S. troops in Korea during the war

Several Supreme Court cases tested whether the act violated First Amendment guarantees of freedom of speech and association. Eugene Dennis and others were members of the Communist Party in the 1940s. After they were arrested and convicted under the Smith Act of making speeches threatening national security, they appealed to the Supreme Court. In *Dennis et al.* v. *United States* (1951), the Court ruled that their First Amendment rights had not been violated because the speeches presented a clear and present danger of overthrowing the government by force.

In *Yates* v. *United States* (1957), the Court shifted its position on the Smith Act. It decided that any idea could be advocated as long as the speaker did not urge people to commit dangerous acts.

McCarran Act In 1950, Congress passed the *McCarran Act (Internal Security Act)*. It was aimed at "Communist-front" organizations—groups that did not admit to Communist affiliations but were accused of receiving Communist support or harboring Communist members. The law required all Communist and Communist-front organizations to file membership lists and financial statements. It also prohibited the (1) employment of Communists or members of Communist-front organizations in defense plants, and (2) entry into the United States of Communists or former Communists.

House Un-American Activities Committee (HUAC)

In the 1940s, a special committee of the House of Representatives—the *House Un-American Activities Committee (HUAC)*—held hearings on the subject of disloyalty.

A labor organizer, John Watkins, was called before HUAC and answered questions about his own dealings with Communist groups. He refused, however, to give information about other persons on the grounds that it was not relevant to HUAC's work. Watkins was convicted of violating a federal law against refusing to answer a congressional committee's questions. In 1957, he appealed to the Supreme Court. In *Watkins* v. *United States*, the Court ruled that a witness at a congressional hearing may refuse to answer any question that does not relate to the committee's lawmaking task.

Hiss Case In 1945, Alger Hiss, a member of the State Department, accompanied Franklin Roosevelt to the Yalta Conference. He then became director of a private world peace organization. In 1948, Whittaker Chambers, a former Communist, testified before HUAC that Hiss had been a Communist spy in the 1930s and had given Chambers secret government documents. Hiss denied the accusations but was convicted of **perjury** (lying under oath) and sentenced to five years in prison.

Rosenbergs Case

The Soviet Union tested its first atomic bomb in 1949. In 1950, Julius and Ethel Rosenberg were charged with passing secrets about the U.S. atomic bomb to the Soviets. Found guilty of conspiracy to commit espionage, the Rosenbergs maintained their innocence and appealed to the Supreme Court and President Eisenhower. Despite worldwide appeals on their behalf, they were executed in 1953.

Oppenheimer Case

Dr. J. Robert Oppenheimer was one of the physicists who built the atomic bomb in 1945. He later opposed U.S. development of a hydrogen bomb because he feared an uncontrolled arms race and the ultimate destruction of the world. Because of his public stand, the government accused Oppenheimer of being a Communist and a security risk. In 1954, it withdrew his security clearance.

McCarthyism

During the Korean War years (1950–1953), U.S. Senator Joseph McCarthy of Wisconsin intensified American distrust of Communists and fear of subversion.

Portraying himself as a defender of U.S. security, McCarthy conducted Senate committee hearings in which he accused government officials, actors, writers, educators, and others of being "Communist sympathizers." Their constitutional rights were disregarded, and many lost their jobs. New jobs were difficult to find because businesses would **blacklist** (refuse to hire) those under investigation.

In 1954, McCarthy began to investigate the Army, whose members he demanded the right to question in committee. The hearings, unlike earlier ones, were televised. Between April and June 1954, a TV audience of 20 million watched the Army-McCarthy Hearings. Seeing the senator in action—interrupting and bullying witnesses and making reckless charges—many were offended. As the public turned against him, McCarthy lost both supporters and power. In December 1954, the Senate voted to **censure** (officially criticize) him for conduct damaging to the reputation of the Senate. The term "McCarthyism" has come to mean "the use of reckless and unfair accusations in the name of suppressing political disloyalty."

Cold-war Politics

China had two governments—Mao's Communists on the mainland (the People's Republic of China) and Jiang's Nationalists on Taiwan. Each claimed legitimacy. Through the 1950s and 1960s, the United States recognized only the Nationalists.

In the same period, the Nationalists represented China in the UN, despite Soviet attempts to unseat them in favor of Mao's Communists.

Truman's Loss of Popularity

As the 1952 presidential election drew near, voters' complaints against the Truman administration grew:

- Negotiations for a Korean armistice had been stalemated for more than a year.
- Inflation, caused by war expenses and Truman's failure to settle a steelworkers' strike, was hurting the economy.
- Communists gained control of China in 1949, and Republicans blamed Democrats for that development.
- According to Senator McCarthy, many Communists had infiltrated the government.
- Some of Truman's political friends were suspected of corruption.
- Truman had removed the popular General MacArthur from command in Korea.

All these problems led to the victory of the Republican presidential candidate, Dwight D. ("Ike") Eisenhower, over the Democratic candidate, Governor Adlai Stevenson of Illinois.

Stalemate and Truce in Korea

The war in Korea dragged on, with high casualties and no decisive victories. There was a stalemate near the 38th Parallel. In 1952, Republican presidential candidate Eisenhower had promised, if elected, to "go to Korea" and end the fighting. He did so in 1953, and soon afterward, a truce established the 38th Parallel as the official line between North and South Korea. An armistice was signed in June 1953.

IN REVIEW

1. Describe *one success* and *one failure* of U.S. foreign policy in Asia between 1945 and 1955.
2. Explain how the United States responded to the Communist threat at home.
3. Identify and explain the significance of *each* of the following: Mao Zedong, Jiang Jieshi, Yalu River, Point Four Program, Smith Act, HUAC, *Watkins* v. *United States*, Alger Hiss case, Rosenbergs' trial, J. Robert Oppenheimer, McCarthyism.

CHAPTER REVIEW

MULTIPLE-CHOICE QUESTIONS

1 Following World War II, Eleanor Roosevelt was most noted for her
(1) support of racial segregation in the United States military
(2) role in creating the United Nations Universal Declaration of Human Rights
(3) opposition to the Truman administration
(4) efforts to end the use of land mines

Base your answer to question 2 on the quotation below and on your knowledge of social studies.

> ...I believe that it must be the policy of the United States to support free peoples who are resisting attempted subjugation [control] by armed minorities or by outside pressures.
>
> I believe that we must assist free peoples to work out their own destinies in their own way.
>
> I believe that our help should be primarily through economic and financial aid which is essential to economic stability and orderly political processes....
>
> —PRESIDENT HARRY TRUMAN, SPEECH TO CONGRESS (TRUMAN DOCTRINE), MARCH 12, 1947

2 The program described in this quotation was part of the foreign policy of
(1) détente
(2) containment
(3) neutrality
(4) colonialism

3 The Truman Doctrine was originally designed to
(1) stop the proliferation of nuclear weapons
(2) contain communism by giving aid to Greece and Turkey
(3) use the United Nations as a tool to eliminate threats posed by the Soviet Union
(4) rebuild Southeast Asia by extending economic aid

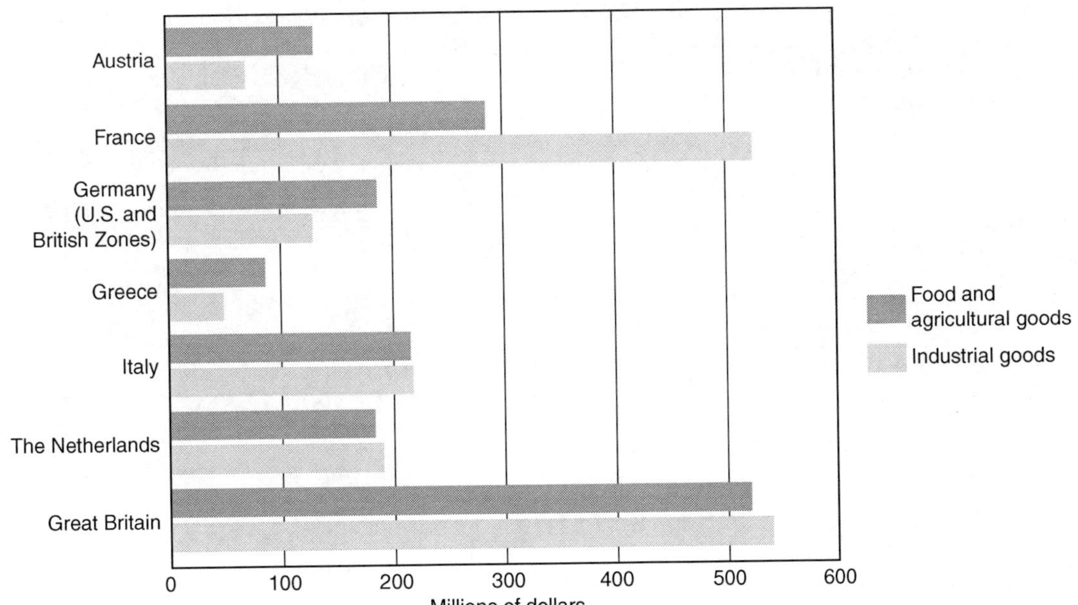

Base your answer to question 4 on the graph above and on your knowledge of social studies.

4 Information provided by the graph indicates that the Marshall Plan tried to prevent the spread of communism in Europe by
(1) providing military aid to France and Great Britain
(2) restoring economic stability throughout Western Europe
(3) encouraging domestic revolutions in Europe
(4) making European nations dependent on the United Nations

Base your answer to question 5 on the cartoon at the right and on your knowledge of social studies.

5 Which event of 1948–1949 is illustrated by this cartoon?
(1) Berlin Airlift
(2) collapse of the Berlin Wall
(3) reunification of Germany
(4) allied invasion on Normandy

6 The primary reason for the formation of the North Atlantic Treaty Organization (NATO) in 1949 was to
(1) maintain peace in the Middle East
(2) block the German Nazi threat in Europe
(3) protect Western Europe from the Soviet Union
(4) increase United States influence in Asia

7 "There shall be a loyalty investigation of every person entering the civilian employment of any department or agency of the Executive Branch of the Federal Government."

—THE TRUMAN LOYALTY ORDER, MARCH 22, 1947

President Harry Truman issued this Executive order in response to the
(1) fear of Communist Party influence in government
(2) election of Socialist Party representatives to Congress
(3) discovery of spies in defense industries
(4) arrest and trial of high-ranking government employees for terrorism

8 What was a cause for the investigations of the House Un-American Activities Committee in the late 1940s and the investigations of a Senate committee headed by Joseph McCarthy in the early 1950s?
(1) the belief that there were Communist agents in the federal government
(2) excessive spending by the United States military
(3) the corruption and bribery of members of Congress
(4) actions of President Harry Truman that might have led to his impeachment

9 Which situation resulted from Senator Joseph McCarthy's search for Communists within the United States during the 1950s?
(1) Thousands of American citizens who believed in communism were either jailed or deported.
(2) The reputations of many people were ruined by false accusations of disloyalty.
(3) Many high-ranking government officials were exposed as spies of the Soviet Union.
(4) Organized groups of Communists began a wave of violent political terrorism.

10 Since the 1950s, the term *McCarthyism* has been applied to events that are related to
(1) the basic rights of citizens to own and carry guns
(2) the violent activities of international terrorists
(3) reckless accusations unsupported by evidence
(4) questionable methods used to finance political campaigns

THEMATIC ESSAYS

1 **THEME:** *Containment of Communism.* After World War II, the United States under President Truman faced the new challenge of expanding communism.

TASK: Describe *two* methods by which the administration halted or contained the spread of communism in Europe and the rest of the world. For *each* method:
- explain the program
- illustrate the program as it applied to a specific area or nation
- describe the ultimate impact of the program on limiting the spread of communism.

Consider the Truman Doctrine, Marshall Plan, Point Four Program, and formation of NATO as possible examples.

2 **THEME:** *Security and Democracy.* During the late 1940s and the 1950s, the threat of global communism made many Americans fear that traitors were seriously undermining the interests and well-being of the United States.

TASK: Complete both of the following tasks:
- Describe *two* examples of federal involvement in a hunt for Communists within American society.
- Show how, *in at least one case*, a constitutional value or individual right was

sacrificed in pursuit of the Communist menace. (You may use an example already used in the first part or choose a new example.)

DOCUMENT-BASED QUESTION

*Study each document and answer the question that follows it. Then read the **Task** and write your essay. Include references to most of the documents and additional information you retain about U.S. history and government.*

Historical Context: After World War II, two superpowers waged a cold war for global dominance. An early test of will was over Korea. The fighting there led to a dispute between President Truman and General MacArthur, the result of which was MacArthur's dismissal.

Document 1: President Truman, as quoted in *The New York Times*, April 12, 1951:

> So far . . . a limited war in Korea [has] prevented aggression [leading to] general war. . . . We have taught the enemy a lesson. He has found out that aggression is not cheap or easy. . . .
>
> We do not want . . . the conflict . . . extended. We are trying to prevent a world war—not start one. . . .
>
> But you may ask: "Why can't we take other steps to punish the aggressor?" . . .
>
> If we were to [bomb Manchuria and China and assist Chinese Nationalist troops], . . . we would . . . risk . . . a general war, . . . we would become entangled in a vast conflict, . . . and our task would become immeasurably more difficult all over the world.
>
> What would suit . . the Kremlin [Soviet Union] better than for our military forces to be committed to a full-scale war in Red China?

Question: Why did President Truman wish to fight a "limited war" in Korea?

Document 2: General MacArthur, as quoted in *The New York Times*, April 19, 1951:

> . . . The Communist threat is a global one. Its successful advance in one sector threatens . . . every other sector. . . .
>
> I made it clear that . . . not . . . to destroy the enemy build-up . . . [not] to utilize [the] friendly Chinese force . . . on Formosa . . . not . . . to blockade the China coast . . . , and [without] hope of major reinforcements, . . . the military standpoint forbade victory. . . .
>
> War's very object is victory, not prolonged indecision.
>
> In war there can be no substitute for victory.

Question: Why did General MacArthur disagree with President Truman's conduct of the Korean War?

Document 3: President Truman in the *Congressional Record*, April 10, 1951:

> With deep regret I have concluded that General . . . MacArthur is unable to give this wholehearted support to the policies of the United States . . . and . . . United Nations. . . . I have, therefore, relieved [him] of his commands. . . .
>
> Full and vigorous debate on matters of national policy is . . . vital [to] our free democracy. It is fundamental, however, that military commanders must be governed by the policies . . . issued to them [as] provided by our laws and Constitution. In time of crisis, this consideration is particularly compelling.

Question: Why did Truman remove MacArthur from his command in Korea?

Korean War, 1950–1953

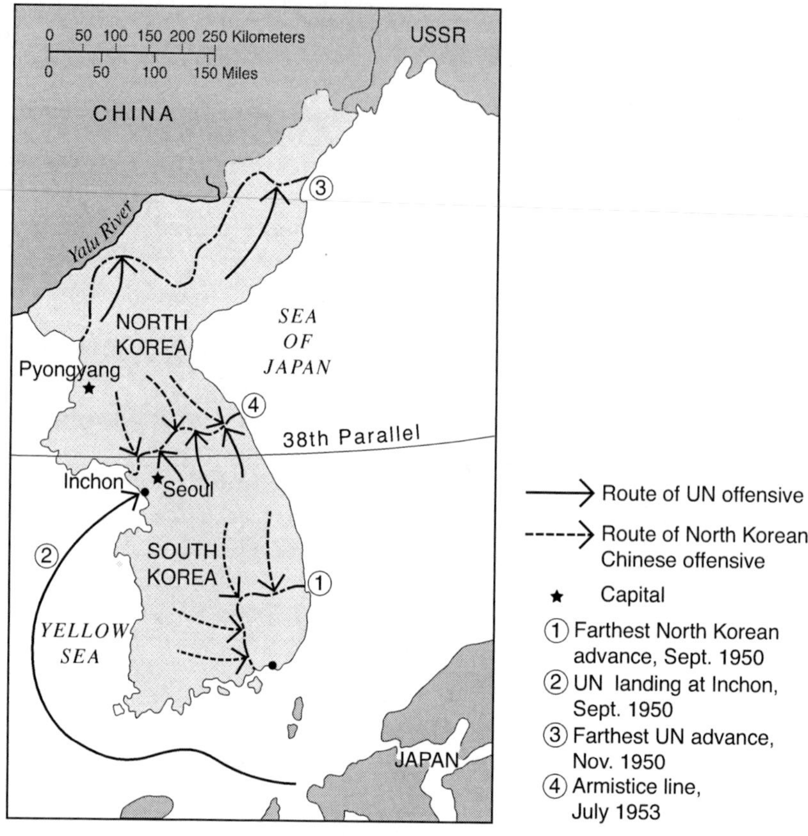

DOCUMENT 4: Refer to the map above.

QUESTION: What was the result of the Korean War?

TASK: Using the documents and your knowledge of U.S. history and government, write an essay in which you:

- describe the conflicting strategies of Truman and MacArthur regarding the Korean War.
- evaluate the wisdom of Truman's dismissal of MacArthur in light of the results of the war and the president's constitutional powers as commander in chief.

UNIT VI
The World in Uncertain Times

CHAPTER 16
Containment and Consensus: 1945–1960

DOCUMENTS AND LAWS
Plessy v. *Ferguson* (1896) • *Brown* v. *Board of Education of Topeka* (1954)
Interstate Highway Act (1956) • Civil Rights Act of 1957 • Voting Rights laws (1957–1960)
Eisenhower Doctrine (1958)

EVENTS
End of the Korean War (1953) • Commonwealth status for Puerto Rico (1952)
Establishment of SEATO (1954) • Bus boycott in Montgomery, Alabama (1955–1956)
Suez Crisis (1956) • Polish and Hungarian uprisings (1956) • Soviet launch of *Sputnik* (1957)
Desegregation of public schools, Little Rock, Arkansas (1957) •
Soviet downing of U-2 spy plane (1960)

PEOPLE
John Foster Dulles • Orval Faubus • Oveta Culp Hobby • Martin Luther King, Jr.
Nikita Khrushchev • Thurgood Marshall • Gamal Abdel Nasser • Rosa Parks • Jackie Robinson
Earl Warren

OBJECTIVES

- To describe U.S. foreign policy of the postwar period under Eisenhower.
- To understand how Eisenhower's domestic policies exemplified moderate conservatism.
- To describe early victories in the African-American struggle for civil rights.
- To examine changes in American society in the 1950s.

Emerging Power Relationships

Beginning in the 1950s, the world was divided into three main political-economic groups:

- *first world:* anti-Communist nations in the West
- *second world:* the Soviet Union, its satellites, and allies
- *third world:* underdeveloped, nonindustrial nations such as the newly independent nations of Asia and Africa and some Latin American countries.

The United States extended foreign aid to third-world countries to promote economic growth and thereby contain communism.

East/West

In 1949, after the Chinese Communists under Mao Zedong defeated the Chinese Nationalists led by Chiang Kai-shek, the Western powers feared a Chinese-Soviet alliance. Given China's large population and Soviet industrial and military strength, such an alliance would be formidable. The United States, which had historically allied itself with China against its Asian neighbors—in particular, Japan—now sought to enhance its relationship with Japan in order to contain China and the Soviet Union.

Moreover, with the formation of NATO in 1947, the United States and the Western European nations faced off against Soviet aggression. The Marshall Plan also aimed at resistance against Communist influence by helping countries in Western Europe rebuild their economies.

North/South

Except for Australia and New Zealand, the industrialized nations occupy the Northern Hemisphere. Most developing countries lie to the south, near the equator. A huge economic gap exists between the **developed nations** (industrialized ones) and the **developing nations** (those still developing industries)—sometimes also known as the **third world**. (This last term has not been used much since the end of the cold war in 1990.)

After World War II, the United States and other developed countries aided developing countries with loans, grants, and *technical assistance* (expert advice). The Soviet Union also provided aid to developing nations in an effort to compete with the United States for influence in the third world. Despite this aid, the gap between rich and poor nations widened as a result of high rates of population growth. Populations in the poorer regions of the world tend to grow much faster than elsewhere.

Eisenhower's Foreign Policy

End of the Korean War In 1953, six months after Dwight Eisenhower became president, North and South Korea agreed to a permanent truce. The war had been fought not for total victory but to contain Chinese and Soviet power. Today, the 38th Parallel still separates South and North Korea.

Projected World Population Growth, 2000–2050

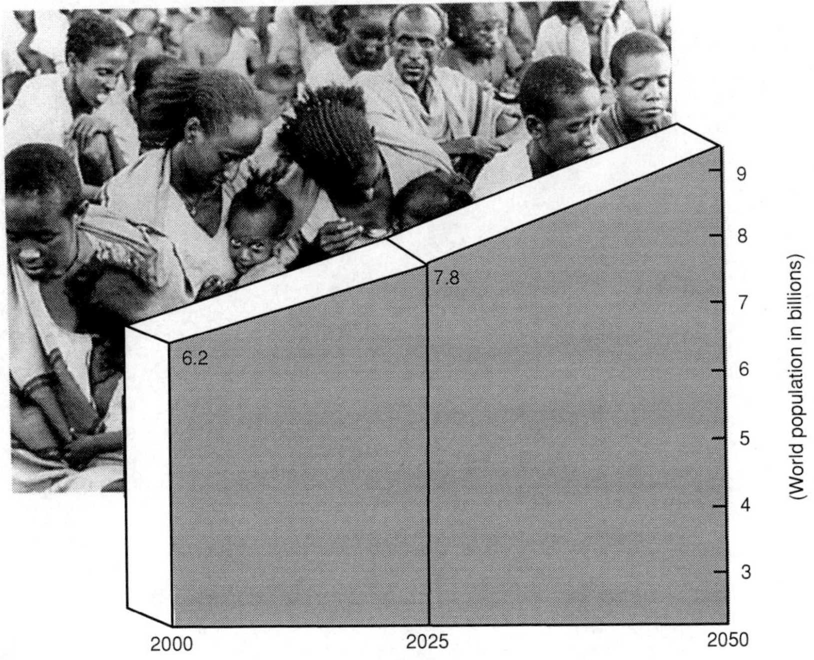

Much of the projected world population growth will be in developing countries.

Domino Theory and Massive Retaliation To impress upon the Soviet Union U.S. determination to stop the spread of communism, John Foster Dulles, Eisenhower's secretary of state, announced that any Soviet aggression would be met by **massive retaliation**. That is, the United States might resort to a policy of nuclear-weapons use called **brinkmanship**.

As the French pulled out of French Indochina in 1954, Dulles developed the **domino theory**: Southeast Asia was a lineup of dominoes ready to topple; if Vietnam fell to communism, Cambodia, Laos, and Thailand would be likely to fall too. Remember that 1954 was only five years after China had fallen to the Communists and four years after South Korea had almost fallen to a Communist invasion.

"Atoms for Peace" By 1953, both the United States and the Soviet Union had A-bomb and H-bomb capabilities. Realizing that nuclear war would destroy the world, Eisenhower proposed an "atoms for peace" plan to the UN in 1953. Under this plan, nations would pool their nuclear resources for peaceful purposes, especially the production of electricity. However, the Soviet Union refused to participate.

U-2 Incident In 1960, the Soviet Union shot down a U.S. spy plane, the U-2. After initial denials, Eisenhower admitted that U-2 planes were commonly used for spying. As a result of the U-2 incident, Soviet leader Nikita

Cold-War Military Alliances—NATO and the Warsaw Pact

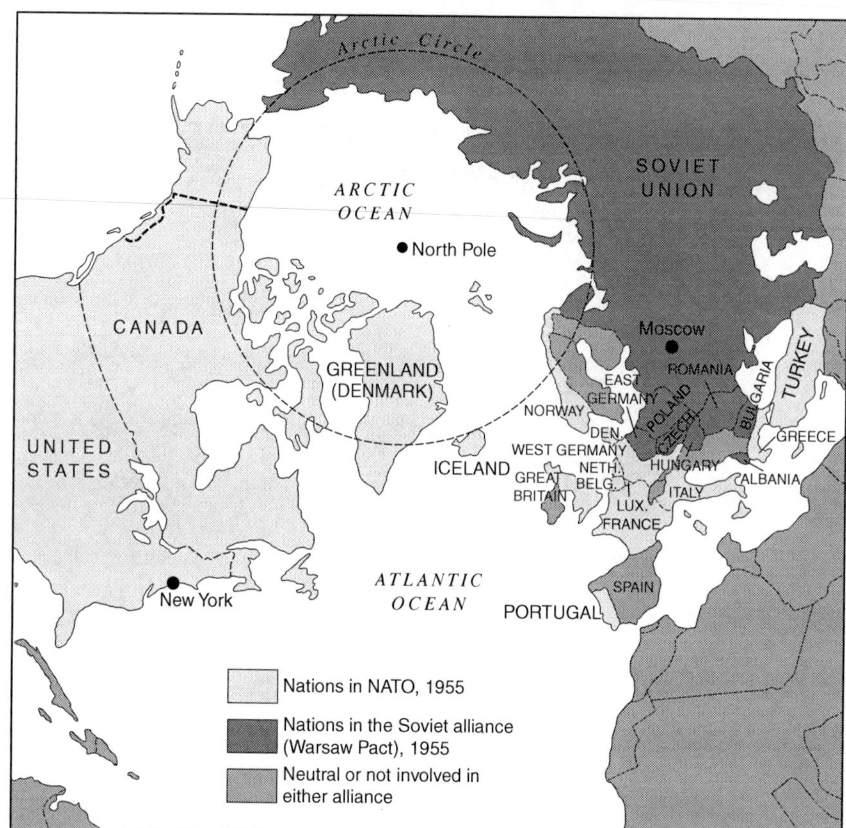

Khrushchev canceled a summit conference with Eisenhower, and cold-war tensions increased.

SEATO In 1954, the United States formed the *Southeast Asia Treaty Organization (SEATO)*, an alliance similar to NATO in Europe. Members were Britain, France, the United States, Australia, New Zealand, Pakistan, Thailand, and the Philippines (granted independence from the United States in 1946). SEATO was disbanded in 1977.

The U.S. alliances in Asia and Europe were based on the assumption that the Soviet Union masterminded Communist movements throughout the world. Thus, Americans viewed communism as a single force. In the 1960s and 1970s, however, U.S. policy makers realized that Chinese Communists and North Korean Communists differed in their goals from Soviet Communists.

Aswan Dam/Suez Canal In 1956, Egypt's leader, General Gamal Abdel Nasser, asked the United States for help in building the Aswan Dam along the Upper Nile River. Its purpose was to generate electricity and irrigate the desert. After the United States refused, Nasser turned to the Soviets, who agreed to help. Nasser then proclaimed the **nationalization** of the Suez Canal route from the Mediterranean Sea through Egypt to the Red Sea. (Nationalization is the government takeover of property formerly owned by a colonial power or private company.) To regain the canal, Britain and France, its former owners—joined by Israel—launched an attack on Egypt. Eisenhower, worried that the Soviet Union might enter the conflict as Egypt's ally, condemned the attack. As a result, the invading forces withdrew, UN peacekeepers moved in, and the Suez Canal remained under Egyptian control.

Polish and Hungarian Uprisings In 1956, anti-Soviet riots broke out in Poland and Hungary. The Soviet Union agreed to a slight loosening of control in Poland. In Hungary, however, Soviet tanks rolled into the capital city of Budapest and crushed the uprising.

Despite urgent requests for help, Eisenhower sent no military assistance to the Hungarian "freedom fighters." In response to NATO, the Soviets had formed a military alliance known as the *Warsaw Pact* with its satellites. To avoid war, Eisenhower chose not to challenge the pact by interfering in a country within the Soviet sphere of influence. The Soviet Union was equally careful not to challenge NATO.

Eisenhower Doctrine The resentment felt by most Arab nations because of U.S. support of Israel led to growing Soviet influence in the Middle East. In 1957, Eisenhower—determined to contain this influence—stated that the United States would send troops to *any* Middle Eastern nation that asked for help against communism. This *Eisenhower Doctrine* was first applied in Lebanon in 1958. The presence there of U.S. troops helped that country avert a Communist takeover.

Sputnik In 1957, the Soviet Union took the world by surprise by launching *Sputnik*, an artificial satellite that orbited Earth. Both Eisenhower and his successor, John F. Kennedy, wanted to show that U.S. space technology was superior to that of the Soviets. Under their leadership, Congress committed vast resources to the race for space. Between 1957 and 1963, the United States launched many satellites, began training astronauts for Earth-orbiting missions, and spent large sums on science education.

IN REVIEW

1. Define *each* of the following terms: developed and developing nations, domino theory, brinkmanship, nationalization, Suez Crisis.
2. Explain how *each* of the following built on and extended the policy of containment: massive retaliation, SEATO, the Eisenhower Doctrine.
3. For *each* Soviet action listed, state how the United States responded: forcibly putting down a 1956 revolt in Hungary; launching *Sputnik* in 1957; shooting down a U-2 spy plane in 1960.

Domestic Politics

In the 1952 presidential election, Eisenhower had easily defeated his Democratic opponent, Governor Adlai Stevenson of Illinois. In 1956, Eisenhower won a second term, defeating Stevenson by an even greater margin.

Eisenhower Peace

Peacetime Economy Eisenhower's domestic policies were mostly conservative—notably, laissez-faire for businesses and an increase in states' rights.

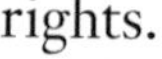

In the early 1950s, oil wells off the coasts of Texas, Louisiana, and California became very productive. The states claimed power to regulate and tax any oil drilled near their coastlines. President Truman had argued that such offshore oil rights were under the authority of the federal government. Eisenhower, however, sided with the states. In 1953, he gave them power to control oil rights within their territorial waters.

Eisenhower criticized the federal-run Tennessee Valley Authority power projects, which he called "creeping socialism."

While favoring businesses, Eisenhower disagreed with conservative Republicans who wished to cut back social programs begun by Democrats. To show his concern for people's welfare, Eisenhower persuaded Congress to enact the following laws and programs:

"The Helicopter Era"
from *Herblock: A Cartoonist's Life* (Times Books, 1998)

- increased the minimum wage from 75 cents to $1 an hour
- increased Social Security benefits for retired persons and extended coverage to more workers
- created the Cabinet-level Department of Health, Education, and Welfare, with a woman, Oveta Culp Hobby, as its secretary
- provided government loans for students to attend college.

Interstate Highway Act In 1956, Eisenhower persuaded Congress to legislate the building of 42,000 miles of interstate highways linking major cities. (He said they would also be useful as well to the military in national emergencies.) The billions of federal dollars spent benefited the automobile, tourist, trucking, and housing industries, among others.

Suburbanization New highways increased the number of suburbs outside cities. Suburbanites drove between their homes and city jobs or became railroad commuters.

Warren Court President Eisenhower appointed Earl Warren, governor of California, as chief justice of the United States. Under Warren (served 1953–1969), the Supreme Court made landmark decisions concerning the Bill of Rights (discussed on pages 300–302).

Farewell Address After serving two terms as president, Eisenhower left office as one of America's most popular presidents. In his "Farewell Address," Ike warned of the growth of a **military-industrial complex** in which *defense contractors* (those who build military equipment and machines) had increasing influence in Congress.

Civil Rights and Constitutional Change

Eisenhower, like Truman, found himself involved in the African-American struggle for equal rights. Having fought to liberate peoples in Asia and Europe during World War II, African Americans felt that it was time for them to gain freedom from racial discrimination at home.

Jackie Robinson The first African American to play on a major league baseball team, Jackie Robinson joined the Brooklyn Dodgers (now the Los Angeles Dodgers) in 1947. At first, Robinson endured racial insults from some whites in the crowd, some teammates, and opposing ballplayers. He also had to stay in segregated motels and rooming houses when his team was playing out-of-town games.

His athletic talents and determination to keep calm won him the admiration of millions. In 1962, Robinson was the first of many African Americans elected to the Baseball Hall of Fame. His breaking of the color barrier in major league baseball quickly led to integration on other teams. It was not until 1955, however, that Elston Howard became the first African American to play for the New York Yankees. After retirement, Robinson continued the fight for racial equality.

Brown* v. *Board of Education of Topeka The 1954 Supreme Court decision in *Brown* v. *Board of Education of Topeka* was a turning point in the civil rights movement. This landmark case came to the Court shortly after Earl Warren was appointed chief justice.

In *Plessy* v. *Ferguson* (1896), the Court had held that railroads, schools, hotels, and other facilities could be segregated if they were "separate but equal"—that is, if the facilities for whites and blacks were roughly the same. One justice, John Harlan, disagreed. In his dissenting opinion, Harlan argued that segregation threatened personal liberty and equal rights.

However, the standard of "separate but equal" was used for many years to justify racial segregation.

In the early 1950s, public schools in Topeka, Kansas, were segregated. An African-American student, Linda Brown, happened to live closer to a white elementary school than to the nearest black one. The white school refused her father's attempt to enroll Linda there. Brown, aided by the NAACP, sued the Topeka Board of Education. A lower federal court rejected the suit on "separate but equal" grounds. The NAACP then appealed this case to the Supreme Court, combining it with four other cases.

Thurgood Marshall, an African-American lawyer employed by the NAACP, represented the plaintiffs. Marshall used legal arguments as well as psychological evidence uncovered by Kenneth Clark, an African-American psychologist. Clark's studies had shown that African-American children felt inferior because of segregation.

The Court, in a reversal, declared that segregated schools could not be equal because of the psychological damage that they inflicted on minority children. The justices unanimously agreed that segregation deprived children of equal educational opportunities and that Topeka's schools, and similar ones, violated the Fourteenth Amendment's guarantee of equal protection.

Shortly afterward, the Court ruled that segregated school systems had to be desegregated. Despite the ruling, some Southern states were slow to desegregate their schools. In urban areas, housing patterns remained an obstacle to school integration. In 1967, Thurgood Marshall was appointed to the Supreme Court.

Launching the Civil Rights Movement

As the 1950s progressed, civil rights workers also challenged segregated buses, lunch counters, and movie theaters.

Montgomery Bus Boycott Montgomery, Alabama, was a typical Southern city in that it required African Americans to sit in the rear of a bus. In 1955, Rosa Parks, an NAACP official returning home from work, refused to give up her seat to a white passenger. She was arrested and charged with violating segregation laws. Martin Luther King, Jr., a young Baptist minister, organized an African-American boycott of the city's buses. After more than a year, during which the boycott hurt the bus system and business in general, Montgomery agreed to desegregate its transportation system.

After *Brown* v. *Board of Education of Topeka* ended *de jure* segregation in education, many people wanted a similar ruling applied to transportation. The Montgomery bus boycott highlighted the issue nationally. In 1956, the Supreme Court ruled that segregation in transportation was unconstitutional.

Little Rock, Arkansas: Federal troops protect African-American students attending a formerly all-white high school.

Forceful School Desegregation By 1957, the Little Rock, Arkansas, Board of Education had a desegregation plan and ordered a white high school to admit a few African Americans. Governor Orval Faubus, however, stated that troops were needed to keep order and then posted the Arkansas National Guard around the school to stop the African Americans from entering. A federal court reaffirmed the students' right to enter and prohibited the governor from interfering. Faubus removed the troops after a white mob had stepped in to prevent African Americans from entering.

Faubus's actions challenged the authority of the federal government and the Supreme Court. Eisenhower, using his authority as commander in chief, called the Arkansas National Guard into federal service and ordered it to protect African Americans as they entered the school. He also sent U.S. soldiers to Little Rock to keep order and prevent further trouble.

Civil Rights Act of 1957 African Americans in Southern states were often prevented from voting. Moreover, many African Americans knew that they risked their lives and property by appearing at a polling place.

In 1957, Congress enacted a civil rights law calling on the Justice Department to stop illegal practices that prevented African Americans from voting. In 1960, another civil rights law called for federal "referees" to intervene when voting rights were denied. Although these laws—the first such laws since Reconstruction—were too weak to really protect African-American voters, they paved the way for stronger legislation in the 1960s.

Strategy of Nonviolence Hoping to desegregate businesses such as restaurants, African-American students engaged in civil disobedience. Beginning in 1960, the *Student Nonviolent Coordinating Committee (SNCC)* organized **sit-ins** throughout the South. In a sit-in, African Americans would enter a segregated restaurant and sit at the counter. When refused service, they would remain in their seats. Many were arrested, but sit-ins, combined with boycotts, led to desegregation in Dallas, Atlanta, and Nashville.

IN REVIEW

1. Identify and explain the significance of *each* of the following: Interstate Highway Act, Jackie Robinson, Rosa Parks, sit-ins, Civil Rights Act of 1957.
2. Summarize the background, facts, and Supreme Court decision in *Brown* v. *Board of Education of Topeka*. Explain its long-term significance.

The People

Because of the needs of the military, Americans during World War II had put off buying many goods because they were not available. After the war, though, Americans spent a lot of money on the things they had lived without during the Great Depression and World War II. These purchases marked a new kind of middle-class society. The urge to acquire more and more possessions became known as **consumerism.**

Postwar Consumption

In the postwar years, millions of Americans bought cars. Automobile sales spurred the growth of the steel, rubber, and glass industries. Spending on travel, restaurants, and motels increased. The gasoline required for auto trips was plentiful and cheap.

Since cars had enabled people to live in suburbs, suburban developments mushroomed. Middle-income families filled their roomy suburban homes with the latest appliances.

Television, developed in the 1920s, became widely available in the early 1950s. By 1953, more than half of U.S. households had at least one set. TV entertainment profoundly influenced American society.

For one thing, television intensified consumerism. Every show had a commercial sponsor—a company that paid for the show and then advertised its products to a huge audience. TV was a visual medium, and its ads were more effective than radio ads in promoting sales.

Television influenced American tastes and habits. Most people seemed to prefer light entertainment—sports, comedy shows, game shows, soap operas, and adventure movies—to more serious educational programs. As people watched more and more TV, they spent less time doing such meaningful things as reading books or taking family outings. Critics of television believed (and still believe) that it had a negative effect on the values and habits of children and teenagers. On the other hand, for those who were interested, TV offered excellent cultural programs—plays, concerts, news

Baby Boom—and Baby Bust: U.S. Birthrate, 1940–1988

The *birth rate* is the number of births per 1,000 women aged 18 to 44.

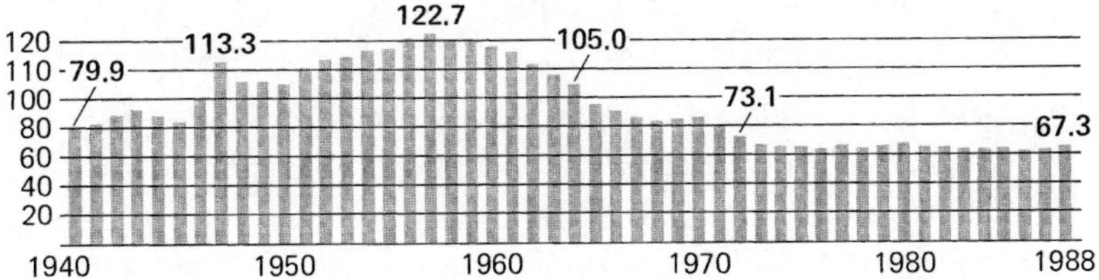

commentary, and documentaries. Many of these programs could be found on National Educational Television stations.

Baby Boom The postwar prosperity influenced married couples to have larger families. Between 1945 and 1960, some 50 million babies were born. The dramatic increase in the birthrate was known as the **baby boom**. It increased sales of homes, cars, and appliances as well as toys, fad items, and teen clothing. Communities had to build more schools. Today, these baby boomers are impacting the Social Security and Medicare systems, since many are or will soon be eligible for these benefits.

Migration and Immigration

As white middle-class Americans moved to the suburbs, African Americans from the South and new immigrants from Latin America moved into cities. By the 1950s, African Americans and Hispanics had become significant and growing minorities in the North.

Suburban Mass Production Builders created entire suburban communities. One, established in Levittown, New York, used the same design for all of its houses so that they could be **prefabricated** (build standard parts in a factory and then put them together on the building site). Prefabrication meant lower costs. Thus, returning soldiers, aided by government loans, were able to buy affordable homes.

Cities in Decline The increase in urban populations raised troubling issues for city governments. In general, the new populations were poorer than the middle-income groups that they were replacing. Inevitably, there was a decline in the tax base within the cities just as the need for greater services soared. By the 1970s, many cities such as New York City would be close to bankruptcy and desperately needed federal aid.

New Immigration Patterns Most Latin American newcomers came from Mexico, Cuba, and Puerto Rico.

Poor Mexicans sought economic opportunity in the United States. They came as *braceros* (laborers) to harvest crops in California, Texas, and other

Southwestern states. While many entered in compliance with immigration laws, many others crossed the border illegally.

Puerto Rico had become a U.S. territory in 1898 as a result of the Spanish-American War. In 1917, Congress granted Puerto Ricans full U.S. citizenship. In 1952, their island was given commonwealth status; that is, Puerto Ricans elected their own governors and did not pay U.S. federal taxes. As U.S. citizens, Puerto Ricans may enter or leave the United States at will. After World War II, many of them settled in New York and other Northeastern cities in search of jobs, which were scarce back home.

Fidel Castro's Communist revolution in Cuba (1959) caused hundreds of thousands of Cubans to flee to the United States. They settled in Miami and other Florida cities. Most Cuban immigrants had middle- or upper-income backgrounds and readily found employment in the United States.

IN REVIEW

1. Define consumerism, baby boom, Levittown, *bracero*.
2. Explain the significance of television as a force for change in American society.
3. Describe the new immigration patterns of the 1950s.

CHAPTER REVIEW

MULTIPLE-CHOICE QUESTIONS

1 In foreign affairs, the domino theory was mainly applied to
(1) United States involvement in Latin America
(2) Japanese expansion in East Asia
(3) the Communist threat in Southeast Asia
(4) the movement for national independence in Africa

2 The Eisenhower Doctrine (1957) was an effort by the United States to
(1) gain control of the Suez Canal
(2) take possession of Middle East oil wells
(3) find a homeland for Palestinian refugees
(4) counter the influence of the Soviet Union in the Middle East

3 **"*Sputnik* Launch Propels Soviets Ahead in Space Race"**

In 1957, the United States government responded to the event described in this headline by
(1) reducing military spending
(2) building a joint space station with the Soviet Union
(3) constructing President Ronald Reagan's "Star Wars" defense system
(4) providing funds to improve the educational system in the United States

Base your answer to question 4 on the following diagram and on your knowledge of social studies.

4 Which development following World War II caused the urban-suburban pattern shown in the diagram?

Urban-Suburban Pattern of American Life

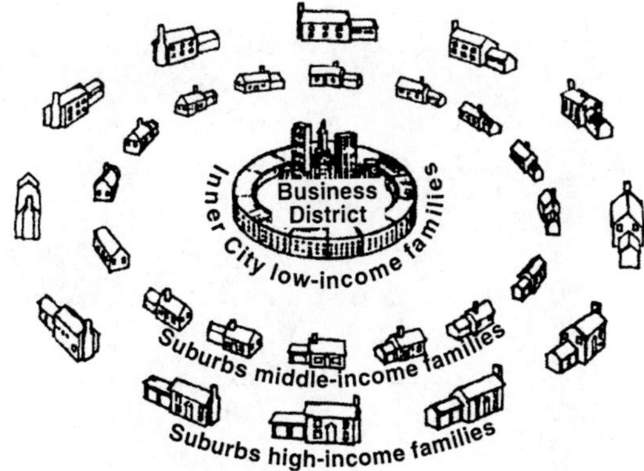

(1) increase in the number of farms
(2) expansion of highways and automobile ownership
(3) movement of most factories to rural areas
(4) decline in the number of middle-income families

5 In a farewell message to the American public, President Dwight D. Eisenhower warned of the growth of the "military-industrial complex." This term refers to the
(1) influence of defense contractors on Congress
(2) threat from the Soviet Army
(3) internal danger from Communist spies
(4) economy's dependence on oil imported from the Middle East

6 "We conclude that in the field of public education the doctrine of 'separate but equal' has no place. Separate educational facilities are inherently unequal."
—*Brown* v. *Board of Education* (1954)

Which constitutional idea was the basis for this Supreme Court decision?
(1) protection against double jeopardy
(2) equal protection of the law
(3) freedom of speech
(4) right of assembly

7 Rosa Parks was honored at the March on Washington for her part in
(1) bringing about the Montgomery bus boycott
(2) integrating Little Rock Central High School
(3) forming the Student Nonviolent Coordinating Committee
(4) organizing lunch counter sit-ins in Greensboro, North Carolina

Base your answer to question 8 on the statement below and on your knowledge of social studies.

> ...Whenever normal agencies prove inadequate to the task and it becomes necessary for the Executive Branch of the Federal Government to use its powers and authority to uphold Federal Courts, the President's responsibility is inescapable.
>
> In accordance with that responsibility, I have today issued an Executive Order directing the use of troops under Federal authority to aid in the execution of Federal law at Little Rock, Arkansas. This became necessary when my Proclamation of yesterday was not observed, and the obstruction of justice still continues....
>
> —President Dwight D. Eisenhower, September 24, 1957

8 The situation described in this statement grew out of efforts to
(1) uphold the Voting Rights Act
(2) pass a constitutional amendment ending poll taxes
(3) enforce the decision in *Brown* v. *Board of Education of Topeka*
(4) extend the Montgomery bus boycott to Little Rock

9 What was the significance of the use of Federal marshals to protect African-American students in Little Rock, Arkansas, in 1957?

(1) It was the first time martial law had been declared in the United States.
(2) It led to Federal takeover of many Southern public schools.
(3) It strengthened control of education by state governments.
(4) It showed that the Federal Government would enforce court decisions on integration.

Base your answer to question 10 on the map below and on your knowledge of social studies.

10 The information on the map supports the conclusion that African-American migration between 1940 and 1970 was mainly from the
(1) urban areas to rural areas
(2) South to the North
(3) Mountain states to the West Coast
(4) Sun Belt to the Great Plains

THEMATIC ESSAYS

1 **Theme:** *U.S. Foreign Policy, 1945–1960.* U.S. commitment to contain communism resulted in a period of peace with tension.

Task: Complete *both* of the following tasks:

- Describe *one* example of how the United States promoted peace or avoided potential conflict.
- Describe *one* incident that increased cold-war tensions.

Consider the end of the Korean War, the policies of John Foster Dulles, development of the H-bomb, "atoms for peace," the U-2 incident, new alliances such as NATO and SEATO, the Suez Crisis, the anti-Communist uprising in Hungary, the Eisenhower Doctrine, and the launching of *Sputnik* by the Soviet Union. You are *not* limited to these examples.

2 **Theme:** *The United States in the 1950s: Conformity and Change.* Some historians view Americans of the 1950s as conformists. Others view the period as a time of great change in U.S. society.

African-American Migration, 1940–1970

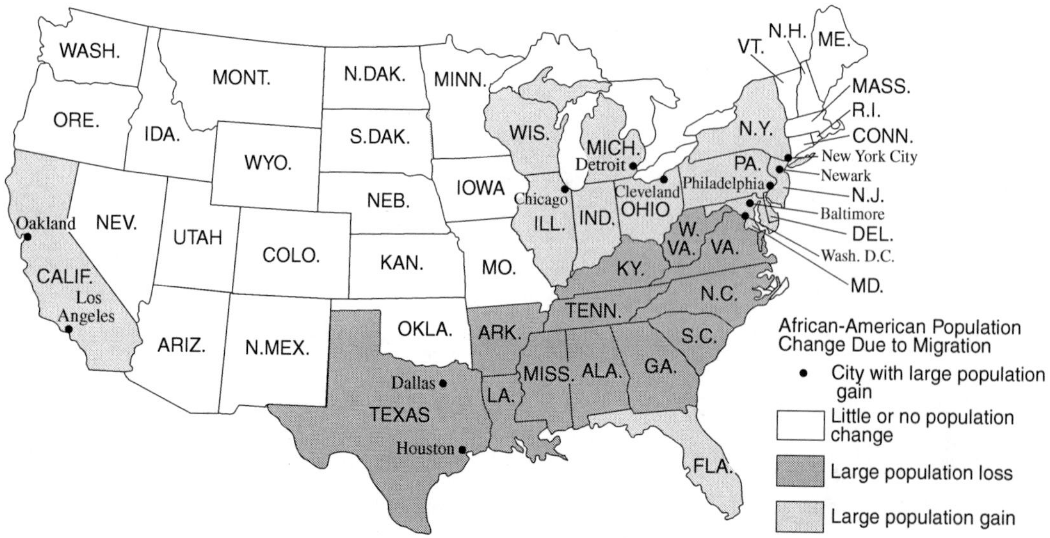

Task: Complete *both* of the following tasks:

- Describe *one* way in which Americans sought to conform.
- Demonstrate *one* example of how change was taking place simultaneously with conformity.

You may use, but are not limited to, the interstate highway system, suburban development, early civil rights actions, television, the automobile, consumerism, the baby boom, the decline of cities, and immigration patterns.

DOCUMENT-BASED QUESTION

Study each document and answer the question that follows it. Then read the **Task** *and write your essay. Include references to most of the documents and additional information you retain about U.S. history and government.*

Historical Context: In spite of some small gains by African Americans during the late 1940s and 1950s, implementation of equal rights for black people would be a long and difficult process.

Document 1: Refer to the inset photograph below.

Question: What does the photo show about the armed services in the 1950s?

Document 2: Refer to the other photograph below.

Question: How did Jackie Robinson serve as a symbol of hope to many African Americans?

Document 3: Refer to the reading by Chief Justice of the United States Earl Warren in 1954, *Brown* v. *Board of Education, Topeka, Kansas.*

Former prisoners of war returning from Korea: The integrated U.S. Army of the 1950s

Jackie Robinson of the Brooklyn Dodgers—first African American in baseball's major leagues

> ...Compulsory school attendance laws and the great expenditures for education both demonstrate... the importance of education to our democratic society. It is required in ...our most basic public responsibilities, even...the armed forces. It is the very foundation of good citizenship. ...[It awakens] the child to cultural values...[prepares] for later professional training, and [helps in adjustment] to [the] environment.... [I]t is doubtful that any child [can] succeed in life [without] the opportunity of an education. Such an opportunity... must be made available to all on equal terms.
>
> ...Does segregation...in public schools..., even though the physical facilities...may be equal, deprive... the minority group of equal educational opportunities? We believe that it does.

QUESTION: What was the Chief Justice saying about segregated school facilities?

DOCUMENT 4: Refer to the photograph below.

QUESTION: How did Rosa Parks help promote integration in Montgomery, Alabama?

Crowd of whites protest integration of Little Rock Central High School.

DOCUMENT 5: Refer to the photograph above.

QUESTION: Why was it difficult to integrate Central High School in Little Rock, Arkansas?

TASK: Using the documents and your knowledge of U.S. history and government, write an essay in which you:

- give *one* example of how hope for a better future was provided for African Americans in the late 1940s and in the 1950s.
- show how, in spite of the gains made, the average African American in the 1950s was still a second-class citizen.

Rosa Parks in the front of a Montgomery, Alabama, bus when Southern segregation laws required African Americans to sit in the back

CHAPTER 17
Liberalism at Home: 1961–1969

DOCUMENTS AND LAWS
Vocational Rehabilitation Act (1920) • New Frontier (1961–1963) • *Mapp* v. *Ohio* (1961)
Baker v. *Carr* (1962) • *Engel* v. *Vitale* (1962) • *Abington School District* v. *Schempp* (1963)
Gideon v. *Wainwright* (1963) • *Escobedo* v. *Illinois* (1964) • Civil Rights Act of 1964
Twenty-fourth Amendment (1964) • Great Society legislation (1964–1968)
Voting Rights Act of 1965 • *Miranda* v. *Arizona* (1966)
Tinker v. *Des Moines School District* (1969)
P.A.R.C. v. *Commonwealth of Pennsylvania* (1971)
Equal Employment Opportunity Act (1972)
Mills v. *Board of Education of District of Columbia* (1972) • Title IX (1972)
Equal Rights Amendment • *Roe* v. *Wade* (1973)
Vocational Rehabilitation Act, amended (1973)
Education for all Handicapped Children Act (1975)
Kaiser Aluminum and Chemical Corporation v. *Weber* (1979)
Regents of the University of California v. *Bakke* (1978) • Americans with Disability Act (1990)

EVENTS
Assassination of Medgar Evers (1963) • Assassination of President Kennedy (1963)
Civil rights march in Birmingham, Alabama (1963) • March on Washington (1963)
Assassination of Malcolm X (1965)
Civil rights march from Selma to Montgomery, Alabama (1965)
National Organization for Women (NOW) founded (1966)
Assassination of Martin Luther King, Jr. (1968) • AIM protest in Washington, D.C. (1972)
AIM protest at Wounded Knee (1973) • Defeat of Equal Rights Amendment (1982)

PEOPLE/GROUPS
Bella Abzug • Black Panthers • Stokely Carmichael • Rachel Carson • Cesar Chavez
Eldridge Cleaver • James Farmer • Freedom riders • Betty Friedan • Lyndon B. Johnson
John F. Kennedy • Robert Kennedy • James Meredith • Elijah Muhammad • Sonia Sotomayer
Gloria Steinem • Robert Weaver

OBJECTIVES

- To understand the social and political changes of the 1960s.
- To compare presidents Kennedy and Johnson as leaders.
- To note African Americans' gains in the civil rights movement.
- To describe other movements for social justice by the disabled, women, Hispanic Americans, and Native Americans.
- To analyze landmark Supreme Court cases that redefined the rights of the accused.

Kennedy Years

In his 1961 inaugural address, President John F. Kennedy showed a determination to champion liberty against **totalitarianism** (all-controlling political dictatorship such as Soviet communism). He appealed to the idealism of American youth: "Ask not what your country can do for you. Ask what you can do for your country."

Kennedy's *New Frontier* program included proposals for federal aid to education, greater Social Security benefits, assistance to Appalachia (a poor rural region stretching from Pennsylvania to Alabama), protection of African-American civil rights, and public health insurance for the elderly.

Domestic Policy Although both houses of Congress had Democratic majorities, Kennedy was able to pass only a few of his programs:

- funds for urban renewal (rebuilding rundown city neighborhoods)
- funds to aid the poor of Appalachia and other "distressed areas."

Other programs were rejected:

- grants to states for school construction and teachers' salaries
- Medicare (public health insurance) for elderly Americans
- a new civil rights law enabling the government to act boldly against discrimination and segregation.

Such important programs would be adopted during Lyndon Johnson's administration (1963–1969).

Desegregation

Interstate Buses The success of the Montgomery bus boycott and *Brown* v. *Board of Education* (discussed in Chapter 16) led to a new tactic in the civil rights movement: **freedom rides**. By crossing state lines on interstate buses, white and black freedom riders highlighted that segregation existed in interstate commerce (as defined in the Constitution) and, therefore, was not a matter of local law. After violent confrontations in which Southern whites attacked the riders, Robert Kennedy, the president's brother and U.S. attorney general, persuaded the Interstate Commerce Commission (ICC) to desegregate the buses.

University of Mississippi In 1962, a young African American, James Meredith, tried to enroll at the all-white University of Mississippi. Told by the governor not to enroll and threatened by a crowd of whites, Meredith stood firm. Kennedy ordered 400 federal marshals to the university to protect

CORE freedom riders faced attacks on their buses as well as other grave personal dangers.

Meredith. He became the first African American to graduate from this university. Soon, other Southern colleges and universities began admitting African Americans.

Martin Luther King, Jr. The Montgomery bus boycott led to the emergence of Martin Luther King, Jr., as a national leader of the civil rights movement.

King believed that nonviolent **civil disobedience** (refusal to obey unjust laws) would prevail against segregation. He effectively used this strategy to challenge segregation laws.

In 1963, King led a peaceful march through Birmingham, Alabama, to protest segregation there. The police attacked the marchers with dogs, water from fire hoses, and electric cattle prods. King and other marchers were arrested.

Writing from jail, King explained his action: "I submit that an individual who breaks [an unjust] law . . . and who willingly accepts the penalty of imprisonment in order to arouse the conscience of the community . . . is . . . expressing the highest respect for law."

Medgar Evers Medgar Evers was an NAACP leader who organized economic boycotts, marches, and picket lines. In 1963, Byron De La Beckwith, a white supremacist, assassinated Evers. In two trials, all-white juries could not reach a verdict. Years later, in 1994, Beckwith was sentenced to life in prison.

March on Washington In 1963, King and other civil rights leaders organized the March on Washington to alert Congress to the need for stronger civil rights laws. More than 200,000 participated and heard King's powerful "I Have a Dream" speech, a portion of which follows:

Martin Luther King, Jr., in Washington, D.C., 1963, where he delivered his "I Have a Dream" speech

> ...I have a dream that one day this nation will rise up and live out the true meaning of its creed: "We hold these truths to be self-evident; that all men are created equal." I have a dream that one day on the red hills of Georgia the sons of former slaves and the sons of former slave owners will be able to sit down together at the table of brotherhood.
>
> ...I have a dream that my four little children will one day live in a nation where they will not be judged by the color of their skin but by the content of their character....
>
> ...With this faith we will be able to work together, to pray together, to struggle together, to go to jail together, to stand up for freedom together, knowing that we will be free one day.

Kennedy Assassination

President Kennedy was shot and killed on November 22, 1963, while campaigning in Dallas, Texas. The police arrested Lee Harvey Oswald, but two days later, while in police custody, a local nightclub owner killed Oswald. A group known as the Warren Commission was organized to investigate the assassination of President Kennedy. It concluded that Oswald acted alone in the killing of Kennedy. However, the Commission's findings have been challenged by later studies, and thus a mystery still surrounds Kennedy's death. Did Oswald act alone or were others involved in the crime?

Rights of Disabled Citizens

A disabled person is someone with a physical or mental impairment that substantially alters a major life activity. Popular attitudes toward disability were once characterized by ignorance, fear, and superstition.

In the 19th century, attitudes became more humane. For example, Dorothea Dix (active 1840–1860) argued that the mentally disabled should be put in humane mental hospitals, not prisons.

"Normalization" In the early 20th century, a policy called "normalization" aimed to help the disabled enter mainstream society and lead more normal lives. The *Vocational Rehabilitation Act* (1920) was the first major federal program to assist disabled veterans of World War I with counseling, guidance, job training, and placement. The *Social Security Act* (1935) made the law permanent and provided federal funds.

Activism (1966–1990)

In 1962, Kennedy created a *President's Council on Mental Retardation*. It called attention to the job needs and capabilities of disabled persons and encouraged businesses to hire them.

During the Kennedy administration, a sports program—the Special Olympics—was started for intellectually disabled children and adults.

Litigation The U.S. Supreme Court has been involved in the effort to protect the rights of children.

- *P.A.R.C.* v. *Commonwealth of Pennsylvania* (1971). A U.S. district court ruled that Pennsylvania could not prevent mentally disabled children from participating in free public education. Equal protection under the law required state programs for educating mentally disabled children.
- *Mills* v. *Board of Education of District of Columbia* (1972). The Supreme Court established that children between 7 and 16, even if emotionally or mentally disabled, must be included in regular classes unless the school district provides a special program.

Legislation Congress passed several acts to protect the rights of disabled children.

- *Education of the Handicapped Act* (1966). In 1965, the *Elementary and Secondary Education Act (ESEA)* set up special funding known as Title I to meet the needs of economically disadvantaged students. The 1966 amendment also provided grants for disabled children.
- *Vocational Rehabilitation Act* (1973). This amendment to the original act of 1920 prohibited discrimination against the physically disabled in any

federal program or state program supported by federal funds. It provided for ramp accesses in public buildings, specially equipped buses for passengers in wheelchairs, suitable bathroom facilities in public places, and sign-language interpretations of public television programs.

- *Education for All Handicapped Children Act* (1975). This law provided for testing to identify disabilities, a list of rights for disabled children and their parents, and funds to assist state and local school districts in providing special education.
- *Americans With Disabilities Act* (1990). This law protected 43 million mentally and physically impaired Americans against discrimination. It required businesses to facilitate employment of disabled persons by providing "reasonable accommodations"—restructuring jobs, changing workstation layouts, and altering equipment. All new public accommodations had to be accessible to the disabled. In existing facilities, barriers to services were to be removed if "readily achievable."

Dependence to Independence

Activism by Veterans Veterans wounded in Vietnam held demonstrations to show that doors and stairs of courthouses, schools, and other public buildings made access difficult for people in wheelchairs. The federal government then required public buildings to have at least one entrance for wheelchairs, to make some telephone booths and toilets accessible to the disabled, and to design buses so that passengers in wheelchairs could board.

An hydraulic lift makes it possible for this young man to ride a city bus.

Deinstitutionalization The mentally ill were often kept in state mental hospitals for years with little or no treatment. In 1975, the Supreme Court ruled that such people who were not dangerous could not be confined against their will. New medicines and federal aid to local communities were supposed to provide support for the mentally ill. Many of those released, however, lacked skills and could not find jobs. By the late 1980s, many of them were living on the streets.

Mainstreaming Disabled students had often been placed in special schools. Many believed that such segregation damaged a child's self-image and ability to learn. A series of laws and court decisions during the 1970s mandated **mainstreaming**—providing special education services in regular classrooms so that disabled and all other children could be educated together. Special classrooms or schools were to be used only if a student's disability was too severe for mainstreaming.

IN REVIEW

1. Summarize and evaluate the domestic agenda of the Kennedy administration.
2. Define and evaluate the philosophy of Martin Luther King, Jr., as it has been used to protest unjust laws.
3. How did Congress act to protect the educational rights of disabled students in the 1960s and 1970s? Students should cite at least one law.

Johnson's Great Society

Vice President Lyndon Johnson succeeded Kennedy as president in 1963. Johnson, a more experienced politician, shared Kennedy's belief in liberal reforms. To realize his domestic program, the *Great Society,* Johnson got Congress to pass more important legislation than any other president since Franklin D. Roosevelt. Johnson was elected president in his own right in 1964.

Expanding Kennedy's Social Programs

War on Poverty/VISTA. Johnson announced an "unconditional" *War on Poverty,* a series of recommendations to Congress. As a first step, Congress passed the *Economic Opportunity Act* (1964), which authorized $1 billion for antipoverty programs. Congress also set up *VISTA* (*Volunteers in Service to America*). Modeled on the Peace Corps, VISTA sent volunteers to poor rural and urban areas of the country, including Native-American reservations, to teach and lend technical support.

Medicare To help senior citizens pay for hospital care, doctor care, and other medical needs, Congress established *Medicare,* which became part of

VISTA volunteer maps conditions of buildings in Cleveland, Ohio, in 1972

the Social Security system in 1964. People 65 or older were insured for much of the cost of health care. States also received *Medicaid*—federal grants to pay the medical bills of needy persons.

Education The *Elementary and Secondary Education Act* (1965) authorized $1.3 billion for educational programs such as *Head Start*—a program that gives instruction to disadvantaged preschool children.

The *Higher Education Act* (1965) authorized scholarships to low-income students qualified for college.

Environmental Issues In response to the environmental movement inspired by Rachel Carson's *Silent Spring* (discussed on page 387), Congress enacted several laws to control pollution and protect land, air, and water. The *Clean Air Act of 1963* funded state conferences to call attention to air quality and pollution. In 1965, the *Water Quality Act* attempted to establish clean-water standards. Also in 1965, the *Motor Vehicle Air Pollution Control Act* mandated the federal government to set automobile emission standards.

Civil Rights Movement

Without President Johnson's leadership, the Civil Rights Act of 1964 and the Voting Rights Act of 1965 (discussed on pages 299–300) would not have passed. In 1966, he appointed as secretary of Housing and Urban Development (HUD) Robert C. Weaver—the first African American to serve in a president's Cabinet. In 1967, Johnson appointed Thurgood Marshall to the Supreme Court—the first African American to serve there.

Black Protest, Pride, and Power

Activism With Nonviolence The following organizations in the civil rights movement were moderate in their methods and goals. They achieved political and economic equality through nonviolence:

- *National Association for the Advancement of Colored People (NAACP)* (discussed in Chapter 10).
- *Urban League.* This organization sought to end discrimination in employment and housing and to increase job opportunities for African Americans.
- *Student Nonviolent Coordinating Committee (SNCC).* Students who joined this organization participated in sit-ins and other peaceful demonstrations against Jim Crow laws in the South.
- *Southern Christian Leadership Conference (SCLC).* Founded in 1957 by Martin Luther King, Jr., SCLC coordinated African Americans' efforts to end segregation in the South. Its nonviolent protests included boycotts, sit-ins, and marches.
- *Congress of Racial Equality (CORE).* Founded during World War II, CORE, under the leadership of James Farmer, conducted freedom rides in the 1960s. White and black Americans took long-distance bus trips to check that terminals in the South were not segregated. Though attacked by racist mobs, members responded with **passive resistance** (noncooperative opposition to something without the use of violence).

Black Muslims/Black Panthers In the mid-1960s, more radical leaders—Eldridge Cleaver, Stokely Carmichael, and Angela Davis—were dissatisfied with the pace of progress. They called for "black power" and spoke of racial revolution. Two groups committed to black power were the *Black Muslims* and the *Black Panthers.*

Black Muslims are a group of African-American followers of Islam. Their founder, Elijah Muhammad, advocated (1) a separate African-American state within the United States, and (2) pride in being black. A leading Black Muslim, Malcolm X, formed his own group in 1963. He told his followers to obey the law but also urged them to fight back against physical abuse.

Organized in 1966, the Black Panthers advocated force to achieve "black power." They formed a semi-military organization, wore uniforms, and carried rifles. They also demanded "better education, better medical care, and better housing." Their chief spokesperson and minister of information was Eldridge Cleaver.

Montgomery, Alabama, civil rights marcher attacked by police dog, 1965

Civil Unrest There was strong and even violent opposition from white defenders of segregation. More than 30 African-American churches were bombed during the 1960s. In 1963, the bombing of a Baptist church in Birmingham, Alabama, killed four African-American girls.

In 1964, three young activists—James Chaney, a Southern black, and two white Jewish students from New York, Andrew Goodman and Michael Schwerner—tried to register African-American voters in Mississippi and were killed by unknown assailants. The Ku Klux Klan was suspected, but at the time no one was convicted of the murders. Many years later, in 2005, Edgar Ray Killen was found guilty of manslaughter and sentenced to 60 years in jail.

To rally support for registering African Americans in Alabama, Martin Luther King, Jr., in 1965, organized a long-distance march from Selma to the state capital, Montgomery. The marchers were beaten by the police and harassed by hostile crowds. President Johnson sent federal troops to protect them, although one marcher, Viola Liuzzo, was killed shortly after reaching Birmingham.

In Northern cities, African Americans, many of them unemployed and living in poor, crowded neighborhoods, realized that civil rights laws would not immediately solve their problems. The bombing of black churches and murdering of civil rights workers fueled anger and distrust of whites, which erupted in riots. The 1965 Watts riot in Los Angeles lasted six days and resulted in 34 deaths and $200 million worth of property damage. In the summers of 1966 and 1967, similar outbreaks occurred in more than 167 cities, including Detroit, Michigan, and Newark, New Jersey.

Investigating the rioting, the Kerner Commission noted that the United States was becoming two "separate but unequal" societies, one black and one white. It recommended government programs to relieve urban poverty and to increase job opportunities for African Americans.

White person protesting the speed of African Americans' civil rights gains
from *Straight Herblock* (Simon & Schuster, 1964)

Assassinations of Civil Rights Leaders Three African-American leaders were assassinated during the 1960s. Medgar Evers was killed by white racists in 1963. In 1965, Malcolm X was killed by three Black Muslim opponents. Martin Luther King, Jr., was killed in 1968. News of King's death touched off riots in many cities. A Southern white, James Earl Ray, was convicted of the crime.

Legislation

Civil Rights Act of 1964 This law authorized the U.S. attorney general to file lawsuits over civil rights violations and prohibited various forms of **racial discrimination** (treating someone differently because of race). It prohibited the following:

- discrimination in restaurants, hotels, and gas stations
- discrimination in government-operated facilities such as parks and pools
- discrimination in federal projects such as urban renewal and antipoverty programs
- discrimination by employers of 100 or more workers and by labor unions of 100 or more members (later reduced to 25).

In effect, the act abolished Jim Crow laws and practices.

In *Heart of Atlanta Motel, Inc.* v. *United States* (1964), a motel owner challenged Congress's right to outlaw discrimination in motels and hotels. The Court ruled that Congress had the right under the powers of the interstate commerce clause of the Constitution.

Twenty-fourth Amendment The Twenty-fourth Amendment (1964) prohibited a poll tax in federal elections (for president, vice president, and Congress). It especially benefited Southern African Americans, many of whom were too poor to pay poll taxes. Soon after ratification of the amendment, many states abolished the poll tax in state and local elections too.

Voting Rights Act (1965) This law prohibited literacy tests as means of barring African Americans from voting and authorized federal registrars to help blacks register in areas where they had been afraid to do so. Within a year, the number of registered Southern blacks increased by about 50 percent.

Supreme Court Decisions (1950–1995)

Educational Equity In *Sweatt* v. *Painter* (1950), the Supreme Court had declared that a black student, Herman Sweatt, must be accepted by the University of Texas law school because the only African-American law school in the state was unequal to the white law schools. In that same year, a black student at the University of Oklahoma challenged being seated apart from white students in classes and in the cafeteria. The Court ruled in *McLaurin* v. *Oklahoma State Regents* (1950) that a state may not treat a student differently because of race.

Brown v. *Board of Education of Topeka* (1954) had ended *de jure* segregation in education. In 1964, the Court ruled that schools in Prince Edward County, Virginia, could not use public funds to support private schools for white students.

In the 1970s, the Supreme Court challenged *de facto* segregation in the North, stemming from housing patterns. In several cases, the Court ruled that busing should be used to desegregate neighborhood schools. This ruling led to some violence by whites.

Affirmative Action Under Johnson, the government adopted a policy of **affirmative action**. To ensure that past discrimination did not continue, the government encouraged businesses to increase job opportunities for women and minorities. It also cut off financial aid to colleges and universities without affirmative action programs. Businesses without such programs lost their government contracts.

One of the first affirmative-action-in-education decisions of the Court was *Regents of the University of California* v. *Bakke* (1978). The university had twice rejected the application of Allan Bakke, a white man, even though his entrance examination scores were higher than those of many who had been admitted. The university argued that it had set aside 16 out of 100 openings for minority students to fulfill affirmative action goals. Bakke sued the university for violating the equal-protection clause of the Fourteenth Amendment.

Ruling in favor of Bakke, the Court declared that the university's approach to affirmative action was unconstitutional because it involved racial

U.S. Supreme Court Building

quotas. It said, however, that race could be one factor—but only one—in deciding whom to admit.

Student Rights In *Engel* v. *Vitale* (1962) the parents of several pupils in New York schools objected to a prayer composed by the New York State Board of Regents and meant to be **nondenominational** (favoring no religious group in particular). The board had recommended that students voluntarily recite the prayer in classrooms at the beginning of each day. The Supreme Court ruled that the practice violated separation of church and state.

***Abington School District* v. *Schempp* (1963)** Pennsylvania required that at least ten Bible verses be read in public schools each day. The Schempp family sued the Abington School District in Pennsylvania, claiming that Bible readings were against their religious beliefs. The Court ruled that Bible readings in public school violated the First Amendment's guarantee against establishment of religion.

***Tinker* v. *Des Moines School District* (1969)** The Supreme Court decided that students could not be penalized for wearing black armbands to school in protest against the Vietnam War. Students do not "shed their Constitutional rights to freedom of speech or expression at the schoolhouse gate."

Preferential Employment In 1971, the Court ruled against racial discrimination in employment. A power company in North Carolina required applicants without high school diplomas to take intelligence tests. The Court declared that such a requirement violated the Civil Rights Act of 1964 and the Fourteenth Amendment, which called for equality under law.

Kaiser Aluminum and Chemical Corporation v. *Weber* (1979) involved an affirmative action plan to correct racial imbalance in the workforce. The workers at Kaiser had been almost exclusively white. The steelworkers' union and the company agreed to develop a training program in which half of the trainees would be African American. Brian Weber, a white worker, sued Kaiser because he had been rejected for the program even though he had more **seniority** (years of service) than the African Americans selected.

The Court ruled that Kaiser's affirmative action plan was reasonable because it was temporary and did not deprive white workers of their jobs.

The Court did not always favor affirmative action. In a case involving the firefighters of Memphis, Tennessee, it ruled that African-American workers hired to reduce racial imbalance could be laid off first if they had less seniority than white coworkers. In 1995, the Court ruled against favoritism toward women and minority businesspeople bidding on government contracts.

Voting Rights/Legislative Reapportionment In *Baker* v. *Carr* (1962), the Supreme Court ruled that all legislative districts must have approximately the same number of persons ("one person, one vote"). Thus, voting districts in African-American areas could no longer contain more people than voting districts in white areas. As a consequence of this decision, the number of representatives from urban areas increased, which improved minority representation in state legislatures.

Modern Women's Movement

The Nineteenth Amendment gave women the vote but not equal rights in the workplace. After World War II, many women left their jobs to make way for ex-servicemen returning to the workforce. During the 1950s, most middle-income women preferred to stay at home and care for their families while their husbands provided the family income. Such traditional views were challenged in the 1960s by **feminists** (those in favor of women's rights and opposed to political, economic, and social inequality between men and women).

Kennedy Commission/Civil Rights Act of 1964 In 1963, Kennedy established a commission to investigate and review the role of U.S. women, with Eleanor Roosevelt as first chairperson. One goal of the Civil Rights Act of 1964 was to ban job discrimination on the basis of sex.

Title IX (1972) Title IX, which aimed to promote equal treatment in schools for female staff and students, stated that "no person in the United States shall, on the basis of sex, be excluded from participation in, be denied the benefits of, or be subjected to discrimination under any education program or activity receiving federal financial assistance." One consequence was that schools and colleges greatly increased sports programs for females.

"How Come No Founding Mothers?" A cartoonist's view of women's complaints about their exclusion from history

NOW (1966–Present) In 1966, feminist leaders formed the *National Organization for Women (NOW)*. Its goals included equal pay for equal work, day-care centers for the children of working mothers, and the passage of antidiscrimination laws. It also aimed to increase awareness about how men unfairly dominate women's lives.

Many NOW members, experienced in the civil rights movement, organized marches and demonstrations. NOW also supported female candidates for office and lobbied for changes in laws. NOW spokespersons such as Gloria Steinem and Bella Abzug became famous. In the 1970s, Abzug represented a New York City district in Congress. Steinem founded *Ms.*, a magazine focused on feminist issues. NOW still works for equal pay for equal work and such issues as a woman's right to abortion. It is politically strong on both state and national levels.

Shifting Roles and Images In 1963, Betty Friedan wrote *The Feminine Mystique*, which questioned the assumption that women were happiest at home and challenged women to redefine their roles. Friedan argued that women were not the "weaker sex" but as capable as men, and deserved equal opportunity to pursue high-level jobs. Friedan's book energized the women's rights movement.

Equal Rights Amendment In 1972, Congress proposed the *Equal Rights Amendment (ERA)* to the Constitution. It stated: "Equality of rights under the law shall not be denied or abridged by the United Sates or any state on account of sex." For ten years, NOW and other feminists campaigned for the ratification against strong opposition. The amendment failed to win support from the required 38 states.

Many NOW lawyers argued that discrimination against women violated the equal protection clause of the Fourteenth Amendment, according to which no state may "deny to any person within its jurisdiction the equal protection of the laws." Thus, government support of all-male public schools such as Stuyvesant High School in New York City was successfully challenged.

***Roe* v. *Wade* (1973)** A pregnant woman in Texas wanted an abortion, which was prohibited by state law. The U.S. Supreme Court ruled the law unconstitutional because it violated a woman's constitutional right to privacy. It further ruled that a woman could choose to have an abortion during the first six months of pregnancy. During the last three months, however, a state may prohibit an abortion to protect the fetus (unborn child)—considered a person at this stage, according to the court.

Roe v. *Wade* sparked an ongoing controversy. Supporters argue that the right to privacy applies to a woman's body. Opponents argue that a fetus is a person as pregnancy begins and has a right to life.

Equality in the Workplace Friedan and other feminists charged that male employers tended to discriminate against female workers. Median (average) income for men in the mid-1960s was $7,500 a year, compared to $5,600 for women. Men were more likely to obtain high-level positions and gain admittance to professional schools.

The *Equal Employment Opportunity Act* (1972) required equal pay for equal work and banned discriminatory practices in hiring, firing, promotions, and working conditions.

Many women confront a "glass ceiling"—an invisible barrier of discrimination in private corporations—that limits their attaining the highest positions. Women who raise families part-time rather than work full-time rarely reach the high-level positions. Increasingly, however, women are taking leadership roles in both government and business. Madeleine Albright, Condoleezza Rice, and Hillary Clinton have been secretary of state. There are women on the Supreme Court and women serving as chief executive officers of major corporations.

Domestic Abuse In the last decades of the 20th century, many women turned to the courts for protection against domestic abuse. Private foundations and women's shelters, which provide a place to seek help, have also reduced women's acceptance of domestic abuse.

Hispanic-American Activism

Hispanic Americans began to organize a movement for "brown power" in the 1960s.

Organized Farm Labor Like thousands of Mexican Americans in the Southwest, Cesar Chavez had worked long hours for low pay as a migrant farm laborer. Employers often exploited such workers. Unfortunately, with no permanent residences, they were extremely difficult to organize until Chavez succeeded in establishing the *United Farm Workers.*

From 1965 to 1970, Chavez's union struggled for *La Causa*—better pay and greater respect from California's grape growers. The union struck employers and urged Americans to boycott California grapes. Chavez insisted on complete nonviolence. Eventually, his tactics won major concessions. In 1970, the largest grape growers in California signed a contract with Chavez's union.

Cuban and Haitian Immigration By the 1950s, the U.S. Hispanic population had become a significant and growing minority. Castro's 1959 revolution in Cuba made hundreds of thousands of Cubans flee to the United States, mainly to Florida cities. This immigration continued into the 1980s.

Throughout the 1960s, "Papa Doc" Duvalier ruled Haiti. He formed a private military force and brutally put down all opposition. As a result, there was a surge in immigration from Haiti, primarily to Florida and New York. Continuing oppression and poverty in the 1980s increased illegal immigration from Haiti.

Political Involvement Hispanic-American involvement in politics has increased in states with large Hispanic minorities—such as Florida, Texas, California, and New York. In the 1980s, Miami elected its first Cuban-born mayor, Xavier Suarez, and Florida elected a Hispanic-American governor, Bob Martinez. In 1988, President Reagan appointed Lauro Cavazos as secretary of education. Hispanic Americans such as Nathan Quinones, Joseph Fernandez, and Ramon Cortines all served as chancellor (chief executive officer) of New York City's school system. In New Mexico, a Hispanic, Bill

Cesar Chavez (with sign) leads a United Farm Workers' boycott of table grapes in 1969.

Richardson was elected governor. President Obama's selection of Sonya Sotomayer as the first Hispanic appointee to the Supreme Court was another milestone.

Native-American Activism

Grievances and Goals In the 1960s, Native Americans from various reservations joined forces to assert "red power." The *National Congress of American Indians* complained that the *Bureau of Indian Affairs* (*BIA*) had failed for decades to raise Indians' standard of living. According to a 1960 study, they had a life expectancy of only 46 years, compared with 70 years for the population as a whole. More than other ethnic minorities, Indians suffered from malnutrition and unemployment. Activists demanded the following rights:

- greater freedom on reservations (less supervision by the BIA)
- return of fishing and hunting rights that Native Americans once enjoyed —even if state game laws had to be changed
- greater economic assistance against poverty
- fulfillment of broken U.S. treaties guaranteeing Native-American land claims.

Occupation of Alcatraz In 1969, a small group took control of Alcatraz Island in San Francisco Bay, the site of a former federal prison. The occupiers asserted that an 1860s treaty gave them the right to seize federal lands no longer in use. But their main purpose was to highlight injustice toward Native Americans. In time, the occupiers numbered more than 600, who called themselves "Indians of All Nations." After two years, communications and electricity were cut and most of the Indians left. The federal government removed the rest. They had, however, publicized their grievances.

Wounded Knee In 1972, the radical *American Indian Movement (AIM)* occupied the BIA offices in Washington, D.C., and demanded that the government honor historical treaties. In 1973, more than 200 armed members gained control of Wounded Knee, South Dakota. (An earlier conflict there is discussed on page 162.) During their two-month occupation, they demanded that old treaty rights be reinstated. They won no concessions, but they prepared the way for later court victories by several Native-American tribes. In 1975, Congress passed the *Indian Self-Determination and Education Act*, designed to increase self-government by reservation inhabitants and their control over education.

Victories in Court Through the 1970s, Native Americans sued for lands promised them by treaties. One court granted the Narragansett Indians of Rhode Island the return of 1,800 acres. In another suit, the Penobscots of Maine won thousands of acres and millions of dollars. The Sioux of South

Dakota won still another case, in which the court ruled that 7 million acres of land had been taken illegally from their ancestors.

Rights of the Accused

Conservatives accused the Supreme Court under Chief Justice Earl Warren of interfering with state police powers. Liberals argued that fair police procedures are required by the Fourth, Fifth, and Sixth amendments.

***Mapp v. Ohio* (1961)** This case involved the Fourth Amendment's protection against "unreasonable searches and seizures." An Ohio court had convicted Dollree Mapp of a crime on the basis of evidence obtained without a search warrant. The Court ruled that wrongly obtained evidence cannot be admitted during a trial.

***Gideon v. Wainwright* (1963)** This case involved the Sixth Amendment's guarantee that the accused shall "have the assistance of counsel for his defense." Accused of breaking into a Florida poolroom, Clarence Gideon could not afford a lawyer. Florida provided lawyers for defendants only in *capital cases* (those punishable by death). The Court ruled that Gideon was tried unfairly because a state must provide lawyers to poor defendants in all criminal cases.

***Escobedo v. Illinois* (1964)** This case also involved the right of an accused person to counsel. The Illinois police arrested Danny Escobedo as a murder suspect. During questioning, the police refused Escobedo's request for a lawyer. Statements that he made were later used at his trial to convict him. The Court ruled that Escobedo's right to counsel under the Sixth Amendment had been violated.

***Miranda v. Arizona* (1966)** Ernesto Miranda did not ask to see a lawyer when questioned by the Arizona police. After two hours, he signed a written confession of kidnapping and rape. The Court's decision stated: "Prior to any questioning, the person must be warned that he has a right to remain silent, that any statement he makes may be used as evidence against him, and that he has a right to the presence of an attorney." The police now read "Miranda rights" to arrested suspects before they are questioned.

IN REVIEW

1. Identify the goals of reformers in *each* of the following movements: (a) women's rights, (b) rights of Hispanic Americans, and (c) rights of Native Americans.
2. How did the civil rights movement influence the demands for equality on the part of Hispanic Americans and Native Americans?
3. Select *three* landmark Supreme Court cases of the Warren Court, and for each case, (a) identify the constitutional issue involved and (b) summarize the Court's decision.

CHAPTER REVIEW

MULTIPLE-CHOICE QUESTIONS

1 "...there are two types of laws: There are *just* laws and there are *unjust* laws. I would be the first to advocate obeying just laws. One has not only a legal but a moral responsibility to obey just laws. Conversely, one has a moral responsibility to disobey unjust laws."

—MARTIN LUTHER KING, JR.

This statement is a justification of the concept of
(1) cultural pluralism
(2) ethnic assimilation
(3) reverse discrimination
(4) civil disobedience

2 "I have a dream that one day this nation will rise up and live out the true meaning of its creed: 'We hold these truths to be self-evident; that all men are created equal.'"

—MARTIN LUTHER KING, JR., WASHINGTON, D.C., 1963

Which step was taken following this speech to advance the dream of Martin Luther King, Jr.?
(1) desegregation of the Armed Forces
(2) ruling in *Plessy* v. *Ferguson*
(3) elimination of the Ku Klux Klan
(4) passage of new civil rights acts

3 A major purpose of the Americans With Disabilities Act is to
(1) eliminate physical barriers for persons with disabilities
(2) create separate but equal facilities for all persons
(3) encourage political participation by persons with disabilities
(4) decrease government welfare payments for persons with disabilities

Base your answer to question 4 on the following cartoon and on your knowledge of social studies.

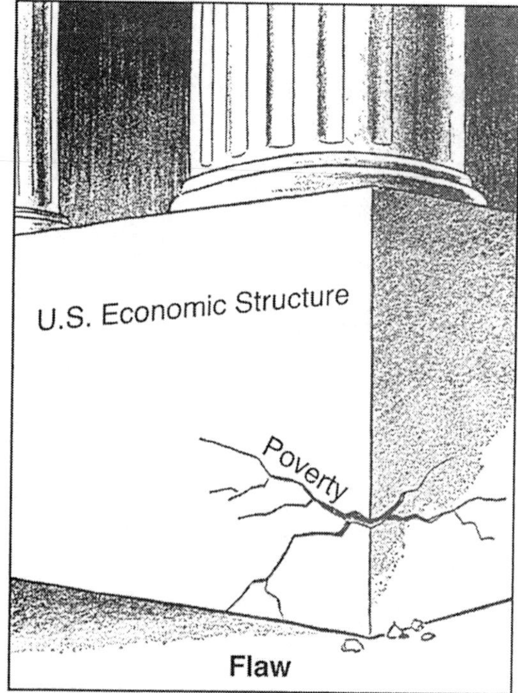

Source: Robert Palmer, *The Springfield Leader and Press* (adapted)

4 Which federal government program was designed to solve the problem illustrated in this cartoon?
(1) Great Society
(2) Peace Corps
(3) New Federalism
(4) Dollar Diplomacy

Base your answer to question 5 on the chart below and on your knowledge of social studies.

African-American Voter Registration

	Years	
State	*1960*	*1966*
Alabama	66,000	250,000
Mississippi	22,000	175,000
N. Carolina	210,000	282,000
S. Carolina	58,000	191,000
Tennessee	185,000	225,000

5 The changes shown in the chart were most directly the result of the
(1) enactment of voting-reform laws by these Southern states
(2) Supreme Court decision in *Brown* v. *Board of Education*
(3) passage of the Voting Rights Act of 1965
(4) executive branch's resistance to protecting the civil rights of minorities

6 The program that promotes preference in hiring for African Americans and other minorities to correct past injustices is known as
(1) Title IX
(2) open admissions
(3) affirmative action
(4) Head Start

7 "No person in the United States shall, on the basis of sex, be excluded from participation in, be denied the benefits of, or be subjected to discrimination under any education program or activity receiving Federal financial assistance,..."
—TITLE IX, 1972

The passage of this law affected women across the nation by
(1) granting them the right to own property
(2) guaranteeing them the same wages as male workers
(3) increasing their opportunities to participate in school sports
(4) allowing them the right to seek elective offices

8 The Supreme Court decision in *Roe* v. *Wade* (1973) was based on the constitutional principle of
(1) protection of property rights
(2) freedom of speech
(3) right to privacy
(4) freedom of religion

9 As a result of the Supreme Court ruling in *Miranda* v. *Arizona* (1966), a person accused of a crime is entitled to
(1) a speedy trial
(2) reasonable bail
(3) a reading of his or her rights at the time of arrest
(4) protection against cruel or unusual punishment

10 The police enter an individual's home without invitation or a warrant and seize evidence to be used against the individual. Which Supreme Court decision may be used to rule this evidence inadmissible in court?
(1) *Baker* v. *Carr*
(2) *Gideon* v. *Wainwright*
(3) *Mapp* v. *Ohio*
(4) *Roe* v. *Wade*

THEMATIC ESSAYS

1 **THEME:** *Federal Activism.* From the 1950s through the 1970s, the U.S. government took an active role in creating change and reform, which benefited many people.

TASK: Complete *both* of the following tasks:

- Choose *one* example of federal legislation and *one* Supreme Court decision from the 1950s through the 1970s. Explain how *each* created positive change for a specific group.
- Evaluate the degree of success of *each* of the examples selected.

Examples of federal legislation involve the disabled, voting rights, health care, civil rights, and poverty.

Examples of Supreme Court decisions involve integration, student rights, rights of the accused, voting, and affirmative action.

You are not limited to these suggestions. Specific names of the federal law and Supreme Court case are not necessary so long as detailed descriptions are given.

2 **THEME:** *Public Opinion and the Civil Rights Movement.* In the 1960s, public opinion influenced the federal government to begin ensuring greater equality for African Americans.

TASK: Complete all *three* of the following tasks:

- Describe *two* specific examples of how civil rights leaders used public opinion to promote greater equality for African Americans.
- Describe how the media (television, radio, newspapers, etc.) helped promote or influence pubic opinion about the civil rights movement.
- Evaluate the degree of success of *either* example that you described.

You may use, but are not limited to, integration of facilities, voter registration, equality of educational opportunity, and the March on Washington.

DOCUMENT-BASED QUESTION

Study each document and answer the question that follows it. Then read the ***Task*** *and write your essay. Include references to most of the documents and additional information you retain about U.S. history and government.*

HISTORICAL CONTEXT: The civil rights movement utilized a variety of tactics to create a more equitable society.

DOCUMENT 1: From Martin Luther King, Jr.'s "Letter From a Birmingham Jail," April 1963:

> Nonviolent direct action seeks to create such a crisis and establish such creative tension [that] a community that has consistently refused to negotiate is forced to confront the issue. It seeks so to dramatize the issue that it can no longer be ignored.... [Creating tension]... may sound rather shocking.... I am not afraid of the word tension. I have earnestly worked and preached against violent tension, but ...constructive nonviolent tension... is necessary for growth.

QUESTION: Why did King recommend nonviolent direct action?

DOCUMENT 2: Refer to the drawing below.

1963 drawing of African Americans on a nonviolent civil rights march

QUESTION: Why would the artist have agreed or not agreed with Martin Luther King, Jr.'s "Letter From a Birmingham Jail" (excerpted above)?

DOCUMENT 3: From Stokely Carmichael, "What We Want," 1966:

> But our vision is not merely of a society in which all black men have enough to buy the good things of life. When we urge that black money go into black pockets, we mean the communal pocket...into the community...to benefit it.... We want to see black ghetto residents demand that an exploiting store keeper sell them, at minimal cost, a building or a shop that they will own and improve

> cooperatively . . . [by means of] a rent strike, or a boycott, and a community so unified . . . that no one else will move into the building or buy at the store. The society we seek . . . is not a capitalist one. It is a society in which . . . community and humanistic love prevail.

QUESTION: What new tactics did Carmichael suggest that African Americans use?

DOCUMENT 4: Refer to the photograph above.

QUESTION: What happened to many people in the South who demanded civil rights?

DOCUMENT 5: Statement by the minister of defense of the Black Panthers, May 2, 1967:

> The Black Panther Party . . . calls upon . . . people in general and . . . black people in particular to . . . note . . . the racist California Legislature which is . . . considering . . . keeping the black people disarmed and powerless [while] racist police agencies . . . are intensifying the terror, brutality, murder, and repression of black people.
>
> Black people have begged, prayed, petitioned, demonstrated, . . . to get the *racist* power structure . . . to right the wrongs . . . perpetrated against black people. . . . these efforts have been answered by . . . repression, deceit, and hypocrisy. As [U.S.] aggression . . . escalates in Vietnam, the police agencies [here] escalate the repression of black people. . . . Vicious police dogs, cattle prods, and increased patrols [are a] familiar sight. . . . City Hall turns a deaf ear to the pleas of black people. . . .
>
> . . . [T]he time has come for black people to arm themselves against this terror before it is too late.

QUESTION: How did the Black Panther Party feel African Americans should respond to conditions in the United States?

TASK: Using the documents and your knowledge of U.S. history and government, write an essay in which you:

- describe different tactics suggested by various civil rights activists as the 1960s progressed.
- explain why civil rights leaders changed strategies at various times during the 1960s.

CHAPTER 18
Limits of Power: The Continuing Cold War (1961–1974)

DOCUMENTS AND LAWS
Nuclear Test-Ban Treaty (1963) • Tonkin Gulf Resolution (1964) • Pentagon Papers (1971)
War Powers Act (1973)

EVENTS
NASA created (1958) • Bay of Pigs invasion (1961) • Berlin Wall built (1961)
Cuban Missile Crisis (1962) • Vietnam War (1965–1975)
Assassination of Robert Kennedy (1968) • Tet Offensive (1968)
Democratic Convention of 1968 • Election of 1968
War protest march in Washington, D.C. (1969) • *Apollo 11* astronauts walk on moon (1969)
Kent State incident (1970) • U.S. withdrawal from Vietnam (1973)
North Vietnamese victory (1975)

PEOPLE/GROUPS
Neil Armstrong • Fidel Castro • Daniel Ellsberg • John Glenn • Hippies • Ho Chi Minh
Abbie Hoffman • Hubert Humphrey • Robert Kennedy • Nikita Khrushchev • Henry Kissinger
Lyndon B. Johnson • Eugene McCarthy • MIAs • Richard Nixon • POWs • Alan Shepard • SDS
Vietcong • George Wallace

OBJECTIVES

- To understand various public pressures that affect the American political system.
- To recognize the limitations of modern war technology in dealing with nationalistic uprisings.
- To analyze the foreign policy of John F. Kennedy.
- To explore U.S. involvement in Vietnam through the presidencies of John F. Kennedy, Lyndon Johnson, and Richard Nixon.

Cold War Crises

President John F. Kennedy continued the policy of containment that had begun during the Truman administration (discussed on page 260). In his "Inaugural Address" (1961), Kennedy said, "Let every nation know, whether it wishes us well or ill, that we shall pay any price, bear any burden, meet any hardship, support any friend, oppose any foe to assure the survival and the success of liberty."

Bay of Pigs

In 1959, Fidel Castro had overthrown Cuba's military dictator, Fulgencio Batista. The United States approved the change until Castro seized

American-owned properties in Cuba and established a Communist regime. Cuba soon fell under Soviet influence.

President Eisenhower had approved U.S. assistance to Cuban exiles planning to invade Cuba and oust Castro. Kennedy also supported the assistance. But he rejected supporting the invasion with U.S. air power. In April 1961, the Cuban invasion was launched in an area known as the *Bay of Pigs.* Its failure was an embarrassment for the Kennedy administration.

Vienna Summit/Berlin Wall

In 1955, West Germany had joined NATO, and East Germany, the Warsaw Pact. Because West Germany became more prosperous than Soviet-controlled East Germany, many East Germans fled to West Germany. Shortly after Kennedy's inauguration, Nikita Khrushchev threatened to sign a Soviet treaty with East Germany that would allow the East German Communists to cut off all the food shipped to West Berlin by land. Kennedy and Khrushchev met to discuss the issue in a summit conference in Vienna, Austria, but they came to no agreement.

In August 1961, the Soviets and East Germans built the *Berlin Wall* to prevent East Berliners from escaping to West Berlin. Kennedy traveled to West Berlin to assure the people there that any threat against them would also be a threat against the United States. In a highly applauded speech, he assured West Berliners of American support by saying, "Ich bin ein Berliner" (I am a Berliner).

The Caribbean and Central America

Cuban Missile Crisis

Cuba is only 90 miles from Florida. In October 1962, U.S. spy planes discovered Soviet nuclear missiles in Cuba. Kennedy sent U.S. ships into Cuban waters to blockade the coast and intercept Soviet ships. He demanded that Soviet ships carrying missiles to Cuba turn around and that the missiles already in Cuba be removed. Many Americans feared a nuclear war if Khrushchev disregarded Kennedy's demands.

But Khrushchev complied. In return, Kennedy publicly agreed never again to support an invasion of Cuba. Privately, he agreed to remove U.S. missiles from Turkey. The *Cuban Missile Crisis* was considered Kennedy's greatest success, as the Bay of Pigs invasion had been his greatest failure. Afterward, the Soviet Union and the United States became more cautious with each other.

Latin America

Kennedy developed a Marshall-like plan to promote economic growth in Latin America and contain the spread of communism from Cuba. This *Alliance for Progress* gave Latin American nations, excepting Cuba, $20 billion over ten years. Latin America, however, lacked Western Europe's democratic traditions, and most of the aid funded the ruling class rather than the poor. Congress allowed the program to die out.

Peace Corps

Another foreign aid program, the *Peace Corps*, sent volunteers to help people in Africa, Asia, and Latin America by teaching them literacy and modern methods of agriculture and health care. The Peace Corps tried to build goodwill for the United States through person-to-person contacts in developing countries.

Race to the Moon

The Soviet launch of *Sputnik* in 1957 spurred President Eisenhower to sign the *Space Act of 1958*, which created the *National Aeronautics and Space Administration (NASA)* to compete with the Soviets in space. In 1961, Soviet cosmonaut Yuri Gagarin became the first human to orbit Earth in outer space. Less than a month later, a NASA rocket lifted astronaut Alan Shepard into space but not into orbit. In 1962, astronaut John Glenn orbited Earth for five hours.

In 1961, Kennedy announced that the United States would be the first nation to land a human on the moon. In July 1969, *Apollo 11* carried Michael Collins, Neil Armstrong, and Edwin Aldrin, Jr., to the moon, as millions around the world watched on TV. As Neil Armstrong set foot on the lunar surface, he said, "That was one small step for a man, one giant leap for mankind." Kennedy's promise had been kept.

Astronaut Edwin E. Aldrin, Jr., walking on the moon, 1969

Nuclear Test-Ban Treaties

The Cuban Missile Crisis had influenced President Kennedy's decision to seek a *Nuclear Test-Ban Treaty.* By 1963, U.S.-Soviet relations had improved. The superpowers signed such a treaty agreeing to end nuclear-weapons testing in the atmosphere, outer space, and underwater. Underground tests were permitted. In 1967, another treaty banned putting nuclear weapons in orbit around Earth, on the moon, or on planets. A "hot line" established a direct telegraph link between the U.S. president and the Soviet premier so that they could communicate quickly in a crisis. Both Kennedy and Khrushchev recognized the need to avoid direct military conflicts, which could lead to the destruction of a nuclear war.

United States and Communism in Indochina

(*Note*: To review the domino theory and its application to French Indochina during the Eisenhower administration, see page 275.)

President Eisenhower believed that a U.S. failure to respond to the Communist challenge in Indochina would damage the credibility of U.S. commitments elsewhere in the world.

Vietnam Civil War

Vietnam lies just south of China. It was a French colony beginning in the late 1800s. During World War II, it was occupied by Japan. After the Japanese occupiers left in 1945, nationalist leader Ho Chi Minh proclaimed independence from French colonial rule. But the French opposed Vietnamese

Vietnam War

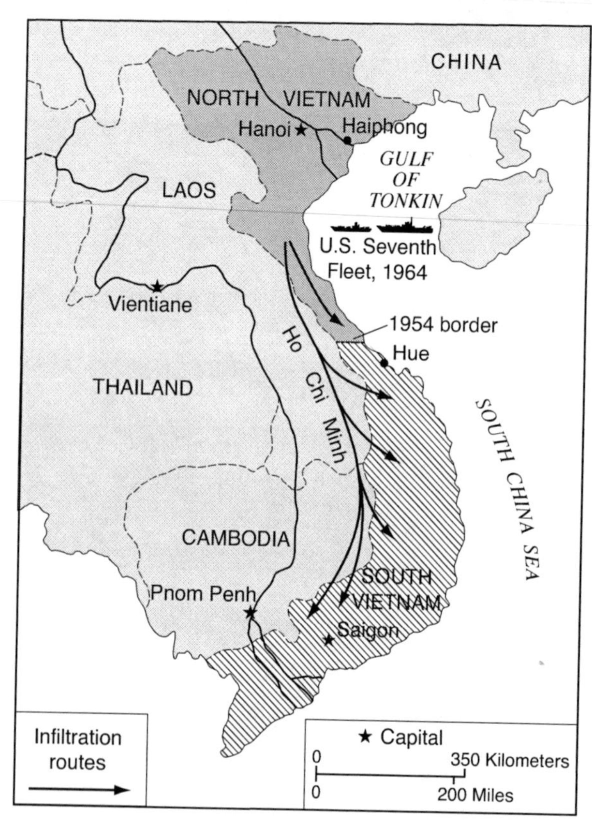

independence and regained military control. As a result, Ho, a Communist, directed **guerrilla warfare** (surprise attacks by small bands of raiders) against the French from northern Vietnam. In such warfare, advanced technology has only limited effectiveness.

U.S. Involvement

After a major defeat at Dien Bien Phu in 1954, the French withdrew from French Indochina (Cambodia, Laos, and Vietnam). In each country, Communists competed with other factions to win control.

In 1954, a conference about Indochina was held in Geneva, Switzerland. The United States attended only as an observer. French, Vietnamese, and other diplomats agreed to divide Vietnam at the 17th Parallel into a Communist north and a non-Communist south. Within two years, elections were supposed to be held to unite the country under one government.

The elections were never held as a civil war broke out in the south between supporters of Ho and those of South Vietnam's government led by Ngo Dinh Diem. To contain Ho's faction, Eisenhower increased U.S. support of South Vietnam by sending U.S. advisers to train South Vietnam's loyal soldiers.

Deeper Involvement Under Kennedy President Kennedy continued Eisenhower's policy of giving South Vietnam military aid and increasing the number of advisers from 2,000 in 1961 to 16,000 in 1963. Hoping to fortify Diem against a Communist takeover, Kennedy urged him to fight poverty and make democratic reforms. Instead, Diem tried to crush Buddhist opposition with violence, which provoked greater opposition. In 1963, Diem was assassinated by South Vietnamese military leaders.

IN REVIEW

1. How did the Peace Corps reflect Kennedy's words when he said, "Ask not what your country can do for you. Ask what you can do for your country"?

2. How did Kennedy and Khrushchev succeed in reducing cold-war tensions?
3. Explain how *each* of the following created a cold-war crisis for Kennedy: (a) Bay of Pigs invasion, (b) Berlin Wall, (c) Cuban Missile Crisis, (d) Vietnam.

Johnson and the "Americanization" of the War

In 1963, President Johnson promised "no wider war" in Vietnam, but in 1964 he concluded that South Vietnam was losing to the *Vietcong* (Communist guerrillas in South Vietnam). To counter North Vietnam's strong support of the Vietcong and fearing a Communist takeover of Indochina, Johnson began an "Americanization" of the war by sending in U.S. troops.

In August 1964, there were inaccurate reports of North Vietnamese gunboat attacks on two U.S. ships in the Gulf of Tonkin, near North Vietnam. Based on these reports, Johnson asked Congress for increased military aid to South Vietnam. Congress responded with the *Tonkin Gulf Resolution.* It authorized the president "to take all necessary measures to repel any armed attack against the forces of the United States and to prevent further aggression." Johnson now had power to use armed force in Vietnam however he wanted to, thus expanding presidential power. Like the Korean War, the Vietnam War began and was fought without a formal declaration of war by Congress.

Escalation/Tet Offensive In 1965, Johnson sent combat troops to Vietnam and bombed targets in the north. The U.S. troop count rose from 184,000 in 1965 to 536,100 in 1968. This steady **escalation** (buildup of forces) was intended to lead to a quick U.S. victory. It was also meant to prevent a takeover of much of Asia by Communist China and the Soviet Union.

In January 1968, Communist forces made major gains in South Vietnam and were about to capture the capital, Saigon. Although this so-called *Tet Offensive* was pushed back, it demonstrated Communist strength and forced the Americans to anticipate a long war.

Debating the War

Arguments for the War To answer American doubts about U.S. involvement in Vietnam, Johnson, in a 1965 speech, offered the following reasons:

- Since 1954, the United States had pledged to help South Vietnam.
- Ending U.S. commitments to South Vietnam would make U.S. commitments elsewhere untrustworthy.
- A Communist victory in South Vietnam would threaten neighbors in Southeast Asia and foster Communist aggression throughout the region (the domino theory).

- Communist China was supporting North Vietnam's war effort as part of "a wider pattern of aggressive purposes."

Arguments Against the War Opponents of U.S. involvement offered the following arguments:

- Communist North Vietnam did not take orders from China or the Soviet Union. In fact, Vietnam was a historic enemy of China. North Vietnam was actually fighting for nationalistic reasons.
- The distant war was not vital to U.S. security, nor were Vietnam's resources vital to the U.S. economy.
- A long land war in Asia involving U.S. troops was too costly.
- The South Vietnamese government was corrupt and undemocratic.
- South Vietnam's army was incapable of winning against the Vietcong guerrillas and the disciplined North Vietnamese troops.
- Thousands of Americans were being killed and wounded.

Student Protests

Draft Protesters/Political Radicals Many people felt that the Vietnam War was not a worthwhile cause and that the enemy posed no threat to the United States.

College students opposed to the war adopted various protest strategies. The majority marched in peaceful, legal antiwar demonstrations. Radical groups such as *Students for a Democratic Society (SDS)* occupied college

"Snow White and the Seven Experiments": 1970 cartoon targeting U.S. hypocrisy in supporting Asian military regimes

buildings and chanted defiant slogans. Some students publicly set fire to their draft cards. Others sought conscientious objectors status. Still others moved to Canada to escape the draft.

By 1966, the nation was sharply divided between "doves" (those opposed to war) and "hawks" (those advocating even greater use of military power in Vietnam).

Cultural Radicals As 1968 began, a new youth movement arose. Its members were against the war and preached love and nonviolence. Their lifestyle, known as the **counterculture**, placed a high value on personal honesty and creativity, and generally opposed the norms of American culture—marriage, patriotism, and business. The more extreme members were known as "hippies" and "flower children." Some of them united as "families," often living in rural **communes**.

1968: Year of Turmoil

The president and his advisers insisted that U.S. and South Vietnamese forces would eventually win. TV news reports, however, showed that most South Vietnamese villages were controlled by the Vietcong. Members of the press spoke of a "credibility gap" between the government's and the public's view. Opposition to the war increased.

"The Strategists," one for total commitment in Vietnam, the other for total noninvolvement—and both unrealistic

Johnson and Reelection In the presidential campaign of 1968, young people supported an antiwar candidate, Senator Eugene McCarthy of Minnesota. John Kennedy's brother, Robert, also announced his candidacy for the Democratic nomination. In a television address to the American people, Johnson announced an end to the bombing of North Vietnam and the start of peace negotiations. To prevent politics from compromising the peace plan and in recognition of his growing unpopularity, he said that he would not seek or accept nomination for reelection.

Assassination of Robert Kennedy In June 1968, U.S. Senator Robert Kennedy was killed by an Arab nationalist named Sirhan Sirhan. Many believed that had he lived and won the presidency, he might have helped overcome social and political divisions between young and old and between whites and nonwhites.

Democratic Convention The 1968 Democratic National Convention took place in Chicago. Vice President Hubert Humphrey beat out Eugene McCarthy for the nomination. The well-known radicals Abbie Hoffman and Bobby Seale led protests against the Democrats' choice. The Chicago police overreacted to the protests and verbal abuse, and their harsh treatment of the demonstrators was televised.

Election of Richard Nixon The violence associated with the Democratic convention and Humphrey's support of the war helped the Republicans and their candidate, Richard Nixon. A third-party candidate from Alabama, George Wallace, took away thousands of Southern votes from both major candidates. In one of the closest elections in U.S. history, Nixon won the presidency.

Social Impact of the Vietnam War The Vietnam War created deep divisions within American society. Many veterans of World War II felt that Americans should serve their country with pride; they reviled the actions of radical students and the counterculture. And returning Vietnam veterans were offended not to receive a traditional and enthusiastic welcome-home.

Opponents of the war felt a responsibility to protest against a war that they considered immoral and purposeless. They challenged the trustworthiness of elected officials and the U.S. policy of acting as "policeman of the world."

War in Vietnam: The Nixon Years

As promised, Johnson sent diplomats to Paris to discuss peace with the North Vietnamese. The talks continued under Nixon, as did the war.

Nixon and his national security adviser, Henry Kissinger, proposed a pullout from South Vietnam by both North Vietnamese and U.S. troops at the same time. The North Vietnamese rejected this proposal.

"Vietnamization" and Heavy Bombing

Student protests took place at colleges around the country, including Columbia and the University of California at Berkeley. As a result, Nixon announced a gradual withdrawal from Vietnam of U.S. troops while the South Vietnamese troops were being trained to carry on the war alone. He called this strategy "Vietnamization." Meanwhile, he secretly ordered U.S. bombing raids in Cambodia to cut off land routes there used by the North Vietnamese to move troops and materials south.

More Protests As the war stretched on, many who had supported it joined the antiwar movement. On October 15, 1969, dissidents participated in a peaceful nationwide protest. One month later, more than 250,000 protesters marched from the Washington Monument to the White House.

In 1970, news of the U.S. bombing of Cambodia led to protests on many college campuses. At Kent State University in Ohio, four students were killed and several wounded when the National Guard opened fire to break up a peaceful demonstration.

"Middle Course"—State Department Vietnam policy of commitment, but not full commitment

Pentagon Papers In 1971, Daniel Ellsberg, an official in the Department of Defense, released to several newspapers, including *The New York Times*, a secret Pentagon study of U.S. involvement in Vietnam. Fearing that the study would damage support at home for the war, Nixon demanded that *The Times* refrain from publishing it. In *New York Times* v. *United States*, the Supreme Court denied the claim that national security was at stake and ruled that, under the First Amendment's guarantee of freedom of the press, newspapers had the right to publish the Pentagon Papers.

Withdrawal From Vietnam In 1972, as more U.S. troops left Vietnam, Nixon ordered the continuous bombing of North Vietnam, including, for the first time, its capital, Hanoi. In addition, the harbor of Haiphong was mined to cut off shipments of oil and other supplies. Still, South Vietnamese forces lost ground to the Communists.

Meanwhile, U.S.–North Vietnamese negotiations continued, and in early 1973, South Vietnam, North Vietnam, and the United States agreed on the following terms of cease-fire:

- The last U.S. troops (fewer than 50,000) would leave Vietnam.
- North Vietnamese forces in South Vietnam would remain there.
- South Vietnam's government would remain in place until elections could be held.
- The Vietcong would return all American prisoners of war (*POWs*) and fully account for Americans missing in action (*MIAs*).

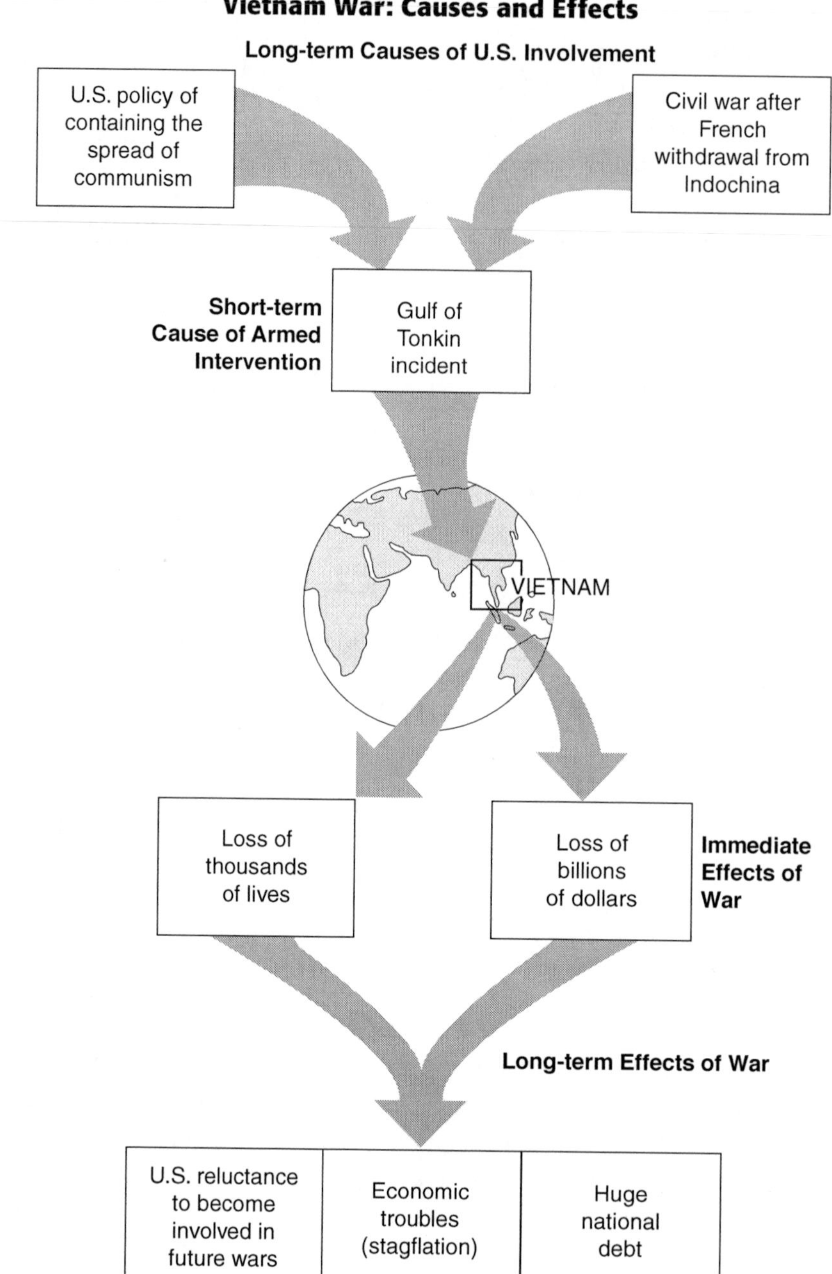

U.S. involvement in Vietnam ended in 1973, but the Vietnam War continued for almost two more years.

North Vietnamese Victory South Vietnam's government survived until 1975, when a combined force of Vietcong and North Vietnamese swept into Saigon and won control of all of Vietnam. Cambodia and Laos also fell to

Communist forces. The defeat of South Vietnam, despite U.S. military aid and fighting power, demonstrated limitations of U.S. power.

Consequences of the Vietnam War

Casualties and Costs About 58,000 Americans died in the Vietnam War, and 365,000 were wounded. A memorial wall in Washington, D.C., lists the names of the dead. It is a reminder of the service and sacrifice of those who serve in the armed forces.

Some soldiers who were imprisoned and tortured or overwhelmed by combat suffered from **post-traumatic stress disorder** (recurring flashbacks and nightmares). Others developed medical problems that were probably caused by Agent Orange, a chemical used to kill vegetation that gave cover to the Vietcong. Some veterans became dependent on drugs.

Government spending on the war was so great that it put a strain on the U.S. economy as Congress, for political reasons, would not raise taxes. Simultaneous huge spending on domestic programs (Johnson's Great Society) forced the government to borrow billions more. The **national debt** (accumulation of debts owed to purchasers of government bonds) soared to record heights, and inflation was a problem during and after the war.

Impact on Foreign Policy Although active antiwar protesters were a minority, millions of Americans came to doubt the wisdom of U.S. involvement in a distant conflict. Distrust of government policies grew, and the policy of containment came in for sharp criticism. For many years, both the American people and Congress would be reluctant to become involved in another foreign conflict.

War Powers Act Many members of Congress regretted enactment of the Tonkin Gulf Resolution and the ability of a president to commit troops overseas. To limit the president's power, Congress in 1973 passed the *War Powers Act*, with the following major provisions:

- Within 48 hours of sending troops into combat, the president must inform Congress of the reasons for the action.
- If troops fight abroad for more than 90 days, the president must obtain Congress's approval for continued fighting or must bring the troops home.

IN REVIEW

1. Identify the following and explain the significance of *each*: Tonkin Gulf Resolution, "Americanization," Tet Offensive, "doves," "hawks," "hippies," "credibility gap," "Vietnamization," Pentagon Papers, War Powers Act.
2. Summarize the arguments for and against the Vietnam War.
3. Evaluate the short-term and long-term effects of the Vietnam War on the United States.

CHAPTER REVIEW

MULTIPLE-CHOICE QUESTIONS

1 President John F. Kennedy supported the 1961 Bay of Pigs invasion of Cuba as an effort to
(1) remove a Communist dictator from power
(2) stop the flow of illegal drugs to the United States
(3) support Fidel Castro's efforts for reform
(4) rescue hostages held by Cuban freedom fighters

Base your answers to questions 2 and 3 on the map below and on your knowledge of social studies.

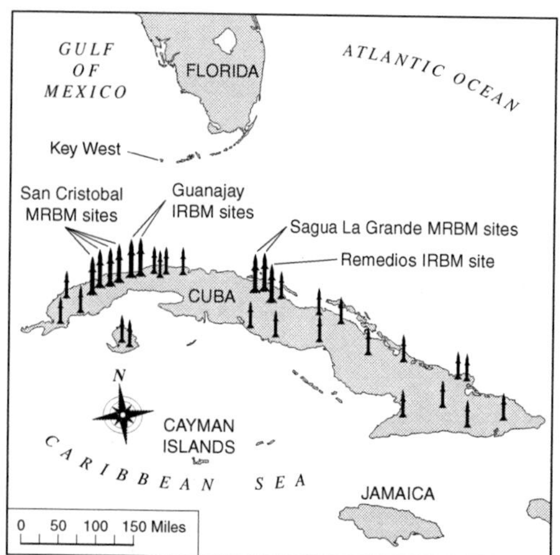

2 President John F. Kennedy attempted to deal with the situation shown on the map by
(1) bombing all the missile sites simultaneously
(2) imposing a naval blockade to isolate Cuba from the Soviet Union
(3) allowing the Soviet Union to keep some missiles in Cuba if the remainder were removed
(4) landing an invasion force on the Cuban mainland

3 What was the main reason for President Kennedy's action toward Cuba?
(1) Cuba is located close to the United States.
(2) The United States needed to protect business investments in Cuba.
(3) The cost of building missile defense bases in Florida was high.
(4) Cuba threatened to seize United States merchant ships in the Caribbean.

4 The Peace Corps was established by President John F. Kennedy in an effort to provide
(1) support to developing nations of the world
(2) job training for the unemployed
(3) markets for consumer goods
(4) teachers for inner-city areas

5 The immediate impact of the 1957 launch of *Sputnik I* was that it
(1) forced the United States to find new sources of fuel
(2) focused attention on the need to regulate the uses of outer space
(3) heightened the space race as a form of Cold War competition
(4) ended the period of peaceful coexistence between the United States and the Soviet Union

6 The Cuban missile crisis (1962) influenced President John F. Kennedy's decision to
(1) negotiate the limited Nuclear Test Ban Treaty with the Soviet Union
(2) reduce the nation's commitment to the North Atlantic Treaty Organization (NATO)
(3) forbid Americans to trade with and travel to Latin America
(4) send Peace Corps volunteers to aid developing countries

7 One reason the United States became involved in the Vietnam War was to
(1) prevent the spread of communism in Indochina
(2) reduce French influence in Vietnam
(3) stop China from seizing Vietnam
(4) support the government of North Vietnam

8 The United States experience in the Vietnam War supports the idea that the outcome of a war
(1) is determined mainly by technological superiority
(2) is dependent on using the greatest number of soldiers
(3) is assured to countries dedicated to democratic ideals
(4) can be strongly affected by public opinion

9 The war in Vietnam led Congress to pass the War Powers Act of 1973 in order to
(1) affirm United States support for the United Nations
(2) strengthen the policy of détente
(3) increase United States participation in international peacekeeping operations
(4) assert the role of Congress in the commitment of troops overseas

10 The case of John Peter Zenger (1735) and *New York Times Co.* v. *United States* (1971) both involved a government's attempt to limit
(1) freedom of religion
(2) freedom of the press
(3) the right to bear arms
(4) the right to counsel

THEMATIC ESSAYS

1 **Theme:** *The United States Versus Communism in Asia.* The United States, originally founded on the principle of achieving independence, found itself in the role of a great power attempting to prevent the independence of a colonial people.

Task: Complete *both* of the following tasks:
- Describe how the United States became involved in Vietnam after 1954.
- Show how the spread of communism in Asia led the United States to a major commitment in Vietnam.

In answering the first part, you may refer to the rise of Vietnamese nationalism during World War II, the war between Vietnamese nationalists and French imperialists, and the peace treaty signed at Geneva in 1954.

In answering the second part, you may discuss how the U.S. government was influenced by the rise of Mao Zedong, the Korean War, the domino theory, and the unpopularity of the South Vietnamese government.

2 **Theme:** *The Vietnam War and U.S. Domestic Policies.* The Vietnam War had an impact on the United States in ways not foreseen when it entered the conflict. As a result of extended U.S. participation in Vietnam, there were significant changes at home.

Task: Complete *both* of the following tasks:
- Describe *two* ways in which the war changed the United States.
- Show how *one* of the changes you discussed had a lasting impact on the United States.

You may discuss, but are not limited to, the effects of the war on the election of 1968; Johnson's Great Society program; and the attitude of (a) the American public toward government, (b) soldiers who fought in the war, and (c) high school and college students.

U.S. Troop Buildup in Vietnam, 1964–1968

DOCUMENT-BASED QUESTION

*Study each document and answer the question that follows it. Then read the **Task** and write your essay. Include references to most of the documents and additional information you retain about U.S. history and government.*

HISTORICAL CONTEXT: Committing troops to the war in Vietnam became one of the most hotly protested federal actions in U.S. history. Many Americans, particularly high school and college students, questioned the wisdom of U.S. involvement.

DOCUMENT 1: Refer to the map above.

QUESTION: Why were many Americans fearful of a Communist victory in Vietnam?

DOCUMENT 2: Refer to the graph below.

Asia in 1954

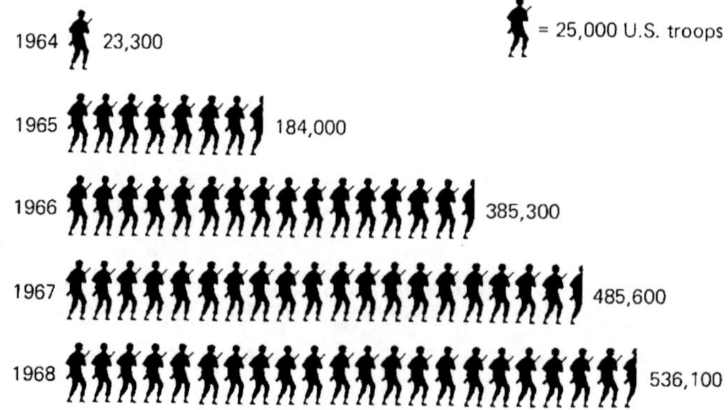

QUESTION: How did the United States become further involved in Vietnam between 1964 and 1968?

DOCUMENT 3: Refer to the map below.

Vietnam War

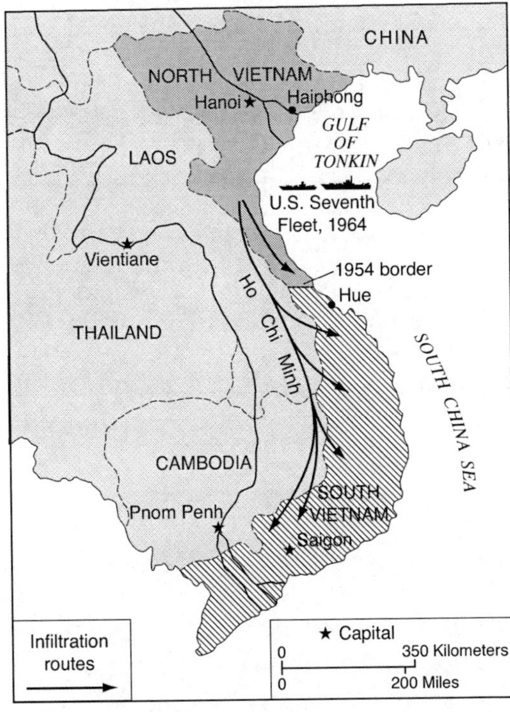

QUESTION: What were the Communist North Vietnamese able to do throughout South Vietnam?

DOCUMENT 4: From an undated handbill entitled "An Appeal to the Conscience of the American People":

> Opponents of the administration's policies point out that the many Saigon governments have been military dictatorships.
>
> None of [them] were elected by the Vietnamese people. The United States refused to permit the elections provided by the Geneva Agreement of 1954 and installed Ngo Diem. South Vietnam has been ruled by [U.S.-supported] military dictatorship... ever since. Opposed by the majority of the people of South Vietnam, it has changed 14 times since January 1964.

QUESTION: Why did the writer oppose U.S. support of South Vietnam (Saigon)?

DOCUMENT 5: From President Johnson's State of the Union message, January 12, 1966:

> We will stay because a just nation cannot leave to the cruelties of enemies a people who have staked their lives and independence on America's solemn pledge [during three U.S. presidencies].
>
> We will stay because in Asia—and around the world—are countries whose independence rests... on confidence in America's word and... protection. To yield to force... would weaken that confidence,... undermine the independence of many lands, and ... [provoke] aggression. We would have to fight in one land, and then... in another—or abandon much of Asia to... Communists.

QUESTION: Why did Johnson feel that the United States should maintain its commitments in Vietnam?

TASK: Using the documents and your knowledge of U.S. history and government, write an essay in which you:

- explain the arguments supporting and opposing U.S. involvement in Vietnam.
- give specific reasons why one of the two sides had the better argument.

CHAPTER 19
A Decade of Moderation: 1969–1980

DOCUMENTS AND LAWS
Clean Air Act (1970) • Twenty-sixth Amendment (1971) • SALT I (1972)
Clean Water Act (1972) • Seabed Agreement (1972) • *United States* v. *Nixon* (1974)
Panama Canal treaties (1977) • Camp David Accords (1978)

EVENTS
Arab-Israeli wars (1948–1973) • Environmental Protection Agency (EPA) established (1970)
Watergate break-in (1972) • First oil crisis (1973) • Nixon's resignation (1974)
Indian Self-Determination and Education Assistance Act (1975)
U.S. diplomatic recognition of Communist China (1979) • Second oil crisis (1979)
Iranian hostage crisis (1979–1981) • Soviet invasion of Afghanistan (1979)

PEOPLE
Spiro Agnew • Menachem Begin • Warren Burger • Harry Blackmun • Leonid Brezhnev
Jimmy Carter • Gerald Ford • Ayatollah Khomeini • George McGovern
Mohammad Reza Pahlavi (Shah of Iran) • William Rehnquist • Anwar Sadat

OBJECTIVES

- To assess the impact of the Watergate Affair on the presidency.
- To understand that periods of upheaval often lead to conservative reactions.
- To compare and contrast the domestic policies of presidents Nixon, Ford, and Carter.
- To identify and evaluate presidential responses to foreign policy challenges.
- To explain how global interdependence influences domestic policies.

Nixon Presidency

Richard Nixon—Dwight Eisenhower's vice president—was elected president in 1968 in the midst of anti–Vietnam War protests and growing distrust of government policies. His popularity increased while in office, and he easily won reelection in 1972.

Domestic Policies and Events

Modified Great Society Programs Nixon's policies were more conservative than Kennedy's or Johnson's. Judging many Great Society programs to be wasteful and impractical, he reduced expenditures on education, housing, job training, and welfare assistance. He persuaded Congress, for example, to

President Nixon's Inauguration, January 20, 1969

eliminate the *Office of Economic Opportunity*, which had administered many programs for aid to the poor.

In other ways, Nixon expanded the government's role. He backed creating the *Occupational Safety and Health Administration (OSHA)* to inspect workplaces for acceptable safety and health standards.

He also agreed to set up the *Drug Enforcement Agency (DEA)* as part of the Justice Department. It still coordinates efforts to reduce domestic sales and use of illegal drugs. Its agents are sometimes assigned to foreign governments attempting to curb illegal drug exports into the United States.

In 1970, the Sierra Club and other environmental groups organized a nationwide "Earth Day" to raise Americans' consciousness and exert pressure for tougher antipollution laws. Nixon persuaded Congress to establish the 1970 *Environmental Protection Agency (EPA)*. This agency had the power to enforce 15 federal programs already enacted for protecting the environment. Under the *Clean Air Act of 1970*, the EPA could set standards for monitoring the quality of the air. Under the *Clean Water Act of 1972*, it could assist state and local government projects for cleaning polluted rivers and lakes. In addition, DDT, a pesticide fatal to wildlife, was banned.

Nixon expanded the 1964 *food stamp program* for providing the poor with coupons for food. This program of the Department of Agriculture also provides subsidized school lunches for poor children and meals for the elderly poor.

Nevertheless, Nixon's policies tended to be conservative. He proposed a *New Federalism* to give states greater freedom in using federal funds. In effect, he asked the federal government to "share" its revenues with state and local governments. In 1971, Congress approved bills for **revenue sharing** that permitted a state or community to use federal funds as it wished.

Chief Justice Earl Warren announced his retirement from the Supreme Court in 1969. The Warren Court had been in the forefront of major social changes (discussed in Chapter 17). After two of Nixon's nominees to replace Warren were rejected by the Senate, Nixon selected a conservative judge, Warren Burger, who was approved. When three new vacancies on the Court arose, the judges who won Senate approval were Harry Blackmun, a moderate from Minnesota, Lewis Powell, and William Rehnquist, who held conservative views.

Moon Landing In 1969, Neil Armstrong and Edwin Aldrin, Jr., walked on the moon. For President Nixon, their feat was a welcome change from demonstrations against the Vietnam War.

Native-American Self-Determination In an attempt to improve conditions for Native Americans, Nixon returned to the Taos people of New Mexico their traditional lands and increased the number of Native-American employees in the Bureau of Indian Affairs. In 1975, after Nixon left office, Congress passed the *Indian Self-Determination and Education Assistance Act*, which increased Native Americans' control of their own education and government.

Twenty-sixth Amendment Beginning in the late 1960s, many young Americans argued that if they were old enough to fight in Vietnam, they were old enough to vote. In 1971, ratification of the Twenty-sixth Amendment gave U.S. citizens 18 years or older this right.

Title IX In 1972, Congress passed an education act that included a provision known as *Title IX*. Its purpose was to make gender discrimination in educational programs illegal (discussed also on page 302).

Nixon's Internationalism

As vice president, Nixon had expressed hostility toward the Soviet Union, China, and other Communist nations. As president, however, he attempted to ease cold-war tensions and scale back U.S. military commitments. In forming foreign policy, Nixon was advised by Henry Kissinger, his chief national security adviser and, later, secretary of state.

Kissinger and *Realpolitik* As a result of the Vietnam War, both Nixon and Kissinger questioned the role of the United States as a police officer patrolling the world. Kissinger argued that U.S. foreign policies should support the national self-interest. This focus on international political realities rather than ideals is known as **realpolitik**. Nixon attempted to apply it so as to reshape U.S. relations with major Communist powers.

Nixon Doctrine In 1969, as anti–Vietnam War protests grew, Nixon announced the *Nixon Doctrine*. To avoid U.S. involvement in future wars in

Chairman Mao and President Nixon meeting in China, 1972

Asia, the nations there would have to carry the main burden of their own defense. They could no longer rely on the United States for massive military aid or large numbers of ground forces.

U.S.–Chinese Relations After Mao Zedong's Communist government took over the Chinese mainland in 1949, the United States continued to recognize the Nationalist government, which had fled to Taiwan (discussed on page 263).

During the 1960s, Mao's government began denouncing the Soviet Union, an action that negated the American belief that all Communist countries followed identical policies and formed a **monolith** (single, undivided force). China's suspicions of the Soviet Union prompted Nixon and Kissinger to try and establish normal relations with the People's Republic of China.

In 1972, Nixon surprised the world by announcing his plan to visit China and seek an understanding with its leaders. There followed a major shift in U.S. policy: decreased support for Nationalist China and increased trade with mainland China. China and the United States soon exchanged performing groups and athletic teams. They did not, however, exchange ambassadors until 1979, when the United States formally recognized the People's Republic as the official government of China. The People's Republic also replaced Taiwan as the official government of China on the Security Council of the UN.

U.S.-Soviet Détente Nixon pursued a foreign policy of **détente** (relaxation of tensions) with the Soviet Union. A major goal of détente was to limit production of nuclear weapons, which had placed a burden on the budgets of both countries. During Nixon's first term, the U.S.-Soviet *Strategic Arms Limitations Talks* (*SALT I*) resulted in an arms race breakthrough—fixed limits on intercontinental (long-range) ballistic missiles, or ICBMs; and antiballistic (defensive) missiles, or ABMs.

"Let's talk about not watering them": U.S. and Soviet diplomats negotiate nuclear arms reduction.

In 1972, Nixon and Soviet Premier Leonid Brezhnev met in Moscow. They signed the SALT I agreement. Nixon also agreed to end a 1949 ban against shipping U.S. goods to the Soviet Union. To ease a severe Soviet food shortage, Nixon offered (and Congress later approved) the sale of $750 million worth of U.S. wheat. This "grain deal" pleased Soviet officials and American farmers alike. In 1972, the two nations joined 100 others in signing the *Seabed Agreement*, a pledge never to install nuclear weapons on the ocean floor.

Middle East Negotiations In October 1973, Arab nations of the Middle East attacked Israel in an attempt to regain the territories lost during the Arab-Israeli war of 1967. The United States supported Israel, while the Soviet Union backed Syria. Kissinger then traveled to the Middle East to arrange a cease-fire. At stake was not only the security of Israel but also U.S.-Soviet relations. A cease-fire was arranged after Israeli troops had successfully invaded Egypt, but a new crisis arose. Angered by U.S. support of Israel, several Arab nations announced an embargo on oil shipments to the United States and its Western allies.

Presidency in Crisis

Watergate Affair During the campaign for the 1972 presidential election, the Democrats nominated Senator George McGovern of South Dakota. The Democratic Party National Committee's headquarters was in a Washington, D.C., office building known as the Watergate. To get information about Democratic campaign plans, five men tried to break into the Watergate office. A watchman called the police, and the burglars were arrested.

President Nixon won reelection by a huge margin, but, as his second term began, the Watergate Affair broke. Throughout 1973, news reports suggested that the break-in had been planned by the White House staff and, perhaps, even by the president. The *Federal Bureau of Investigation (FBI)* began to investigate, and two reporters from the *Washington Post* revealed that certain officials close to the president might have planned the break-in. Most dramatic was a Senate committee's televised investigation of members of the president's White House staff.

A witness testified before the U.S. Senate Watergate Investigating Committee in 1973.

Meanwhile, Nixon repeatedly stated that he had no previous knowledge of the break-in and had attempted no cover-up.

United States v. Nixon The Senate committee then learned that the president had taped every conversation in his White House office. It requested the tapes as evidence. Nixon released some and offered summaries and transcripts of others. He refused, however, to turn over certain tapes, claiming **executive privilege**. He argued that he would violate the separation of powers if he gave the tapes to a Senate committee or a special prosecutor.

In *United States* v. *Nixon* (1974), the Supreme Court ruled that due process of law is more important than executive privilege. The president then released the tapes, which revealed that, shortly after the break-in, Nixon and his chief aides had tried to protect those responsible for the crime. Since it is illegal to cover up a crime, Nixon's actions, if proved in court, would also be crimes.

Impeachment Process and Resignation Impeachment is a two-part process. First, a majority of the House of Representatives must charge a federal official such as the president, with misconduct. Second, two-thirds of the Senate must find the accused guilty, after which dismissal from office is automatic. The Chief Justice of the United States presides during the Senate trial. As in the case of *The New York Times* v. *United States* (1971), the Supreme Court essentially ruled that no president is above the law.

In 1974, a committee of the House of Representatives voted to recommend Nixon's impeachment. At the urging of Republican advisers, Nixon appeared on television on August 8 and announced that he would resign and turn over the presidency to Gerald Ford, whose appointment as vice president had been approved by Congress shortly before the Watergate Affair began. Ford's appointment had been the first time that the Twenty-fifth Amendment (1967) had been used to fill a vice presidential vacancy (see the section "Ford Presidency," which follows).

Assessment Beginning with Franklin Roosevelt, presidential power had grown significantly, especially in time of war (World War II, Korean War, Vietnam War). In 1973, historian Arthur Schlesinger, Jr., warned about this growth in power, noting that Johnson and Nixon seemed to ignore the concerns of both Congress and the American people.

The Watergate Affair and Nixon's resignation brought an end to the "imperial presidency," as Schlesinger had called abuse of executive power. Congress, the Supreme Court, and an independent press had checked Nixon, and Americans were relieved to see that the system of checks and balances was working well. Nixon served as an example to subsequent presidents not to overstep the limits of their constitutional power, and that scandal can destroy the reputations of otherwise effective presidents.

IN REVIEW

1. Identify and explain the significance of *each* of the following: OSHA, DEA, EPA, revenue sharing, Twenty-sixth Amendment, realpolitik, détente, SALT I.
2. Describe how Nixon changed U.S. foreign policy with regard to China and the Soviet Union.
3. Explain how the system of checks and balances applied to the Watergate Affair.

Ford Presidency

Gerald Ford was in an unusual situation when he took the oath of office as the new president. He had not been elected to either the vice presidency or the presidency. Rather, he had been appointed to replace Spiro Agnew, who had resigned the vice presidency as part of a plea agreement for bribe-taking while serving as governor of Maryland and as vice president.

In his "Inaugural Address," Ford promised to restore trust in the government. He selected former governor of New York Nelson Rockefeller as vice president. A Senate committee conducted a long and probing investigation of Rockefeller before recommending his approval.

While in office, Ford followed moderately conservative policies.

Domestic Policy Issues

Pardon for Nixon A month after becoming president, Ford pardoned Nixon for any crime he committed in the Watergate Affair. (Article II, Section 2, of the Constitution gives the president power to pardon wrongdoers and release them from punishment.) Others on Nixon's staff were less fortunate. Former Attorney General John Mitchell and key White House aides were convicted and imprisoned for the cover-up and perjury.

First Energy Crisis Between 1973 and 1974, the price of a barrel of oil jumped from $3 to $11 as a result of the oil embargo by Arab nations. Because factory machines cannot operate without oil, the increase affected the price of almost all manufactured products and led to inflation in the U.S. economy. In addition, the U.S. automobile industry suffered as consumers turned to smaller, fuel-efficient imports from Japan and Europe.

The embargo made Americans realize how dependent they had become on oil from the Middle East, where price and output were controlled by the *Organization of Petroleum Exporting Countries (OPEC).* Japan and Western Europe were also almost totally dependent on OPEC oil. Worldwide, oil prices soared. This first **energy crisis** also led to long lines at gas stations.

"You're like a bunch of… of… of… CAPITALISTS!": Uncle Sam outraged at OPEC's control of the oil market

OPEC lifted the embargo in 1974 but continued to limit production to keep prices high. The government urged Americans to conserve energy at home and on the road. After the crisis, however, the nation became even more dependent on foreign oil.

Carter Presidency

The 1976 presidential election pitted President Ford against Jimmy Carter, a former governor of Georgia. In a close election, Carter emerged with 297 electoral votes to Ford's 240.

Carter proved to be a hardworking and honest president, dedicated to human rights. But his leadership disappointed many people. While urgently pressing Congress to pass certain laws, he was unable to inspire the Democratic majority to vote for them. Three other major issues, however, further decreased his popularity: (1) ineffectual response to a second energy crisis in 1979, (2) failure to win release of American hostages in Iran, and (3) stagflation.

Domestic Policy Issues

Amnesty In 1977, under his authority as chief executive, Carter extended **amnesty** (general pardon) to Vietnam War draft evaders, many of whom had fled to Canada. Many Americans who had lost a loved one in the war were opposed. Nevertheless, Carter's move brought to a close the issue of how draft evaders should be treated.

Second Oil Crisis Political unrest in the Middle East has often led to higher oil prices. In 1979, a revolution in Iran caused a major cutback in its oil production. Oil prices climbed from about $11 to $40 a barrel and shocked the global economy. Again, there were long lines at gas stations, and motorists had to pay more than a dollar a gallon (compared to 80 cents before the shortage). In 1980, urged on by the president, Congress voted $20 billion to develop synthetic fuels whose availability would not be affected by OPEC policies or upheavals in the Middle East.

The Environment Environmental concerns increased during the 1970s. In 1979, the partial meltdown of a nuclear power plant at Three Mile Island, Pennsylvania, reminded Americans that even peaceful use of nuclear energy could release dangerous amounts of radioactive materials into the atmosphere. Pollutants that caused acid rain and radioactive wastes were also placing the environment at risk.

Stagflation Spending on the Vietnam War and domestic programs in the 1960s coupled with an oil embargo by OPEC members in the 1970s, led to a unique economic hardship in the United States called **stagflation** (persistent inflation combined with relatively high unemployment). During the Carter administration, stagflation was characterized by an inflation rate of 13 percent or more and an unemployment rate of 8.5 percent or more. Stagflation was difficult to resolve since government policies aimed at reducing unemployment levels, such as increased government spending, tended to increase consumer prices (inflation). As a result, stagflation remained a persistent problem throughout President Carter's term of office.

Foreign Policy Issues

Middle East in Turmoil After World War II, constant unrest in the Middle East challenged U.S. policy makers to balance three main interests:

- support for Israel
- support for Arab states to ensure a steady flow of oil to the West
- containment of Soviet influence in the region.

Arab-Israeli Conflicts Israel fought four wars with its Arab neighbors. First, from 1948 to 1949 Arab states attacked the newly established state of Israel but failed to crush its independence. Second, in the Suez Crisis of 1956, Israel, France, and Great Britain attacked Egypt after it had nationalized the Suez Canal. U.S. condemnation halted the attack, and Israel withdrew its forces (discussed on page 276). Third, in 1967 Israel defeated Jordan, Syria, and Egypt in the "Six-Day War" and occupied the neighboring territories of the Golan Heights (taken from Syria), the Sinai Peninsula and Gaza Strip (taken from Egypt), and the West Bank of the Jordan River, including East Jerusalem (taken from Jordan). Israel stated that it would continue to occupy these territories, which it viewed as buffer zones, until Israel was recognized by its Arab neighbors.

Finally, the Yom Kippur War broke out in October, 1973. Egypt and Syria, seeking to win back territories lost in 1967, attacked Israel on the Jewish holy day of Yom Kippur. After initial Arab victories, Israel drove back both nations in a successful counterattack. The United States, fearful of a Soviet intervention, negotiated a cease-fire.

Middle East Mediation In 1978, Carter persuaded Egypt's president, Anwar Sadat, and Israel's prime minister, Menachem Begin, to discuss peace at Camp David, Maryland. The leaders then announced an agreement—the *Camp David Accords*—resolving the problems dividing their countries. In 1979, Egypt and Israel signed a treaty providing for the following:

- Israel's return of the Sinai Peninsula to Egypt
- Egypt's formal recognition of Israel as an independent nation
- a pledge by Israel and Egypt to respect the border between them.

Sadat was condemned by fellow Arabs, and Begin came in for harsh Israeli criticism. Nevertheless, Sadat and Begin both received the Nobel Peace Prize in 1978. Sadat's peace policy was to cost him his life: In 1981, he was assassinated by Muslim extremists.

Soviet Invasion of Afghanistan In 1979, the Soviet Union invaded Afghanistan, a Muslim nation located on its southern border. The invasion was an attempt to crush a rebellion against the Soviet-backed Communist government there.

Carter immediately suspended the U.S.-Soviet détente that had existed since 1972. Fearing that the Soviets might use Afghanistan as a base to seize oil fields in the Persian Gulf, Carter retaliated by cutting back U.S. grain

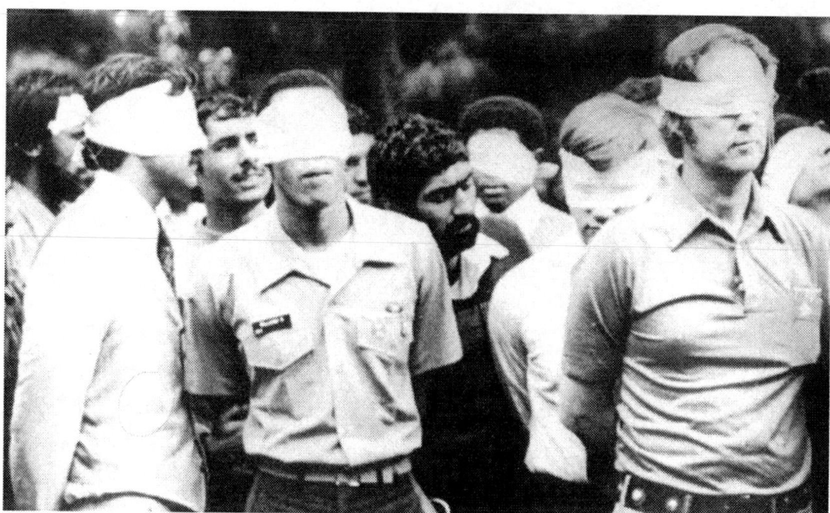

Blindfolded American hostages being held in Iran, 1979

shipments to the Soviet Union. He also announced that U.S. athletes would not participate in the 1980 Summer Olympics in Moscow.

Iranian Hostage Crisis Since 1953, the United States had supported Iran's monarch, Shah Mohammad Reza Pahlavi. In return for U.S. military aid, the United States used Iran as a base for spying on the Soviet Union. Meanwhile, the shah angered fundamentalist Muslims by modernizing the country in opposition to strict Muslim laws and customs. He also employed secret police to suppress this opposition.

In 1979, an important fundamentalist leader, Ayatollah Khomeini, led a successful revolution, forcing the shah into exile. Carter angered Iranian revolutionaries by allowing the ailing shah to enter the United States for medical treatment. In violation of international law, some of the revolutionaries invaded the U.S. Embassy in Iran's capital, Teheran, seized 62 Americans, and took 52 of them as **hostages** (persons held until ransom is paid or demands met). The revolutionaries demanded the return of the shah for trial. Carter refused and, in turn, demanded the hostages' release.

In April 1980, with pressure mounting on the president to take action, Carter ordered a military rescue. Unfortunately, helicopters carrying U.S. troops over Iran broke down, causing the rescue effort to fail.

Changing Relations With Panama Ever since Panama gained its independence from Colombia in 1903, it had a special relationship with the United States. The United States owned and operated the Panama Canal as well as the bordering Canal Zone. Many Panamanians objected to U.S. influence in their country.

In the late 1970s, Carter recognized that nationalism in Panama required changes in the U.S. presence. He negotiated two treaties with Panama. The first transferred ownership of the canal and the bordering zone to Panama in the year 2000. In the second, Panama and the United States agreed that the canal would always be neutral territory, and that the United States could defend it by military force, if necessary.

"I-took-Panama" Teddy Roosevelt does a double take in outrage at President Carter's Panama Canal "give-away."

Carter and Human Rights

During his presidency (1977–1981), Carter insisted that the United States use its influence to stop other governments from abusing their citizens and denying them their rights as humans. For Carter, friend and foe alike should respect basic human rights.

Military regimes in Argentina and Chile arrested thousands of people suspected of being dissidents. They were either imprisoned without trial or killed. El Salvador's friendly government and Nicaragua's hostile Communist regime both mistreated their dissenting citizens. At Carter's urging, Congress reduced or eliminated economic aid to these and other oppressive countries.

Oppressed peoples were perhaps best helped by being admitted into the United States as refugees from tyranny. From the end of the Vietnam War in 1975 into the 1990s, a steady stream of refugees fled reprisals by the Communist government in Vietnam. During Carter's presidency, thousands of Cubans fled Castro's dictatorship and thousands of Haitians escaped from the harsh laws and extreme poverty in their country. Many Americans wanted to turn these "boat people" away, but Carter let them stay. Like President Woodrow Wilson, he had a strong belief that moral principles should guide U.S. foreign policy.

Pessimism as the Carter Administration Ends

Carter lost the 1980 election, in part because of the situation in Iran. On January 20, 1981—the day Carter left office—Iran announced the release of the hostages. The hostage crisis, which took place only a few years after the Vietnam War, was a second blow to U.S. prestige. Many Americans wondered whether the United States was declining as a world power.

IN REVIEW

1. Explain the significance of the Ford presidency.
2. How did Carter respond to *each* of the following issues: Soviet invasion of Afghanistan, Iranian hostage crisis, anti-U.S. feelings in Panama?
3. Evaluate the appropriateness of President Carter's emphasis on human rights in the conduct of U.S. foreign policy.

CHAPTER REVIEW

MULTIPLE-CHOICE QUESTIONS

1 President Richard Nixon's visit to the People's Republic of China in 1972 was significant because it
(1) convinced the Chinese to abandon communism
(2) brought about the unification of Taiwan and Communist China
(3) reduced tensions between the United States and Communist China
(4) decreased United States dependence on Chinese exports

Base your answers to questions 2 and 3 on the cartoon below and on your knowledge of social studies.

2 The cartoonist is expressing the opinion that
(1) the United States should place tariffs on goods from Communist nations
(2) most Americans favor trading with both China and Cuba
(3) American foreign trade policies are sometimes inconsistent
(4) democratic nations should receive preferential trade agreements

Jeff Danziger, New York Times Syndicate

3 What is the explanation for the situation shown in the cartoon?
(1) Strong anti-Castro sentiment existed in Congress.
(2) China had met all United States human rights demands.
(3) Castro refused to allow Cuba to trade with the United States.
(4) The United States was dependent on food imports from China.

4 The easing of cold war tensions between the United States and the Soviet Union during the 1970s was called
(1) containment (3) neutrality
(2) détente (4) isolationism

5 Which presidential action best represents the policy of détente?
(1) John F. Kennedy's order for the Bay of Pigs invasion against Cuba
(2) Lyndon B. Johnson's escalation of the Vietnam War
(3) Richard Nixon's Strategic Arms Limitations Talks (SALT) with the Soviet Union
(4) George Bush's military action to remove Iraqi forces from Kuwait

6 The Supreme Court ruling in *United States* v. *Nixon* (1974) was significant because it directly
(1) increased the power of the legislative branch
(2) showed that the Court controlled the executive branch
(3) limited the president's power of executive privilege
(4) weakened the principle of federalism

7 What was the primary reason Richard Nixon resigned his presidency?
(1) He was convicted of several serious crimes.
(2) He was facing impeachment by the House of Representatives.
(3) His reelection was declared invalid by the Supreme Court.
(4) His actions in Cambodia and Laos were exposed in the *Pentagon Papers.*

8 Which action did President Gerald Ford take in an attempt to end the national controversy over the Watergate affair?
(1) pardoning Richard Nixon
(2) declaring a war on poverty
(3) declining to run for reelection
(4) asking Congress to impeach Richard Nixon

9 Which situation in the 1970s caused the United States to reconsider its dependence on foreign energy resources?
(1) war in Afghanistan
(2) oil embargo by the Organization of Petroleum Exporting Countries (OPEC)
(3) meetings with the Soviet Union to limit nuclear weapons
(4) free-trade agreements with Canada and Mexico

10 A major result of the Camp David Accords was the
(1) establishment of diplomatic relations between Egypt and Israel
(2) creation of permanent United States military bases in Latin America
(3) commitment of United States combat troops to Bosnia
(4) end of the cold war in Europe

THEMATIC ESSAYS

1 **THEME:** *Stagflation During the 1970s.* President Carter was confronted with the issue of stagflation. The high unemployment levels and inflation associated with stagflation were not all of his making but were nevertheless difficult to resolve.

TASK: Complete *all three* of the following tasks:

- Explain why decreased spending by the government and the increased cost of oil would result in a decline in production and employment that caused economic recession.
- Explain why the OPEC oil embargo took place.

- Demonstrate why the oil embargo resulted in rising prices (inflation).

2 **THEME:** *The United States in an Interdependent World.* Events of the 1970s showed that nations were becoming increasingly interdependent. This meant that after years of trying to be neutral or isolationist, the United States would have to adopt new strategies for existing in a constantly changing global environment.

TASK: Complete *all three* of the following tasks:

- Describe *two* examples from the 1970s of the federal government being forced to respond to events in other parts of the world.
- Show how *both* examples illustrate that the United States must adapt to a new interdependent world.
- Suggest *one* strategy that the federal government can adopt to coexist in a world that is more interdependent than ever before.

You may discuss, but are not limited to, the Iranian Revolution, OPEC oil embargo, the Soviet invasion of Afghanistan, and economic and political conditions of neighbors in Latin America and the Caribbean.

DOCUMENT-BASED QUESTION

Study each document and answer the question that follows it. Then read the ***Task*** *and write your essay. Include references to most of the documents and additional information you retain about U.S. history and government.*

HISTORICAL CONTEXT: In spite of diplomatic successes, President Nixon's second term was plagued by the Watergate Affair, which erupted during the 1972 presidential election campaign.

DOCUMENT 1: From Article I of the House Judiciary Committee's proposed impeachment document of Richard Nixon, 1974:

> ... Richard M. Nixon, in violation of his constitutional oath faithfully to execute the office of President... and... preserve, protect, and defend the Constitution..., and in violation of his constitutional duty to take care that the laws be faithfully executed, has prevented, obstructed, and impeded the administration of justice, in that:
>
> On June 17, 1972, and prior thereto, agents of the Committee for the Re-election of the President committed unlawful entry of the headquarters of the Democratic National Committee... [to secure] political intelligence. Subsequent thereto, Richard M. Nixon... engaged personally and through his subordinates and agents, in [conduct] designed to delay, impede, and obstruct the investigation of such unlawful entry; to cover up, conceal and protect those responsible; and to conceal the existence and scope of other unlawful covert activities.

QUESTION: Why was the House Judiciary Committee recommending that Nixon be impeached?

DOCUMENT 2: From President Nixon's address to the nation, January 23, 1973:

> Good evening. I have asked for this radio and television time tonight for the purpose of announcing that we today have concluded an agreement to end the war and bring peace with honor in Vietnam and in Southeast Asia....
>
> We must recognize that [this] is only the first step toward... peace. All parties must now see to it that this is a peace that lasts, and... heals, and a peace that not only ends the war... but contributes to the prospects of peace in the whole world....

Question: What announcement did Nixon make to the nation on January 23, 1973?

Document 3: Refer to the photograph below.

In Moscow, National Security Adviser Henry Kissinger and President Nixon share a toast to détente, while Premier Brezhnev (center) chats with diplomats.

Question: Why did Nixon travel to the Soviet Union?

Document 4: Refer to the cartoon at the top of the next column.

Question: What does the cartoon say about Nixon's ability to carry out foreign affairs? (Nixon is the figure on the left; the other figure is Secretary of State Henry Kissinger.)

Task: Using the documents and your knowledge of U.S. history and government, write and essay in which you:

- describe *two* examples of the conduct of foreign affairs during the Nixon administration.
- describe how Nixon increasingly had to concern himself with the Watergate Affair.
- evaluate the effect that the Watergate Affair had on Nixon's conduct of foreign affairs.

CHAPTER 20
The Triumph of Conservatism: 1981–1992

DOCUMENTS AND LAWS
Immigration Act of 1965 • SALT II (1979) • Economic Recovery Tax Act (1981)
SDI (1983–1993) • Social Security Reform Act (1983) • *New Jersey* v. *TLO* (1985)
Gramm-Rudman-Hollings Act (1985) • Immigration Reform and Control Act (1986)
Tax Reform Act (1986) • INF Treaty (1987) • *Texas* v. *Johnson* (1989)
Cruzan v. *Director, Missouri Department of Health* (1990)
Planned Parenthood of Southeastern Pennsylvania, et al. v. *Casey* (1992)
Vernonia School District v. *Acton* (1995)

EVENTS
GATT conferences (1947–1995) • Civil war in El Salvador (1979–1991)
Civil war in Nicaragua (1979–1990) • Iran–Iraq War (1980–1988) • Election of 1980
Terrorist attack on U.S. marines in Lebanon (1983) • Invasion of Grenada (1983)
Iran-Contra Affair (1984–1992) • U.S. embargo of South Africa (1986–1991)
Savings and Loan Bailout (1989) • War on Drugs (1989) • Berlin Wall dismantled (1989)
Eastern European nations hold free elections (1989) • U.S. invasion of Panama (1989)
Reunification of East and West Germany (1990) • Persian Gulf War (1990–1991)
Civil war in Bosnia (1991–1995) • Collapse of Soviet Union (1991)
First non-apartheid elections in South Africa (1994)

PEOPLE/GROUPS
Leonid Brezhnev • George H. Bush • Jimmy Carter • Contras • F. W. de Klerk • Mikhail Gorbachev
Gray Panthers • Saddam Hussein • Jesse Jackson • Nelson Mandela • Walter Mondale
Manuel Noriega • Oliver North • Ronald Reagan • Sandanistas • Desmond Tutu • Boris Yeltsin
Palestine Liberation Organization

OBJECTIVES

- To assess the impact of Reagan's conservatism on domestic policies.
- To understand the impact of Supreme Court decisions on schools.
- To evaluate how the government responded to problems of farmers, the poor, new wave of immigrants, and the elderly.
- To explain the effects of U.S. foreign policy in the Caribbean, Central America, and Soviet Union.
- To identify forces and events leading to the end of the cold war and dissolution of the Soviet Union.
- To examine domestic events during the presidency of George H. Bush.

Ronald Reagan, former movie star and two-term governor of California, defeated Jimmy Carter in the 1980 presidential election. Reagan was an extremely popular president. An experienced entertainer, he could use television to project a pleasing personality. He believed in reducing taxes and spending on social programs, and increasing spending on defense. His policies had a positive effect on business and a negative effect on the poor. In the election of 1984, Reagan overwhelmingly defeated Democratic challenger Walter Mondale, Carter's former vice president.

Reagan and the Growth of Conservatism

A major issue during the Reagan presidency was whether the federal government or the state governments had prime responsibility for combating crime, improving schools, and providing for the general welfare. The Republican presidents (Nixon, Ford, Reagan, and, later, George H. Bush) believed that the chief responsibility lay with state and local authorities. Reagan adopted Nixon's New Federalism (discussed on page 329) and urged states to take more responsibility for social and economic problems.

Cartoonist's view of Washington's "new look" in the 1980s: The White House and Capitol have only right wings (they are very conservative).

Throughout the 1980s, as the federal government trimmed its budget and cut back social programs, the states increased spending on everything from police salaries to hospitals. Citizens raised objections, however, to paying higher taxes. Candidates for election added to the public outcry by promising not to raise taxes at the federal or state level.

Supply-Side Economics

When President Ford replaced Nixon in 1974, the U.S. inflation rate climbed to a frightening 11 percent. Under Carter, it increased to 13 percent. Government spending on the Vietnam War and high oil prices caused by the Arab oil embargo were largely responsible. The failures of the Ford and Carter administrations to control inflation was a big reason why neither won a second term.

Reagan's solution for inflation was called **supply-side economics**. According to this conservative theory, the economy would benefit if the government spent less and businesses spent more. Cuts in federal taxes would leave businesses with more money to invest and consumers with

"Trickle-Down Economics"—What point is the cartoonist making about Reagan's tax reforms?

more income to buy goods and services. At the same time, there would be major cuts in welfare programs, which Reagan considered wasteful. Some economists compared Reagan's supply-side economics to Hoover's trickle-down theory (discussed on page 223).

In 1981, Reagan persuaded Congress to enact the largest income tax cut in history. The *Economic Recovery Tax Act (ERTA)* reduced personal income taxes by 25 percent over three years and gave corporations generous tax credits.

The Federal Reserve's anti-inflation policy of high interest rates caused inflation to drop to 6 percent in 1982 and down below 4 percent in 1983. A severe business recession also lowered inflation. By late 1982, about 11 percent of the labor force was out of work. Prosperity returned in 1984, and low inflation continued for the remainder of the decade.

Tax Policy In 1986, Reagan urged Congress to pass the *Tax Reform Act*. Previous tax laws had divided taxpayers into several brackets according to earned income. The higher the taxable income, the higher the percentage of income paid in taxes. The new law created only two tax brackets. Lower-income people were taxed at 15 percent of taxable income and upper-income people at 28 percent.

Instead of being taxed at 50 percent, as formerly, people with very high incomes paid just 28 percent. Thus, someone with an income of $1 million was in the same tax bracket as a person earning $30,000 a year. The wealthy benefited most from the new tax law. However, the new law did close a few "loopholes" in the old tax code so that the wealthy could not deduct as much from their taxable income as before.

Budget Deficits Every year, the executive branch submits a budget to Congress. When spending exceeds income, there is a **budget deficit**. In the opposite case, there is a **budget surplus**.

Beginning with the Great Depression of the 1930s, the government has usually ended its **fiscal year** (budget year) with a deficit. It has made up the difference by borrowing millions, even billions, of dollars annually. This debt was manageable through the early 1960s. After the Vietnam War ended in 1973, however, the accumulation of yearly budget deficits amounted to a national debt exceeding $500 billion. By 1981 when Reagan submitted his first budget, the debt had climbed to nearly $1 trillion.

Effects of "Reaganomics" Critics called Reagan's economic policy "Reaganomics." The combination of tax cuts and increased spending for defense led to record deficits. By the end of the 1980s, the national debt had risen to more than $2 trillion. By 1990, interest payments on the national debt cost the government about $150 billion annually. Partly because of the debt burden, the government was unable to fund adequately national needs such as highway repair and health care.

Business Deregulation

During the Progressive Era in the early 1900s, regulatory agencies were established to protect consumers. More consumer protection laws were passed in the 1960s. Moreover, the government under Carter and Reagan deregulated the economy by getting rid of some of the government rules that controlled business competition.

Carter urged Congress to deregulate four industries: oil, natural gas, airlines, and trucking. Government controls had kept the prices of oil and natural gas low for consumers. Carter phased out such price controls to encourage the search for new sources of oil and natural gas. He also persuaded Congress to eliminate the *Civil Aeronautics Board (CAB)*, which had regulated airline routes and rates for 40 years. Thus, U.S. airlines began to compete free of all restrictions except those imposed by federal safety standards. Rapid change marked the airline industry: new airlines were started; some old airlines went out of business. Profits and ticket prices fell, while a greater number of people flew.

Reagan ordered regulatory agencies in the executive branch to grant businesses greater freedom. He weakened some agencies by appointing opponents of regulation to head them. Business mergers increased during the Reagan years because antitrust laws were not enforced. Reagan also speeded up deregulation of the oil industry.

Reduced Federal Involvement in the Environment and Civil Rights

Reagan reduced support for environmental measures because he believed that environmental laws resulted in high costs for businesses and high prices for consumers. Laws protecting wildlife were poorly enforced. **Strip mining** —ground-level mining of minerals that leaves the landscape scarred and ridden with debris—increased as a method for extracting coal.

Reagan's policy of reduced federal involvement and increased support of "states' rights" also weakened civil rights legislation. Federal support for busing and affirmative action decreased. Congress did, however, establish Martin Luther King, Jr., Day as a national holiday.

Reverend Jesse Jackson (with his daughter) campaigned for president in 1984.

Effect on Minorities A disproportionate share of the poor are from minority groups. Reagan's cuts in social programs meant that such groups as African Americans and Hispanic Americans did not benefit economically from the so-called Reagan Revolution. The income gap between white and black Americans increased.

Nevertheless, due in large part to increased voter registration that resulted from passage of the Voting Rights Act in 1965, African Americans and Hispanic Americans made political progress. African Americans were elected as mayors in Atlanta, Detroit, Chicago, Los Angeles, and Philadelphia. Hispanic Americans were elected as mayors in San Antonio and Miami, and as governors in New Mexico and Florida.

In the 1990s, the Reverend Jesse Jackson, a civil rights activist, won a strong following as an African-American leader. He also reached out to other minorities, women, and discontented farmers and workers, referring to this multiracial, multicultural blend of people as the "Rainbow Coalition." In 1984 and 1988, Jackson campaigned for the Democratic presidential nomination and came closer to being a presidential candidate than any other nonwhite American ever had to this point. In 2008, the color line would be broken when Barack Obama was elected president.

U.S. Supreme Court and the Schools

The following Supreme Court cases focus on the extent to which the Bill of Rights applies to students in school:

***New Jersey* v. *TLO* (1985)** A high school freshman found smoking in the school bathroom was made to open her purse. School officials found wrapping paper that could be used for cigarettes or marijuana, a list of students who owed her money, and a large amount of cash. The student was sentenced to one year of probation. The Court ruled that the school acted reasonably to maintain discipline; reasonable suspicion for searches and seizures in school need not be based on the "probable cause" provision of the Fourth Amendment.

***Vernonia School District* v. *Acton* (1995)** The Supreme Court ruled that a school district can conduct random testing of urine for evidence of drug use. The majority opinion held that the Fourth Amendment protects only against intrusions upon legitimate expectations of privacy. The state may exercise a greater degree of supervision over public school students than over adults since schools act in place of the parents. Thus, public school students have a lesser expectation of privacy than members of the general public and the Fourth Amendment right to privacy is not violated. The Court held that although the tests were searches under the Fourth Amendment, they were reasonable in light of the schools' interest in preventing teenage drug use. Since student athletes were already required to take medical tests, a drug test need not be based on suspicion of drug use among individual students.

IN REVIEW

1. Identify the following: supply-side economics, Tax Reform Act of 1986, budget deficits, national debt, and deregulation.
2. Summarize Reagan's economic policies. Why are they sometimes known collectively as the Reagan Revolution?
3. According to the Supreme Court ruling in *Vernonia School District* v. *Acton*, how does the Bill of Rights apply to students in school and to adult citizens elsewhere?

New Approaches to Old Problems

Many problems of the 1980s and 1990s had their roots in the past. But the new conservatism proposed new solutions.

Hard Times for Farmers

Between 1940 and 1970, farmers doubled wheat production per acre and increased production of all crops per acre by 66 percent. At the same time, the number of farms and farmers declined. In 1994, about 2.5 percent of Americans were farmers, compared to 38 percent in 1900. The decline of the small family farm was closely linked to mechanization. Expensive equipment increased productivity on large and medium-size farms. But owners of small farms were unable to buy such equipment and could not compete. By 1995, most farm acreage was controlled by large agricultural corporations.

Farm Subsidies A **subsidy** is a grant of government money to a private enterprise. Since the Great Depression, the government had paid subsidies

Mechanization has resulted in fewer but larger farms.

to farmers during years when crop prices were low. Laws enacted in 1973 and 1977 established **target prices** for crops such as wheat, corn, and cotton. If the market price fell below the target price, the government paid farmers the difference. This policy encouraged farmers to produce more crops. The government also paid farmers for using less of their land to raise crops. By the mid-1990s, many in Congress complained that farm price supports were too expensive.

Good Times in the 1970s Farming is a business of ups (high demand, high prices) and downs (low demand, low prices). In the 1970s, prices for farm products were high, partly because of increased exports to the Soviet Union and other nations. Encouraged by the government, farmers borrowed money to modernize farms and increase production. Gains in productivity were spectacular.

Hard Times in the 1980s World demand for American crops declined in the 1980s. Farmers received low prices for what they could sell and were left with millions of tons of unsold grain. Carter's embargo on the sale of grain to the Soviet Union contributed to the problem (discussed on pages 337–338). With high debts and declining income, thousands of family farms went bankrupt.

In the 1980s, Reagan initiated two programs to help farmers. The first was "Payment in Kind" (PIK). To reduce the oversupply that had led to reduced prices, farmers who did not plant on their land were paid in surplus crops held by the government. A second program entailed government cash payments to farmers for not planting. These programs helped farmers but increased the federal budget deficit because they were costly. In the 1990s, grain exports again helped increase farm income.

Poverty in an Affluent Society

In the 1950s, many Americans had incomes high enough to sustain a prosperous lifestyle. There were, however, millions of Americans still living in poverty. Then between 1960 and 1969, the number of poor Americans dropped from 40 million to 24 million, largely because of Johnson's War on Poverty.

In the 1970s, stagflation (discussed on page 336) led to renewed increases in the poverty rate. In the 1980s, larger numbers of homeless people appeared on city streets. Poverty was especially strong among children, single women with dependent children, African Americans, Native Americans, Latinos, migrant farmworkers, and unemployed factory and mine workers. Increased poverty helped raise the crime and school dropout rates, as did the wide availability of crack, a new illegal drug that was inexpensive and highly addictive.

The escalating defense budget reduced social programs to beggar status.

As social scientists pointed out, the wealthiest fifth of the population commanded an ever greater share of total national income. The widening income gap between rich and poor was viewed as a serious danger to American democracy.

In 1981, Reagan argued that financial aid to the poor (except the "truly needy") made them permanently dependent on the government. Many Americans concerned about high taxes and budget deficits supported his efforts to cut back federal poverty programs. Critics blamed the cuts in welfare programs for the increasing number of homeless. Others argued that the poor might represent a new and permanent "underclass" in American society that no amount of government aid could rescue.

New Wave of Immigrants

In the 1980s (as in the 1880s), a new wave of immigrants rapidly changed the U.S. population. They came not from Western Europe but from Latin America, the Soviet Union, Eastern Europe, the Middle East, and other parts of Asia.

Immigration Act of 1965 Between 1921 and 1965, U.S. immigration laws had favored Western European nationalities. The *Immigration Act of 1965* ended the old quota system and set the following criteria for yearly admission of immigrants:

- no more than 20,000 from any one country
- no more than 120,000 from the Western Hemisphere
- no more than 170,000 from outside the Western Hemisphere
- preference given to skilled workers, professionals, and those with family ties to U.S. citizens.

A 1953 law gave the president authority to admit refugees from political oppression. Ford used it to admit hundreds of thousands of Vietnamese, Laotians, and Cambodians after their countries fell to communism.

Illegal Immigrants In addition to the millions of legal immigrants, millions crossed the U.S. border illegally. Others overstayed their visas. American employers often were glad to hire some illegal immigrants because, having

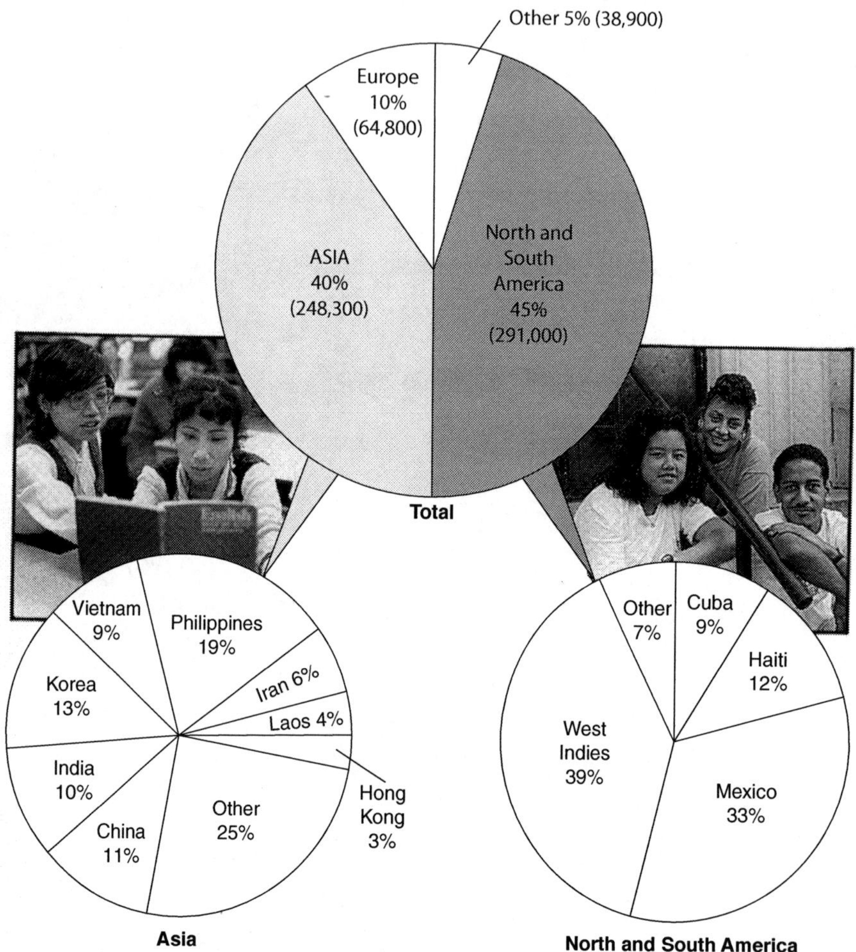

fled from extreme poverty, they were willing to work for lower wages than U.S. citizens. Labor unions feared that they would work for less than the minimum wage.

Members of Congress who wanted to curb illegal immigration used two arguments: (1) illegal aliens paid no taxes, placed a strain on city services, and increased the cost of city government; (2) tolerance of illegal aliens was unfair to immigrants who had waited years to enter the United States legally.

Immigration Reform In 1986, with Reagan's approval, Congress enacted the *Immigration Reform and Control Act*, or *Simpson-Mazzoli Act.* It placed heavy fines on employers who knowingly hired illegal aliens. Illegal aliens who had arrived before 1982 were allowed to remain as legal residents.

Opponents of the law argued that employers would fear hiring Hispanic-American legal residents because absolute proof of legality might be hard to obtain. In reality, the act has failed to stop the flow of illegal immigrants across the Mexican-U.S. border.

Encouraging Immigration Social scientists point out some benefits of increased immigration:

- Immigrants buy goods and services.
- They pay taxes.
- Some create jobs rather than take them away.
- In the event that a decrease in the native birthrate creates a labor shortage, skilled workers from abroad will be needed.
- The diverse backgrounds of immigrants enrich U.S. culture.

Changing Demographic Patterns

In 2004, people aged 65 and over (the elderly or "senior citizens") represented 12.4 percent of the population, compared with only 5.5 percent in 1930.

Increased Life Expectancy In 1900, such common diseases as tuberculosis, influenza, and polio had no cures. Over the next 60 years, medical science brought them under control. In 1928, Sir Alexander Fleming discovered penicillin. This antibiotic and many other drugs developed since have accounted for major gains in **life expectancy** (the number of years that a newborn is expected to live). Americans born in 1928 were expected to live to their mid-50s. In contrast, those born in 2005 can expect to live into their late 70s and early 80s.

As the number of elderly increased, so did their political influence. For millions of senior citizens of the 1970s and 1980s, the most important political issue was the future of Social Security. They organized pressure groups such as the *American Association of Retired Persons (AARP)* and the *Gray*

Panthers. They pressured Congress for higher monthly checks to keep pace with inflation and for improved benefits under Medicare, which pays hospital and doctor bills for people 65 and over. In 1975, Congress passed a law linking Social Security benefits to the cost of living. The new provision was known as a **cost-of-living adjustment (COLA).**

Social Security System The increased benefits were extremely expensive. Congress, therefore, passed two laws:

- In 1977, the Social Security tax was raised. This tax, collected from workers' paychecks and from employers, goes into a fund that pays benefits to retired workers.
- The *Social Security Reform Act* (1983) saved the system from financial collapse by speeding up planned increases in Social Security taxes. In addition, the age when recipients were to receive benefits gradually rose from 65 to 67. Benefits for some higher-income retirees were also subject to partial taxation.

Ever since the reform of 1983, money coming into the Social Security system has covered benefits paid out to the elderly. Despite this, concern remains about the viability of the Social Security system. Social scientists predict that as huge numbers of baby boomers (Americans born in the late 1940s and in the 1950s) retire, the Social Security system will run a deficit in the 2030s unless further reforms are instituted. There are not enough young workers to support the system the way it is now constituted.

IN REVIEW

1. How did Reagan attempt to solve (a) the farmers' dilemma and (b) poverty in an affluent society?
2. Why were some Americans opposed to illegal immigrants and others in favor of them?
3. What are the political, economic, and social implications of an increasingly elderly population?

United States: Global Power Broker

Presidents of the Progressive Era (Theodore Roosevelt, Woodrow Wilson, and William H. Taft) had intervened in the political affairs of the Dominican Republic, Haiti, and Nicaragua. These interventions caused lasting resentments among Latin Americans. In the 1930s, Franklin Roosevelt adopted the *Good Neighbor Policy* of nonintervention in Latin America's internal affairs. After World War II, U.S. leaders followed both the interventionist and "good neighbor" paths at the same time. While they offered

Latin America economic assistance as a means of thwarting Soviet influence there, they did not hesitate to intervene militarily at times.

Central America and the Caribbean

Reagan chose to oppose communism through containment. He believed that U.S. military intervention was warranted when U.S. interests were threatened, even if such intervention meant the loss of Latin American goodwill.

Grenada Invasion Grenada, an island nation in the Caribbean, had a population of 94,000. A few hundred Americans were attending medical school there in 1983 when Communist forces overthrew Grenada's democratic government. Believing that the students were in danger, Reagan sent in U.S. troops, who quickly defeated the Cuba-backed Communists and restored democratic rule.

Aid to El Salvador During the 1980s, civil war raged in the Central American nation of El Salvador. Fearing that the rebels might set up a Communist state, Reagan persuaded Congress to vote more than $600 million in military aid for El Salvador's government. Nevertheless, the civil war continued until 1991, when UN negotiators arranged a cease-fire and a peace settlement.

Aid to Nicaraguan "Contras" In nearby Nicaragua, U.S. aid helped a rebel group, the "*contras*," fight Nicaragua's Communist government, the "*Sandinistas*," who came to power in 1979. In 1982 and 1983, Reagan persuaded Congress to supply financial and military aid to the contras. In 1984, Congress granted financial aid but rejected military aid, only to reverse itself in 1986 and approve $160 million in military aid.

The civil war ended in 1990 when the Sandinistas permitted a free election, which they lost. The United States then provided aid to the new, moderately conservative government, and the contras returned to civilian life.

"Adopt a Contra"—critical view of undercover U.S. aid for military insurgents trying to overthrow Nicaragua's government

The Iran-Contra Affair In 1986, the press discovered that U.S. officials had broken a law banning sale of U.S. weapons to Iran. Many suspected that the arms sale was in exchange for the release of American hostages held in Lebanon. Indeed, the press called it the "arms-for-hostages deal." The money from the illegal arms sale secretly went to Nicaraguan contras in an operation carried out by Oliver North, a presidential aide and Marine lieutenant colonel. Questioned by a congressional committee, North testified that President Reagan knew nothing about this Iran-contra connection. Some Americans, however, compared the scandal to the Watergate Affair and were concerned about a possible loss of faith in elected leaders.

U.S. Marines in Lebanon

Lebanon, a country north of Israel, is inhabited by various Christian and Muslim groups. In the 1960s, the *Palestine Liberation Organization* (*PLO*) moved its primary base of operations to Beirut after its expulsion from Jordan for attempting to overthrow the government there. During the 1970s, Muslims outnumbered Christians, and Palestinians in Lebanon's refugee camps began to protest the government's pro-Western policies. In 1975, a civil war erupted between the Christians, on one side, and the Palestinians and other Muslims, on the other side.

In 1982, Israel sent troops to Lebanon to retaliate for PLO terrorist attacks on Israel. Israel bombarded Beirut, winning a Palestinian withdrawal from the Lebanese capital. The PLO was forced to relocate its operations to Tunis, Tunisia. In 1982, Reagan sent U.S. troops to Lebanon to help keep peace. The next year, though, a terrorist bomb killed 241 U.S. Marines stationed near Beirut. As a result, Reagan soon removed all U.S. troops from the country.

Syria took control of much of Lebanon, while Israeli troops occupied a southern strip of the country as a security zone against attacks on northern Israel. During the 1980s and 1990s, militant groups in Lebanon launched rocket attacks and suicide raids against Israel, which retaliated with commando raids into Lebanon.

Economic Competition, Cooperation, Boycott

Beginning in the 1970s, the United States became less concerned with Communist expansion in Asia and more so with economic competition from Japan.

Japan By the early 1970s, Americans were buying many Japanese goods—automobiles, motorcycles, cameras, TVs, and radios. American consumers benefited from these high-quality imports, but U.S. manufacturers worried about losing business, while labor unions worried about losing jobs.

By the 1980s, the United States worried about it large trade imbalance (less exports than imports) with Japan.

After 1947, most nations, including the United States, had participated in conferences called the *General Agreement on Tariffs and Trade (GATT)*, which worked toward lowering tariffs among member nations. Reagan favored low U.S. tariffs too. High protective tariffs might trigger tariff wars that would hurt both the U.S. and the global economies. At the same time, the United States had to continually pressure Japan to change its trade policies, which placed quotas on the number of foreign goods that Japanese businesses could buy.

South Africa

During the Carter administration, U.S. policy toward Africa shifted from containment of communism to opposition to racial injustice, specifically in South Africa.

The British had taken control of South Africa after defeating the Afrikaners (Dutch settlers) in the *Boer War* (1899–1902). The Afrikaners, however, outnumbered the British settlers, won control of the government in 1948, and broke ties with Britain in 1961.

The Afrikaner government practiced **apartheid** (strict racial segregation), which separated South Africa into four racial groups: whites, blacks, Asians, and "coloreds" (those of mixed ancestry). Blacks had to live apart from the other groups, could not vote, and could work only in the lowest-paying occupations. They were required to carry identification passes and could enter white areas only for limited periods of time. Many blacks were even moved to "tribal homelands"—regions where, in fact, most had never lived before.

A black South African showed his identity pass under apartheid.

The populations of most nations viewed South African apartheid as an insulting carryover from when white Europeans ruled much of Africa and Asia. Third world members of the UN voted for resolutions condemning apartheid and calling on UN members to stop trading with South Africa.

Until the 1980s, many U.S. businesses and universities invested in South Africa's gold, diamond, and uranium mines. However, as its ruthless methods to enforce apartheid were increasingly reported on television and dramatized in movies, many U.S. college students and others demonstrated against this injustice. South Africa's Episcopal archbishop, Desmond Tutu, visited U.S. cities to urge a ban on trade with South Africa. In 1986, Congress passed such an embargo over Reagan's veto.

South Africa began to change its policies in 1990. A new president, F. W. de Klerk, promised to integrate parks and beaches and to permit blacks to vote. In 1990, the black leader Nelson Mandela, imprisoned for 27 years for opposing apartheid, was released. On a U.S. tour, Mandela urged Americans to continue the embargo until apartheid ended. In 1991, however, President George H. Bush, Reagan's successor, persuaded Congress to lift the embargo, noting that progress had been made toward ending apartheid.

In 1994, the first South African elections were held in which all races could vote. Mandela's party—the *African National Congress (ANC)*—won a majority of seats in the legislature, and Mandela became the first black president. This transition to multiracial democracy ended U.S. boycotts of South Africa and increased cooperation between the two nations.

U.S.-Soviet Relations

From 1974 to 1989, the cold war went through three phases. First, Ford and Carter tried to improve U.S.-Soviet relations by continuing Nixon's détente. Second, during Reagan's first term as president (1981–1985), relations between the superpowers grew hostile again. Third, Mikhail Gorbachev became the Soviet leader in 1985 and eventually permitted Eastern European countries to shake off Soviet control. In the Soviet Union as well as in Eastern Europe, many aspects of communism were abandoned as unworkable.

Arms Limitation Efforts The 1972 SALT I agreement applied to defensive missiles (discussed on page 332). In 1979, President Carter and Soviet Premier Leonid Brezhnev signed SALT II. This treaty limited offensive missiles by establishing a ceiling on how many long-range missiles could be installed on airplanes and submarines. Early in 1980, Carter withdrew the treaty from congressional consideration because of the Soviet invasion of Afghanistan.

"Star Wars" Reagan, in his 1980 campaign for the presidency, promised to increase military spending. In his first year in office, he asked Congress for huge increases in the defense budget—$1.5 trillion over five years—for new bombers, submarines, and missiles. Congress approved most of the president's program.

Reagan's most ambitious proposal, set forth in a 1983 speech, was for a "space shield"—the *Strategic Defense Initiative (SDI).* To critics, it sounded like something out of the popular movie *Star Wars.* The weapons would orbit

"Star Wars": Reagan's planned missile-defense shield seen as a costly computer game

Earth and supposedly shoot down launched Soviet missiles before they could reach U.S. targets. Though skeptical, Congress voted funds to explore the idea. Then, U.S.-Soviet relations improved, and in 1991, the Soviet Union collapsed. In 1993, after ten years of research and an outlay of $30 billion, President Bill Clinton, George H. Bush's successor, eliminated the SDI program. However, President George W. Bush later renewed the program.

Gorbachev and Soviet Relations In 1985, the Soviet Communist Party selected a new leader, Mikhail Gorbachev. Relatively young and energetic, he proposed sweeping reforms to revitalize the Soviet system.

First, he told the Soviet people not to fear speaking their minds about public issues. This ***glasnost*** (openness) reversed years of an opposite policy of state arrests and imprisonment for frankness.

Perestroika (restructuring), a policy for economic reform, encouraged local bureaucrats and factory managers to make their own decisions rather than relying on orders from the government. Gorbachev also wanted to develop privately owned businesses run for profit. In reality, perestroika was a mixture of private enterprise and government welfare.

Gorbachev realized that the Soviet economy could not improve while a large percentage of the nation's resources went for the armed forces. Reagan's arms buildup was putting the United States far ahead in the arms race, and the Soviet Union could no longer afford to compete. Gorbachev and Reagan met three times to discuss arms control and other issues. In 1987, at their third meeting, they signed the *Intermediate-range Nuclear Forces Treaty (INF Treaty).* (Intermediate-range missiles can travel hundreds of miles, compared with long-range ICBMs, which can cross oceans.) The treaty provided that all intermediate-range missiles in Europe be removed and dismantled by 1990.

Thus, the Reagan years were characterized by improved relations with the Soviet Union and growing American power and prestige. Domestically, there were reduced taxes, greater federal deficits, and increasing deregulation. Legislation provided temporary solutions to problems posed by illegal immigration and to financial pressures posed by a growing number of people eligible for Social Security.

IN REVIEW

1. Identify and explain *each* of the following: Grenada, Sandinistas, contras, Iran-Contra Affair, tariff war, apartheid, Nelson Mandela, SALT II, SDI, Mikhail Gorbachev, *glasnost*, *perestroika*, and INF Treaty.
2. Explain how *each* of the following posed a challenge to U.S. foreign policy: El Salvador, Nicaragua, civil war in Lebanon, South Africa.
3. To what extent did Reagan's foreign policy represent a return to traditional cold-war politics?

George H. Bush Presidency

When George H. Bush succeeded Reagan as president, he continued his predecessor's conservative policies into the 1990s.

Election of 1988

Demographics Bush's election demonstrated the political importance of suburbanites. As the more affluent moved to the suburbs, they identified with Republican issues such as lowering taxes, reducing spending, and curbing crime (including the sale and use of illegal drugs). Bush won over many former Democrats by promising to address these issues. He depicted his Democratic opponent, Michael Dukakis, as being soft on crime, and easily defeated him.

Domestic Issues

Bush, like Reagan, called for states to assume a larger role in domestic programs.

Environment Many environmentalists complained of how slow the federal government was to clean up the 1989 *Exxon Valdez* oil spill (discussed on page 388). They also complained that enforcement of such environmental measures as the Clean Air Act was weakened as well. Business interests countered that environmental laws should not be too restrictive because they can make U.S. businesses less competitive with foreign ones.

Economy A 1980s business boom was marked by heavy consumer spending, high interest rates, and low savings. In 1991, however, the economy slipped into a recession, and the unemployment rate rose to 7 percent. Hoping to increase consumer and business borrowing, the Federal Reserve Board reduced the **discount rate** (interest the Fed charged to member banks).

Tax Increases/ Deficit Reduction The federal debt continued to rise. Congress reacted by passing the *Gramm-Rudman-Hollings Act* (1985), which mandated that the federal budget had to be balanced by the early 1990s. If Congress failed to reduce deficits to zero, the law provided for automatic budget cuts in all executive departments.

President George H. Bush

In 1990, Bush broke his 1988 campaign promise by approving an increase in taxes. He and Congress also worked out cuts in federal spending. The income tax rate for the wealthy was raised from 28 to 31 percent. Federal excise taxes on cigarettes, alcoholic beverages, and gasoline went up. Cuts were made in military and social programs. The resulting economic slowdown and his violation of his pledge not to raise taxes hurt President Bush's standing with the American public.

Savings and Loan Bailout The failure of hundreds of **savings and loan associations (S & Ls)** further burdened the economy. S & L owners had made unwise and, perhaps, illegal investments and loan decisions. Since the government had insured savings in such bankrupt businesses, it was obligated to pay back depositors. To recover its losses, the government created the Resolution Trust Corporation in 1989, which took over and tried to sell S & L property. The bailout cost taxpayers more than $300 billion.

U. S. Supreme Court Decisions

- *Texas* v. *Johnson* (1989). A citizen had burned a U.S. flag in public as an act of protest. The Supreme Court ruled that the First Amendment right to freedom of speech applied to this act, and, therefore, Texas's law against **desecrating** (treating disrespectfully) the flag was unconstitutional. In 2000, the U.S. Senate failed to pass a proposed constitutional amendment outlawing the burning of the U.S. flag.
- *Cruzan* v. *Director, Missouri Department of Health* (1990). Nancy Cruzan had been injured in an automobile accident and was lying in a Missouri

hospital with no evidence of brain function. Her parents wanted to terminate her life-support system, but the hospital refused. The Court ruled that a state may require clear evidence—for example, a living will —that a person did not wish to be sustained by life support in such an extreme situation.

- *Planned Parenthood of Southeastern Pennsylvania, et al.* v. *Casey* (1992). Five Pennsylvania abortion clinics challenged a state law requiring girls under 18 to obtain parental consent for an abortion. Upholding the law as constitutional, the Court empowered the state to limit (but not ban) abortions.

Families in Crisis In 1966, the divorce rate was twice as high as it had been in 1950. Two out of every five 16-year-olds born during the 1970s saw their parents break up. By the 1990s, half of all marriages would end in divorce.

In the 1970s and 1980s, married women sought outside employment in record numbers. Sixty percent of them were in the labor force by 1990, compared with 25 percent in 1950. (Thousands of single mothers also held jobs.) Some worked to make full use of their talents. Growing numbers, though, worked because one income did not pay family expenses. This increase in working mothers led to an increase in day care centers and nurseries.

Drug Abuse Illegal drugs had been a domestic problem since the late 1940s. In the 1960s, increasing numbers of college students smoked marijuana. Teenagers and even preteens were used by organized crime to buy and sell illegal drugs. The use of crack in the 1980s only aggravated the problem. In 1989, Bush declared a "war on drugs" that entailed spending more than $7 billion a year.

Drug addiction was partly responsible for increases in violent crime and property crime (burglary, larceny, and auto theft). In the 1980s, the rate of violent crime went up by nearly 30 percent.

Unknown in the United States before 1981, **AIDS (acquired immunodeficiency syndrome)** caused more than 200,000 deaths by the mid-1990s. The two most common causes of infection were sharing of needles to inject a drug into the bloodstream and sexual contact.

Foreign Policy Issues

Invasion of Panama In the late 1980s, Manuel Noriega came to power in Panama. Two U.S. grand juries indicted him for being involved in smuggling illegal drugs into the United States. In December 1989, President George H. Bush ordered a surprise invasion of Panama to drive Noriega from power and prevent his taking control of the Panama Canal. Noriega was captured, brought to the United States for trial, convicted in a federal court for drug trafficking, and sentenced to imprisonment.

Free elections established a new Panamanian government friendly to the United States, which gave it aid. Other Latin American countries condemned the U.S. invasion as an act of aggression.

Collapse of Communism In June 1989, Poland held free elections, and the Communists lost. Soviet leader Mikhail Gorbachev accepted the result.

The people of Hungary, Czechoslovakia, and Romania demanded free elections. Eventually in most of Eastern Europe, the people voted to replace communism with democratically elected governments.

Fall of the Berlin Wall/German Reunification In November 1989, both East and West Germans tore down the Berlin Wall. The collapse of communism in Eastern Europe was directly influenced by the fall of the Berlin Wall.

Germany was officially reunited in October 1990. The new German government pledged never again to take military action against its European neighbors.

End of the Cold War Bush and Gorbachev held their first summit conference in 1989, a major step toward ending the cold war. The United States promised food and economic aid to the Soviet Union, both powers agreed to dismantle nuclear weapons systems in Europe, and the Soviets agreed to support the U.S. policy against Iraq.

Berliners celebrating the fall of the Berlin Wall, 1989

Dissolution of Soviet Union In December 1991, the Soviet Union ceased to exist as a single nation for the following reasons:

- *Economic failure.* Burdened by large military costs, the Soviet economy had steadily declined. Fewer consumer goods reached the marketplace, forcing consumers to wait in long lines to buy whatever goods were available. Critics called for an end to the old economic system—communism.
- *Yeltsin's rise to power.* In 1987, a radical reformer, Boris Yeltsin, broke with Gorbachev and resigned from the Communist Party (the only legal one). In 1991, Yeltsin was elected president of the Russian Republic. In August 1991, conservative Communists tried to oust Gorbachev and seize control. The **coup** (seizure of power) failed when many of Moscow's citizens, led by Yeltsin, blocked the path of Soviet troops, who refused to attack the crowd.
- *Independence for the republics.* In 1991, all 15 republics in the Soviet Union demanded independence. In December, the presidents of Russia, Ukraine, and Belarus declared that the Soviet Union was "dead" and formed the *Commonwealth of Independent States (CIS)*, open to all republics. Shortly afterward, Gorbachev resigned.

Effects on U.S. Foreign Policy

The cold war ended officially in February 1992 when Bush and Yeltsin met to work out deep cuts in their arsenals of long-range missiles. Yeltsin gave assurances that nuclear missiles of the former Soviet Union would remain under central control. The United States and other Western nations pledged emergency aid for the Russian economy in the form of low-interest loans.

Another effect of the end of the cold war was the reduction in U.S. defense spending as a percentage of the budget in the 1990s.

Crisis in Bosnia Founded after World War I, Yugoslavia consisted of six republics, of which Serbia was the most powerful. In 1991, the republic of Bosnia declared independence, which the United States recognized in 1992. Bosnia's population was made up of Bosnian Muslims, Serbian Orthodox Christians, and Croatian Roman Catholics.

Serbs felt that their dominance of Yugoslavia was threatened by Serbian independence. Many Bosnian Serbs, unwilling to be a minority within the new state, opposed independence. As civil war broke out among the three groups in Bosnia, Serbs engaged in **ethnic cleansing** (expulsion or massacre of Muslims and non-Serbs from areas under Bosnian Serb control).

Persian Gulf Crisis In the 1980s, the four major producers of Middle Eastern oil were Saudi Arabia, Kuwait, Iran, and Iraq—all located on the Persian Gulf. Between 1980 and 1988, Iraq won small gains in territory during the Iran-Iraq War.

Cartoon showing that rising oil prices cause pain and hardship for many consumers

Shortly after that war, Iraq's military dictator, Saddam Hussein, accused Kuwait of taking an unfair share of oil revenues. In August 1990, Hussein claimed that Kuwait was part of Iraq and invaded and occupied it. The price of gasoline and heating oil soared in the United States. To pressure an Iraqi withdrawal, the UN voted to place an embargo on Iraqi oil. This drop in the oil supply led to even higher fuel prices.

The Iraqi invasion of Kuwait alarmed world leaders. This act of aggression by a strong nation against a weak one opened the way for an Iraqi conquest of Saudi Arabia and, possibly, domination of the other Middle Eastern countries.

President George H. Bush announced a defensive effort called *Operation Desert Shield* and sent U.S. troops to Saudi Arabia. They were joined by forces from a UN-supported coalition of 28 nations, including Britain, France, Saudi Arabia, Syria, Turkey, and Egypt.

Members of the Security Council voted a series of resolutions: Iraq's unconditional withdrawal from Kuwait, an international embargo on trade with Iraq, and the use of force if Iraqi troops did not leave Kuwait by January 15, 1991. Both houses of Congress authorized Bush to send U.S. troops into combat in the Persian Gulf.

After the deadline expired, *Operation Desert Storm* went into effect: thousands of planes from allied bases in Saudi Arabia made massive air strikes against military targets in Iraq and Kuwait. After more than a month of bombing attacks, U.S. and allied tanks swept across the desert toward Kuwait City and into Iraq and overwhelmed Iraqi forces. Hussein withdrew from Kuwait, and Bush announced victory. As with the Korean and Vietnam wars, there had been no formal U.S. declaration of war.

As part of the cease-fire agreement, Iraq agreed to eliminate all its poison gas and germ warfare capabilities and let UN observers inspect the sites. To enforce the agreement, the UN imposed trade **sanctions** (penalties) until Iraq complied with all terms. To prevent Hussein from ordering air attacks on Iraq's minority Kurdish population in the north, the United

States created safe havens for the Kurds inside Iraq and established a "no-fly zone" in the north.

The Persian Gulf War liberated Kuwait and prevented Hussein from controlling the region's oil prices and supplies. It also demonstrated military cooperation between the nations of Western Europe and the United States. Even Russia had supported U.S. resolutions in the UN. Criticized for not removing Hussein, though, President Bush stated that the goal had been only to liberate Kuwait.

IN REVIEW

1. Identify *each* of the following and explain its significance: savings and loan bailout, ethnic cleansing, Operation Desert Storm.
2. For *each* of the following Supreme Court cases, identify the constitutional issue involved and summarize the decision: (a) *Texas* v. *Johnson*; (b) *Cruzan* v. *Director, Missouri Department of Health*; and (c) *Planned Parenthood of Southeastern Pennsylvania, et al.* v. *Casey*.
3. Discuss the role of economics and political leadership in bringing about an end to the cold war.

CHAPTER REVIEW

MULTIPLE-CHOICE QUESTIONS

1 "In this present crisis, government is not the solution to our problems.... It is my intention to curb the size and influence of the Federal establishment and to demand recognition of the distinction between the powers granted to the Federal Government and those reserved to the States or to the people. All of us need to be reminded that the Federal Government did not create the States; the States created the Federal Government."

—PRESIDENT RONALD REAGAN, FIRST INAUGURAL ADDRESS, JANUARY 20, 1981

Which action did the Reagan administration take based on the belief expressed in these statements?
(1) It increased government spending on social programs.
(2) It reduced defense spending.
(3) It increased corporate and personal income taxes.
(4) It reduced government regulation of business.

2 President Ronald Reagan's supply-side economic policy was successful in
(1) increasing government spending on social programs
(2) lowering tax rates on personal and business income
(3) reducing defense spending
(4) enforcing stricter environmental regulations

3 In the Supreme Court cases *New Jersey* v. *T.L.O.* and *Tinker* v. *Des Moines School District*, the Court ruled that
(1) individual student rights are more important than a safe school environment

(2) students can be expelled from school without a hearing
(3) civil liberties can be both protected and limited in schools
(4) the Bill of Rights does not apply to minors

4 Over the past thirty years, an objective of United States immigration policy has been to
(1) reduce the number of illegal immigrants
(2) keep out immigrants from former Communist nations
(3) return to an open immigration policy
(4) encourage emigration from Western Europe

Base your answers to questions 5 and 6 on the graph below and on your knowledge of social studies.

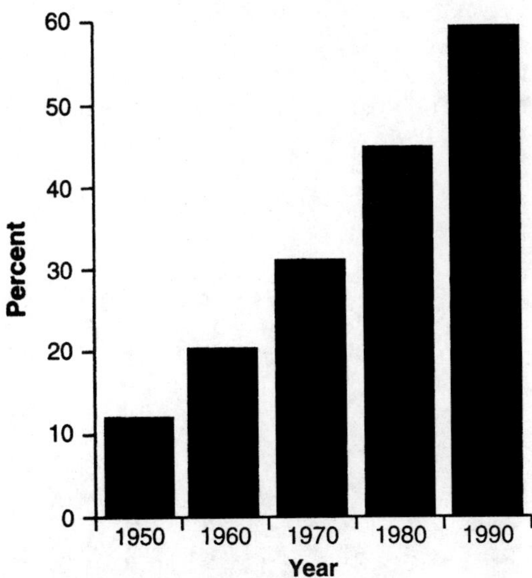

Source: *1996 Green Book,* U.S. Department of Labor, Bureau of Labor Statistics (adapted)

5 Which statement is most clearly supported by the information in the graph?
(1) More children were under age 6 in 1990 than in 1950.
(2) Since 1990, women have made up more than half of the workforce.
(3) The gap between male and female incomes has declined.
(4) Fewer women are staying home to raise their young children.

6 A candidate for public office would likely conclude from a study of this graph that the public would favor increased government support for
(1) additional foreign aid
(2) health care facilities
(3) child day-care centers
(4) colleges and universities

7 The beginning of the collapse of communism in Eastern Europe is most closely associated with the
(1) fall of the Berlin Wall
(2) admission of Warsaw Pact nations to the North Atlantic Treaty Organization (NATO)
(3) intervention of the North Atlantic Treaty Organization (NATO) in Yugoslavia
(4) formation of the European Union

8 Which event led directly to the end of the cold war?
(1) reunification of Germany
(2) formation of the European Union
(3) breakup of the Soviet Union
(4) creation of the North Atlantic Treaty Organization (NATO)

9 Since the Russian people rejected communism in the early 1990s, the United States has provided support to the new nation by
(1) creating a military alliance with Russia
(2) destroying most United States nuclear weapons
(3) opposing the independence of the other Russian republics
(4) giving foreign aid to Russia in the form of low interest loans

10 One way in which the Korean War, the Vietnam War, and the Persian Gulf War are similar is that in all three wars
(1) the goal was to defeat the Soviet Union
(2) the United States was primarily interested in protecting oil supplies
(3) the United States was fighting without allies
(4) no formal declaration of war was made by Congress

THEMATIC ESSAYS

1 **THEME:** *"Reaganomics," a Conservative Revolution.* Ronald Reagan's presidency marked a change in federal economic policy that has been called a "conservative revolution."

TASK: Complete *all* of the following tasks:
- Describe *two* aspects of Reaganomics.
- Describe *two* specific examples of how Reagan applied Reaganomics to the U.S. economy.
- Show a specific effect of *one* of the applications on a specific group.

You may use, but are not limited to, various federal social programs, taxation, federal regulation of business and industry, and relations with organized labor.

2 **THEME:** *Presidential Popularity*: Success in foreign affairs does not always guarantee a president's re-election. This statement reflects the presidency of George H. Bush, who, despite U.S. military victories and the dissolution of the Soviet Union, would lose the election of 1992.

Task: Complete *all* of the following tasks:
- Describe *two* military victories achieved by the United States during the presidency of George H. Bush.
- Explain why many Americans credited President Reagan with the dissolution of the Soviet Union rather than President Bush.
- Discuss *two* domestic issues that undermined the popularity of President Bush.

For the first part, you may wish to use the invasion of Panama and the Persian Gulf War.

For the second part, you may wish to discuss President Reagan's increased military spending and the Strategic Defense Initiative.

For the third part, you may wish to discuss the 1991 recession, the federal deficit, and tax increases.

DOCUMENT-BASED QUESTION

*Study each document and answer the question that follows it. Then read the **Task** and write your essay. Include references to most of the documents and additional information you retain about U.S. history and government.*

HISTORICAL CONTEXT: Many people credit or blame Reagan for changing the nature of the United States and the world.

DOCUMENT 1: Refer to the cartoon below.

QUESTION: What does the cartoon say about Reagan's budget priorities?

Document 2: From a 1982 address by President Reagan concerning political developments in Central America:

> My fellow Americans, I must speak to you tonight about a mounting danger in Central America that... will grow worse... if we fail to take action now.
>
> ... With over a billion dollars in Soviet-bloc aid, the Communist Government of Nicaragua has launched a campaign to subvert and topple its democratic neighbors.
>
> Using Nicaragua as a base, the Soviets and Cubans can... threaten the Panama Canal, interdict our vital Caribbean sea lanes, and, ultimately, move against Mexico. Should that happen, [millions of Latins] would begin fleeing north into the cities of the southern United States, or to wherever some hope for freedom remained.
>
> The United States Congress has before it... an aid package of $100 million for the more than 20,000 freedom fighters struggling to... eliminate this Communist menace at its source.... We are not asking for a single dime in new money. We are asking only to be permitted to switch a small part of our present defense budget—to the defense of our own southern frontier....

Question: What was President Reagan asking Congress and the American people to do regarding the Sandinista government in Nicaragua?

Document 3: Refer to the cartoon at the top of the next column.

Question: What difficulties were going on at the Reagan-Gorbachev summit meeting?

Document 4: Refer to the cartoon below.

Question: What was the cartoonist saying about spending priorities of the Reagan administration?

Document 5: Refer to the following table.

National Debt, 1970–1998 (billions of dollars)

Year	*Debt*	*As Percent of Gross Domestic Product*
1970	$ 380.9	38.7
1975	541.9	35.9
1980	909.0	34.4
1982	1,137.3	36.4
1984	1,564.6	42.3
1986	2,120.6	50.3
1988	2,601.3	54.1
1990	3,206.5	58.5
1992	4,002.1	67.6
1994	4,643.7	70.0
1996	5,181.9	68.0
1998	5,478.7	65.2

QUESTION: What happened to the national debt during the Reagan years (1981–1989)?

DOCUMENT 6: Refer to the following photo.

QUESTION: What does the photo show about the economy of the Soviet Union prior to its collapse?

The average Soviet shopper in the 1980s faced severe shortages of food and consumer goods.

TASK: Using the documents and your knowledge of U.S. history and government, write an essay in which you:
- describe and evaluate the success of Reagan's foreign and domestic policies.
- explain what have been the long-term results of Reagan's foreign and domestic policies on the United States.

CHAPTER 21
Toward a Postindustrial World: 1993–2001

DOCUMENTS AND LAWS
AmeriCorps (1993) • Brady Bill (1993) • Family and Medical Leave Act (1993) • NAFTA (1994)
U.S.-Cuban agreement on immigrants (1994) • Welfare Reform Act (1996)
Nuclear Non-Proliferation Treaty (1970) • START II (1993)

EVENTS
Three Mile Island nuclear accident (1979) • Chernobyl nuclear accident (1986)
Exxon Valdez oil spill (1989) • Tiananmen Square Massacre (1989)
Contract With America (1994) • U.S. withdrawal from Somolia (1994)
Dayton Peace Treaty (1995) • Impeachment and trial of Bill Clinton (1998–1999)
Decoding of human genome (2000)

PEOPLE/GROUPS
Madeleine K. Albright • Yasir Arafat • Jean-Bertrand Aristide • Daniel Bell • Bill Clinton
Hillary Rodham Clinton • Dianne Feinstein • Ruth Bader Ginsburg • Al Gore, Jr. • Alan Greenspan
Hamas • Kim Jong Il • Slobodan Milosevic • NRA • Vladimir Putin • Yitzhak Rabin • Janet Reno

OBJECTIVES

- To examine changes in domestic policy during the Clinton administration.
- To evaluate presidential responses to challenges in Haiti, the Middle East, Bosnia, Yugoslavia, Iraq, North Korea, and Russia.
- To explain how the United States is changing from an industrial to a postindustrial nation.
- To describe changes in technology and their impact on the United States and the rest of the world.
- To recognize how the nations of the world are closely linked economically by trade and electronic communications.

Clinton Presidency

Citing the Gulf War victory and the end of the cold war as achievements and blaming the Democratic majority in Congress for stalling his economic programs, President George H. Bush sought reelection in 1992. Former Arkansas governor Bill Clinton and running mate Senator Albert Gore, Jr., blamed economic ills on Bush and promised a change. Clinton was elected that year, and he also won reelection in 1996, over Senator Robert Dole.

Domestic Issues

Social Concerns The election of a Democratic president, which ended 12 years of Republican leadership, marked a shift from Reagan-Bush conservatism. In his first term, Clinton worked with Democratic majorities in both houses to achieve the *Family and Medical Leave Act* (1993). It granted employees 12 weeks of unpaid leave to care for newborn infants and family members who are ill. Clinton won congressional approval for a program called *AmeriCorps* (1993), which enlisted young people in community service projects. With varying degrees of success, he also dealt with a number of domestic issues:

Health Care Clinton's wife, Hillary Rodham Clinton, headed a task force to reform the health care system. The plan had two main objectives: to guarantee insurance coverage for all Americans and to prevent the costs of medical care from consuming increasingly more of the national wealth. Small businesses and the insurance industry vigorously opposed the plan and gained the strong support of the majority of Congress. By mid-1994, it was clear that Congress would not pass Clinton's health care reform bill. In addition, international problems took the administration's focus away from health care reform.

Education Since the early 1970s, educators have reported low levels of student performance on standardized tests. Conservatives urged a "back

Cartoon contrasting American students' poor skills with the highly developed ones of students in other lands

to basics" approach (more math, reading, and writing). Liberals proposed restructuring schools so that teachers, parents, and students could take part in decision making. In the mid-1990s, setting improved national standards in education was widely debated. Clinton favored them and increased federal aid to schools. Influenced by the president's proposals, states began to raise local standards too.

Welfare Reform At times, President Clinton supported Republican positions. In 1996, he signed into law the *Welfare Reform Act*, which sharply cut federal spending on welfare programs. Instead, the federal government provided states with **block grants** (financial aid with few guidelines on their use) and required welfare recipients to work. The now Republican-led Congress (discussed on page 374) supported the bill, with only liberal Democrats objecting. As the program was implemented, welfare costs dropped.

Stability of Social Security Ever since the reform of 1983, money coming into the Social Security system has covered benefits paid out to the elderly. But social scientists predicted trouble for the system by the 2030s, when the number of senior citizens will have increased to the extent that the declining number of younger workers cannot fund the system. Because of the looming impact of the baby boomers on the Social Security system, Congress passed legislation to gradually raise the age for collecting full Social Security benefits from 65 years of age to 67. Despite this, concern remains about the financial viability of the Social Security system.

Gays in the Military Early in his presidency, Clinton removed the long-standing ban against homosexuals serving in the armed forces. To make the military more comfortable with the change, he stipulated that gays must remain silent about their sexual preferences (the "don't ask, don't tell" policy). This policy produced controversy in both the military and civilian sectors.

Progress for Women Clinton appointed a number of women to top posts. For example, in 1993, Janet Reno became the attorney general and Ruth Bader Ginsburg was appointed to the Supreme Court. In 1997, Madeleine K. Albright was appointed secretary of state.

Women also won more elected positions. Barbara Boxer and Dianne Feinstein of California, Carol Moseley Braun of Illinois, and Patty Murray of Washington won Senate seats. The number of women in the House increased from 28 to 47.

Despite progress for women in politics, equal pay for women in non-government employment remained a major goal of the women's rights movement.

The Economy

Budget Deficits and the Federal Debt Before the federal government can spend money, it must have a budget listing proposed government expenditures. In order to pay for these expenditures, the government taxes its citizens and corporations. When the federal government spends more than it takes in, the budget is in deficit, and the government must borrow money to make up the difference. It does this by selling bonds. Money owed over the long term gets added to our **national debt** (the amount our government actually owes) and must repay over time, with interest.

From 1970 to 2000, the national debt skyrocketed from $300 billion to more than $5.5 trillion. Much of the increase in the federal debt during the Reagan and Bush administrations was due to deficit spending. Under the Clinton administration, though, the budget deficit was reduced, and there were several years of budget surpluses. Since then, however, the federal debt has continued to increase.

In order to slow down the pace of the increase, one of Clinton's first acts as president was to submit to Congress a budget that increased taxes. The measure increased the top income tax rate to 36 percent, increased the federal tax on gasoline slightly, and cut spending. The measure passed Congress.

By 1994, a significant decline in unemployment signaled the recession's end. The economy appeared to be healthy. In 1997, Congress voted to increase the minimum wage. The economy still improved, and a budget surplus helped to increase President Clinton's popularity.

Republican Midterm Victories For some Americans, Clinton was too liberal on social issues. For others, his failed national health plan was a sign of weak leadership. As a result, midterm elections of 1994 gave Republicans control of both the House and the Senate for the first time in 40 years.

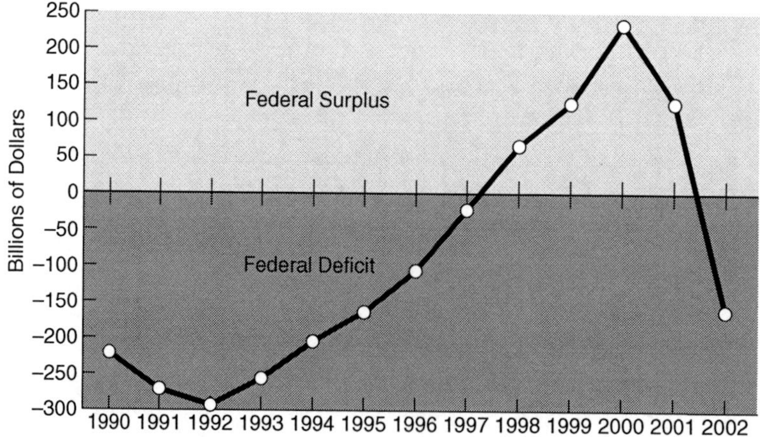

The Republican election platform, known as the *Contract With America*, included a balanced budget amendment, term limits for Congress, and welfare reform. It also outlined a smaller central government, with many functions and powers transferred to the states. Republicans hoped to cut spending by reducing the federal bureaucracy. Clinton opposed major portions of the Contract With America for fear that they would hurt the poor and the middle class and favor only the rich.

Stock Market Trends From 1987 through the end of the 1990s, the stock market surged forward in a strong bull market. In 1987, the Dow Jones average (a grouping of 30 major companies) had stood at 2,000. By 1999, it had increased to more than 10,000. A major reason for the increase was the growth in new technology businesses. A second reason was the mergers and acquisitions that led to **downsizing** (laying workers off) in major corporations and the corporations' increased profits.

As wealth increased, Alan Greenspan, Chair of the Federal Reserve, gradually increased interest rates in an attempt to slow the economy and prevent inflation. Reassured by the lowest unemployment rate in 40 years, the public kept up the economic boom by spending for all types of products.

Politics

Whitewater Investigations As governor of Arkansas, Clinton and his wife had taken loans from an Arkansas bank and purchased land in the Whitewater region of Arkansas. The value of this land was expected to increase greatly. Questions, however, arose regarding the loans and land purchase. A special U.S. Senate Whitewater Committee was set up to determine if Clinton had acted improperly and violated the law.

After more than a year, the committee reached no specific conclusions about the president's conduct. Attorney General Janet Reno appointed a special prosecutor to investigate further.

President Clinton presents his proposals for a national health plan at a town meeting.

Impeachment, Trial, and Acquittal In 1998, the special prosecutor turned from Whitewater to Clinton's sexual involvement with a young woman on the White House staff. The president denied involvement with this White

House intern. Evidence, however, was uncovered that Clinton was involved with her. Thus, his denial under oath led to a call for impeachment.

In December 1998, the Republican-controlled House of Representatives voted for impeachment. The accusations, which focused not on the sexual affair but on the president's testimony, led to charges of perjury and **obstruction of justice** (attempting to influence others to conceal the truth). The proceedings then moved to the Senate for trial, with Chief Justice Rehnquist presiding. On February 12, 1999, the Senate, by a narrow margin, acquitted Clinton, and he remained in office. Bill Clinton and Andrew Johnson were the only two presidents to be impeached by the House, and both were acquitted by the Senate.

Gun Control Opponents of gun control cite the Second Amendment's provision that "the right of the people to keep and bear arms shall not be infringed." Proponents of gun control claim that the amendment refers only to a "well regulated militia." In 1993, Congress passed the *Brady Bill*, which called for a five-day waiting period and a background check by local officials before a handgun could be sold. (James Brady had been wounded in an assassination attempt on President Reagan in 1981.) In 1996, however, the Supreme Court, citing the division of powers between the federal and state governments, ruled that Congress could not require local officials to conduct background checks.

As violence involving guns increased, the gun control issue became more controversial. In April 1999, for instance, two teenagers shot and killed 12 fellow students and a teacher and wounded 30 others at Columbine High School, Littleton, Colorado. The *National Rifle Association (NRA)*, the main lobbying group opposed to gun control, argued that people rather than guns kill people. Others argued that guns must be made more difficult to obtain. An assault weapons bill, signed into law by President Clinton in 1994, was not renewed by Congress in 2004.

Nov. 18, 1988

"Soft Money"

from *Herblock: A Cartoonist's Life* (Macmillan Publishing Co., 1993)

Campaign Finance Reform Americans have long been concerned about how much the two major parties spend on elections. In 1974, a federal law established disclosure requirements for federal campaign contributions and set specific limits on donations to individual candidates. However, it allowed unlimited contributions to political parties and organizations for party-building and issue education. Such contributions are called **soft money**. In spite of restrictions, soft money is often used to benefit specific candidates. The 1974 law also began public financing of presidential elections and created a *Federal Election Commission.* In 1976, however, the Supreme Court, in *Buckley* v. *Valeo,* declared that mandatory spending limits on federal candidates and on those who support federal candidates reduce (1) freedom of expression as guaranteed in the First Amendment and (2) the ability to communicate political ideas. The ruling pointed out that "every means of communicating ideas in today's mass society requires the expenditure of money."

A new campaign finance law limiting some soft money contributions was passed by Congress in 2002, but it was overturned by the Supreme Court in 2010.

U.S.–Middle East Relations

Palestinian Problem After Israel's 1948 and 1967 victories, Palestinian refugees were resettled in camps in Syria, Lebanon, and Jordan. Their poverty and strong feelings of nationalism gave rise to the Palestine Liberation Organization (PLO), which aimed to eliminate the state of Israel and create a Palestinian homeland there. Its main weapon was **terrorism** (systematic use or threat of violence to achieve political goals). The PLO attacked Israeli settlements, buses, beaches, and airplanes, and even made anti-Israeli assaults abroad.

Intifada More than a million Palestinians lived in the Israeli-occupied Gaza Strip and West Bank. Beginning in 1987, youths protested by throwing rocks, and Israeli troops sometimes retaliated with gunfire. This **intifada**, or uprising, attracted international attention.

Changing Relations In 1979, Egypt and Israel signed the first Arab-Israeli peace agreement (discussed on page 337). In a 1993 breakthrough, Israeli Prime Minister Yitzhak Rabin and PLO leader Yasir Arafat signed a "land for peace agreement":

- Palestinians gained self-rule in the Gaza Strip and the West Bank town of Jericho.
- The PLO recognized Israel and pledged to end terrorism.

In 1994, Jordan and Israel officially ended five years of war. In 1995, Israel agreed to expand Palestinian self-rule in the West Bank. The PLO reconfirmed Israel's right to exist and undertook to strengthen Palestinian antiterrorism measures.

Extremists challenged this peace process. In 1995, an Israeli shot and killed Rabin. A new Palestinian resistance movement, *Hamas,* used terror bombing and suicide attacks against Israelis to disrupt peace efforts. The difficult movement toward peace continued with Presidents Clinton and

Invasions in the Middle East, 1973–2003

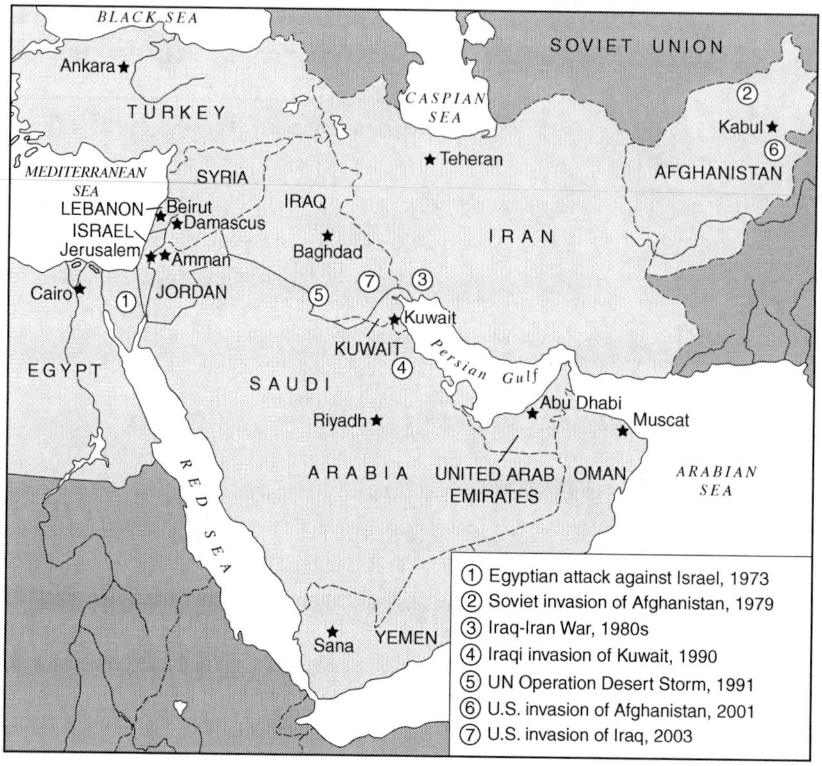

① Egyptian attack against Israel, 1973
② Soviet invasion of Afghanistan, 1979
③ Iraq-Iran War, 1980s
④ Iraqi invasion of Kuwait, 1990
⑤ UN Operation Desert Storm, 1991
⑥ U.S. invasion of Afghanistan, 2001
⑦ U.S. invasion of Iraq, 2003

George W. Bush working with different Israeli prime ministers and moderate Palestinian leaders.

United States in the Global Economy

NAFTA In 1994, in a commitment to globalization, Clinton completed negotiations begun by Bush for the *North American Free Trade Agreement (NAFTA)* with Mexico and Canada. This treaty immediately eliminated tariffs on some goods and phased out others. Thus, U.S., Canadian, and Mexican businesses gained a much larger market, with 380 million potential customers. This expanded market, it was hoped, would increase production and create jobs. Moreover, better economic conditions in Mexico might reduce illegal immigration to the United States. Many Canadian and U.S. workers, however, feared that if businesses moved to Mexico, where wages were lower, Mexicans would get more of their jobs. NAFTA was supported by big businesses but criticized by labor unions, many farmers, and environmentalists.

GATT After World War II, the major economic powers set up the *General Agreement on Tariffs and Trade (GATT)* to reduce and limit trade barriers and settle trade disputes. Periodic negotiations had further lowered tariffs among GATT members. In 1995, GATT changed its name to the *World Trade Organization (WTO).* Now with 149 members, it is the major body overseeing international trade. Both GATT and NAFTA have contributed to increased participation of the United States and most other countries in the global economy.

In 1999, the WTO met in Seattle, Washington, to promote increased global trade. Thousands of protesters, however, demonstrated against it. In their view, the WTO promoted unrestricted trade among large multinational corporations at the expense of workers' rights and the environment.

In response, President Clinton asked the WTO to include in its agenda more protection of labor rights and the environment. But most developing countries feared that linking trade with labor and environmental standards would burden their economies or be used by others as an excuse to boycott their goods.

Critics of the WTO also said that it infringed on national sovereignties because it was empowered to settle trade disputes and impose sanctions on countries found in violation of the group's agreements. Supporters maintained that free trade led to greater global prosperity.

Farm Subsidies For many years, developing countries had been critical of U.S. government subsidies paid to some American farmers. These subsidies kept the prices of farm product low and prevented developing nations from profitably selling their agricultural goods in the United States. In the United States, large-scale farmers and agribusinesses lobbied the government to maintain the subsidies. In 2004, the United States along with other developed countries reached a tentative agreement with the developing nations to reduce farm subsidies, particularly to cotton farmers. However, in 2005, negotiations for further reductions slowed.

Trade With China With its 1.3 billion people, China is the greatest potential market in the world for American goods. Its violations of human rights, however, have been a stumbling block to full-scale U.S.-Chinese trade.

Between 1978 and 1989, China's Communist leaders adopted several economic reforms:

- The Chinese people were encouraged to set up small businesses.
- The country was opened to Western tourists and businesses.
- Advice from the West on improving the economy was welcomed.

In the spring of 1989, Chinese troops fired on some 100,000 student demonstrators gathered in Tiananmen Square in the capital, Beijing. They had been peacefully urging the government to make democratic reforms. The massacre and arrest of thousands of students were telecast around the world. President George H. Bush criticized the massacre but did not carry out the economic sanctions against China voted by Congress. Clinton continued Bush's policy after Chinese leaders ordered the arrest of more Chinese dissidents. Despite protests from human rights groups, both Bush and Clinton believed that increased trade with a prospering China would lead to a better human rights policy there.

Trade With the Asian Pacific Rim During the 1980s and 1990s, trade and industry grew rapidly in most of the Asian Pacific Rim countries—including South Korea, Japan, Thailand, Singapore, Malaysia, and Taiwan. Their clothing, shoes, electric appliances, and steel sold well in foreign markets. In the late 1990s, an economic downturn in the Pacific Rim made their products cheaper for Americans to buy. While American consumers benefited from the lower prices, the competition forced many American manufacturers out of business and caused many American workers to lose their jobs. As a result, some Americans called for higher duties on imports from Japan and other Pacific Rim countries.

Problems With Latin America Traditional Latin American imports to the United States have been coffee, bananas, copper, and tin. In the 1990s, television sets, oil, and textiles were added to the list. In 1999, the U.S. trade deficit with South and Central America reached $13 billion, as U.S. workers continued to complain about the loss of jobs in the United States.

The United States does not trade with Cuba. To damage Fidel Castro's Communist government, the United States in 1962 imposed a trade embargo. Because Cuba's main trading partners were Communist nations, the Soviet Union's collapse in 1991 badly damaged Cuba's economy. Soon thousands of Cubans fled poverty and dictatorship by attempting to enter the United States illegally. As the number of "boat people" rose, the United

U.S. Interventions in Latin America in the 1980s and 1990s

States decided to intercept and turn back boats leaving Cuba. In 1994, a U.S.-Cuban agreement ended the illegal exodus and raised the yearly quota of Cubans allowed to enter the United States legally.

U.S. Interventionism

Somalia During the last year of the George H. Bush presidency, the United States provided humanitarian aid to Somalia, an African nation suffering from famine and civil war. U.S. forces joined a UN force trying to end the civil war. In 1994, after significant multinational casualties, the United States withdrew. As a result, the Clinton administration became more cautious about committing American troops on foreign soil. By 1995, all UN troops had left Somalia, where war and famine continued.

Haiti In 1990, Father Jean-Bertrand Aristide was elected president of Haiti. Less than a year later, a military coup ousted Aristide, who fled to the United States. In retaliation, the UN in 1993 imposed an oil and arms embargo on Haiti. Large numbers of Haitians tried to reach the United States by boat. U.S. officials returned some to Haiti, held others in detention centers, and allowed still others to emigrate to welcoming countries.

Finally the Haitian military, under threat of a UN invasion, agreed to recognize Aristide as president. U.S. troops restored order, and in October 1994 Aristide resumed the presidency. Haiti's democracy and its economy, though, remained unsettled.

Bosnia In 1994, Bosnian Muslims and Croatians created a Muslim-Croat confederation even though Bosnian Serbs controlled more than 70 percent of Bosnia. Heavy Muslim-Serb fighting continued. In 1995, the balance of power shifted, NATO launched heavy air strikes at Bosnian Serb targets, and a Croat-Muslim offensive recaptured significant territory. In 1995, after nearly four years of civil war, the leaders of Bosnia, Croatia, and Serbia signed a peace treaty in Dayton, Ohio. It divided Bosnia into two **autonomous** (self-governing) regions: a Muslim-Croat federation controlling 51 percent of the country and a Serb republic holding 49 percent. About 60,000 NATO troops, including a large U.S. force, stayed on as peacekeepers to prevent another civil war. A UN tribunal brought charges against suspected war criminals.

Yugoslavia Ethnic and religious conflicts also led to war in Kosovo, a Yugoslavian province with a population of roughly 90 percent Albanian Muslims and 10 percent Serbian Orthodox Christians. Until 1989, Kosovo had its own elected officials and Albanian-language schools. Then, Slobodan Milosevic, the Yugoslavian president, forced Kosovo's elected officials to step down and reinstated Serbo-Croatian as the official language there. When Albanians demanded full independence, Serbian officials countered with violence. In 1996, ethnic Albanians formed the Kosovo Liberation Army (KLA) and conducted a guerrilla war for Kosovo's independence. Milosevic authorized dozens of executions of ethnic Albanians in Kosovo and burned thousands of their homes. Full-scale war erupted.

Fearful of Serbian "ethnic cleansing" in Kosovo, as had happened earlier in Bosnia, the UN and the United States called for an immediate cease-fire, threatening air strikes as the alternative. The Albanians signed the peace plan, but the Serbs rejected the provision calling for a NATO peacekeeping force in Kosovo. NATO, with President Clinton's support, then launched a massive air war against Yugoslavian and Serbian forces in Kosovo between March and June 1999. In retaliation, the Serbs terrorized Albanians, thousands of whom fled to Albania and Macedonia. In May 1999, the UN war crimes tribunal indicted Milosevic for "crimes against humanity." In June, he accepted a peace plan that included NATO occupation. A 50,000-member multinational force entered Kosovo, and refugees began returning home.

Iraq After Iraq's 1991 defeat in the Persian Gulf War, UN inspection teams were to monitor Iraq's destruction of missiles and chemical and biological weapons. Iraq, however, refused access to some sites. In 1998, Iraq ordered the inspectors to leave, and the United States and Britain bombarded Iraqi military targets.

North Korean Nuclear Capability In North Korea, the Communist regime of Kim Il Sung and his son and successor, Kim Jong Il, survived the collapse of communism elsewhere. In the early 1990s, North Korea was suspected of developing nuclear weapons. It denied the charge but refused UN inspection of its nuclear power plants. Under threat of UN economic sanctions, North Korea in 1994 froze its nuclear program in exchange for two light-water reactors and economic and diplomatic concessions. (Light-water reactors are used to produce nuclear power but are difficult to use in the production of nuclear weapons.) U.S.-North Korean relations remained clouded by suspicions that North Korea was secretly building nuclear weapons.

U.S.-Russian Relations Russia became an independent state in 1991 as the Soviet Union came to an end. The United States and other Western nations pledged emergency economic aid to Russia, which began a series of economic reforms.

In 1991, the United States and Russia signed START I, which aimed at a two-thirds reduction in each side's strategic nuclear weapons, and the Russian parliament ratified it in 2000. The United States also worked with Russia to dismantle hundreds of stockpiled Russian nuclear weapons.

Russia and the United States differed on a number of issues, however. The United States objected to Russia's use of force among its own people. In 1994, for example, Russia sent troops into the Muslim region of Chechnya after it declared its independence. On December 31, 1999, Boris Yeltsin resigned as Russia's president, naming Vladimir Putin as his successor. Putin, who had been largely responsible for Russia's defeat of Chechnya, won the 2000 presidential election.

Other areas of disagreement included Russia's opposition to including Eastern European countries in NATO, Russia's desire to end economic sanctions against Iraq, and Russia's objection to NATO's bombing of its traditional ally, Yugoslavia.

Chechen women protest the killing of their leader by a Russian missile.

Economic and Military Organizations

European Union The European Union (EU) originated in the 1950s from an effort by six Western European nations to reduce trade barriers. By 2011, the EU had a total of 27 members, 17 of which use a common currency, the euro. A central bank coordinates monetary policy. The economic power of the EU makes it a strong trading rival to the United States as well as a strong trading partner.

North Atlantic Treaty Organization With the collapse of the Soviet Union in 1991 and the end of the cold war in 1992, NATO members created a rapid deployment force to react to local crises. A multinational NATO force was deployed in Bosnia in 1995 and in Kosovo in 1999. In March 1999, the Czech Republic, Hungary, and Poland officially joined NATO, the first former members of the Warsaw Pact to do so. Seven more nations in Eastern Europe were added in 2004. Nevertheless, Russia objected to the inclusion in NATO of countries bordering its nation.

IN REVIEW

1. Describe (a) *three* social concerns, (b) *three* economic concerns, and (c) *two* political concerns that arose during the Clinton administration.
2. Summarize the issues involved in the (a) movement for campaign finance reform and (b) the impeachment of Clinton.
3. Explain how *three* of the following posed a challenge to U.S. foreign policy during the 1990s: (a) Middle East, (b) Somalia, (c) Haiti, (d) Bosnia, (e) Kosovo, (f) Iraq, (g) Russia.

Changes in the Postindustrial Age

The Industrial Revolution began about 1750 and, in a sense, persists today. By the 1950s, however, a revolutionary era of new technology and economic systems was under way. This era is called the *information age* or **postindustrial age.** We are still in it.

Manufacturing: Energy Sources, Materials, Automation

Nuclear Power The industrial age relied on burning coal and oil for energy. Scientists, however, predicted that people might use up all the oil sometime in the 21st century. And burning coal results in more pollution than burning other common fuels. So scientists began to look for new sources of energy.

Energy and heat can be created by splitting uranium atoms. In the 1950s, the U.S. government and electric power companies hoped that nuclear power plants might produce cheap and efficient energy in the future without polluting the air with smoke. However, there is an inherent danger—accidents might release harmful substances into the atmosphere. An additional problem is getting rid of nuclear waste in the form of radioactive by-products.

New Sources of Energy Scientists have experimented with using the sun as an energy source. Trapping its rays to heat a home or run a small automobile would be environmentally safe. But would it be practical? So far, devices to harness **solar energy** have had only limited use because of the

Nuclear Reactor Orders, 1965–1978

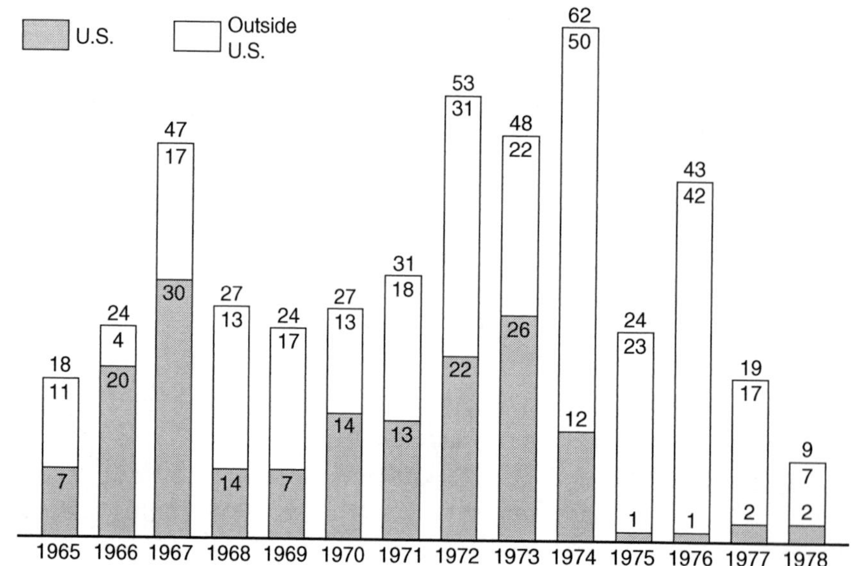

costs involved. The same is true of modern windmills and other technological applications for tapping the winds, tides, and underground heat.

Plastics and Light Metals In the postindustrial world, many items—calculators, computers, compact discs, watchbands, car seats, cameras, radios, and carpets—are made entirely or in part of various plastics that did not exist before 1900.

The production of aluminum on a wide scale became practical in the early 1900s. Aluminum foil first appeared in 1947. Thereafter, manufacturers began to use aluminum to make many other things. Aluminum cans replaced glass bottles in the 1960s. In the 1970s, cars made from aluminum alloys were produced. Because of their lighter weight, they used less gas and were thus cheaper to run and less polluting to the environment.

Automation In the 1950s and 1960s, the U.S. economy made spectacular gains in productivity, largely because of **automation**—the manufacturing method in which one set of machines regulates other machines. Through automation, goods are assembled rapidly and with a minimum of human labor or error. Automation, however, has been a worry for factory workers because it reduces the number of jobs that require little education or skill.

Computerization

Electronic devices called computers helped make automation possible. To help the U.S. military, ENIAC, a 30-ton computer, was operational in February 1946.

This "first-generation" computer was replaced in the 1960s by a more powerful version. Instead of the vacuum tube of the 1940s, its basic electronic element was the transistor. Less than one-tenth the size of the vacuum tube, the transistor performed the same functions with greater speed and reliability.

In 1969, a smaller and more compact element—a thin square **microchip** of silicon imprinted with electronic circuits—replaced the transistor. Thus, smaller computers began to process and store more information at higher speeds and for less cost.

In the 1960s, a social scientist, Daniel Bell, observed that in a postindustrial society "information is power" and that the computer enabled people to collect more information than ever before. Computer discs were used to store **data** (information) that was formerly printed on paper. They then transmitted the data to other computers over telephone lines or through electronic signals bounced off space satellites. By 1990, the personal computer was used as a tool of word processing and classroom instruction. Consumers began to use the Internet to purchase all types of goods and services. To some extent, e-mail and texting replaced telephone calls and letter writing.

One problem with computerized applications was the possibility for

"I never tire of looking at them"
from *Herblock on All Fronts* (New American Library, 1980)

businesses and government to invade personal privacy. For a small user fee, almost anyone can access a database listing people who had, for example, been arrested or failed to pay a debt.

The Internet has led to a new type of industry, as companies create Web sites that enable users to retrieve information and buy and sell products and services. The Internet and World Wide Web are contributing to **globalization**, the expanding ability of individuals and corporations everywhere to communicate and do business with one another. As a result of U.S. leadership in developing the Internet, English is becoming the world's major language.

Widespread use of computers has led critics to point out a number of associated problems. How can computerized communications be kept private? Is there a limit to the amount of data a user needs or can absorb? Will commercial computer applications lead to a frenzy of overconsumerism? And how can computer programs be safeguarded against harmful electronic "viruses" that skilled but unethical users design and disseminate through the World Wide Web?

Genetics Great strides have been made in **genetics** (science of the heredity of living organisms). By the late 1990s, scientists were able to **clone** (reproduce from one parent without fertilization) sheep and some other animals. They could also produce new forms of genetically altered soybeans and corn. In 2000, scientists researching **genomes** (genetic makeup of organisms) were able to identify the complete sequence of human DNA. They could thus detect genes that may cause such diseases as cancer and Alzheimer's.

Corporate Structures

Public firms that have operations in more than one country are known as **multinational corporations (MNCs)**. (Large examples include General Motors and IBM.) They may maintain headquarters in U.S. cities but have manufacturing plants in developing countries, where labor is cheaper. By the 1990s, hundreds of U.S. companies operated in multiple countries. Multinational businesses have vastly increased world trade and opened world markets for U.S. goods and services. Unfortunately, when U.S. firms set up factories abroad, it often results in the closing of U.S. factories and the loss of manufacturing jobs at home. Also, it is more difficult to regulate firms that have operations in other countries.

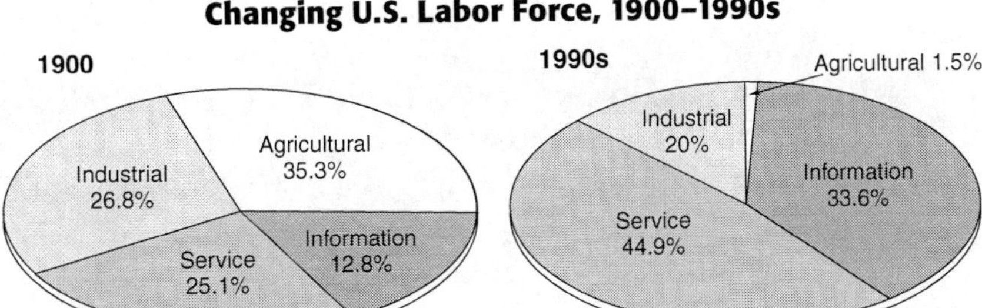

Employment By the second half of the 20th century, most Americans were involved in delivering services of some kind rather than in making products. By 1993, only one out of five workers in the labor force produced goods in a factory or on a farm. Four out of five workers either dealt with information (creating, transmitting, or storing it) or performed a service, such as selling clothes or providing transportation.

Problems of the Postindustrial Era

Since the mid-1900s, technological and industrial growth has created environmental problems.

Pollution

Nuclear Waste Disposal and Accidents Waste materials from nuclear plants present special risks to the environment because they are radioactive. Moreover, there is the possibility that an accident might cause the nuclear core of a power plant to burn through its protective walls. In the event of such a **meltdown**, the area for miles around could become radioactive. In 1979, a less serious accident occurred at the nuclear power plant at *Three Mile Island*, Pennsylvania. There was no meltdown, but many people, frightened by the possibility, began to oppose building more nuclear plants. Opposition increased in 1986, when the nuclear power plant near the Soviet city of *Chernobyl* caught fire. Winds carried radioactive smoke across Europe.

Chemicals and Fossil Fuels In the 1960s, Americans became aware that industrial wastes and exhaust fumes were damaging the natural environment. In 1962, Rachel Carson published a book, *Silent Spring*, in which she identified the pesticide DDT, a chemical spray to kill insects, as the cause of the deaths of many birds and fish. She also explained that the extinction of wildlife would cause further damage to the entire environment. In response to Carson's book, an environmental movement gained strength.

Sewage and factory waste polluted reservoirs of drinking water as well as such bodies of water as the Hudson River in New York and the Great Lakes. In 1989, the oil tanker *Exxon Valdez* spilled more than ten million gallons of oil off the Alaskan coast. Much of the nearby marine life died. The cleanup took years. In 2010, the British Petroleum (BP) oil spill in the Gulf of Mexico added to the concerns of Americans regarding drilling in deep water (discussed more on page 417).

Depletion of Ozone The **ozone layer**, a band of gas high above Earth, blocks the sun's ultraviolet light, which can cause skin cancer and other damage to human tissue. Aerosol sprays, Styrofoam materials, and chemicals used in refrigerators and air conditioners emit an ozone-destroying gas into the atmosphere. Canada, the United States, and the nations of Western Europe have banned production of damaging substances.

Global Warming The chief environmental debate in the postindustrial era has been between those who believe that climate change or global warming is increasing and those who believe its dangers are overstated. Former Vice President Al Gore is outspoken in his belief that global warming would negatively impact future generations. He stated that we are "continuing to dump 90 million tons of global warming pollution in the atmosphere every 24 hours." Most of these come from fossil fuels and deforestation. As a result, average temperatures have increased globally over the last century and in the first decade of the new century. The chief concern is pollutants such as carbon dioxide that trap heat from the sun and increase temperatures (the **greenhouse effect**). As a result, many scientists believe that glaciers will melt, sea levels will rise, land near oceans will flood, sever storms will occur more frequently, and agricultural output will be disrupted.

Opponents argue that increasing temperatures are part of a normal cycle and that human activity has little to do with climate change. They believe that the meltdown rate of glaciers is vastly overstated and point to the cold weather in the United States during the winter of 2010 as evidence to support their position.

Acid Rain Threatening the world's lakes, rivers, and streams, **acid rain** is caused mainly by factory chemicals and automobile exhaust fumes that enter the air as vapor and fall to Earth in acid-rich rain. In bodies of water thus polluted, fish die and plant growth is stunted. Wind currents carry this form of pollution hundreds and even thousands of miles. Half the acid rain that falls in Canada originates in the United States. As a result, environmentalists have been successful in the passage of federal laws requiring industries to reduce smokestack emissions.

Waste Disposal Plastic, glass, and aluminum items are not **biodegradable**, that is, they do not decompose readily when thrown away. Finding ways to dispose of them has become a major problem. Many communities recycle such items so that materials can be reused or turned into other products. Moreover, production of light metals such as aluminum consumes huge amounts of energy. To reduce these energy requirements, efforts are being made to reuse aluminum products. From 1960 to 1990, both total waste and recycling increased.

Energy Use and Depletion of Resources

Between 1960 and the mid-1990s, energy use in the United States more than doubled. This rise in consumption spurred an increase in domestic production of crude oil as well as increased reliance on imported oil. As U.S. oil reserves ran low, the nation became ever more dependent on foreign petroleum. At the turn of the century, prices of imported oil rose significantly. This led to expanded efforts to find oil in shale and the use of deepwater oil rigs that drill down thousands of feet beneath the surface of water bodies, such as the Gulf of Mexico.

IN REVIEW

1. Identify *two* characteristics of a postindustrial society that distinguish it from an industrial society.
2. Define multinational corporation and explain how it depends on modern technology.
3. Define and explain the significance of greenhouse effect, ozone layer, and acid rain.

CHAPTER REVIEW

MULTIPLE-CHOICE QUESTIONS

1 The aging of the baby boom generation will most likely result in
(1) an increase in Social Security spending
(2) a decrease in health care costs
(3) a decrease in infant mortality in the United States
(4) a balanced federal budget

Base your answer to question 2 on the chart below and on your knowledge of social studies.

2 The data in this chart support the conclusion that between 1960 and 1990
(1) government failed to pass laws that granted women equal access to jobs
(2) the earnings gap between men and women was only slightly improved
(3) women's earnings consistently increased faster than those of men
(4) most higher paying jobs were still not legally open to women

Base your answer to question 3 on the cartoon at the top of the next column and on your knowledge of social studies.

3 The cartoonist is critical of computers mainly because
(1) important personal records are frequently lost

A 1998 Herblock Cartoon, copyright by The Herb Block Foundation

(2) personal information may no longer be private
(3) computers are becoming more difficult to use
(4) computer technology becomes obsolete too quickly

Median Earnings of Men and Women in the United States, 1960–1990

Year	*Women*	*Men*	*Women's Earnings as a Percent of Men's*	*Earnings Gap (in Constant 1990 Dollars)*
1960	$ 3,257	$ 5,368	60.7%	$ 8,569
1970	5,323	8,966	59.4	11,529
1980	11,197	18, 612	60.2	11,776
1990	19,822	27,678	71.6	7,856

Source: Bureau of the Census

4 In the late 1990s, increasing public concern about the role of money in politics led to
(1) all candidates receiving an equal amount of money
(2) a ban on all private campaign contributions
(3) attempts to reform campaign financing
(4) the widespread defeat of incumbent congressional candidates

5 President Bill Clinton supported the North American Free Trade Agreement (NAFTA) primarily as a way to
(1) normalize trade relations with Cuba
(2) stimulate economic growth in the United States
(3) restrict the flow of drugs into the United States
(4) increase the United States trade deficit

6 In the late 1990s, congressional opposition to granting a more favorable trade status to China was based primarily on China's
(1) persecution of Hong Kong residents
(2) high-priced exports
(3) history of unstable governments
(4) disregard for human rights

7 The United States intervened in Haiti and Bosnia during the 1990s to
(1) gain access to new markets
(2) acquire colonies for an economic empire
(3) stop conflicts within those nations
(4) disrupt international drug trafficking

8 The loss of jobs in manufacturing industries has been caused by the introduction of
(1) radio and television
(2) automobiles and airplanes
(3) automation and computers
(4) improved medicine and space travel

9 Since 1980, most new jobs in the United States have been in
(1) education
(2) heavy industry
(3) service industries
(4) civil service

10 One way in which some environmentalists want the United States Government to protect lakes and forests from acid rain is by
(1) requiring factories to use coal rather than other forms of energy
(2) spraying lakes and forests with protective chemicals
(3) replacing nuclear energy with fossil fuels
(4) requiring industries to reduce their smokestack emissions

THEMATIC ESSAYS

1 **THEME:** *Presidential Decision Making in the 1990s.* The president of the United States must make decisions that affect the prosperity and security of the nation.

TASK: Complete *all* of the following tasks:
- Describe *two* such problems faced by President Clinton.
- Discuss the way in which the president attempted to resolve *each* issue.
- Evaluate the relative success or failure of *each* of the two decisions.

In your discussion you may wish to use examples such as the North American Free Trade Agreement (NAFTA), national health care, and crises in such nations as Somalia, Bosnia, Kosovo, and Haiti.

2 **THEME:** *The Computer and Society.* The development of the computer has changed how we live and work.

TASK: Complete *both* of the following tasks:

- Show *two* ways in which the computer has changed U.S. society.
- Describe *one* problem and *one* benefit resulting from the changes you described.

You may use, but are not limited to, access to information, improved communication, and convenience. Problems include privacy, information overload (access to more information than necessary), overconsumerism, and electronic "viruses."

DOCUMENT-BASED QUESTION

*Study each document and answer the question that follows it. Then read the **Task** and write your essay. Include references to most of the documents and additional information you retain about U.S. history and government.*

HISTORICAL CONTEXT: Beginning around the 1950s, the United States and other industrial nations underwent changes that indicated the emergence of a postindustrial world. In the new millennium, the impact of postindustrialism is being felt worldwide. This new world will create demands on U.S. leadership and new problems for which leaders will have to find innovative solutions.

DOCUMENT 1: From the magazine *L'Express*, Paris, France, May 17, 1976:

> The Russians depend on American agriculture in order to feed themselves, and without American technology, Siberia would remain barren. The European leftists who demonstrated against the Vietnam War were dressed in jeans and listened to Bob Dylan every night.

QUESTION: How has the new technology increased U.S. influence throughout Europe and the world?

DOCUMENT 2: Babatunde Jose, Jr., as quoted in *Sunday Tide*, Port Harcourt, Nigeria, July 3, 1976:

> Though [the United States] has not been a major participant in the African scene, she has nonetheless demonstrated her desire to help in the building up of the continent. American technological, scientific, educational, and cultural aid is what Africans want from America. We want the cooperation of [the United States] in the development of our friendships. What we Africans do not want, however, is American imperialism and domination.

QUESTION: How can U.S. technological assistance be both helpful and harmful to many African nations?

DOCUMENT 3: Refer to the cartoon below.

Reprinted with special permission of King Features Syndicate.

QUESTION: What does the cartoon say about the typical U.S. consumer's response to global warming?

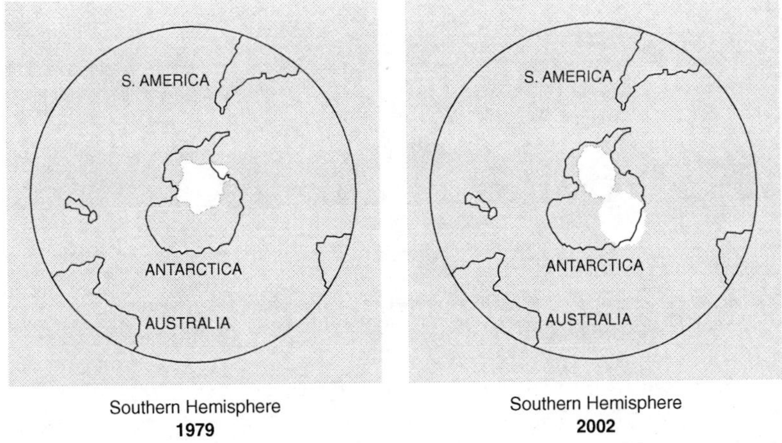

Hole in the Antarctic Ozone Layer, 1979–2002

DOCUMENT 4: Refer to the maps above.

QUESTION: What is happening to the protective ozone layer above Antarctica?

TASK: Using the documents and your knowledge of U.S. history and government, write an essay in which you:

- explain how U.S. influence has expanded as the world has moved through the early stages of postindustrialism.
- describe *three* postindustrial problems facing the United States and the rest of the world. At least *one* problem should be different from those referred to in the documents.
- show how the United States can lead in solving a problem that you described.

CHAPTER 22
A New Century: 2000–Present

DOCUMENTS AND LAWS
USA Patriot Act (2001) • No Child Left Behind Act (2002) • *Kelo* v. *City of New London* (2005)
Hamdan v. *Rumsfeld* (2006) • Medicare Prescription Drug Benefit Program (2006)
Economic Stimulus Act (2008) • Bailout of AIG (2008)
Emergency Stabilization Act (2008) • American Recovery and Reinvestment Act (2009)
Bailout of General Motors and Chrysler (2009) • "Cash for Clunkers" (2009)
Citizens United v. *Federal Elections Commission* (2010) • *Florida* v. *Powell* (2010)
Jobs Bill (2010) • Affordable Care Act (2010) • New START Treaty (2010)

EVENTS
Elections of 2000 and 2004 • September 11, 2001, attacks • Afghanistan invasion (2001)
Second Iraq War (2003) • *Columbia* disaster (2003) • Hurricane Katrina (2005)
Recession of 2007–2009 • Elections of 2008 and 2010 • Haiti earthquake (2010)
BP oil spill (2010)

PEOPLE/GROUPS
Mahmoud Abbas • Iyad Allawi • Nuri al-Maliki • Al Qaeda • Hamid Karzai
Jean-Bertrand Aristide • Ben Bernanke • Osama bin Laden • George W. Bush • Raúl Castro
Hillary Clinton • Robert Gates • Timothy Geithner • Alan Greenspan • Hezbollah • Elena Kagan
Hamid Karzai • Kim Jong Il • Dmitri Medvedev • Barack Obama • Nancy Pelosi • David Petraeus
René Préval • Al Qaeda • John Roberts • Ariel Sharon • Sonia Sotomayor • Tea Party

OBJECTIVES

- To examine domestic issues during the George W. Bush and Barack Obama presidencies.
- To analyze the U.S. role in the global economy.
- To evaluate presidential responses to challenges in Haiti, the Middle East, Afghanistan, Bosnia, Yugoslavia, Iraq, Iran, North Korea, and Russia.

Elections of George W. Bush in 2000 and 2004

In the presidential election of 2000, the Democratic candidate, Vice President Albert Gore, Jr., faced Republican rival Governor George W. Bush of Texas (and son of ex-president George H. Bush). There was no clear winner, due to the close race in Florida, whose 25 electoral votes proved to be decisive. An automatic machine recount of ballots there was triggered, as required by state law.

For weeks, the results of the 2000 presidential election remained in doubt. The election was finally decided by an appeal to the U.S. Supreme

Presidential Election 2000

Political Party	*Presidential Nominee*	*Electoral College Vote*	*Electoral College Vote Percent*	*Popular Vote Number*	*Popular Vote Percent*
Republican	George W. Bush	271	50.4	50,456,062	47.9
Democratic	Albert Gore, Jr.	266	49.4	50,996,582	48.4
Green	Ralph Nader	0	0.0	2,858,843	2.7

Court. The Court, in a controversial decision, *Bush* v. *Gore*, ruled 5–4 that the Florida recount had to stop in order to meet the state schedule to select Electoral College members, and that the recounting was violating the equal protection clause of the Fourteenth Amendment. Gore then conceded the race. This contest, like the election of 1876, demonstrated that a candidate may win the election despite losing the popular vote. Some critics of the Electoral College system have called for a constitutional amendment mandating a nationwide popular vote for president and vice president.

In November 2004, in running for reelection, President Bush defeated Senator John Kerry of Massachusetts after a bitter and costly campaign. President Bush called his Democratic opponent a "flip-flopper" on the issues and accused him of lacking the leadership to fight the war on terror. Senator Kerry said the president had mismanaged the war in Iraq and the battle against terrorism, and that the Bush tax cuts for the wealthy should be repealed. Other issues in the campaign included health care, Social Security, jobs, the economy, and "moral" values and social issues such as funding stem-cell research and banning same-sex marriages. The Republican Party in 2004 also expanded its majorities in Congress to 55 seats in the Senate and 232 seats in the House.

George W. Bush Presidency

Shock quickly spread on the morning of September 11, 2001, as pictures of terrorist attacks on America were viewed across the nation. Islamic extremists had hijacked four large passenger airplanes. Two of the planes were flown into the World Trade Center in New York City, killing nearly 3,000 people, including several hundred heroic police officers and firefighters trying to rescue those trapped in the collapsing towers. A third plane was flown into the Pentagon, the nation's military headquarters, killing nearly 200 people, while a fourth plane, bound for Washington, D.C., crashed into a field in Pennsylvania after its passengers had fought with the terrorists on board.

The 19 hijackers were followers of Osama bin Laden, a wealthy Saudi, who directed a terrorist network called *Al Qaeda* ("the Base"). Al Qaeda members were thought to have previously bombed U.S. embassies in East Africa in 1998 and attacked the U.S.S. *Cole* in Yemen in 2000.

War on Terrorism

Speaking after September 11, President George W. Bush said that the nation would search out Al Qaeda, Osama bin Laden, and terrorists across the globe and hold any nation protecting them accountable. He asked Congress to enact antiterrorist legislation and to provide funds to aid the reconstruction of New York City.

Congress passed the *USA Patriot Act* in October 2001, giving the government greater power and suspending the civil liberties of accused terrorists. The act was renewed in 2006, although some aspects of the act were questioned by civil libertarians. To coordinate government efforts against terrorism, an Office of Homeland Security was established (made the Department of Homeland Security in 2003).

9/11 Commission Report President George W. Bush appointed a bipartisan commission to investigate the events that led to the September 11 attacks. The commission concluded in 2004 that government agencies had missed or ignored terrorist activities in the United States. The report called for greater coordination of intelligence agencies, including the FBI, CIA, and the Department of Homeland Security.

Foreign Policy

The events and issues discussed in this section include the foreign policies of both President George W. Bush and President Barack Obama, who was elected in 2008. (For the election of Barack Obama, see page 412.)

Afghanistan

In October 2001, the U.S. government demanded that the fundamentalist Taliban government of Afghanistan end its protection of Al Qaeda members and their leader, Osama bin Laden. When the Taliban rejected the U.S. demand, U.S. air strikes were launched. The United States formed an alliance with Afghans fighting against the Taliban, and U.S. troops were deployed in the country. By December, the Taliban's control had ended, but bin Laden remained at large. Hamid Karzai, a Pashtun (the dominant ethnic group in the country), was named head of Afghanistan's interim government, and in 2002 he formally became president.

The United States maintained troops in Afghanistan to combat the remaining Taliban and Al-Qaeda fighters. About 30 other nations also contributed NATO-led peacekeeping forces. In 2004, a new constitution was written, and Afghanistan's first democratic presidential elections were held. Ten million Afghans, more than a third of the country, registered to vote, including more than 40 percent of the eligible women. Karzai was declared the winner and was inaugurated, but Afghanistan remained an unsettled nation with regional warlords, fundamentalists, and the Taliban opposed to democracy.

The Taliban continued to attack U.S. troops, and Taliban militants began infiltrating southern Afghanistan from Pakistan, terrorizing local villagers, and attacking Afghan and U.S. troops. In 2006, NATO troops took over military operations in southern Afghanistan from the U.S.-led coalition. Attacks by the Taliban intensified, with militants crossing into eastern Afghanistan from Pakistan's tribal areas.

In 2008, Allied deaths in Afghanistan reached the highest number since the war had begun in 2003. As a result, Obama in 2009 approved a request by the military to send an additional 30,000 troops to Afghanistan.

A U.S. soldier talks with Afghan students in a village near the Pakistan border.

In 2009, provincial and presidential elections were again held. More than 30 candidates challenged the incumbent, Hamid Karzai. Although a UN-backed commission overseeing the election found widespread evidence of fraud, Karzai was eventually declared the winner and began his second five-year term as president. By 2010, more than 1,200 U.S. military personnel had died in combat. In addition, the war had cost an estimated $300 billion.

War Against Iraq

After September 11, U.S. government officials became concerned that Iraq's possible possession of **weapons of mass destruction** (nuclear, biological, and chemical ones) could lead to their use in support of global terrorism. In his 2002 State of the Union address, President George W. Bush referred to an "axis of evil": Iraq, Iran, and North Korea, which he claimed had been developing nuclear weapons. The U.S. plan for a preemptive attack on Iraq was opposed by many, including France, Germany, and Russia. Without a UN resolution of support, a U.S.-led coalition launched Operation Iraqi Freedom in March 2003. Within three months, conventional military action ended with the defeat of the Iraqi military forces. Later in the year, Iraqi dictator Saddam Hussein was captured. In 2006, he was convicted of crimes against humanity by an Iraqi court and hanged in Baghdad.

Rebuilding The efforts of the United States and its coalition partners to rebuild Iraq and develop a democratic system immediately came under constant attack by guerrilla and terrorist forces representing the old regime and religious fundamentalists.

U.S. policies in Iraq were subject to much controversy. After the war, the United States conducted extensive searches for weapons of mass destruction but found no evidence of them. Then photographs of U.S. soldiers mistreating Iraqis at the Abu Ghraib prison led to an investigation that showed official neglect.

Some success was achieved in developing a democratic government based on Islamic law in Iraq. In 2005, the work of an interim government resulted in a referendum in which Iraqis approved a constitution and an election to select their first permanent parliament since the overthrow of Saddam Hussein. In 2006, Nuri al-Maliki was approved as prime minister, representing a Shiite coalition. The challenge remained to avoid civil war and get the major religious and ethnic groups—Shiites, Sunnis, and Kurds—to work together.

With the unrelenting postwar violence in Iraq, opposition grew in the United States to continued involvement. While recognizing the good in ending the Iraqi dictatorship and efforts to establish a democratic society, opponents protested the escalating human, financial, and political costs to the United States.

By the end of 2006, U.S. military deaths topped 3,000. To stem ongoing sectarian violence and increasingly deadly attacks by insurgents and militias, President Bush in 2007 named Lt. Gen. David Petraeus as the top commander in Iraq and announced that the United States would begin a "surge" of some 30,000 troops to Iraq. Although U.S. troop deaths for all of 2007 totaled the highest for any year since the war began, the surge proved to be a success, and military and civilian casualties dropped steadily from mid-2007 through 2008. At the end of 2008, Iraq's parliament approved a status of forces agreement with the United States that governed the U.S. presence in Iraq through 2011. The pact called for the removal of U.S. troops from Iraqi cities by the summer of 2009, and the withdrawal of all U.S. combat troops by December 31, 2011.

As 2009 began, Iraq held local elections to create provincial councils. The elections were notable for their lack of violence. In June 2009, as a signal of the United States' diminishing role in Iraq and in compliance with the status of forces agreement between the United States and Iraq, U.S. troops completed their withdrawal from Iraqi cities and transferred the responsibility of securing the cities to Iraqi troops. In addition, President Obama announced his intention in 2010 that he would withdraw most U.S. troops out of Iraq that summer. Approximately 50,000 troops are to remain there for smaller missions and to train Iraqi soldiers.

U.S. combat troops leaving Iraq in 2010

In 2010, new parliamentary elections were held in Iraq. A secular coalition led by former prime minister Iyad Allawi won the most seats, narrowly edging out Prime Minister Nuri al-Maliki. By 2010, approximately 4,400 U.S. service members had died in combat and roadside bombings. In addition, the war had cost an estimated $700 billion.

Iran

There has been hostility between the United States and Iran since the establishment of an Islamic state there and the U.S. hostage crisis of 1979–1980. The Iranians oppose any U.S. involvement in the Middle East, and U.S. leaders are concerned about Iranian efforts to develop nuclear weapons. In 2003, an investigation by the *International Atomic Energy Agency* (*IAEA*) revealed a secret Iranian nuclear program, which the Iranians claimed was for peaceful purposes.

The war in Iraq contributed to a new period of tensions between the United States and Iran. The Bush administration accused the Iranian regime of seeking to build nuclear weapons, aiding Shiite militias in Iraq, and supplying rockets to Hezbollah fighters (a political and paramilitary organization based in Lebanon) for use against Israel.

The diplomatic conflict between the United States and Iran increased further in 2009 by disclosures that Iran had been secretly enriching uranium at an underground uranium-enrichment plant, and by Iranian tests of medium-range missiles capable of reaching Israel and U.S. and European military bases in the Persian Gulf region. Iranian officials acknowledge the existence of the facility but maintain it is for peaceful purposes.

North Korea

In 2002, the Communist government led by dictator Kim Jong Il admitted that it was pursuing a secret nuclear weapons program, in violation of past agreements. Later that year, North Korea expelled UN weapons inspectors from the country, and in 2003 it announced that it was officially withdrawing from the *Nuclear Non-Proliferation Treaty* (*NPT*). This treaty, designed to limit the spread of nuclear weapons, came into force in 1970. It is a widely accepted arms control agreement with 189 nations having signed on to it as of 2010. Under NPT, all nuclear materials used for peaceful purposes must be declared to the IAEA, whose inspectors have access to the facilities for monitoring and inspections. There are five declared nuclear states —the United States, Britain, France, Russia, and China—and three states with nuclear weapons that have refused to sign the NPT—India, Pakistan and Israel. Iran remains a signatory but has repeatedly been found to be in violation of its obligations.

Between 2003 and 2009, meetings of officials from six nations—the United States, North Korea, China, Russia, South Korea, and Japan—have been unsuccessful in getting North Korea to stop its nuclear weapons program. During this time, North Korea has followed a fluctuating course, alternately stopping and resuming its nuclear program in order to win further concessions from the United States.

In 2009, North Korea tested a long-range missile. Although the launch was a failure, the international community condemned the test. North Korea responded by dropping out of talks to end its nuclear program. Two more weapons tests followed: an underground nuclear test and a short-range missile test. As a result, the UN Security Council approved new sanctions against North Korea, banning all weapons exports from North Korea and the import of all but small arms. The resolution, which was unanimous, called upon all members of the international community to stop and search North Korea's ships for weapons.

Middle East Conflict The search for a peaceful solution to the conflict between Israel and the Palestinians continued. In 2003, President George W. Bush proposed a "road map for peace" that called for the removal of Israeli settlements from the occupied territories and for ending the Palestinian Authority's violence against Israel. However, the road map failed to achieve its goal. Continued terrorist attacks resulted in Israel building a controversial security barrier that divided Israeli and Palestinian areas in order to keep out suicide bombers.

In April 2004, Israeli Prime Minister Ariel Sharon announced a unilateral Israeli withdrawal from the Gaza Strip. The death of Palestinian leader Yasir Arafat led to the first free elections for Palestinians. Their new president, Mahmoud Abbas, called for peace with Israel. In February 2005, Abbas and Sharon declared a cease-fire to halt acts of violence. Israel completed its withdrawal from Gaza in 2005.

In January 2006, democratic Palestinian elections in Gaza resulted in an unexpected landslide victory for Hamas over the ruling Fatah Party. Hamas, classified as a terrorist organization by the United States, called for Israel's destruction and refused to renounce violence. In June 2006, after Hamas militants killed two Israeli soldiers and kidnapped another, Israel launched air strikes and sent ground troops into Gaza. Fighting continued over the summer, with Hamas firing rockets into Israel, and Israeli troops reoccupying Gaza.

In July 2006, Israel became involved in war on a second front. Hezbollah guerrillas from Lebanon entered Israel and captured two Israeli soldiers. In response, Israel launched a major military attack. Hezbollah, with weapons mostly supplied by Iran and funneled through Syria, retaliated with hundreds of rockets and missile strikes, proving to be a much more powerful enemy than Israel had anticipated. A cease-fire was finally arranged by the UN in August, and a UN peacekeeping force was deployed as a buffer along the countries' borders. An exchange of gunfire between Israeli and Lebanese soldiers broke out in 2010, the first conflict between these two armed forces.

A dispute between Hamas and Fatah over recognizing Israel and other issues led to tensions that erupted into actual fighting in 2006. Continuing clashes led to Hamas's seizure of control in Gaza, which then led Abbas to install a new government in the West Bank without Hamas.

In 2008, Hamas again launched rockets from Gaza into Israel, which retaliated with air strikes. Israel targeted Hamas fighters, weapons stockpiles, rocket-firing positions, and smuggling tunnels. After more than a week of intense air strikes, Israeli troops crossed the border into Gaza, launching a ground war against Hamas. After several weeks of fighting, more than 1,300 Gazans and about a dozen Israelis had been killed. Since the ground war ended, however, relatively few rockets have been fired into Israel.

Caribbean

A number of old problems with some of its Caribbean neighbors still commanded U.S. attention.

Haiti The government of President Jean-Bertrand Aristide lost public and military support in 2004 because of continued high unemployment and poverty rates. After widespread rioting, U.S. troops took Aristide into exile, and a 15-nation UN peacekeeping force endeavored to maintain peace under an interim president and prime minister. After numerous delays, Haiti held elections in 2006, in which former prime minister René Préval was elected president.

In 2010, a devastating earthquake struck Haiti near Port-au-Prince, the country's capital. The earthquake leveled many sections of the city, destroying government buildings along with countless homes and businesses. International aid poured in, and the scope of the damage highlighted the need to improve Haiti's infrastructure and lift it out of poverty—the country is the poorest in the Western Hemisphere.

Cuba Since the Cuban Revolution of 1959, the United States has maintained a trade embargo on Cuba that makes it illegal for U.S. corporations and individuals to do business with Cuba. The United States has stated it will continue the embargo so long as the Cuban regime continues to refuse to move toward democratization and greater respect for human rights.

Fidel Castro, Cuba's Communist leader, resisted changes even though his nation's economy weakened after the demise of the Soviet Union. Since the 1990s, the United States has discouraged Cubans from sailing to the United States. In 2004, the George W. Bush administration limited the amount of money Cuban Americans can send to their families in Cuba.

In 2008, Fidel Castro ended 49 years of power after he fell ill and announced his retirement. He was succeeded by his brother, Raúl Castro. In 2009, President Barack Obama stated that the United States sought a new beginning with Cuba and lifted all restrictions on the ability of Cuban Americans to visit family members in Cuba and to send them money.

China

Relations between the People's Republic of China and the United States have generally been stable, especially following the September 11 attacks when China offered strong support for the war on terrorism and in preventing nuclear proliferation. For example, concerned over North Korea's nuclear capabilities, China sponsored the six-nation talks to resolve the nuclear dispute with North Korea and has opposed North Korea's decision to withdraw from the Nuclear Non-Proliferation Treaty. However, there are concerns with regard to human rights in China. The United States believes that China has a long way to go in making the kind of changes that will protect the rights and liberties of all its citizens.

During the past three decades, China had the fastest-growing economy in the world. China's economy is now the second largest in the world, after the United States. In addition, China is the world's largest trading nation, the largest exporter of goods, and the second largest importer of goods.

China and the United States have become major trade partners. In 2008, the U.S. trade deficit with China set a record, becoming the largest in the world between any two countries. The deficit meant that the United States imported billions of dollars more in goods and services from China than it exported there. In addition, China had become the top creditor to the United States, overtaking Japan as the biggest holder of U.S. treasury bonds. In 2010, hoping to increase American exports to China and create more jobs, the Obama administration emphasized the need for China to revalue its currency in order to reduce its exports, encourage imports, and focus on its domestic growth.

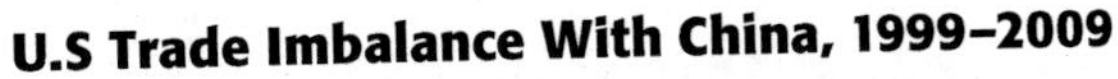

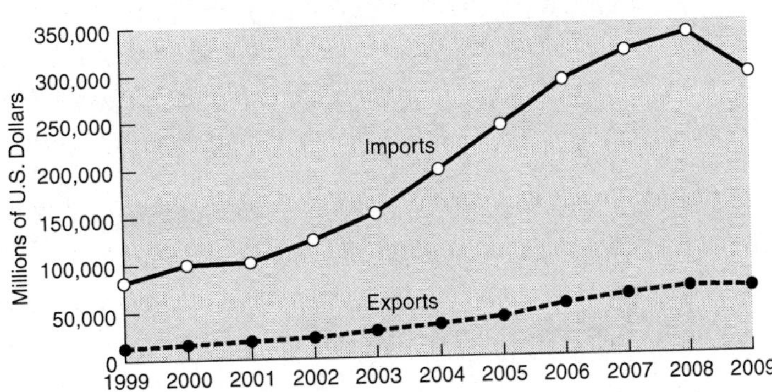

Russia

As you recall, in 2000 Vladimir Putin won the presidential election in Russia. During the presidencies of Vladimir Putin and George W. Bush, the United States and Russia began to have serious disagreements.

In 2002, Bush withdrew the United States from the Anti-Ballistic Missile Treaty in order to move forward with plans for a missile defense system. Putin called the decision a mistake. In addition, Russia strongly opposed the 2003 U.S. invasion of Iraq as well as the expansion of NATO into Eastern Europe. For its part, the United States expressed concern over Putin's reversal of democratic reforms and suppression of free speech in Russia.

In 2008, Dmitri Medvedev was elected president of Russia, and Putin became prime minister. Later that year, fighting broke out between Georgia (one of the former republics of the Soviet Union that had gained independence in 1991) and two breakaway regions of Georgia. Russia sent hundreds of troops to support the breakaway regions, launched air strikes, and occupied two Georgian cities. After a week of military action, a cease-fire agreement between Russia and Georgia was signed. Medvedev broke diplomatic ties with Georgia, officially recognized the two breakaway regions as independent, and pledged military assistance from Russia. The moves increased tensions between Russia and the United States.

U.S.-Russian relations became further strained when President George W. Bush signed agreements to build an anti-missile defense system in Poland and the Czech Republic. Bush planned the system to counter potential incoming ballistic missiles launched from states such as Iran. However, Russia strongly opposed the anti-missile system, claiming it targeted its nuclear arsenal and was a threat to its own defenses. Despite these disagreements, Russian President Medvedev and U.S. President Obama issued a joint statement in April 2009 that promised a fresh start in U.S.-Russian relations. In September 2009, President Obama canceled the plan to build a missile defense shield in Europe, declaring that any potential threat to Europe from Iran can be countered with U.S. and sea-based missile defense systems.

In 2010, President Obama announced a new nuclear strategy that set limits under which the United States would use nuclear weapons. Known as the *Nuclear Posture Review*, the United States for the first time made a specific commitment not to use nuclear weapons against non-nuclear states that are in compliance with the Nuclear Non-Proliferation Treaty, even if these states attacked the United States with biological or chemical weapons, or launched a cyberattack. President Obama's strategy was to create incentives for countries to give up any nuclear ambitions.

Also in 2010, the United States and Russia achieved a major breakthrough in arms control negotiations by reaching an agreement to reduce their stockpile of nuclear weapons. Known as the *New START Treaty*, the nuclear arms pact replaced the 1991 Strategic Arms Reduction Treaty, which expired in 2009. Both countries agreed to reduce the number of **strategic warheads** (long-range nuclear weapons) and land-, air- and sea-based launchers (delivery vehicles such as missiles, bombers, and submarines) held by each side. The treaty, ratified by the U.S. Senate in December 2010, also reestablished inspection procedures that had expired in 2009.

IN REVIEW

1. Discuss how the September 11 attacks affected the George W. Bush presidency in the area of homeland security.
2. The United States became involved in a war in Afghanistan in 2001 and one in Iraq in 2003. (a) Explain a major reason for U.S. involvement in *each* conflict. (b) Explain the extent to which the United States has achieved its goals in *each* of the conflicts.
3. Why has the United States become increasingly concerned with both Iran and North Korea?

Domestic Issues

We will look at domestic issues in separate sections, one for each president.

Taxes, Deficits, and the Economy

Cutting taxes has been a major goal of the Republican Party since the Reagan administration. In 2001, George W. Bush requested and a Republican Congress passed a $1.35 trillion tax cut spread over the next ten years. It was

Jeff Danziger, New York Times Syndicate

hoped that this would stimulate an economy that had slowed down from the collapse of technology stocks and the closing or **downsizing** of many companies. In 2002 and 2003, further tax cuts were made in the face of a weak economy and increased unemployment. Capital gains taxes were cut and the child-care tax credit was increased.

Opposition to the tax cuts was based on a belief that they favored the wealthy, increased the federal budget deficit, and added to the national debt. One-third of all tax cuts went to those in the top 1 percent of taxpayers. Many Democrats would have preferred to see more direct aid to the poor and unemployed.

To stimulate the economy, the Federal Reserve Bank lowered the **discount rate** (interest charged to banks) to 1 percent by 2003. Mortgage rates fell to record lows, and home buying and consumer spending increased. By 2004, employment had risen, and the Federal Reserve slowly began to raise the discount rate to avoid inflation. By the end of 2005, the rate had risen to 4 percent.

The Economy Falters The second Bush administration (2005–2009) saw the emergence of major problems. Housing prices increased at a rapid rate, which led to speculation. People bought homes expecting prices to continue upward, and many bought homes they could not afford. Banks offered **variable-rate mortgages** (ones that permitted buyers to pay a low interest for a number of years, only to find that interest rates rose sharper later). Often, banks did not take the time to check the earnings and income records of borrowers, creating a situation where many buyers could not make their mortgage payments. Banks took many of these mortgages, bundled them together into bonds and other debt obligations, and resold them to other banks, investors, and financial institutions. These bundled financial instruments often got good ratings, even though it was apparent that many individual mortgages on which they were based would never be paid back. This speculation came to be known as the **housing bubble** because, just as a bubble will get bigger and bigger but then break, the same would happen with housing prices.

In 2007, defaults on mortgages began to increase significantly. Borrowers were unable to pay back their loans. Banks foreclosed on many more homeowners than in the past. Newly built homes stood empty, and a large number of resales came on the market. As housing prices slipped even farther, more homeowners defaulted. Banks that had focused on home mortgages were threatened with bankruptcy as loans went unpaid. With new bank loans unavailable, consumers who had financed purchases with second mortgages and home equity loans cut back on their purchases, leading to more unemployment. The stock market fell as companies suffered reduced sales and profits. Even established companies, such as the insurance giant

American International Group (AIG), almost went out of business. They had sold insurance called ***credit default swaps*** on many of these bundled mortgage-backed securities and were unable to pay when the mortgage default rate increased substantially. With higher unemployment and a decline in business investment, consumer spending, home building, and housing prices, the nation fell into a recession. By 2008, unemployment rates had increased to 8 percent and threatened to climb higher.

Another issue linked to higher unemployment was **outsourcing**. Corporations shifted production or services from the United States to countries where labor costs were lower. Thus, China, India, Indonesia, and other countries benefited from the outsourcing of jobs that had previously been done in the United States, including working in call centers and motor vehicle assembly plants.

Efforts to Halt the Recession

In 2008, the Bush administration recognized the need for action to combat the economic crisis and took several steps in an attempt to halt the recession.

Congress passed the *Economic Stimulus Act* to provide $152 billion in tax incentives for businesses, tax rebates for low-and middle-wage earners, and higher limits imposed on mortgages guaranteed by the government.

To reduce foreclosures and bank failures, the Federal Housing Authority took over two government chartered (but privately owned) agencies that purchased, guaranteed, and resold home mortgages. These agencies, the *Federal National Mortgage Association* (*Fannie Mae*) and the *Federal Home Loan Mortgage Corporation* (*Freddie Mac*), were on the brink of becoming insolvent. This expanded guarantee cost the government approximately $800 billion.

The American International Group was provided with $85 billion to keep it from going bankrupt and defaulting on the insurance it had sold on the mortgage-backed bonds. AIG's bankruptcy would have resulted in the loss of thousands of jobs.

While it was "bailing out" AIG, the government encouraged banks thought to be healthier to take over weaker financial institutions that were about to go bankrupt. For example, Bank of America took over the investment and brokerage house Merrill Lynch, and JPMorgan Chase took over Washington Mutual and Bear Stearns. However, the investment bank and brokerage house Lehman Brothers was allowed to go bankrupt.

In the hope of keeping larger, "too-big-to-fail" banks from going bankrupt, Congress passed the *Emergency Stabilization Act*, which provided $700 billion to help offset the reduced value and price of many of the assets held by these banks. This program was called the *Troubled Asset Relief Program* (*TARP*), and it provided a financial cushion for banks until they could sell some of their troubled assets or see them increase in value.

Congress was not alone in attempting to revive the economy. Fearing

During the credit crisis of 2007–2010, the U.S. government encouraged healthy banks to take over financial institutions that were about to go bankrupt. Bank of America, for example, took over Merrill Lynch.

a depression, the Federal Reserve, which supervises the banking system, provided money to banks by dropping the interest rate it charges to zero, purchasing mortgages and government bonds from banks, and setting up a new, temporary loan facility from which banks and other financial institutions could borrow additional funds. The chair of the Federal Reserve, Ben Bernanke, believed that this action would help to avoid a 1930s-type depression.

Despite these efforts, the Bush administration was unable to halt the slide into a recession, though the actions taken likely avoided a depression. However, these additional government outlays led to a growing budget deficit and an increasing national debt.

Education

President George W. Bush stressed the importance of education and in 2002 signed the No Child Left Behind Act. The law mandated stricter education standards and new testing requirements. It also permitted students to transfer from a school with low test scores to one with a higher success rate. The Supreme Court issued a key ruling affecting education when it approved spending taxpayer money for vouchers to pay tuition at private or religious schools. President Bush supported this decision because it gave students more choices, but opponents believed it violated the principle of separation of church and state and would also weaken public schools by diverting funds from them.

Supreme Court Decisions

During his eight years in office, President George W. Bush appointed two Supreme Court Justices: Chief Justice John Roberts and Associate Justice Samuel Alito. Their appointments led to a nine-member court with four justices generally considered "liberal," four justices generally considered "conservative," and one justice, Anthony Kennedy, generally viewed as a swing vote but was often conservative. Important decisions of the Court in the first years of the 21st century included the following:

- *Gutter* v. *Bollinger* (2003) reaffirmed the 1978 *Bakke* decision that racial quotas were illegal but that race could be a factor in college admissions at the University of Michigan.
- *Virginia* v. *Black, et al.* (2003) ruled that acts such as cross burning could be viewed as free speech as long as there was no intent to threaten people's lives.
- *U.S.* v. *Booker* and *U.S.* v. *Fanfan* (2005) ruled that mandatory sentencing guidelines, set by Congress, were to be viewed only as guidelines. Federal judges were free to use or ignore them.
- *Kelo* v. *City of New London* (2005) ruled that a local government had the right to use **eminent domain** to take over private property that presented no problems or blight and to sell the property to private developers if the sale benefited the community.
- *U.S.* v. *Gonzalez Lopez* (2006) ruled that a defendant has a Sixth Amendment right to a lawyer of his choice and cannot be forced to accept another lawyer.
- *Hudson* v. *Michigan* (2006) ruled that evidence seized in a raid does not have to be suppressed if the officers have a warrant but do not provide sufficient time for the person to respond to their knock on the door before they enter the premises.
- *Hamdan* v. *Rumsfeld* (2006) ruled that detainees held at Guantánamo could not be tried at military tribunals without congressional authorization. They also ruled that rights provided under the Geneva Convention had to be applied.
- *Parents* v. *Seattle* (2007) ruled that it is unconstitutional to assign students to schools strictly on the basis of race. It also ruled that districts that had not intentionally discriminated were not required to desegregate their schools.

Medicare and Prescription Drugs

The first major addition to Medicare benefits since its passage in 1965 was made when President George W. Bush and Congress agreed on a program to provide prescription drugs at lower-than-retail prices for Medicare recipients. The program went fully into effect in 2006. As part of this new addition, Medicare pays most of the initial cost of drugs. After this initial period, recipients pay the full cost for drugs in what has been termed the "donut hole" until they have spent sufficient funds for Medicare to again step in and pay most of the cost. While supporters of the act argued that many senior

This cartoon appeared during the debate on the prescription drug law

Dana Summers/*The Orlando Sentinel,* 1999, by permission Tribune Media Services

citizens need the help to combat high drug prices, opponents argued that the federal expenditures add to the budget deficit.

As a result of increased Medicare benefits, improved medical care, and higher life expectancy, government spending is expected to increase significantly as the baby boomers reach the age of 65 and qualify for Medicare. The high birthrate of this generation has led to what has been called the "graying of America." It is anticipated that those age 65 or older will increase from 40 million in 2010 to 55 million in 2020, and then to 86.7 million in 2050. This would translate into a 147 percent increase in the 65-and-over population between 2000 and 2050. By comparison, the population as a whole would increase by only 49 percent over the same period.

Environmental Issues

President George W. Bush had definite positions on a number of environmental issues. The president called for:

- Voluntary industrial compliance with the Kyoto Protocol (1997) on greenhouse gases
- "Clean skies" legislation to reduce factory pollution, but excluding carbon dioxide emissions
- Increased logging in the national forests to reduce fire risks
- Limited oil drilling in the Arctic National Wildlife Refuge in Alaska to reduce reliance on foreign oil.

Several environmental groups opposed each of the above positions. They wanted the U.S. Senate to ratify the Kyoto Protocol. They favored clean air acts that limited carbon dioxide emissions. They wanted to restrict logging in national forests to protect wildlife and limit erosion. And they favored no drilling for oil in the Arctic National Wildlife Refuge.

Hurricane Katrina On August 29, 2005, 145-mph winds and torrential rains swept onto the U.S. mainland coast near Buras, Louisiana. Over the next several days, the Gulf Coast of the United States was hit by perhaps the greatest natural disaster in the nation's history. The areas most affected by this Category 5 hurricane (the highest and most severe category) were the coastal areas of Louisiana and Mississippi, including the major city of New Orleans.

The city itself created a unique problem because much of it is below sea level. The U.S. Army Corp of Engineers had built levees to control floodwaters, but they were not sufficient for this storm. All residents of New Orleans were ordered to evacuate before the storm hit, but the city's large low-income population lacked the means to leave. When the levees broke, major government efforts were needed for quick evacuation and rescue of people trapped in the flooded city. But federal, state, and local relief efforts were slow to arrive and were never enough.

More than a million people were displaced from their homes and communities by Hurricane Katrina. Almost 2,000 people lost their lives. The cost of rebuilding was estimated at $200 billion. New Orleans briefly resembled a developing nation. Relief workers found a city in which many people lacked shelter, food, water, electricity, and medical services. For weeks afterward, residents sought missing family members. Thousands of now homeless persons were relocated within Louisiana and to other states across the country. The absence of an effective relief effort by the Bush administration left many Americans wondering whether the administration could deal quickly and effectively with another major disaster or terrorist attack.

Space Exploration

Following the *Columbia* space shuttle disaster in 2003, which killed all seven astronauts on board, serious concerns were raised about the cost and safety of manned flights. In 2004, President George W. Bush proposed a manned flight to the moon by the year 2020 in preparation for a manned trip to Mars later. NASA began preparing for these.

Immigration Reform

During President Bush's second term, it appeared that immigration laws might be reformed. Concern about the number of illegal immigrants in the United States and the need for some means of legalizing temporary workers led many Americans to believe that the time was ripe for change. However, increasing concern over the number of illegal immigrants and opposition to any plan to legalize those who had come illegally ended the possibility of a new approach. In 2006, many immigrants across the nation protested against a planned fence to be built on the Mexican border and against charging illegal immigrants as felons.

IN REVIEW

1. Explain the significance of *three* of the following: (a) *Bush* v. *Gore*, (b) the 9/11 Commission, (c) budget deficits, (d) No Child Left Behind Act, (e) Hurricane Katrina, (f) the "housing bubble."

2. In what way was President George W. Bush's economic plan for the nation in his first term of office similar to that of President Ronald Reagan in his first term of office?
3. People argue about the role of government in the economy. Describe *three* actions taken by the Bush administration to fight the recession and discuss whether or not the government was right to take these actions.

Barack Obama Administration

In 2006 Democrats won back the House of Representatives and the Senate. There was a growing unease about the wars in Iraq and Afghanistan as well as scandals involving Republican leaders. As a result, Nancy Pelosi, a leading Democrat from California, became the first woman to serve as Speaker of the House of Representatives. The midterm victory ended 12 years of Republican control of the House.

Election of Barack Obama (2008) As the presidential election of 2008 drew near, Republicans faced the problem of a weakening economy. The Republican nominee for the presidency was John McCain, a long-serving senator from Arizona and a Vietnam War hero. The Democrats nominated Barack Obama, a first-term senator from Illinois. Obama had won the nomination over Hillary Clinton after a long and grueling season of primary contests throughout the nation. In the election, Senator Obama won 52 percent of the popular vote and 365 electoral votes compared to 46 percent and 173 electoral votes for Senator McCain. For the first time, an African American was elected president of the United States. In addition, Democrats increased their Senate and House seats, giving them a 60–40 advantage in the Senate and a huge majority in the House of Representatives.

One outcome of the election was the growing popularity of John McCain's running mate, Governor Sarah Palin of Alaska. After the election, she resigned as governor and increased her speaking engagements and television appearances. Her greatest popularity is with Americans who identify themselves as conservatives.

The Economic Crisis Continued

The Obama administration was confronted by a continuing decline in jobs, housing sales, consumer spending, and business investment that had begun under the Bush administration in 2007–2008.

Soon after taking office, President Obama and his economic team took actions to improve the economy. The first step was a second stimulus act, the *American Recovery and Reinvestment Act (2009)*, which provided $787 billion

President Barack Obama with his secretary of state, Hillary Rodham Clinton

for construction, incentives to hire workers, additional funding for states to avoid layoffs, and expanded unemployment benefits.

In September 2009, with the auto industry on the brink of collapse, $82 billion was provided to General Motors and Chrysler to modernize their production and distribution facilities, reduce debt levels, and decrease their number of models. In return, the government received shares of stock in the two companies. Ford Motors refused the offer to participate.

Aid to the auto industry was followed by aid to buyers of automobiles. The government initiated a $3 billion "*Cash for Clunkers*" program to encourage consumers to turn in their old cars for new, more efficient cars. It was also hoped that this program would reduce carbon dioxide levels in the atmosphere.

With the economy still in recession, a $15 billion *Jobs Bill* was passed in March 2010 to encourage private industry to hire workers who had been laid off for more than 60 days. In addition, $20 billion from unused stimulus funds was shifted to road building in the hope of increasing employment. Unemployment, however, remained at high levels. The spending on programs to stop the economic decline together with reduced tax collections due to the recession drove up the federal debt to more than $13 trillion from the $5.5 trillion during the Clinton administration.

Major Appointments

After securing the nomination for president, Barack Obama selected Senator Joseph Biden from Delaware as his running mate. Biden had competed against Obama in the primaries for the nomination.

Upon taking office, President Obama had to make decisions with regard to important positions in his Cabinet. For secretary of defense, the President appointed Robert Gates, who had served in that position in the previous administration. This allowed for continuity during a time of war. Hillary Clinton accepted the position of secretary of state. Timothy Geithner, head of the Federal Reserve Bank of New York, accepted the position as secretary of the treasury.

When it came time to select a new chair of the Board of Governors of the Federal Reserve System, the President reappointed Ben Bernanke, demonstrating confidence in his efforts to increase liquidity in the banking system and provide support for the economy.

In 2009, President Obama appointed Sonia Sotomayor to fill a vacancy in the Supreme Court. Raised in the Bronx, Justice Sotomayor became the first Latino and only the third woman appointed to the Court. A fourth was added in 2010 after another vacancy developed on the Supreme Court. President Obama nominated and the Senate confirmed Elena Kagan, also from New York City. Supreme Court nominees often cause controversy as their past decisions or positions on controversial issues are thoroughly scrutinized. This was no different with Obama's appointees to the Court.

In addition to the appointment of women to important government positions, women continued to make new gains in sports. For example,

Members of the U.S. Supreme Court: (front row, from left) Justices Clarence Thomas and Antonin Scalia, Chief Justice John G. Roberts, Justices Anthony Kennedy, Ruth Bader Ginsburg, (second row) Sonia Sotomayor, Stephen G. Berger, Samuel Anthony Alito, Jr., and Elena Kagan.

the number of women participating in high school sports increased from 294,000 in 1972 to 2.8 million in 2004. This increase was due in large part to the passage by Congress of Title IX, in 1972 (discussed on page 302).

Supreme Court Decisions

The Supreme Court decided in *Citizens United* v. *The Federal Elections Commission* (2010) that corporations and labor unions are entitled to the same free speech protections as individuals. Thus, there are no limits on the amount of money they may spend on advertisements to support candidates for political office.

In *Florida* v. *Powell* (2010), the Supreme Court ruled that there is no requirement that an arrested individual be read each of the Miranda rights as long as the person is advised that he or she is entitled to a lawyer before answering any questions.

Affordable Care Act

A major priority for the newly elected president was passage of a health care bill, which Congress had debated for many months. In major speeches, President Obama noted the lack of insurance for more than 43 million Americans and the rising cost of health care coverage. Republicans strongly opposed the bill, claiming that it was too expensive and would lead to a government takeover of the health care industry. Democrats countered that there were too many uninsured people and that health care was a right. Finally, in March 2010, President Obama signed the *Affordable Care Act* into law. Key elements included:

- coverage for 30 million uninsured people beginning in 2014
- a requirement that all Americans have health insurance beginning in 2014
- Medicaid coverage for families with incomes below $29,000
- no denial of insurance for people with pre-existing conditions
- no cancellation of policies for those who are ill
- tax credits to help families with incomes below $88,000 pay for insurance
- capping out-of-pocket expenditures for a family at $11,900
- allowing children under the age of 26 to remain on a parent's policy.

To help pay for this expanded coverage, individuals who earn above $200,000 or families that earn over $250,000 will pay a special Medicare tax. In 2018, Congress is expected to pass a tax on "Cadillac health plans." A major effort is to take place to save $500 billion over ten years by eliminating "waste, fraud and abuse" in Medicare. Finally, an additional tax is to be placed on medical devices.

During the long battle for health care, Obama's approval ratings declined. In addition, the loss of a long-held Democratic Senate seats after the death of Edward Kennedy of Massachusetts and Robert Byrd of West Virginia, the growth of a *Tea Party Movement*, which called for fiscal restraint and less government, and the loss of several gubernatorial elections for Democratic candidates indicated that passage of the health care bill did not come without a price.

Financial Reform

In July 2010, Congress passed the *Wall Street Reform and Consumer Protection Act.* The new law was fallout from the practices of the "too-big-to-fail" banks and other financial institutions. The act aims to end future bailouts by taxpayers and to protect consumers from unfair practices by financial institutions.

In order to ensure financial stability, one provision of the law limits bank trading or investments in private funds to no more than 3 percent of a bank's capital. A second provision sets up clear lines of responsibility for regulating banks. For example, state banks with less than $50 billion in assets will be regulated by the FDIC. National banks with less than $50 billion in assets will be regulated by the Office of the Comptroller of the Currency. All other banks will be under the supervision of the Federal Reserve System. The Federal Insurance Office will have the authority to seize big, failing companies.

A third provision sets up a consumer protection bureau, the Office of Thrift Supervision, to make sure that consumers receive clearly written, understandable, and accurate statements when applying for credit cards, debit cards, and mortgages. Fees will have to be justified by costs.

The law also sets up the Financial Services Oversight Council composed of major regulators to identify risks to the economy posed by new financial practices and activities of large corporations. The new law seeks to end the lack of oversight of financial institutions that led to the practices and products that paved the road to the recession of 2007–2009.

Space Exploration

Pictures taken by unmanned spacecraft demonstrated that water may have existed on the surface of Mars millions of years ago and that ice may lie deep under the surface. Despite the nation's interest in space, there were serious doubts about the costly manned flight program as well as the overall costs of space exploration. In April 2010, President Obama announced that the shuttle program would be ended after the last planned flights to the International Space Station in 2011. However, private companies would be encouraged to continue these efforts, while NASA would focus on robotic missions to asteroids after 2025 and Mars by the mid-2030s.

BP Oil Disaster of 2010

Seeking oil and building wells in deepwater areas had become economically viable as oil prices rose due to increased demand for energy in 2009 and 2010. In April 2010, the oil company British Petroleum (BP) suddenly found itself with a major oil leak from a drilling rig explosion in the Gulf of Mexico. Each day, thousands of gallons of oil poured into the Gulf, edging toward the shores of Louisiana, Mississippi, Alabama, Texas, and Florida. Those who relied on fishing for a livelihood were suddenly unemployed. Tourism suffered as many tourists wanted to avoid beaches that they assumed were polluted with tar balls. The environmental and financial costs were difficult to assess. Despite the efforts of BP, the unwanted flow continued into midsummer as early attempts to plug the leak and fully cap the well failed. In a major speech in June 2010, President Obama noted that 30,000 people in the affected states as well 17,000 members of the National Guard were working to clean up the beaches and stop oil from spreading and doing even more damage to the coastline and wildlife. He said it was time for America to end its reliance on fossil fuels and move aggressively toward alternative sources of energy, such as wind and solar power.

Elections of 2010

The 2010 national and state elections were marked by a sweeping Republican victory. In the national elections, Republicans captured control of the House of Representatives, winning over 60 seats, the largest turnaround in the House since the 1948 elections. Republicans also gained 6 seats in the Senate, but fell short of control. The Republicans also surged at the state level, gaining a majority of the nation's governorships and legislative chambers.

"Lame Duck" Congress Called into session for the last time in December 2010, the "lame duck" Congress, still dominated by the Democrats, passed significant legislation, often with the support of Republicans. The tax cuts of the George W. Bush era (discussed on pages 405–406) were extended for all income groups. These tax cuts were part of a package that included an extension of unemployment benefits, reduced payroll taxes, and an estate tax that was lower than past levels. In a further example of bipartisanship, Congress repealed the "Don't Ask, Don't Tell" policy of the armed forces. Now gays and lesbians could serve openly in the armed forces for the first time. Congress also passed a bill to help pay for the ongoing health needs of people who responded to help victims of the 9/11 attack on the World Trade Center in New York City. These bills were supported and signed into law by President Obama. The U.S. Senate also ratified the New START Treaty at this time (discussed on pages 404–405).

IN REVIEW

1. Explain how the elections of 2006, 2008, and 2010 changed leadership of the legislative and executive branches of government.
2. Discuss the key features of *each* of the following; (a) American Recovery and Reinvestment Act, (b) aid to the auto industry, (c) "Cash for Clunkers," (d) Jobs Bill of 2010.
3. For *each* of the following, list the position to which he or she was appointed by President Obama: (a) Hillary Rodham Clinton (b) Timothy Geithner (c) Ben Bernanke (d) Sonya Sotomayor.
4. List *three* provisions of the Affordable Care Act and explain why you favor or oppose each.

CHAPTER REVIEW

MULTIPLE-CHOICE QUESTIONS

1 The dispute over counting Florida voter ballots in the presidential election of 2000 was settled by
(1) an order of the governor of Florida
(2) an agreement between the candidates
(3) a vote of the United States Senate
(4) a United States Supreme Court decision

2 The disputed elections of 1876 and 2000 were similar because in both contests the
(1) winner was chosen by a special electoral commission
(2) states were required to hold a second election
(3) winner of the popular vote did not become president
(4) election had to be decided in the House of Representatives

3 Which event led to the other three?
(1) United States overthrow of the Taliban in Afghanistan
(2) passage of the Patriot Act
(3) September 11, 2001, terrorist attacks against the United States
(4) creation of the Department of Homeland Security

Base your answer to question 4 on the chart below and on your knowledge of social studies.

Number of Americans Age 85 and Older

Year	*Millions*
1900	0.1
1950	0.6
1960	0.9
2000	4.2
2010	6.1
2020*	7.3

*Projected
Source: Federal Interagency Forum on Aging-Related Statistics

4 Which statement is most clearly supported by information in the chart?
(1) Elderly men outnumber elderly women.

(2) In 1960, more than 10 percent of Americans were age 85 or older.
(3) The number of Americans living past the age of 85 is increasing.
(4) In 1900, only 1 million Americans were age 85.

5 The economic policies of President Ronald Reagan (1981–1989) and President George W. Bush (2001–2009) are similar in that both
(1) balanced the federal budget
(2) expanded welfare programs to end poverty
(3) used tax cuts to encourage economic growth
(4) decreased military spending

Base your answer to question 6 on the cartoon below and on your knowledge of social studies.

6 What is the main idea of this cartoon?
(1) The president is responsible for helping hurricane victims.
(2) Members of the Supreme Court can often ignore political issues.
(3) Nominating a justice to the Supreme Court often creates controversy.
(4) The Constitution should be amended so that Supreme Court Justices are elected.

7 **"Gasoline Prices Soar in 2008"**
"U.S. Oil Consumption and Imports Continue to Rise"
"OPEC Votes to Reduce Oil Production"

Which conclusion is most clearly supported by these headlines?
(1) The United States exports more oil than it imports.
(2) Energy policies are not affected by domestic events.
(3) The demand for alternative energy sources is declining.
(4) United States dependence on foreign oil is a major problem.

Supreme Court Nominee

Source: Joe Heller, *Green Bay Press-Gazette*, July 20, 2005 (adapted)

* 8 **"Additional 30,000 U.S. troops to Afghanistan"**
"New sanctions against North Korea"
"U.S. and Russia agree to reduce stockpile of nuclear weapons"

These events occurred during the presidency of
(1) George H. Bush
(2) Bill Clinton
(3) George W. Bush
(4) Barack Obama

* 9 A primary issue that the Affordable Care Act, signed into law by President Obama, tries to address is the
(1) increasing cost of medical care
(2) shortage of prescription drugs
(3) safety of medical procedures
(4) reorganization of hospitals

*10 The American Recovery and Reinvestment Act of 2009, enacted under President Obama, is an example of
(1) the increased power of the states to deal with economic problems
(2) a reliance on laissez-faire capitalism to combat continuing inflation
(3) direct federal involvement in the U.S. economy to address the problems of a recession.
(4) decreased support for the concerns of minority groups

**These last questions are simulated Regents questions, since no actual questions on recent events were available at the time of the writing of this book.*

THEMATIC ESSAYS

1 **THEME:** *Presidential Decisions on Foreign Policy.* Presidents of the United States must often make decisions regarding emergencies and issues that have serious implications for or are crucial to the security of the United States or other nations.

TASK: Complete *all* of the following tasks:

- Describe *one* foreign policy problem faced by President George W. Bush and *one* foreign policy problem faced by President Barack Obama.
- For *each* problem, discuss the president's options and the final decision he made.
- Evaluate the implications of *each* president's decision.

In your discussion of President George W. Bush, you may wish to use an example such as the attacks of September 11, the invasion of Afghanistan, or the invasion of Iraq.

In your discussion of President Barack Obama, you may wish to use the war in Iraq, the war in Afghanistan, or the agreement with Russia to reduce nuclear weapons.

You are *not* limited to these suggestions.

2 **THEME:** *Presidential Decisions on Domestic Issues.* Presidents are confronted with situations they do not anticipate and that will affect the economy and the well-being of the American people.

TASK: Complete *both* of the following tasks:

- Describe *one* domestic problem faced by President George W. Bush and *one* domestic problem faced by President Barack Obama.
- For *each* problem, discuss the president's decision and why that decision was made. Discuss whether or not you agree with each decision and explain why.

In your discussion of George W. Bush, you may wish to use an example such as Hurricane Katrina, the housing crisis, or the recession.

In your discussion of Barack Obama, you may wish to use an example such as the economic crisis, health care reform, or the BP oil disaster.

You are *not* limited to the above suggestions.

President George W. Bush speaks to firefighters, police officers, and rescue workers at Ground Zero in New York City, September 14, 2001.

DOCUMENT-BASED QUESTION

*Read each document and answer the question that follows it. Then read the **Task** and write your essay. Include references to most of the documents along with additional information you retain on U.S. history and government.*

HISTORICAL CONTEXT: During the first decade of the 21st century, the United States has confronted many serious problems and issues. These include the terrorist attacks on 9/11/01, the invasion of Iraq, the financial crisis, the debate over a national health care bill, and the BP oil disaster.

DOCUMENT 1: Refer to the photograph above.

QUESTION: Why was the president of the United States speaking to rescue workers at Ground Zero on September 14, 2001?

DOCUMENT 2: Refer to the photograph below.

QUESTION: Based on the photo, describe what happened in Iraq in 2003.

U.S. troops in Baghdad take cover during a gun battle after a rocket attack in August 2003.

DOCUMENT 3: From President George W. Bush, Speech to the Nation, October 10th, 2008:

> So my administration worked with Congress to quickly pass a $700 billion financial rescue package. This new law authorizes the Treasury Department to use a variety of measures to help banks rebuild capital—including buying or insuring troubled assets and purchasing equity of financial institutions. The Department will implement measures that have maximum impact.

QUESTION: What was one reason for the financial rescue package discussed above by President Bush?

DOCUMENT 4: Read the excerpt below and then answer the question that follows:

> What this plan will do is make the insurance you have work better for you. Under this plan, it will be against the law for insurance companies to deny you coverage because of a preexisting condition. As soon as I sign this bill, it will be against the law for insurance companies to drop your coverage when you get sick or water it down when you need it the most. They will no longer be able to place some arbitrary cap on the amount of coverage you can receive in a given year or in a lifetime. We will place a limit on how much you can be charged for out-of-pocket expenses, because in the United States of America, no one should go broke because they get sick....

—PRESIDENT BARACK OBAMA, SPEECH TO A JOINT SESSION OF CONGRESS, SEPTEMBER 9TH, 2009

QUESTION: What was one reason for the president's support of a national health care reform bill?

DOCUMENT 5: From President Barack Obama, Speech to the Nation on the BP oil spill, June 15, 2010:

> Already, this oil spill is the worst environmental disaster America has ever faced. And unlike an earthquake or a hurricane, it's not a single event that does its damage in a matter of minutes or days. The millions of gallons of oil that have spilled into the Gulf of Mexico are more like an epidemic, one that we will be fighting for months and even years.... We cannot consign our children to this future. The tragedy unfolding on our coast is the most painful and powerful reminder yet that the time to embrace a clean energy future is now. Now is the moment for this generation to embark on a national mission to unleash America's innovation and seize control of our own destiny.

QUESTION: What does President Obama see as the problem and the mission?

TASK: Using the documents and your knowledge of U.S. history and government, write an essay in which you:

- describe *two* problems confronted by the United States in the first decade of the 21st century.
- discuss a solution for *each* of the two problems you selected.
- explain the outcome you anticipate from your suggested solutions to the problems.

Glossary

abolition pre–Civil War reformers' goal of ending slavery

acid rain pollution caused when industrial and exhaust fumes in air dissolve in water vapor and fall as precipitation

acquired immunodeficiency syndrome (AIDS) disease transmitted by a virus entering a person's body, as when drug users share needles or through sexual contact

affirmative action increased educational and job opportunities for women and minorities to make up for past discrimination

American System Henry Clay's idea of imposing high tariffs to provide funds for internal improvements (roads, bridges, and canals) and to protect domestic industries

amnesty general pardon granted to a large group

anarchist person who advocates the abolition of all governments

animism religion in which humans seek security and prosperity by pleasing nature spirits

annexation takeover by one nation of another nation or part of it

apartheid strict racial segregation formerly enforced by South Africa's white minority government against blacks and other racial groups

appeasement yielding to an aggressor's demands to avoid armed conflict

appellate jurisdiction higher court's authority to review a case tried in a lower court

arbitration impartial judgment in a dispute such as one between labor and management

assembly line arrangement of workers and machines in which products being manufactured pass (often on a moving belt) from one operation to the next

asylum government protection of a person fleeing danger or mistreatment elsewhere

Australian ballot voting method in which a state-printed ballot is marked in secret

automation manufacturing method in which one set of machines regulates other machines

autonomous self-governing (but not independent)

baby boom dramatic increase in the U.S. birthrate between 1945 and 1960

bail money or credit allowing an arrested person's release from jail pending trial

belligerent nation involved in war

bicameral having two houses, as a legislature

bill of rights written list of personal liberties expressed as actions that a government may not take

biodegradable subject to natural decomposition

bipartisanship two major political parties acting together

Black Codes post–Civil War laws by Southern state conventions to limit the civil rights of African Americans

blacklist organized refusal by businesses to hire persons suspected of being pro-union or Communist sympathizers

blitzkrieg violent, surprise German offensive during World War II, characterized by speed and mobility

block grant federal financial aid to states, given with few guidelines on its use

blockade attempt by a nation's forces, usually a navy, to cut off access to another nation's ports, coastline, or other vital area

bootlegger supplier of illegal alcoholic beverages

boycott refusal to buy or sell goods or services in order to change a policy

breach of contract failure to carry out terms formally agreed to

brinkmanship pushing a dangerous confrontation to the limits of safety in order to achieve a desired outcome

budget plan of income and spending

budget deficit situation when expenditures exceed revenues

budget surplus situation when revenues exceed expenditures

bull market economic condition when public confidence in stocks causes their prices to soar

Cabinet presidential advisory group composed mostly of heads of executive departments

capital buildings and equipment for producing goods and services; money to buy such buildings and equipment

capitalism economic system marked by privately owned businesses competing for profits
carpetbagger during Reconstruction, Northerner in the South seeking private gain
cash-and-carry principle method of purchase by which a buyer pays in full and is responsible for transporting the goods; in particular, purchase by World War II belligerents of nonmilitary goods from the United States during its neutral period
cattle drive movement of a large group of cattle a long distance by foot
caucus meeting of party leaders to select candidates for office
censure official reprimand of a member of Congress
census official count of population, taken in the United States every ten years
checks and balances system by which one government branch may obstruct or defeat policies and decisions of the other branches
chief executive head of the executive branch
circuit court group of courts with jurisdiction to review district court decisions
civil disobedience purposeful refusal to obey laws regarded as unjust
clone to reproduce from one parent without fertilization
closed shop workplace in which an employer must hire only dues-paying union members
coalition alliance for joint action
codes of fair practices rules on maximum work hours, minimum wages, productivity, and prices drawn up together by businesses and labor groups
cold war period of U.S.-Soviet rivalry from 1945 to 1991, marked by espionage, hostile propaganda, the arms race, and the race in space
collective bargaining process by which workers and employers work out differences about wages, hours, and working conditions
commune rural community of counterculture "families"
company town company-owned settlement near the site of a large plant whose workers depend on it for employment
concurrent powers those exercised jointly by the federal and state governments
conference committee group of senators and representatives meeting to achieve a compromise between similar but differing bills
confirmation Senate approval of a chief executive's appointment
conservation wise management and careful use of the natural environment
conspicuous consumption lavish spending habits to indicate social prestige
constituency group of voters represented by an elected legislator
constitution written plan of government
consumerism inclination of the general public to buy more and more products
containment U.S. cold-war policy of preventing Soviet power and influence from spreading to non-Communist nations
cooperative business owned and operated by those who buy its products or services
corporation business chartered by a state and owned by shareholders who invest in it
cost-of-living adjustment (COLA) automatic increase in Social Security benefits when inflation increases the costs of goods and services
cotton gin device that separates seeds from cotton mechanically
counterculture beginning in the late 1960s, lifestyle of young Americans that emphasized honesty and creativity and was opposed to such cultural norms as marriage, patriotism, and business
coup small group's sudden, violent overthrow of a government
craft worker laborer with a trade skill
credit time allowed for payment for goods or services sold on trust
credit default swap insurance on bundled mortgage-backed securities

data information
data base computerized information file
***de facto* segregation** separation of races that exists because of circumstances, such as housing patterns, rather than law
***de jure* segregation** separation of races authorized or required by law
debt moratorium temporary halt on the payment of debts
deficit spending government spending more money than it takes in
delegated powers those given to the federal government by the Constitution
demobilization reduction of armed forces after a war's end
democracy government in which the people rule directly or through elected representatives
depression severe economic decline marked by business failures, high unemployment, and low production and prices
desecrate to treat something disrespectfully
détente relaxation of U.S.-Soviet tensions during the cold war

developed nation an industrialized country that has a generally high standard of living
developing nation one that has a largely agricultural economy and is not heavily industrialized
dictatorship government in which all power is concentrated in one person or a small group
direct primary state election to choose party candidates by popular vote before the general election in November
disarmament removal of weapons from a nation or nations
discount rate interest charged by the Federal Reserve Board to member banks
disenfranchisement cancellation of voting rights
dissenter person opposed to a policy or cause supported by the majority
dissenting opinion written explanation of why a minority of Supreme Court justices disagree with the majority's ruling
domino theory in the 1950s, U.S. State Department belief that Southeast Asia's nations were like dominoes, ready to topple once any one of them was taken over by Communists
double jeopardy being tried twice on the same charge
downsizing laying off some of a business's workers and closing plants or departments
draft compulsory enrollment for military service

elastic clause grant by the Constitution to Congress of power not specifically stated in order to make "necessary and proper" laws
elector member of a political group selected by voters to be part of the Electoral College
Electoral College group of state officials casting ballots for a president and vice president
embargo government order forbidding shipment of goods to another nation or group of nations
eminent domain government-sanctioned takeover of private property
energy crisis acute shortage of oil leading to an increase in oil prices
entrepreneur person who assumes the risk of organizing a business in hopes of profit
erosion wearing away of Earth's surface by wind, rain, or ice
escalation steady buildup of something, such as armed forces
espionage spying
ethnic cleansing use of force and terror to expel from an area a minority group
ethnicity common cultural bond uniting a large group of people
Euro the currency of the majority of the nations in the European Union
excise tax one set on the sale of a domestic product
executive privilege argument that a president can withhold information from the legislative and judicial branches
extradition return of a person accused of crime to the state where the crime was committed

fad vivid, usually frivolous, form of social expression of short duration
fascism government characterized by militarism, extreme nationalism, and a one-party dictatorship
federal system one in which power is shared by central and state governments
federalism principle by which political power is divided equally between central and state governments
feminist person in favor of women's rights and opposed to political, economic, and social inequality between men and women
filibuster attempt to stop passage of a Senate bill by talking or threatening to talk indefinitely
fiscal year 12-month period of a budget
foreclosure repossession by a bank of property of a resident unable to repay a loan
freedman former slave (male or female)
freedom ride civil rights protest of the 1960s in which participants took interstate bus rides to spur desegregation of public transportation
frontier imaginary dividing line between settlements and wilderness

genetics science of the heredity of living organisms
genocide extermination or attempted extermination of an entire national, ethnic, or religious group
genome genetic makeup of an organism
gerrymandering drawing voting district borders so as to give a voting advantage to one political party
ghetto urban neighborhood inhabited mostly by people of one nationality or ethnic group
glasnost Gorbachev policy to grant Soviet citizens more freedom of speech and the press
globalization expanding ability of people and corporations everywhere to communicate and do business with one another
graduated income tax one that takes proportionately more from high-income individuals
"grandfather clause" in post–Civil War South, ruling that any male citizen could vote without restriction whose male ancestors could vote in 1867, when African Americans had not yet gained citizenship and the right to vote

grand jury citizen panel to determine whether enough evidence exists to indict a person for a crime
greenhouse effect the trapping of solar heat by gases in the atmosphere
guerrilla warfare surprise attacks by small bands of raiders

holding company business combination owning a majority of stock in member companies and therefore able to dictate common policy
Holocaust systematic killing of Jews and other groups by Nazi officials during World War II
"Hooverville" during the Great Depression, cluster of temporary dwellings for the homeless
hostage person held prisoner until ransom is paid or demands are met
housing bubble the sudden end of constantly rising costs of real estate, resulting in a fast decline in prices

ideology belief system
impeachment accusation of wrongdoing against a government official
imperialism national policy of acquiring foreign territories or exercising control over them
implied powers federal powers derived from the elastic clause
impressment forcing people into military service, especially seamen of one country into another's navy
indemnity payment to cover damages and deaths
indentured servant person agreeing to work for a number of years in exchange for passage to a British colony
indictment formal statement by a grand jury charging a person with a criminal offense
Industrial Revolution period from about 1750 to the present marked by the invention of machines and systems to mass-produce goods
industrial worker factory laborer
inflation continuing rise in prices
initiative voters' power to propose ideas for new laws
injunction court order directing that an action be carried out or stopped
installment plan method of purchase by which partial payment is made immediately and the remainder paid out periodically
interchangeable parts separate elements of a manufactured product that are made exactly alike to ease assembly and repair
interlocking directorship placing of the same persons on executive boards of several companies as a means of limiting competition
interstate commerce trade crossing state lines
interstate compact agreement between states for mutual assistance
intervention the interference of one country in the internal affairs of another
intifada widespread uprising by Palestinians living in Israeli-occupied territory
island-hopping military policy of seizing control of only some islands from an enemy, with the goal of striking at the center of the enemy's realm
isolationism noninvolvement with foreign governments or multinational organizations

Jim Crow laws in post–Civil War South, state and local laws denying African Americans free access to public facilities
joint-stock company organization in which merchants buy shares and the resulting capital is invested in business projects
judicial review Supreme Court's power to determine whether an act of Congress is constitutional
jurisdiction authority to hear and decide judicial cases in an area

laissez-faire economic theory that businesses should not be regulated by government
landmark decision judicial ruling that marks a turning point or sets a precedent in law
law of supply and demand economic theory that when supply of an item is low, sellers can charge a high price, and that as supply increases, prices decrease as a result of competition
libel writing a false and unfavorable opinion about someone
life expectancy average number of years a newborn is expected to live
literacy test state requirement that a voter demonstrate the ability to read and write
lobbyist professional advocate seeking to encourage a policy or influence a law favorable to a special-interest group
loose construction belief that the Constitution's elastic clause gives the federal government unstated powers
loyalty check during Truman administration, FBI or Civil Service Commission search to uncover whether a person had ever belonged to a subversive organization
lynch to kill someone by hanging without a trial

mainstreaming education of disabled and nondisabled children together so as to provide special education services in regular classrooms

manifest destiny early 19th-century belief that the United States was bound to expand westward to the Pacific and dominate North America
mass production manufacture of goods in large quantities by machine
massive retaliation during the cold war, an announced U.S. threat to meet Soviet aggression with a nuclear-weapons bombardment
meltdown accident in which the nuclear core of a power plant burns through protective walls, allowing radioactive substances to escape into the environment
mercantilism economic theory by which a colony supplies raw materials to the home country, which uses them to make goods to be sold in the colony for profit
merger business combination in which two or more companies are united
microchip tiny square of silicon imprinted with electronic circuits and their connections and capable of storing and processing data at high speed
military-industrial complex close ties between a nation's armed forces and the defense industries
militarism nation's policy of glorifying its armed forces and aggressive spirit
mission religious settlement to convert native people and offer humanitarian services
mobilization assembly of equipment and personnel in preparation for war duty
monolith single, undivided force
monopoly exclusive control over the supply of a product or service
mortgage money borrowed against the value of property
muckraker writer, especially in the Progressive Era, who exposed conditions needing reform
multinational corporation (MNC) company operating plants, offices, or both in several countries

national debt accumulation of debts owed to purchasers of government bonds
national guard state force of citizen volunteers to serve in the military or natural emergencies
nationalism loyalty to one's nation and support of its interests; militant patriotism
nationalization government takeover of property formerly owned by a colonial power or private company
nativist one who believes that foreigners are a threat to the majority culture and should be barred from entering the country
natural rights theory that people are born with certain rights, such as of liberty and property
neutrality policy of taking no sides in a war involving other nations
nominating convention meeting of party delegates to select candidates for office
nomination party's selection of a candidate for elected office
nondenominational favoring no religious group in particular
nuclear power energy produced by using heat given off by radioactive substances
nullification cancellation of a law; also belief that a state can invalidate a federal law it considers unconstitutional

obstruction of justice improper influence exerted on others to conceal the truth
ordinance regulation made by a local government
original jurisdiction authority of a court to be first to hear and try a case
outsourcing shifting a company's production or services to another country, usually to save money
ozone layer band of gas high above Earth that blocks the sun's ultraviolet light

pacifist opponent of all wars
pardon chief executive's power to forgive a convicted person's crime
parity equality, as of two nations' armed forces; price for farm products based on a price in an earlier base period
parliament assembly of nobles, clergy, and commoners who make a nation's laws; (cap.) two-house British legislature
partnership multiple business ownership entailing liability for all debts for each partner
passive resistance endurance of violence without retaliation
peaceful assembly nonviolent demonstration by a group
perestroika Gorbachev's economic policy of introducing elements of capitalism
perjury lying under oath
petit jury citizen panel that hears trial testimony and decides on a verdict
petition written request for a change in government policy
philanthropist person who uses wealth to fund humanitarian endeavors
plantation large farm with many workers
plateau flat or gently rolling expanse at high elevation
platform pre-election statement of a party's principles and policies

pocket veto automatic veto when a bill remains unsigned by the president and Congress adjourns fewer than ten days after passing it

pogrom sudden violent attack on a helpless minority community

political action committee (PAC) group funded by an organization to financially support political candidates favoring the organization's interests

political machine organized control of elected officials by party leaders

poll tax payment formerly required for voting in some states

polygamy having multiple marriage partners

pooling agreement between competing businesses to fix prices, divide markets, and share profits

popular sovereignty in pre–Civil War period, decision of voters in a territory to prohibit or allow slavery

popular vote ballots cast by the people

population density measure of concentration of people in a given area

postindustrial age era after the industrial age when information and service providers dominate economies

post-traumatic stress disorder condition characterized by nightmares, irritability, depression, and guilt, caused by extreme stress; battle fatigue

power of the purse power to approve or reject proposed taxes

prefabricate to assemble a building from large parts put together in a factory

primary election preliminary procedure by which voters choose between candidates for party nomination

productivity rate at which goods are manufactured

progressive late-1800s to early-1900s reformer dedicated to moderate political and social change through governmental action

propaganda facts, ideas, and rumors spread to help one's cause and harm opposing ones

proprietorship single business ownership entailing liability for all debts

protectorate nation whose foreign policy is dictated by a foreign power

provisioning plantation large Northern farm producing food and lumber for West Indies sugar plantations

psychoanalysis treatment of mental or emotional problems through free association, reliving of troubling experiences, and recall of dreams

racial discrimination denying someone equal opportunity because of race

racism prejudice and discrimination based on the supposed superiority of one group over others

railhead end of a cattle drive where cattle are loaded onto trains

ratification formal approval

rationing government-imposed limits on food and other necessities for civilians during wartime

realpolitik foreign policy based on international political realities rather than ideology

reapportionment process by which a change in state population might result in a gain or loss of House seats

rebate former practice among competing railroads of refunding some of a large corporation's shipping charges

recall procedure by which voters can remove an elected official before expiration of his/her term

recession period of business decline (less severe than a depression)

Red Scare a time of hysteria and intolerance in 1919 America connected with a fear of terrorist bombings

redistricting redrawing the lines that separate legislative or congressional districts

referendum voters' power to mark ballots for or against a proposed law

refugee person fleeing life-threatening conditions or persecution in the home country

regional agency official group administering operations crucial to neighboring states

renewable resource energy source that can be used without being diminished, such as solar power or wind power

reparations payments made to compensate others for wrongdoings or losses

reprieve chief executive's power to postpone a convicted person's punishment

republic government in which the people elect representatives to make and execute laws

reservation land set aside for use by one or more Native-American tribes

reserved powers under the Constitution, powers retained by the states

revenue sharing letting state and local governments decide how to spend federal grants

rules of succession procedure setting the order in which government officials replace the chief executive in case of illness or death

salutary neglect pre–1763 British colonial policy of overlooking trade violations and allowing self-government

sanction action such as a trade restriction taken against a nation by one or more other nations to enforce adherence to international law

satellite in post–World War II period, country dominated by the Soviet Union
savings and loan association (S & L) cooperative that holds members' savings as dividend-bearing shares and invests in home mortgages
scalawag during Reconstruction, Southerner who cooperated with occupying Northerners
scapegoat person who bears the blame for others
search warrant judges' written permission to search suspects' properties
secession state's separation of itself from previous ties and obligations to a federal union
secondary boycott refusal by strikers to buy products from companies doing business with their employer
sectionalism strong loyalty to one region within a nation
segregation separation of people on the basis of race
self-determination right of people with a common culture or nationality to form an independent nation
seniority privileges acquired by length of service
separation of powers division of governmental authority and duties among legislative, executive, and judicial branches
settlement house community center to aid city dwellers, especially poor immigrants
share part-ownership in a business, based on the amount invested; stock
sharecropper farmer paying for use of a landlord's land with a portion of the annual crop
sit-down strike a labor action that involves occupying a business and refusing to leave
sit-in a demonstration such as sitting at a segregated lunch counter and refusing to leave
slum poor urban neighborhood of run-down buildings
social Darwinism theory that people, social groups, and businesses advance by means of free competition and that the stronger triumph over the weaker
socialism economic system based on public, rather than private, ownership of the means of production
soft money unlimited contribution to a political organization for party-building and issue education, sometimes misdirected to benefit a specific candidate
solar power energy derived directly from the sun
sovereignty independence
special-interest group organization formed to exert pressure on lawmakers' decisions; lobby
speculation making risky investments in hopes of high profits
sphere of influence area dominated by a foreign power
spiritual religious song of an emotional nature
spoils system appointing people to government jobs on the basis of party loyalty rather than qualifications
stagflation high unemployment coupled with inflation
standing committee permanent House or Senate group specializing in a particular area of law
state militia group of volunteer soldiers for the common defense
stock part-ownership in a business, based on the amount invested; share
stockholder one who owns stock; also called **shareholder**
strategic warhead long-range nuclear weapon
strict construction belief that federal powers are limited to those specified in the Constitution
strip mining ground-level mining of minerals that leaves the landscape scarred and ridden with debris
subcommittee one made up of only some of the members of a larger committee
subsidy government grant to a private enterprise
suburb residential community outside a city but near enough to allow residents to commute to city jobs
subversive person attempting to weaken or overthrow a government
suffrage the ability to vote
summit conference meeting of heads of state to discuss affairs of mutual interest
supply-side economics policy of reducing federal taxes so as to give more money to businesses for investment and consumers for spending
supremacy clause part of U.S. Constitution stating that it and other U.S. laws take precedence over state and local laws
sweatshop small manufacturing establishment with unsafe and unsanitary conditions

target price farm goods price considered fair by the federal government; if the market price decreases, a farmer is paid a subsidy to make up the difference
tariff tax on imports
temperance movement organized effort to limit or ban sales of alcoholic beverages
tenant farmer person working another's land and paying rent in cash or crops
tenement multifamily urban dwelling with few amenities
territorial integrity keeping one's borders free from foreign intervention

terrorism systematic use or threat of violence to achieve political goals
third world developing nations of Asia, Africa, and Latin America that were not aligned with either NATO countries or the Communist bloc
totalitarianism political dictatorship that tries to control every aspect of citizen's lives
town meeting an annual assembly of self-governing village inhabitants, especially popular in New England
trust business combination of companies in the same field for the purpose of reducing competition or creating a monopoly
trust buster government executive dedicated to breaking up monopolies

ultimatum final demand not subject to negotiation
unwritten constitution traditions that have become part of the U.S. political system, such as political parties and the president's Cabinet

variable rate mortgage one whose interest rate changes over time
veto chief executive's power to refuse to sign a bill into law
vigilante member of a self-appointed police force, especially on the Western frontier

weapons of mass destruction nuclear, chemical, or biological ones
work ethic traditional belief that hard work is morally good and will be rewarded with material success
writ of habeas corpus written document that requires a prisoner to be brought before a judge

yellow dog contract company policy that requires workers to agree not to join a union as a condition of employment
yellow journalism newspaper's emphasis on scandals, crimes, and other shocking events to lure more readers
Yiddish Germanic language of many Central and Eastern European Jews

zoning local government regulations specifying business and home locations, land use, and allowable acreage for building sites

Index

Abbas, Mahmoud, 401, 402
Abington School District v. *Schempp*, 301
Abolitionists, 74, 79–80
Abortion, 304
Abraham Lincoln Brigade, 241
Abu Ghraib prison, 398
Abzug, Bella, 303
Accused, rights of, 25–26, 29, 307
Acid rain, 388
Adams, John, 12; presidency of, 45, 58–59, 61
Adams, John Quincy, 64; in election of 1824, 41
Adams, Samuel, 12, 23
Addams, Jane, 171
Affirmative action, 300–301, 302
Affordable Care Act, 415–416
Afghanistan: Soviet invasion of, 337–338, 358; U.S. policies toward, 396–398
Africa: culture of, 7–8; slavery in, 4–5
African Americans: in American Revolution, 13; Back to Africa movement and, 173; Black movement and, 172–173; civil rights and, 117, 251; in Civil War, 103–104; in Colonial population, 8; in Congress, 115; education of, 279–281; emancipation of, 103; in Great Depression, 224; Harlem Renaissance and, 216–217; industrial and vocational training for, 117; Jim Crow laws and, 208; Ku Klux Klan and, 213; as mayors, 348; migration of, 148, 208, 283; in military service, 161, 248; music of, 217; New Deal and, 232–233; race riots and, 208; rights of, 180; on segregation, 117; in sports, 279; voting rights of, 281, 298, 299–300; women, 148; in World War I, 208; in World War II, 244. *See also* Civil rights movement
African National Congress, 358
Agnew, Spiro T., 334
Agricultural Adjustment Act, 227, 229
Agriculture: *braceros* in, 283–284; inventions in, 136; of Native Americans, 3; organization of, 135–137; plantation, 3, 8; post-Civil War, 110; revolution of, 136; in World War II, 209–210. *See also* Farmers; Farming
AIDS (acquired immune deficiency syndrome), 362
Alamo, 93
Alaska: gold in, 139; purchase of, 114
Albany Plan of Union, 6, 7
Albright, Madeleine K., 304, 373
Aldrin, Edwin E., Jr., 314, 315, 330
Alger, Horatio, 130
Alien Act, 58–59, 80
Alito, Samuel Anthony, Jr., 408, 414
Allawi, Iyad, 400
Alliance for Progress, 314
Amending U.S. Constitution, 48–49. *See also* names of amendments.
American Association of Retired Persons (AARP), 353
American Federation of Labor (AFL), 133–134, 228
American Indian Movement (AIM), 306
American International Group (AIG), 407
Americanization, 153, 161
American Party, 96
American Protective Association, 149
American Railway Union, 134
American Recovery and Reinvestment Act, 412–413
American Red Cross, 101
American Revolution, 5, 8; African Americans in, 13; battles of, 10, 12; causes of, 9–10; leaders of, 12; revolutionary ideology in, 11–12
Americans with Disabilities Act, 294
American System, 91–92
AmeriCorps, 372
Amnesty Act, 118
Amnesty to Vietnam War draft evaders, 336
Anarchists, 133, 199
Anderson, Marian, 232
Animism, 7–8
Anthony, Susan B., 171
Antiballistic missiles, 331, 404
Anti-Defamation League, 173
Antietam, Battle of, 100, 103
Anti-Federalists, 22, 23
Antitrust movement, 132, 176, 178
Apartheid, 357–358
Apollo 11, 314
Appalachian Mountains, 9–10
Appeals process, 44–45
Appomattox Court House, 100
Arab-Israeli conflicts, 332, 337, 401–402, 377–378
Arab-Israeli peace agreement, 377
Arafat, Yasir, 377, 401
Arctic National Wildlife Refuge, 410
Aristide, Jean-Bertrand, 381, 402
Arkansas, 375
Armour, Philip, 169
Arms, right to keep and bear, 25
Armstrong, Neil, 314, 330
Army-McCarthy Hearings, 266–267
Articles of Confederation, 7, 14–15, 19
Asia, trade with, 113–114
Assembly, freedom of, 25, 28
Assembly line, 125, 126, 211
Aswan Dam, 276–277
Atlantic Charter, 243
Atomic bomb, 261, 275; dropping on Hiroshima, 246–247
Atoms for Peace, 275
Attucks, Crispus, 10
Australian ballot, 175
Austria, 201; as member of EEC, 261
Austria-Hungary, 195, 201
Automation, 385
Automobiles: "Cash for Clunkers" program and, 413; production of, 125–126, 211

Baby boom, 283
"Back to Africa" movement, 173
Bail, 3, 27
Baker, Josephine, 216–217
Baker v. *Carr*, 50, 302
Banking, reforms in, 103, 227, 361, 407, 416
Barbed wire, 159
Barnard, Henry, 78
Barton, Clara, 101
Basie, Count, 233
Batista, Fulgencio, 312–313
Bay of Pigs, 312–313
Begin, Menachem, 337
Belarus, 364
Belgium: formation of European Coal and Steel Community, 261; as member of NATO, 262
Bell, Alexander Graham, 128
Bell, Daniel, 385
Bell, John, 97
Berger, Stephen G., 414
Berlin: airlift, 260–261; division of, after World War II, 258; wall, 313, 363
Bernanke, Ben, 408, 414
Bessemer process, 127
Bethune, Mary McLeod, 232
Bicameral legislative branch, 14
Biden, Joseph, 414
Bill of rights, 20, 25–28; English, 3, 14
Bin Laden, Osama, 395–396

Birmingham, Alabama: church bombing in, 298; coal mining and, 128; mills in, 114, 125
Birth control, 172
Black Codes, 116
Blacklist, 135, 267
Blackmun, Harry, 330
Black power, 297
Black Tuesday, 222
Blake, Eubie, 217
Bleeding Kansas, 96
Blitzkrieg, 242
Block grants, 373
Boat people, 339, 380–381
Boer War, 357
Bolsheviks, 198
Bonaparte, Napoleon, 90
Bonus Army, 224
Booth, John Wilkes, 105
Bootleggers, 214
Bosnia, crisis in, 364, 381
Bosnia-Herzegovina, in World War I, 195
Boston: in American Revolution, 10, 11, 12; Democratic politics in, 149; immigrants in, 147–148
Boston Massacre, 10
Boston Tea Party, 10
Boxer Rebellion, 188
Box Henry, 74
Boycotts, 10, 251
Braceros, 283–284
Brady Bill, 376
Brandeis, Louis, 169
Breckinridge, John C., 97
Brezhnev, Leonid, 332, 358
British Petroleum oil disaster, 388, 417
Brown, John, 79, 80, 96, 97
Brown v. *Board of Education*, 279, 280, 290, 300
Bryan, William Jennings, 191, 215; in election of 1896, 138–139
Buchanan, James, 98
Buckley v. *Valeo*, 377
Budget deficit/surplus, 346, 374
Bull market, 210, 222
Bull Moose Party, 178
Bunker Hill, Battle of, 11
Bureau of Indian Affairs, 306, 330
Burgoyne, John, 12
Burr, Aaron, 41, 59
Bush, George H.: in election of 1988, 360; presidency of, 360–366, 379–381
Bush, George W., 404; in election of 2000, 41, 394–395; in election of 2004, 395; presidency of, 358–359, 395–411
Bush v. *Gore*, 395
Businesses, 130–131; boom of, 210; deregulation of, 347; increasing inequities in, 169–170; regulation of, 139, 171, 176–177, 178
Byrd, Robert, 416

Cabinet, 39; under Washington, George, 56–59
Calhoun, John C., 80–81
California, 82; Compromise of 1850 and, 82; gold rush of, 94–95; Mexicans in, 198; movies in, 213; Spanish missions in, 91; Watts riot in, 298
Calloway, Cab, 233
Campaign finance reform, 376–377
Camp David Accords, 337
Canada: as member of NATO, 262; in underground railroad, 74, 75; U.S. border with, 93
Canals, major, in the North, 70
Canal zone, 192–193
Capital cases, 307
Capitalism, 125. *See also* Corporations; Entrepreneurs
Carmichael, Stokely, 297
Carnegie, Andrew, 127, 129–130, 134, 147, 168, 169
Carpetbaggers, 112
Carranza, Venustiano, 194
Carson, Rachel, 296, 387
Carter, Jimmy: in election of 1980, 344–345; presidency of, 335–339, 347, 357, 358
Cash-and-carry principle, 241
"Cash for Clunkers" program, 413
Castro, Fidel, 284, 312–313, 380, 402–403
Castro, Raúl, 403
Cather, Willa, 150
Catholics: Coughlin, Charles and, 231; missions of, 3; as target of Ku Klux Klan, 213
Catt, Carrie Chapman, 171
Cattle frontier, 158, 159
Caucuses, 76
Cavazos, Lauro, 305
Central Intelligence Agency (CIA), 39
Central Pacific Railroad, 114, 152
Chambers, Whittaker, 266
Chaney, James, 298
Chaplin, Charlie, 213
Chavez, Cesar, 304–305
Chechnya, 382–383
Checks and balances, 24, 47–48, 111–112
Chernobyl, 387
Chiang Kai-shek, 274
Chicago: Democratic politics in, 149; growth of, 159; immigrants in, 148; nightclubs in, 217; settlement houses in, 171
Children: as slaves, 73; in workforce, 71, 146, 148, 169, 175, 228
China: Communism in, 262, 267, 274; immigration from, 152; imperialism and, 187; Japanese invasion of, 241; Korean War and, 264; under Mao Zedong, 263, 267, 274, 331; as member of Security Council, 256, 331; territorial integrity of, 187; Tiananmen Square in, 379–380; trade with, 379–380, 403; U.S. relations with, 262, 331, 379–380, 403
Chinese Exclusion Act, 152, 156
Chrysler Corporation, 413
Churchill, Winston, 243, 257, 260
Circuit courts, 44
Cities: life in, 144–146, 150; reform in, 174
Citizenship, 111
Citizens United v. *The Federal Elections Commission*, 415
Civil Aeronautics Board, 347
Civil disobedience, 281–282, 291
Civilian Conservation Corps, 226
Civil liberties: Civil War and, 100–101; threats to, 213–214
Civil Rights Act: of 1866, 116; of 1875, 116; of 1957, 281; of 1964, 296, 299, 302
Civil rights cases, 117
Civil rights movement: African Americans and, 251; desegregation and, 290–292; under Eisenhower, 279, 281–282; federal involvement in, 347–348; Japanese-American, 248; under Johnson, 296–297; launching, 280–282; Native-American, 162; under Truman, 251, 279
Civil War: Spanish, 241; Vietnam, 315
Civil War (1861–1865): African Americans in, 103–104; battles of, 99–100; beginning of, 98; causes of, 69; consolidation after, 126; costs of, 110; home front in, 100–101; impacts of, 113–114; resources of North and South in, 102; wartime policy in, 102–103. *See also* North; South
Clark, Kenneth, 280
Clark, William, 90
Clay, Henry, 41, 64, 76–77, 81, 91, 98
Clayton Antitrust Act, 178
Clean Air Act: of 1963, 296, 360; of 1970, 329
Clean skies legislation, 410
Clean Water Act, 329
Cleaver, Eldridge, 297
Cleveland, Grover: in election of 1892, 138; presidency of, 135, 178, 188
Clinton, Hillary, 304, 414; in election of 2008, 412; as Secretary of State, 413
Clinton, Bill: impeachment, trial, and acquittal, 43, 375–376; presidency of, 359, 371–383
Coal, 127–128
Coercive Acts, 10
Cold war: containment in, 262–264; crises in, 312–315; détente in, 331–332, 337–338; Domino Theory in, 275; end of, 363, 364; at home, 264–267; Kennedy, John F. and, 312–315; origins of, 258–259; politics of, 267–268
Collective bargaining, 133
Collins, Michael, 314
Collin v. *Smith*, 28

Colonies: assemblies in, 6; business and property laws, 6–7; charters and self-government, 6; policies in, 9; settlement of, 5. *See also* American Revolution
Columbia (space shuttle), 411
Columbine High School, 376
Columbus, Christopher, 3
Committees of Correspondence, 12
Common Market, 261
Common Sense (Paine), 11
Commonwealth of Independent States, 364
Communes, 319
Communism: in China, 262, 267, 274; collapse of, in Eastern Europe, 363; in Cuba, 284; in Indochina, 315–317; in North Korea, 400–401; in Russia, 213; U.S. views of, 208, 276; in Yugoslavia, 260
Compromise: of 1850, 82; of 1877, 119
Comptroller of the Currency, 416
Concord, Battle of, 10–11
Concurrent powers, 48
Congress, U.S., 35–39; African Americans in, 115. *See also* House of Representatives, U.S.; Senate, U.S.; names of laws
Congress for Industrial Organization (CIO), 228
Congressional Reconstruction, 110–111
Congress of Racial Equality (CORE), 297
Connecticut Plan, 20
Conservation, 177
Conservatism, 168, 307, 345–354
Conspicuous consumption, 147
Constitution, U.S.: amending, 22, 48–49; basis of, 2, 26; checks and balances in, 24, 47–48; executive branch in, 21; interstate relations of, 22; judicial branch in, 22; legislative branch in, 21; as "living document," 48–49; main parts of, 20–24; Preamble of, 21; ratification of, 22; separation of powers in, 21–22, 46–47; strengths of, 23–24; strict construction of, 58; supremacy clause of, 22; unwritten, 56; weaknesses of, 24
Constitutional Convention, 19–20
Constitutional Union Party, 97
Constitutions, state, 14
Consumer protection, 176, 282
Containment, 260, 262–264, 416
Continental Army, 12
Continental Congress, 14; First, 11, 12; Second, 11, 12
Contract With America, 375
Contras, 355
Coolidge, Calvin, 209, 222
Cooperatives, 133, 137
Cornwallis, Lord, 13
Corporations, 126; concentration in, 130–131, 210
Cortines, Ramon, 305
Cotton gin, 72
Coughlin, Charles, 231
Council of National Defense, 196
Counterculture, 319
Craft workers, 133, 147
Crawford, William H., 41
Crazy Horse, 162
Crisis (magazine), 173
Crittenden Proposal, 98
"Cross of Gold" speech, 139
Cruzan v. *Director, Missouri Department of Health*, 361–362
Cuba: Bay of Pigs in, 312–313; Communists in, 284; immigrants from, 284, 305; in Spanish-American War, 190; U.S. relations with, 380–381, 402–403
Cuban Missile Crisis, 314, 315
Cullen, Countee, 216
Cultural pluralism, 155
Cultural values, 215–217
Culture, popular, 150. *See also* Entertainment; Literature; Movies; Music
Custer, George Armstrong, 162
Czechoslovakia: collapse of Communism in, 363; creation of, 201; German occupation of, 241, 242
Czech Republic: anti-missile defense system in, 404; as member of NATO, 383

Darrow, Clarence, 215
Darwin, Charles, 146, 214–215
Davis, Angela, 297
Dawes Act, 161
Dayton, Ohio, peace treaty in, 381
D-day, 246
DDT, 329, 387
Debs, Eugene V., 134–135
Declaration of Independence, 2, 11–12
Deere, John, 136
De facto segregation, 251, 300
Deficit spending, 225, 374
De jure segregation, 251, 280, 300
De Klerk, F. W., 358
Delaware, ratification of Constitution by, 23
Delegated powers, 47
De Lôme, Dupuy, 189
Democracy: colonial, 6; defined, 1; expanding and contracting, 179–180; representative, 2; slavery and, 8
Democratic Party, 64; convention of 1968, 320; immigrant support for, 153
Democratic-Republicans, 58, 60, 64
Demographic patterns, 353–354
Denmark: as member of EEC, 261; as member of NATO, 262; in World War II, 242
Dennis et al. v. *United States*, 265
Depression, Great, 221–224
Desegregation, 290–292
Destroyers-for-Bases Agreement, 242
Détente, 331
Detroit, Michigan, race riots in, 298
Developed and developing nations, 274
Dewey, George, 190
Dewey, Thomas E., 251
Dictaphone, 168
Dictatorships, 101, 240–243
Dien Bien Phu, 316
Diphtheria, 150
Direct primary, 175
Disabled citizens, rights of, 293–295
Disarmament, 200, 202, 243, 331–332, 358, 382, 404–405, 417
Discount rate, 361, 406
Diseases, 150, 193, 353, 362
Displaced persons, 257
Division of powers in government, 230
Dix, Dorothea, 78, 101, 293
Dole, Robert, 371
Dollar diplomacy, 193
Domestic abuse, 304
Dominican Republic, 192, 194
Domino theory, 275, 317
Double jeopardy, 26
Douglas, Stephen, 95; debate between Lincoln, 96–97; in election of 1860, 97
Douglass, Frederick, 73, 74, 79–80
Downsizing, 375, 406
Draft, 104; protesters of, 318; riots and, 104; in World War I, 199; in World War II, 244
Drake, Edwin, 128
Dred Scott v. *Sanford*, 82–83
Drug Enforcement Agency, 329
Du Bois, W. E. B., 117, 172, 173
Due process of law, 27, 169, 333
Dugouts, 160
Dulles, John Foster, 275
Dust Bowl, 224
Duvalier, "Papa Doc," 305

Earhart, Amelia, 232
Earth Day, 329
Eastern Europe: independence of, 363; new nations of, 201; Soviet control of, 258, 259–260
East Germany, 260
Economic Opportunity Act (1964), 295
Economic Recovery Tax Act, 346
Economic Stimulus Act, 407, 412–413
Economy: under Bush, George H., 360–361; under Bush, George W., 406–408; under Carter, 336; under Eisenhower, Dwight D., 278; faltering of, 406–407; under Ford, 335; in Great Depression, 221–223; joint-stock companies, 6; mercantilism, 6–7; under Obama, 412–413; postwar consumption, 282–283; regional, 212; supply-side, 345–347; trickle-down theory, 346
Edison, Thomas, 128
Education: of African Americans, 279–281; back to basics approach, 372–373; Bible reading in, 28;

Education *(continued)*
Elementary and Secondary Education Act and, 293; evolution and, 214–215; Great Society programs for, 296; growth of public, 145; mainstreaming in, 295; No Child Left Behind Act and, 408; reform of, 78; rights of students in, 348–349; Title IX and, 302–303, 330, 415
Education for All Handicapped Children Act, 294
Education of the Handicapped Act, 293
Edward I (King of England), 3
18-year-olds, voting rights for, 330
Eighteenth Amendment, 30, 173, 214
Eighth Amendment, 27, 29, 30
Einstein, Albert, 246
Eisenhower, Dwight D., 43; in election of 1952, 267, 278; presidency of, 264, 266, 268, 274–282, 313, 315–316; as Supreme Allied Commander in Western Europe, 246
Eisenhower Doctrine, 277
El Alamein, Battle of, 246
Elastic clause, 36, 49, 90
El Caney, Battle of, 190
Elderly, political influence of, 353–354, 410
Elections: of 1800, 41, 59–60; of 1824, 41; of 1828, 75; of 1832, 77; of 1860, 97; of 1864, 104; of 1876, 119; of 1892, 138–139; of 1896, 138–139; of 1900, 175; of 1912, 41, 178; of 1920, 208–209; of 1948, 251; of 1952, 267, 278; of 1968, 319–320, 328; of 1972, 328; of 1980, 339, 344–345; of 1984, 345; of 1988, 360; of 1992, 371; of 1996, 371; of 2000, 41, 394–395; of 2004, 395; of 2008, 412; of 2010, 417–418; primary, 40; reforms in, 376–377
Electoral College, 40–41, 43, 395
Elevators, 146
Eleventh Amendment, 27, 30
Elkins Act, 176
Ellington, Duke, 217, 233
Ellsberg, Daniel, 321
El Salvador, aid to, 355
Emancipation Proclamation, 103
Embargo, 61
Emergency Banking Act, 225
Emergency Quota Act, 157
Emergency Stabilization Act, 407
Eminent domain, 409
Energy: crisis of, 335; sources of, 127–128, 384; use of, 389
Engel v. *Vitale*, 28, 301
English Bill of Rights, 3, 14
Enlightenment, 2
Entertainment, 213, 217
Entrepreneurs, 129–130, 144
Environment: Bush, George W. on issues of, 410; concerns over, 336; Federal involvement in, 347
Environmental Protection Agency, 329
Equal Employment Opportunity Act, 304
Equal Rights Amendment, 303–304
Era of Good Feelings, 63–64
Escalation, 317
Escobedo v. *Illinois*, 29, 307
Espionage, 199, 259
Ethiopia, Italian takeover of, 241
Ethnic cleansing, 364, 382. *See also* Holocaust
Ethnicity, 153
Ettor, Joseph, 135
Euclid, Ohio, Village of, v. *Ambler Realty Company*, 212
Europe: U.S. isolationism toward, 239–240; U.S. neutrality toward, 239–240, 241; U.S. trade with, 113
European Central Bank, 262
European Coal and Steel Community, 261
European Community, 261–262
European Economic Community, 261
European immigrants, difficulties for, 5
European Union, 262, 383. *See also* Common Market
Evers, Medgar, 291, 299
Evolution, 214–215
Excise tax, 58
Executive branch, 2, 14, 21. *See also* President
Executive Order 9066, 248
Executive privileges, 333
Exxon Valdez oil spill, 360, 388

Factory system, 145
Fair Employment Board, 251
Fair Labor Standards Act, 228
Family and Medical Leave Act, 372
Farmer, James, 297
Farmers: on the Great Plains, 159; in 1920s, 209; ranchers versus, 158; tenant, 115; Western move by, 168. *See also* Agriculture; Farming
Farming: decline in income, 208; organized labor and, 304–305; owners of, 115; Reagan policies on, 349–351; scientific, 162; sharecroppers in, 115; subsidies of, 379
Fascism, 240, 241, 257
Fatah Party, 401, 402
Faubus, Orval, 281
Faulkner, William, 233
Federal Bureau of Investigation, 264, 332
Federal courts: life tenure of judges in, 45; organization of, 44
Federal Deposit Insurance Corporation, 227
Federal Election Commission, 377
Federal Emergency Relief Administration, 225
Federal Farm Board, 223
Federal Housing Administration, 227, 407
Federal Insurance Office, 416
Federalism, 22, 47
The Federalist (Madison, Hamilton, and Jay), 22
Federalists, 22, 58–60, 62, 63
Federal Judiciary Act, 44
Federal National Mortgage Association, 407
Federal Reserve System, 179, 406, 414
Federal system, 22
Federal Trade Commission, 178
Feminists, 302–304
Ferdinand, Francis, 195
Fernandez, Joseph, 305
Field, Cyrus, 186
Fifteenth Amendment, 27, 30, 111, 115
Fifth Amendment, 25–26, 27, 29–30, 307
Filibuster, 36
Filipino Rebellion, 191
Fillmore, Millard, 98
Financial Services Oversight Council, 416
Finland: independence of, 201; as member of EEC, 261
Fireside chats, 232
First Amendment, 8, 28, 29, 199, 301, 361
First Continental Congress, 11, 12
First National Bank, 57, 58, 71
Fitzgerald, F. Scott, 216
Flappers, 215
Fleming, Alexander, 353
Florida v. *Powell*, 415
Flynn, Elizabeth Gurley, 135
Food and Drug Administration, 197–198
Food stamp program, 329
Foraker Act, 190
Force Act, 117
Ford, Gerald R., 334–335
Ford, Henry, 125–126, 211
Ford Motors, 413
Foreclosures, 136, 210, 406
Forest Reserve Act, 177
Fort McHenry, 62
Fossil fuels, 127–128, 387
Fourteen Points, 200
Fourteenth Amendment, 27, 30, 117; in defining U.S. citizenship, 111; due process of law and, 169; equal protection clause of, 300, 303–304, 395; laissez-faire theory and, 130; preferential employment and violation of, 302; segregation as violation of, 280
Fourth Amendment, 28–29, 307, 349
France: formation of European Coal and Steel Community, 261; French and Indian War and, 4; as member of NATO, 262; as member of SEATO, 276; as member of Security Council, 256; monarchy in, 2; revolution in, 61; in World War II, 242

Franklin, Benjamin, 12; Albany Plan of Union, 6; as delegate to Constitutional Convention, 19
Free blacks in North, 71–72
Freedmen, 116
Freedmen's Bureau, 116, 117
Freedom rides, 290
Free states, 81–82, 95–96, 99
Frémont, John Charles, 96
Freud, Sigmund, 215
Frick, Henry Clay, 134
Friedan, Betty, 303, 304
Frontier, closing of, 9–10
Fugitive Slave Act, 82
Fulton, Robert, 70
Furman v. *Georgia*, 29

Gable, Clark, 234
Gadsden Purchase, 95
Gagarin, Yuri, 314
Garland, Judy, 234
Garrison, William Lloyd, 79, 80
Garvey, Marcus, 173
Gates, Robert, 414
Gays: in the military, 373, 417; in World War II, 248
Gaza, 402
Geithner, Timothy, 414
General Agreement on Tariffs and Trade, 357, 378–379
General Motors, 228, 386, 413
Genetics, 386
Genocide, 248
Gentlemen's Agreement, 156
Georgia, 404; settlement of, 5, 7
Germany: division of, after World War II, 248–249, 258, 260; immigrants from, 74; loss of colonies, 200; nonaggression pact with Soviet Union, 242; reunification of, 363; in World War I, 195, 197, 198, 200, 202; in World War II, 240, 241, 246, 248
Gerrymandering, 50
Gettysburg, Battle of, 100
Gettysburg Address, 103
Ghettos, 153
Gibbons v. *Ogden*, 46
GI Bill of Rights, 250
Gideon v. *Wainwright*, 29, 307
Gilded Age, 147
Ginsburg, Ruth Bader, 373, 414
Glasnost, 359
Glass ceiling, 304
Glass-Steagall Act, 227
Glenn, John, 314
Globalization, 127, 386
Global warming, 388
Glorious Revolution, 3
Goethals, George W., 193
Gold: in Alaska, 139; in California, 94–95
Goldman, Emma, 199
Gompers, Samuel, 133
Goodman, Andrew, 298
Goodman, Benny, 233
Good Neighbor Policy, 354–355
Gorbachev, Mikhail, 359, 363, 364
Gore, Albert, Jr.: in election of 1992, 371; in election of 2000, 41, 394–395; global warming and, 388
Gorgas, William C., 193
Graduated income tax, 138, 178
Gramm-Rudman-Hollings Act, 361
Grandfather clauses, 119
Grand jury, 26
Grange movement, 136–137
Grant, Ulysses S., 100, 118
The Grapes of Wrath (Steinbeck), 233
Gray Panthers, 353–354
Great Britain: colonial policy of, 9; French and Indian War and, 4; immigrants from, 74; Industrial Revolution in, 125; limitations on government, 2–3; as member of EEC, 261; as member of NATO, 262; as member of SEATO, 276; as member of Security Council, 256; monarchy in, 2; Monroe Doctrine and, 64; Native Americans and, 3–4; Oregon and, 93; retaliation of, 10; rights of citizens, 8–9; taxation and, 10; in war against the colonists, 12–13; War of 1812 and, 61–62; in World War I, 195, 196, 198, 200; in World War II, 242, 243
Great Compromise, 20
Great Depression, 221–224
The Great Gatsby (Fitzgerald), 216
Great Plains, 158
Great Society, 295–296, 328–329
Greece: immigrants from, 149; as member of EEC, 261; Truman Doctrine and, 260
Greenhouse effect, 388
Greenspan, Alan, 375
Gregg v. *Georgia*, 29
Grenada invasion, 355
Guerrilla warfare, 316
Gun control, 376
Gutter v. *Bollinger*, 409

Habeas corpus: in England, 3; U.S. suspension of, 101
Haiti, 194; as American protectorate, 192; Duvalier, "Papa Doc," ruling of, 305; earthquake in, 402; immigration from, 305; U.S. relations with, 381, 402
Hamas, 377, 401, 402
Hamdan v. *Rumsfeld*, 409
Hamilton, Alexander, 71; as delegate to Constitutional Convention, 19; as Federalist, 22; as Secretary of Treasury, 56–57
Hampton, Lionel, 233
Handy, W. C., 217
Haralson, Jeremiah, 115
Harding, Warren G.: death of, 209; in election of 1920, 208–209; presidency of, 202
Harlan, John Marshall, 120, 279–280
Harlem Renaissance, 216–217
Harpers Ferry raid, 96
Hawaii, acquisition of, 188
Hawley-Smoot Tariff, 223
Hay, John, 187
Hayes, Rutherford B., 119
Haymarket bombing, 133
Haywood, "Big Bill," 135
Head Start, 296
Healthcare, 150; Clinton's effort to reform, 372; Obama's reform of, 415–416
Hearst, William Randolph, 150, 170, 188–189
Heart of Atlanta Motel, Inc. v. *United States*, 299
Hellman, Lillian, 233
Hemings, Sally, 73
Hemingway, Ernest, 216
Henry, Patrick, 12, 23
Henry Street Settlement, 171
Hepburn Act, 176
Hezbollah, 400, 401
Hideki Tojo, 249
Higher Education Act, 296
Hiroshima, dropping of atomic bomb on, 246–247
Hispanics: activism of, 304–306; migration of, 283; in politics, 305–306, 348
Hiss, Alger, 266
History of the Standard Oil Company (Tarbell), 170
Hitler, Adolf, 240; Germany under, 240–242; pact with Stalin, 242, 245; suicide of, 246
Ho Chi Minh, 315–316
Hoffman, Abbie, 320
Holding companies, 131
Holmes, Oliver Wendell, Jr., 28
Holocaust, 248
Homeland Security, U.S. Department of, 396
Home Owners' Loan Corporation, 227
Homestead Act, 103, 136, 158
Homesteaders, 160
Homestead Strike, 134
Hoover, Herbert, 231; as head of Food Administration, 197–198; presidency of, 198, 222, 223
Hoovervilles, 224
Hope, Bob, 244
Hostages, U.S., in Iran, 338, 339
House of Burgesses, 6
House of Representatives, U.S., 35, 37; committees in, 37, 38; election of 2006 and, 412; election of 2010 and, 417; HUAC in, 265–266. *See also* Congress, U.S.; Senate, U.S.
Housing bubble, 406
Howard, Elston, 279
How the Other Half Lives (Riis), 171
Hudson v. *Michigan*, 409
Huerta, Victoriano, 194
Hughes, Langston, 216, 217
Hull House, 171

Human rights, 257, 339
Humphrey, Hubert, 320
Hundred Days, 225
Hungary, 201; anti-Soviet riots in, 277; collapse of Communism in, 363; as member of NATO, 383
Hurricane Katrina, 410–411
Hussein, Saddam, 365–366, 398
Hydrogen bomb, 261, 266, 275

IBM, 386
Immigrants: Chinese, 152, 156; Cuban, 284; difficulties for, 5; Haitian, 305; illegal, 352–353; Irish, 74–75; Italian, 149, 151; Japanese, 156; Jewish, 134; new wave of, 351–353; in 1920s, 208; patterns of settlement of, 147–148; as target of Ku Klux Klan, 213; Western move by, 168; in workforce, 114
Immigration: changes in, 151–157; Cuban and Haitian, 305; limits on, 156; by nationality, 154; new, 154; new patterns in, 283–284; pre-Civil War, 74–75; reasons for, 153; reform of, 353, 411
Immigration Restriction Act, 157
Impeachment, 21, 43; Clinton and, 375–376; Nixon and, 333–334; trial of Johnson, Andrew, and, 111–112
Imperialism, 127; China and, 187; Panama and, 192; Nicaragua and, 193, 355
Imperial presidency, 334
Implied powers, 36
Impressment, 61
Indentured servants, 5
Indian Removal, 77
Indian Reorganization Act, 162, 233
Indian Self-Determination and Education Assistance Act, 306, 330
Indochina, Communism in, 315–317. *See also* Vietnam War
Industrial Revolution, 124–127
Industrial Workers of the World, 135
Industry: post-civil war growth of U.S., 125–132; workers and, 132–135. *See also* Antitrust movement; Businesses; Labor unions
Inflation, 138; increase in, 345; post World War II, 249
Initiative, 138, 175
Inland Waterways Act, 177
Installment buying, 150, 211
Insular Cases, 191
Interchangeable parts, 71
Interlocking directorships, 178
Intermediate-range Nuclear Forces Treaty, 359
Internal Security Act, 265
International Atomic Energy Agency, 400
International Court of Justice, 257
International Ladies' Garment Workers' Union, 134
International Space Station, 416–417
Internet, 386
Interstate commerce, 36, 137, 139
Interstate Commerce Commission, 137, 139, 176, 290
Interstate Highway Act, 278
Interstate relations, 22, 51
Intifada, 377
Intolerable Acts, 10
Iran-Contra Affair, 356, 400
Iranian hostage crisis, 338, 339
Iran-Iraq War, 364
Iraq: invasion of Kuwait, 365; U.S. wars against, 364–366, 398–400, 404
Ireland: immigrants from, 74–75, 149; as member of EEC, 261
Iron Curtain, 260
Iroquois Confederacy, 6, 7
Island hopping, 246
Isolationism: ending of, with UN, 257; George Washington and, 60–61; Monroe Doctrine and, 64; U.S. abandonment of, 243; as U.S. policy toward Europe, 239–241, 243
Israel: Middle East conflict and, 277, 332, 401–402; Palestine Liberation Organization and, 377–378
Italy: formation of European Coal and Steel Community, 261; immigrants from, 149, 151; as member of NATO, 262; under Mussolini, 240, 241; Paris Peace Conference and, 200

Jackson, Andrew: in election of 1824, 41; in election of 1828, 75; presidency of, 75–76; War of 1812 and, 62, 64
Jackson, Helen Hunt, 161
Jackson, Jesse, 348
James, Henry, 150
James II (King of England), 3
Jamestown, Virginia, 3, 5, 6
Japan: attack on Pearl Harbor, 243, 245; immigration from, 156; invasion of China, 241; opening of, 114, 186–187; U.S. occupation of, 247–248; U.S. relations with, 356–357; in World War II, 241, 246
Japanese Americans: civil rights of, 248; as immigrants, 156
Jay, John, 22
Jazz, 150, 217
Jefferson, Thomas, 12; as author of Declaration of Independence, 2, 11–12; in election of 1800, 41, 59; opposition to Hamilton's financial plan, 57; presidency of, 45, 61, 89–90; as Secretary of State, 56; views of, 59, 73
Jews: Hitler and, 240; Holocaust and, 248; immigrants, 134, 149, 153; Ku Klux Klan and, 213
Jiang Jieshi, 263, 267
Jim Crow laws, 116, 117, 208
John (King of England), 2
Johnson, Andrew: impeachment of, 43, 111–112, 376; plan for reconstruction, 110
Johnson, James Weldon, 216
Johnson, Lyndon Baines, 43; election of 1968 and, 319; presidency of, 295–297, 317–320, 328, 351
Johnson, Tom, 174
Joint-stock companies, 6
Jolson, Al, 213
Jones, Samuel, 174
Joplin, Scott, 150
Joseph, Chief, 162
JPMorgan Chase, 407
Judicial branch, 2, 14, 22
Judicial review, 45–46
Judiciary, New York State, 51
Judiciary Act, 45
The Jungle (Sinclair), 171

Kagan, Elena, 414
Kaiser Aluminum and Chemical Corporation v. *Weber*, 302
Kansas-Nebraska Act, 95–96, 97
Karzai, Hamid, 397, 398
Katz v. *United States*, 29
Kelley, Florence, 169
Kellogg-Briand Pact, 202
Kelo v. *City of New London*, 409
Kennan, George, 260
Kennedy, Anthony, 408–409, 414
Kennedy, Edward, 416
Kennedy, John F., 43, 277; assassination of, 292, 302; presidency of, 290–291, 293, 312–315, 316
Kennedy, Robert, 290; assassination of, 319
Kennedy Commission, 302
Kent State University, incident at, 321
Kern, Jerome, 216
Kerner Commission, 299
Kerry, John, 395
Key, Francis Scott, 62
Khomeini, Ayatollah Ruhollah, 338
Khrushchev, Nikita, 276, 313, 314, 315
Killen, Edgar Ray, 298
Kim Il Sung, 382, 400–401
Kim Jong Il, 382
King, Martin Luther, Jr.: assassination of, 299; founding of SCLC, 297; March on Washington and, 291–292; national holiday for, 347; Selma to Montgomery March and, 298
Kissinger, Henry, 320, 330, 331, 332, 343
Knights of Labor, 133
Knights of the White Camellia, 112
Know-Nothings, 75, 96, 149
Knox, Henry, 57
Korea. *See* Korean War, North Korea
Korean War (1950–1953), 263, 266; end of, 268, 274–275. *See also* North Korea
Korematsu v. *United States*, 248
Kosovo, war in, 381–382
Ku Klux Klan, 112, 113, 117, 118, 213, 298
Kurds, 398

Kuwait, Iraqi invasion of, 365
Kyoto Protocol, 410

Labor: changes in, 387; illegal immigrants and, 353; organization of, 132–135; relations under Truman, 250–251
Labor unions, 133–134, 135, 228, 305, 353
La Causa, 305
La Follette, Robert, 174
Laissez-faire, 125, 130, 209, 210
Land-grant colleges, 136
Latin America: human rights and, 339; U.S. relations with, 63–64, 193, 314, 338–339, 362, 380–381
Law of supply and demand, 136
Lawrence Strike, 135
Laws, procedures for making, 37–38
Lazarus, Emma, 155
League of Nations, 200, 201–202, 240
Lebanon, U.S. marines in, 356
Lee, Robert E., 100
Legislative branch, 2, 14, 21, 50
Lehman Brothers, 407
Lend-Lease Act, 243
Levittown, New York, 283
Lewis, John L., 228
Lewis, Meriwether, 90
Lewis, Sinclair, 216
Lexington, Battle of, 10–11
Liberals, 213–214, 307
The Liberator, 80
Liberty League, 231
Life expectancy, 150, 353–354
Liliuokalani, Queen, 188
Lincoln, Abraham: assassination of, 105, 110; Civil War strategy of, 100; debate between Douglas and, 96–97; in election of 1860, 97; leadership of, 104–105; reconstruction plan of, 110; second term of, 104
Lincoln, Mary Todd, 105
Lindbergh, Charles A., 213
Literacy test, 119, 156
Literature, 150, 216, 233
Liuzzo, Viola, 298
Lobbyists, 39
Local governments, 51–52
Lochner v. *New York*, 169
Locke, John, 2, 11
Lodge, Henry Cabot, 201–202
Long, Huey, 231
Long Island, New York, 212
Loose construction of Constitution, 58
Louisiana, French territory, 7
Louisiana Purchase, 89–91
Loyalty checks, 264
Lusitania (British liner), 196
Luxembourg: formation of European Coal and Steel Community, 261; as member of NATO, 262
Lynchings, 104, 173

MacArthur, Douglas A.: Korean War and, 264; occupation of Japan and, 247–248
Machine guns in World War I, 198
Madison, James: as delegate to Constitutional Convention, 19; as Federalist, 22; opposed to Hamilton's financial plan, 57; as Secretary of State, 45; War of 1812 and, 61–62
Magna Carta, 2
Mahan, Alfred Thayer, 186
USS *Maine*, sinking of, 189
Mainstreaming in education, 295
Main Street (Lewis), 216
Malaria, 193
Malcolm X, 297; assassination of, 299
a-Maliki, Nuri, 398, 400
Manchuria: Japanese invasion of, 241; as Japanese sphere of influence, 187
Mandela, Nelson, 358
Manhattan Project, 246
Manifest destiny, 91, 92–95
Mann, Horace, 78
Mao Zedong, 263, 267, 274, 331
Mapp v. *Ohio*, 29, 307
Marbury v. *Madison*, 45–46
March on Washington, 291
Marshall, George, 260
Marshall, John, 45–46, 77
Marshall, Thurgood, 280, 297
Marshall Court, 45–46, 69
Marshall Plan, 260, 261, 274
Martinez, Bob, 305
Mary (Queen of England), 3
Maryland: court case in, 46; slavery in, 7
Massachusetts: in American Revolution, 10–11, 12; colony, 6; ratification of Constitution by, 23
Mather, Cotton, 130
Mayflower Compact, 6
McCain, John, 412
McCarran Act, 265
McCarthy, Eugene, 319
McCarthyism, 266–267
McClellan, George B., 100, 104
McClure's, 170
McCormick, Cyrus, 136
McCulloch v. *Maryland*, 46
McGovern, George, 332
McKinley, William: in election of 1896, 139; in election of 1900, 175; presidency of, 188, 189, 190, 191
McLaurin v. *Oklahoma State Regents*, 300
Meade, George G., 100
Meat Inspection Act, 171
Medicaid, 296
Medicare, 295–296, 354, 409–410, 415
Medvedev, Dmitri, 404
Melting pot theory, 155
Mentally ill, institutions for, 78
Mercantilism, 6–7
Meredith, James, 290–291
Mergers, 131
Merrill Lynch, 407, 408
Mexico, 82; revolution in, 194; U.S. war with, 82, 94–95, 160
Middle class, 147; influence of, 169–170; political reform and, 174
Middle East: Carter and, 336–338; negotiations of, 332; U.S. relations with, 377–378, 401–402. *See also* Israel and names of other Middle East nations
Midway, Battle of, 246
Military, U.S.: demobilization of, 249, 250; gays in, 373, 417; during Reconstruction, 116; segregation in, 248. *See also* names of wars
Military-industrial complex, 279
Miller, Glenn, 233
Mills v. *Board of Education of District of Columbia*, 293
Milosevic, Slobodan, 381–382
Miners: in West, 94–95, 168; in Alaska, 139
Minimum wage, 169, 374
Mining, 125, 158
Minorities: cuts in social programs on, 348; in Great Depression, 224; in World War I, 198; in World War II, 248. *See also* Civil rights movement
Miranda v. *Arizona*, 29, 307, 415
Missing in action (MIAs), 321
Missions, Spanish, 91
Mississippi, University of, 290–291
Mississippi River, 89–90
Missouri Compromise, 64, 81, 83, 95
Missouri River, 158
Mitchell, John, 335
Mondale, Walter, 345
Monopolies, 131
Monroe Doctrine, 63–64; Roosevelt corollary to, 191–192
Montesquieu, Baron, 2
Montgomery bus boycott, 280, 291–292
Moon, landing on, 314, 330
Morgan, J. P., 169
Mormons, 91
Morrill Land Grant Act, 136
Morse Code, 186
Mortgages, 210, 227; defaults on, 406
Moseley-Braun, Carol, 373
Motor Vehicle Air Pollution Control Act, 296
Mott, Lucretia, 78
Mountain men, 91
Movies, 213, 233–234
Ms. (magazine), 303
Muckrakers, 170
Muhammad, Elijah, 297
Muir, John, 176, 177
Muller v. *Oregon*, 169
Multinational corporations, 386
Munich Conference, 242
Municipal reform, 174
Munn v. *Illinois*, 137
Murray, Patty, 373
Music, 150, 216, 233
Muslim-Croat confederation, 381
Mussolini, Benito, 240, 241
My Antonia (Cather), 150

Nagasaki, dropping of atomic bomb on, 247
Napoleon Bonaparte, 90; wars of, 61
Nasser, Gamal Abdel, 276–277
Nast, Thomas, cartoon by, 149
Nation, Carrie, 173, 214
National Aeronautics and Space Administration (NASA), 39, 314
National Association for the Advancement of Colored People (NAACP), 173, 297
National Banking Act, 103
National Congress of American Indians, 306
National debt, 323, 346, 374
National guard, 50–51
National Industrial Recovery Act, 227
Nationalists, Chinese, 267, 274; flight to Taiwan, 263
Nationalization of Suez Canal, 277
National Labor Relations Board, 228
National Organization for Women, 303
National Prohibition Act, 214
National Recovery Administration, 227
National Recovery Association, 229, 233
National Republicans, 64
National Rifle Association, 376
National Woman Suffrage Association, 78
National Women's Trade Union League, 133
Native Americans, 77; activism of, 306–307; contact with Europeans, 3–4; governments of, 7; in Great Depression, 224; Hurons, 4; Iroquois, 4; New Deal and, 233; origins, 3; self-determination of, 330; Western settlement and, 95, 160–162
Nativism, 75, 155, 213–214, 224, 248
Natural rights, 2
Nazi Party, 240
Netherlands: formation of European Coal and Steel Community, 261; as member of NATO, 262
Neutrality, 60, 239–242
Neutrality Acts, 241, 242
Newark, New Jersey, race riots in, 298
New Deal, 225–232; African Americans and, 232–233; controversies in, 229–232; Native Americans and, 233; opposition to, 230–231; support for, 231–232; unemployment and, 225–227; women and, 232
New Federalism, 329, 345
New Freedom, 178
New Frontier, 290
New Jersey, 12, 298; at Constitutional Convention, 20; ratification of Constitution by, 23
New Jersey Plan, 20
New Jersey v. *TLO*, 348–349
Newlands Reclamation Act, 177
New Mexico, Mexicans in, 198
New Orleans: breakdown of levees in, 411; jazz in, 217
Newspapers, selling, 170
New York: in American Revolution, 12; constitution of, 14; decline in population of, 283; government of, 50–51; ratification of Constitution by, 23; reforms in, 175
New York City: Democratic politics in, 149; garment industry in, 169; growth of, 125; immigrants in, 147, 148; libraries in, 169; nightclubs in, 217; opera in, 150; settlement houses in, 171; slums in, 151; tenements in, 146
New York Journal, 170
The New York Times v. *United States*, 321, 333
New York World, 170
Ngo Dinh Diem, 316
Niagara Movement, 173
Nicaragua: U.S. aid to contras in, 355; U.S. intervention in, 193
9/11 Commission Report, 396
Nineteenth Amendment, 27, 30, 179, 216, 302
1920s, politics and economics of, 208–210
Ninth Amendment, 30
Nixon, Richard M., 328; election of, 320; granting of pardon to, 335; impeachment process and, 333–334; presidency of, 320–323, 328–332; resignation of, 43, 333–334; Watergate Affair and, 332–334
Nixon Doctrine, 330–331
No Child Left Behind Act, 408
Nomination of candidates, 40, 76
Noriega, Manuel, 362
Norris, Frank, 171
North, 70; abolition of slavery in, 14; economic policies of, 71; factory system of, 71; family life of, 71; free blacks of, 71–72; geography of, 70; slavery in, 7, 8; technology of, 70; urban problems of, 71. *See also* Civil War (1861–1865)
North, Oliver L., 356
North Africa in World War II, 245–246
North American Free Trade Agreement (NAFTA), 378
North Atlantic Treaty Organization (NATO), 262, 277, 383; bombing of Yugoslavia by, 383; expansion of, 404; formation of, 274; members of, 262, 313, 383
Northern Securities Company v. *United States*, 176
North Korea, 403; nuclear capability of, 382; U.S. relations with, 400–401
North Star, 79–80
Northwest Ordinance, 14–15
Norway: as member of NATO, 262; in World War II, 242
Nuclear Non-Proliferation Treaty, 400, 403, 404
Nuclear power, 384; waste disposal and accidents and, 387
Nuclear Test-ban Treaty, 315
Nullification, 46, 59, 81
Nuremberg Trial, 248–249

Obama, Barack, 348, 399, 403; election of, 412; presidency of, 404–405, 412–418
Occupational Safety and Health Administration (OSHA), 329
The Octopus (Norris), 171
Office of Economic Opportunity, 329
Office of Price Administration, 244
Oglethorpe, James, 5
Oil, 128; crisis, 336; discovery of, 125; refining of, 129
Oil spills: BP, 388, 417; *Exxon Valdez*, 360, 388
Open Door Policy, 187, 243
Operation Desert Shield, 365
Operation Desert Storm, 365
Operation Iraqi Freedom, 398
Oppenheimer, J. Robert, 266
Ordinance of Nullification, 81
Oregon: Nez Percé people of, 162; reforms in, 175
Oregon Country, 91, 93–94
Organization of Petroleum Exporting Countries (OPEC), 335
Original jurisdiction, 44
O'Sullivan, Mary Kenney, 133
Oswald, Lee Harvey, 292
Outsourcing, 407
Oveta Culp Hobby, 278
Ozone, 388

Pacifists, 199
Pahlavi, Mohammed Reza, 338
Paine, Thomas, 11
Pakistan as member of SEATO, 276
Palestine Liberation Organization (PLO), 356, 377–378
Palin, Sarah, 412
Palmer, A. Mitchell, 156–157
Panama: building canal in, 192–193, 339; U.S. invasion of, 362; U.S. relations with, 338–339
P.A.R.C. v. *Commonwealth of Pennsylvania*, 293
Parents v. *Seattle*, 409
Paris: nightclubs in, 217; peace conference in, 200
Parity, 202, 227
Parks, Rosa, 280
Parliament, British, 3
Partnerships, 126
Passive resistance, 297
Paul, Alice, 171
Payment in Kind, 350
Payne-Aldrich Tariff, 177
Peace Corps, 295, 314
Pearl Harbor, 243, 245
Pelosi, Nancy, 412
Penicillin, 353
Penn, William, 4, 5
Pennsylvania: coal mining in, 127–128; colony of, 4, 5; oil in, 128; ratification of Constitution

by, 23; steel industry in, 114, 125; Whiskey Rebellion in, 58. *See also* Philadelphia
Pentagon, terrorist attacks on, 395
Pentagon Papers, 321
Perestroika, 359
Perkins, Frances, 232
Permanent Court of International Justice, 202
Perry, Matthew, 114, 186
Pershing, John J., 198
Persian Gulf crisis and war, 364–366, 382
Petit jury, 26
Petraeus, David, 399
Philadelphia: in American Revolution, 12; Constitutional Convention in, 19–20; immigrants in, 147; nightclubs in, 217
Philippines: as member of SEATO, 276; in Spanish-American War, 191
Pickford, Mary, 213
Pierce, Franklin, 98
Pilgrims, 3–4, 6, 148
Pinchot, Gifford, 177, 178
Plains Indians, 160–161
Planned Parenthood of Southeastern Pennsylvania, et al. v. *Casey*, 362
Plantations, 3, 7, 8, 72
Platforms, 138
Platt Amendment, 190, 191
Plessy v. *Ferguson*, 119–120, 279
Plymouth, Massachusetts, 6
Pocahontas, 3
Pocket veto, 38
Pogroms, 153
Poison gas in World War I, 198
Poland, 242; anti-missile defense system in, 404; anti-Soviet riots in, 277; collapse of Communism in, 363; German invasion of, 242; immigrants from, 149; independence of, 200; as member of NATO, 383; occupation of, 258
Political action committees (PACs), 39
Political machines, 149–150
Political parties, 58. *See also* specific parties
Polk, James Knox, 93
Poll tax, 119, 299
Pollution, 296, 329, 336, 347, 387–389, 410
Polygamy, 50, 91
Pooling, 130–131
Popular culture, 150, 213, 217, 233–234
Popular sovereignty, 82
Population distribution, 154; census and, 35
Populist Party, 137–139
Portugal: as member of EEC, 261; as member of NATO, 262
Postindustrial age: changes in, 384–387; problems of, 387–389
Post Office, U.S., 199
Potsdam Conference, 257, 259
Poverty, 295, 351. *See also* Great Depression; Recession
Powell, Lewis, 330
Power of the purse, 6
Powers: delegated, 47; division of, 47; implied, 36; reserved, 47–48
Preamble of U.S. Constitution, 20, 24
Prescription drugs, 409–410
President, 21; executive privileges of, 333; growth of powers in, 43, 334; roles of, 37, 39–41; succession of, 42. *See also* specific names of presidents
President's Council on Mental Retardation, 293
Press, freedom of, 8, 25, 28
Préval, René, 402
Primary election, 40
Prisoners of war (POWs), 321
Privacy, Fourth Amendment right to, 349
Proclamation of 1763, 10
Productivity, 126
Progressive Party, 178
Progressives, 168–170, 177, 180
Prohibition, 173, 214
Propaganda, 196
Proprietorship, 126
Protectorates, 190
Psychoanalysis, 215–216
Public Works Administration, 226
Puerto Rico: in Spanish-American War, 190; as U.S. territory, 284
Pulitzer, Joseph, 150, 170, 188–189
Pullman sleeping car, 134, 168
Pullman Strike, 134–135
Punishments, cruel and unusual, 27, 29
Pure Food and Drug Act, 171
Puritans, 5, 148–149
Putin, Vladimir V., 383, 404

al-Qaeda, 396, 397
Quakers, 4, 5, 148
Quartering, protection against, 25
Quinones, Nathan, 305

Rabin, Yitzhak, 377
Race riots, 208
Radical Republicans, 110–111, 115, 116–117
Railroads, 114, 127, 159, 176
Rainbow Coalition, 348
Ranching, 158, 159
Randolph, Edmund, as attorney general, 57
Ratification: of amendments, 48–49; of U.S. Constitution, 19, 22
Rationing, 244
Ray, James Earl, 299
Reagan, Ronald, 345; in election of 1980, 344–345; presidency of, 345–360
Reaganomics, 347
Real estate boom, 211–212, 406
Realpolitik, 330
Reapportionment, 35, 302
Rebates, 129
Recall, 175
Recession, 208; efforts to halt, 407–408
Reconstruction: end of, 118–120; plans of, 110–111, 112, 115–117
Reconstruction Finance Corporation, 223
Redistricting, 50
Red Scare, 156–157
Referendums, 138, 175
Refugees, 257
Regents of the University of California v. *Bakke*, 300–301; decision of, 409
Rehnquist, William, 330, 376
Religion: freedom of, 25; in pluralistic society, 148–150; slavery and, 73
Reno, Janet, 373, 375
Reparations, 200, 202
Representative democracy, 2
Republics, 1–2
Republican Party: after Reconstruction, 112; birth of, 97; cutting taxes as goal, 405–406; midterm victories in 1994, 374–375; midterm victories in 2010, 417; rise of, 96
Republicans, Radical, 110–111
Reservations, 95, 161
Reserved powers, 47–48
Resettlement Act, 77
Resolution Trust Corporation, 361
Revels, Hiram, 115, 116
Revenue sharing, 329
Revere, Paul, 10
Rice, Condoleezza, 304
Richardson, Bill, 305–306
Richmond, Virginia, 100
Rights of English citizens, 8–9
Riis, Jacob, 151, 171
Road building, 70
Roaring Twenties, 211, 233
Robber barons, 130
Roberts, John G., 408, 414
Robeson, Paul, 216
Robinson, Jackie, 279
Rockefeller, John D., 169; creation of trusts by, 131; entrepreneurship of, 129–130; Gilded Age and, 147; Tarbell's investigation of, 170
Rockefeller, Nelson, as vice president, 334
Rocky Mountains, 90, 158
Roe v. *Wade*, 304
Rolfe, John, 3
Romania, collapse of Communism in, 363
Roosevelt, Eleanor, 232–233, 257, 302
Roosevelt, Franklin Delano, 43; Atlantic Charter and, 243; brain trust of, 225; court-packing proposal of, 229; declaration of war, 243; Good Neighbor Policy of, 354–355; illness of, 232; meeting at Yalta, 257; New Deal of, 225–232; presidential power and, 334; "Quarantine" speech of, 241; terms served, 49, 230; at Yalta Conference, 266
Roosevelt, Theodore, 43, 156; in election of 1912, 41, 178;

Roosevelt, Theodore *(continued)*
as muckraker, 170; presidency of, 175–177, 191–192, 354; as Rough Rider, 190; in state government, 175; Washington, Booker T., and, 173
Roosevelt Corollary to Monroe Doctrine, 191–192
Rosenberg, Ethel and Julius, 266
Rough Riders, 190
Rousseau, Jean-Jacques, 2
Rules Committee, 38
Russia: CIS and, 364; immigrants from, 149, 152; U.S. relations with, 382–383, 404–405; revolutions in, 197, 198, 213; in World War I, 195. *See also* Soviet Union
Russo-Japanese War, 187
Ruth, Babe, 213

Saar Basin, 200
Sacajawea, 90–91
Sacco, Nicola, 213–214
al-Sadat, Anwar, 337
Salutary neglect, 8
Samoa, 188
Sandinistas, 355
Sanger, Margaret, 172
San Juan Hill, Battle of, 190
Santa Anna, Antonio López de, 93
Saratoga, Battle of, 12
Savings and loan associations, 361
Scalawags, 112
Scalia, Antonin G., 414
Schechter Poultry Corp. v. *United States*, 229
Schenck v. *United States*, 28, 199
Schlesinger, Arthur, Jr., 334
School District of Abington Township v. *Schempp*, 28
Schools. *See* Education
Schwerner, Michael, 298
Scopes, John, 214–215
Scott, Dred, 82, 96, 97
Seabed Agreement, 332
Seale, Bobby, 320
Search warrants, 25, 29
Secession, 62, 99
Second Amendment, 25, 29
Secondary boycott, 251
Second Bank of the United States, 71, 76
Second Continental Congress, 11, 12
Sectionalism, 64, 69–74, 76, 79–82, 95–98, 99–105
Securities and Exchange Commission (SEC), 227
Sedition Act (1798), 58–59, 80
Sedition Act (1918), 199
Segregation, 103, 208; African-Americans positions on, 117; *de facto*, 251, 300; *de jure*, 251, 280, 300; in military, 248
Selective Service Act, 199
Self-determination, 200
Senate, U.S.: Army-McCarthy Hearings in, 266–267; committees in, 37, 38, 375; facts on, 35–37; League of Nations and, 201–202, 240; Versailles Treaty and, 201–202. *See also* Congress, U.S.; House of Representatives, U.S.
Senators: direct election of, 179; popular election of U.S., 139
Seneca Falls Convention, 78, 171
Seniority, in workplace, 302
Separate but equal, 119–120, 280
Separation of church and state, 25, 28
Separation of powers, 21–22, 24, 46–47
September 11, 2001, terrorist attacks, 395–396
Settlement houses, 171
Seventeenth Amendment, 30, 139, 179
Seventh Amendment, 30
Seward, William, purchase of Alaska and, 114
The Shame of the Cities (Steffens), 170
Sharecroppers, 115
"Share Our Wealth" program, 231
Sharon, Ariel, 401
Shay's Rebellion, 15
Shepard, Alan, 314
Sherman, William T., 100
Sherman Antitrust Act, 132, 176
Shiites, 398
Showboat (play), 216
Sicily, Allied invasion of, 246
Sierra Club, 329
Silent Spring (Carson), 296
Sinclair, Upton, 171
Sioux people, 161–162, 306–307
Sit-down strikes, 228
Sit-in, 281–282
Six-Day War, 337
Sixteenth Amendment, 27, 30, 139
Sixth Amendment, 25–26, 28–29, 30, 307, 409
Skyscrapers, 146
Slavery: at Constitutional Convention, 20; democracy and, 8; in the North, 7, 14; religion and, 73; in the South, 7, 72–74, 81–82, 97; Thirteenth Amendment and, 110; Western expansion and, 95–96. *See also* Abolitionists; African Americans
Slaves: child, 73; global trade of, 4–5; women, 72–73
Slums, 145
Smalls, Robert, 115, 116
Smith, Adam, 125, 130
Smith, Alfred E., 231
Smith, Bessie, 217
Smith, Joseph, 91
Smith Act, 264–265
Social classes, 146–147
The Social Contract (Rousseau), 2
Social Darwinism, 146, 169, 186
Socialism, 135, 199; creeping, 230, 278
Social justice movement, 171
Social Security, 293, 296; under Eisenhower, Dwight D., 278; reforms in, 227, 354; stability of, 373
Sod houses, 160
Solar energy, 384–385
Solid South, 119
Somalia, U.S. intervention in, 381
Sotomayor, Sonia, 306, 414
The Souls of Black Folk (Du Bois), 117
South: during and after Reconstruction, 115–117; role of cotton in, 72; secession of, 97–98; slavery in, 7, 72–74, 99. *See also* Civil War (1861–1865); Desegregation
South Africa, U.S. relations with, 357–358
South Carolina: secession of, 97–98; slavery in, 7, 8
Southeast Asia Treaty Organization (SEATO), 276
Southern Christian Leadership Conference (SCLC), 297
Soviet Union: A-bomb and H-bomb tests of, 261; aid to developing nations, 274; invasion of Afghanistan and, 337–338, 358; as member of Security Council, 256; nonaggression pact with Germany, 242; satellites of, 258, 259–260; U.S. relations with, 331–332, 358–360; in World War II, 245. *See also* Russia
Space exploration, 277; *Columbia* space shuttle, 411; moon landing and, 314, 330; under Obama, 416–417; Soviet, 277, 314
Spain: Civil War in, 241; contact with Native Americans, 3; as member of EEC, 261; missions of, 91; war with United States, 188–191, 193
Spanish-American War, 188–191, 193
Special-interest groups, 38–39
Special Olympics, 293
Speculation, 58, 210
Speech, freedom of, 25, 28
Spencer, Herbert, 146
Spheres of influence, 187
The Spirit of Laws (Montesquieu), 2
Spirituals, 73
Spoils system, 76
Sports and recreation, 150
Sputnik, 277, 314
Square Deal, 175–176
Stagflation, 336, 351
Stalin, Joseph, 259; pact with Hitler, 242, 245; at Yalta, 257
Stalingrad, Battle of, 245
Stamp Tax, 10
Standard Oil Company, 129
Standing committees, 37
Stanford, Leland, 169
Stanton, Edwin, 112
Stanton, Elizabeth Cady, 78, 171
"The Star-Spangled Banner," 62
Star Wars (movie), 358–359
States: admission of new, 49–50; constitutional governments of, 14; militias of, 25; reforms of, 174–177; rights of, 27, 98
Statue of Liberty, 155

Steam locomotive, 127
Steel, 127; plows made of, 159; trusts, 131
Steffens, Lincoln, 170
Steinbeck, John, 233
Steinem, Gloria, 303
Stevens, Thaddeus, 115
Stevenson, Adlai, 267, 278
Stewardship theory, 175–176
Stewart, James, 234
Stimulus Act, 407, 412–413
Stocks and stockholders, 126
Stock Market: crash of, 222, 225; reforms in, 227; trends in, 375
Stowe, Harriet Beecher, 79
Strategic Arms Limitations Talks (SALT I), 331–332, 358
Strategic Arms Limitations Talks II (SALT II) Treaty, 358
Strategic Arms Reduction Talks (START I) Treaty, 364, 382
Strategic Arms Reduction Treaty II (START II or New START), 404–405, 417
Strategic Defense Initiative (SDI), 358–359
Strict construction of U.S. Constitution, 58
Strikes, 133, 134–135, 249; sit-down, 228
Strip mining, 347
Strong, Josiah, 186
Student Nonviolent Coordinating Committee (SNCC), 281, 297
Students for a Democratic Society (SDS), 318
Suarez, Xavier, 305
Submarines: in World War I, 196, 198, 240
Subsidies, 349–350
Suburban development, 211–212
Suez Canal, 276–277, 337
Suffrage. *See* Voting rights
Suffragists, 160, 171–172, 216
Sumter, Fort, 98
The Sun Also Rises (Hemingway), 216
Sunnis, 398
Supply-side economics, 345–347
Supreme Court, U.S.: Burger, 330; court-packing proposal for, 229–230; jurisdiction of, 44; justices of, 44; landmark decisions of, 28-29; National Recovery Association and, 229; Obama's appointments to, 414; Roberts, 408–409; schools and, 348–349; Taney, 83; Warren, 330. *See also* names of cases
Sweatshops, 134
Sweatt v. *Painter*, 300
Sweden as member of EEC, 261
Swift, Gustavus, 169
Syria: Lebanon and, 356; Soviet support for, 332

Taft, William Howard: in election of 1912, 41; presidency of, 43, 177–178, 193, 354
Taft-Hartley Act, 250
Taiwan, 267
Taliban, 396–397
Tammany Hall, 149–150
Taney, Roger, 83
Tarbell, Ida, 170
Target prices, 350
Tariffs, 57, 96, 97, 103, 223, 357, 378–379; of Abominations, 80–81; of 1833, 81; Payne-Aldrich, 177; Underwood, 178
Tax Reform Act, 346
Tea Party Movement, 416
Tecumseh, 61
Telegraph, 128, 186
Telephone, 128, 168
Television, 282–283
Temperance movement, 78, 173
Temple, Shirley, 233–234
Tenant farmers, 115
Tenements, 71, 146, 153
Tennessee Valley Authority (TVA), 228–229, 230, 233, 278
Tenth Amendment, 27, 30, 47–48
Tenure of Office Act, 111–112
Terrorism, 377; Ku Klux Klan and, 118
Tet Offensive, 317
Texas: independence and annexation, 92–93; Mexicans in, 92, 198; war with Mexico and, 94
Texas v. *Johnson*, 28, 361
Thailand as member of SEATO, 276
Third Amendment, 25, 29
Thirteenth Amendment, 27, 30, 104, 110
38th Parallel, 263, 264, 268, 274
Thomas, Clarence, 414
Thomas, Norman, 231
Three Mile Island, Pennsylvania, 336, 387
Thurmond, Strom, 251
Tiananmen Square, 379–380
Tilden, Samuel J., 119
Tinker v. *Des Moines Independent School District*, 28, 301
Title I, 293
Title IX, 302–303, 330, 415
Tobacco, 3, 7; trust, 131
Tonkin Gulf Resolution, 317, 323
Tories, 12
Totalitarianism, 290
Town meetings, 6
Townsend, Francis, 231
Trade: with Asia, 113–114, 380; with China, 379–380; compromises on at Constitutional Convention, 20; with Europe, 113. *See also* Tariffs
Trail of Tears, 77
Transcontinental railroad, 114
Transportation: advances in, 127; investment in, 126
Treaty of 1846, 93
Trenton, New Jersey, 12
Trial courts, 44
Triangle Shirtwaist Company, fire in, 134
Trickle-down theory, 346
Troubled Asset Relief Program (TARP), 407
Truman, Harry S., 43; Doctrine of, 260; in election of 1948, 251; presidency of, 246–247, 249, 250–251, 257, 263–264, 267, 278, 279
Trusts, 131–132; busting of, 176, 177
Tubman, Harriet, 79
Turkey, Truman Doctrine and, 260
Turner, Frederick Jackson, 160
Turner, Nat, 73
Tuskegee Institute, 117
Tutu, Desmond, 358
Twain, Mark, 150
Twelfth Amendment, 27, 30, 59–60
Twentieth Amendment, 30
Twenty-fifth Amendment, 30, 42, 334
Twenty-first Amendment, 30, 214
Twenty-fourth Amendment, 30, 299–300
Twenty-second Amendment, 30, 42, 49, 230
Twenty-seventh Amendment, 27, 31
Twenty-sixth Amendment, 27, 31, 330
Twenty-third Amendment, 30
Two Treatises of Government (Locke), 2
Typewriters, 168

U-2 incident, 275–276
Ukraine, 364
Uncle Tom's Cabin (Stowe), 79
Underground Railroad, 74, 75, 79
Underwood Tariff, 178
Unemployment, 208; increased, 407–408; New Deal and, 225–227
Union Pacific Railroad, 74–75
Unions. *See* Labor unions
United Farm Workers, 305
United Mine Workers, 228
United Nations (UN): creation of, 256–257; Middle East conflict and, 401–402; North Korea and, 382, 400–401; Operation Desert Shield/Storm and, 365–366; organization of, 256–257, 263
United Nations (UN) High Commissioner for Refugees, 257
United States: invasion of Iraq, 404; as member of SEATO, 276; as member of Security Council, 256; relations with Soviet Union, 358–360; trade with China, 403
U.S. v. *Booker*, 409
United States v. *E. C. Knight*, 132
U.S. v. *Fanfan*, 409
U.S. v. *Gonzales Lopez*, 409
United States v. *Nixon*, 333
Universal Declaration of Human Rights, 257
Universal Negro Improvement Association, 173
Urban League, 297
USA Patriot Act, 396
U.S.S. *Cole*, attack on, 396

Valentino, Rudolph, 213
Valley Forge, Pennsylvania, 12

Vanderbilt, Cornelius, 169
Vanzetti, Bartolomeo, 213–214
Veblen, Thorstein, 147
V-E day, 246
Vera Cruz, Mexico, 194
Vernonia School District v. *Acton*, 349
Versailles, Treaty of, 200–201, 240, 241
Vesey, Denmark, 73
Vetoes, 37
Vicksburg, 100
Vienna Summit, 313
Vietnamization, 320
Vietnam War, 315–317; consequences of, 323; Eisenhower and, 316; end of, 346; Johnson and, 317–320; Kennedy and, 316; Nixon and, 320–323; North Vietnamese victory, 322–323; public opinion on, 317–319; social impact of, 320; U.S. withdrawal from, 321–322
Villa, Pancho, 194
Virginia: Civil War in, 100; at Constitutional Convention, 20; ratification of Constitution by, 23; slavery in, 7
Virginia Plan, 20
Virginia v. *Black, et al.*, 409
Vocational Rehabilitation Act: of 1920, 293; of 1973, 293–294
Volstead Act, 214
Voltaire, 2
Volunteers in Service to America (VISTA), 295
Voting rights: for African Americans, 281, 298, 299–300; for 18-year-olds, 330; reapportionment and, 302; universal, 76; for women, 160, 171–172, 216
Voting Rights Acts, 296, 300, 348

Wabash, St. Louis, and Pacific Railway v. *Illinois*, 137
Wagner Act, 228
Wald, Lillian, 171
Wallace, George C., 320
Wallace, Henry, 251
War Hawks, 61–62
War Industries Board, 197
War of 1812, 61–62
War on Poverty, 295
War Powers Act, 323
Warren, Earl, 28, 279, 292, 307, 330
Warsaw Pact, 277, 313, 383
Washington, Booker T., 117, 172
Washington, George, 12, 13; advice against permanent alliances, 60, 195; army of, 13; Cabinet under, 56–59; French Revolution and, 61; as head of Constitutional Convention, 19; terms served, 49
Washington Naval Conference, 202
Washington Square (James), 150
Watergate Affair, 332–334, 335, 356
Water Quality Act, 296
Watkins, John, 266
Watkins v. *United States*, 266
Watt, James, 125
Watts riot (1965), 298
The Wealth of Nations (Smith), 125
Weapons of mass destruction (WMDs), 398
Weaver, James, 138
Weaver, Robert C., 232, 296–297
Weber, Brian, 302
Webster, Daniel, 98
Welfare Reform Act, 373
Wells-Barnett, Ida B., 173
Western settlement, 9–10, 90–91, 158; motives for, 91–92; Native Americans and, 160–162; slavery and, 95–96
West Germany, 248–249, 260; formation of European Coal and Steel Community, 261. *See also* Berlin
Westinghouse air brake, 168
Weyler, Valeriano, 189
Wharton, Edith, 150, 216
Whig Party, 96
Whiskey Rebellion, 58
Whitewater investigations, 375
Whitney, Eli, 71, 72
Willard, Frances, 173
William (King of England), 3
Wilson, Teddy, 233
Wilson, Woodrow: in election of 1912, 41; Fourteen Points of, 200; presidency of, 43, 156, 178–180, 193–196, 200–201, 239–240, 339, 354
Windmills, 159
Wisconsin, reforms in, 174–175
The Wizard of Oz, 234
Women: African-American, 148; changing roles of, 216; in Civil War, 101; equal pay for, 373; exclusion from A.F. of L., 133; in factory system, 71; frontier, 160; government appointments of, 373; in Great Depression, 224; New Deal and, 232; on plantations, 72; rights of, 78, 171–173; as slaves, 72–73; social and political change and, 168, 169; voting rights for, 160, 171–172, 179, 216; in workforce, 69, 114, 227, 362; working-class, 148; in World War I, 197, 198, 207–208; in World War II, 244
Women's movement, 302–304
Workplace: children in, 146, 148, 169; equality in, 304; immigrants in, 114; women in, 114, 146, 148, 168, 169, 216, 227, 362
Works Progress Administration, 227, 233
World Court, 202
World Trade Center, terrorist attack on, 395
World Trade Organization (WTO), 379
World War I: African Americans in, 208; airplanes in, 198; causes of, 195–197; decision for, 197; draft for, 199; fighting the, 198; impact of, 207–208; impact on economy, 222; minorities in, 198; mobilization, 197–198; peace conference after, 200–201; reparations and, 200, 202; start of, 239–240; submarines in, 240; U.S. entrance into, 180; women in, 197, 198, 207–208
World War II: African Americans in, 244; Allied strategy and leadership, 245–246; causes of, 240–243; demobilization in, 249; draft in, 244; economy following, 249–250; financing, 244; Germany in, 242, 245–246; Italy in, 241; Japan in, 241, 243, 246; Jews in, 240; military and civilian deaths in, 249; mobilization for, 244; North Africa in, 245–246; rationing in, 244; Soviet Union in, 245; start of, 242; U.S. in, 243–248, 264; women in, 244
Wounded Knee, 162, 306
Writ of habeas corpus, 37, 100

XYZ Affair, John Adams and, 61

Yalta Conference, 257, 258, 259, 266
Yates v. *United States*, 265
Yellow dog contract, 135
Yellow fever, 193
Yellow journalism, 170, 188–189
Yellow peril, 156
Yeltsin, Boris, 364, 383
Yom Kippur War (1973), 337
Yorktown, Battle of, 13
Young, Brigham, 91
Yugoslavia, 381–382; Bosnian crisis and, 364; Communists in, 260; NATO's bombing of, 383

Zenger, John Peter, 8
Zimmermann Telegram, 197
Zoning, 212

Acknowledgments

Picture Credits

Cover iStockphoto/Nyul **7** Ben Franklin, *Philadelphia Gazette*, May 9, 1754 **10** Courtesy, American Antiquarian Society **21** Stock Montage, Inc. **23** & **36** Library of Congress **42** *both:* AP/Wide World Photos **46** Corbis-Bettmann **57** Corbis-Bettmann **62** The Nelson-Atkins Museum of Art, Kansas City, Missouri **67** New-York Historical Society **79** *Stowe:* © Corbis-Bettmann; *Douglass:* Corbis-Bettmann/UPI; *Tubman and Brown:* © Hulton-Getty/Liaison Agency; *Garrison:* Corbis **86** *bottom:* Woolaroc Museum, Bartlesville, Oklahoma **87** *top:* Historical Pictures Service **88** © Hulton-Getty/Liaison Agency **90** North Wind Picture Archives **93** *Punch* (London), 1846 **97** Corbis-Bettmann **104** Corbis-Bettmann **108** *bottom: Yankee Doodle*, 1847 **113** Archives of the Rutherford B. Hayes Library **116** *both:* © Hulton-Getty/Liaison Agency **117** © Corbis-Bettmann **122** *Harper's Weekly*, November 16, 1867 **123** Corbis-Bettmann **126** New-York Historical Society **129** *left:* Corbis-Bettmann; *right:* Library of Congress **131** Library of Congress, redrawn by Amsco **142** © Corbis-Bettmann **143** Culver Pictures **147** *left:* Corbis-Bettmann; *right:* Corbis-Bettmann/UPI **149** North Wind Picture Archives **151** Library of Congress **156** New York Public Library, Prints Division, Astor, Lenox, and Tilden Foundations **162** © Hulton-Getty/Liaison Agency **166** *top:* Gamma Liaison Network © Roger Viollet, Gamma Presse **168** © Amsco School Publications **170** North Wind Picture Archives **172** *top*: Library of Congress; *bottom left:* North Wind Picture Archives; *bottom right:* Corbis-Bettmann **176** Library of Congress **184** *bottom:* Library of Congress **189** © Amsco School Publications **193** Louis Dalrymple, *Judge*, 1895 **197** National Archives **205** Library of Congress **206** *Los Angeles Daily Times*, 1917 **209** Fitzpatrick in the *St. Louis Post-Dispatch* **214** *top:* Library of Congress; *bottom*: *The Best of H. T. Webster* (Simon & Schuster, 1953) **219** © Amsco School Publications, 2010 **220** © Hulton-Getty/Liaison Agency **230** Library of Congress **235** Fred O. Seibel Collection, University of Virginia **237** Library of Congress **240** Corbis-Bettmann **242** © *Straight Herblock* (Simon & Schuster, 1964) **244** Historical Pictures Service **255** Orr in *Scottish Daily Record* [Glasgow], 1941 **261** Jay N. Darling, *Des Moines Register*, 1945 **263** Joseph Parrish, *Chicago Tribune*, 1949 **265** National Archives **278** *Herblock's Special for Today* (Simon & Schuster, 1958) **281** Corbis-Bettmann/UPI **287** *top:* © Corbis-Bettmann; *bottom:* Corbis-Bettmann/UPI **288** *top:* Corbis-Bettmann/UPI; *bottom:* © Corbis-Bettmann **291** Corbis-Bettmann/UPI **292** © Corbis/Bettmann **294** ©Bob Daemmrich/The Image Works **296** Action VISTA/Ohio **298** Black Star **299** *Straight Herblock* (Simon & Schuster, 1964) **301** Library of Congress **303** Dana Fradon © 1972 The New Yorker Magazine, Inc. **305** AP/Barry Sweet **310** Illingworth © *London Daily Mail* **311** Corbis-Bettmann/UPI **315** National Aeronautics and Space Administration **318** Corky Trinidad, *Honolulu Star-Bulletin*, 1970 **319** Bill Mauldin © 1966 *Chicago Sun-Times* **321** Cal Alley, *The Commercial Appeal* (Memphis, Tenn.), 1968 **329** National Archives **331** Black Star © 1998 C. W. Owen **332** Bissell, *The Tennessean* **333** AP Photos **335** Dennis Renault, *Sacramento Bee*, 1974 **338** Corbis-Bettmann/UPI **339** © Valtman/Rothco **343** *left:* © Corbis-Bettmann; *right:* Tony Auth, *Philadelphia Inquirer*, 1974 **345** King Features Syndicate, Inc. **346** Len Boro/Rothco **348** AP/Mark Elias **350** United Nations Photo **351** Bill Mauldin, *Chicago Sun Times* **352** *left:* Laima Druskis, Photo Researchers, Inc.; *right:* David M. Grossman, Photo Researchers, Inc. **355** Oliphant © Universal Press Syndicate **357** United Nations Photo **359** Doug Marlette, *Charlotte Observer* **361** AP/Mark Duncan **363** D. Aubert, Sygma **365** Borgman, *Cincinnati Enquirer*, Reprinted with special permission King Features Syndicate **368** © Mazotta/Rothco **369** *top:* Hy Rosen, *Albany Times-Union*, New York/Rothco; *bottom:* Bill Mauldin, *Chicago Sun-Times* **370** AP/Wide World Photos **372** By permission of Chuck Assay and Creators Syndicate, Inc. **375** White House Photo **376** From *Herblock: A Cartoonist's Life* (Macmillan Publishing Co., 1993) **383** J. Abraityte, Sygma **386** From *Herblock on All Fronts* (New American Library, 1980) **397** AP/Emilio Morenatti **399** AP/Maya Allenruzzo **408** AP/Paul Sakuma **413** AP/Ron Edmonds **414** Steve Petteway, Collection of the Supreme Court of the United States **421** *top:* Getty Images/The White House; *bottom:* Getty Images

Text Acknowledgments

217 "One Way Ticket" from THE COLLECTED POEMS OF LANGSTON HUGHES by Langston Hughes, edited by Arnold Rampersad with David Roessel, Associate Editor, copyright © 1994 by the Estate of Langston Hughes. Used by permission of Alfred A. Knopf, a division of Random House, Inc. Reprinted by permission of Harold Ober Associates Incorporated. Copyright © 1994 by The Estate of Langston Hughes.

United States History and Government
June 2016

Part I

Answer all questions in this part.

Directions (1–50): For each statement or question, record on your separate answer sheet the *number* of the word or expression that, of those given, best completes the statement or answers the question.

1 Which geographic features had the most significant positive influence on settlement patterns and economic development in the British North American colonies?

(1) rivers and harbors
(2) mountains and plateaus
(3) forests and deserts
(4) prairies and lakes

2 The Erie Canal played a large role in the settlement of the Midwest because it provided a link between the Atlantic Ocean and the

(1) Gulf of Mexico
(2) Great Lakes
(3) Missouri River
(4) Pacific Ocean

3 During the 1600s and 1700s, the fundamental goal of British mercantilism was to

(1) prohibit all exports of raw materials from the colonies
(2) encourage economic competition with the American colonies
(3) develop manufacturing within the colonies
(4) maintain a favorable balance of trade for Great Britain with its colonies

4 The Proclamation of 1763 was issued by Great Britain after the French and Indian War primarily to

(1) promote colonial settlement beyond the Appalachian Mountains
(2) limit conflict between Native American Indians and colonial settlers
(3) encourage colonial economic ties with France
(4) force French settlers to leave British territory

Base your answer to question 5 on the passage below and on your knowledge of social studies.

> ...Small islands not capable of protecting themselves, are the proper objects for kingdoms to take under their care; but there is something very absurd, in supposing a continent to be perpetually governed by an island. In no instance hath nature made the satellite larger than its primary planet, and as England and America, with respect to each other, reverses the common order of nature, it is evident that they belong to different systems: England to Europe, America to itself....
>
> — Thomas Paine, *Common Sense*

5 The argument presented in this passage was intended to

(1) urge colonists to accept the Albany Plan of Union
(2) provide a reason for ratification of the Constitution of the United States
(3) convince American colonists to declare their independence
(4) persuade France to aid the United States in the Revolutionary War

6 What was one effect of the Three-fifths Compromise?

(1) Slave states gained additional congressional representation.
(2) The number of justices on the Supreme Court was established.
(3) Presidential appointments were assured easy confirmation.
(4) A two-house legislature was created.

Base your answer to question 7 on the passage below and on your knowledge of social studies.

> ...No political truth is certainly of greater intrinsic [essential] value, or is stamped with the authority of more enlightened patrons of liberty, than that on which the objection is founded. The accumulation of all powers, legislative, executive, and judiciary, in the same hands, whether of one, a few, or many, and whether hereditary, self-appointed, or elective, may justly be pronounced the very definition of tyranny....
>
> — James Madison, *The Federalist*, Number 47

7 Which constitutional principle was established to protect American citizens from the tyranny suggested in this quotation?

(1) due process of law
(2) States rights
(3) popular sovereignty
(4) separation of powers

Base your answer to question 8 on the passages below and on your knowledge of social studies.

> Each state retains its sovereignty, freedom and independence, and every power, jurisdiction and right, which is not by this confederation expressly delegated to the United States, in Congress assembled.
>
> — Article II, Articles of Confederation

> The powers not delegated to the United States by the Constitution, nor prohibited by it to the states, are reserved to the states respectively, or to the people.
>
> — 10th amendment, United States Constitution

8 The purpose of each of these provisions is to

(1) determine the division of power between state and central governments
(2) create a process for allowing amendments
(3) grant the central government power to control the states
(4) limit the power of the executive branch

---

9 **"President Jackson Vetoes Bill Rechartering Bank of United States"**

"Taney Court Overturns Missouri Compromise"

"Senate Approves NATO Treaty"

Which concept is best illustrated by these headlines?

(1) federalism
(2) direct democracy
(3) checks and balances
(4) westward expansion

10 What was a major demand of the Antifederalists during the debate over ratification of the United States Constitution?

(1) continuation of slavery
(2) right to habeas corpus
(3) inclusion of a bill of rights
(4) reduction in the number of representatives in Congress

11 Which headline would be considered an example of the unwritten constitution?

(1) **"President Nixon Vetoes War Powers Act"**
(2) **"Congress Approves President Reagan's Tax Cuts"**
(3) **"Congress Votes to Impeach President Bill Clinton"**
(4) **"President Obama Names Hillary Clinton to Cabinet"**

12 What was a common goal of the Proclamation of Neutrality (1793), the Embargo Act (1807), and the Monroe Doctrine (1823)?

(1) forcing Great Britain to grant independence to Canada
(2) avoiding conflicts with European nations
(3) providing wartime aid to European nations
(4) encouraging independence movements in Latin America

Base your answer to question 13 on the map below and on your knowledge of social studies.

Railroads in 1840 and 1860

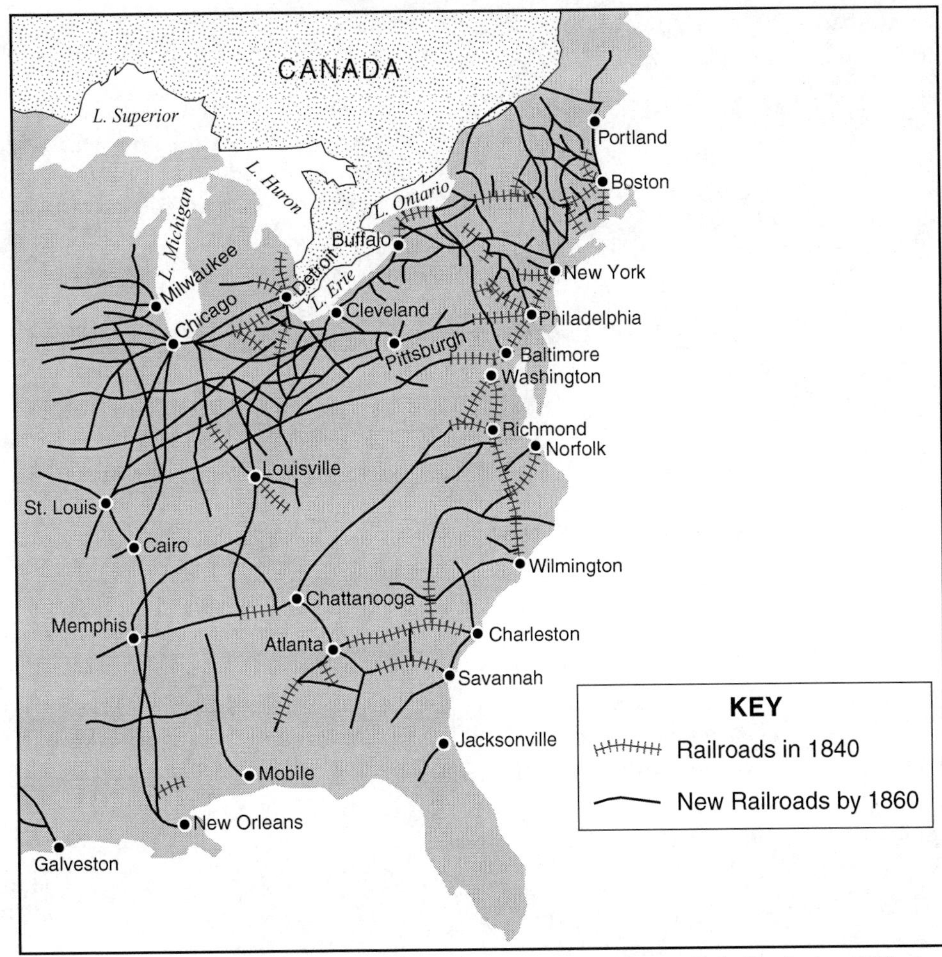

Source: Kownslar and Frizzle, *Discovering American History*, Holt, Rinehart and Winston (adapted)

13 The information provided by the map best supports the conclusion that

(1) the South's transportation system was more efficient
(2) most railroads were owned and operated by the United States government
(3) the transcontinental railroad linked the West and the South
(4) the North had transportation advantages by the start of the Civil War

---

14 The Supreme Court decisions in *Marbury* v. *Madison* (1803), *McCulloch* v. *Maryland* (1819), and *Gibbons* v. *Ogden* (1824) are similar in that each resulted in the

(1) development of new political parties
(2) admission of new slave states
(3) strengthening of the power of the federal government
(4) expansion of the rights of corporations

15 The Missouri Compromise of 1820 and the Compromise of 1850 were attempts by the federal government to

(1) limit immigration from Europe
(2) reduce the conflict over slavery
(3) settle border disputes with Mexico
(4) control the migration of settlers to new western territories

16 The Homestead Act of 1862 was important to the expansion of the United States because it provided

(1) land for agricultural colleges
(2) assistance to sharecroppers in the South
(3) free land to settlers in the West
(4) land grants for construction of transcontinental railroads

17 After the Civil War, a significant cause of the conflict between President Andrew Johnson and the Radical Republicans in Congress was disagreement over

(1) the plans for restoring Southern states to the Union
(2) a proposal to repeal the Emancipation Proclamation
(3) reduction of the army and the navy to prewar levels
(4) congressional efforts to pay the Confederate war debt

18 In the late 1800s, which idea was used most often to justify the elimination of business competition?

(1) conservation
(2) Manifest Destiny
(3) Social Darwinism
(4) populism

19 Poll taxes, literacy tests, and grandfather clauses were used in the South after 1890 to

(1) support the goals of the Freedmen's Bureau
(2) deny suffrage rights to African Americans
(3) undermine the "separate but equal" ruling of the Supreme Court
(4) enforce the amendments enacted during the Civil War and Reconstruction

20 The importance of *Northern Securities Co.* v. *United States* (1904) is that the Supreme Court

(1) used the Sherman Antitrust Act to break up a monopoly
(2) ruled child labor laws unconstitutional
(3) upheld the right of women to vote
(4) established regulations for the New York Stock Exchange

Base your answer to question 21 on the statement below and on your knowledge of social studies.

> …the policy of the government of the United States is to seek a solution which may bring about permanent safety and peace to China, preserve Chinese territorial and administrative entity, protect all rights guaranteed to friendly powers by treaty and international law, and safeguard for the world the principle of equal and impartial trade with all parts of the Chinese Empire.…
>
> — Secretary of State John Hay, Circular Letter, July 3, 1900

21 This excerpt from John Hay's Circular Letter became part of the

(1) Open Door policy
(2) Roosevelt Corollary to the Monroe Doctrine
(3) policy of Dollar Diplomacy
(4) Kellogg-Briand Pact

---

22 In the early 1900s, Progressives succeeded in strengthening federal control over the money supply by

(1) passing the Clayton Antitrust Act
(2) creating the Federal Reserve System
(3) enacting the Underwood Tariff bill
(4) establishing the gold standard

23 What was the purpose of states adopting initiative, referendum, and recall during the Progressive Era?

(1) supporting new political parties
(2) increasing the power of voters over the political process
(3) reestablishing property qualifications for voting
(4) extending voting rights to immigrants

Base your answer to question 24 on the cartoon below and on your knowledge of social studies.

IF CAPITAL AND LABOR DON'T PULL TOGETHER

Source: John McCutcheon, *Chicago Tribune*, 1919 (adapted)

24 Which statement most accurately describes the main argument made in this 1919 cartoon?

(1) Labor and management have the same economic goals.
(2) The federal government should take ownership of major industries.
(3) Organized workers are more productive than nonunion workers.
(4) Disputes between labor and the leaders of business are hurting the economy.

---

25 Which action by Germany prompted the United States to enter World War I?

(1) attacking British shipping
(2) forming an alliance with Austria-Hungary
(3) resuming unrestricted submarine warfare
(4) invading France

26 The United States Supreme Court in *Schenck* v. *United States* (1919) ruled that freedom of speech may be limited during national emergencies when the speech

(1) threatens the principle of States rights
(2) conflicts with national economic policies
(3) interferes with a presidential campaign
(4) presents a clear and present danger to the nation

Base your answer to question 27 on the photograph below and on your knowledge of social studies.

Dust Bowl, 1936

Source: Farm Security Administration

27 The situation shown in this photograph occurred in which region?
(1) Ohio River valley
(2) Great Plains
(3) Rocky Mountains
(4) Northeast

Base your answer to question 28 on the chart below and on your knowledge of social studies.

Consumer spending (in billions) on selected items and total value of stock, 1929–1933

	1929	1933
Food	$19.5	$11.5
Housing	$11.5	$7.9
Clothing	$11.2	$5.4
Automobiles	$2.6	$0.8
Medical care	$2.9	$1.9
Philanthropy	$1.2	$0.8
Value of shares on the New York Stock Exchange	$89.7	$22.2

Source: *Historical Statistics of the United States*

28 Which conclusion is best supported by the information on the chart?
(1) Business advertising had succeeded in selling more products.
(2) Violence by labor had increased throughout the country.
(3) Economic conditions had become worse.
(4) The stock market had recovered in 1933.

Base your answer to question 29 on the passage below and on your knowledge of social studies.

> ...Of all the Nations of the world today we are in many ways most singularly blessed. Our closest neighbors are good neighbors. If there are remoter [distant] Nations that wish us not good but ill, they know that we are strong; they know that we can and will defend ourselves and defend our neighborhood.
>
> We seek to dominate no other Nation. We ask no territorial expansion. We oppose imperialism. We desire reduction in world armaments....
>
> — President Franklin D. Roosevelt, Address at Chautauqua, NY, August 14, 1936

29 Which policy is President Franklin D. Roosevelt supporting in this speech?
(1) neutrality in foreign relations
(2) a growth in military spending
(3) an increase in foreign aid
(4) formation of military alliances

Base your answers to questions 30 through 32 on the cartoon below and on your knowledge of social studies.

Do We Want a Ventriloquist Act in the Supreme Court?

Source: *Waterbury Republican*, February 14, 1937

30 This 1937 cartoon is criticizing President Franklin D. Roosevelt's plan to

(1) reduce the number of federal courts
(2) impeach current Supreme Court justices
(3) give states the power to appoint Supreme Court justices
(4) increase the number of justices on the Supreme Court

31 One reason President Franklin D. Roosevelt proposed the plan shown in the cartoon was that the Supreme Court had

(1) challenged his right to run for a third term
(2) rejected several important Cabinet appointments
(3) ruled against laws to protect the rights of minorities
(4) declared parts of key New Deal programs unconstitutional

32 Many members of Congress opposed the plan shown in the cartoon because it would

(1) reduce the power of the president
(2) upset the system of checks and balances
(3) destroy the system of federalism
(4) cost too much to implement

Base your answer to question 33 on the photograph and poster below and on your knowledge of social studies.

Source: "Women workers chipping paint," Marinship Corp., National Archives, 1942

Source: Office of War Information, 1943

33 Photographs and posters showing scenes similar to these were used by the federal government to

(1) support the goal of equal pay for equal work
(2) discourage women from taking jobs from men with families
(3) recruit women to fill wartime manufacturing jobs
(4) encourage women to accept combat roles

---

34 The Servicemen's Readjustment Act of 1944 (GI Bill) was responsible for

(1) building United States military bases in allied countries throughout the world
(2) providing education and home loan benefits for soldiers returning from World War II
(3) maintaining the size of the active duty military at its pre–World War II level
(4) sending the United States economy into a post–World War II recession

35 President Harry Truman's decision to drop atomic bombs on Japan was based on the belief that the action would

(1) save American lives by avoiding an invasion of Japan
(2) force Germany and Italy to lay down their arms
(3) help create a military alliance with China
(4) persuade the Soviet Union to surrender

Base your answer to question 36 on the cartoon below and on your knowledge of social studies.

Source: Edwin Marcus, c. 1947, Library of Congress (adapted)

36 Which United States effort is the Soviet Union responding to in this cartoon?

(1) a commitment to rebuild the League of Nations
(2) a plan to join with other nations to reduce military spending
(3) an effort to improve United States–Soviet relations
(4) an attempt to stabilize the economy of Western Europe

---

37 **"Greece Receives U.S. Aid to Fight Communists"**
"U.S. Military Airlifts Supplies to Berlin"
"U.S. Troops Sent to Defend South Vietnam"

These headlines best illustrate the United States commitment to a policy of

(1) détente
(2) isolationism
(3) containment
(4) imperialism

38 • Alger Hiss conviction
• Rosenberg trial
• McCarthy hearings

These post–World War II events are most closely associated with the fear of

(1) an increase in immigration from the Soviet Union
(2) labor conflicts in United States cities
(3) an expansion of communism into Cuba
(4) a communist threat inside the United States

39 The 1957 launch of *Sputnik* by the Soviet Union embarrassed the United States because it

(1) allowed the Soviets to place missiles in Turkey
(2) revealed that the Soviets had nuclear weapons
(3) appeared that the United States had failed to keep up in scientific achievement
(4) confirmed the United States use of U-2 spy planes

40 "…And so, my fellow Americans: ask not what your country can do for you—ask what you can do for your country.

My fellow citizens of the world: ask not what America will do for you, but what together we can do for the freedom of man…."

— President John F. Kennedy, Inaugural Address, January 20, 1961

President Kennedy sought to achieve the goal described in this speech through support for the formation of the

(1) Peace Corps
(2) World Bank
(3) Organization of American States (OAS)
(4) South East Asia Treaty Organization (SEATO)

Base your answer to question 41 on the poster below and on your knowledge of social studies.

Source: Another Mother for Peace

41 This poster from 1967 is an expression of

(1) support for the foreign policy of the president
(2) support for increased financing of environmental programs
(3) opposition to health care reform for seniors and the poor
(4) opposition to United States involvement in Vietnam

---

42 Which title best completes the partial outline below?

I. ____________________

A. *Heart of Atlanta Motel* v. *United States* (1964)
B. Voting Rights Act of 1965
C. Fair Housing Act of 1968

(1) Latino Women Gain Equal Pay
(2) Civil Rights Movement Achieves Victories
(3) Native American Indians Regain Land Rights
(4) Persons With Disabilities Win Educational Opportunities

43 In *New York Times* v. *United States* (1971) and *United States* v. *Nixon* (1974), the Supreme Court placed limits on the

(1) authority of federal judges
(2) exercise of freedom of religion
(3) powers of the president
(4) right of Congress to declare war

44 Which statement accurately describes a result of the 1993 adoption of the North American Free Trade Agreement (NAFTA)?

(1) Tariff barriers were reduced between the three largest nations of North America.
(2) A single currency was created for the nations of North America.
(3) Immigration restrictions between North American nations were eliminated.
(4) The United States stopped importing oil from other North American nations.

Base your answer to question 45 on the cartoon below and on your knowledge of social studies.

Source: Jeff Stahler, *Columbus Dispatch*, March 7, 2009 (adapted)

45 Which situation related to the Great Recession in 2008 and 2009 is addressed in this cartoon?

(1) crisis in home foreclosures
(2) growth of federal budget deficits
(3) shortage of health care facilities
(4) decline in the financial stability of Social Security

---

46 **"Congress Passes Alien and Sedition Acts"**
"Lincoln Suspends Writ of Habeas Corpus"
"Roosevelt Authorizes Internment of Japanese Americans on West Coast"

Which conclusion is best supported by these headlines?

(1) Immigrants are a danger to the welfare of the United States.
(2) Perceived threats to national security sometimes result in limits on civil liberties.
(3) Foreign policy is greatly affected by domestic conflicts.
(4) The power of the federal government is weakened by risks to national security.

47 In the 1880s and the 1920s, low prices for United States agricultural products were the result of

(1) the overproduction of staple crops
(2) a shortage of usable farm land
(3) competition from cheaper imported goods
(4) inflationary monetary policies

48 One way in which the Progressive movement of the early 1900s and the women's rights movement of the 1960s are similar is that each resulted in

(1) restrictions on immigration
(2) limits on labor union activities
(3) passage of reform legislation
(4) a return to laissez-faire economic policies

49 One way in which President Franklin D. Roosevelt's New Deal and President Lyndon B. Johnson's Great Society are similar is that both programs

(1) made civil rights for African Americans a major goal
(2) drew wide support and few critics
(3) helped to end major depressions
(4) attempted to improve the lives of the poor and the aged

Base your answer to question 50 on the graph below and on your knowledge of social studies.

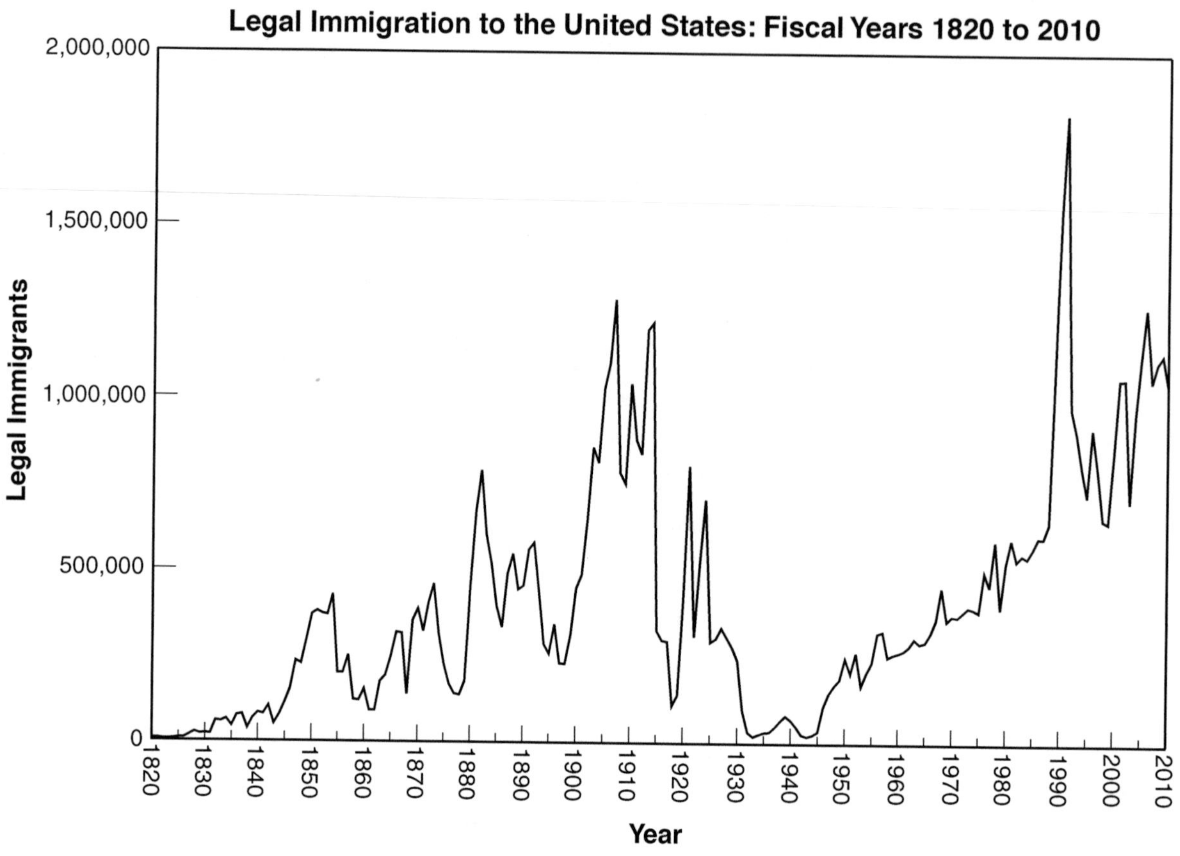

Source: U.S. Department of Homeland Security (adapted)

50 The low level of immigration between 1930 and 1945 is most directly related to

(1) passage of the Chinese Exclusion Act
(2) the Great Depression and World War II
(3) the Cold War and the civil rights movement
(4) improvements in living standards in Europe and Asia

This page left blank intentionally.

GO ON TO THE NEXT PAGE ⇨

Answers to the essay questions are to be written in the separate essay booklet.

In developing your answer to Part II, be sure to keep these general definitions in mind:

(a) **describe** means **"to illustrate something in words or tell about it"**

(b) **discuss** means **"to make observations about something using facts, reasoning, and argument; to present in some detail"**

Part II

THEMATIC ESSAY QUESTION

Directions: Write a well-organized essay that includes an introduction, several paragraphs addressing the task below, and a conclusion.

Theme: Reform Movements

During the period from 1820 to 1933, individuals and groups participated in major reform movements to bring social, political, and economic changes to American society. These reform movements achieved varying degrees of success.

Task:

Select ***two*** major reform movements during the period from 1820 to 1933 and for ***each***

- Describe the historical circumstances that led to the reform movement
- Discuss the extent to which the movement achieved its goal

You may use any major reform movement during the period from 1820 to 1933. Suggestions you might wish to consider include the abolition movement, the woman's suffrage movement, the temperance movement (prohibition), the consumer protection movement, the labor movement, and the conservation movement.

You are *not* limited to these suggestions.

Guidelines:

In your essay, be sure to:

- Develop all aspects of the task
- Support the theme with relevant facts, examples, and details
- Use a logical and clear plan of organization, including an introduction and a conclusion that are beyond a restatement of the theme

NAME ____________________ SCHOOL ____________________

Part III

DOCUMENT-BASED QUESTION

This question is based on the accompanying documents. The question is designed to test your ability to work with historical documents. Some of these documents have been edited for the purposes of this question. As you analyze the documents, take into account the source of each document and any point of view that may be presented in the document. Keep in mind that the language used in a document may reflect the historical context of the time in which it was written.

Historical Context:

Throughout the history of the United States, wars have been fought to protect national security and promote the national interest. These wars have affected the United States and American society in many different ways. These wars include the ***Spanish-American War (1898)***, the ***Korean War (1950–1953)***, and the ***Persian Gulf War (1991)***.

Task: Using the information from the documents and your knowledge of United States history, answer the questions that follow each document in Part A. Your answers to the questions will help you write the Part B essay in which you will be asked to

Select ***two*** wars mentioned in the historical context and for ***each***

- Describe the historical circumstances that led to United States involvement in the war
- Discuss the effects of the war on the United States and/or on American society

In developing your answers to Part III, be sure to keep these general definitions in mind:

(a) describe means "to illustrate something in words or tell about it"

(b) discuss means "to make observations about something using facts, reasoning, and argument; to present in some detail"

Part A
Short-Answer Questions

Directions: Analyze the documents and answer the short-answer questions that follow each document in the space provided.

Document 1

War Message to Congress

…The grounds for such intervention may be briefly summarized as follows:

First. In the cause of humanity and to put an end to the barbarities, bloodshed, starvation, and horrible miseries now existing there, and which the parties to the conflict are either unable or unwilling to stop or mitigate [lessen]. It is no answer to say this is all in another country, belonging to another nation, and is therefore none of our business. It is specially our duty, for it is right at our door.

Second. We owe it to our citizens in Cuba to afford them that protection and indemnity [security] for life and property which no government there can or will afford, and to that end to terminate the conditions that deprive them of legal protection.

Third. The right to intervene may be justified by the very serious injury to the commerce, trade, and business of our people and by the wanton [unlimited] destruction of property and devastation of the island.…

The issue is now with the Congress. It is a solemn responsibility. I have exhausted every effort to relieve the intolerable condition of affairs which is at our doors. Prepared to execute every obligation imposed upon me by the Constitution and the law, I await your action.…

Source: President William McKinley, Message to Congress, April 11, 1898

1 What are ***two*** reasons President William McKinley is asking Congress to declare war? [2]

(1)____

____

Score

(2)____

____

Score

Document 2a

DECLINED WITH THANKS.

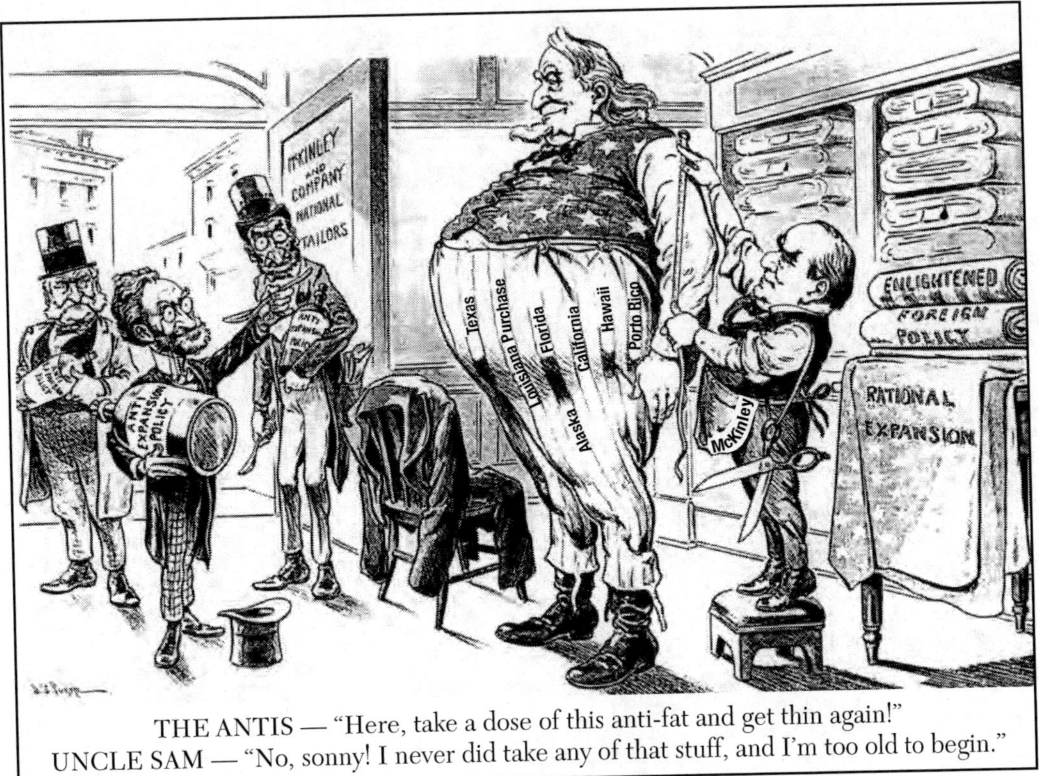

THE ANTIS — "Here, take a dose of this anti-fat and get thin again!"
UNCLE SAM — "No, sonny! I never did take any of that stuff, and I'm too old to begin."

Source: J. S. Pughe, *Puck*, September 5, 1900 (adapted)

Document 2b

...In the forcible annexation of the Philippines our nation neither adds to its strength nor secures broader opportunities for the American people.

Even if the principle of conquest were permissible under American public law, the conquest of territory so remote from our shores, inhabited by people who have no sympathy with our history or our customs, and who resent our attempt to overthrow their declaration of independence, would be a tax [burden] upon our military and naval strength the magnitude of which cannot now be determined.

Who can estimate in money and men the cost of subduing and keeping in subjection eight millions of people, six thousand miles away, scattered over twelve hundred islands and living under a tropical sun?...

Source: William Jennings Bryan, "Will It Pay?," Bryan et al., *Republic or Empire? The Philippine Question*, The Independence Company, 1899

2 Based on documents *2a* and *2b*, what are ***two*** ways the United States might be affected by the Spanish-American War? [2]

(1)____

____

Score

(2)____

____

Score

Document 3

...The transformation of America from a provincial to a world power began in the 1890s. When Theodore Roosevelt took office, the first and most important steps had already been taken. By going to war with Spain and keeping the Philippines in 1898, America had joined the more ambitious industrialized world powers. With the Platt Amendment in 1901, Congress declared to the world its continued independence from European colonial ambitions. In his presidency Roosevelt supported both the expansion that had taken place and the limitations Congress imposed upon it, and never envisioned any further American expansion. He regarded the taking of Panama as a fulfillment of the most direct American strategic interest, as a way of denying Europe a foothold in Central America, and at the same time assuring full mobility for a two-ocean navy....

Source: Richard H. Collin, *Theodore Roosevelt, Culture, Diplomacy, and Expansion: A New View of American Imperialism*, Louisiana State University Press, 1985

3 According to Richard Collin, what was ***one*** effect the Spanish-American War had on the United States? [1]

____

____

Score

Document 4

...Korea is a small country, thousands of miles away, but what is happening there is important to every American.

On Sunday, June 25th, Communist forces attacked the Republic of Korea.

This attack has made it clear, beyond all doubt, that the international Communist movement is willing to use armed invasion to conquer independent nations. An act of aggression such as this creates a very real danger to the security of all free nations.

The attack upon Korea was an outright breach of the peace and a violation of the Charter of the United Nations. By their actions in Korea, Communist leaders have demonstrated their contempt for the basic moral principles on which the United Nations is founded. This is a direct challenge to the efforts of the free nations to build the kind of world in which men can live in freedom and peace....

Furthermore, the fact that Communist forces have invaded Korea is a warning that there may be similar acts of aggression in other parts of the world. The free nations must be on their guard, more than ever before, against this kind of sneak attack....

Source: President Harry Truman, Radio and Television Address to the American People on the Situation in Korea, July 19, 1950

4 According to President Harry Truman, what is ***one*** reason the United States should be concerned about the situation in Korea? [1]

____

____

Score

Document 5

> ...And so the true brutality of the war never really penetrated the American cultural consciousness. An estimated 33,000 Americans died in it. Another 105,000 were wounded. The South Koreans lost 415,000 killed and had 429,000 wounded. Both the Chinese and North Koreans were exceptionally secretive about their casualties, but American officials put their losses at roughly 1.5 million men killed. The Korean War momentarily turned the Cold War hot, heightening the already considerable (and mounting) tensions between the United States and the Communist world and deepening the chasm between the United States and Communist forces asserting themselves in Asia. Those tensions and divisions between the two sides in the bipolar struggle [taking opposing positions] grew even more serious after American miscalculations brought China into the war. When it was all over and an armed truce ensued, both sides claimed victory, though the final division of the country was no different from the one that had existed when the war began. But the United States was not the same: its strategic vision of Asia had changed, and its domestic political equation had been greatly altered....

Source: David Halberstam, *The Coldest Winter: America and the Korean War*, Hyperion, 2007

5 According to David Halberstam, what were ***two*** effects the Korean War had on the United States? [2]

(1)____

____

Score

(2)____

____

Score

Document 6a

Source: Tim Kane, Heritage Foundation, 2006 (adapted)

Document 6b

...There is another subject that has to be addressed here today. When the guns fell silent, some asked what our forces in Korea had done for freedom, after all, for after all, the fighting began at the 38th parallel and ended at the 38th parallel. I submit to you today that looking back through the long lens of history, it is clear that the stand America took in Korea was indispensable to our ultimate victory in the cold war. Because we stood our ground in Korea, the Soviet Union drew a clear lesson that America would fight for freedom....

Because we have continued to stand with our democratic ally South Korea, with 37,000 American troops standing watch on the border today [2000], just as we have since 1953, we have kept the peace. And because of all that, there is now a chance for a different future on the Korean Peninsula....

Korea helped remind us of a few other lessons, too, that our people and all our rich diversity are our greatest strength, that a fully integrated military is our surest hope for victory, that our freedom and security depends on the freedom and security of others, and that we can never, ever, pull away from the rest of the world....

Source: President Bill Clinton, Remarks on the Observance of the 50th Anniversary of the Korean War, June 25, 2000

6 Based on these documents, what were ***two*** effects the Korean War had on the United States? [2]

(1)______________________________

Score

(2)______________________________

Score

Document 7

Just two hours ago, allied air forces began an attack on military targets in Iraq and Kuwait. These attacks continue as I speak. Ground forces are not engaged.

This conflict started August 2nd when the dictator of Iraq invaded a small and helpless neighbor. Kuwait—a member of the Arab League and a member of the United Nations—was crushed; its people, brutalized. Five months ago, Saddam Hussein started this cruel war against Kuwait. Tonight, the battle has been joined....

Our objectives are clear: Saddam Hussein's forces will leave Kuwait. The legitimate government of Kuwait will be restored to its rightful place, and Kuwait will once again be free. Iraq will eventually comply with all relevant United Nations resolutions, and then, when peace is restored, it is our hope that Iraq will live as a peaceful and cooperative member of the family of nations, thus enhancing the security and stability of the Gulf....

President George H. W. Bush

Source: President George H. W. Bush, Address to the Nation Announcing Allied Military Action in the Persian Gulf, January 16, 1991 (adapted)

7 According to President George H. W. Bush, what is ***one*** reason the United States began air strikes in Iraq in January of 1991? [1]

____

____

Score

Document 8a

...As a result of servicewomen's performance during Operation Desert Storm, the last of the laws restricting women's service were lifted by the middle of the decade. In 1992, Congress repealed the restriction banning servicewomen from flying in aircraft engaged in combat missions. In 1993, they lifted the restriction banning women from serving aboard combat vessels. By the turn of this [21st] century, women comprised almost 14 percent of active military duty personnel and were reaching the highest levels of the military....

While issues of equal opportunity for women in the military still remained, the distance between the servicewomen of 1999 and the Army nurses of 1901 who served their country before they could even vote was staggering....

Source: Women in Military Service for America Memorial Foundation

Document 8b

...Although the Persian Gulf War was brief, its impact was no less traumatic than other wars. From the time the Persian Gulf War ended in 1991 to now [2009], veterans have reported a number of physical and mental health problems.

Studies examining the mental health of Persian Gulf War veterans have found that rates of PTSD [Post-Traumatic Stress Disorder] stemming from the war range anywhere from almost 9% to approximately 24%. These rates are higher than what has been found among veterans not deployed to the Persian Gulf....

Source: Matthew Tull, *Rates of PTSD in Veterans*, about.com, July 22, 2009 (adapted)

8 Based on these documents, what were ***two*** effects the Persian Gulf War had on American society? [2]

(1)____

____

Score

(2)____

____

Score

Document 9

The undefeated Saddam Hussein of 1991

...The 2003 U.S. invasion and occupation of Iraq can't be viewed in isolation. The chain of events began more than a decade earlier with the botched close of the 1991 [Persian] Gulf War and then it continued in the U.S. effort to contain Saddam Hussein in the years that followed. "I don't think you can understand how OIF"—the abbreviation for Operation Iraqi Freedom, the U.S. military's term for the 2003 invasion and occupation of Iraq—"without understanding the end of the '91 war, especially the distrust of Americans" [by Iraqis] that resulted, said Army Reserve Maj. Michael Eisenstadt, an intelligence officer who in civilian life is an expert on Middle Eastern security issues.

The seeds of the second president Bush's decision to invade [in 2003] were planted by the unfinished nature of the 1991 war, in which the U.S. military expelled Iraq from Kuwait but ended the fighting prematurely and sloppily, without due consideration by the first president Bush and his advisors of what end state they wished to achieve. In February 1991, President Bush gave speeches that encouraged Iraqis "to take matters into their own hands and force Saddam Hussein the dictator to step aside." U.S. Air Force aircraft dropped leaflets on fielded Iraqi units urging them to rebel. On March 1, Iraqi army units in Basra began to do just that....

Source: Thomas E. Ricks, *Fiasco: The American Military Adventure in Iraq*, The Penguin Press, 2006 (adapted)

9 According to Thomas E. Ricks, what was ***one*** effect the 1991 Persian Gulf War had on the United States? [1]

____

____

Score

Part B
Essay

Directions: Write a well-organized essay that includes an introduction, several paragraphs, and a conclusion. Use evidence from *at least* ***four*** documents in your essay. Support your response with relevant facts, examples, and details. Include additional outside information.

Historical Context:

Throughout the history of the United States, wars have been fought to protect national security and promote the national interest. These wars have affected the United States and American society in many different ways. These wars include the ***Spanish-American War (1898)***, the ***Korean War (1950–1953)***, and the ***Persian Gulf War (1991)***.

Task: Using the information from the documents and your knowledge of United States history, write an essay in which you

> Select ***two*** wars mentioned in the historical context and for ***each***
> - Describe the historical circumstances that led to United States involvement in the war
> - Discuss the effects of the war on the United States and/or on American society

Guidelines:

In your essay, be sure to

- Develop all aspects of the task
- Incorporate information from *at least* ***four*** documents
- Incorporate relevant outside information
- Support the theme with relevant facts, examples, and details
- Use a logical and clear plan of organization, including an introduction and a conclusion that are beyond a restatement of the theme

United States History and Government
January 2017

Part I

Answer all questions in this part.

Directions (1–50): For each statement or question, record on your separate answer sheet the *number* of the word or expression that, of those given, best completes the statement or answers the question.

1 New England's geographic features most directly influenced the region's development of

(1) industry
(2) sugar mills
(3) large plantations
(4) tenant farming

2 • Colonists protest the Stamp Act.
• Sons of Liberty groups are formed.
• Crates of tea are thrown into Boston Harbor.
• Parliament passes Coercive Acts.

These events helped lead to the

(1) French and Indian War
(2) Revolutionary War
(3) Whiskey Rebellion
(4) War of 1812

3 Which heading best completes the partial outline below?

I. ____________________
A. National government unable to levy direct taxes
B. No single national currency
C. Lack of an elected chief executive

(1) Weaknesses of the Articles of Confederation
(2) Strengths of the Continental Congress
(3) Provisions of the United States Constitution
(4) Influence of Treaties with European Governments

4 During the debate over ratification of the United States Constitution, Antifederalists argued that a bill of rights should be added to

(1) preserve the interests of slaveholders
(2) list the responsibilities of citizens
(3) protect individual liberties
(4) ensure federal supremacy

Base your answer to question 5 on the passage below and on your knowledge of social studies.

> Congress shall make no law respecting an establishment of religion, or prohibiting the free exercise thereof; or abridging the freedom of speech, or of the press; or the right of the people peaceably to assemble, and to petition the Government for a redress of grievances.
>
> —First amendment, United States Constitution

5 What is one impact of this amendment on American society?

(1) Congress cannot mandate a national religion.
(2) Religious groups cannot lobby Congress.
(3) Members of the press cannot hold public office.
(4) The Supreme Court cannot limit free speech during wartime.

---

6 The Supreme Court can influence the actions of the other two branches of the federal government by

(1) vetoing legislation
(2) pardoning criminals
(3) exercising judicial review
(4) impeaching the president

7 In 1790, the first census of the United States was taken in order to

(1) create immigration quotas
(2) determine each state's representation in Congress
(3) establish the number of appointed federal judges
(4) justify funding for public education

8 Which group benefited the most from the United States acquisition of the port of New Orleans?

(1) farmers in the Ohio River valley
(2) Native American Indians in the Southwest
(3) fur trappers in the Hudson River valley
(4) gold miners in northern California

9 A major reason for the issuance of the Monroe Doctrine (1823) was to

(1) improve trade relations with Asia
(2) gain new colonies in Latin America
(3) acquire land to build a canal in Central America
(4) limit European influence in the Western Hemisphere

10 A major reason for President Andrew Jackson's policy toward the Cherokee Nation was to

(1) provide Native American Indians with better farmland
(2) enforce the United States Supreme Court decision in *Worcester* v. *Georgia* (1832)
(3) obtain land from Native American Indians for white settlers
(4) gain the political support of Native American Indians

11 Which quotation best represents the idea of Manifest Destiny?

(1) "American interests are best served by strict isolationism."
(2) "The passage of protective tariffs will encourage industrial development."
(3) "Immigration is the key to the nation's economic growth."
(4) "The United States has a duty to spread American ideals westward."

12 . . ."We hold these truths to be self-evident: that all men and women are created equal; . . ."

—Seneca Falls Convention, 1848

Which document most influenced the authors of this statement?

(1) Mayflower Compact
(2) Albany Plan of Union
(3) Declaration of Independence
(4) Articles of Confederation

13 The Homestead Act (1862) encouraged the settlement of the West because it provided

(1) forty acres of land and a mule to formerly enslaved persons
(2) land to people who would live on it for at least five years
(3) mining claims for prospectors seeking gold and silver
(4) land to companies to build transcontinental railroads

14 What was one major result of the North's victory in the Civil War?

(1) The power of the Supreme Court was limited.
(2) Slave owners were compensated for their losses.
(3) The influence of corporations on government was reduced.
(4) The supremacy of the national government was upheld.

15 One way in which Andrew Carnegie and John D. Rockefeller are similar is that they both

(1) served in the United States Congress
(2) treated their workers with respect
(3) gave large sums of money to charitable causes
(4) made fortunes in the automobile industry

16 During the late 1800s, the use of child labor in United States factories was most opposed by

(1) parents
(2) nativists
(3) labor unions
(4) factory owners

17 In the late 1800s, an increased demand for raw materials and a desire for new markets contributed to the United States adopting a policy of

(1) imperialism
(2) pacifism
(3) collective security
(4) isolationism

18 ". . .You come to us and tell us that the great cities are in favor of the gold standard; we reply that the great cities rest upon our broad and fertile prairies. Burn down your cities and leave our farms, and your cities will spring up again as if by magic; but destroy our farms and the grass will grow in the streets of every city in the country. . . ."

—William Jennings Bryan, 1896

In the late 19th century, farmers attempted to address the issue raised by William Jennings Bryan by

(1) supporting the Populist Party
(2) demanding higher tariffs
(3) providing jobs for the unemployed
(4) lobbying Congress to cut income taxes

19 What was one result of the Supreme Court decision in *Plessy* v. *Ferguson* (1896)?

(1) Public schools were integrated nationwide.
(2) Civil rights for African Americans were strengthened.
(3) Northern states were forced to segregate public facilities.
(4) The "separate but equal" doctrine was established.

20 One major result of the Spanish-American War was that the United States

(1) formed an alliance with England
(2) gained recognition as a world power
(3) repealed the Monroe Doctrine
(4) decreased the size of its navy

21 A common goal of Lincoln Steffens, Frank Norris, and Ida Tarbell was to

(1) encourage government officials to decrease the regulation of business
(2) publicize the achievements of the captains of industry
(3) create a demand for new political parties to replace the two major parties
(4) increase public awareness of social, political, and economic problems

22 During the Progressive Era, direct primary elections were adopted to

(1) raise additional campaign funds for candidates
(2) increase the power of voters in the political process
(3) strengthen the role of political machines
(4) expand the power of the federal government

23 President Theodore Roosevelt was called a trustbuster because he

(1) directed the building of the Panama Canal
(2) encouraged conservation of natural resources
(3) supported legal action against business monopolies
(4) resigned from the Republican Party

24 What was President Woodrow Wilson's stated policy toward the warring nations of Europe prior to United States entry into World War I?

(1) neutrality
(2) containment
(3) internationalism
(4) dollar diplomacy

25 Which statement about the United States economy during the 1920s is true?

(1) Federal regulation of business was strengthened.
(2) The purchase of stocks steadily declined.
(3) Mass production increased the supply of consumer goods.
(4) Republican Party presidents supported unemployment insurance.

Base your answer to question 26 on the cartoon below and on your knowledge of social studies.

Source: Clifford Berryman, *Washington Star*, August 31, 1930

26 This cartoon is portraying a situation that resulted from the

(1) public rejection of the New Deal
(2) economic downturn of the late 1920s
(3) failure of the Civilian Conservation Corps
(4) opposition to the Treaty of Versailles

27 President Franklin D. Roosevelt believed that declaring a bank holiday and creating the Federal Deposit Insurance Corporation (FDIC) would aid the nation's banking system by

(1) restricting foreign investments
(2) eliminating government regulation of banks
(3) restoring public confidence in banks
(4) granting tax relief

Base your answer to question 28 on the passage below and on your knowledge of social studies.

> . . . I see one-third of a nation ill-housed, ill-clad, ill-nourished.
>
> It is not in despair that I paint you that picture. I paint it for you in hope—because the Nation, seeing and understanding the injustice in it, proposes to paint it out. We are determined to make every American citizen the subject of his country's interest and concern; and we will never regard any faithful, law-abiding group within our borders as superfluous. The test of our progress is not whether we add more to the abundance of those who have much; it is whether we provide enough for those who have too little. . . .
>
> —President Franklin D. Roosevelt, Second Inaugural Address, January 20, 1937

28 President Franklin D. Roosevelt addressed the situation described in this speech by

(1) reducing the influence of labor unions
(2) supporting programs to aid the poor and unemployed
(3) promoting the interests of big business
(4) adopting the trickle-down economic theory

---

29 The Neutrality Acts of 1935 and 1937 were enacted by Congress to

(1) help the United States recover from the Great Depression
(2) stop Nazi Germany from conquering Europe
(3) aid the Americans who fought in the Spanish Civil War
(4) prevent the United States from being drawn into another world war

30 "Yesterday, December 7, 1941—a date which will live in infamy—the United States of America was suddenly and deliberately attacked by naval and air forces of the Empire of Japan. . . ."

—President Franklin D. Roosevelt, Address to Congress, December 8, 1941

In this statement, President Roosevelt was addressing Congress about the

(1) sinking of merchant ships in the Atlantic Ocean
(2) D-Day invasion of France
(3) bombing of Pearl Harbor
(4) air raids on the Panama Canal

31 During World War II, the federal government was accused of violating constitutional rights by

(1) signing the Yalta Agreement
(2) implementing a draft to expand the armed forces
(3) relocating Japanese Americans to internment camps
(4) initiating the secret Manhattan Project

Base your answer to question 32 on the posters below and on your knowledge of social studies.

Source: N.C. Wyeth, U.S. Department of the Treasury, 1942

Source: Weimer Pursell, Office of Price Administration, 1943

32 These World War II posters encouraged Americans to

(1) demand higher wages
(2) enlist in the armed services
(3) purchase new automobiles
(4) support home-front war efforts

---

33 Which standard of justice was applied to Nazi leaders who were tried at Nuremberg after World War II?

(1) Military attacks on civilian populations are legal.
(2) Individuals can be held personally responsible for war crimes.
(3) Military officers are not accountable for crimes if they were obeying orders.
(4) Only the League of Nations can determine international law.

34 What was the purpose of the Berlin airlift?

(1) supplying West Berlin with necessities during the Soviet blockade
(2) helping defeat the German military
(3) assisting people trying to escape from East Berlin
(4) forcing the Soviet Union to end its occupation of East Germany

35 During the 1960s, members of the Student Nonviolent Coordinating Committee (SNCC) used sit-ins primarily to

(1) protest high college tuition costs
(2) promote passage of clean air laws
(3) support voting rights for 18-year-old citizens
(4) challenge racially segregated public facilities

36 What was a major result of the Cuban missile crisis of 1962?

(1) Fidel Castro was removed from power.
(2) Steps were taken to relax Cold War tensions.
(3) United Nations forces invaded Cuba.
(4) Trade between Cuba and the United States increased.

37 President Kennedy created the Peace Corps in the 1960s to

(1) fight revolutionaries in democratic nations with military force
(2) improve economic conditions in developing countries
(3) rebuild United States cities through urban renewal
(4) overthrow Soviet control in Eastern Europe

38 Which statement about the Vietnam War is an opinion?

(1) President Lyndon B. Johnson's escalation of the war was a mistake.
(2) United States forces withdrew from Vietnam during the presidency of Gerald Ford.
(3) Disagreement over the war divided the American public.
(4) The Vietnam War had been the longest military conflict in United States history.

39 The SALT I and SALT II agreements of the 1970s tried to improve Cold War relations between the United States and the Soviet Union by

(1) encouraging space exploration
(2) increasing cultural exchanges
(3) lowering barriers to trade
(4) limiting nuclear weapons

40 What was a major achievement of the presidency of Jimmy Carter?

(1) uniting East Germany and West Germany
(2) negotiating the peace accord between Egypt and Israel at Camp David
(3) ending United States dependence on imported oil
(4) rescuing United States hostages in Iran

41 President Ronald Reagan supported supply-side economics through reduced tax rates to

(1) encourage economic growth
(2) create more public-works jobs
(3) increase government regulation of business
(4) decrease defense spending

42 The North American Free Trade Agreement (NAFTA) and the General Agreement on Tariffs and Trade (GATT) were created primarily to

(1) support environmentalism
(2) maintain mutual defense
(3) improve public health worldwide
(4) promote economic interdependence

Base your answer to question 43 on the cartoon below and on your knowledge of social studies.

Source: Nick Anderson, *Louisville Courier-Journal,* December 22, 2005

43 This cartoon illustrates that actions taken during times of crisis have sometimes led to concerns about the functioning of

(1) federalism
(2) salutary neglect
(3) checks and balances
(4) bicameral legislatures

44 The decisions of the Supreme Court under Chief Justice John Marshall and under Chief Justice Earl Warren demonstrate that

(1) the Supreme Court can greatly influence economic and social change
(2) chief justices have little influence over the rest of the Supreme Court
(3) Supreme Court decisions must be approved by the president
(4) states can overturn decisions of the Supreme Court

45 ". . . Under a government which imprisons any unjustly, the true place for a just man is also a prison. . . ."

—Henry David Thoreau

Which leader's reform efforts reflect the idea in this statement by Thoreau?

(1) Booker T. Washington's support for vocational education
(2) Jane Addams's establishment of Hull House
(3) Rachel Carson's books about the environment
(4) Martin Luther King Jr.'s advocacy of civil disobedience

Base your answer to question 46 on the graph below and on your knowledge of social studies.

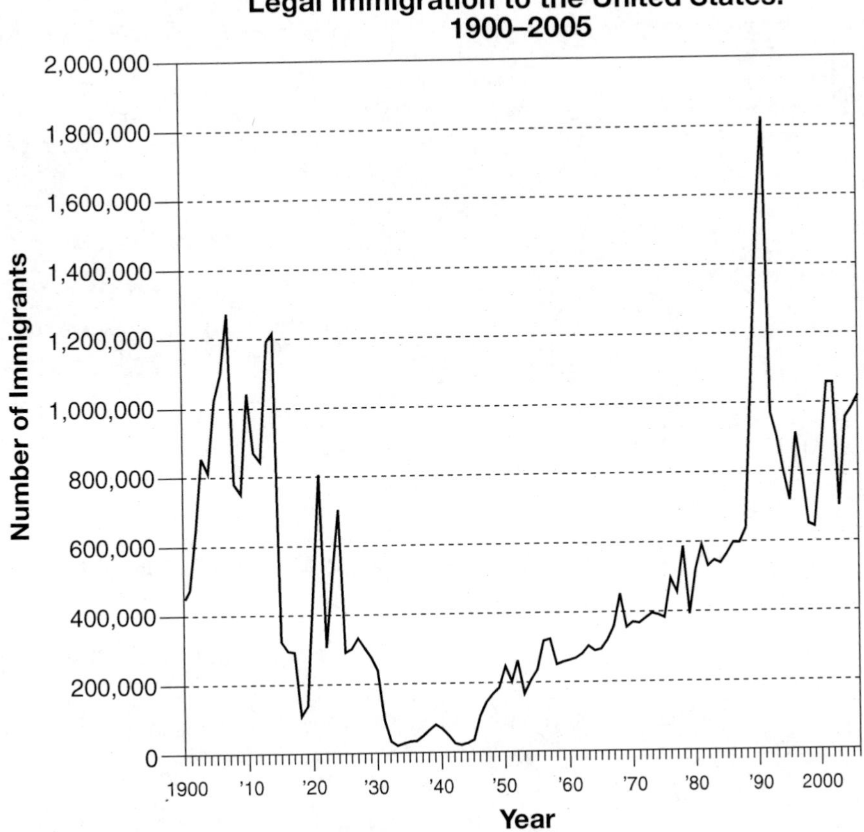

Source: U. S. Department of Homeland Security (adapted)

46 Which statement is best supported by the information provided in this graph?

(1) Each year since 1950, immigration has increased.
(2) Quotas favored immigration from southern and eastern Europe.
(3) Immigration declined during world wars and economic hard times.
(4) Every year since 1920, at least one million people have come to the United States.

---

47 One way in which President Abraham Lincoln's suspension of habeas corpus (1861), the Espionage Act (1917), and the USA Patriot Act (2001) are similar is that these actions

(1) enforced international treaties
(2) expanded political cooperation
(3) encouraged economic development
(4) restricted civil liberties during wartime

48 The Harlem Renaissance was influenced by the

(1) migration of African Americans from the rural South to the urban North
(2) passage of federal laws outlawing racial discrimination in public facilities
(3) racial integration of the military during World War I
(4) use of affirmative action after World War II

Base your answers to questions 49 and 50 on the graph below and on your knowledge of social studies.

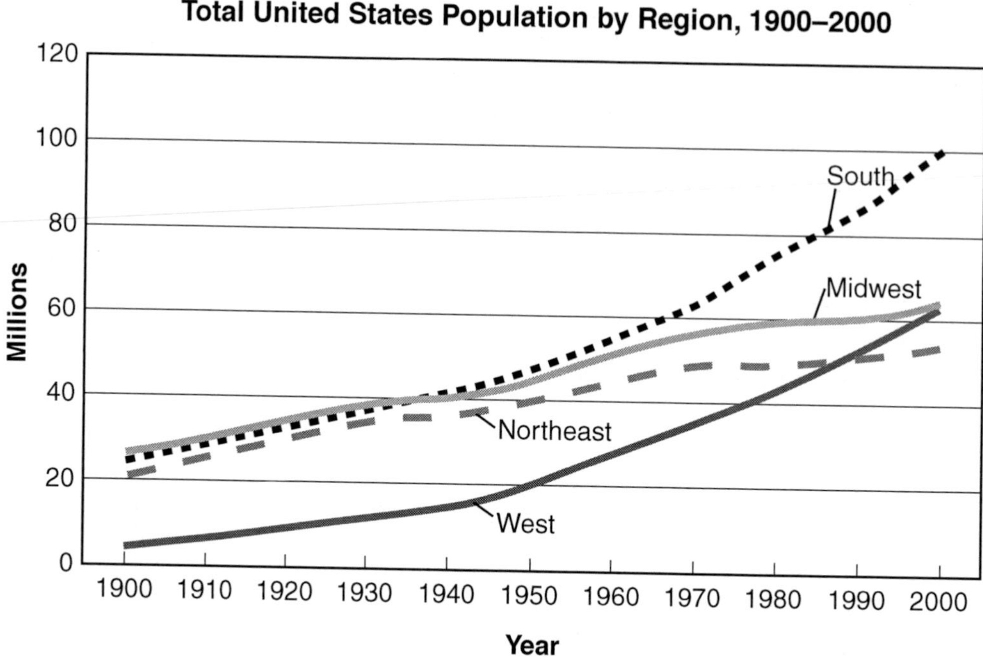

49 Which section of the country gained the most population in the years shown on the graph?

(1) South
(2) Midwest
(3) Northeast
(4) West

50 What is one effect the population changes shown in the graph have had on national politics?

(1) reducing the number of senators from the Midwest
(2) increasing the representation of the South and West in Congress
(3) enhancing the chances for election of presidential candidates from the Northeast
(4) strengthening the Democratic Party's control of the South

---